Walking in
Italy

Helen Gillman
Sandra Bardwell
Stefano Cavedoni
Nick Tapp

Walking in Italy

1st edition

Published by
Lonely Planet Publications ABN 36 005 607 983
Head Office: Locked Bag 1, Footscray, Victoria 3011, Australia
Branches: 150 Linden Street, Oakland CA 94607, USA
                10a Spring Place, London NW5 3BH, UK
                1 rue du Dahomey, 75011 Paris, France

Printed by
The Bookmaker International Ltd
Printed in China

Photographs by

Sandra Bardwell	Stefano Cavedoni
Ugo Esposito	Dott. Sandro Privitera
Nick Tapp	Consorzio Turistico Val Gardena

Front cover: The northern Alpi Apuane in the late afternoon from the summit ridge of Pania della Croce (Nick Tapp)

First Published
June 1998

National Library of Australia Cataloguing in Publication Data

Walking in Italy.

   Includes index.
   ISBN 0 86442 542 2.

   1. Hiking - Italy - Guidebooks. 2. Italy - Guidebooks.
   I. Gillman, Helen. (Series: Lonely Planet walking guide).

914.504929

Helen Gillman

Helen works as a freelance journalist and editor, based in Italy. For many years she worked as a journalist in Australia (her country of birth), before moving to Italy in 1990. Helen is the coordinating author of Lonely Planet's *Italy* guide and has also written the Italy chapter in Lonely Planet's *Mediterranean Europe* and *Western Europe* shoestring guides. Helen is also the coordinating author of this book. She wrote the introductory chapters and helped Stefano with the planning and some of the research for the Toscana and Dolomiti chapters.

Sandra Bardwell

Having written a PhD thesis on the history of national parks in Victoria, Sandra has been writing ever since. She was born in Melbourne and, after graduating, worked as an archivist and then as historian for the National Parks Service and its successors. She has been a dedicated walker since joining a bushwalking club in the early 1960s and became a bushwalking guru through her column in the Melbourne *Age* and as the author of several guidebooks on the subject. In 1989 Sandra and her husband retired to the Highlands of Scotland, where they are now settled in a village near Loch Ness. She works for Historic Scotland as a monument warden, writing about everything from prehistoric burial cairns to 20th century wartime defences. She has walked extensively in Scotland, England and Wales – and in Italy, having yielded to the temptation to contribute part of this book.

Stefano Cavedoni

Stefano is an actor and writer. In the late 1970s, while he was still a university student, Stefano's career in the Italian entertainment industry was launched with a bang when his rock band, Skiantos, achieved some success. After this, he wrote and performed humorous one-man shows. But, while on the stage, he was secretly thinking about travel, forests and mountains. He researched and wrote up the walks for the Dolomiti, Volcanoes and Sardegna chapters, as well as the Chianti Classico and Medieval Hills walks in the Toscana chapter. Stefano has also worked on Lonely Planet's *Italy* guide.

Nick Tapp

Nick first picked up a rucksack while at university and was instantly converted. The career in medicine never eventuated but the outdoor habit stuck, and he has since walked, skied and climbed in Australia, New Zealand, Nepal, North and South America and Italy. Over the years, while cobbling together a degree in English and philosophy and a graduate diploma in Spanish, Nick has sold outdoor gear, operated ski lifts, led a school outdoor activities group and done a brief stint as a cabaret singer in Peru. His first gig in publishing, at *Wild* and *Rock* magazines, began in the packing room and ended in the editor's chair. Now he is editor in charge of Lonely Planet's walking guide series.

From the Publisher

This book was edited in Melbourne, Australia, by Justin Flynn. Justin was helped by Joyce Connolly, Michelle Glynn, Tom Smallman, Anne Mulvaney, Nick Tapp and Richard Plunkett. Lindsay Brown, Geoff Stringer and Clem Lindenmayer helped out with the Flora & Fauna section. Andrew Smith coordinated the mapping, design and layout with the assistance of Chris Klep, Anna Judd, Indra Kilfoyle, Verity Campbell, Glenn van der Knijff and Leanne Peak. Thanks also to Dr David R Shlim for the Traumatic Injuries section in the Health, Safety & First Aid chapter, Simon Bracken for the cover design, Trudi Canavan and Ann Jeffree for the illustrations, Paul Piaia for the climate charts and Quentin Frayne for help on the language section.

Walking Disclaimer

Although the authors and publisher have done their utmost to ensure the accuracy of all information in this guide, they cannot accept any responsibility for any loss, injury or inconvenience sustained by people using this book. They cannot guarantee that the tracks and routes described here have not become impassable for any reason in the interval between research and publication.

The fact that a trip or area is described in this guidebook does not mean that it is safe for you and your walking party. You are ultimately responsible for judging your own capabilities in the light of the conditions you encounter.

Warning & Request

Things change. Prices go up, schedules change, good places go bad and bad places go bankrupt – nothing stays the same. So, if you find things better or worse, recently opened or long since closed, please tell us and help make the next edition even more accurate and useful.

We value all of the feedback we receive from travellers. Julie Young coordinates a small team who read and acknowledge every letter, postcard and email, and ensure that every morsel of information finds its way to the appropriate authors, editors and publishers.

Everyone who writes to us will find their name in the next edition of the appropriate guide and will also receive a free subscription to our quarterly newsletter, *Planet Talk*. The very best contributions will be rewarded with a free Lonely Planet guide.

Excerpts from your correspondence may appear in new editions of this guide; in our newsletter, *Planet Talk*; or in updates on our Web site – so please let us know if you don't want your letter published or your name acknowledged.

Contents

Map Legend

BOUNDARIES

━━━━━━━━━━━━ .... International Boundary

━━━━━━━━━━━━ .... Provincal Boundary

ROUTES

━━━━━━━━━━━━ ....Freeway

━━━━━━━━━━━━ .... Primary Road

━━━━━━━━━━━━ .... Secondary Road

━━━━━━━━━━━━ ....City Road

━━━━━━━━━━━━ ....City Street

━ ━ ━ ━ ━ .... 4WD Track

━ ━ ━ ━ ━ .... Walking Track

━━━━━━━━━━━━ .... Described Walk

━ ━ ━ ━ ━ .... Ferry Route

╫──╫──╫──╫── .... Chair Lift or Cable Car

AREA FEATURES

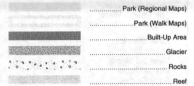

.... Park (Regional Maps)

.... Park (Walk Maps)

.... Built-Up Area

.... Glacier

.... Rocks

.... Reef

HYDROGRAPHIC FEATURES

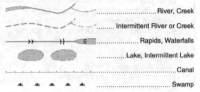

.... River, Creek

.... Intermittent River or Creek

.... Rapids, Waterfalls

.... Lake, Intermittent Lake

....Canal

.... Swamp

SYMBOLS

✪ CAPITAL	.....National Capital	✝	...................Airfield	✕	........................Mine
◉ Capital	....Provincial Capital	⚲	...................Beach	▲	........Mountain, Hill
● City	.... City	⌒	.... Cave	)(	.........................Pass
● Town	.... Town	⛪	.... Church	★	.... Police Post
● Village	.... Village	⌇	.... Cliff	✉	........Post Office
		—500—	.... Contour	100	.... Route Number
		⋈	.... Gate	⁚⁚	....................Ruins
🄰	..........Camping Area	⊕	.... Hospital	◎	...................Spring
🄱	Refugio (un-manned)	❶	Information	☎	Telephone
🄲	... Refugio (manned)	🄻	.... Lookout	♣	.... Transport

Note: not all symbols displayed above appear in this book

The Walks	Duration	Standard	Season
Western Alps			
Alp Money	5½-6 hours	medium	July-Sept
Vallone del Grand Nomenon	8-8½ hours	hard	July-Sept
Piano del Nivolet	7½-8 hours	medium	July-Sept
The Rifugio Walk	6½-7 hours	hard	July-Sept
Best of the Alta Via 2	6 days	hard	July-Sept
Lake District			
Monte Baldo	6½-7 hours	medium	May-Oct
Valle del Singol	6½-7 hours	medium-hard	May-Oct
Monte Grona	5-5½ hours	medium-hard	May-Oct
Sass Corbee	3-3½ hours	easy	May-Oct
Il Rogolone	4-4½ hours	easy	May-Oct
Valle Cannobina	7½-8 hours	hard	May-Oct
Monte Carza	7½-8 hours	hard	May-Oct
Dolomiti			
Parco Naturale Sciliar & Alpe di Siusi	3 days	medium	July-Sept
Northern Dolomiti	5-6 days	easy-medium	July-Sept
Parco Naturale delle Dolomiti d'Ampezzo	4 hours	easy	July-Sept
Parco Naturale Dolomiti di Sesto	2 x 1 day	easy	July-Sept
Alpi Marittime			
Lago di Valscura Circuit	5-6 hours	easy-medium	July-Sept
Terme di Valdieri to Entracque	4 days	hard	July-Sept
Marguareis Circuit	2 days	medium-hard	July-Sept
Liguria			
Sentiero Azzurro	2½-5 hours	easy-medium	all year
Sentiero Rosso	6-8 hours	medium	all year
Portovenere to Levanto Combination	2 days	easy-medium	all year
Promontorio di Portofino Circuit	4½-5½ hours	easy-medium	all year
Volcanoes of Southern Italy			
Vesuvio Long Circuit	3½ hours	easy-medium	all year
Vesuvio Short Circuit	2 hours	easy-medium	all year
Stromboli Circuit	2-3 days	hard	all year
Vulcano	3-4 hours	easy	all year
Mt Etna – Ascent to the Craters	9½-11½ hours	medium	Apr-Oct
Mt Etna Circuit	3 days	medium	Apr-Oct
Amalfi Coast & Sorrento Peninsula			
Monte dell'Avvocata	7-7½ hours	hard	all year
Valle delle Ferriere	5½-6 hours	medium	all year
Capo Muro	8½-9 hours	hard	all year
Sentiero degli Dei	5-5½ hours	medium	all year
Punta Penna	4½-5 hours	easy	all year
Punta Campanella	5-5½ hours	medium	all year
Toscana			
Chianti Classico	3 days	easy	all year
Medieval Hills	3 days	easy	all year
Pizzo d'Uccello	2½ days	medium	July-Sept
Procinto, Monte Forato & Pania della Croce	2 days	medium	July-Sept
Sardegna			
Golfo di Orosei	3 days	medium	all year
Tiscali-Gorropu	3 days	medium	all year
Capo Testa	3 hours	easy	all year

SWITZERLAND

AUSTRIA

HUNGARY

Dolomiti p170

Trentino-
Alto-Adige

Western Alps
p104

Lake District p134

Valle
d'Aosta

Lombardia

Trento

Friuli-
Venezia
Giulia

SLOVENIA

Piemonte

Milano

The Veneto

Torino

Venezia

CROATIA

Alpi Marittime & Liguria p198

FRANCE

Liguria

Emilia-Romagna

Genova

Firenze

BOSNIA
HERCEGOVINA

LIGURIAN
SEA

Toscana

Le
Marche

Umbria

A
D
R
I
A
T
I
C

Corsica
(FRANCE)

Toscana (Tuscany) p297

Abruzzo

S
E
A

ROMA

Lazio

Molise

Campania

Puglia

Napoli

Basilicata

Amalfi Coast &
Sorrento Peninsula
p 275

Sardegna

TYRRHENIAN

SEA

Calabria

Sardegna (Sardinia) p331

Volcanoes of
Southern Italy p233

IONIAN

SEA

Italy (colour country map)
between pp 16 & 17
Domestic Airfares p 98
Index of all maps p 368

Palermo

Sicilia

TUNISIA

MEDITERRANEAN

SEA

MALTA

0   75   150 km

**Walking Regions
Map Index**

Introduction

The key to using this guide effectively is to regard it as an introduction to walking in a country which offers a truly dazzling array of possibilities. Test your skills at high altitudes in the Alps, tackle very scenic day walks in the Western Alps or try challenging longer walks in the less-visited Alpi Marittime.

Even well-travelled walkers gasp when they first set eyes on the spectacular Dolomiti (Dolomites) and those looking for a challenge won't be disappointed. There are lower altitude mountain walks in the Alpi Apuane in Toscana (Tuscany) and in the Lake District further north. You can ramble past olive groves, vineyards and ancient churches in the gentle hills of Chianti; stroll along the coast of Liguria and visit the enchanting villages of the Cinque Terre; head south to meander along the ancient paths and stairways of the

Amalfi Coast, one of the world's most spectacular coastlines; or, if adventure appeals, explore the 'wilds' of Sardegna (Sardinia).

For something really different, you can climb a few of Europe's most active volcanoes: Vesuvio near Napoli (Naples); Stromboli and Vulcano in the Isole Eolie (Aeolian Islands); and Mt Etna, which looms majestically on the eastern coast of Sicilia (Sicily).

This guide aims to give you a taste of walking in Italy. We haven't tried to cover the whole country; rather, we have presented a selection of walks which we think are among Italy's best. There is something for those who want to experience Italy's very generous historical, cultural and artistic offerings on foot. And there are plenty of suggestions for people who want to sample Italy's wonderful *cucina* (cooking) and *vino* (wine) along the way.

Facts about Italy

HISTORY

Italy's strategic position in the Mediterranean made it a target for colonisers and invaders, whose comings and goings over thousands of years have left a people with a diverse ethnic background. But it also gave the Romans, and later the Christian church, an excellent base from which to expand their respective empires. Italy's history is therefore a patchwork of powerful empires and foreign domination, and from the fall of the Roman Empire in 476 AD until the formation of the Kingdom of Italy in 1861, the country was never a unified entity.

The following is a brief outline of the main events in Italian history. See Lonely Planet's *Italy* guide for a more detailed history of the country, otherwise see under Books in the Facts for the Walker chapter for some suggestions on further reading.

c. 70,000 BC – Palaeolithic Neanderthals living on the Italian peninsula.

c. 4000 BC – Neolithic humans start to establish settlements across the peninsula.

c. 1800 BC – Start of the Bronze Age. Italy has been settled by several Italic tribes, including the Ligurians, the Veneti, the Apulians, the Siculi and the Sardi.

12th century BC – The Etruscan people migrate to the Italian peninsula from the Aegeo-Asian area.

8th century BC – Greek settlements established in southern Italy, first on the island of Ischia in the Bay of Naples, followed by others along the peninsula's southern coast and on Sicilia (Sicily). These independent city-states will become known as Magna Graecia (Greater Greece).

753 BC – Traditional date for the foundation of Roma (Rome) by Romulus on 21 April.

7th & 6th centuries BC – Etruscan civilisation at its peak. The nation is based on large city-states, among them Caere (Cerveteri), Tarquinii (Tarquinia), Veii (Veio), Felsina (Bologna), Perusia (Perugia), Volaterrae (Volterra), Faesulae (Fiesole) and Arretium (Arezzo), collectively known as the Etruscan League. During the 6th century, seven Etruscan kings rule Roma.

509 BC – Foundation of the Roman Republic.

5th century BC – Decline of Etruscan civilisation.

413 BC – Athens attacks Syracuse and is defeated in one of the great maritime battles in history.

312 BC – The Via Appia (Appian Way), known as the Regina Viarum (Queen of Roads), is started.

264-241 BC – First Punic War fought between Roma and Carthage over control of Sicilia. Carthage, which has settlements on Sicilia, controls the Mediterranean's maritime traffic in competition with Greece and strongly opposes Roma's expansion. Roma is victorious.

241-218 BC – Roma manages to expel the Gauls from the Italian peninsula, consolidating the frontiers of Italy as we now know them.

218 BC – Hannibal launches his famous offensive, using elephants to cross the Alps, and sparks the Second Punic War with Roma. Hannibal crushes Roman troops in bloody battles as he moves down the peninsula – around Lago di Trasimeno in what is now Umbria and at Cannae in what is now Puglia (Apulia).

202 BC – Hannibal is defeated by the Roman general Scipio at Zama in North Africa.

149-146 BC – The Third Punic War deals the final blow to Carthage. Roma razes the city, destroys all evidence of Carthaginian civilisation and enslaves more than 50,000 survivors.

91 BC – A revolt of the allied peoples of the peninsula against Roma, known as the Social War, is resolved by force. As a result, Roma grants citizenship to the Etruscan people, as well as to all of the Italic peoples on the peninsula.

73-71 BC – A Thracian slave named Spartacus escapes from a school for gladiators at Capua and sparks a second, more bloody Social War. His aim is to secure freedom for his fellow slaves. Eventually joined by some 70,000 runaway slaves, Spartacus is later killed by Roman forces, and some 6000 of his followers are crucified, lining the Appian Way from Capua to Roma.

60 BC – Pompey, Crassus and Julius Caesar form an unconstitutional triumvirate to control the Senate, effectively ending any semblance of government for and by the people.

52 BC – Pompey takes the title of sole consul and dictator, supported by Julius Caesar. Caesar declares southern Britain a part of Roma.

48 BC – Pompey murdered in Egypt. Caesar returns to Roma as consul and dictator.

44 BC – Julius Caesar is murdered on 15 March. It is said that among his murderers are more of his friends than his enemies, including Brutus, his adopted son. Marc Antony is consul for one year following Caesar's death.

27 BC – Caius Octavian, Caesar's adopted son and heir, is declared Roma's first emperor, adopting the title of Augustus, the Grand One. Augustus will rule for more than 40 years, a period of great advancement in engineering, architecture, administration, military arts and literature.

14 AD – Augustus is succeeded by his stepson, Tiberius.

54-68 – The empire is ruled by obviously deranged Nero, best known for the burning of Roma and his persecution of the Christians.

72 – Emperor Vespasian starts the Colosseum in the former grounds of Nero's Golden House.

98-117 – The Roman Empire reaches its point of greatest expansion under the Emperor Trajan.

313 – Emperor Constantine converts to Christianity and makes the Edict of Milan, which officially recognises the Christian religion.

324 – Constantine moves the capital of the empire from Roma to the northern shore of what is now Turkey. The city becomes known as Constantinople (present-day Istanbul).

364 – The ruling brothers Valentinian and Valens divide the empire into a western and an eastern half, a division later formalised by the Emperor Theodosius I in 395.

452 – Attila the Hun invades Italy.

476 – The last Western Roman emperor, Romulus Augustulus, is deposed by the Gothic invader Odovacar.

488-526 – Rule of the Ostrogothic emperor Theodoric, based in Ravenna, marks a period of relative peace in Italy.

527 – The Eastern Roman emperor Justinian and his wife Theodora embark on a reconquest of Roma.

c. 568 – Lombard invasion of Italy.

c. 440 – Pope Leo I cites the Donation of Constantine, which gave the western empire as a gift to the papacy. The document supposedly will be exposed as a forgery during the Renaissance.

590 – Pope Gregory I is elected.

754 – The Franks invade Italy, led by King Pepin, and establish the Papal States.

800 – Pepin's son Charlemagne is crowned emperor in St Peter's Basilica in Roma by Pope Leo III.

831 – Muslim Arabs invade and settle in Sicilia.

962 – The Saxon King Otto I is crowned emperor in Roma and founds the Holy Roman Empire.

11th century – The Normans begin arriving as mercenaries to fight the Arabs in southern Italy.

1091 – The Normans conquer Sicilia.

1095 – The First Crusade is launched.

1130 – The Norman Roger II is crowned king of Sicilia and southern Italy.

1220 – Norman rule in Sicilia gives way to Germanic claims when Frederick II is crowned Holy Roman Emperor. The grandson of Holy Roman Emperor Frederick I (Barbarossa) and son of Constance de Hauteville, heir to the Norman throne, Frederick presides over an exotic, multi-cultural court and becomes known as Stupor Mundi (Wonder of the World).

1232 – Beginning of the Inquisition.

1268 – The French Charles of Anjou takes control of the Kingdom of Sicilia after defeating and beheading Frederick II's grandson, Conradin.

12th to 14th centuries – The city-states evolve in northern Italy and the regional divisions begin to take shape.

1282 – Sicilian Vespers. Sicilians rise up against the Angevins and declare an independent republic. Five months later Peter of Aragon takes control, effectively dividing the south between the Spanish in Sicilia and the French in Napoli.

13th century – Dante Alighieri writes the *Divina Commedia* (Divine Comedy), confirming the Italian vernacular as a serious medium for poetic expression.

13th & 14th centuries – The artist Giotto di Bendone revolutionises painting and helps nurture the forces which spawn the Renaissance. Dominican monk St Thomas Aquinas significantly influences Christian doctrine with his *Summa Theologiae*, which seeks to bridge the gap between the Christian belief in God and Aristotle's respect for the validity of reason.

1305-77 – During a period known as the Babylonian Captivity, the popes reside at Avignon in France. Roma becomes a battleground as its powerful families fight for control of the city.

1347-48 – The Black Death kills more than one third of Italy's population.

1388-1417 – The Great Schism: a period when there are two rival popes, one based in Roma, the other in Avignon.

1451 – Cristoforo Colombo is born in Genova (Genoa).

1453 – Constantinople falls to the Turks, marking the end of the Byzantine Empire.

15th century – Dawn of the Renaissance, a period of unparalleled creativity and visionary accomplishments in all aspects of political, cultural and social life. Lorenzo de' Medici, who rules Firenze (Florence) from 1469 to 1492, is the greatest art patron of the Renaissance. Among the many artists who enjoy his patronage are Michelangelo and Botticelli.

1506 – Pope Julius II employs Donato Bramante to design the new St Peter's Basilica.

1508 – Michelangelo is commissioned to paint the ceiling of the Sistine Chapel.

1527 – The Sack of Roma by Charles V.

1542 – Establishment of the Holy Office, the ruthless final court of appeal in heresy trials.

16th century – The Counter-Reformation; the response of the Church to the Reformation, a movement which aimed to reform the church and led to the rise of Protestantism.

1582 – Pope Gregory XIII introduces Gregorian calendar, fixing 1 January as the first day of the year.

1651 – Giovanni Bernini completes his Baroque masterpiece, the *Fontana dei Fiumi* (Fountain of the Rivers) in Piazza Navona, Roma.

1701-14 – The War of Spanish Succession, resulting in control of Italy passing from Spain to Austria.

18th century – The Enlightenment.

1796 – Napoleon invades Italy.

1804 – Napoleon declares himself Emperor of France and establishes the Kingdom of Italy, naming himself king.

1815 – Napoleon is defeated at Waterloo and the Congress of Vienna restores the prerevolutionary map of Italy, as well as the country's monarchs.

1830 – Giuseppe Mazzini founds the nationalist movement, Young Italy, and later leads a number of abortive uprisings throughout the country.

1848 – Count Camillo Benso di Cavour and Cesare Balbo publish their *Statuto*, which in 1861 will become the constitutional basis for the Kingdom of Italy. Giuseppe Garibaldi returns to Italy from South America and the Italian unification movement gains momentum.

1860 – Leading his Expedition of One Thousand, Garibaldi takes Sicilia and Napoli.

1861 – The Kingdom of Italy is declared and Victor Emmanuel II is proclaimed king. Cavour is appointed prime minister of Italy's first parliament, but dies six months later.

1866 – Venezia (Venice) is wrested from Austria and joins the Kingdom of Italy.

1870 – Roma is reclaimed from Napoleon III and declared the capital of Italy. The pope refuses to acknowledge the Kingdom of Italy.

1914 – WWI, the Great War, breaks out in Europe.

1915 – Italy enters the war mid-year as an ally of France, Britain and Russia.

1919 – Following the end of the Great War, the Conference of Versailles gives Italy Trieste and the South Tyrol (now known as Alto Adige). The area of Trentino is restored to Italy. In the same year, Benito Mussolini founds the Fascist Party.

1921 – Following violent general elections, the Fascist Party wins 35 of the 135 seats in parliament.

1922 – The March on Roma by 40,000 Fascist militia. King Victor Emmanuel invites Mussolini to form a government.

1924 – Following an election campaign marked by violence and intimidation, the Fascist Party wins national elections with 64% of the vote.

1925 – Mussolini expels opposition parties from parliament.

1929 – Mussolini and Pope Pius XI sign the Lateran Pact, under which Catholicism is declared the sole religion of Italy and the Vatican is declared an independent state.

1935 – Italy invades Abyssinia (present-day Ethiopia) and, one year later, annexes the country.

1936 – Mussolini and Hitler form Roma-Berlin Axis.

1940 – Italy enters WWII as an ally of Germany.

1943 – Allied troops land on Sicilia on 10 July. Two weeks later, following a vote by the Fascist Grand Council condemning Mussolini's conduct of the war, the dictator is arrested and the king and parliament take control. The king signs an armistice with the Allies and declares war on Germany. Mussolini is rescued by German troops from a prison on the Gran Sasso and the Republic of Salò is declared. However, northern Italy is effectively controlled by the Germans.

1944-45 – The Allied armies move up the Italian peninsula. The Italian Resistance fights German troops in the north of the country.

1945 – Mussolini and his mistress, Clara Petacci, are captured and shot by partisans in Milano (Milan) in April. Italy is liberated by the end of May.

1946 – Following a referendum, the monarchy is abolished and a republic is established. The newly-formed Democrazia Cristiana (Christian Democrats) win elections.

1957 – Italy is a founding member of the European Economic Community.

1968 – Student uprising and the formation of revolutionary groups.

1969 – A bomb explodes in a bank in Milano's Piazza Fontana, killing 16 people. Neo-Fascist terrorists are blamed.

1970s – The *Anni di Piombo* (Years of the Bullet). Left-wing terrorists, notably the Brigate Rosse (Red Brigades), as well as right-wing terrorists are active throughout the decade.

1978 – Former Prime Minister Aldo Moro is kidnapped and murdered by the Brigate Rosse.

1980 – Right wing extremists are held responsible for a bomb explosion at Bologna train station, in which 84 people die.

1992 – *Tangentopoli*, a massive corruption scandal breaks, eventually implicating many of the country's most important politicians and businesspeople. Anti-Mafia judges Giovanni Falcone and Paolo Borsellino are assassinated by the Mafia in Sicilia.

1993 – The Sicilian godfather, Salvatore 'Toto' Riina, is arrested after 24 years on the run. Bombs planted by the Mafia in Milano, Firenze and Roma kill several people and damage historic monuments, including the Galleria degli Uffizi.

1994 – Voters express their disgust with the extent of the corruption revealed by the Tangentopoli scandal and vote in a new right-wing coalition government. Media magnate Silvio Berlusconi is appointed prime minister.

1995 – Berlusconi's government collapses after only nine months in power.

1996 – A left-wing coalition government is elected. Romano Prodi becomes prime minister.

1997 – Mafia boss Toto Riina is sentenced to life imprisonment for his role in the deaths of judges Falcone and Borsellino.

GEOGRAPHY

Italy's boot shape makes it one of the most recognisable countries in the world, with the island of Sicilia appearing at the toe of the boot and Sardegna (Sardinia) situated in the middle of the Tyrrhenian Sea to the west of the mainland.

The country is bounded by four seas, all part of the Mediterranean Sea. The Adriatic Sea separates Italy from Slovenia, Croatia and Montenegro; the Ionian Sea laps the southern coasts of Piemonte, Basilicata and Calabria; and to the west of the country are the Ligurian and Tyrrhenian seas. Coastal areas vary from the cliffs of Liguria and Calabria to the generally level Adriatic coast.

More than 75% of Italy is mountainous, with the Alps stretching from the Golfo di Genova (Gulf of Genova) to the Adriatic Sea north of Trieste and dividing the peninsula from France, Switzerland, Austria and Slovenia. The highest Alpine peak is Mont Blanc (Monte Bianco) on the border with France, standing at 4807m, while the highest mountain in the Italian Alps (Le Alpi) is Monte Rosa (4634m) which rests on the Swiss border.

The Alps are divided into three main groups – western, central and eastern – and undoubtedly are at their most spectacular in the Dolomiti (Dolomites) in the eastern Alps in Trentino-Alto Adige and the Veneto.

The Appennini (Apennines) form a backbone extending for 1220km from Liguria, near Genova, to the tip of Calabria and into Sicilia. The highest peak is the Corno Grande (2914m) in the Gran Sasso d'Italia group in Abruzzo. Another interesting group of mountains, the Alpi Apuane (Apuan Alps), is found in north-west Toscana (Tuscany) and forms part of the sub-Appennini. These mountains are composed almost entirely of marble and, since Roman times, have been mined almost continuously. Michelangelo selected his blocks of perfect white marble at Carrara in the Alpi Apuane.

Lowlands, or plains, make up less than a quarter of Italy's total land area. The largest plain is the Pianura Padana (Po valley), bounded by the Alps, the Appennini and the Adriatic Sea. The plain is heavily populated and industrialised, and through it runs Italy's largest river, the Po, and its tributaries, the Reno, Adige, Piave and Tagliamento rivers. Other, smaller plains include the Tavogliere di Puglia and the Pianura Campana around Vesuvio (Mt Vesuvius).

GEOLOGY

Italy has a complex geological history, characterised by marked environmental and climatic changes. Around 100 million years ago the area now occupied by the peninsula was covered by a tropical sea, the Tethys, which separated the Euro-Asiatic and African continental plates. As the ocean began to recede, various types of materials were deposited, including limestones, dolomites and sandstones, as well as the extensive coral reefs to the north-east from which the Dolomiti mountain range were later formed (see the Coral Reefs at 3000m boxed text in the Dolomiti chapter). Although earlier volcanic activity resulted in the formation of the original nucleus of the Alpine chain and other mountains further south, the crucial moment came around 40 million years ago when the African and European continental plates collided. The collision forced the respective borders of the plates, and part of the bed of the Tethys, to fold and rise up, beginning the formation of the Alpine and Appennini chains. The Alps rose up relatively quickly, at first forming an archipelago of tropical islands in the Tethys Sea. The curvature of the Alpine and Appennini chains, as well as the transverse orientation of the peninsula itself in the Mediterranean basin, reflect the manner in which the continental plates collided.

Both mountain chains underwent significant erosion, resulting in huge deposits of sand, gravel and clay at their feet and in part preparing the way for the development of land areas including Toscana. It is interesting to note that around six million years ago, when both the Alps and the Appennini were still largely submerged, the Straits of Gibraltar closed up completely. As a result, the

Mediterranean Sea, which was all that remained of the vast Tethys, began to dry up.

The Straits of Gibraltar reopened around two million years ago, allowing the Atlantic Ocean to refill the Mediterranean. Some scholars have suggested that this ancient geological event could have given rise much later to the Atlantis myth, as well as the biblical story of Noah and the great flood.

By around two million years ago, after much modelling by the combined forces of continental plate movement and erosion, the Italian peninsula had almost arrived at its present-day form. The level of the sea continued to rise and fall with the alternation of ice ages and periods of warm climate, until the end of the last Ice Age around 10,000 to 12,000 years ago.

During periods of expansion, vast glaciers caused the formation of the glacial valleys of the Alps. Glacial valleys are characterised by a wider, more gentle formation than valleys formed by water erosion. There are more than 1000 glaciers in the Alps, remnants of the last Ice Age, which are in a constant state of retreat. The best known in the Italian Alps is the Marmolada glacier on the border of Trentino and the Veneto, a popular spot for summer skiers.

Rock Varieties

Even though Italy is not a large country, it has a great variety of rock types. The Alps are largely formed of crystalline rocks, such as granite and porphyry, and there are also sedimentary rocks, such as limestone, dolomite and sandstone, in the eastern and pre-Alps. Sedimentary rocks are also found throughout the Appennini and in Sicilia and Sardegna. Crystalline and volcanic rocks predominate in Sardegna. Volcanic rocks are also common in Sicilia and along the Tyrrhenian side of the country, consistent with the volcanic activity in these parts of Italy. The country's plains are mainly formed from mixed deposits of gravel, sand and clay.

Earthquakes & Volcanoes

A fault line runs through the entire Italian peninsula, from eastern Sicilia, following the Appennini up into the Alps of Friuli-Venezia Giulia in the north-east of the country. The fault line corresponds to the collision point of the European and African continental plates and means that a good part of the country is subject to seismic activity. Central and southern Italy, including Sicilia, are subject to sometimes devastating earthquakes. The worst this century was in 1908, when Messina and Reggio di Calabria were destroyed by a seaquake registering seven on the Richter scale. Almost 86,000 people were killed by the quake and subsequent tidal wave. In November 1980 an earthquake south-east of Napoli destroyed several villages and killed 2570 people. A more recent earthquake in the central Appennini in September 1997, affecting Umbria and the Marche, killed 10 people and caused part of the vaulted ceiling of the Basilica di San Francesco d'Assisi, in Assisi, to collapse, destroying important frescoes.

Italy has six active volcanoes: Stromboli and Vulcano (in the Aeolian Islands); Vesuvio, the Campi Flegrei (Phlegraean Fields) and the island of Ischia (near Napoli); and Etna (in Sicilia). Stromboli and Etna are among the world's most active volcanoes, while Vesuvius has not erupted since 1944 – a source of concern for scientists, who estimate that it should erupt every 30 years. Etna's most recent major eruption occurred in 1992, when a trail of lava on its eastern flank threatened to engulf the town of Zafferana Etnea. Related volcanic activity produces thermal and mud springs, notably at Viterbo in Lazio and in the Aeolian Islands. Etna gave cause for alarm in early January 1998, when there were minor earth tremors and a series of explosions at the South-East Crater – a small amount of lava even flowed from the crater. At the time of research experts were unable to say if the activity heralded any bigger events. The Phlegraean Fields near Napoli is an area of intense volcanic activity, including hot springs, gas emissions and steam jets. See the Volcanoes of Southern Italy chapter for more detailed information about Italy's volcanoes.

CONSORZIO TURISTICO VAL GARDENA

CONSORZIO TURISTICO VAL GARDENA

CT VAL GARDENA

CONSORZIO TURISTICO VAL GARDENA

NICK TAPP

NICK TAPP

DOTT. SANDRO PRIVITERA

Gentians (top left) are common in Alpine areas; orange lilies (top right) are found throughout southern Europe. Chamois (middle left) and marmots (centre) are wary of intruders; ibex (middle right) may allow walkers to approach. The rowan (bottom left) bears red berries in autumn; *Amanita muscaria* (bottom right) is a poisonous fungus common on Mt Etna.

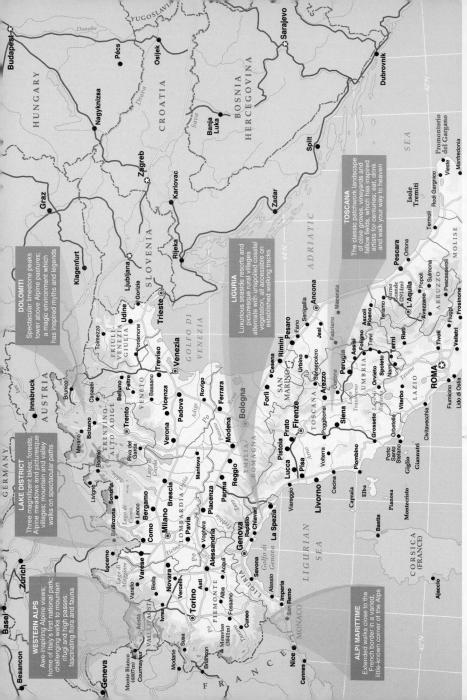

WESTERN ALPS
Awe-inspiring Alpine views;
home of Italy's first national park;
challenging walks to mountain
rifugi and high passes;
fascinating flora and fauna

LAKE DISTRICT
Three magnificent lakes; forests,
Alpine meadows and picturesque
villages; mountain and valley
walks on spectacular paths

DOLOMITI
Spectacular limestone peaks
tower above Alpine pastures;
a magic environment which
has inspired myths and legends

LIGURIA
Luxurious seaside resorts and
picturesque rural villages
alternate with unspoiled coastal
vegetation, all accessible on
established walking tracks

TOSCANA
The classic patchwork landscape
of olive groves, vineyards and
fallow fields, which has inspired
artists for centuries; eat, drink
and walk your way to heaven

ALPI MARITTIME
Extended walks close to the
French border in a varied,
little-known corner of the Alps

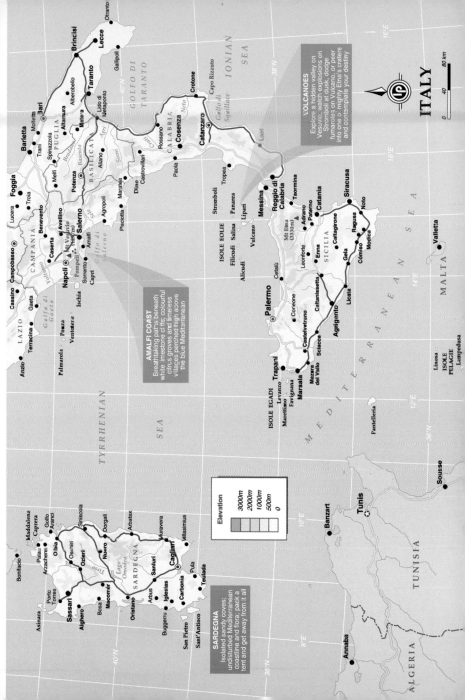

ITALY

VOLCANOES
Explore a hidden valley on Vesuvio, watch explosions on Stromboli at dusk, dodge fumaroles on Vulcano, or peer into one o' mighty Etna's craters and contemplate your destiny

AMALFI COAST
Breathtaking paths beneath white limestone cliffs; colourful citrus groves and timeless villages perched high above the blue Mediterranean

SARDEGNA
Isolated sandy coves; undisturbed Mediterranean coastline and flora; pack a tent and get away from it all

Elevation
3000m
2000m
1000m
500m
0

0   40   80 km

ITALY (labels)

Otranto, Brincisi, Lecce, Taranto, Gallipoli, GOLFO DI TARANTO, IONIAN SEA, Crotone, Capo Rizzuto, Golfo di Squillace, Catanzaro, Rossano, Cosenza, CALABRIA, Neto, Aiaro, Loci, Tropea, Stromboli, Panarea, Lipari, ISOLE EOLIE, Salina, Filicudi, Alicudi, Vulcano, Messina, Reggio di Calabria, Taormina, Palmi, Catania, Adrano, Mt Etna (3350m), SICILIA, Leonforte, Enna, Siracusa, Noto, Ragusa, Cómiso, Modica, Gela, Caltagirone, Cefalù, Caltanissetta, Corleone, Castelvetrano, Sciacca, Licata, Agrigento, Mazara del Vallo, Marsala, Trapani, ISOLE EGADI, Levanzo, Marettimo, Favignana, Palermo, Linosa, ISOLE PELAGIE, Lampedusa, Fantellaria, MALTA, Valletta, MEDITERRANEAN SEA

Brincisi, Lecce, Taranto, Bari, Mollete, Altamura, Alberobello, Lido di Metaponto, Matera, Spinazzola, Trani, Barletta, PUGLIA, Altamura, Melfi, Foggia, Troia, Lucera, BASILICATA, Potenza, Benevento, Campobasso, CAMPANIA, Avellino, Caserta, Napoli, Mt Vesuvio (1277m), Pompei, Salerno, Golfo di Salerno, Sorrento, Amalfi, Capri, Ischia, Agropoli, Piecotta, Maratea, Castrovillari, Aliano, Dino, Paola, Pacia

LAZIO, Cassino, Gaeta, Golfo di Gaeta, Terracina, Anzio, Palmarola, Ponza, Ventotene, TYRRHENIAN SEA

Maddalena, Caprera, Palau, Arzachena, Golfo Aranci, Olbia, Bonifacio, Asinara, Porto Torres, Sassari, Alghero, Ozieri, Osimi, Nuoro, Macomér, Bosa, Oristano, SARDEGNA, Lago Omodeo, Tirso, Santuri, Arbus, Iglesias, Buggerru, San Pietro, Carbonia, Sant'Antioco, Teulada, Pula, Cagliari, Villasimius, Muravera, Arbatax, Dorgali, Siniscola

TUNISIA, Tunis, Banzart, Annaba, ALGERIA, Sousse

38°N, 40°N, 8°E, 10°E, 12°E, 14°E, 16°E, 18°E, 36°N

UGO ESPOSITO

A spectacular night-time eruption on Mt Etna. Etna, with four live craters near its summit as well as hundreds of major and secondary cones, is one of six active volcanoes in Italy. Because of the volatile and dangerous nature of volcanoes, walkers should seek out the latest information regarding safety and observe restrictions on access to craters.

CLIMATE

Situated in the temperate zone and jutting deep into the Mediterranean, Italy is regarded by many tourists as a land of sunny, mild weather. The country's climate is, however, quite variable, because of the length of the peninsula and the fact that it is largely mountainous. In the Alps temperatures are lower and winters are long and severe. Generally the weather is warm enough for walking at high altitudes from July to September, although rainfall can be high in September. While the first snowfall is usually in November, light snow sometimes falls in mid-September and the first heavy falls can occur in early October.

The Alps shield northern Lombardia (Lombardy) and the Lakes area, including Milano, from the extremes of the northern European winter and Liguria enjoys a mild Mediterranean climate similar to southern Italy because it is protected by both the Alps and the Appennini. The Appennini cause considerable climatic difference between the opposite sides of the peninsula.

Toscana's reasonably mild climate should permit you to walk almost year round. Try to avoid walking in July and August, when it can be very hot. As you travel towards the tip of the boot, temperatures and weather conditions become milder.

Roma, for instance, has an average temperature in the mid-20s (Celsius) in July/August, although the impact of the *sirocco*, a hot, humid wind blowing from Africa, can produce stiflingly hot weather in August,

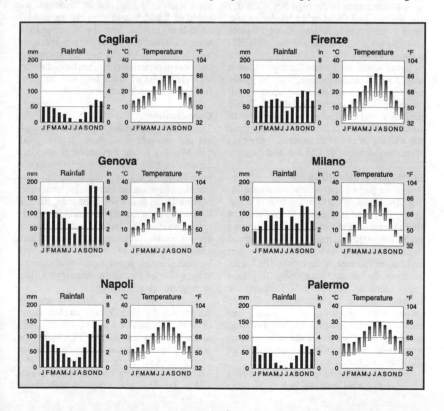

Italy's Climatic Zones

Italy has six main climatic regions, mainly determined by mountain influence:

Alpine Region The climate is strongly influenced by altitude, with long, cold winters and short, cool summers. Rainfall is greater in summer especially in the pre-Alpine areas.

Po Region Winters are cold and often snowy, and summers are warm and sultry. Rainfall is highest in spring and autumn and fog is frequent. The climate is milder in the pre-Alpine area.

Adriatic Region The climate has a continental character because the Adriatic Sea has little influence, due to the fact that its waters are too shallow to trap the summer heat. Winters are characterised by cold north-east winds.

Appennini Region The climate also has continental tendencies. Winters are cold and snowy. Rain is abundant from autumn to spring, and always heavier on the Tyrrhenian slopes.

Ligurian-Tyrrhenian Region This has a maritime climate with frequent, heavy rain (less in summer). Winters are cool and there is a narrow annual temperature range.

Mediterranean Region Summers are hot and dry. Rainfall is heavy, especially in winter, and there is a limited annual temperature range.

---

with temperatures in the high 30s (Celsius) for days on end. Winters are moderate and snow is very rare in Roma, although winter clothing (or at least a heavy overcoat) is still a requirement.

In the south, Sicilia and Sardegna have a mild Mediterranean climate, with long, hot and dry summers and moderate winters with an average temperature of around 10˚C. These regions are also affected by the sirocco in summer. Summer is definitely not the time for walking in any of these areas. Temperatures can rise above 40˚C in July and August.

ECOLOGY & ENVIRONMENT

Whatever part of Italy you are walking in, you'll be struck by the dramatic beauty of the country's varied landscapes. Since Etruscan times humans have had a significant impact on the environment, resulting in widespread destruction of original forests and vegetation and their replacement with crops and orchards. Aesthetically the result is not always displeasing – much of the beauty of Toscana, for instance, lies in the interaction of olive groves with vineyards, fallow fields and stands of cypress and pine. Even soil erosion caused by overuse of the land can become an interesting feature of the landscape – as illustrated by the *calanchi* of Toscana.

Walkers in search of real wilderness might end up being a bit frustrated in Italy. Even in areas such as the interior of Sardegna, the wilds of Calabria and Abruzzo or at high altitude in the Alps, there always seems to be some evidence that someone was there not long before you. Usually this 'evidence' is in the form of litter: many Italians have the very annoying habit of discarding and dumping rubbish when and where they like.

Conservation

The Italian government's record on ecological and environmental issues is not good. The Ministry for the Environment was only created in 1986, and many environmental laws are not adequately enforced. Environmental groups say the increase in the number of devastating floods which have hit parts of northern Italy in recent years are due not only to increased rainfall, but also to deforestation and excessive building near rivers. From 1984 to 1995, 20% of new houses were built without planning permits and environmental groups blamed this on the ministry's failure to regulate urban planning.

Surprisingly, there are still some areas of Italy which the World Wide Fund for Nature (WWF) has classified as wilderness areas, although they constitute 20.8% of the country. Most of these unspoiled areas are above 2000m, largely in the Alps (for example, the Gran Paradiso in Valle d'Aosta, and in Trentino-Alto Adige), which means that mountain walkers are the visitors most likely to enjoy Italy's unspoiled nature. Areas such as Sicilia and Puglia have precious few remaining untouched areas, however almost 40% of Sardegna is classified as wilderness, including the stunning Supramonte-Barbagia-Gennargentu area. The downside is that there are now virtually no protected areas on the island.

Environmental organisations active in Italy include:

Lega Ambiente (Environment League)
 (☎ (06) 86 26 81), Via Salaria 403, 00199, Roma
World Wide Fund for Nature (WWF)
 (☎ (06) 84 49 71), Via Garigliano 57, 00198, Roma
Lega Italiana Protezione Uccelli (LIPU, the Italian Bird Protection League)
 (☎ (06) 39 73 09 03), Piazzale Clodio 13, Roma

National Parks & Reserves

Italy's national parks and nature reserves cover about 1.2 million hectares, or a little more than 4% of the country. There are 17 national parks, plus three more in the process of being instituted, and 421 smaller nature reserves, natural parks and wetlands. Together they account for almost two million hectares of protected land (6.63% of the country). Italy's environmentalists have been campaigning for years to bring the protected areas up to 10% of the country. They have had some success. In the period from 1922 to 1991, only five national parks were created in Italy and their management left a lot to be desired. However, a law on protected areas passed in 1991, allowed for the creation of 14 new national parks. A few of these are shrouded in controversy and are yet to be realised; others have been created but management infrastructure is still to be established.

The five so-called historical national parks are Parco Nazionale del Gran Paradiso, Parco Nazionale d'Abruzzo, Parco Nazionale del Circeo, Parco Nazionale dello Stelvio and Parco Nazionale della Calabria. The new parks include Parco Naturale della Val Grande (Piemonte), Parco Nazionale delle Dolomiti Bellunesi (Veneto), Parco Nazionale delle Foreste Casentinesi (Emilia-

Romagna), Parco Nazionale dei Monti Sibillini (Le Marche/Umbria), Parco del Gran Sasso-Laga (Abruzzo), Parco Nazionale della Maiella (Abruzzo), Parco Nazionale del Vesuvio (Campania), Parco Nazionale del Cilento (Campania), Parco Nazionale del Gragano (Puglia), Parco Nazionale del Pollino (Basilicata/Calabria) and Parco Nazionale dell'Aspromonte (Calabria).

Parco Nazionale del Gran Paradiso This was Italy's first national park, created in 1922 after the country's King Victor Emmanuel II gave his personal hunting reserve to the state. The park incorporates about 70,000 hectares of Alpine valleys and peaks and straddles the regions of Valle d'Aosta and Piemonte. An original priority of the park was the preservation of the ibex, which had been hunted almost to extinction (see Italy's First National Park boxed text in the Western Alps chapter for more detailed information about this park).

Parco Nazionale d'Abruzzo Established in 1923, with a former royal hunting reserve as its nucleus, this park now incorporates about 40,000 hectares of the Appennini (plus an external protected area of 60,000 hectares). This park has become a model of modern park management, demonstrating that local residents can participate in and benefit from nature conservation. Efforts to reintroduce animals once threatened with extinction, including the Marsican brown bear, the Appennini wolf, the chamois and even the European lynx are having varying degrees of success.

Parco Nazionale del Circeo This coastal wetlands reserve south of Roma was established in 1934. However, neglect and real estate speculation almost led to its demise in the 1970s. Despite laws protecting the reserve, local government bodies continued to grant permits for building within its boundaries. A great deal of effort has been put into recuperating this tiny park (only 8400 hectares) and it is a haven for a wide variety of water birds.

Parco Nazionale dello Stelvio Established in 1935 to protect the Alpine environment of the majestic Ortles-Cevedale group, the Stelvio is Italy's largest national park. The Ortles-Cevedale group includes some of Italy's highest mountains, including Ortles itself (3905m) and the Gran Zebru (3859m). The park straddles the regions of Lombardia and Trentino-Alto Adige.

Parco Nazionale della Calabria This park is made up of three separate areas in the Calabrian Appennini: the Sila Grande, the Sila Piccola and the Aspromonte. It was established in 1968. The geographical separation of the three areas created serious difficulties for the park's management, problems compounded by the lack of local support for the protection of the environment. In the Aspromonte alone, it is estimated that there are 20 hunters per square kilometre. In 1991, the Aspromonte section of the park was extended and instituted as one of Italy's 14 new national parks.

Endangered Species
The alteration of the environment, combined with the Italians' passion for *la caccia* (hunting), has led to many native animals and birds becoming extinct, rare or endangered. Hunters are a powerful lobby group in Italy: they continue to win the day in regular referenda on whether hunting should be banned.

In the 20th century, 13 species have become extinct in Italy, including the Alpine lynx, aquila di mare (white-tailed eagle) and the crane. Under laws progressively introduced in this century, many animals and birds are now protected. The WWF has released a *Lista Rossa* (Red List) of threatened vertebrates in Italy. The 120-page document claims that 60% of Italy's vertebrates are at risk.

Among those which are very slowly making a comeback after being reintroduced in the wild are: the brown bear, which survives only in the Brenta area of Trentino; the Marsican bear, which has been reintroduced in Abruzzo; and the lynx, which is extremely rare and found mainly in the area around Tarvisio in Friuli-Venezia Giulia. Efforts are also underway to reintroduce the lynx in Abruzzo. Wolves are slightly more common, although you will still be very hard pressed to spot one in the wild. There is a large enclosure at Civitella Alfadena in Abruzzo National Park, where you'll be able to see some wolves.

There are only about 100 otters left in Italy and most live protected in Parco Nazionale del Cilento, in Campania. Another extremely rare animal is the monk seal: only about 10 are thought to survive in sea caves on the east coast of Sardegna. The magnificent golden eagle was almost wiped out by hunters and now numbers about 300 couples spread throughout the country. A colony of griffon vultures survives on the western coast of Sardegna near Bosa. The bearded vulture was reintroduced in the Alps in the past decade (see 'Gipeto – The Bearded Vulture' boxed text in the Western Alps chapter for more information about this bird, known in Italy as the *gipeto).*

POPULATION & PEOPLE
The population of Italy is 58.3 million, according to 1995 estimates. The birth rate was put at 10.89 per thousand in 1995, one of the lowest in Europe and below the EU average of about 12 per thousand – surprising given the Italians' preoccupation with children and family.

Heavily populated areas include those around Roma, Milano and Napoli, Liguria, Piemonte (Piedmont) and parts of Lombardia, the Veneto and Friuli-Venezia Giulia. The most densely populated spot in Italy – in fact the most populous in the world after Hong Kong – is Portici, a suburb of Napoli located directly under Vesuvio.

There is only a small minority of non-Italian-speaking people, which includes German speakers and speakers of the ancient Ladin language in Alto Adige (in the province of Bolzano) and a tiny French-speaking minority in the Valle d'Aosta.

The Ladin language and culture trace their ancestry to around 15 BC, when the people

continued on page 39

Flora & Fauna of Italy

ALPINE FLORA

Several Ice Ages over the last million years repeatedly forced cold-resistant highland plants to move down to lower areas in order to survive. Following the last Ice Age, new plants steadily re-colonised the Alps, so the Alpine flora actually consists of relatively recent arrivals. For this reason there are few highly-specialised plants in the Alps.

In the mountains the growing season (essentially the snow-free period) becomes shorter with increasing altitude, and therefore Alpine plants take longer to recover from any setback in their growth cycle. Walkers should always consider this, and take particular care to avoid damaging the fragile flora of the Alps.

Vegetation Zones

Hiking up from valley floor to mountain summit, walkers will notice that the vegetation changes in stages, becoming progressively smaller in stature and more sparsely distributed. Botanists describe the Dolomiti environment according to five zones:

Lower Montane (up to 1400m) This is the pasture zone which has always supplied winter forage and which is still used today, regardless of the steep slopes. The pastures are frequently interrupted by wooded patches which are characterised by the red spruce *(Picea excelsa)*, by a few beeches *(Fagus)* and by silver firs *(Abies alba)*. In higher areas, soil-poor and sunny, the Scots pine *(Pinus sylvestris)* begins to appear.

Upper Montane (1400m to 1700m) Characterised by the red spruce, sometimes together with or alternate to the European larch *(Larix decidua)*, with the rare presence of the green alder *(Alnus viridis)* and, on the right terrain, the scots pine.

Subalpine (1700m to 1900m) Predominantly populated by the European larch, sometimes along with the red spruce, but often with the arolla pine *(Pinus cembra)*.

Alpine (1900m to 2200m) The transitional zone between the woods and the Alpine prairie, characterised by underbrush formations made up for the most part of alpenroses *(Rhododendron ferrugineum)*, dwarf pine *(Pinus mugo)*, bilberry *(Vaccinium myrtillus)*, green alder and numerous species of willow. In some areas at this altitude, there can even be some isolated, twisted larches and arolla pines.

High Alpine (2200m to 2800m) Here we find the pioneer Alpine vegetation rich in species, with many native grasses and more than 100 common wild flowers. Plants rooted in the rock face and boulders, almost always perennial, small, low to the ground with deep roots and very brightly coloured flowers. The acid or basic composition of the fine layer of soil determines the occurrence of the species growing in a given area.

Mountain Trees

The original tree cover of extensive areas of the Alps and Pre-Alps was cleared over the centuries to make way for pasturelands. However, at altitudes around 2000m, you begin to reach the 'true' Alpine pastures – areas above the tree line. The average tree line (timberline) in the Italian Alps varies widely – from 1700 to 2300m above sea level. Many tree species are essentially Eurasian – that is, they range from Western Europe into Siberia. Some of the trees most commonly encountered in the mountains of Italy are described below.

Arolla Pine (Pino Cembro) Like the larch, the arolla pine (*Pinus cembra*) is a true high-mountain tree that grows only at upper elevations, and is rarely found below 1300m. Arolla pine has a similar form to other mountain pines (such as *Pinus montana*), but uniquely it has five needles on each bunch rather than the two of other Italian mountain pine species. The purplish-brown cones contain resinous edible nuts that provide an important food source for birds, squirrels and foxes. The arolla pine can withstand the extreme conditions well above the normal forest line, with the highest specimens found at around 2850m! Under the harsh conditions of these high-altitude environments the tree takes on a twisted and weathered form, yet may live to a thousand years of age with a 1.5m-thick trunk.

Beech (Faggio) The beech *(Fagus sylvatica)* is one of Italy's most abundant broad-leaf trees. Preferring moist locations in the montane zone, beech form almost pure-stand forests in practically every region. The trees are easily identified by their smooth, pearl-grey bark, often attaining a height of 45m and an age of 300 years. Beech forests are rich ecosystems and make attractive areas for walking. The oily beech nuts provide an important source of food for many birds and animals, particularly squirrels, pheasants and wild boar. The oval-shaped leaves of the beech are light-green in spring, dark-green in summer and golden-brown in autumn, when they fall in a thick carpet over the forest floor; covering foot tracks, beech leaves can create a slippery (and potentially dangerous) walking surface for the unwary walker.

European Larch (Larice) Unique among Italian conifers, the European larch *(Larix decidua)* is a dooiduous tree that turns a striking golden colour before the first autumn storms strip the needles from the branches. If the needles fall into a lake, an interesting phenomenon may sometimes be observed where the needles are rolled together to form so-called 'larch-balls'. In order to thrive, larch demands sunny and dry conditions, and is therefore very common in areas with a 'continental' climate. This highland species grows right up to the tree line, often in beautiful open stands with a heather underbrush. Larch wood is harder and more weather resistant than any other type of timber, and for centuries it has been a favoured building material among mountain communities.

Mountain Maple (Acero Oppio) The mountain maple *(Acer pseudoplatanus)* sometimes reaches an age of 500 years and a height of 40m. Its characteristic form is a broadly-spread crown above a thick and gnarled old trunk. The mountain maple prefers moist sites between the high-montane and Alpine zones, where it frequently colonises old screeslides. Being a particularly hardy tree it is often planted along roadsides, and in autumn its large leaves turn a striking golden yellow.

Also known as the Swiss stone pine, the arolla pine is originally from the Carpathian Mountains in southern Romania.

European larch trees provide the wood from which Venetian turpentine is produced.

The red and yellow male flowers of the red spruce are distinguishable from the more brightly coloured purple varieties of female flowers.

Mountain Pine (Pino Cembro) Another larger conifer of the high mountains is the mountain pine *(Pinus montana)*. This tree may grow to 20m in height, frequently occupying rocky ground or stabilised talus slopes where it may form pure stands. The mountain pine has oval-shaped cones with two-needle branchlets.

Red Spruce (Abete Rosso) The red spruce *(Picea excelsa)*, also called Norway spruce, is a densely foliated conifer whose cones point downwards. Foresters and farmers have favoured this useful and fast-growing tree for centuries, and as a result the red spruce is ubiquitous throughout Italy's Alpine areas, where it forms closed forests at altitudes of up to 1800m. The red spruce has shown itself to be particularly susceptible to damage by acid rain and the bark beetle.

Silver Fir (Abete Bianco) The silver fir *(Abies alba)* is similar in appearance to, but somewhat less common than, the red spruce. Although it prefers rather lower altitudes – rarely growing above 1200m – the silver fir's range also overlaps with the red spruce and the two species are often found together. The silver fir is most easily distinguished from the red spruce by its cones, which protrude upwards like candles, and by the slight whitish tinge to its branches and trunk.

Sweet Chestnut (Castagno) The sweet chestnut *(Castanea sativa)* is an attractive, large tree with slightly serrated and elongated leaves, developing hairy capsules that split open in autumn to release the ripe brown nuts. Rich in carbohydrates, sweet chestnuts were a staple food for many mountain-dwellers, who would bake bread using flour ground from the dried nuts. The chestnut tree grows throughout Italy at altitudes of 300m to 1000m.

Alpine Heathland Plants

Alpenroses or Alpine Rhododendrons (Rododendro) Alpine rhododendrons typify the high-Alpine landscape perhaps more than any other species of plant. Two species of rhododendron grow in the Italian Alps, the rust-leaved alpenrose *(Rhododendron ferrugineum)* and the hairy alpenrose *(R. hirsutum)*, often forming lovely rolling Alpine heaths at altitudes up to 2500m. Easily the more common of the two is the rust-leaved alpenrose, which is partially protected and is found mainly in the central Alps; its flowers are dark-red and it has smooth-sided leaves whose undersides are a rusty-brown colour. The less common hairy alpenrose, which is protected, has bright-red blooms and grows in limestone soils; the undersides of its leaves are green.

Bilberry (Mirtillo) A relative of the cultivated blueberry, the bilberry *(Vaccinium myrtillus)* is a heavily branched shrub reaching up to half a metre in height. It is a true Alpine species whose natural distribution is generally well above 1500m, where it often grows interspersed with larch or mountain pine forest if not above the tree line. Rich in vitamin C, the berries have a tangy flavour which tempts many a walker to stop and pick. In autumn the leaves of the bilberry turn a rusty-red hue, giving a melancholic feel to the highland slopes.

The bilberry is originally a native of the UK. Its fruits are often gathered for making crostate (tarts) and jam.

Dwarf Pine (Pino Mugo) The dwarf pine *(Pinus mugo)* grows mostly above the tree line, typically forming semi-prostrate thickets up to 2m high on exposed Alpine slopes. It has thick, deep-green needles in tufts of two. Being well adapted to harsh conditions, this large, hardy shrub has been successfully planted in coastal land-stabilisation programmes. The dwarf pine can also be found down to 1500m, however, where it grows to be a largish tree of up to 20m that looks rather similar to the mountain pine. Due to the patchy nature of its distribution, the dwarf pine has developed into several subspecies.

Dwarf Willows (Salice) Some of the most interesting plants of the Alpine heaths are the half-dozen or so dwarf willows *(Salix* spp) which grow in sheltered sites over 1500m above sea level and can be found up to 2500m or more. The lesser willow *(S. herbacea)* has pale green, thinly serrated leaves about 2cm in length. It's one of the smallest trees in the world, rarely exceeding 5cm in height. The blunt-leaved willow *(S. retusa)* has small, shiny leaves and may reach 80cm or more, often growing up larger rocks which remain warm after nightfall.

The dwarf pine is commonly used to consolidate snow drifts and in so doing prevent avalanches.

Alpine Wild Flowers

The Alps have a florescent diversity and splendour equalled by few other mountain regions of the world. Amateur botanists can delight in learning to recognise the scores of different species of Alpine flora. Each species comes into bloom at a particular time (and/or at different elevations), so from spring to mid summer (May to late July) the Alpine slopes always offer something interesting. There are numerous species of anemones buttercups, daisies, gentians, lilies and orchids to name just a few.

A very incomplete selection of Alpine wild flowers appears below.

Alpine Aster (Astro Alpino) The Alpine aster *(Aster alpinus)* is a small daisy-like wild flower found only in limestone regions, typically on cliffs or well-drained mountain slopes. It blooms throughout the summer months, and the flowers have elongated bluish petals radiating around a strikingly yellow centre.

Alpine Poppy (Papavero Alpino) The Alpine poppy *(Papaver alpinum rhaeticum)*, sometimes called the Rhaetian poppy, is found only in the western Alps at elevations above around 2000m. The flower buds hang in a 'nodding' position before opening out into attractive white blooms. It is protected.

Bearded Bellflower (Campanella Barbuta) Another resident of the Alpine zone is the bearded bellflower *(Campanula barbata)*, which grows up to 3000m above sea level. It blooms throughout the summer, and its bell-shaped lilac-blue flowers and elongated leaves are covered with coarse, stiff hairs. Preferring slightly acid soils, the bearded bellflower is fairly common on mountain pastures.

Edelweiss (Stella Alpina) The edelweiss *(Leontopodium alpinum)* prefers sunny and remote mountainsides up to 3500m and blooms from July to September. The entire plant, including the delicate star-shaped flowers, is covered

The Alpine aster is drought tender but still favours the harsh growing conditions of stony ground.

The deeply serrated leaves of the globeflower resemble those of the maple tree.

The flowers of the drought-tender martagon lily are characterised by dark spots on the lighter, more colourful background..

with a white felt-like coating that protects it against dehydration. The edelweiss is quite rare nowadays, and although walkers often still can't resist picking it, this Alpine flower is strictly protected.

Glacier Buttercup (Ranuncolo dei Ghiacciai) The glacier buttercup *(Ranunculus glacialis)*, also called the glacial crowfoot, is probably the hardiest Alpine wild flower of all. Seldom seen below 2000m, the glacier buttercup can survive at elevations of well over 4000m, establishing itself on scree slopes, moraine rubble or crevices in cliffs. The glacier buttercup has five white petals which gradually turn pink. It is protected.

Globeflower (Botton d'Oro) Favouring very moist or even waterlogged sites, the globeflower *(Trollis europaeus)* grows to 60cm in height and is commonly seen along meandering streams in the highland pastures. Blooming in early summer, with its cupped, yellow flowers it bears a passing resemblance to some buttercup species.

Martagon Lily (Martagone) The martagon lily *(Lilium martagon)* has mauve, pink or white petals curled back in a form reminiscent of a sultan's turban. Although not especially common, the martagon lily is one of the Alps' most flamboyant Alpine wild flowers, and blooms in June and July. It is protected.

Noble Wormwood (Genipì Bianco) Although not especially common, noble wormwood *(Artemisia mutellina)* is found throughout the Alps, from the Alpi Marittime through to the eastern Alps. It is a small, delicate plant with numerous little yellow flower buds that typically grows on steep, rocky mountainsides. When rubbed between the fingers the plant gives off an intense, aromatic odour. The noble wormwood has medicinal properties (an infusion made from the leaves is a cure for stomach upsets) and its bitter essence is the flavouring used in vermouth.

Purple Gentian (Genziana Purpurea) Another of the well-represented Alpine wild flowers of the genus *Gentiana*, the purple gentian has fleshy bell-shaped velvet-purple coloured flowers clustered at the end of the single stem up to 60cm high. The purple gentian is found sporadically on mountain pastures and in Alpine heaths, and its roots contain bitter medicinal substances similar to the those of the yellow gentian.

Spring Gentian (Genziana Primaticcia) Spring gentians *(Gentiana verna)* are one of the most attractive and widespread smaller Alpine wild flowers. They are those shy sparkles of violet-blue hiding amongst the Alpine herb fields or pastures. Spring gentians grow close to the ground in clusters and are best seen from April to early June. They are protected.

Thorny Thistle (Cirsio Spinosissimo) Rather common in the Alps, the thorny thistle *(Cirsium spinosissimum)* is often the first larger plant encountered as you descend from the bare high-Alpine slopes into the vegetation line. Growing up to 120cm tall, the thorny thistle has a pale yellow crown with long, spiny leaves. In autumn it dies back and starts to decay, giving off an odour distinctly reminiscent of sour socks.

White Crocus (Zafferano Selvatico) One of the mountain world's real early bloomers is the white crocus *(Crocus vernus)*, an Alpine saffron species. Beginning in March at its lowest elevations of around 1000m, this hardy plant pops its purplish-white flowers straight through the melting spring snows, and until other later species come into flower whole fields are dominated by the white crocus. Such a sight is enough to fill every springtime walker's heart with joy.

Yellow Alpine Pasqueflower (Anemone) Reasonably common on mountain meadows is the yellow alpine pasqueflower *(Pulsatilla sulphurea)*, a pretty Alpine anemone. The plant grows to about 25cm and produces a large, single six-petal flower that blooms from late spring until midsummer. The flower matures into a white, hairy ball that looks vaguely like the head of a dandelion.

Yellow Gentian (Genziana Maggiore) The yellow gentian *(Gentiana lutea)* has an appearance quite unlike other Alpine gentian species, which are mostly small and have bluish flowers. A single plant may reach 70 years of age, each season producing a new thick succulent stem up to 100cm high which dies back again in autumn. The yellow gentian has long leathery cupped leaves and bunched bright yellow flowers. For centuries an astringent essence has been produced from the roots for medicinal purposes.

A late bloomer, the yellow gentian takes 10 years to reach maturity before flowering for the first time.

MEDITERRANEAN FLORA

The plant life of Italy's Mediterranean areas is quite extensive, even though the environment has been subject to extensive interference over the centuries. The forests which once blanketed the foothills of the south of the country have been replaced by a scrub known as the *macchia*, an often very fragrant mix of small trees, shrubs and flowering plants.

Trees

Carob Tree (Carrubo) The carob tree *(Ceratonia siliqua)* is an evergreen typical of the Mediterranean, which grows in coastal areas and up to 500m above sea level. It produces a sweet, edible fruit which is used in the confectionery industry, and as treats for horses.

Cluster Pine (Pino Marittimo) This very picturesque pine tree *(Pinus pinaster)* inspired Respighi's *Pines of Rome*. It is originally a coastal Mediterranean tree, and is a very popular species in the many pine forests which line Italy's beaches. However, its preferred environments are hills and low mountains. It has broad branches, which grow high up on the trunk, giving the tree its characteristic appearance. It has very long needles and elongated pine cones.

Holly (Agrifoglio) The holly tree *(Ilex aquifolium)* is particularly beautiful in winter, with its dark green, spiny leaves and bright red berry-like fruit. It grows in clay soils in forest areas and produces small, white, highly perfumed flowers in April-May. Male and female flowers appear on different trees and the fruit grows on the female tree in summer. The rampant collection of holly branches during the Christmas

In exposed coastal locations, strong winds can cause the cluster pine to take on very picturesque twisted forms.

One of the greatest features of the olive tree is its longevity – specimens can commonly live for 1500 years or more.

period has had a major impact on the tree, which is now on the protected species list of several Italian regions.

Oak Tree (Quercia) A number of types of oak tree grow in Italy. The roverella *(Quercus pubescens)* is considered a pioneer species because of its ability to grow in degraded, poor soils – although it prefers sunny, warm and dry slopes. It reproduces easily, but grows to be not much higher than a bush. The bark of the cork oak (sughera; *Q. suber*) is the most important source of cork (a most important product in this wine-producing country!). It grows mainly in the Appennini, reaching heights of more than 20m. Its spongy light-grey bark is around 5cm thick and can be stripped every six to 12 years. The holm oak (leccio; *Q. ilex*) is typical of the Mediterranean macchia, growing along the coast and up to 600m above sea level. It grows best in warm, dry areas, but has also adapted to the salty winds of the coast and the pollution of city areas. It is an evergreen and a lovely effect is created when the new, lighter coloured leaves appear in spring, mingled with the older, darker leaves.

Olive (Olivastro or Oleastro) This small tree *(Olea europea* ssp *oleaster)* is believed to be the progenitor of today's cultivated olive tree, transported in ancient times from Syria. Its leaves are small and oval-shaped, while those of the cultivated olive tree are large and long, and it produces olives which have very little flesh and contain only a very small amount of oil.

Stone Pine (Pino Domestico) The stone pine *(Pinus pinea)* was imported into Italy in the dim, dark past – much to the delight of Italians, who place great value on its seed, the edible pine nut (pinolo). The tree is, in fact, cultivated largely because of the nuts, since its wood is too light and not resistant enough to be valued as timber.

Willow (Salice) This fast-growing pioneer plant grows along watercourses and colonises bare ground, helping to consolidate river banks and unstable ground. The white willow (salice bianco; *Salix alba*) is very well adapted to growing along watercourses, its flexible branches and elongated leaves offering little resistance to flowing water. It also grows on plains and in mountains up to 900m.

Bushes & Shrubs

Broom (Ginestra) There are several species of broom found in Italy, which have in common a tremendous adaptability and a vivacious yellow flower. The ginestra comune (*Spartium junceum*) is an evergreen shrub with long, thin branches. Its bright yellow flowers bloom from May to August and have a lovely perfume. Due to its adaptability, the plant is often used to consolidate the earth in areas subject to landslide.

Cistus (Cisto) There are 16 species of cistus in Italy, all with large pink or white flowers, which are similar to the wild rose. Cistus is found throughout the Mediterranean and is a typical plant of the macchia. The flowers of the cisto di Montpellier or cisto marino *(Cistus monspeliensis)* contain a strong-odoured balsamic resin which in the past was used for medicinal purposes and today is used in perfume-

One of the most widespread species of the genus, the Montpellier cistus also grows along the north coast of Africa and in the Canary Islands.

making. A pretty plant, with its bunches of white or pink flowers, the cistus grows mainly in coastal areas.

Common Hawthorn (Biancospino) Common hawthorn *(Crataegus monogyna)* is a fast-growing prickly bush which can grow at altitudes up to 900m and is often found in forests of oak trees. In dry soils it is smaller and often grows with broom and cistus to form the classic Mediterranean macchia. The spiny branches of the hawthorn offer a safe haven for nesting birds, while its small, white, perfumed flowers attract insects and its small, dark red fruit, which is rich in vitamin C, provides winter sustenance for birds.

Everlasting (Elicriso) There are 25 species of everlasting found in the Mediterranean basin. A hardy plant, which grows well in arid, stony areas, the everlasting produces densely globular clusters of golden yellow flowers which are very durable and are popular in dried flower arrangements. The elicriso italico *(Helichrysum italicum)* grows mainly in the macchia in rocky areas along the coast. It is a twisted, tormented-looking plant, and its long, grey unrolled leaves have a curry-like smell when crushed.

Juniper (Ginepro) There are several species of juniper found in Italy. One, the ginepro nano *(Juniperus nana)* is found in mountain zones as high as 3000m. It is a small bush, forming dense, cushion-like ground cover, which can be as high as 50cm and extend for metres. It has needle-like, curved leaves. The ginepro coccolone *(J. oxycedrus)* is found throughout the Mediterranean area and grows mainly in arid coastal areas. It is a large bush which grows very slowly and is very long-lived. Its flowers appear in January and the reddish-brown fruit grows the following year. The fruit is a food source for animals.

Lentisk (Lentisco) *(Pistacia lentiscus)* is found widely throughout the Mediterranean basin, growing mainly in coastal areas, where it forms part of the macchia. The lentisk is an evergreen bush, with dark green, leathery leaves. The whole plant has strong acrid odour of resin. Its yellow or reddish-brown flowers bloom from March to June.

Myrtle (Mirto) Another principal plant of the macchia, the myrtle *(Myrtus communis)* grows mainly along the coast in hot, arid areas. It is found throughout the Mediterranean and into Asia Minor. It is a very aromatic plant, with both its leaves and flowers heavily perfumed. The plant's essential oil is extracted for use in perfume-making. Its fruit is also very aromatic and is used to flavour grappa. The myrtle bush blooms in July/August, its flowers are milky white in colour.

Oleander (Oleandro) The oleander *(Nerium oleander)* is a very attractive bush (or small tree) used widely in the south of Italy as a border plant on main roads. Its branches almost all grow from the base of the trunk, giving the bush a very distinctive appearance. It is an evergreen – its leaves dark on top and light underneath. Its flowers are pink or white in colour (cultivated species also produce apricot, yellow and fuschia coloured flowers) and heavily perfumed. The whole plant, particularly the flowers and fruit, is poisonous.

The five-petalled flowers of the myrtle are followed in spring by the blue-black berries used to make grappa.

The strawberry tree is originally from Killarney in Ireland, and its name is considered an Irish joke as the fruit bears little resemblance to a strawberry.

Strawberry Tree (Corbezzolo) The strawberry tree *(Arbutus unedo)* is one of the most characteristic of the Mediterranean plants and is usually found in the macchia along with plants such as the lentisco, erica arborea, fillirea and oleastro. It was in fact selected as Italy's national plant last century after unification. The strawberry tree is an evergreen bush, which can grow very high. It has a short, strong trunk and very contorted branches. Its leaves are shiny and an elongated oval shape and it has pretty white flowers, which appear in autumn. Its reddish-orange fruit, which grow in small bunches, are edible, but not very tasty – they are used to make marmalade and grappa.

Tree Heath (Erica Arborea) Another plant typical of the Mediterranean macchia, the tree heath *(Erica arborea)* is an evergreen shrub which can grow to 7m high. It is a very attractive plant, with small off-white, slightly scented flowers and mid-green leaves.

Flowers

Orchid (Orchide) There are more than 80 species of orchid in Italy, although many are threatened with extinction. The orchid is a delicate plant which reacts badly to any disturbance in its environment – a bad way to be in Italy where few areas remain untouched. Orchids are perennial herbs which have simple stems and leaves, and are characterised by beautiful flowers with three, usually brightly coloured sepals and three petals. One of the petals is always more prominent than the others – this is the labellum, or lip, which is long, fringed or sack-like. Among the more interesting orchids in Italy are those of the genus *Ophrys*, which have a lip resembling a female insect; male insects are tricked into trying to mate with the flower, thus carrying pollen from one plant to another. One of these is the bee orchid (vesparia; *Ophrys apifera*), whose lip resembles a bumblebee – it is a velvety dark brown with yellow markings.

ALPINE FAUNA

As with the flora, many animals that now inhabit the Alpine region migrated there after the Ice Ages. Some, such as the snow hare and snow grouse, came from Arctic regions, while others, like the marmot, were originally inhabitants of Central Asia.

Below is a list of native fauna of interest to walkers. It's worth noting how many species of native animal became extinct in Italy, some of which have since been reintroduced. These include the wolf, the brown bear, the lynx and the bearded vulture – although it is very unlikely that you'll come across any of these animals while walking in the Alps.

Mammals

Large Predators
Brown Bear (Orso Bruno) Being true symbols of wilderness, bears demand a habitat of extensive forest with steep-sided slopes (preferably cliffs) as a protective retreat. While members of the order Carnivora, brown bears *(Ursus arctos)* are primarily vegetarians, eating

Owing to their large size and appetite, brown bears demand a habitat that is rich and abundant in the berries and roots that they devour.

mainly berries and roots, although they also hunt small prey (like marmots) and feed on carrion.

Having now enjoyed protection for more than half a century, Western Europe's populations of wild bears have increased dramatically – with small but resilient populations of brown bears existing in the Trentino region, as well as in the area of the Parco Nazionale d'Abruzzo, where there are approximately 100 bears. An adult brown bear stands about one metre tall when on all fours and has a body length of around 2m. They weigh an average of 375kg.

Lynx (Lince) The largest native European cat species, the lynx *(Lynx lynx)* reaches a maximum length of 1.5m from its head to the tip of its tail. This handsome feline has pointed ears ending in paintbrush-like tufts, a spotted ginger-brown coat and a short thick tail with a black tip. Originally found throughout the Alps and the Appennini, the lynx had been completely wiped out by the beginning of the 20th century. However, it is being re-released into the wild and is once again part of the natural ecosystem in areas including Tarvisio in the eastern Alps and the Parco Nazionale del Gran Paradiso in the western Alps, where it inhabits high rocky areas during the summer and comes down to the valleys in winter. There is also a project to reintroduce the lynx in the Parco Nazionale d'Abruzzo. With a territorial range of up to 300 sq km, lynx typically prey on birds and small mammals, including the roe deer (capriolo). They present absolutely no danger to humans and are totally protected.

Wolf (Lupo) No other animal has been hated and persecuted by man as much as the wolf *(Canis lupus)*. Hunted almost to extinction throughout Europe, its natural habitat and prey seriously degraded, the wolf has gained a new image as a victim. Intensive efforts led by the WWF are under way in Italy to save the animal, including programmes of reintroduction to areas such as the Parco Nazionale d'Abruzzo. There are only between 350 and 400 wolves left in Italy, living in the most isolated, mountainous areas – although illegal hunting is reducing even those low numbers by up to 30 a year. It is very unlikely you'll come across one in the wild – at least not in the near future.

Small Predators

Badger (Tasso) Despite being a member of the stoat and marten family, the badger *(Meles meles)* is more an omnivorous scavenger, as much accustomed to feeding on seeds and fruits as snails, birds or small mammals. Badgers are outstanding diggers, building surprisingly complex burrows, with several entrances and sleeping chambers. A social animal, the badger lives in family groups, visiting and overnighting in neighbouring burrows. Legendary for its cleanliness, the badger leaves no remains of its prey after feeding and – hikers take note! – carefully buries its excrement in neat funnel-shaped holes. Although they produce small litters only sporadically, badgers have few natural enemies and reach a comparatively old age.

Marten (Martora) Cousins of weasels and stoats, several species of these small omnivorous hunters live in Italy. The adaptable stone marten *(Martes foina)* is brown except for

Typically a solitary animal, the lynx hunts by stalking its prey and then using its superior speed to pounce and capture it.

In addition to avoiding the clutches of brown bears, martens also have to be wary in the winter months of cages placed to trap them for their pelts.

Widespread immunisation of red foxes through-out Europe has substantially lessened the prevalence of rabies in this species.

a white patch on the collar and ranges from lowland areas to well above the tree line. The stone marten has settled in urban areas, where it may nest in the crevices of buildings or disused pipes etc. The tree marten *(M. martes)* is almost identical to the stone marten, but inhabits undisturbed montane forests. An excellent climber, the tree marten preys mainly on squirrels and mice, but also feeds on nuts, berries, insects and birds.

Red Fox (Volpe) The red fox *(Vulpes vulpes)* is found throughout Italy and is often seen by walkers. This intelligent opportunist can adapt to widely varying environments – from remote Alpine to densely populated urban – although it thrives in areas of mixed field and forest. The fox may dig its own burrow, but prefers to enlarge an existing rabbit warren and may even co-inhabit the burrow of a badger. In April or May the vixen produces a litter of up to six whelps, which she takes with her on the hunt after just one month. Mice are the staple prey of foxes, but they'll eat anything from frogs to beech nuts.

Stoat (Ermellino) This smallest predator hunts rabbits, mice or birds. Living in forested areas, the stoat *(Mustela erminea)* has a reddish-brown summer coat that turns a snow-white for the winter season (when the animal is referred to as an ermine). The stoat kills its prey by biting deeply into the back of the head with its sharp teeth. For better observation of their surroundings, stoats often stop and sit up on their hind legs in a 'begging' position.

Large Herbivores
Chamois (Camoscio) A member of the antelope family, the chamois *(Rupicapra rupicapra)* is another animal characteristic of the Alpine zone. Adapted to the mountain environment at least as well as the ibex, chamois are excellent climbers and jumpers, with spread hooves to avoid sinking into the snow. The animals have short crook-shaped horns and a summer coat of reddish-brown with a black stripe along the spine. Their diet consists of lichen, grass, herbs or pine needles.

Although generally shy, chamois are quite abundant in Alpine regions and mountain walkers have an excellent chance of spotting them.

A small population of pure-bred ibex of Italian origin were used as the basis for repopulating the ibex communities of the Alpine region.

Ibex (Stambecco) A true mountain species, ibex *(Capra ibex)* have an outstanding adaptation to the Alpine environment. These long-horned beasts normally stay well above the tree line, moving to the warmer south-facing mountain-sides in winter. Ibex are related to domesticated goats, and will occasionally breed with farm animals if unable to find a mate in the wild. Once relentlessly hunted for the (supposed) medicinal properties of the flesh and horns, by the early 19th century there were almost no ibex left in Italy. A small group of less than 100 remained on the Gran Paradiso, which later became the nucleus of a programme of reintroduction of the ibex throughout the Alps. The Parco Nazionale del Gran Paradiso was created in 1922 at the initiative of Italy's King Victor Emmanuel II, whose main objective was the preservation of the ibex. There are now about 6000 ibex in the park and a further 16 or so groups throughout the Alps.

Less timid and more curious than chamois, ibex are the most frequently sighted game animal in the Alps. Feeding

on Alpine herbs, grasses and lichens, ibex are typically seen in small herds on craggy mountain ridge tops, from where they can survey the surrounding slopes. As long as walkers stay on their downhill side, ibex will generally allow you to approach within a reasonable distance.

Re
fo
na
nu
tir
ot
re
de
st
fa

R
((
te
a
ir
b

V
in
a
c
a

...ually eradicated from the ... hunting until migrations ...brought it back to a com-

Wild boar are common in Italy and it is possible that walkers will come across them. Wallowing holes and turned-up ground left by foraging animals are an unmistakable indication of their presence. Wild boar are unpopular with farmers, whose crops they sometimes raid; foresters, however, value wild boar highly, since they destroy tree pests and prepare the ground for natural seeding.

Smaller Mammals

Alpine Marmot (Marmotta) Living in colonies of around 50 individuals, marmots *(Marmota marmota)* prefer sunny, grassy slopes between 1300m and 2700m. In June, females give birth to two to four young, which reach maturity within just two months. Marmots build extensive burrow systems, and with the first snowfalls seal off the burrow entrance with grass and stones before beginning a long winter hibernation. During this time they survive exclusively on fat reserves built up over the summer.

Extremely alert and wary, at the slightest sign of danger marmots let out a shrill whistling sound to warn other members of the colony, which immediately head for the underground shelter. Due to their slim and agile form in spring and early summer marmots can be difficult to spot; they are most easily observed in the autumn when slowed down by their heavy fat reserves. A pair of binoculars and a discreet manner of approach are the best tricks for observing marmots in the wild.

Red Squirrel (Scoiattolo) The red squirrel *(Sciurus vulgaris)* is protected in Italy, but it is not as difficult as you might think to spot these small arboreal rodents in coniferous forests, parks and gardens up to an altitude of 1800m. This shy creature rarely leaves the treetops, where it largely feeds on pine or beech nuts. In autumn, squirrels

In the past, Alpine marmots often formed the basis of family meals in the Alpine regions of Italy.

The Alpine chough is distinguished from the red-billed chough by its yellow feet and bill and its smaller size.

bury the nuts as food reserves, but winter snows make these storage spots hard to find. Since some seeds stay in the ground to germinate, squirrels make an important contribution to the regeneration of their forest habitat.

Snow Hare (Lepre Variabile) The snow hare *(Lepus timidus)* inhabits the Alpine zone from 1600m right up to 3400m. Somewhat smaller than the lowland subspecies, in summer the snow hare has reddish-brown fur with white-tinged ears and feet, but in winter the entire coat turns snowy-white. Widely distributed throughout the Alps, it typically feeds on twigs and grasses found in Alpine heathlands. Snow hares are solitary and nocturnal creatures, and are therefore seen only sporadically.

Birds

Alpine Chough (Gracchio) The Alpine chough *(Pyrrhocorax graculus)* and the red-billed chough (gracchio corallino; *P. pyrrhocorax)*, the former with pitch-black feathers, a yellow beak and feet and the latter with coral-coloured beak and feet, are both found at up to 4000m. A relative of the common crow, this hardy opportunist is an ever-present companion throughout the mountains. They are often seen swooping around mountain-top restaurants in search of discarded food scraps, but walkers should refrain from deliberately feeding them. The birds normally feed on worms, insects or berries.

Bearded Vulture (Gipeto Barbuto) With a wingspan measuring up to 2.8m and a body length of more than 1m, the bearded vulture *(Gypaetus barbatus)* is Europe's largest bird of prey. This bird, also known as the lammergeier, was mercilessly persecuted as a supposed predator of sheep, and finally became extinct in Italy. Having been reintroduced into the wild only in the last decade, the bird still occupies a tenuous niche in the Alpine habitat.

The bearded vulture typically preys on marmots or hares, but finds plenty to eat during the long Alpine winter when animals are killed by avalanches or fall to their death due to icy conditions. In March, when such carrion is most plentiful, the vulture raises its brood. Living in strongly-bonded pairs, bearded vultures generally nest on exposed cliff ledges to allow for better takeoff. The birds vigorously defend their territory – an area as large as 80 sq km – against intruding fellow species, and territorial fights commonly end in the death of one of the birds.

The plumage of the bearded vulture is slate-black in colour, apart from a darker stripe by its eyes. Unlike other vulture species, its head is completely covered with feathers, with a tuft of bristle-like plume under the chin. Even from a relatively close distance, the bearded vulture is hard to distinguish from the golden eagle.

Black Woodpecker (Picchio Nero) The largest European woodpecker, the black woodpecker *(Dryocopus martius)* is found in fir and hardwood forests at altitudes of 1000m to 1800m and feeds on insects that live in the bark of trees. It has black feathers and is capped with red. Building its nest in tree cavities, it is very timid and difficult to spot.

Capercaillie (Gallo Cedrone) The capercaillie *(Tetrao urogallus)* is the largest of the Alpine tetraonidae. The male

Boasting a wingspan of 2.8m, the bearded vulture is a ferocious-looking sight.

has a beautiful black plumage. They live in the woods at between 1300m and 1800m and eat bilberries and other berries in the summer, fir needles and buds in winter, and are prey to night predators such as owls and foxes.

Eagle Owl (Gufo Reale) The largest of the night predators, the eagle owl *(Bubo bubo)* lives on rocky cliff faces and hunts birds and rodents at between 1000m and 1800m in the thick of the forest. It is yellow-brown in colour, with dark brown or black markings, and has a flat head with tufts above its ears. The eagle owl is a skilled predator which catches its prey on the wing. It is difficult to spot, but it is easier to find its compact egg-shaped droppings with the bones, skin and feathers of its prey.

Golden Eagle (Aquila Reale) Although sometimes called the king of the Alps, the golden eagle *(Aquila chrysaetos)* was once less common in the Alpine zone. This majestic bird actually took refuge in the mountains to escape human persecution in its original lowland habitat. With a wingspan of up to 2.5m, the eagle can be observed gliding around the highest peaks seeking its prey. Marmots are the bird's staple food, but it also regularly attacks larger animals trapped in snowdrifts or injured by falls. The golden eagle is now fully protected throughout Italy.

Hazel Grouse (Francolino di Monte) The most visible of the tetraonids, the hazel grouse *(Testrastes bonasia)* lives in the dense and humid fir and hardwood forests between 1300m and 1800m. It eats insects, berries, leaves and, in winter, also wood. It is the preferred prey of the marten, but is also hunted by foxes and birds of prey.

Nutcracker (Nocciolaia) A member of the crow family, this bird *(Nucifraga aryocatactes)* has dark brown feathers, spotted with white, and a dark brown cap. It has an undulating way of flying and feeds on the nutritious seeds of the arolla pine. It lives above the tree line. It is likely that you will see this bird while walking.

Snow Finch (Fringuello Alpino) Like the snow grouse, the small white, black and brown-coloured snow finch *(Montifringilla nivalis)* is an exclusively Alpine bird. Never venturing below the tree line even in winter, it nests in very high sites up to 3000m – anywhere from sheltered nooks in mountain huts to crevices on sheer mountain walls. Normally eating insects and seeds, the snow finch (which is really a member of the sparrow family) has a tendency to scrounge for food scraps around sites frequented by humans.

Snow Grouse (Pernice Bianca) The snow grouse *(Lagopus mutus)*, also known as the ptarmigan, is a true mountain species well adapted to the Alpine zone – it is able to live year-round at altitudes of 2000m to 2800m. In winter, the bird digs itself an insulating cavity in the snow, wandering the exposed, snow-free slopes in search of food during the day. Like the stoat and the mountain hare, the snow grouse camouflages itself for the winter by turning from a sprinkled brown to a snowy-white colour. With the sprouting of the mountain vegetation in spring, the snow grouse feeds on the protein-rich new shoots, moving progressively up the mountainside as the summer awakens.

The snow finch has adapted very well to the presence of humans, resorting to scavenging at human sites when food is scarce.

The snow grouse has adapted to the harshness of the Alpine environment by developing protection mechanisms to survive through the winter months.

Reptiles

Snakes
Adder (Marasso) & Common Viper (Vipera Comune)
The adder *(Vipera berus)* and the common viper *(Vipera aspis)* are the only poisonous snakes in the Alps. They are dangerous only when disturbed and live in various habitats, from the rocks to the marshes, from the valley floor to as high as 3000m. From about 40cm to 100cm long, they have a distinctive triangular head and a dark zigzag line along their grey-green bodies.

Coluber (Biacco-Biacco) This nonpoisonous constrictor snake *(Coluber viridiflavus carbonarius)* is among the largest in Europe – it can reach 2m in length. It is green with bluish-black spots and tends to attack and bite if disturbed. It can live as long as 30 years and is found as high as 2000m.

Natrix (Natrice Viperina) The natrix *(Natrix maura)* is an innocuous inhabitant of wetlands and a skilled swimmer, and can easily be mistaken for an adder. It is longer and slimmer than the adder and of a more uniform colour, with shades from grey to brown to yellow.

Lizards (Lucertole)
Slowworm (Orbettino) Easily mistaken for a snake is the copper-coloured slowworm *(Anguis fragilis)*, a common, legless lizard that prefers a moist environment close to forest clearings. The spotted brown mountain lizard *(Lacerta vivipara)* grows to a length of 15cm, and can live up to an altitude of 3000m.

Long and slender, the slowworm closely resembles a snake, even to the point of having a forked tongue.

MEDITERRANEAN FAUNA

Many of the animals already discussed in the section on Alpine fauna are also found in Italy's Mediterranean zone. These animals include the fox, badger, deer, wild boar and squirrel. In reality, not that many wild animals remain in Italy's more populous areas – most have been hunted relentlessly – but you might spot a wild boar, a fox or a squirrel while walking.

Mammals

Hedgehog (Riccio) The hedgehog *(Erinaceus europaeus)* is an insectivore found widely throughout the country. It lives in forests and cultivated fields, and often builds its nests near farmhouses so as to benefit from the extra food available. It is often willing to accept food from humans. The hedgehog grows to up to 27cm long and its back and sides are covered with 2cm-long prickles.

Mediterranean Mouflon (Muflone) The mouflon *(Ovis musimon)* is almost extinct in its natural habitat – Sardegna and Corsica. However, there have been efforts to save the species by establishing it in the Alps and other high mountain areas of Europe.

Monk Seal (Foca Monaca) The monk seal *(Monachus monachus)* is a marine mammal, now extremely rare, perhaps even extinct in Italian waters. The last known colony

The mouflon is now listed in the International Union for the Conservation of Nature (IUCN) Red Data Book of threatened species.

is located near Cala Gonone on Sardegna's eastern coast and it is believed that not more than 10 seals survive – if that! The monk seal's demise has been directly related to the degradation of coastal areas, largely due to major tourist developments. In the past it was also killed regularly by fishermen.

Porcupine (Istrice) The crested porcupine (*Hystrix africae-australis*) was probably brought to Italy from Africa by the ancient Romans. An Old World porcupine (as distinct from the New World porcupines found in America), the istrice has a variety of bristles and long, heavy quills covering its head, body and tail, which it rattles when frightened. Some of its quills can be as long as 40cm. The istrice is considered a delicacy by Italians, and as a result it has been hunted almost to extinction. However, efforts are under way to protect the animal and it is possible that you'll see one while walking.

Wild Cat (Gatto Selvatico) A stunningly beautiful animal, the wild cat (*Felis silvestris*) is larger than the domestic cat and is found in Sardegna – although they are also known to exist in Alpine forests and in semiwilderness areas such as on Mt Etna in Sicilia. It has a coat of thick yellow-grey fur with tabby markings and a tail which is shorter than that of a domestic cat. The wild cat is characterised by four black stripes on its forehead which continue back to its neck, where the middle two stripes form a single, wide black stripe down the cat's back. It is a night hunter and very difficult to spot during the day.

The black-winged stilt has a yelping call and flies with its very long legs trailing behind it.

Birds

Bonelli's Eagle (Aquila dei Bonelli) *Hieraaetus fasciatus* is a beautiful, well-proportioned bird which lives in open, rocky areas. It has a light-coloured breast, contrasted with dark wings. It can have a wingspan of up to 1.6m, distinguishing it from a fully grown golden eagle, which can have a wingspan up to 2.5m. When hunting, its wings are flat and its tail feathers closed. Bonelli's eagle hunts small mammals and birds, including other birds of prey.

Black-Winged Stilt (Cavaliere d'Italia) Once almost extinct in Italy, the black-winged stilt *(Himantopus himantopus)* is now returning in large numbers to the country's wetlands. A very elegant bird, it has a long, fine beak and very long, bright red legs. Its back and the top feathers of its wings are black, while the rest of its body is white. The black-winged stilt uses its long beak to scavenge for insects and molluscs on the swamp bottom.

Common Barn Owl (Barbagianni) This very interesting-looking bird *(Tyto alba)* is a night hunter. It is only about 30cm high, but has a wingspan of about 1m. Its feathers are ash-grey and ochre in colour, with darker speckled markings. Its facial disk is yellow and heart-shaped. The barn owl hunts rodents, as well as insects, birds and other small animals. It swallows its prey whole and then expels the bones and other indigestible parts in a spherical-shaped mass.

Flamingo (Fenicottero) There are large colonies of pink flamingoes *(Phoenicopterus ruber roseus)* in Sardegna,

Flamingoes typically flock to low-lying fresh-water areas as well as salt pans.

living in salt lakes near the coast just outside Cagliari and on the Sinus Peninsula on the west coast. These long-legged birds are easily recognisable by their characteristic pink plumage.

Griffon Vulture (Grifone) The griffon *(Gyps fulvus)* is one of the largest birds in Italy – its wingspan can reach 2.8m, which gives it an exceptional ability to exploit air currents. Finding a suitable current, the griffon will circle slowly upwards, expending very little energy, reaching heights of up to 5000m. Its eyesight is so acute that it can spot a mouse from 1000m up! The griffon is uniformly brown in colour, with a long neck covered with short, white feathers and a characteristic collar of longer white feathers. The only colony of griffons in Italy is in Sardegna, in the mountains above Bosa on the west coast of the island, where there are approximately 90 pairs.

Hoopoe (Upupa) The very unusual-looking hoopoe *(Upupa epops)* is found throughout Europe. It is a migratory bird, found in Italy only during the summer, when it nests in cavities on rock faces, earth walls, or even in the walls of old buildings. It is very easy to recognise, with its rose coloured body and its wings and tail striped black and white. It has a rose coloured crest, tipped black. It has a long, curved beak, which it uses to excavate its food, mainly invertebrates, from the soil. The hoopoe has an undulating way of flying.

Jay (Ghiandaia) A member of the crow family, jays are among the most alert birds. Their warning screech serves as a danger signal to many animals. Jays have a reddish-brown body, their wings have distinctive bands of bright blue, white and black and they have a crest of barred feathers, which can be raised. Living mainly in deciduous and coniferous forests, jays are rarely far from the trees and sometimes congregate in small noisy communities.

Kestrel (Gheppio) The kestrel is relatively easy to pick out from other hawks by its small size and ability to hover while searching for prey. The male has a reddish-brown flecked back and the female is a rusty colour, with darker bars. Both have black end bands on their tails. It flies with rapid beats of its wings and frequently hovers for long periods. Kestrels are very common in Italy, their habitats extending from hills to coastlines, cultivated fields, light forests and even cities. You will see them with little difficulty.

Peregrine Falcon (Falco Pellegrino) A powerful bird, incapable of being outflown, the peregrine falcon *(Falco peregrinus)* is about the size of a crow, with long, pointed wings and a long tail. Its back is almost black and the upper part of its body is dark grey, in contrast with its underside, which is white, heavily marked with black bars. The adult bird also has dark 'moustaches' on white cheeks. Peregrines fly rapidly, interrupted by long periods of gliding, and kill their prey in the air. When they spot their prey, peregrines drop on it almost vertically with their wings completely closed, reaching incredible speeds. They hunt mainly other birds, such as pigeons.

The griffon vulture is able to cover vast distances with minimal effort by riding on the thermals in the higher altitudes.

continued from page 20

of the Central Alps were forcibly united into the Roman province of Rhaetia. The Romans, of course, introduced Latin to the province, but the original inhabitants of the area, with their diverse linguistic and cultural backgrounds, modified the language to the extent that, by around 450 AD, it had evolved into an independent Romance language, known as Raeto-Romanic.

At one point the entire Tirol was Ladin, but today the language and culture are confined mainly to the Val Gardena and the Val Badia, where about 90% of the locals declared in the 1981 census that they belonged to the Ladin language group. Along with German and Italian, Ladin is taught in schools and the survival of the Ladin cultural and linguistic identity is protected by law.

Italy has traditionally been a country of emigrants, as Italians have left in search of work, travelling mainly to the USA, Argentina, Brazil, Australia and Canada. In recent years, however, it has become a country of immigration. Long coastlines, the country's proximity to Africa and a fairly relaxed attitude to enforcement of immigration laws by Italian authorities has made Italy an easy point of entrance into Europe. It is estimated that more than 1.5 million immigrants now live in Italy.

Italians, however, are still more concerned with the traditional hostility of northern Italians towards southerners. Many northerners are resentful that the richer north in effect subsidises the poorer south. Their concerns are finding a strong voice in the success of the Northern League, which has called for the secession of the north, dubbed Padania, from the rest of the country.

SOCIETY & CONDUCT

It is difficult to make blanket assertions about Italian culture, if only because Italians have only lived as one nation for little more than 100 years. Prior to unification, the peninsula was long subject to a widely varied mix of masters and cultures. This lack of unity also contributed to the maintenance of local dialects and customs.

Indeed it was really only the advent of national TV that began the spread of a 'standard' Italian. Previously it was not unusual to find farmers and villagers who spoke only their local dialect.

Italians at a World Cup soccer match may present a patriotic picture, but most Italians tend to identify more strongly with their region or town than the nation – known to some as *campanilismo* (which loosely translates as an attachment to one's local bell-tower!). An Italian is always first and foremost a Sicilian or

The Mafia

In Italy, the term 'mafia' can be used to describe five distinct organised crime groups: the original Sicilian Mafia, also known as the Cosa Nostra; the Calabrian 'Ndrangheta; the Camorra of Napoli; and two relatively new organisations, the Sacra Corona Unita (United Holy Crown) and La Rosa (the Rose) in Apulia. These groups operate both separately and together.

The Sicilian Mafia has its roots in the oppression of the Sicilian people and can claim a history extending back to the 13th century. Its complex system of justice is based on the code of silence known as *omertà*. Mussolini managed to virtually wipe out the Mafia, but from the devastation of WWII grew the modern version of the organisation, which has spread its tentacles worldwide and is far more ruthless and powerful than its predecessor. It is involved in drug-trafficking and arms deals, as well as finance, construction and tourist development, not to forget public-sector projects and Italian politics.

In the early 1990s, two anti-Mafia judges were assassinated in Palermo in separate bomb blasts. One early result of the feverish anti-Mafia activity that followed was the arrest of Salvatore 'Toto' Riina, the Sicilian godfather. Riina was sentenced to life imprisonment in 1997 for his role in the deaths of Falcone and Borsellino. The man believed to have taken over after Riina's arrest, Giovanni ('The Pig') Brusca, was arrested in May 1996. Giulio Andreotti, a former prime minister and one of the longest serving and most dominant political figures in post-war Italy, was put on trial in Palermo for alleged links with the Mafia. Andreotti was also on trial in Perugia for alleged complicity in the 1979 murder of journalist Carmine Pecorelli. ∎

Toscan, or even a Romano, Milanese or Napolitano, before being Italian.

Confronted with a foreigner, however, Italians will energetically reveal a national pride difficult to detect in the relationship they have with each other.

Stereotypes

Foreigners may think of Italians as passionate, animated people who gesticulate wildly when speaking, love to eat and drive like maniacs but there's a bit more to it than that.

Italian journalist Luigi Barzini defined his compatriots as a hard-working, resilient and resourceful people, who are optimistic and have a good sense of humour. If there is a 'national' stereotype, this is probably closer to the truth. They are passionately loyal to their friends and families – all-important qualities, noted Barzini, since 'a happy private life helps people tolerate an appalling public life'.

Many Italians have a strong distrust of authority. When confronted with a silly rule, an unjust law or a stupid order (and they are confronted with many), they don't complain or try to change it, but rather try to find the quickest way around it.

Family

The family, particularly in the south, remains of central importance in the fabric of Italian society. Most young Italians tend to stay at home until they marry, a situation admittedly partly exacerbated by the lack of affordable housing. Still, modern attitudes have begun to erode the traditions. Statistics show that one in three married couples have no children and one in nine children is born out of wedlock. In Milano, more than one-third of families are headed by a single parent and two-thirds of these by a woman.

Dos and Don'ts

Italians tend to be very tolerant but, in spite of the apparent obsession with (mostly female) nakedness conveyed especially in billboard and TV advertising but it's not as free and easy as all that. In some parts of Italy, particularly in the south, women will be harassed if they wear skimpy or see-through clothing.

However, female walkers should have no hesitation in donning a decent pair of shorts.

In churches you are expected to dress modestly, and those that are major tourist attractions, such as St Peter's in Roma enforce dress codes strictly. The rules are generally more flexible in smaller towns and villages, but if you intend to include church visits (for instance in Toscana), carry a pair of lightweight long pants just in case. Churches are places of worship – if you visit one during a service, try to be as inconspicuous as possible.

RELIGION

Some 85% of Italians professed to be Catholic in a census taken in the early 1980s. Of the remaining 15%, there were about 500,000 evangelical Protestants, around about 140,000 Jehovah's Witnesses and other, small groups, including a Jewish community in Roma and the Waldenses (Valdesi) – Swiss-Protestant Baptists living in small communities in Piemonte. There are also communities of orange-clad followers of the Bhagwan Rajneesh, known in Italy as the *arancioni*.

The big surprise on this front is the growth of the Muslim population, estimated at 700,000, and thus the second greatest religious community in Italy after the Catholics. A fitting symbol for this novelty in the heart of Christendom was the inauguration in 1995 of the first mosque in Roma.

Although the fabric of Italian life is profoundly influenced by the presence of the Catholic church, surprisingly few Italian Catholics practise their religion. Church attendance is low – an average of only 25% attend Mass regularly – and many children are never baptised. But first communion remains a popular event, the majority of Italian couples prefer to be married in a church, and religious festivals are very popular.

There is a full calendar of religious festivals in Italy and it would be well worth your while to time at least one of your walks to coincide with a festival (see the Public Holidays & Special Events section and the 'Festivals' boxed text in the Facts for the Walker chapter).

LANGUAGE

Although many Italians speak some English because they study it in school, English is more widely understood in the north, particularly in major centres such as Milano, Firenze and Venezia, than in the south. Staff at most hotels, pensioni and restaurants usually speak a little English, but you'll be better received if you at least attempt to communicate in Italian.

Italian is a Romance language related to French, Spanish, Portuguese and Romanian. The Romance languages belong to the Indo-European group of languages, which include English. Indeed, as English and Italian share common roots in Latin, you'll recognise many Italian words.

Modern literary Italian began to develop in the 13th and 14th centuries, predominantly through the works of Dante, Petrarch and Boccaccio, who wrote chiefly in the Florentine dialect. The language drew on its Latin heritage and many dialects to develop into the standard Italian of today. Although many dialects are spoken in everyday conversation, standard Italian is the national language of schools, media and literature, and is understood throughout the country.

There are 58 million speakers of Italian in Italy; half a million in Switzerland, where Italian is one of the official languages; and 1.5 million speakers in France, Slovenia and Croatia. As a result of migration, Italian is also spoken in the USA, Argentina, Brazil and Australia.

Visitors to Italy with more than the most fundamental grasp of the language need to be aware that many older Italians still expect to be addressed by the third person formal, ie *lei* instead of *tu*. Also, it is not considered polite to use the greeting *ciao* when addressing strangers, unless they use it first; it's better to say *buongiorno* (or *buonasera*, as the case may be) and *arrivederci* (or the more polite form, *arrivederla*). We have used the formal address for most of the phrases. The informal address appears in brackets. Italian, like other Romance languages, has masculine and feminine forms. These two forms appear separated by a slash, the feminine

form first. For a more comprehensive guide to the language use LP's *Italian phrasebook*.

Pronunciation

Italian is not difficult to pronounce once you learn a few easy rules. Although some of the more clipped vowels, and stress on double letters, require careful practice for English speakers, it is easy enough to make yourself understood.

Vowels

Vowels are generally more clipped than in English:

a	as in 'art'
e	as in 'get'
i	as in 'inn'
o	as in 'dot'
u	as in 'cook'

Consonants

The pronunciation of many Italian consonants is similar to that of English. The following sounds depend on certain rules:

c	as 'k' before 'a', 'o' and 'u'. As the 'ch' in 'choose' before 'e' and 'i'.
ch	as the 'k' in 'kick'
g	as in 'get' before 'a', 'o' and 'u'. As in 'Geoff' before 'e' and 'i'.
gh	as in 'get'
gli	as the 'lli' in 'million'
gn	as the 'ny' in 'canyon'
h	always silent
r	a rolled 'rrr' sound
sc	as the 'sh' in 'sheep' before 'e' and 'i', or as the 'sch' in 'school' before 'h', 'a', 'o' and 'u'.
z	as the 'ts' in 'lights'. As the 'ds' in 'beds' at the beginning of a word.

Note that when 'ci', 'gi' and 'sci' are followed by 'a', 'o' or 'u', the 'i' is not pronounced unless the accent actually falls on it. Thus the name 'Giovanni' is pronounced 'joh-*vahn*-nee'.

Double consonants are pronounced as a

longer, often far more forceful sound than one single consonant.

Stress

Stress often falls on the second-last syllable, as in *spa-ghet-ti*. When a word has an accent, the stress is on that syllable, as in *cit-tà*, 'city'.

Language Problems

Please write it down.	*Può scriverlo, per favore?*
Can you show me on the map?	*Può mostrarmelo sulla carta/pianta?*
I (don't) understand.	*(Non) Capisco.*
Do you speak English?	*Parla (Parli) inglese?*
Does anyone speak English?	*C'è qualcuno che parla inglese?*
How do you say ... in Italian?	*Come si dice ... in italiano?*
What does ... mean?	*Che vuole dire ...?*

Paperwork

name	*nome*
nationality	*nazionalità*
date of birth	*data di nascita*
place of birth	*luogo di nascita*
sex (gender)	*sesso*
passport	*passaporto*
visa	*visto consolare*

Greetings & Civilities

Hello.	*Buongiorno/Ciao.*
Goodbye.	*Arrivederci/Ciao.*
Yes.	*Sì.*
No.	*No.*
Please.	*Per favore/Per piacere.*
Thank you.	*Grazie.*
That's fine/You're welcome.	*Prego.*
Excuse me.	*Mi scusi (Scusami).*
Sorry (forgive me).	*Mi scusi/Mi perdoni.*

Small Talk

What is your name?	*Come si chiama? (Come ti chiami?)*
My name is ...	*Mi chiamo ...*

Where are you from?	*Di dov'è (Di dove sei)?*
I'm from ...	*Sono di ...*
How old are you?	*Quanti anni ha (hai)?*
I'm ... years old.	*Ho ... anni.*
Are you married?	*È sposata/o?*
I'm (not) married.	*(Non) sono sposata/o.*
I (don't) like ...	*(Non) Mi piace ...*
Just a minute.	*Un momento.*

Getting Around

I want to go to ...	*Voglio andare a ...*
What time does ... leave/arrive?	*A che ora parte/arriva ...?*
the boat	*la barca*
the bus (city bus)	*l'autobus*
the bus (intercity)	*il pullman/il corriere*
the train	*il treno*
the aeroplane	*l'aereo*
the first	*il primo*
the last	*l'ultimo*
one-way ticket	*un biglietto di solo andata*
return ticket	*un biglietto di andata e ritorno*
1st class	*prima classe*
2nd class	*seconda classe*
platform number	*binario numero*
station	*stazione*
ticket office	*biglietteria*
timetable	*orario*
train station	*stazione*
The train has been cancelled/delayed.	*Il treno è soppresso/in ritardo.*
I'd like to rent ...	*Vorrei noleggiare ...*
a car	*una macchina*
a bicycle	*una bicicletta*
a motorcycle	*una motocicletta*

Directions

Where is ...?	*Dov'è ...?*
Go straight ahead.	*Si va/(Vai) sempre diritto.*
Turn left.	*Gira a sinistra.*
Turn right.	*Gira a destra.*

at the next corner	*al prossimo angolo*
at the traffic lights	*al semaforo*
behind	*dietro*
in front of	*davanti*
far	*lontano*
near	*vicino*
opposite	*di fronte a*

Around Town

I'm looking for ...	*Cerco ...*
a bank	*un banco*
the church	*la chiesa*
the city centre	*il centro (città)*
the ... embassy	*l'ambasciata di ...*
my hotel	*il mio albergo*
the market	*il mercato*
the museum	*il museo*
the post office	*la posta*
a public toilet	*un gabinetto/ bagno pubblico*
the telephone centre	*il centro telefonico*
the tourist infomation office	*l'ufficio di turismo/ d'informazione*

| I want to exchange some money/ travellers cheques. | *Voglio cambiare del denaro/degli assegni per viaggiatori.* |

beach	*la spiaggia*
bridge	*il ponte*
castle	*il castello*
cathedral	*il duomo/la cattedrale*
church	*la chiesa*
island	*l'isola*
main square	*la piazza principale*
market	*il mercato*
mosque	*la moschea*
old city	*il centro storico*
palace	*il palazzo*
ruins	*le rovine*
sea	*il mare*
square	*la piazza*
tower	*la torre*

Accommodation

I'm looking for a ...	*Cerco un ...*
hotel	*albergo*
guesthouse	*pensione*
youth hostel	*ostello per la gioventù*

Where is a cheap hotel?	*Dov'è un albergo che costa poco?*
What is the address?	*Cos'è l'indirizzo?*
Could you write it down, please?	*Può scriverlo, per favore?*
Do you have any rooms available?	*Ha camere libere?*
I'd like ...	*Vorrei ...*
a bed	*un letto*
a single room	*una camera singola*
a double room	*una camera matrimoniale*
room with two beds	*una camera doppia*
a room with a bathroom	*una camera con bagno*
to share a dorm	*un letto in dormitorio*

How much is it per night/per person?	*Quanto costa per la notte/ciascuno?*
Can I see it?	*Posso vederla?*
Where is the bathroom?	*Dov'è il bagno?*
I'm/We're leaving today.	*Parto/Partiamo oggi.*

Food

breakfast	*prima colazione*
lunch	*pranzo/colazione*
dinner	*cena*
restaurant	*ristorante*
grocery store	*un alimentari*

What is this?	*(Che) cos'è?*
I'd like the set lunch.	*Vorrei il menu turistico.*
Is service included in the bill?	*È compreso il servizio?*
I'm a vegetarian.	*Sono vegetariana/o.*

Shopping

I'd like to buy ...	*Vorrei comprare ...*
How much is it?	*Quanto costa?*
I don't like it.	*Non mi piace.*
Can I look at it?	*Posso dare un'occhiata?*
I'm just looking.	*Sto solo guardando.*
Do you accept credit cards/ travellers cheques?	*Accetta carte di credito/assegni per viaggiatori?*
It's cheap.	*Non è cara/o.*
It's too expensive.	*È troppo cara/o.*
more	*più*
less	*meno*
smaller	*più piccola/o*
bigger	*più grande*

Time & Dates

What time is it?	*Che ora è?/Che ore sono?*
It's 8 o'clock ...	*Sono le otto ...*
in the morning	*di mattina*
in the afternoon	*di pomeriggio*
in the evening	*di sera*
today	*oggi*
tomorrow	*domani*
yesterday	*ieri*
Monday	*lunedì*
Tuesday	*martedì*
Wednesday	*mercoledì*
Thursday	*giovedì*
Friday	*venerdì*
Saturday	*sabato*
Sunday	*domenica*
January	*gennaio*
February	*febbraio*
March	*marzo*
April	*aprile*
May	*maggio*
June	*giugno*
July	*luglio*
August	*agosto*
September	*settembre*
October	*ottobre*
November	*novembre*
December	*dicembre*

Numbers

0	zero
1	uno
2	due
3	tre
4	quattro
5	cinque
6	sei
7	sette
8	otto
9	nove
10	dieci
11	undici
12	dodici
13	tredici
14	quattordici
15	quindici
16	sedici
17	diciassette
18	diciotto
19	diciannove
20	venti
21	vent'uno
22	ventidue
30	trenta
40	quaranta
50	cinquanta
60	sessanta
70	settanta
80	ottanta
90	novanta
100	cento
1000	mille
2000	due mila
one million	un milione (di)

Health

I need a doctor.	*Ho bisogno d'un medico/dottore.*
I'm ill.	*Mi sento male.*
It hurts here.	*Mi fa male qui.*
I'm ...	*Sono ...*
diabetic	*diabetica/o*
epileptic	*epilettica/o*
asthmatic	*asmatica/o*
I'm allergic ...	*Sono allergica/o ...*
to antibiotics	*agli antibiotici*

to penicillin	*alla penicillina*	tampons	*tamponi*

antiseptic	*antisettico*
aspirin	*aspirina*
condoms	*preservativi*
contraceptive	*anticoncezionale*
diarrhoea	*diarrea*
medicine	*medicina*
sunblock cream	*crema/latte solare*
	(per protezione)

Emergencies

Help!	*Aiuto!*
Call a doctor!	*Chiami (Chiama) un dottore/medico!*
Call the police!	*Chiami (Chiama) la polizia!*
Go away!	*Vai via! (informal)*

Facts for the Walker

PLANNING

When to Walk

The range of walks presented in this book is designed to permit year-round walking in Italy: the Alps, Appennini (Apennines) and Alpi Apuane in summer; and all other areas, with the exception of the volcanoes, basically year-round. It's handy to remember that August is the month when just about everyone in Italy is on holiday either at the beach or in the mountains, along with huge numbers of European holidaymakers. July and September are the best months for hiking in the Alps and Appennini (like everything else, walking trails and *rifugi* (mountain huts, refuges) are crowded in August). During these months the weather is generally good, although you should always allow for cold snaps. Rifugi are usually open from late June to mid-late September for hikers.

The hottest months (July and August) are not the ideal time for walking in areas such as Toscana (Tuscany) (apart from the Alpi Apuane) and are certainly best avoided if you're planning to walk in Sicilia (Sicily) or Sardegna (Sardinia), or to tackle the volcanoes.

In winter there is snow on Mt Etna (3330m) and even in summer there can be strong, freezing winds near the summit. It doesn't snow on the other volcanoes, so winter is a good time to tackle them. However, autumn and spring are ideal. The Amalfi Coast and the Cinque Terre walks could be done during July and August, as long as you avoid walking during the hottest hours of the day. A mild climate from central Italy to Sicilia usually makes winter a reasonable time to walk in these areas, but in recent years parts of the south, including Sicilia have all been hard hit by freezing conditions, heavy rain and snow in winter. Spring and autumn are probably the safest bets for all areas, except for the Alps and higher areas of the Appennini. Another important thing to consider is the length of the days at different times of the year. Italy has daylight saving from March to the end of October and daylight can stretch out to around 9 pm in July. In winter it can get dark as early as 5 pm. See under Climate in the Facts about Italy chapter for more information.

Types of Walks

Walking in Italy is generally a pretty organised affair. Italians tend to prefer well-marked trails which are well served by rifugi or hotels – rather than treks in wilderness areas where they'll need to carry a tent, cooking facilities and food. In heavily frequented areas such as the Alps, the Appennini, the Alpi Apuane and Chianti (in Toscana) facilities are usually pretty good and it is easy to plan a walk with public transport and/or accommodation at the be-ginning and end. As you head further south you'll find that walking facilities tend to be less well organised: there are fewer rifugi and trails are not always well marked.

On Etna there is a system of unstaffed rifugi which are open to walkers, but they have little more than a table and a spot to put down your sleeping bag. However, trails are well maintained and local mountain guides are highly organised. In contrast, if you venture up Stromboli or into the interior of Sardegna without a guide you run a real risk of getting lost and, if you have problems, you'll be pretty much on your own.

That said, the beauty of choosing Italy for a walking holiday is the very fact that it offers an extraordinary variety of options. In this book, we have tried to offer something for everyone, while also highlighting the fact that in Italy you can walk for its own sake, or combine walking with cultural, artistic and even gourmet pursuits. You could add walking to a holiday at some of the country's most famous beach resorts, in Liguria, on the Amalfi Coast, or in the Aeolian Islands in Sicilia. You could be daring and follow the volcanoes route, which includes walks to the summits of two of Europe's most active volcanoes–Etna and Stromboli. The challenges presented by the Alps will satisfy the most demanding trekkers, although there are also Alpine walks detailed which can be tackled by completely inexperienced walkers and families with young children. Walkers in Chianti will come across more castles, ancient churches, farmhouses, wineries and fantastic little restaurants than they'll care to count. Fans of orienteering can test their skills and try not to get lost in the wilds of Sardegna – make sure you carry a compass.

Maps

Small-Scale Maps Michelin has a series of good foldout country maps. No 988 covers the whole country on a scale of 1:1,000,000. Or you can consider the series of area maps at 1:400,000. Nos 428 to 431 cover the mainland, No 432 covers Sicilia and No 433 covers Sardegna. These cost L10,000 apiece in Italy. The Touring Club Italiano (TCI) also publishes a decent map covering Italy, Switzerland and Slovenia at 1:800,000.

Road Atlases If you are driving around Italy, the AA's *Big Road Atlas – Italy*, available in the UK for UK£9.99, is scaled at 1:250,000 and includes 39 town maps. In Italy, de Agostini's *Atlante Stradale d'Italia* (1:600,000) contains city plans and sells for L24,500. For L43,000 the same publisher offers the more comprehensive *Atlante Turistico Stradale d'Italia* (1:250,000). The Touring Club Italiano publishes an *Atlante Stradale d'Italia* (1:200,000), divided into three parts – Nord, Centro and Sud. Each costs L34,000.

Walking Maps The maps in this book show the general routes of the main walks in each chapter. They should be used in conjunction with the more detailed maps recommended for use in each area. Excellent commercially-produced hiking maps of walking trails are available for the Alps, Appennini and most other parts of Italy where there are established walking trails.

It is strongly recommended that you use the largest scale maps possible – usually

1:25,000. These have extensive detail of topographical features, showing altitude, gradients, rivers and streams, as well as all trails (marked and unmarked), rifugi, towns, villages, groups of farmhouses and any other buildings in the area.

The best hiking maps are the 1:25,000 scale series published by Tabacco, which mainly cover the north of the country. Kompass also publishes 1:25,000 scale maps of various parts of Italy. Edizioni Multigraphic Firenze produces a series of walking maps concentrating mainly on Toscana and the Appennini.

The Istituto Geografico Centrale in Torino (Turin) produces maps for the Lakes District, the Western Alps and the Alpi Marittime and Liguri. Many of these maps are available in major bookshops in the cities (some are listed here), although the selection might not be extensive. It is more likely that you will find a full selection of the maps you need in the areas where you plan to walk. They are usually sold at *edicole* (newsagencies), *tabacchi* (tobacconists), sports stores and other outlets, and cost around L8000 to L12,000 each.

For some walks in this book, it is necessary to use specialised 1:25,000 IGM (Istituto Geografico Militare) maps in areas where no commercial maps exist. These are the official maps of the Italian territory and are in the process of being updated. The new series is available only for certain areas of the country, such as Sardegna. It is indicated throughout this book when it is necessary to use these maps. They can be purchased at a number of specialist bookstores in Italy's major cities (see information following). You can also order them directly by fax from the Istituto Geografico Militare (☎ (055) 27 75 446; fax 41 04 10), Via di Novoli 93, Firenze (Florence) (it is due to move soon to a new address at Via Filippo Strozzi 10). Within Europe you can pay on delivery of the maps, however if you're ordering from overseas you will need to pay before they send them out.

Bookstores in major cities where you will find a good selection of maps, as well as IGM maps, and guidebooks, include:

Roma (Rome)
    Feltrinelli International (☎ (06) 482 78 73), Via
    V E Orlando 84
    Libreria all'Orologio (☎/fax (06) 68 80 66 59),
    Via del Governo Vecchio 7, 00186 (stocks IGM
    maps)
    Libreria del Viaggiatore (☎ (06) 68 80 10 48),
    Via del Pellegrino 70
Milano (Milan)
    Luoghi e Libri (☎/fax (02) 738 83 60), Via
    Mameli 8 (also has IGM maps)
    Nuova Libreria Dante (☎ (02) 87 70 34), Via
    Dante 12
Torino (Turin)
    La Montagna (☎/fax (011) 562 00 24), Via Sacchi
    28
    Libreria Il Giromondo (☎ (011) 473 28 15), Via
    Carena 3 (both bookstores have IGM maps)
Firenze (Florence)
    Feltrinelli International (☎ (055) 29 21 96), Via
    Cavour 12
Napoli (Naples)
    Yamm (☎ (081) 552 63 99; fax 552 97 82), Via
    G Summonte 10 (stocks IGM maps)

What to Bring

Depending on where and when you are planning to walk, your essential items will vary.

Clothing & Footwear If you are planning to walk in the Alps or other mountain areas, you are going to need to be well prepared. A high number of walker deaths at high altitudes are attributed to inadequate clothing or footwear. Even on the shortest, most popular trails at the height of summer, sudden weather changes can bring freezing conditions, where five minutes earlier there had been blazing sunshine. Make sure you have good walking boots, a warm jacket and plenty of water. It is essential that your boots are already worn in and advisable that they are waterproof – many these days are made with a combination of leather and waterproof Gore-Tex.

A useful tip is to wear clothing which can easily be layered. You might start your walk in the morning sunshine and finish it in the midst of an afternoon thunderstorm, progressing from a T-shirt and lightweight cotton pants to a pile jacket, covered by a waterproof wind jacket and waterproof pants, topped perhaps with a plastic poncho.

Layering and stripping off items of clothing is an 'occupational hazard' of mountain walking.

In heavy rain, even with a waterproof wind jacket and poncho, you are still likely to get wet (most people will also sweat a lot when wearing a plastic poncho). Some walkers carry an umbrella, which can be strapped to a backpack, or used as a walking stick.

You should in any case be carrying a change of clothing in your pack: a useful tip is to pack clothing in individual plastic bags to ensure everything stays dry even if your pack gets soaked. Make sure you wear a sun hat; at high altitude you can get sunburned very quickly.

For warm weather walking in areas such as Toscana, Liguria, the Amalfi Coast and further south, you are obviously going to need to carry a lot less. The weather is more stable, so you are unlikely to risk hypothermia in August if you don't have a pile or wind jacket. However, it still advisable to have one on hand, particularly for the volcanoes and even for the Amalfi Coast, where afternoon thunderstorms are common during summer. Lightweight, comfortable walking shoes are still essential. You'll be fine with a good pair of runners (training shoes) for walking in Chianti, but in most other areas a more solid shoe is advisable.

Equipment A compass and altimeter will be essential on some walks, particularly in Sardegna, and very useful on many others. Camping gear, including a tent, sleeping bag, insulation and portable stove, could prove useful in more remote areas such as Sardegna and Sicilia, particularly if you are on a tight budget. However, it should be noted that wild camping is usually not permitted in Italy. Another drawback might be the difficulty in obtaining fuel for some portable stoves. The author who covered the Western Alps, Lakes District and Amalfi Coast chapters said she was able to find Coleman gas (butane) for her stove only in the Valle d'Aosta. Camping Gaz is usually available in sports stores. Some people carry stoves

Equipment Checklist

The following is a list of items which it is highly recommended you carry on high-altitude treks of one day or more:

☐ comfortable, waterproof walking boots (already worn in)

☐ comfortable backpack with waterproof liner

☐ warm jumper or pile jacket

☐ windproof and waterproof jacket with hood (Gore-Tex or similar fabric)

☐ waterproof overpants

☐ change of T-shirt, underwear and socks

☐ short and long pants

☐ gloves, wool or pile hat, or headband, and scarf

☐ sun hat or visor

☐ lightweight, energy-producing food

☐ water bottle (at least 1L per person)

☐ lightweight thermal blanket or polythene survival bivouac bag (for emergencies)

☐ torch (flashlight) and extra batteries

☐ whistle (for emergencies)

☐ maps, guides and compass

☐ notebook and pencil

☐ barometer/altimeter

☐ basic medical kit (see the Medical Kit Checklist in the Health, Safety & First Aid chapter)

☐ pocket knife, tissues

☐ sunglasses with UV lenses, sunscreen

☐ sleeping bag or sheet. Also bring along a pair of slippers or thongs (flip flops) to wear at the rifugio

☐ camera, film and binoculars

For the Camper

These items are necessary if you're planning on camping rather than staying at rifugi.

☐ tent with pegs, poles, guy ropes and fly

☐ sleeping bag

☐ insulation mat (foam or air-filled)

☐ groundsheet

☐ towel, soap and toilet paper

☐ minimal unbreakable cooking, eating and drinking utensils

☐ portable stove, fuel and matches

☐ spare shoes/boots or sneakers

which run on unleaded petrol, or on white spirit.

For walking in the Alps you are unlikely to need camping gear, since there is an extensive network of rifugi. Your most important piece of equipment will be your backpack. If you will be using the same pack for both travelling and walking, be sure that it is comfortable, with shoulder and waist straps that can be adjusted. A smaller daypack, again with adjustable straps, is very useful for shorter walks. Outside pockets on backpacks are very useful for stowing those items which you might need to get to quickly, such as your camera, sunglasses etc.

Buying Locally The best advice is to bring whatever you need with you. There are two reasons for this; you can never assume that you will easily find exactly what you are looking for; and, walking equipment is expensive in Italy. If you need gas or fuel for a portable stove, you won't be able to pack it if you're travelling by plane. Should you need to buy any equipment on arrival, the following is a brief list of outlets:

Roma
    Cisalfa, Largo Brindisi 3/8 (just next to the exit from the San Giovanni Metro stop)
    Adventure Centre, Via Derna 12 (far from the city centre off Via Libia)
Torino
    Ronco Alpinismo, Corso Montegrappa 31 (take tram No 1 from Porta Nuova or Porta Susa)
    Perero Sport, Corso Dante 51
Milano
    La Montagna Sport, Via Lazzaretto 14 (from the central train station, take the yellow line of the MM and get off at Piazza Repubblica

SUGGESTED ITINERARIES

Unless you are a regular visitor to Italy, you'll want to leave some time to see at least the main sights, particularly the cities of Roma, Firenze and Venezia (Venice). If you have plenty of time on your hands, consider planning an extended itinerary in each of the areas where you'll be walking.

If you're walking in Toscana, the routes proposed in this book will take you to several historical towns, including San Gimignano

Highlights
The authors nominated the following as some of the highlights of their walks in Italy – you might have other ideas, but these are a good guide to the best of the best:

- The Parco Naturale Fanes-Senes-Braies, Dolomiti.
- The eastern coast of Sardegna.
- Watching the volcanic explosions at the summit of Stromboli by night.
- Watching the sunrise, from near the summit of Mt Etna.
- The view of the Gran Paradiso and Monte Bianco from Col di Entrelor, a pass at just more than 3000m, between Valsavarenche and Val di Rhêmes, in Valle d'Aosta.
- The view of the Alps from the summit of Monte Bregagno (2100m) in the Lake District.
- View of distant snowcaps in the Alps from the summit of Pizzo d'Uccello (Alpi Apuane).
- The village of Vernazza in the Cinque Terre (Sentiero Azzurro).
- Close encounters with *stambecchi* (ibex) and *camosci* (chamois) in the Alpi Marittime.
- The smell of the *vendemmia* (grape harvest) in the villages of the Cinque Terre.
- The Punta Marguareis circuit through the limestone country of Parco Naturale Alta Valle Pesio.
- Walking along the Amalfi Coast.

and Volterra. To undertake the main walk through Chianti, you will actually depart from Firenze and end up in Siena, so make sure you set aside time to visit both towns. You could tack on a few extra days and also visit Pisa and Lucca (which is close to the Alpi Apuane). If you really like the idea of spending your time in Toscana, you could even consider renting a villa in Chianti. See the Toscana chapter for information on how to do this.

The volcanoes route will take you down into the south of Italy, to the Campania region and Sicilia. If you plan to climb Vesuvio, you are probably also considering walking along the Amalfi Coast. Napoli is literally in the shadow of Vesuvio and is definitely worthy of a few days' investigation. From there you could you could easily spend a week or more taking in the wonders of the ancient cities of Pompeii, Bolzano (Herculaneum) and, further south, Paestum; the captivating islands of Capri, Ischia and Procida; the seaside resort of Sorrento and the Amalfi Coast itself; and the royal palace of Caserta.

If you head down to Sicilia, the volcanoes route will take you to the Aeolian Islands, off the island's north-east coast, and to Mt Etna, which looms over Catania. Consider adding a week or two to your itinerary and, after climbing Etna, visit the spectacular hilltop town of Taormina, then head along the coast to Syracuse (you can afford to give Catania a miss). Continue around the coast, visiting the Baroque towns of Noto and Ragusa, then spend a day at Agrigento to visit the famous Greek temples, Sicilia's most important archeological site. If you're pressed for time, catch a train or bus across the island to Palermo and take a few days to explore the remains of what was once the grandest city in Europe, not to mention a former Arab emirate and seat of a Norman kingdom! Detours along the way could include Enna and the Villa Romana del Casale near Piazza Armerina, or Marsala, Trapani and the Egadi islands.

If you're heading north to walk in the Alps or in the Lake District, leave time for Verona, Padova and Venezia – all three are relatively close to the Dolomiti. At a push, one day is enough for each of Verona and Padova, but at least three days is advised for Venezia.

TOURIST OFFICES
Local Tourist Offices
The quality of tourist offices in Italy varies dramatically. One office might have enthusiastic staff but no useful printed information, while indifferent and even rude staff in another might keep a gold mine of brochures hidden under the counter.

Three tiers of office exist: regional, provincial and local. The names of tourist boards vary throughout the country, but they all offer basically the same services.

Regional offices are generally concerned with promotion, planning, budgeting and other projects far removed from the daily concerns of the humble tourist. Provincial offices are known either as the Ente Provinciale per il Turismo (EPT) or, more commonly, as the Azienda di Promozione Turistica (APT) and usually have information on both the province and the town. They can be particularly helpful with information about transport between the provinces and major cities. Local offices generally only have information about the town you're in and go by various names. Increasingly common is Informazioni e Assistenza ai Turisti (IAT), but you may also come across Azienda Autonoma di Soggiorno e Turismo (AAST) offices. These are the places to go if you want specific information about local bus routes, museum opening times etc.

The provincial and local tourist offices will usually have information about walking trails and rifugi and might even have maps (although usually not with the detail of commercial maps). This is generally the case in areas where walking is a popular activity, particularly in the Alps and areas such as Toscana and the Amalfi Coast.

Most tourist offices will respond to written and telephone requests for information about accommodation, transport and walking trails.

Tourist offices are generally open from Monday to Friday between 8.30 am and 12.30 or 1 pm and from 3 to around 7 pm. Hours are usually extended in summer, when some offices also open on Saturday afternoons or on Sundays.

Information booths at most major train stations and some smaller stations tend to keep similar hours, but in some cases only operate in summer. Many will help you find a hotel.

English, and sometimes French or German, is spoken at offices in larger towns and major tourist areas. German is of course spoken in Alto Adige. Printed information is generally provided in a variety of languages.

The addresses and telephone numbers of relevant local and provincial are listed throughout this book.

Tourist Offices Abroad

Information on Italy is available from the Italian State Tourist Office in the following countries:

Australia
   Alitalia (☎ (02) 247 1308), Orient Overseas Building, Suite 202, 32 Bridge St, Sydney 2000
Canada
   (☎ (514) 866-7667) 1 Place Ville Marie, Suite 1914, Montreal, Quebec H3B 3M9
UK
   (☎ (0171) 408 1254; (0891) 600280) 1 Princes St, London W1R 8AY
USA
   (☎ (212) 245-4822) 630 Fifth Ave, Suite 1565, New York, NY 10111
   (☎ (310) 820-2977) 124000 Wilshire Blvd, Suite 550, Los Angeles, CA 90025
   (☎ (312) 644-0990) 401 North Michigan Ave, Suite 3030, Chicago, IL 60611

Compagnia Italiana di Turismo (CIT), Italy's national travel agency, also has offices throughout the world (known as CIT or Citalia outside Italy). It can provide extensive information on travelling in Italy and also organises walking tours. CIT can also make train bookings, including sector bookings (such as Roma-Napoli), and sells Eurail passes and discount passes for train travel in Italy. CIT offices include:

Australia
   (☎ (02) 9267 1255) 263 Clarence St, Sydney 2000
   (☎ (03) 9650 5510) Level 4, 227 Collins St, Melbourne 3000
Canada
   (☎ (514) 845-4310) 1450 City Councillors St, Suite 750, Montreal, Quebec H3A 2E6
   (☎ (416) 927-7712) 111 Avenue Rd, Suite 808, Toronto M5R 3I8
France
   (☎ 01 44 51 39 00) 5 Blvd des Capucines, Paris 75002
Germany
   (☎ (0221) 20 70 90) Komödienstrasse 49, Köln D-50667

UK
  (☎ (0181) 686 0326) Marco Polo House, 3-5
  Lansdowne Rd, Croydon, Surrey CR9 1LL
USA
  (☎ (212) 697-2497) 342 Madison Ave, Suite 207,
  New York, NY 10173
  (☎ (310) 338-8615) 6033 West Century Blvd,
  Suite 980, Los Angeles, CA 90045

VISAS & DOCUMENTS

Passport

Citizens of the 15 European Union (EU) member states can travel to Italy with their national identity cards alone. People from countries that do not issue ID cards, such as the UK, must have a valid passport. All non-EU nationals must have a full valid passport.

If you've had the passport for a while, check that the expiry date is at least some months off, otherwise you may not be granted a visa (if you need one). If you travel a lot, keep an eye on the number of pages you have left in the passport. US consulates will generally insert extra pages into your passport if you need them, but others tend to require you to apply for a new passport. If your passport is nearly full when you are preparing to leave home and you are likely to have this trouble, do yourself a favour and get a new one before you leave.

Visas

EU citizens can enter Italy freely and stay for as long as they like. Citizens of many other countries, including the US, Canada, Australia, New Zealand, Japan and South Africa do not need a visa if entering as tourists for up to three months. Since passports are often not stamped on entry, that three-month rule can generally be interpreted flexibly, since no-one can prove how long you have been in the country. The only time you are likely to have your passport stamped is when entering by air – although even at Roma's airport there's a good chance it won't be. If your passport has been stamped and you wish to stay longer, you can play safe by leaving the country and re-entering – in that case you will have to make sure a new entry stamp goes into the passport, as it's likely you won't be stamped out either.

Italy is now a member of the Schengen Area – a group of EU countries including France between which there is free movement without passport controls. For EU nationals, this means that you don't need to produce a passport or identity card when entering or leaving the country (if you are a citizen of an EU country).

Photocopies

Make photocopies of all important documents, especially your passport. This will help speed replacement if they are lost or stolen. Other documents to photocopy might include your airline ticket and credit cards. Also record the serial numbers of your travellers cheques (cross them off as you cash them in). All this material should be kept separate from the documents concerned, along with a small amount of emergency cash. Leave extra copies with someone reliable at home. If your passport is stolen or lost, notify the police and obtain a statement, and then contact your embassy or consulate as soon as possible.

Permesso di Soggiorno

Visitors are technically obliged to report to a *questura* (police station) if they plan to stay at the same address for more than one week, to receive a *permesso di soggiorno*. Tourists who are staying in hotels, youth hostels etc are not required to do this, because proprietors are required to register all guests with the police.

A permesso di soggiorno only becomes a necessity (for non-EU citizens at any rate) if you plan to study, work (legally) or live in Italy. Obtaining one is never a pleasant experience. It involves enduring long queues, rude police officers and the frustration of arriving at the counter (after a two hour wait) to find that you don't have all the necessary documents.

Basically, if you're in Italy for a holiday only, you really shouldn't need to worry about this formality. If you need more detailed information, see Lonely Planet's *Italy* guide, or contact an Italian consulate in your country.

Travel Insurance

Don't, as they say, leave home without it. You may never need it, but you'll be glad you've got it if you get into trouble. These papers, and the international medical aid numbers that generally accompany them, are valuable documents, so treat them like air tickets and passports. Keep the details (photocopies or hand written) in a separate part of your luggage. Make sure that you read the fine print to ensure that your walking activities will be covered by the policy.

Driving Licence & Vehicle Papers

If you want to rent a car or motorcycle, you will generally need to produce your driving licence. Certainly you will need to produce it if pulled over by the police or *carabinieri*, who, if it's a non-EU licence, may well want to see an International Driving Permit. This is available from automobile clubs throughout the world and usually valid for 12 months, and must be kept with your proper licence.

If driving your own vehicle in Italy you need an International Insurance Certificate, also known as a Green Card (Carta Verde). Your third party insurance company will issue this. For further details, see the Car & Motorcycle section in the Getting There & Away chapter.

Hostel Card

A valid HI hostelling card is required in all associated youth hostels (Associazione Italiana Alberghi per la Gioventù) in Italy. You can get this in your home country or at youth hostels in Italy. In the latter case you apply for the card and must collect six stamps in the card at L5000 each. You pay for a stamp on each of the first six nights you spend in a hostel. With six stamps you are considered a full international member.

Student & Youth Cards

An International Student Identity Card (ISIC) or similar card will get you discounted entry prices into some museums and other sights, and is an asset in the search for cheap flights out of Italy. It can also come in handy for cinema, theatre and other travel discounts.

Some travel agents may issue cards with certain discounted air tickets without even asking to see proof of student status. More legitimately, the cards are available from many student and budget travel offices, including the following:

Australia
STA Travel (head office) (☎ (03) 9347 6911), 224 Faraday St, Carlton 3053
Canada
Travel Cuts (☎ (416) 977-3703), 187 College St, Toronto
Voyages Campus (☎ (514) 398-0647), Université McGill, 3480 Rue McTavish, Montreal
UK
Cards are best obtained from STA and Campus Travel offices – see Air in the Getting There & Away chapter.
USA
CIEE (☎ (212) 661-1414), 205 East 42nd St, New York; (☎ (213) 208-3551) 1093 Broxton Ave, Los Angeles; (☎ (415) 421-3473) 312 Sutter St, San Francisco

Similar cards are available to teachers (ITIC). They are good for various discounts and carry a travel insurance component.

You can get information on travel problems, medical or legal emergencies and the like on an international free ISIC/ITIC help line. Dial the UK on ☎ (0181) 666 9205. Cardholders can reverse the charges.

If you're aged under 26 but not a student you can apply for a Federation of International Youth Travel Organisations (FIYTO) card or Eurocard (in the UK known as the Under 26 Card), which gives much the same discounts as ISIC.

The head office of FIYTO is in Denmark, at Islands Brygge 81, DK-2300 Copenhagen S, where you can write to request a brochure. Otherwise, the organisations listed earlier for the USA and Canada will issue the cards.

Both cards are issued by student unions, hostelling organisations and some youth travel agencies (like Campus Travel in the UK). They don't always automatically entitle you to discounts, but you won't find out until you flash the card.

In Italy, any office of the Centro Turistico Studentesco e Giovanile (CTS) will issue

ISIC, ITIC and Eurocards if you join the CTS itself for L43,000.

CONSULATES & EMBASSIES
Italian Consulates & Embassies Abroad
The following is a selection of Italian diplomatic missions abroad. It's important to bear in mind that Italy maintains consulates in additional cities in many of the countries listed below:

Australia
    (☎ (02) 9392 7900) Level 45, The Gateway, 1 Macquarie Place, Sydney
    (☎ (03) 9867 5744) 509 St Kilda Rd, Melbourne
Austria
    (☎ (01) 713 5671) Ungargasse 43, Vienna
Belgium
    (☎ (02) 537 19 34) Rue de Livourne 38, Brussels
Canada
    (☎ (416) 977-2569) 136 Beverley St, Toronto
    (☎ (514) 849-9544) 3489 Drummond St, Montreal
Croatia
    (☎ (051) 48 46 118) Meduliceva Ulica 22, Zagreb
Denmark
    (☎ 39 62 68 77) Gammel Vartov Vej 7, Hellerup
France
    (☎ 01 44 30 47 00) 17 rue du Conseiller Collignon, Paris
Germany
    (☎ (0228) 82 00) Karl Finkelnburgstrasse 49-51, Bonn
Greece
    (☎ (01) 361 7260) Odos Sekeri 2, Athens
Japan
    (☎ (03) 3453-5291) Mte 2-chome 5/4, Tokyo
Netherlands
    (☎ (020) 624 0043) Herengracht 581, Amsterdam
New Zealand
    (☎ (04) 473 53 39) 34 Grant Rd, Thorndon, Wellington
Norway
    (☎ 22 55 22 33) Inkognitosten 7, Oslo
Slovenia
    (☎ (061) 126 2194) Snezniska Ulica 8, Ljubljana
South Africa
    (☎ (012) 43 55 41) 796 George Ave, Pretoria
Spain
    (☎ (91) 577 65 29) Calle Lagasca 98, Madrid
Sweden
    (☎ (08) 24 58 05) Oakhill Djurgarden, Stockholm
Switzerland
    (☎ (031) 352 41 51) Elfenstrasse 14, Bern
Tunisia
    (☎ (01) 32 18 11) 3 Rue de Russie, Tunis

UK
    (☎ (0171) 312 2209) 14 Three Kings Yard, London
USA
    (☎ (213) 820-0622) 12400 Wilshire Blvd, West Los Angeles
    (☎ (212) 737-9100) 690 Park Ave, New York
    (☎ (415) 931-4924) 2590 Webster St, San Francisco

Foreign Consulates & Embassies in Italy
Foreign embassies are all based in Roma, although many countries maintain consulates in other big cities. The following are all in Roma (telephone area code 06).

Australia
    (☎ 85 27 21) Via Alessandria 215
Austria
    (☎ 844 01 41) Via Pergolesi 3
    Consulate: (☎ 855 29 66) Viale Liegi 32
Belgium
    (☎ 360 95 11) Via dei Monti Parioli 49
Canada
    (☎ 44 59 81) Via G B de Rossi 27
    Consulate: (☎ 45 59 84 21) Via Zara 30
Croatia
    (☎ 33 25 02 42) Via SS Cosma e Damiano 26
Denmark
    (☎ 320 04 41) Via dei Monti Parioli 50
Finland
    (☎ 85 22 31) Via Lisbona 3
France
    (☎ 68 60 11) Piazza Farnese
    Visas: (☎ 68 60 11) Via Giulia 251
Germany
    (☎ 88 47 41) Via Po 25c
Greece
    (☎ 854 96 30) Via Mercadante 36
Ireland
    (☎ 697 91 21) Piazza di Campitelli 3
Israel
    (☎ 322 15 42) Via Michele Mercati 14
Japan
    (☎ 48 79 91) Via Sella 60
Netherlands
    (☎ 322 11 41) Via Michele Mercati 8
New Zealand
    (☎ 440 29 28) Via Zara 28
Norway
    (☎ 57 17 03) Via Terme Deciane 7
Slovenia
    (☎ 808 10 75) Via L Pisano 10
South Africa
    (☎ 85 25 41) Via Tanaro 14
Spain
    (☎ 683 21 68) Largo Fontanella Borghese 19
    Consulate: (☎ 687 14 01) Via Campo Marzio 34

Sweden
(☎ 44 19 41) Piazza Rio de Janeiro 3
Switzerland
(☎ 80 95 71) Via Barnarba Oriani 61
Consulate: (☎ 80 95 71) Largo Elvezia 15
Tunisia
(☎ 860 30 60) Via Asmara 5-7
Consulate: (☎ 87 18 80 06) Via Egadi 13
UK
(☎ 482 54 41) Via XX Settembre 80a
USA
(☎ 4 67 41) Via Vittorio Veneto 119a-121

For other foreign embassies in Roma and consulates in other cities, look under 'Ambasciate' or 'Consolati' in the telephone book or, in Roma, in the English *Yellow Pages*. Tourist offices will also generally have a list.

CUSTOMS

You can import, without paying duty, two still cameras and 10 rolls of film; a movie or TV camera with 10 cartridges of film; a portable tape recorder and 'a reasonable amount' of tapes; a CD player; a pair of binoculars; sports equipment, including skis; one bicycle or motorbike (not exceeding 50cc); one portable radio and one portable TV set (both may be subject to the payment of a licence fee) and personal jewellery.

Limits on duty-free imports include: up to 200 cigarettes; 50 cigars; 2L of wine and 1L of liquor. There is no limit on the amount of lire you can import.

MONEY

A combination of travellers cheques and credit cards is the best way to take your money.

Since you are likely to be combining some normal sightseeing with walking trips, this section will discuss the costs involved in visiting the main cities and tourist destinations, as well as for the actual walks.

Costs

Italy isn't cheap. Accommodation charges and high entrance fees for many museums and monuments keep daily expenditure high. A *very* prudent backpacker might scrape by on around L60,000 a day, but only by staying in youth hostels, eating one simple meal a

day (at the youth hostel), making sandwiches for lunch, travelling slowly to keep transport costs down and minimising the number of museums and galleries visited.

One rung up, you can get by on L100,000 per day if you stay in the cheaper pensioni or small hotels, and keep sit-down meals and museums each to one a day. Lone travellers may find even this budget hard to maintain, since single rooms tend to be pricey.

If money is no object, you'll find your niche in Italy. Realistically, a traveller wanting to stay in comfortable lower to mid-range hotels, eat two square meals a day, not feel restricted to one museum a day and be able to enjoy the odd drink and other minor indulgences should reckon on a minimum daily average of L200,000 to L250,000 a day – possibly more if you are driving.

For the walker, costs will really depend on where and when you are walking. In Chianti, you'll be hard pressed to keep to a tight budget. Accommodation and food costs are high and budget options are difficult to come by. On mountain walks, your main costs will also be for food and a bed, but up there your options are even more limited. At rifugi you'll pay an average of L25,000 for a bed (perhaps in a dormitory), plus at least L30,000 for a meal. In many areas you can save by camping and preparing your own food.

A basic breakdown of costs per person during an average day for the bottom to lower middle-range traveller could be: accommodation L20,000 (youth hostel) to L50,000 (single in pensione or per person in comfortable double); breakfast L3000 (coffee and croissant); lunch (sandwich and mineral water) L5000; bottle of mineral water L1500; public transport (bus or underground railway in a major town) up to L5000; entrance fee for one museum up to L12,000; cost of long-distance train or bus travel (spread over three days) L15,000 to L20,000; and sit-down dinner L14,000 to L30,000.

Savings Budget travellers can save by staying in youth hostels (open to people of all ages) or camping grounds. If you're travelling in a group and staying in pensioni or hotels, always ask for triples or quads. The cost per person drops with each extra person you have in a room.

In Italian bars, prices can double (sometimes even triple) if you sit down and are served at the table. Stand at the bar to drink your coffee or eat a sandwich – or buy a sandwich or slice of pizza and head for the nearest piazza. Read the fine print on menus (usually posted outside eating establishments) to check the cover charge (coperto) and service fee (servizio). These can make a big difference to the bill and it is best to avoid restaurants that charge both.

If travelling by train and you have time to spare, take a regionale or diretto: they are slower but cheaper than the Intercity trains, for which you have to pay a supplement. See the Getting Around chapter for information about these different types of trains and about various discounts on train travel.

Carrying Money

Petty theft is a problem throughout Italy, and tends to get worse the further south you travel. Keep only a limited amount of your money as cash, and the bulk in more easily replaceable forms such as travellers cheques or plastic. If your accommodation has a safe, use it. If you must leave money and documents in your room, divide the former into several stashes and hide them in different places. Lockable luggage is a good deterrent.

On the streets of the main cities, keep as little on you as necessary. The safest thing is a shoulder wallet or under-the-clothes money belt or pouch. External money belts tend to attract attention to your belongings rather than deflect it. If you eschew the use of any such device, keep money in your front pockets and watch out for people who seem to brush close to you – there is an infinite number of tricks employed by teams of delinquents, whereby one distracts your attention and the other deftly empties your pockets.

Cash

There is little advantage in bringing foreign cash into Italy. True, exchange commissions

are often lower than for travellers cheques, but the danger of losing the lot far outweighs such petty gains.

It is worth bringing some lire with you into the country (especially those arriving by air) to avoid the hassles of changing money on arrival.

Travellers Cheques

These are a safe way to carry money and easily cashed at banks and exchange offices throughout Italy. Always keep the bank receipt listing the cheque numbers separate from the cheques and keep a list of the numbers of those you have already cashed – this will reduce problems in the event of loss or theft. Check the conditions applying to such circumstances before buying the cheques.

If you buy your travellers cheques in lire (which you should only do if your trip is to be restricted to Italy alone), there should be no commission charge when cashing them. Most hard currencies are widely accepted, although you may have occasional trouble with the New Zealand dollar. Buying cheques in a third currency (such as US dollars if you are not coming from the USA), means you pay commission when you buy the cheques and again when cashing them in Italy.

Get most of the cheques in largish denominations to save on per-cheque exchange charges.

If you are using the better known cheques, such as Visa, American Express (Amex) and Thomas Cook, then you will have little trouble in Italy. Amex, in particular, has offices in all the major Italian cities and agents in many smaller cities. If you lose your Amex cheques, you can call a 24 hour toll free number (☎ 167-87 20 00) anywhere in Italy.

Take along your passport when you go to cash travellers cheques.

Credit/Debit Cards & ATMs

Carrying plastic (whether a credit or debit card) is the simplest way to organise your holiday funds. You don't have large amounts of cash or cheques to lose, you can get money after hours and on weekends, and the exchange rate is better than that offered for travellers cheques or cash exchanges. By arranging for payments to be made into your card account while you are travelling, you can avoid paying interest.

Major credit cards, such as MasterCard, Visa, Eurocard, Cirrus and Euro Cheques cards, are accepted throughout Italy.

They can be used for many purchases (including in many supermarkets) and in hotels and restaurants (although pensioni and smaller trattorie and pizzerie tend to accept cash only). Credit cards can also be used in ATMs (bancomat) displaying the appropriate sign or (if you have no PIN) to obtain cash advances over the counter in many banks – Visa and MasterCard are among the most widely recognised for such transactions. Check charges with your bank, but as a rule there is no charge for purchases on major cards and a 1.5% charge on cash advances and ATM transactions in foreign currencies.

It is not uncommon for ATMs in Italy to reject foreign cards. Don't despair or start wasting money on international calls to your bank. Try a few more ATMs displaying your credit card's logo at major banks before assuming the problem lies with your card rather than with the local system.

If your credit card is lost, stolen or swallowed by an ATM, you can telephone toll free to have an immediate stop put on its use. For MasterCard the number in Italy is ☎ 1678-6 80 86, or make a reverse-charges call to St Louis in the USA on ☎ 314-275 66 90; for Visa, phone ☎ 1678 2 10 01 in Italy. Otherwise, call ☎ 1678-2 20 56 to have any card blocked.

Amex is also widely accepted (although not as common as Visa or MasterCard). Amex's full-service offices (such as in Roma and Milano) will issue new cards, usually within 24 hours and sometimes immediately, if yours has been lost or stolen. Some Amex offices have ATMs that you can use to obtain cash advances if you have made the necessary arrangements in your own country.

The toll-free emergency number to report a lost or stolen Amex card varies according to where the card was issued. Check with Amex in your country or contact Amex in Roma on ☎ (06) 7 22 82, which itself has a 24 hour cardholders' service.

International Transfers

One reliable way to send money to Italy is by 'urgent telex' through the foreign office of a large Italian bank, or through major banks in your own country, to a nominated bank in Italy. It is important to have an exact record of all details associated with the money transfer, particularly the exact address of the Italian bank where the money has been sent. The money will always be held at the head office of the bank in the town to which it has been sent. Urgent-telex transfers should take only a few days, while other means, such as by telegraphic transfer, or draft, can take weeks.

It is also possible to transfer money through Amex and Thomas Cook. You will be required to produce identification, usually a passport, in order to collect the money. It is also a good idea to take along the details of the transaction. It is inadvisable to send cheques by mail to Italy, because of the unreliability of the country's postal service.

A more recent and speedy option is to send money through Western Union (toll free ☎ 1670-13839). This service functions in Italy through the Mail Boxes Etc chain of stores, which you will find in the bigger cities. The sender and receiver have to turn up at a Western Union outlet with passport or other form of ID and the fees charged for the virtually immediate transfer depend on the amount sent.

On the Walk

Most small towns in Italy have banks and ATMs which will accept foreign cards, so if you're walking in Toscana, Campania or Liguria you shouldn't have any trouble getting cash. However, when actually on a walk, it might be a good idea to carry enough cash to get you through, unless you have been able to check in advance that the places where you plan to stay and eat accept credit cards or cheques. Credit cards and cheques are not usually accepted at mountain rifugi, so you'll need to carry enough cash to get you from one bank or bancomat to the next. Calculate that for dinner and a bed in a rifugio, you'll need around L60,000 per day. Lunch and snacks at other rifugi along the way could add another L20,000 or more to your daily expenses.

Currency

Italy's currency is the lira (plural: lire). The smallest note is L1000. Other denominations in notes are L2000, L5000, L10,000, L50,000, L100,000 and L500,000. Coin denominations are L50, L100 (two types of silver coin), L200 and L500. You might occasionally find yourself in possession of *gettoni* (telephone tokens). They are legal tender and have the same value as a L200 coin, but are being withdrawn from circulation.

Italy hopes to be included in the first intake of countries when European Monetary Union is introduced in 1999. The lire, along with other European currencies including the deutschmark and the French franc, will be replaced by the euro.

Remember that, like other Continental Europeans, Italians indicate decimals with commas and thousands with points.

Currency Exchange

Australia	A$1	=	L1200
Canada	C$1	=	L1250
France	FF1	=	L295
Germany	DM1	=	L985
Japan	¥100	=	L1400
New Zealand	NZ$1	=	L1040
United Kingdom	UK£1	=	L2940
USA	US$1	=	L1790

Changing Money

If you need to change cash or travellers cheques, be prepared to queue (this is when you'll wish you had a credit card to stick in the nearest friendly ATM!).

You can change money in banks, at the post office or in special change offices. Banks are generally the most reliable and tend to offer the best rates. However, you should look around and ask about commissions. These can fluctuate considerably and a lot depends on whether you are changing cash or cheques. While the post office charges a flat rate of L1000 per cash transaction, banks charge L2500 or even more. Travellers cheques attract higher fees. Some banks charge L1000 *per cheque* with a L3000 minimum, while the post office charges a maximum L5000 per transaction. Other banks will have different arrangements again, and in all cases you should compare the exchange rates too. Exchange booths often advertise 'no commission', but the rate of exchange can often be inferior to that in the banks.

Balanced against the desire to save on such fees by making occasional large transactions should be a fear of pickpockets – you don't want to be robbed the day you have exchanged a huge hunk of money to last you weeks!

Tipping & Bargaining

You are not expected to tip on top of restaurant service charges, but it is common practice to leave a small amount. If there is no service charge, the customer might consider leaving a 10% tip, but this is by no means obligatory. In bars, Italians often leave any small change as a tip, often only L100 or L200. Tipping taxi drivers is not common practice, but you should tip the porter at higher class hotels.

Bargaining is common throughout Italy in flea markets, but not in shops. While bargaining in shops is not acceptable, you might find that the proprietor is disposed to give a discount if you are spending a reasonable amount of money. It is quite acceptable to ask if there is a special price for a room in a pensione if you plan to stay for more than a few days.

Receipts

Laws aimed at tightening controls on the payment of taxes in Italy mean that the onus is on the buyer to ask for and retain receipts for all goods and services. This applies to everything from 1L of milk to a haircut. Although it rarely happens, you could be asked by an officer of the Fiscal Police (Guardia di Finanza) to produce the receipt immediately after you leave a shop. If you don't have it, you may be obliged to pay a fine of up to L300,000.

POST & COMMUNICATIONS
Stamps & Post Offices
Stamps (francobolli) are available at post offices and authorised tobacconists (look for the official tabacchi sign: a big 'T', often white on black). Since letters often need to be weighed, what you get at the tobacconist's for international air mail will occasionally be an approximation of the proper rate. Main post offices in the bigger cities are generally open from around 8 am to at least 5 pm. Many open on Saturday mornings too. Tobacconists keep regular shopping hours.

Postal Rates
The cost of sending a letter air mail (via aerea) depends on its weight and where it is being sent. Letters up to 20g cost L1350 to Australia and New Zealand, L1250 to the USA and L750 to EU countries (L850 to the rest of Europe). Postcards cost the same. Aerograms are a cheap alternative, costing only L850 to send anywhere. They can be purchased at post offices only.

Sending letters express (espresso) costs a standard extra L3000, but may help speed a letter on its way.

If you want to post more important items by registered mail (raccomandato) or by insured mail (assicurato), remember that they will take as long as normal mail. Raccomandato costs L3400 on top of the normal cost of the letter. The cost of assicurato depends on the weight of the object, and is not available to the USA.

Express Mail Urgent mail can be sent by Express Mail Service (EMS), also known as CAI Post. A parcel weighing 1kg will cost L37,000 in Europe, L56,000 to the USA and Canada, and L83,000 to Australia and New Zealand. EMS is not necessarily as fast as private services. It will take four to eight days for a parcel to reach Australia and two to four days to reach the USA. Ask at post offices for addresses of EMS outlets.

Sending Mail
An air mail letter can take up to two weeks to reach the UK or the USA, while a letter to Australia will take between two and three weeks. Postcards will take even longer because they are low-priority mail.

The service within Italy is no better: local letters take at least three days and up to a week to arrive in another city. A 1988 survey on postal efficiency in Europe found that same-day and next-day delivery basically don't exist in Italy. Sending a letter express (see Postal Rates earlier) can help.

In Roma you can avoid this frustration by using Vaticano (the Vatican) post office in St Peter's Square. It has an excellent record for prompt delivery but doesn't accept poste restante mail.

Receiving Mail
Poste restante is known as fermo posta in Italy. Letters will be held at the counter of the same name in the main post office in the relevant town. Poste restante mail should be addressed as follows:

> John SMITH,
> Fermo Posta,
> 37100 Verona
> Italy

Amex card or travellers cheque holders can use the free client mail-holding service at Amex offices in Italy. You can obtain a list of these from Amex offices inside or outside Italy. Take your passport when you go to pick up mail.

Telephone
The orange public pay phones liberally scattered about Italy come in at least four types. Increasingly the most common accept only telephone cards (carte/schede telefoniche), although you will still find plenty that accept cards and coins (L100, L200 and L500). Rare now are the ones that accept only gettoni, tokens worth L200. Some card phones now also accept special Telecom

credit cards and even commercial credit cards. Among the latest generation of pay phones are those that also send faxes. If you call from a bar or shop, you may still encounter old-style metered phones, which count *scatti*, units used to measure the length of a call.

Phones can be found in the streets, train stations, some big stores as well as in Telecom offices. Some of the latter are staffed, and a few have telephone directories for other parts of the country. Where these offices are staffed, it is possible to make international calls and pay at the desk afterwards. Addresses of telephone offices are listed throughout the book.

You can buy phonecards at post offices, tobacconists, newspaper stands and from vending machines in Telecom offices. To avoid the frustration of trying to find fast-disappearing coin telephones, always keep a phonecard on hand. They come with a value of L5000, L10,000 and L15,000.

Mobile Phones GSM is the European digital standard for mobile phones. (GSM is also the standard in Australia, New Zealand and many Asian countries – but not Japan). If you want to take your phone with you, check with your carrier on whether or not you need to make any special arrangements.

Costs Rates, particularly for long distance calls, are among the highest in Europe. There are four different rates for local and national phone calls, and two to three rates for international calls. Cheapest rate for domestic calls is from 10 pm to 8 am. It is a little more complicated for international calls, but basically the cheapest off-peak time is 11 pm to 8 am and most or all of Sunday, depending on the country called.

A local call *(comunicazione urbana)* from a public phone will cost L200 for three to six minutes, depending on the time of day you call (8.30 am to 1 pm from Monday to Friday is peak call time).

Rates for long-distance calls within Italy *(comunicazione interurbana)* depend on the time of day and the distance involved. At the worst, one minute will cost about L580 in peak periods.

If you need to call overseas, beware of the cost – even a call of less than five minutes to Australia after 11 pm will cost around L15,000 from a private phone (more from a public phone). Calls to most of Europe cost about L800 per minute, although closer to L1200 from a public phone.

Travellers from countries that offer direct dialling services paid for at home country rates (such as AT&T in the USA and Telstra in Australia) should think seriously about taking advantage of them.

Domestic Calls Telephone codes all begin with 0 and consist of up to four digits. Codes are provided throughout the guide. The code is followed by a number of anything from four to eight digits. Drop the 0 when calling in the same town or area. The above does not include mobile phone numbers and free phone numbers *(numeri verdi)*, which usually begin with 167 or 1678). For directory inquiries, dial ☎ 12.

Important telephone area codes include: Roma 06, Milano 02, Firenze 055, Napoli 081, Cagliari 070, Venezia 041 and Palermo 091.

International Calls Direct international calls can easily be made from public telephones using phonecards. Dial 00 to get out of Italy, then the relevant country and city codes, followed by the telephone number. Useful country codes are: Australia 61, Canada and USA 1, New Zealand 64, and the UK 44. Codes for other countries in Europe include: France 33, Germany 49, Greece 30, Ireland 353 and Spain 34. Other codes are listed in Italian telephone books.

To make a reverse charges (collect) international call from a public telephone, dial ☎ 170. For European countries dial ☎ 15. All operators speak English.

Easier, and often cheaper, is using the Country Direct service in your country. You dial the number and request a reverse charges call through the operator in your country. Numbers for this service include:

Australia (Telstra)	☎ 172 10 61
Australia (Optus)	☎ 172 11 61
Canada	☎ 172 10 01
France	☎ 172 00 33
New Zealand	☎ 172 10 64
UK (Telecom)	☎ 172 00 44
UK (Mercury)	☎ 172 05 44
UK (Auto BT)	☎ 172 01 44
USA (AT&T)	☎ 172 10 11
USA (MCI)	☎ 172 10 22
USA (Sprint)	☎ 172 18 77
USA (IDB)	☎ 172 17 77

For international directory inquiries call ☎ 176.

International Phone Cards Several private companies now distribute international telephone cards, mostly linked to US phone companies such as Sprint and MCI. You call the number provided, which connects you with a US-based operator, through whom you can then place your international call at rates generally lower (by as much as 40% compared with standard peak hour rates) than the standard Italian rates. A recorded message will tell you before your call goes through how much time you have left on the card for that call. The cards come in a variety of unit 'sizes', and are sold in some bars and tobacconists in the bigger cities – look out for signs advertising them.

Calling Italy from Abroad The country code for Italy is 39. Always drop the initial 0 from area codes.

Fax, Telegraph & Email
Fax There is no shortage of fax offices in Italy, but the country's high telephone charges make faxes an expensive mode of communication. To send a fax within Italy you can expect to pay L3000 for the first page and L2000 for each page after, plus L50 a second for the actual call. International faxes can cost L6000 for the first page and L4000 per page thereafter, and L100 a second for the call. You can imagine what this can mean with a slow fax machine at

peak rates! Some Telecom public phones can also send faxes.

Telegraph Telegrams can be sent from post offices or dictated by phone (☎ 186) and are an expensive, but sure, way of having important messages delivered by the same or next day.

Email Italy has a growing number of Internet cafes, where you can send and receive emails, surf the Net etc. These allow you to log in to the net for an average L10,000 to L15,000 an hour and permit you to send email. To receive emails, you need to have a personal mail box, which requires a subscription for a certain number of hours. It is also possible to log into your own email account in your home country. Get all of the necessary information before leaving home. This type of cafe can be found in several of the bigger cities, including:

Roma
　Xplorer Cafe (☎ 324 17 57), Via dei Gracchi 85, near Vaticano. Cost is L12,000 an hour to have access to an email service.
　Itaca Multimedia (☎ 686 14 64; fax 689 60 96), Via della Fosse di Castello 8, next to the Castel Sant'Angelo. Email access is L15,000 for 30 minutes, or L100,000 for a 10 hour subscription, which includes a personal mail box.
Firenze
　Libreria Cima (☎ 247 72 45), Borgo Albizi 37r. It costs L10,000 an hour, or L35,000 to open an email address for six months.
Milano
　Hard Disk Cafe, Corso Sempione 44 (http://www.hdc.it). To receive email you'd have to log in to your own email address, unless you become a member of the Internet Club, in which case the Hard Disk will provide you with an address. Net time costs L10,000 an hour until 9 pm.

BOOKS
Most books are published in different editions by different publishers in different countries. Fortunately, bookshops and libraries search by title or author, so your local bookshop or library is best placed to advise you on the availability of the following recommendations.

Lonely Planet

Mediterranean Europe on a shoestring and *Western Europe on a shoestring* both include chapters on Italy and are recommended for those planning further travel in Europe. For more comprehensive information about the country, use the *Italy* guide. Also published by Lonely Planet, the *Italian phrasebook* lists the words and phrases you're likely to need while travelling in Italy, and the *Mediterranean Europe phrasebook* does the same in less detail for Italy and other countries in the area. Keep an eye out, too, for Lonely Planet's yet-to-be-released guides to Roma, Firenze and Toscana.

Guidebooks

General The Blue Guide series gives very good detailed information about the art and monuments of Italy. If you can read in Italian, you can't go past the excellent red guides of the Touring Club Italiano.

Walking & Mountaineering Try the guides published by Cicerone Press, Cumbria. Titles include *Walking in the Dolomites* and *Walking in the Central Italian Alps*, both by Gillian Price; *High Level Walks in the Dolomites* by Martin Collins: *Classic Climbs in the Dolomites* by Lele Dinoia and Valerio Casari (translated by Al Churcher); *The Grand Tour of Monte Rosa: A Circuit of the Pennine Alps* by CJ Wright; *Selected Climbs in Northern Italy* by Al Churcher; and *Central Apennines, Walks, Scrambles and Climbs* by Stephen Fox. Other books are *Off the Beaten Track* by Richard Sale, Phil Whitney and Nancy Woodyatt; *Wild Italy: A Traveller's Guide* by Tim Jepson; *The Dolomites – Easy Alpine Walks* by Franz Hauleitner; *Walking and Eating in Tuscany and Umbria* by James Lasdun and Pia Davies.

There is a vast range of walking guides in Italian. The easiest to come by are the Iter Guide *A Piedi* series of books, which are available in bookshops, sports shops and at news stands. Other guides which the authors of this book found particularly useful in their research are recommended in the various chapters.

Travel & Exploration

Three Grand Tour classics are Johann Wolfgang von Goethe's *Italian Journey*, Charles Dickens' *Pictures from Italy* and Henry James' *Italian Hours*. DH Lawrence wrote three short travel books while living in Italy, now combined in one volume entitled *DH Lawrence and Italy*.

Others include: *Venice* by James Morris; *The Stones of Florence* and *Venice Observed* by Mary McCarthy; *On Persephone's Island* by Mary Taylor Simeti; *Siren Land* by Norman Douglas; *The Golden Honeycomb* by Vincent Cronin (travels through Sicily); *A Traveller in Southern Italy* by HV Morton. Although written in the 1960s the latter remains a valuable guide to the south and its people. Morton also wrote *A Traveller in Italy* and *A Traveller in Rome*.

Flora & Fauna

Mediterranean Wild Flowers and *The Alpine Flowers of Britain and Europe* by Marjorie Blamey & Christopher Grey-Wilson are excellent reference books, although too weighty for use in the field. The first has more than 2000 colour illustrations of plants, as well as useful information about habitats. The latter covers the Alps, including the Dolomiti (Dolomites), the Pyrenees and northern Europe. *A Guide to the Vegetation of Britain & Europe* by Oleg Polunin & Martin Walters is a bit technical, but has useful information about habitats. *I Fiori delle Alpi* by Franco Rasetti is published in Italian by the Academia Nazionale dei Lincei, Selciom Editoria. If you want to carry a guide with you on your walk, the illustrated Kompass Guides *Fiori alpini*, *Fiori di prato* and *Animali delle Alpi* are very useful. They are pocket size, cost around L9000 and are also available in English.

General

For a potted history of the country, try *Concise History of Italy* by Vincent Cronin or *History of the Italian People* by Giuliano Procacci. *A History of Contemporary Italy. Society and Politics 1943-1988* by Paul Ginsborg is an absorbing and very well written book which will help Italophiles place the country's modern society in perspective.

Serious readers might like to study some of the classics before heading off, such as Dante's *The Divine Comedy*, Giovanni Boccaccio's *The Decameron* and Niccolò Machiavelli's *The Prince*. More recent names in Italian literature include Italo Calvino, Alberto Moravia, Natalia Ginzburg, Primo Levi, Elsa Morante, Carlo Levi, and Umberto Eco. Here are a few suggestions: *The Leopard* by Giuseppe di Lampedusa; *Christ Stopped at Eboli* by Carlo Levi; *The Name of the Rose* by Umberto Eco; and *The Path to the Nest of Spiders* by Italo Calvino.

For background on the Italian people and their culture, there is the classic by Luigi Barzini, *The Italians*. And not to forget the Mafia, certainly one of the country's most absorbing subjects – *Excellent Cadavers: The Mafia and the Death of the First Italian Republic* by Alexander Stille, is a shocking and absorbing account of the Mafia in Sicilia. It focuses on the years leading up to the assassinations of anti-Mafia judges Giovanni Falcone and Paolo Borsellino in 1992 and the subsequent fall of Italy's 'First Republic'.

ONLINE SERVICES

A good place to start is Excite Reviews (http://www.excite.com). Call it up and key in Italy and it will give you a long selection of sites related to Italy, as well as brief but interesting reviews and ratings. Chiantinet (http://www.chiantinet.it) is an excellent site with lots of useful information about the Chianti area and links to other sites. Alfanet (http://www.alfanet.it) has a Welcome Italy page, with a link to information about Roma. Planet Italy (http://www.planetitaly.com) has interesting information.

NEWSPAPERS & MAGAZINES

The following magazines are published in Italian only. *Montagna* (L9000) has been going for almost 30 years and while it focuses on mountaineering, also has articles about walking. *Trekking* (L9000) has articles about hikes throughout the country. *Airone* is an excellent nature magazine, which focuses

on Italy, but also includes articles about other countries. It is published in Italian and is available at news stands for L7500.

PHOTOGRAPHY & VIDEO
Film & Equipment

A roll of 36 exposures 100 ASA Kodak film costs around L8000. It costs around L18,000 to have 36 exposures developed and L12,000 for 24 exposures. A roll of 36 slides costs L10,000 and L7000 for development.

There are numerous outlets which sell and process films, but beware of poor quality processing. A roll of film is called a *pellicola* but you will be understood if you ask for 'film'. Many places claim to process films in one hour but you will rarely get your photos back that quickly – count on late the next day if the outlet has its own processing equipment, or three to four days if it doesn't. Tapes for video cameras are often available at the same outlets, or can be found at stores selling electrical goods.

Airport Security

Italian authorities claim that x-ray machines at airports are film safe, however, they will permit you to hand carry films.

TIME

Italy operates on a 24 hour clock which will take getting used to for travellers used to a 12 hour clock. Daylight saving time starts on the last Sunday in March, when clocks are put forward one hour. Clocks are put back an hour on the last Sunday in September. Ensure that when telephoning home you make allowances for daylight saving in your own country.

European cities such as Paris, Munich, Berlin, Vienna and Madrid have the same time as Italy. Athens, Cairo and Tel Aviv are one hour ahead. When it's noon in Roma, it's 3 am in San Francisco, 6 am in New York and Toronto, 11 am in London, 7 pm in Perth, 9 pm in Sydney and 11 pm in Auckland.

ELECTRICITY

The electric current in Italy is 220V, 50Hz. Power points have two or three holes, and do not have their own switches, while plugs have two or three round pins. Some power points have larger holes than others. Italian homes are usually full of plug adapters to cope with this anomaly.

Travellers from the USA need a voltage converter (although many of the more expensive hotels have provision for 110V appliances such as shavers).

LAUNDRY

Coin laundrettes, where you can do your own washing, are catching on in Italy. You'll find them in most main cities and towns. A load will cost around L8000. Camping grounds have laundry facilities, but in mountain rifugi and most hotels, you'll need to use the hand basin in your room or bathroom.

WOMEN WALKERS

One of the female authors of this guide did all of her research alone. She spent the good part of two months walking up and down hills and mountains on the Amalfi Coast, in the Valle d'Aosta and in the Lakes District. Her thoughts on women walking alone in Italy are detailed in the boxed text below. While she didn't have any trouble, it has to be said that she did most of her research in 'high traffic' areas of the country, areas which are easily accessible and attract a lot of walkers. This also goes for the Dolomiti, Toscana and Liguria.

Walking alone is not recommended for women in certain parts of the country. This would include parts of Sicilia and very definitely in Sardegna, where the trails can tend to be more isolated and inaccessible. Basically, women should use their common sense: if you must walk alone, try to stick to the more popular trails. Otherwise, try to link up with other walkers when staying in hostels and rifugi.

That said, probably one of the main problems a lone woman walker will have to face is the prospect of being plagued by unwanted attention. Many Italian men find lone fe-males (especially of the foreign variety) completely irresistible and find it difficult to understand why you don't find them equally attractive. They have a type of benevolent-aggressive attitude – they can't decide whether you should be looked after or seduced. Try to be patient and avoid becoming aggressive, as this almost always results in an unpleasant confrontation.

What to Wear

Keep it simple. If you turn up in neon stretch shorts and a bra top, you'll attract a lot of attention – unwanted or otherwise. If you stick to simple, comfortable shorts and a

One Woman's Walk

As I strode past a trio of corpulent, perspiring Italian walkers high above Valsavarenche (in Parco Nazionale del Gran Paradiso) I thought that maybe I could have been more discreet about overtaking these men. Male pride is still, among some at least, easily wounded. Solo women walkers are exceptional in Italy, which came as a surprise after the Highlands of Scotland, where soloists, men and women, are nowadays unremarkable.

Attitudes in Italy seemed to range from awe, if not admiration, to envy. Throughout sojourns at 14 different camp sites, from the Amalfi Coast to Valle d'Aosta, I felt vulnerable only at Lago di Garda, when some rowdy young men were playing cards late at night in a caravan unnervingly close to my small tent, and it was all too obvious by the washing on the makeshift line that its occupant was a woman.

In remote areas and villages, I did sense the disapproval of some older women, and perhaps some men, of my attire – shorts, even though on the baggy side, and of modest length. However, plenty of walkers do wear shorts, so there's no reason to recommend any alternative.

There is little if anything to fear in being a lone woman walker in Italy providing you observe the sensible safety precautions applying to travel anywhere. Perhaps I can say this as someone who is tall, carried an old, weather-beaten rucksack, and perhaps looks fairly anonymous. I was once asked quite unashamedly, by a lively young African woman, whether I was male or female!

Sandra Bardwell

T-shirt, you'll blend in with everyone else. Remember that your clothing should basically conform to the list of essential items in the Planning section earlier in this chapter. Always carry a pair of long pants, just in case you want to visit a church while on your walk: dress rules usually forbid bare legs, and sometimes even bare arms.

WALKING WITH CHILDREN

Many northern Europeans bring their children with them on walking expeditions in the Alps. Some carry babies in specially designed backpacks, and it is not uncommon to spot children as young as six walking at high altitudes. However, if you have never taken your child walking before, don't expect their introduction to it to be trouble-free. It takes a long time and lots of patience to 'train' a child to go on long walks. If you are bringing along inexperienced minors, choose areas where there are short walk options, such as in Toscana, in Liguria and on the Amalfi Coast.

Basically all of the walks except those covered in Sicilia and Sardegna and perhaps the volcanoes route, offer possibilities for families. The Dolomiti, for instance, are a very popular family destination. Cablecars and chair lifts offer easy access to high altitudes and if you plan carefully, you could cover sections of the walks outlined without tiring your kids too much. If you do plan to take the kids walking in the mountains, it is important to ensure that they are well equipped with good walking boots, a light, warm jacket, a hat, gloves and a wind jacket (see Clothing & Footwear in the Planning section earlier in this chapter). It is a good idea to bring a 5m to 6m length of cord/rope with a minimum diameter of 8mm to use in potentially dangerous situations, such as on narrow ledges, or when a short climb may be necessary.

USEFUL ORGANISATIONS

There are numerous local walking clubs throughout Italy, but unless you are able to establish contact through your own local walking organisation, it is unlikely you'll get much help from them. We have included some information about the Club Alpino Italiano (CAI – Italian Alpine Club) in this section, more for background than anything else. The 'club' is actually a network of small, local clubs which maintain walking trails and run rifugi in their respective areas. Walking and related activities are organised primarily for club members.

Mountain Guides Associations

You'll find mountain guides associations throughout the Alps. They usually have offices close to the local tourist office, or actually in the tourist office itself. They offer

---

An Accidental Walker

When our daughter Virginia was still a baby, we used to pop her in a specially designed backpack and take her with us on mountain hikes. She was no trouble at all and usually fell asleep after the first half hour. Unfortunately, once she became too heavy to carry, we didn't put enough effort into her 'training' and now that she is a very independently-minded four-and-a-half-year-old, it is a very tricky business indeed trying to convince her to walk when she doesn't want to. We have found that it is a fine balance: she needs to be in the right mood, not too tired at the beginning of the walk, and there needs to be an incentive (we won't call it a bribe!).

Having another child along, perhaps with a bit more experience, is a great incentive. If there are animals around, they are also a good incentive because they keep her distracted and interested. If not, then there's always the promise of an ice cream at the end of the walk. In fact, we were pleasantly surprised recently when she went on two walks with us on the Amalfi Coast with a minimum of fuss, one of which involved a long climb from Atrani to Ravello, a difference in altitude of almost 200m. Perhaps she's not ready to hit the Dolomiti yet, but we're making progress.

Helen Gillman & Stefano Cavedoni

Italian Alpine Club/Club Alpino Italiano

Walkers visiting Italy cannot help but be aware of the presence of the Club Alpino Italiano (CAI), as owner and manager of mountain rifugi and for its marking of paths. Indeed, the CAI is the major force in the world of Italian walking, mountaineering, trekking and kindred winter activities.

The club was founded in October 1863 in Torino (Turin), following the example set a few years earlier by the establishment of The Alpine Club in London. However, from the outset there was a fundamental difference between the two organisations: would-be members of The Alpine Club had to demonstrate their competence in alpinism, whereas no such requirement applies in Italy – the club is open to all. On the eve of WWI (when the club celebrated its 50th anniversary with an ascent of Gran Paradiso, Italy's highest mountain), the CAI had 7500 members. At the same time, there were only 730 people in The Alpine Club. During the years between the two world wars, the CAI continued to grow and by 1939 had more than 75,000 members. Numbers were halved during WWII but the club quickly recovered and in its centenary had reached 89,000. Growth since 1970 has been phenomenal; the 300,000 mark was passed in 1993. Now the total is considerably more than 305,000. Only the German Alpine Club is larger, while the French equivalent has about 100,000 members.

In Italy the average age of members (in 1994) was 37 and the largest concentration of members is in Lombardia. The greatest strength is among younger people, who make up nearly half the total number. The club is decentralised from its head office in Torino, with more than 450 sections or area groups which are further organised into six regions; this arrangement has opened up opportunities for closer cooperation with local government authorities. Volunteers are the foundation and the strength of the CAI and enable it to undertake a wide range of activities.

It has nearly 800 national instructors in mountaineering, ski mountaineering and touring, climbing, trekking and mountaineering for young people. There are also close to 7000 people on call for the mountain rescue service, and a large corps of technical experts in scientific and other fields. The mountain rescue service in particular is highly regarded internationally and the club's success generally in sustaining the commitment of its volunteer members is the object of admiration.

The club also has a publications programme, notably a prestigious series of mountain guides, which are being updated to better meet modern requirements. Local groups also undertake publication projects, such as the map of the Monti Lattari (see under Maps in The Amalfi Coast chapter).

The club is firmly apolitical and its members' allegiances otherwise embrace the diversity of Italy's colourful political spectrum. Even the appointment of high profile politicians to senior positions has not compromised this stance. Nevertheless, the club does not hesitate to take part in the continuing debate about competitive mountain sports and about environmental issues affecting the mountains. Today it seems the CAI is slightly embarrassed by the potential for conflict between its ownership of the rifugi and its strong environmental protection policy. The commitment to maintaining the inheritance of the rifugi is strong, not the least because the rifugi are generally regarded as the best in the world. The debate continues, about extensions and about new construction. From the outside, it is easy to appreciate the dilemma. The rifugi are clearly magnets for thousands of people, especially young children, which draw them into the mountains – but eroded paths and problems of waste disposal loom large.

Sandra Bardwell

guided treks and climbs and often also run courses in rock climbing or negotiating *ferrate* (cord trails). Some associations are listed in the individual chapters. The following are two of the many associations operating in the Alps:

Scuola Alpina Dolomiten (☎ (0471) 70 53 43; fax 70 73 89), Via Vogelweider 6, Castelrotto
Cortina Alpine Guides Group (☎ (0436) 47 40) Piazzetta San Francesco 5, Cortina

Associazione Italiana Alberghi per la Gioventù (AIG)

The Italian youth hostel association, affili-

ated with Hostelling International (HI), has its head office (☎ (06) 487 1152) at Via Cavour 44, Roma.

DANGERS & ANNOYANCES
Rockfall

The danger presented by rockfalls is most acute in the sparsely vegetated high Alpine zone, where continual melting and freezing produces brittle crags and unstable slopes. Mountaineers are most at risk from falling rocks, but rockfall sometimes causes serious injury or even death to unwary walkers.

Sections of path most obviously exposed

to rockfall lead through steep and eroding mountainsides, or below cliffs fringed by heavy fields of talus. Don't hang around in such places any longer than necessary and keep a watchful eye for 'movements' above as you pass. Rockfalls can also be caused by walkers where trails cross unstable ground. If you accidentally send a loose chunk of rock into motion, shout out a loud warning to any walkers who may be below you. Chamois or ibex sometimes dislodge rocks, so animal watchers should take special care to keep well clear.

Avalanches
Snow avalanches are essentially a winter occurrence, but on certain high Alpine routes very early in the walking season, there may still be a risk from avalanches. Walkers are advised to check with local tourist offices, mountain guides or at rifugi before setting out.

Thunderstorms & Lightning
Thunderstorms accompanied by intense electrical activity are a common occurrence in Italy. In the higher mountain regions storms can strike surprisingly quickly, taking walkers completely unawares. The dangers posed at higher altitudes by the sudden wet and windy conditions are covered under Hypothermia in the Medical Problems & Treatment section in the Health, Safety & First Aid chapter. While the danger is greatest in the mountains, walkers in all of the areas covered by this guide should heed the following safeguards in order to minimise the risk of being hit by lightning.

In open areas where there is no shelter, find a depression in the ground and take up a crouched-squatting position with your feet together. Do *not* lie flat on the ground – if lightning strikes nearby the voltage difference between your head and your feet can reach several thousand volts. Avoid contact with metallic objects – do *not* use an umbrella.

Never seek shelter under objects which are isolated or higher than their surroundings (such as trees or transmission line poles), as these are far more likely to get zapped. Isolated buildings and trees at the edge of a forest are other key targets for lightning bolts. If you find yourself in a forest of regularly high trees, you are relatively safe as long as you keep a fair distance from each tree and away from overhanging branches. If you happen to be standing or swimming in a lake or river when a thunderstorm approaches, get out of the water immediately.

Should anyone actually be struck by lightning, immediately begin first aid measures such as mouth-to-mouth resuscitation and treatment of burns. Get the patient to a doctor as quickly as possible.

Insects
Ticks are found throughout Italy. They live in long grass, bracken and undergrowth. They bury their heads under the host's skin and suck its blood. If you are walking through tick-infested areas wear long pants and carefully check your body, clothing and shoes at the end of the day. Other insects which might cause problems include wasps and *calabroni* (a large wasp), which can provoke acute allergic reactions (see under Insect Bites & Stings in the Health, Safety & First Aid chapter for further information).

Snakes
Italy's only dangerous snake, the viper, is found throughout the country (except in Sardegna). To minimise your chances of being bitten, always wear boots, socks and long trousers when walking through undergrowth where snakes may be present. Don't put your hands into holes and crevices, and be careful when collecting firewood.

Viper bites do not cause instantaneous death, and an antivenene is widely available in pharmacies. Keep the victim calm and still, wrap the bitten limb tightly, as you would for a sprained ankle, and attach a splint to immobilise it. Then seek medical help, if possible with the dead snake for identification. Don't attempt to catch the snake if there is even a remote possibility of being bitten again. Tourniquets and sucking out the poison are now comprehensively discredited.

Hunting

This is not one of the country's most appealing features, but it has a long tradition and hunters jealously protect their rights. Successive referenda aimed at limiting hunters' rights have failed and hunters continue to enjoy privileges including the right to enter private property without the owner's permission. The season is from September to March. You are most likely to encounter hunters in Toscana and Sardegna, but they are active throughout the country. If you stick to walking trails and don't go hiding in bushes, you shouldn't have any problematic or dangerous encounters with hunters, but the sound of guns being fired all around you can be very off-putting. Make a bit of noise to alert them to your presence.

Theft

Theft is one of the main problems for travellers in Italy, but it is mainly confined to the big cities and major tourist destinations. So you're unlikely to be robbed while you're walking in the country or mountains.

However, if you're planning to spend some time sightseeing, take heed of the following advice. Pickpockets and bag-snatchers operate in most major cities and are particularly active in Napoli and Roma. The best way to avoid being robbed in the cities is to wear a money belt under your clothing. (Although this really won't be necessary when you're out on a walking trail.)

You should keep all important items, such as money, passport, other papers and tickets in your money belt at all times. If you are carrying a bag or camera, ensure that you wear the strap across your body and have the bag on the side away from the road to deter snatch thieves, who often operate from motorcycles and scooters. Since the aim of young motorcycle bandits is often fun rather than gain, you are just as likely to find yourself relieved of your sunglasses – or worse, of an earring. Motorcycle bandits are very active in Napoli, Roma, Syracuse and Palermo.

You should also watch out for groups of dishevelled-looking women and children. They generally work in groups of four of five and carry paper or cardboard which they use to distract your attention while they swarm around and riffle through your pockets and bag. Never underestimate their skill – they are lightning fast and very adept. Their favourite haunts are in and near major train stations, at tourist sights (such as the Colosseum) and in shopping areas. If you notice that you have been targeted by a group, either take evasive action, such as crossing the street, or shout *va via!* (go away!) in a loud voice.

Pickpockets often hang out on crowded buses and in crowded areas such as markets. There is only one way to deter pickpockets: simply *do not* carry money or valuables in your pockets, and be careful about your bags.

Be careful even in hotels and don't leave valuables lying around your room. You should also be cautious of sudden friendships, particularly if it turns out that your new-found *amico* or *amica* wants to sell you something. Parked cars are also prime targets for thieves, particularly those with foreign number plates or rental company stickers. Try covering the stickers and leave a local newspaper on the seat to make it look like a local car.

Never leave valuables in your car – in fact, try not to leave anything in the car if you can help it and certainly not overnight. It is a good idea to pay extra to leave your car in supervised car parks, although there is no guarantee it will be completely safe. Throughout Italy, particularly in the south, service stations along the autostradas are favourite haunts of thieves, who can clean out your car in the time it takes to have a cup of coffee. If possible, park the car where you can keep an eye on it. In recent years there have been isolated incidences of armed robberies on the autostrada south of Napoli, where travellers have been forced off the road, or tricked into pulling over, and then robbed at gunpoint.

When driving in cities, you also need to beware of snatch thieves when you pull up at traffic lights. Keep the doors locked, and if you have the windows open, ensure that there is nothing valuable on the dashboard. Car theft is a major problem in the Campania region, particularly in Napoli.

Certainly even the most cautious travellers

are still prey to expert thieves, but there is no need to be paranoid. By taking a few basic precautions, you can greatly lessen the risk of being robbed.

Unfortunately, some Italians practice a more insidious form of theft: short-changing. Numerous travellers have reported losing money in this way. If you are new to the Italian currency, take the time to acquaint yourself with the denominations. When paying for goods, or tickets, or a meal, or whatever, keep an eye on the bills you hand over and then count your change carefully. One popular means of short-changing goes something like this: you hand over L50,000 for a newspaper which costs L2800; you are handed change for L10,000 and, while the person who sold you the paper hesitates, you hurry off without counting it. If you'd stayed for another five seconds, the rest of the change probably would have been handed over without needing to say anything.

In case of theft or loss, always report the incident at the questura within 24 hours and ask for a statement, otherwise your travel insurance company won't pay out.

In case of emergency, you can contact the police throughout Italy on ☎ 113.

BUSINESS HOURS
Business hours vary throughout the country, but generally shops are open Monday to Friday from around 9 am to 1 pm and 3.30 to 7.30 pm (or 4 to 8 pm). In some cities, grocery shops might not reopen until 5 pm and, during the warmer months, they could stay open until 9 pm. They close on Thursday or Monday afternoons (depending on which town you're in) and often on Saturday afternoons. Shops, department stores and supermarkets also close for a half day during the week – it varies from city to city, but is usually either Monday morning or Thursday afternoon. Larger department stores and most supermarkets now have continuous opening hours, from 9 am to 7.30 pm Monday to Saturday. Some even open from 9 am to 1 pm on Sunday.

Banks tend to be open Monday to Friday from 8.30 am to 1.30 pm and 3.30 to 4.30 pm, although hours can vary. They are closed at weekends, but it is always possible to find an exchange office open in the larger cities and in major tourist areas.

Major post offices open Monday to Saturday from 8.30 am to 6 or 7 pm. Smaller post offices generally open Monday to Friday from 8.30 am to 2 pm and on Saturdays from 8.30 am to noon.

Pharmacies are usually open from 9 am to 12.30 pm and 3.30 to 7.30 pm. They are always closed on Sunday and usually on Saturday afternoon. When closed, pharmacies are required to display a list of pharmacies in the area which are open.

Bars (in the Italian sense, ie coffee-and-sandwich places) and cafes generally open from 7.30 am to 8 pm, although some stay open after 8 pm and turn into pub-style places. Restaurants open from noon to 3 pm and 7.30 to 11 pm (later in summer and in the south). Restaurants and bars are required to close for one day each week, which varies.

Museum and gallery opening hours vary, although there is a trend towards continuous opening hours from 9.30 am to 7 pm. Many close on Mondays.

PUBLIC HOLIDAYS & SPECIAL EVENTS
Most Italians take their annual holidays in August, deserting the cities for the cooler seaside or mountains. This means that many businesses and shops close for at least a part of the month, particularly during the week around Ferragosto (Feast of the Assumption) on 15 August. It also means that accommodation in cooler areas can be booked out well in advance. If you want to walk near the sea or in the mountains in August, particularly if you want to stay in rifugi, book early.

National public holidays include:

6 January (Epiphany)
March/April (Easter Monday)
25 April (Liberation Day)
1 May (Labour Day)
15 August (Feast of the Assumption)
1 November (All Saints' Day)
8 December (Feast of the Immaculate Conception)
25 December (Christmas Day)
26 December (Feast of Santo Stefano)

Festivals

February/March/April

Carnevale
During the period before Ash Wednesday many towns stage carnivals and enjoy their last opportunity to indulge before Lent. The carnival, held in Venezia during the 10 days before Ash Wednesday, is the most famous.

Sartiglia
This event is the highlight of carnival celebrations at Oristano in Sardegna on the Sunday and Tuesday before Lent. It involves a medieval tournament of horsemen in masquerade.

Festival of the Almond Blossoms
A traditional historical pageant and fireworks held at Agrigento, Sicilia, in early March.

Le Feste di Pasqua
Holy Week in Italy is marked by solemn processions and passion plays. The week is marked in Sicily by numerous events, including a Procession of the Mysteries at Trapani and the celebration of Easter according to Byzantine rites at Piana degli Albanesi, near Palermo. Women in colourful 15th century costume give out Easter eggs to the public. There is a fascinating procession of the Misteri on the island of Procida in the Bay of Napoli on Good Friday. Another festival is held at Amalfi.

Scoppio del Carro (Explosion of the Cart)
Held in Firenze in the Piazza del Duomo at noon on Easter Sunday, this event features the explosion of a cart full of fireworks – a tradition dating back to the Crusades.

May

Festa di San Domenico e i Serpari (Festival of St Dominic & the Snakes)
On 5 May the townspeople of Cocullo, in Abruzzo, celebrate the feast day of their patron saint, St Dominic, by draping a statue of him with live snakes and carrying it around in a procession.

Festa di San Gennaro
Three times a year (the first Sunday in May, 19 September and 16 December) the faithful gather in Napoli's Duomo to wait for the blood of the saint to liquefy – if the miracle occurs it is a good omen for the city.

Corsa dei Ceri (Candles Race)
In Gubbio, Umbria, townspeople gather on 15 May to race uphill to the town's Basilica di Sant'Ubaldo carrying huge wooden shrines.

Cavalcata Sarda (Sardinian Cavalcade)
Hundreds of Sardi, many on horseback, gather at Sassari in colourful traditional costume on the penultimate Sunday in May to mark a victory over the Saracens in the year 1000.

Maggio Musicale Fiorentino
A music festival held in Firenze in May and June.

June

Historical Regatta of the Four Ancient Maritime Republics
A procession of boats and a race between the four historical maritime rivals – Pisa, Venezia, Amalfi and Genova. The event rotates between the four towns.

Ardia
More dangerous than Siena's Palio (see Il Palio following), this impressive and chaotic horse race at Sedilo in Sardegna on 6 and 7 June celebrates the victory of the Roman Emperor Constantine over Maxentius in 312 AD (the battle was actually at the Ponte Milvio in Roma). A large number of horsemen race around the town while onlookers shoot guns into the ground or air.

Festa di Sant'Antonio
Fans of St Anthony, patron saint of Padua and of lost things, attend the procession of the saint's relics held annually on 13 June.

Festival dei Due Mondi (Festival of Two Worlds)
This major arts festival is held in the beautiful Umbrian hill town of Spoleto in June and July. Created by Gian Carlo Menotti, the festival features music, theatre, dance and art exhibitions.

July

Il Palio
Twice a year, on 2 July and 16 August, jockeys representing Siena's ancient contrade (quarters) gallop around the town's medieval Piazza del Campo in a perilous bareback horse race. The race is preceded by an equally colourful if less breakneck parade of supporters, famed especially for the colourful flag-waving ceremonies. The winning jockey takes Il Palio (the Banner) for his contrada.

Umbria Jazz
Held at Perugia in Umbria in July, this week-long festival features performers from around the world.

August
I Candelieri (Festival of the Candelabra)
On 14 August the townsfolk of Sassari, in Sardinia, dress up in medieval costume to carry huge wooden columns through the town. The festival is held on the Feast of the Assumption to honour a vow made in 1652 to end a plague.
Il Palio
This repeat of Siena's famous horse race is held on 16 August.
Festa del Redentore
Held at Nuoro in Sardegna, this folk festival and parade is attended by thousands of people from all over the island, who dress in traditional regional costume.
International Film Festival
Held at the Lido, Venezia, the festival attracts the international film scene.

September
Regata Storica (Historical Regatta)
This race of gondolas along Venezia's Grand Canal is preceded by a parade of boats decorated in 15th century style. It is held on the first Sunday in September.
Giostra della Quintana
A medieval pageant involving a parade and jousting event with horsemen in traditional costume. Held on the second Sunday in September in Foligno, near Perugia (Umbria).
Festa di San Gennaro
On 19 September the faithful of Napoli gather for the second time to await the miraculous liquefaction of the saint's blood. They gather again on 16 December.

October
Festa di San Francesco d'Assisi
Special religous ceremonies are held in the churches of San Francesco and Santa Maria degli Angeli in Assisi on 3 and 4 October.

November
Festa della Madonna della Salute
Held in Venezia on 21 November, this procession over a bridge of boats across the Canal Grande to the Chiesa di Santa Maria della Salute to give thanks for the city's deliverance from plague in 1630.
Festa di Santa Cecilia
A series of concerts and exhibitions in Siena to honour the patron saint of musicians.

December
Christmas
During the weeks preceding Christmas there are numerous processions, religious events etc. Many churches set up elaborate cribs or nativity scenes known as *presepi*. In the northernmost regions (particularly the province of Alto Adige) each town sets up a Mercantino di Natale, which is the local version of the German/Austrian Christkindlmarkt, where you can happily sip steaming *vino brulé* and buy all sorts of Christmas goodies.

Horsemen in traditional costume gather for the Giostra della Quintana festival in Foligno in September.

Individual towns have public holidays to celebrate the feasts of their patron saints. Some of these are: the Feast of St Mark on 25 April in Venezia; the Feast of St John the Baptist on 24 June in Firenze, Genova and Torino; the Feast of Saints Peter & Paul in Roma on 29 June; and the Feast of San Gennaro (Janarius) in Napoli on 19 September.

Italy's calendar bursts with cultural events ranging from colourful traditional celebrations, with a religious and/or historical flavour, through to festivals of the performing arts, including opera, music and theatre. Religious festivals are particularly numerous in Sicilia and Sardegna, notably Le Feste di Pasqua (Easter Week) in Sicilia.

Major music festivals include Umbria Jazz held in June and Maggio Musicale Fiorentino in Firenze in May, while the Festival of Two Worlds (Festival dei Due Mondi) in Spoleto is worth including in your itinerary. As well as Carnevale in February, Venezia offers an international film festival in September and the Biennale visual arts festival, the latter held every odd numbered year.

The Festivals boxed text on the previous pages contains some of the more interesting and important events, but represent only a fraction of those held in a normal year. Events are listed under the relevant month, with specific dates included only when they are fixed.

WALKING ROUTES
Route Descriptions

The original idea for the selection of walks described in this guide was to include at least one 'long' walk (of more than three days) in each chapter, which could be tackled in its entirety or easily broken into stages. There has been an effort to detail long walks which cover the principal, or most spectacular walking routes in each area: in the Dolomiti, for instance, the Northern Dolomiti route passes through a series of protected areas and incorporates or passes by some of the most spectacular mountains in the region. It hasn't been possible to include long walks in all of the areas covered by the guide, but where they have been described, we have included

information about how to exit from the walk at the end of each day, as well as often detailing alternative shorter (and sometimes longer) routes. We have also included a selection of short walks (half to one day), many of them loops (starting and ending at the same point) and have referred to some of the other options in each area.

The routes described in this book represent only a fraction of the possibilities for walking in Italy. We hope that walkers will use this book as an introduction and a planning tool, as well as a guide to actual walks and, once they become familiar with local circumstances, start planning their own routes to take advantage of the endless number of possibilities.

We have always included information about places to stay at the end of each day: for long walks this is usually a rifugio actually on the route, while for shorter walks it might be a hotel or camping ground in a nearby town. The start and end of almost all walks are easy to reach by public transport.

Levels of Difficulty

It is assumed that walkers are reasonably fit and have some knowledge of how to read a map and use a compass. Previous walking experience is not necessary, but it is advisable that walkers undertake some physical preparation before tackling high altitude walks. Inexperienced walkers should approach with caution walks which include exposed paths, cord trails and sections where it might be necessary to climb. This doesn't mean you shouldn't tackle those walks – just be sure that you are aware of what you might be confronted with in order to avoid potentially dangerous panic attacks (such as when you find yourself on a narrow ledge next to a 200m drop!).

Many of the walks are not at all demanding and could easily be tackled by families, particularly on the Amalfi Coast, in Liguria and around the Lakes. A five-level system has been used to grade the walks in this book: Easy; Easy-Medium; Medium; Medium-Hard; Hard.

Be a Responsible Walker

The following is a checklist of dos and don'ts for responsible walking.

- Don't light fires unless you are absolutely sure that it's safe.
- Don't pick Alpine wild flowers, most of them are protected.
- Don't pick mushrooms if you are in an area where they are reserved for the locals. There will be a sign saying something like *Raccolta dei funghi riservata*.
- Take all of your rubbish away with you, including cigarette butts, unless there are rubbish bins in the area. Don't bury your rubbish.
- Leave the local wildlife alone.
- Don't make too much noise.
- Be careful about where you go to the toilet and be sure to bury your bodily waste.
- Ensure that you close gates after you have passed through.
- Be attentive when passing through fields, particularly during periods of cultivation. Stick to the edges or obvious tracks and don't trample on crops.
- Don't pick grapes or olives on your way through olive groves or vineyards.

Times & Distances

The approximate time needed to complete a walk is given with each walk description. These times are based on actual walking time and don't allow for rest stops, photography or meandering. Any moderately fit person should have no trouble completing walks within the estimated time. However, walking speed is an individual thing and once you factor in time needed to study wildflowers, observe animals and stop for a picnic along the way, a four hour walk quickly extends to six hours or longer. Be sure to calculate in the extra time, so as to avoid being stranded at night. Distances are not quoted for walks: the length of a walk measured in kilometres becomes irrelevant when you're walking in the mountains due to the up-and-down nature of hiking. Even in an area such as Chianti you'll still be walking up and down hills.

Altitude Measurements

In quoting altitude measurements we have relied on those provided by the maps used during our research. These included the best available commercial maps and official Italian military maps (Istituto Geografico Militare (IGM) – see Maps in the Planning section of this chapter) for areas where no commercial maps were available. The authors also used altimeters on occasions to check altitude measurements given on maps. We found that altimeters sometimes gave different readings to those on our maps, and we also found that different maps will give different measurements at the same point, although usually not much different. Measurements have generally been rounded off to the nearest 10m.

Place Names & Terminology

Place names and geographical terms are usually in Italian throughout this book. This includes the use of Italian names for many places which are perhaps better known by their common English names – such as Roma instead of Rome; Firenze instead of Florence; Napoli instead of Naples. Don't worry – you'll get used to it! In some areas, names in local dialect have also been used, particularly when a feature or place is known widely by that name. Things can get a bit confusing in the Dolomiti, where three languages are spoken in some areas – Italian, German and Ladin. In Alto Adige places must be referred to in Italian and German by law. Translations of principal terms used in this book are included on the first mention in each chapter and in the glossary at the back of this book.

Long-Distance Walks

A distinction has been made in this guide between long-distance walks which cross regional or country boundaries, such as the Sentiero d'Italia and the Gran Traversata dell Alpi and 'local' long-distance walks such as the Alte Vie. The country's major long-distance walks have been included in the Long-Distance Walks chapter.

RESPONSIBLE WALKING

Many Italians can have a surprising disregard for the environment (see Ecology & Environment in the Facts about Italy chapter). They litter shamelessly and have been slow to become concerned about conservation issues. Don't follow their example.

Trail Etiquette

It is normal and polite practice to greet other walkers on Alpine paths. A simple 'Hello' or *'Buongiorno'* will do. Germans you meet in the Alps will usually greet you with a brisk *'Grüss Gott'* (hello).

In relation to walks outlined in this guide which pass through private property: at the time of writing it was understood that permission had been granted by owners (since these are generally trails established and marked by local organisations). If for some reason you feel that the situation may have changed, if possible you should approach the owner and ask permission to pass through. In Italy you'll rarely have any problems.

ACCOMMODATION

Throughout this guide, places to stay at the end of each stage of a walk are specifically noted. Sometimes a couple of places may be suggested, whereas in other cases, there may be only one option (such as with mountain rifugi). There has been every effort to plan longer walks (more than one day) bearing in mind accommodation and eating facilities. This means that it may be necessary to walk a long distance one day and then a comparatively short distance the next, in order to ensure a bed for the night.

Reservations

During high season (summer) it is essential that you book a bed at mountain rifugi, otherwise you could find yourself referred on to the next rifugio (which could be hours away), or relegated to sleeping on the floor. Without bookings you will have a lot of problems finding a bed in Chianti year-round and it is strongly recommended that you book at the places detailed in this guide well in advance. A phone call or fax before leaving home is probably the best idea. Summer is high season for tourism throughout the country, and you could encounter problems in the major cities, at beach resorts and in the mountains. It is always a good idea to book a bed at youth hostels.

In Cities & Towns

Hostels Hostels in Italy are called *ostelli per la gioventù* and many are run by the Associazione Italiana Alberghi per la Gioventù (AIG), which is affiliated with Hostelling International (HI). An HI card is not always required, but it is recommended that you have one. Membership cards can be purchased at major hostels, from CTS (student and youth travel centre) offices, from AIG (youth hostel association) offices throughout Italy, and of course from a HI-affiliated office in your home country. Pick up a booklet on Italian hostels, with details of prices, locations etc from the AIG national head office (☎ (06) 487 11 52), Via Cavour 44, Roma.

Nightly rates vary from L13,000 to L24,000 and the cost per night often includes breakfast. If not, breakfast will cost around L2000. In some hostels there is an extra charge for use of heating and hot water, usually around L1000. A meal will cost from L12,000.

Accommodation is in segregated dormitories, although some hostels offer family rooms (at a higher price per person).

Hostels are generally closed from 9 am to 3.30 pm, although there are many exceptions. Check-in is from 6 to 10.30 pm, although some hostels will allow you a morning check-in, before they close for the day (it is best to verify beforehand). Curfew is 10.30 or 11 pm in winter and 11.30 pm or midnight in summer. It is usually necessary to pay before 9 am on the day of your departure, otherwise you could be charged for another night.

Pensioni & Hotels There is often no difference between a *pensione* and an *albergo*; in fact, some hotels use both titles. Hotels and pensioni are graded according to a star system: one star up to five stars. *Locande* (similar to pensioni) and *alloggi*, also known as *affittacamere*, are generally cheaper, but not always and are not given star gradings.

A single room *(camera singola)* is uniformly expensive in Italy, costing from around L40,000. A double room *(camera doppia)* for a room with twin beds, and *camera matrimoniale* for a double bed, ranges from around L60,000. It is much cheaper to share with two or more people. In most parts of Italy, proprietors will charge no more than 15% of the cost of a double room for each additional person.

Tourist offices have booklets listing all pensioni and hotels, including prices (although they might not always be up to date). Ask staff for lists of locande and affittacamere.

Religious Institutions Known as *casa religione di ospitalità*, these institutions offer accommodation in major cities and often in monasteries in the country. The standard is usually good, but prices are no longer low. You can expect to pay about the same as for a one-star hotel, if not more. Information can be obtained through local tourist offices, or through the archdiocese of the relevant city.

On the Walk

Camping Most camping facilities in Italy are major complexes with swimming pools, tennis courts, restaurants and supermarkets. Like hotels, they are graded according to a star system. Prices at even the most basic camping grounds can be surprisingly expensive once you add up the various charges for each person, a site for your tent or caravan and a car, but they generally still work out cheaper than a double room in a one-star hotel. Average prices are L8000 to L12,000 per adult, L6000 to L8000 for children aged under 12 years and from L10,000 for a site. You'll also often have to pay to park your car

and there is sometimes a charge for use of the showers, usually around L1000.

Locations are usually good, ranging from beach or lakeside, to valleys in the Alps. In major cities, camping grounds are often a long way from the historic centres, and the inconvenience, plus the additional cost of needing to use public transport, should be weighed up against the price of a hotel room.

Wild camping is generally not permitted in Italy and you might find yourself disturbed during the night by the carabinieri. But out of the main summer tourist season, free campers who choose spots not visible from the road, don't light fires, and who try to be inconspicuous, shouldn't have too much trouble. Always get permission from the landowner if you want to camp on private property.

Full lists of camping grounds in and near cities and towns are usually available from local tourist offices. In Sicilia and Sardegna the regional tourist boards publish annual booklets listing all facilities throughout the islands. The Touring Club Italiano publishes an annual book listing all camping grounds in Italy, *Campeggi e Villagi Turistici in Italia* (L22,000), and the Istituto Geografico de Agostini publishes the annual *Guida di Campeggi in Europa* (L20,000), both available in major bookshops in Italy.

Rifugi There is an excellent network of mountain rifugi in the Alps, northern Appennini and Alpi Apuane. There are fewer in the Alpi Marittime and they are almost nonexistent in the south of the country, Sicilia and Sardegna. It is a good idea to book ahead (even if only a day ahead) to ensure that there's a bed waiting when you arrive tired and hungry at the end of a long day's walking. Technically, rifugi may not refuse to provide shelter. However, they can send you on to the next rifugio if there is still enough time for you to arrive there before dark. If it is too late to send you on, they will let you sleep on the floor. Some rifugi are privately run, others are owned by the Club Alpino Italiano (CAI – see Useful Organisations). The CAI rifugi tend to be a bit cheaper and are more likely to have dormitory-style accommodation. The average price per person for an overnight stay plus breakfast is L18,000 to around L40,000. Private rooms are also available and meals are always served. The locations of rifugi are marked on good hiking maps and it should be noted that most are open only from July to September. Additional information, including telephone numbers, can be obtained from local tourist offices.

Agriturismo This is a holiday on a working farm and is becoming increasingly popular in Italy. Traditionally the idea was that families rented out rooms in their farmhouses to people who would then actually work on the farm. However, more commonly it is a restaurant in a restored farm complex, with rooms available for rent. All *agriturismo* are operating farms and you will usually be able to sample the local produce.

Agriturismo is well organised in Trentino-Alto Adige, Toscana, Umbria and increasingly so in parts of Sicilia and Sardegna, and local tourist offices will usually have information. For detailed information on all facilities in Italy, contact Agriturist (☎ (06) 68521), Corso Vittorio Emanuele 89, 00186 Roma. It publishes a book with all agriturismo listings throughout the country (L35,000) and is available at the office and in selected bookshops.

FOOD
Regional Food
What the world regards as Italian cooking is really a collection of regional cuisines *(cucine)*. While the eating habits of Italians are now fairly homogeneous, cooking styles continue to vary notably from region to region and significantly between the north and south. Among the country's best known dishes are *lasagne* and *spaghetti bolognese* (eaten in Italy with tagliatelle and called *al ragù*), both from the region of Emilia Romagna.

In Trentino-Alto Adige the cuisine has a heavy Austrian influence, and alongside minestrone and spaghetti, you will find *canerdeli*

(a soup with noodles in it) and Wiener schnitzel. While in Liguria, try *pesto*, a delicious uncooked pasta sauce of fresh basil, garlic, oil, pine nuts and cheese, ground together with a mortar and pestle. Also try the *farinata*, a tart made with chick-pea flour, and the *focaccia*, a flat bread. In Toscana the locals use a lot of olive oil and herbs, and regional specialities are noted for their simplicity, fine flavour and the use of fresh produce. Try the *bistecca fiorentina*, a huge T-bone steak usually 3cm to 4cm thick. It is quite acceptable, and in fact advisable, to order one steak for two people. Among the staples of Tuscan cuisine are small white *cannellini* beans, although all types of beans are widely used. There is also a wide range of soups, from the simple *acquacotta*, which translates as 'cooked water', to the rich *minestrone alla fiorentina*, flavoured with pork and chicken giblets. Don't miss the incredibly rich *panforte*, Siena's famous Christmas fruitcake.

In and around Roma, traditional pasta includes spaghetti *carbonara* (with egg yolk, cheese and bacon) and *alla matriciana* (with a sauce of tomato, bacon and a touch of chilli). Offal is also popular in Roma – if you can stomach it, try the pasta *pajata*, made with the entrails of very young veal, considered a delicacy since they contain the mother's congealed milk.

As you go further south, the food becomes hotter and spicier and the *dolci* (cakes and pastries) sweeter and richer. Don't miss the experience of eating a pizza in Napoli (where it was created), or the *melanzane parmigiana* (eggplant layered with a tomato sauce and mozzarella and baked), another classic Neapolitan dish. A favourite *dolce* in Napoli is *sfogliatelle*, layers of fine pastry with a ricotta filling.

In Sicilia, try the *pesce spada* (swordfish, usually sliced into thick steaks and cooked on an open grill). *Pasta con le sarde* (pasta with sardines) is popular in Palermo. Eggplant is popular in Sicilia, turning up in pasta or as *melanzane alla siciliana*, filled with olives, anchovies, capers and tomatoes.

The Sicilians are masters when it comes

to their dolci. Don't leave the island without trying *cassata*, a rich sponge cake filled with a cream of ricotta cheese, liqueur and candied fruits. Another speciality is *cannoli*, tubes of sweet pastry filled with a rich cream, often made from a mixture of cream cheese, honey and almond paste with bits of candied fruit. Also try the assortment of *paste di mandorle* (almond pastries) and the *zabaione*, native to Marsala.

The *granita* is a drink made of crushed ice with fresh lemon or other fruit juices, or with coffee topped with fresh whipped cream. Another speciality is *marzapane* (marzipan), which Sicilian pastry chefs whip into every imaginable shape. Sicilian gelato is absolutely heavenly.

Sardegna's best known dish is *porcheddu*, baby pig roasted on a spit. Try also the *carte musica*, a thin, crisp bread eaten warm and sprinkled with salt and oil. *Pecorino sardo* is a sharp, aged sheep's cheese which the Sardi sprinkle on their pasta instead of parmigiano.

Where to Eat

When walking in the high mountains, you'll eat almost exclusively in rifugi, where the food is usually hearty and good quality. In the towns and villages you can choose between the following options. A *tavola calda* offers cheap, pre-prepared meat, pasta and vegetable dishes in self-service style and doesn't charge you extra to sit down. A *rosticceria* usually offers cooked meats and other takeaway food. A *pizzeria* will of course serve pizza, but usually also a full menu. An *osteria* is likely to be either a small wine bar offering a small selection of dishes, or a small *trattoria*. A trattoria is basically a cheaper version of a *ristorante*, which in turn tends to have a higher standard of service and a greater range of dishes. Menus are often posted outside and you can check out prices, as well as the cover and service charges. You can buy sandwiches at bars, or have them made in *alimentari* (delicatessen/grocery stores). Pizza by the slice is sold in takeaway outlets usually called *pizza a taglio*. Suggested places to eat are listed throughout this guide.

Pasta al Dente

Cooking good pasta for an Italian is no mean feat. First the pasta has to be of the highest quality, second it has to be cooked for precisely the correct length of time, so that it is *al dente*, which means that it is firm, almost crunchy, an uninitiated eater might observe. Italians almost always add salt to the boiling water before adding the pasta and they never throw in *(buttare)* the pasta until everyone who is going to eat is present. Don't complain if your pasta takes a while to arrive in a restaurant – you'll need to wait the 10 to 12 minutes it takes to cook.

There are heaps of variations of Italian pasta. It comes in a dazzling variety of shapes and sizes, ranging from spaghetti and linguine, to tube pasta such as penne and rigatoni, shell-shaped *(conchiglie)*, bow-shaped *(farfalle*, which means butterflies), corkscrew-shaped *(fusilli)* and many others. Packet, or dried pasta, is made with high quality durum wheat and water. On the other hand, fresh egg pasta *(pasta all'uovo*, or *fatto a mano)* is made with eggs and flour and is used to make stuffed pasta such as tortellini and ravioli, or cut into strips called tagliatelle (thinner strips are also called *taglionini* or *tagliarini)*. Egg pasta is usually served with richer, creamier sauces than those which often accompanies dried pasta, which are most likely to be tomato-based.

Sampling the great variety of pasta sauces you'll find in Italy can make eating a lot of fun during your trip, particularly if you are adventurous enough to try traditional local recipes in the various regions or towns you visit. Pasta sauce ingredients traditionally vary quite dramatically between the north and south of the country. In the north they are richer, often creamy and often use red meat (such as the delicious *ragu* of Bologna, known outside Italy as *bolognese)*, while as you head further south they tend to use more vegetables and, on the coast, lots of seafood. In Apulia, for instance, a typical pasta dish is *orecchiette con cime di rapa*, ear-shaped pasta served with turnip tops which have been sauteed in oil with chilli and garlic. In Sicily, eggplant is a popular addition to tomato-based pasta sauces. See the section on Food in this chapter for some other traditional pasta dishes.

Freshly grated cheese is the magic ingredient for most pasta. Parmesan *(parmigiano)* is the most widely used, particularly in the north. Look for the name *Parmigiano Reggiano* on the rind to ensure you're getting the genuine parmesan, because there is also the similar, but lower quality *Grana Padano*. In Sardegna and around Roma there is a tendency to use the sharp *pecorino*, an aged sheep's cheese, while *ricotta salata* (salted ricotta), is widely used in the south and in Sicilia. ■

Walking Food

For economy and safety it is a good idea to carry some of your own food on walks. If you are walking at high altitudes it is essential that you have emergency supplies. Light, high energy and easy to pack snack foods include mixed nuts, dried fruits and chocolate bars. You will usually be able to pick up daily supplies along the way: some walks will take you through towns and villages, while on others, such as in the Alps, you can buy them at the rifugi, although you'll pay inflated prices.

Buying Food Snack foods, cheeses, sliced meats, bread and fruit can be purchased at supermarkets, alimentari or fresh produce markets (if you can find one). Fresh bread is also available at a *forno* or *panetteria*. Large supermarkets in bigger towns and cities are usually open all day. Alimentari and smaller supermarkets usually close for a few hours in the middle of the day (see Business Hours earlier in this chapter).

Cooking Unless you are planning to use camping grounds, there is really no need to carry your own stove. Most of the walks in this guide are served by rifugi or hotels and even if you choose to stay in camping grounds, there are usually places to eat on site or nearby.

Vegetarian Food

Vegetarians will have no problems eating in Italy. While there are very few restaurants devoted to them, vegetables are a staple of the Italian diet. Most eating establishments serve a good selection of *antipasti* and *contorni* (vegetables prepared in a variety of ways), and the further south you go, the more excellent vegetable dishes you will find.

Food Glossary

This glossary is intended as a brief guide to some of the basics and by no means covers all of the dishes you are likely to encounter in Italy. Names and ingredients of dishes often vary from region to region, and even pizza toppings can change. Most travellers

to Italy will already be well acquainted with the various Italian pastas, which include spaghetti, fettucine, penne, rigatoni, gnocchi, lasagne, tortellini and ravioli. The names are the same in Italy and no further definitions are given here.

Useful Words

bill/cheque	*il conto*
boiled	*bollito*
cooked	*cotto*
cooked over hot coals	*alla brace*
firm (as all good pasta should be)	*al dente*
fried	*fritto*
grilled	*alla griglia*
knife/fork/ spoon/teaspoon	*coltello/forchetta/ cucchiaio/ cucchiaino*
menu	*menù*
plate	*piatto*
raw	*crudo*
restaurant	*ristorante*
roasted	*arrosto*
smoked	*affumicato*
waiter/waitress	*cameriere/a*
well done (cooked)	*ben cotto*

Staples

bread	*pane*
butter	*burro*
cheese	*formaggio*
chilli	*peperoncino*
cooked cornmeal	*polenta*
cream	*panna*
egg/eggs	*uovo/uova*
honey	*miele*
jam	*marmellata*
lemon	*limone*
oil	*olio*
olives	*olive*
pepper	*pepe*
rice	*riso*
rice cooked with wine and stock	*risotto*
salt	*sale*
sugar	*zucchero*
vinegar	*aceto*
wholemeal bread	*pane integrale*

Meat & Fish

anchovies	*acciughe*
beef	*manzo*
chicken	*pollo*
clams	*vongole*
cod	*merluzzo*
crab	*granchio*
cutlet or thin cut of meat, usually crumbed and fried	*cotoletta*
dentex (type of fish)	*dentice*
lamb	*agnello* or *abacchio*
liver	*fegato*
lobster	*aragosta*
mackerel	*sgombro*
mussels	*cozze*
octopus	*polpo*
oysters	*ostriche*
prawns	*gamberi*
rabbit	*coniglio*
sardines	*sarde*
sausage	*salsiccia*
sole	*sogliola*
squid	*calamari*
steak	*bistecca*
swordfish	*pesce spada*
tripe	*trippa*
tuna	*tonno*
turkey	*tacchino*
veal	*vitello*

Vegetables

artichokes	*carciofi*
asparagus	*asparagi*
cabbage	*verza, cavolo*
carrots	*carote*
chicory	*cicoria*
eggplant	*melanzane*
onion	*cipolla*
peas	*piselli*
peppers	*peperoni*
potatoes	*patate*
spinach	*spinaci*
string beans	*fagiolini*

Fruit

apples	*mele*
bananas	*banane*
cherries	*ciliegie*
grapes	*uva*
oranges	*arance*
peaches	*pesche*
pears	*pere*
strawberries	*fragole*

The Menu
Soups & Antipasti

brodo	broth
carpaccio	very fine slices of raw meat
insalata caprese	sliced tomatoes with mozzarella and basil
insalata di mare	seafood, generally crustaceans
minestrina in brodo	pasta in broth
minestrone	vegetable soup
olive ascolane	stuffed, deep-fried olives
prosciutto e melone	cured ham with melon
ripieni	stuffed, oven-baked vegetables
stracciatella	egg in broth

Pasta Sauces

al ragù	meat sauce (bolognese)
arrabbiata	tomato and chilli
carbonara	egg, bacon and black pepper
alla matriciana	tomato and bacon
napoletana	tomato and basil
panna	cream, prosciutto and sometimes peas
pesto	basil, garlic and oil, often with pine nuts
vongole	clams, garlic and oil, sometimes with tomato

Pizzas
All pizzas listed have a tomato and sometimes mozzarella base.

capricciosa	olives, prosciutto, mushrooms, artichokes
frutti di mare	seafood
funghi	mushrooms

margherita	oregano
napoletana	anchovies
pugliese	tomato, mozzarella and onions
quattro formaggi	with four types of cheese
quattro stagioni	the same as a capricciosa, but sometimes with egg
verdura	mixed vegetables (usually zucchini, eggplant and sometimes carrot and spinach)

DRINKS
Nonalcoholic Drinks

Coffee The first-time visitor to Italy is likely to be confused by the many ways in which the locals consume their caffeine. The 'Caffè Society' boxed text on this page is a basic guide, although there can be variations from north to south.

Tea Italians don't drink a lot of tea *(tè)* and generally only in the late afternoon, when they might take a cup with a few *pasticcini* (small cakes). You can order tea in bars, although it will usually arrive in the form of a cup of warm water with an accompanying tea bag.

Water While tap water is reliable throughout the country, most Italians prefer to drink bottled mineral water *(acqua minerale)*. It will be either sparkling *(frizzante)* or still *(naturale)* and you will be asked in restaurants and bars which you would prefer. If you want a glass of tap water, ask for *acqua dal rubinetto*, although simply asking for *acqua naturale* will also suffice.

Alcoholic Drinks

Wine & Spirits Wine *(vino)* is an essential accompaniment to any meal and a popular way to end one. Italians are proud of their wines, and find it hard to believe that anyone else in the world could produce wines as good as theirs.

Wine is reasonably priced and you will rarely pay more than L15,000 for a good bottle of wine, although prices range up to

---

Caffè Society

An *espresso* is a small amount of very strong black coffee. You can ask for a *doppio espresso*, which means double the amount, or a *caffè lungo* (although this can sometimes mean a slightly diluted espresso). If you want a long black coffee (as in a weaker, watered-down version), ask for a *caffè Americano*. If you are in an isolated village in Sardegna (Sardinia) where they have no name for diluted coffee, try asking for an *espresso con molta acqua calda* (coffee with a lot of hot water). A *corretto* is an espresso with a dash of grappa or some other spirit, and a *macchiato* is espresso with a small amount of milk – on the other hand, *latte macchiato* is milk with a spot of coffee. *Caffè freddo* is a long glass of cold black coffee.

Then, of course, there is the *cappuccino*, coffee with hot, frothy milk – if you want it without the froth, ask for a *caffè latte* or a cappuccino *senza schiuma*. Italians tend to drink cappuccino only with breakfast and during the morning. They never drink it after meals or in the evening and, if you order one after dinner, don't be surprised if the waiter asks you two or three times, just to make sure that he or she heard correctly. You will also find it difficult to convince bartenders to make your cappuccino hot, rather than lukewarm. Ask for it *molto caldo* and wait for the same 'tut-tut' response that you attracted when you ordered a cappuccino after dinner. ■

---

more than L30,000 for really good quality. There are three main classifications of wine – *Denominazione d'origine controllata e garantita* (DOCG), *denominazione di origine controllata* (DOC) and *vino da tavola* (table wine) – which will be marked on the label. A DOC wine is produced subject to certain specifications, although the label does not certify quality. DOCG is subject to the same requirements as normal DOC but it is also tested by government inspectors. While there are table wines better left alone, there are also many which are of excellent quality, notably the Sicilian Corvo red and white.

The styles of wine vary throughout the country, so make a point of sampling the local produce in your travels. Try the many varieties of the famous Chianti wines produced in Toscana. Others to try are the white Vernaccia of San Gimignano, the excellent

---

Liqueurs

After dinner try a shot of *grappa*, a very strong, clear brew made from grapes, or an *amaro*, a dark liqueur prepared from herbs. If you prefer a sweeter liqueur, try an almond-flavoured *amaretto* or the sweet aniseed *sambuca*. On the Amalfi Coast and the islands of the Bay of Napoli the fragrant local lemons are used to produce *limoncello*. ∎

Brunello di Montalcino and Vin Nobile di Montepulciano, the Soave in Verona and Valpolicella around Venezia. Piemonte (Piedmont) and Trentino-Alto Adige both produce excellent wines, notably the Barolo in Piemonte. The wines of Orvieto in Umbria are good and in Roma try the local Frascati and other wines of the Castelli Romani. Sicilia is the home of Marsala.

Beer Italy produces its own beer *(birra)* and imports beers from throughout Europe and the world. All of the main German beers are, for instance, available in bottles or cans; British beers and Guinness are often found on tap *(alla spina)* in *birrerie* (bars specialising in beer) and Australians might be pleased to know that you can even find a Foster's and a Castlemaine XXXX. The main local labels are Peroni, Dreher and Moretti and are all very drinkable and cheaper than the imported varieties. There has lately been a proliferation of Irish pubs in Italy.

THINGS TO BUY

Clothing

Italy is synonymous with elegant, fashionable and high-quality clothing. The problem is that most of the better quality clothes are very expensive. However, if you can manage to be in the country during the summer sales in July and August and the winter sales in December and January, you can pick up incredible bargains. By mid-sale, prices are often slashed by up to 60% and 70%. Generally speaking, Roma, Firenze and Milano have the greatest variety of clothing, shoes

and accessories. Main shopping areas are detailed under the relevant cities throughout this book. Fashions tend to be conservative and middle-of-the-range, and cheaper clothing can be downright boring for British, US and Australian travellers accustomed to a wide variety of styles and tastes.

The same applies to shoes. Expect to pay dearly (although still considerably less than at home) for the best quality at shops such as Beltrami and Pollini. Again, prices drop dramatically during the sales, but you can expect to have some difficulty finding shoes to fit if you take a larger size.

Italy is particularly noted for the quality of its leather goods, so plan to stock up on bags, wallets, purses, belts and gloves. At markets such as Porta Portese in Roma you can find some incredible second-hand bargains. The San Lorenzo leather market in Firenze has a vast array of leather goods, including jackets, bags, wallets and belts, although the variety can be limited, and you should check carefully for quality before buying.

Glassware & Ceramics

Some might call the famous and expensive Venetian glass grotesque – and it is certainly an acquired taste. Shops all over Venezia are full of it and if you listen to the claims of the shop assistants, most of it (except for the glass in *their* shop) is not the real thing. If you want to buy Venetian glass, shop around and compare prices and quality. The merchandise at the larger factories is generally not cheaper, but you can be sure it is authentic. And remember you will probably have to pay customs duty on your purchase when you arrive home. Lonely Planet's *Italy* guide has more information on things to buy.

Ceramics and pottery are less costly and more rustic. There is a great diversity of traditional styles throughout Italy, associated with villages or areas, where designs have been handed down over the centuries. Major centres include: Deruta, near Perugia in Umbria; Faenza, in Emilia-Romagna; Vietri sul Mare, near Salerno at the start of the Amalfi Coast; and Grottaglie, near Taranto in Puglua (Apulia). Sicilian pottery is particularly interesting. Caltagirone and Santo Stefano di Camastra are two important ceramic producing towns.

Souvenirs & Handicrafts

The beautiful Florentine paper goods, with their delicate flower design, and Venetian paper goods, with a marbled design, are reasonably priced and make wonderful gifts. Specialist shops are dotted around both cities, although it is possible to buy these paper goods in cartolerie throughout the country.

Popular jewellery tends to be chunky and cheap-looking, but if they can afford it, Italians love to wear gold. The best known haunt for tourists wanting to buy gold in Italy is the Ponte Vecchio in Firenze, lined with tiny shops full of both modern and antique jewellery. Jewellery and ornaments carved from coral can be found at Torre del Greco just out of Napoli, and on the west coast of Sardegna, although overharvesting and pollution threaten this once thriving industry.

Local handicrafts include lace and embroidery, notably on the Isola Maggiore in Lago de Trasimeno, Umbria, and the woodcarvings of the Val Gardena in Trentino-Alto Adige.

Health, Safety & First Aid

The walks detailed in this guide have varying levels of difficulty, ranging from easy walks suitable for families, to more strenuous mountain hikes. It is easy to underestimate the strenuousness of mountain walking, so make sure you are physically prepared (see Physical Fitness in the Predeparture Preparation section). If your walking itinerary takes you into isolated areas, such as in the Alps or Sardegna (Sardinia), be sure that you are prepared for possible medical emergencies (see What to Bring and Dangers & Annoyances in the Facts for the Walker chapter). All walkers should have a good idea of general first aid practices. Before leaving home, consider attending a course in basic first aid.

The quality of medical treatment in public hospitals varies throughout Italy. Basically, the farther north, the better the care. Private hospitals and clinics across the country generally provide excellent services, but are expensive for those without medical insurance. That said, certain treatments in public hospitals may also have to be paid for and in such cases can be equally costly.

Your embassy or consulate in Italy can provide a list of recommended doctors in major cities; however, if you have a specific health complaint, it would be wise to obtain the necessary information and referrals for treatment before leaving home.

For emergency treatment, go straight to the casualty (*pronto soccorso*) section of a public hospital, where you'll also receive emergency dental treatment. In major cities you are likely to find doctors who speak English, or a volunteer translator service. Often, first aid is also available at train stations, airports and ports.

This chapter deals with the basic aspects of everyday health while walking or travelling in Italy. For more information about emergency situations, see Dangers & Annoyances in the Facts for the Walker chapter and Rescue & Evacuation later in this chapter.

The public health system is administered by local centres generally known as Unità Sanitaria Locale (USL), or also Unità Socio Santaria Locale (USSL), usually listed under 'U' in the telephone book (sometimes under 'A' for Azienda USL). Under these headings you'll find long lists of offices – look for Poliambulatorio (polyclinic) and the telephone number for Accetazione Sanitaria. You need to call this number to make an appointment – there is no point in just rolling up. Opening hours vary widely, with the minimum generally being about 8 am to 12.30 pm from Monday to Friday. Some open for a couple of hours in the afternoon and also on Saturday mornings.

Predeparture Preparation

MEDICAL COVER
Citizens of EU countries are covered for emergency medical treatment in Italy on presentation of an E111 form. It is necessary to obtain information about this from your national health service before leaving home. Treatment in private hospitals is not covered. Australia also has a reciprocal arrangement with Italy so that emergency treatment is covered – Medicare in Australia publishes a brochure with the details. The USA, Canada and New Zealand do not have reciprocal arrangements, and citizens of these countries will be required to pay for any treatment in Italy themselves. Advise medical staff of any reciprocal arrangements *before* treatment.

HEALTH INSURANCE
A travel insurance policy to cover theft, loss and medical problems is wise. There is a wide variety of policies and your travel agent will have recommendations. The international student travel policies handled by STA Travel or student travel organisations are usually good value. Some policies offer lower and

higher medical expenses options but the higher one is chiefly for countries like the USA, where medical costs are extremely high. Check the small print. See under Documents in the Facts for the Walker chapter for more information.

Some policies specifically exclude 'dangerous activities' which can include mountain climbing and even trekking. Ask if costs associated with an emergency rescue are covered.

You may prefer a policy that pays doctors or hospitals direct rather than you having to pay on the spot and claim later. If you have to claim later make sure you keep all documentation. Some policies ask you to call back (reverse charges) to a centre in your home country where an immediate assessment of your problem is made.

Check if the policy covers ambulances or an emergency flight home. If you have to stretch out you will need two seats and somebody has to pay for them!

PHYSICAL FITNESS

Mountain walking can be very strenuous, with some walks in the Alps requiring you to ascend as much as 1000m in one day. Without some physical preparation, you are really going to find yourself in trouble. About three months before heading off, start an exercise program that includes at least 20 minutes of physical activity three times a week. This could be jogging, walking or cycling. However, any healthy, reasonably fit person will have little or no trouble tackling the majority of the walks outlined in this book.

IMMUNISATIONS

No immunisations are required for Italy. Discuss your requirements with your doctor, but there are a few vaccinations which you might consider just to be on the safe side.

Plan ahead for getting your vaccinations: some of them require more than one injection, while some vaccinations should not be given together. It is recommended you seek medical advice at least six weeks before travel.

Record all vaccinations on an International Health Certificate, available from your doctor or government health department.

Tetanus This can be a fatal wound infection. Everyone should have these vaccinations. After an initial course of three injections, boosters are necessary every 10 years.

Rabies This disease does exist in Italy, although it is confined to remote areas of the Alps. Rabies is caused by a bite or scratch by an infected animal. Vaccination should be considered if you are in a high risk category – such as handling animals, caving, travelling to remote areas, or for children (who may not report a bite). Pre-travel rabies vaccination involves having three injections over 21 to 28 days. If someone who has been vaccinated is bitten or scratched by an animal they will require two booster injections of vaccine, those not vaccinated require more.

TRAVEL HEALTH GUIDES

Most books on travel health are geared towards the tropics, where health is a major issue. This is not the case in Italy, although you might consider the following:

Travellers' Health, Dr Richard Dawood. Comprehensive, easy to read, authoritative and highly recommended, although it's rather large to lug around.
Travel with Children, Maureen Wheeler, Lonely Planet Publications. Includes basic advice on travel health for younger children.

There are also a number of excellent travel health sites on the Internet. From the Lonely Planet home page there are links to the World Health Organisation and the US Centers for Disease Control & Prevention (http://www. lonelyplanet.com/weblinks/wlprep.htm).

OTHER PREPARATIONS

Make sure you're healthy before you start travelling. If you are going on a long trip make sure your teeth are OK. If you wear glasses take a spare pair and your prescription.

If you require a particular medication take an adequate supply, as it may not be available locally. Take part of the packaging showing the generic name, rather than the brand name, which will make getting replacements easier. It's a good idea to have a legible prescription or letter from your doctor to show that you legally use the medication to avoid any problems.

Medical Kit Checklist

You'll have little trouble finding simple medications such as painkillers and antihistamines and other essentials such as antiseptic creams and bandages in Italy. However, you should take a basic medical kit on your walks, including:

Medications

☐ **antihistamine** cream and pills (such as Benadryl) – useful as a decongestant for colds and allergies, to ease the itch from insect bites or stings, and to help prevent motion sickness. Antihistamines may cause sedation and interact with alcohol so care should be taken when using them; take one you know and have used before, if possible.

☐ **antiseptic** such as povidone-iodine (eg Betadine) – for cuts and grazes.

☐ **aspirin** or paracetamol (acetaminophen in the USA) – for pain or fever.

☐ **betadine antiseptic**

☐ **calamine lotion** or **aluminium sulphate spray** (eg Stingose) – to ease irritation from bites or stings.

☐ **cold & flu tablets** Pseudoephedrine hydrochloride (Sudafed) may be useful if flying with a cold to avoid ear damage.

☐ **loperamide** (eg Imodium) or Lomotil for diarrhoea; prochlorperazine (eg Stemetil) or metaclopramide (eg Maxalon) for nausea and vomiting.

☐ **rehydration** mixture – for treatment of severe diarrhoea; particularly important for travelling with children.

☐ **throat lozenges** eg Strepsils

First Aid Supplies

☐ **adhesive** or **paper tape**
☐ **bandages**
☐ **elasticated support bandages**
☐ **Band-Aids** or similar sticking plaster
☐ **guaze pads**
☐ **sterile alcohol wipes**
☐ **scissors & tweezers**
☐ **safety pins**
☐ **thermometer** (note that mercury thermometers are prohibited by airlines).
☐ **sterile wound dressings**, for lacerations.
☐ **water purifying tablets**
☐ **sunscreen & chap stick**
☐ **insect repellent**

Staying Healthy

Care in what you eat and drink is the most important health rule; stomach upsets are the most likely travel health problem, but in Italy the majority of these upsets will be relatively minor and probably due to overindulgence in the local food.

However, it pays to be careful with certain foods in Italy. In recent years there have been incidences of salmonella poisoning throughout the country related to infected eggs. Therefore foods containing raw or lightly cooked eggs should be avoided. It is a good idea to avoid uncooked shellfish in Italy. There have been isolated outbreaks of cholera in the south of the country in recent years. The simplest way to avoid being affected if such an outbreak occurs is to drink bottled water and eat seafood only if it is well cooked.

WATER

Tap water is safe to drink throughout Italy, although Italians themselves have taken to drinking the bottled stuff. The sign *acqua non potabile* tells you that water is not drinkable (eg in trains and at some camping grounds). Drinking water from drink fountains is safe unless there is a sign telling you otherwise. There are many mineral water springs dotted throughout the country, usually easily identified by the people filling bottles and containers. Water from streams and rivers will almost certainly be polluted. At high altitudes in the Alps, people often drink from mountain springs, but you can never be certain that there are no animals upstream.

Water Purification

The simplest way of purifying water is to boil it thoroughly. Vigorous boiling should be satisfactory; however, at high altitude water boils at a lower temperature, so germs are less likely to be killed. Boil it for longer in these environments.

Chlorine tablets (Puritabs, Steritabs or other brand names) will kill many pathogens, but not giardia or amoebic cysts. Iodine is more effective in purifying water and is available in tablet form (such as Potable Aqua). Follow the directions carefully and remember that too much iodine can be harmful.

Medical Problems & Treatment

ENVIRONMENTAL HAZARDS
Altitude Sickness
Lack of oxygen at high altitudes (over 2500m) affects most people to some extent. The affect may be mild or severe and occurs because less oxygen reaches the muscles and the brain at high altitude, requiring the heart and lungs to compensate by working harder. Symptoms of Acute Mountain Sickness (AMS) usually develop during the first 24 hours at altitude but may be delayed up to three weeks. Mild symptoms include headache, lethargy, dizziness, difficulty sleeping and loss of appetite. AMS may become more severe without warning and can be fatal. Severe symptoms include breathlessness, a dry, irritative cough (which may progress to the production of pink, frothy sputum), severe headache, lack of coordination and balance, confusion, irrational behaviour, vomiting, drowsiness and unconsciousness. There is no hard-and-fast rule as to what is too high: AMS has been fatal at 3000m, although 3500m to 4500m is the usual range.

None of the walks described in this book will take you to such high altitudes, but you might arrive close to 3000m. While you might feel some minor affects, the real risk of AMS to walkers in Italy is fairly remote.

If you have any reason to believe that you have mild symptoms of AMS rest at the same altitude until recovery, usually a day or two. Paracetamol or aspirin can be taken for headaches. If symptoms persist or become worse, however, *immediate descent is necessary*; even 500m can help. Drug treatments should never be used to avoid descent or to enable further ascent.

The drugs acetazolamide (Diamox) and dexamethasone are recommended by some doctors for the prevention of AMS, however their use is controversial. They can reduce the symptoms, but they may also mask warning signs; severe and fatal AMS has occurred in people taking these drugs. In general we do not recommend them for travellers.

To prevent acute mountain sickness:

- Ascend slowly with frequent rests.
- Drink extra fluids. The mountain air is dry and cold and moisture is continually lost as you breathe. Evaporation of sweat may occur unnoticed and result in dehydration.
- Eat light, high-carbohydrate meals for energy.
- Avoid alcohol as it dehydrates.
- Avoid sedatives.

Fungal Infections
When walking – especially if you're back-packing and trying to keep the weight down – it's easy to forget to wash or change clothing as often as you would normally. This can lead to fungal infections. Walkers are most commonly affected by athlete's foot (tinea), which occurs between the toes. Another common complaint is 'crotch rot', a painful rash between the groin and the buttocks caused by the combination of sweating and rubbing as you walk. You get fungal infections such as ringworm from infected animals or other people. Moisture encourages these infections.

To prevent fungal infections wear loose, comfortable clothes, avoid artificial fibres, wash frequently and dry carefully. Always wear thongs (flip flops) in shared bathrooms. If you do get an infection, wash the infected area at least daily with a disinfectant or medicated soap and water, and rinse and dry well. Apply an antifungal cream or powder like tolnaftate (Tinaderm). Try to expose the infected area to air or sunlight as much as possible and wash all towels and underwear in hot water, change them often and let them dry in the sun.

Heat Exhaustion
Dehydration and salt deficiency can cause heat exhaustion. If it is hot and you're exerting yourself, make sure you get sufficient

liquid and salt to replace what you're sweating out. Salt deficiency is characterised by fatigue, lethargy, headaches, giddiness and muscle cramps. You're unlikely to need salt tablets – just a bit extra on your food each day will probably do.

Hypothermia

Too much cold can be just as dangerous as too much heat. Hypothermia occurs when the body loses heat faster than it can produce it and the core temperature of the body falls. It is a real and ever-present threat for mountain walkers and deaths are not uncommon. You should always be prepared for cold, wet and windy conditions, even snow, no matter how warm and clear the weather is when you set out.

It is surprisingly easy to progress from very cold to dangerously cold due to a combination of wind, wet clothing, fatigue and hunger, even if the air temperature is above freezing. It is best to dress in layers; silk, wool and some of the new artificial fibres are all good insulating materials. A hat is important, as a lot of heat is lost through the head. A strong, waterproof outer layer (and a thermal blanket for emergencies) are essential. Carry basic supplies, including food containing simple sugars to generate heat quickly and fluid to drink. (See What to Bring in the Facts for the Walker chapter for a list of essential gear for mountain walking).

Symptoms of hypothermia are exhaustion, numb skin (particularly toes and fingers), shivering, slurred speech, irrational or violent behaviour, lethargy, stumbling, dizzy spells, muscle cramps and violent bursts of energy. Irrationality may take the form of sufferers claiming they are warm and trying to take off their clothes.

To treat mild hypothermia, first get the person out of the wind and/or rain, remove their clothing if it's wet and replace it with dry, warm clothing. Give them hot liquids – not alcohol – and some high-kilojoule, easily digestible food. Do not rub victims, instead allow them to slowly warm themselves. This should be enough to treat the early stages of hypothermia. The early recognition and

treatment of mild hypothermia is the only way to prevent severe hypothermia, which is a critical condition.

Sunburn

It can get pretty hot in Italy during the summer, particularly in the south of the country. You should be extremely careful when walking at high altitude, where you can get sunburnt surprisingly quickly, even through cloud. Use a sunscreen, hat and barrier cream for your nose and lips. Calamine lotion or Stingose are good for mild sunburn. Protect your eyes with good quality sunglasses with UV lenses.

INFECTIOUS DISEASES

Diarrhoea

Simple things like a change of water, food or climate can cause a mild bout of diarrhoea, but a few rushed toilet trips with no other symptoms is not indicative of a major problem.

Diarrhoea caused by contaminated food or water can be more serious. Moderate diarrhoea, involving around half a dozen loose movements in a day, is more of a nuisance. Dehydration is the main danger with any diarrhoea, particularly in children or the elderly as dehydration can occur quite quickly. Under all circumstances *fluid replacement* (at least equal to the volume being lost) is the most important thing to remember. Weak black tea with a little sugar, soda water, or soft drinks allowed to go flat and diluted 50% with water are all good. Keep drinking small amounts often. With severe diarrhoea a rehydrating solution is preferable to replace minerals and salts lost. Oral rehydration salts (ORS) are very useful; you can buy them at pharmacies. Stick to a bland diet as you recover.

Lomotil or Imodium can be used to bring relief from the symptoms, although they do not actually cure the problem. Only use these drugs if you do not have access to toilets eg if you *must* travel. For children under 12 years Lomotil and Imodium are not recommended. Do not use these drugs if the person has a high fever or is severely dehydrated.

If you have diarrhoea with blood or

mucus, diarrhoea with fever, or persistent or severe diarrhoea, seek medical advice.

CUTS, BITES & STINGS

Rabies is passed through animal bites. See Less Common Diseases later in this chapter for details of this disease.

Insect Bites & Stings

Bee and wasp stings are usually painful rather than dangerous. Calamine lotion or Stingose spray will give relief and ice packs will reduce the pain and swelling. However in people who are allergic to them severe breathing difficulties may occur and require urgent medical care. Be particularly careful in Italy of the oversized wasps known as a *calabrone*. Its bite can provoke a severe allergic reaction.

Cuts & Scratches

Wash well and treat any cut with an antiseptic such as povidone-iodine. Where possible avoid bandages and Band-Aids, which can keep wounds wet.

Jellyfish

These are common in Italian waters. Contact with their stinging tentacles is very painful, but not dangerous unless you have an allergic reaction. Dousing in vinegar will deactivate any stingers which have not 'fired'. Calamine lotion, antihistamines and analgesics may reduce the reaction and relieve the pain.

Ticks

You should always check all over your body if you have been walking through a potentially tick-infested area as ticks can cause skin infections and other more serious diseases. If a tick is found attached, press down around the tick's head with tweezers, grab the head and gently pull upwards. Avoid pulling the rear of the body as this may squeeze the tick's gut contents through the attached mouth parts into the skin, increasing the risk of infection and disease. Smearing chemicals on the tick will not make it let go and is not recommended.

Snakes

There is only one poisonous snake in Italy, the viper, and there is an antivenene available. See Dangers & Annoyances in the Facts for the Walker chapter for more information.

TRAUMATIC INJURIES

Trauma is a common cause of death among trekkers and a major cause of evacuation. Trauma results most often from falling off a trail, or having something fall on you while trekking. Many accidents happen during a momentary lapse in judgment: scrambling up or down for a photo, not paying attention to your feet, or trying to climb between trails on steep terrain after taking a wrong turn.

It is important to concentrate when you are walking, and to concentrate even harder towards the end of the day when your legs and mind are both tired: more ankle injuries occur towards the end of the day, when people are tired and can't control their foot placement as well. It is also important to look up and try to assess the risk of rockfall from above. Look for signs of recent rockfall and don't linger in these areas. If you are crossing an obvious landslide or large rockfall area, rest before you start across, and then don't stop in the middle.

Initial Assessment

Trauma usually occurs in a very sudden and unexpected manner, leaving bystanders momentarily stunned. Scrambling to reach someone who has fallen, you may forget some basic rules of safety. Make sure that other members of the group are out of danger, and then be careful to take a route to the victim that doesn't expose that person to further rockfall. If the situation is still very unstable, with continued rockfall, you may have to move the person out of danger before making a complete assessment.

When you and the victim are in a safe spot, you have to make an initial assessment of his or her condition. This can be done quite quickly, and the process of doing this helps you to organise your thoughts and begin to come up with a plan. It is important to approach the person with a set of priorities in mind, rather than be forced to react emotionally as each injury is uncovered. The rule of ABC has been proven to be very useful to help a rescuer move from an overall emotional reaction to a plan of action. ABC stands for 'Airway, Breathing, and Circulation'. If the person is conscious and talking, then obviously the airway and breathing are all right. However, if the person is unconscious it is necessary to immediately check to see whether they are breathing at all or if their breathing is obstructed. You can then check for signs of circulation by feeling for a pulse. In a traumatic fall, if the victim has no respiration or pulse when you reach them, they are dead. Cardiopulmonary resuscitation (CPR) is futile in this situation.

If the person is still alive, but not conscious, or is confused and combative, then they have a head injury. Make note of that, but keep on with your initial assessment. Inspect the head, look for signs of scalp laceration, remember to feel the back of the head as well, and then feel all the rest of the bones in the body briefly, looking for swelling or deformity that might indicate a fracture. If the person is awake, they can generally tell you where they hurt, but do a complete assessment anyway; the person may be unaware of a large cut on their back, for example. Once you have done an initial assessment, you will be aware of their level of consciousness, any large bleeding cuts or bruises, and any signs of broken bones. The next step is to begin to stabilise all these injuries.

Bleeding

Most cuts will stop bleeding on their own, but relatively large arteries may keep pumping blood for a long time, particularly scalp wounds. Put direct pressure with a cloth or dressing over the area that is bleeding, and press relatively hard. Don't keep pulling off the dressing and looking to see if the bleeding has stopped. Apply pressure for five full minutes (use your watch) before you look to see if the bleeding has stopped. You can then tie a dressing over the wound and hopefully move on to assessing other injuries. If you move the patient around, you may

restart the bleeding, so make sure you check the dressing as needed. Large wounds may benefit from cleaning and suturing, even in the field, but this can wait until all other aspects of the situation have been stabilised.

It is not necessary to elevate a limb to stop bleeding, and it is almost never necessary to use a tourniquet on a limb to stop bleeding. Large lacerations can be cleaned and sutured even several days later, so don't feel a great urgency to do a repair unless you are trained to do so and have the appropriate equipment. If you do know how to repair lacerations, do so – infection rates are usually low and the comfort and ease of caring for a wound that has been closed makes it worth taking the risk of closing a wound in a field situation.

Fractures

Broken bones hurt. A conscious person can usually direct your attention to an area of concern. If a limb appears deformed, a fracture is likely. If the bone is broken, but not bent out of place, the person may just have pain in that specific area. There is relatively little urgency to trying to fix a broken bone, since healing will take many weeks at best.

Suspected nondisplaced fractures should be splinted to protect them from further injury. Obviously displaced fractures should be splinted after some attempt is made to straighten out the deformity by pulling gently in a straight line on the hand or foot until the arm or leg straightens out. Have someone else stabilise the joint just above the fracture so you have something to pull against. This will work well on the arm and lower leg, but it will be impossible to hold a broken thigh bone (femur) straight without a special splint. In the case of a broken femur, try to straighten the leg gently, and then tie the injured leg to the good leg to try to hold it in place.

A good splint will keep the broken bone ends from moving around inside, will decrease internal bleeding, and will make the patient much more comfortable. Pad the inside of the splint to protect the skin, and check frequently to make sure that the splint is not cutting off circulation to the hand or foot.

If the broken bone is associated with a laceration of the skin, the fracture is said to be 'compound', which means that the normal problems of the fracture have been 'compounded' by the risk of infection due to exposure to the outside environment. Compound fractures require much more urgent treatment than noncompound (simple) fractures. Most compound fractures need to be thoroughly cleansed as soon as possible in an operating room. Until then, put a sterile dressing soaked in povidone iodine (Betadine) or other disinfectant over the wound, and splint as usual. If you have antibiotics, you should start them immediately. The best choice would be cephalexin (500mg) four times per day.

Internal Injuries

Bleeding from the skin is obvious and can be controlled by direct pressure. Internal bleeding may not be obvious at first, and there is no way to stop this bleeding in the field. You can suspect internal bleeding if the person has a rapid pulse and pale, cool skin after you have otherwise stabilised them. A tender or gradually distending abdomen can mean internal bleeding in the abdomen, usually from the spleen or liver. Bleeding in the chest can be from major arteries, and there is little that you can do to stop it. 'Shock' is a very specific medical term that is often misused by the general public. It refers specifically to the inability of a person to maintain an adequate circulating blood volume. It does not refer to the emotional reaction to an injury. If a person is truly in shock, then evacuation to a hospital is your only hope.

Head Injury

The terms 'unconscious' and 'coma' are vague generalisations. These two terms can describe a wide range of reactions, ranging from temporary amnesia following a blow to the head, to complete unresponsiveness to deep pain. An altered mental state following a blow to the head is due to direct trauma to the brain. Most often this is just a bruise, and the person will improve steadily. However, if a blood vessel is actually torn, blood may accumulate in the closed space of the skull, gradually squishing the brain, causing the person's condition to deteriorate. Thus, it is important to note whether a head-injured person is getting better or worse with time.

Most cases of brief unconsciousness lasting less than a minute are not associated with any serious internal injury to the brain. The person may be confused, combative, or have trouble remembering what is happening to them, but they improve steadily over a number of hours. The medical term for this condition is 'concussion', which simply means a blow to the brain severe enough to cause a brief change in consciousness. A more seriously injured person may not respond to spoken commands, but might be making spontaneous movements, or push your hand away when you touch them. The most seriously injured person will not respond in any way to your touching them or talking to them. Try to note just how an unconscious person is responding when you first see them, and then keep track of whether they appear to be getting worse or better. If they are slowly getting better, you usually can be reassured that they will recover. If they are getting worse, there is very little you can do except to try to get them to advanced medical care, and to be sure that they are in a position that allows them to breathe freely.

OTHER MEDICAL PROBLEMS
Tiredness

Tiredness will be a hassle if you're trying to enjoy a stroll in the Toscan countryside; it could put your life at risk if you're walking in the mountains. If you're tired it can affect your concentration and this can be very dangerous indeed if you're negotiating a narrow path or ledge at 2500m. You should never set out on walks beyond your capabilities. If you feel under the weather, have a day off or, if possible, catch public transport part of the way. Don't push on for hours on end without stopping. Stop for rests every few hours even if only for a few minutes. It is also important to eat properly, so make sure you carry adequate, energy-producing foods on your walk, such as nuts, dried fruit, chocolate, biscuits etc (see under Walking Food in the Facts for the Walker chapter).

Knee Pain

This is likely to be a problem only for mountain walkers making long, steep descents. These put a heavy strain on the knees, since the leg has to bend more sharply in order to compensate for the lower step. As weight is transferred onto the bent knee, the kneecap is pulled backwards against the joint, which can be uncomfortable to say the least.

Walkers can reduce knee strain by developing a proper technique of descent. Take short, controlled steps with the legs in a slightly bent position, placing your heels on the ground before the rest of your foot. Mountain paths usually negotiate very steep slopes in numerous switchback curves to avoid a much steeper direct descent. Some walkers find that tubular bandages help reduce some of the strain, others use hi-tech, strap-on supports. Walking poles are very effective in taking some of the weight off the knees on descents. These are very popular among Alpine walkers, although their long-term use tends to gradually reduce a walker's surefootedness.

Blisters

This is a problem that can be easily avoided. Make sure your walking boots or shoes are well worn in before you set out. At the very least, wear them on a few short walks before tackling a three-day trek. Make sure your boots are not too big or too small, as both can cause blisters. The same goes for socks. Make sure they fit properly. It is a good idea to carry a spare pair of socks so you can change in wet weather. Keep your toenails clipped, but not *too* short. If you do feel a blister coming on, treat it sooner rather then later. Use a simple sticking plaster (Band-Aid) or one of the various 'second skin' spray-on remedies.

Less Common Diseases

The following diseases pose a small risk to travellers, and so are only mentioned in passing. Seek medical advice if you think you may have any of these diseases.

Lyme Disease Lyme disease is a an infection transmitted by ticks which may be acquired throughout North America, Europe and Asia. The illness usually begins with a spreading rash at the site of the tick bite and is accompanied by fever, headache, extreme fatigue, aching joints and muscles and mild neck stiffness. If untreated, these symptoms usually resolve over several weeks but over subsequent weeks or months disorders of the nervous system, heart and joints may develop. Treatment works best early in the illness. Medical help should be sought.

Rabies Rabies is a fatal viral infection present in some isolated areas of the Alps in Italy. Many animals can be infected (such as dogs, cats and bats) and it is their saliva which is infectious.

Medical help should be sought promptly to receive a course of injections to prevent the onset of symptoms and death. Any bite, scratch or even lick from a mammal in an area where rabies does exist should be cleaned immediately and thoroughly. Scrub with soap and running water, and then clean with an alcohol solution. If there is any possibility that the animal is infected, medical help should be sought immediately. Even if the animal is not rabid, all bites should be treated seriously as they can become infected or result in tetanus.

Tetanus Tetanus occurs when a wound becomes infected by a germ which lives in soil and in the faeces of horses and other animals. It enters the body via breaks in the skin. All wounds should be cleaned promptly and adequately and an antiseptic cream or solution applied. Use antibiotics if the wound becomes hot, throbs or pus is seen. The first symptom may be discomfort in swallowing, or stiffening of the jaw and neck; this is followed by painful convulsions of the jaw and whole body. The disease can be fatal. For information on immunisation, see under Tetanus in the Immunisations section earlier in this chapter.

Women's Health

GYNAECOLOGICAL PROBLEMS

Sexually transmitted diseases are a major cause of vaginal problems. Symptoms include a smelly discharge, painful intercourse and sometimes a burning sensation when urinating. Medical attention should be sought and remember in addition to these diseases HIV or hepatitis B may also be acquired during exposure. Besides abstinence, the best thing is to practise safe sex using condoms. Male sexual partners must also be treated.

Antibiotic use, synthetic underwear, sweating and contraceptive pills can lead to fungal vaginal infections, particularly when travelling in hot climates. Maintaining good personal hygiene, and wearing loose-fitting clothes and cotton underwear will help to prevent these infections.

Fungal infections, characterised by a rash, itch and discharge, can be treated with a vinegar or lemon-juice douche, or with yoghurt. Nystatin, miconazole or clotrimazole pessaries or vaginal cream are the usual treatment. If you have a tendency to develop vaginal infections, bring along a supply of your normal treatment in order to avoid the hassle of finding a doctor, getting a prescription etc. While the usual creams and pessaries are available in Italian pharmacies, a prescription may be required.

URINARY TRACT INFECTION

Cystitis, or inflammation of the bladder, is a common condition in women. Symptoms include burning on urination and having to urinate frequently and urgently. Blood can sometimes be seen in the urine. Sexual activity with a new partner or with an old partner who has been away for a while can trigger an infection. The first line of treatment is to drink plenty of fluids, which may resolve the problem. If symptoms persist, they should be treated with an antibiotic because a simple infection can spread to the kidneys, causing a more severe illness. Single dose (non-antibiotic) treatments, called Monuril, are available over the counter at pharmacies in Italy, but they are effective only in the very early stages of mild cystitis. You'll need a prescription for antibiotics, which can be obtained from doctors at the emergency sections of public hospitals.

PREGNANCY

Most miscarriages occur during the first three months of pregnancy. Miscarriage is not uncommon, and can occasionally lead to severe bleeding. The last three months should also be spent within reasonable distance of good medical care. A baby born as early as 24 weeks stands a chance of survival, but only in a good modern hospital. Pregnant women should avoid all unnecessary medication and vaccinations and malarial prophylactics should still be taken where needed. Additional care should be taken to prevent illness and particular attention should be paid to diet and nutrition. Alcohol and nicotine should be avoided.

Rescue & Evacuation

In extreme circumstances, you may require emergency rescue while walking in the mountains. Search and rescue services are well organised in the Alps. However, if you plan to walk in more isolated areas of Sardegna or parts of Sicilia (Sicily) you will most likely be on your own in the event of an emergency. If you are planning to confine yourself to lowland walks, it is far less likely that you'll find yourself in an emergency situation, so you won't need to pay close attention to this section.

Some basic information and guidelines are detailed here, but if you are planning to walk at high altitude or in isolated areas it is essential that you are well prepared in the event of an accident or other potentially life-threatening situations. For example, you might consider taking a short course in life-saving techniques.

BASIC SAFETY

The two basic rules are *be prepared* and *plan carefully*. Carry the necessary clothing, food and equipment, as well as good maps, a compass and altimeter. It is not advisable to walk alone in the mountains: two is considered the minimum number for safe walking. Under no circumstances should walkers leave the marked trail in foggy conditions. With some care you should still be able to follow the marked route in a fog, otherwise wait by the path until visibility improves.

Here are a few basic musts:

- Carry the telephone numbers of local rescue organisations.
- Check the weather forecast.
- Before setting out, advise someone of your planned route (perhaps telephone the proprietor of the rifugio where you plan to spend the night).
- Check that you have the necessary emergency gear: a whistle and a torchlight for giving the alarm, a compass, extra food, a polythene survival 'bivvy' bag or thermal blanket, a basic medical kit etc. See What to Bring in the Facts for the Walker chapter.

You might even consider taking a mobile telephone along.

EMERGENCY

Throughout Italy there are two emergency telephone numbers: ☎ 113 will connect you with the police and ☎ 118 is for an ambulance. In each region there are different organisations responsible for emergency search and rescue. Their phone numbers and addresses are listed throughout the guide.

In the event of an emergency, it is important to remain calm. If you or a companion is injured, first aid might be necessary (see under Traumatic Injuries earlier in this chapter). If you are in the mountains, or an isolated area, consider that even if emergency rescue services are available, it might take hours before help arrives. Use the internationally recognised **emergency signals** to give the alarm. These are: six brief noises or signs (such as a whistle, yell, torchlight etc) per minute (therefore about 10 seconds apart). After a minute's interval, repeat the sequence and continue to do so until someone responds. The response will be three brief noises per minute (every 20 seconds). After a minute's pause, the sequence will be repeated.

If it is necessary to leave the injured person, ensure that they are warm and comfortable in a protected position. Take careful note of where they are (including a map reference) and head for the nearest rifugio or place where you are likely to find a telephone.

SEARCH & RESCUE ORGANISATIONS

Search and rescue services are normally provided by local organisations and the types and conditions of service vary from region to region. In the Alps, emergency services are efficient and well organised. In Trentino, for instance, an emergency helicopter service is provided free of charge. In areas where the service is not free, you'll be required to pay steep fees for the service, so check out your insurance coverage. Members of the Club Alpino Italiano are entitled to free service in all parts of Italy, so it might be worthwhile checking if your local mountaineering club has some type of reciprocal arrangement. In out-of-the-way places in the south of the country, services are not always well organised. On Stromboli, for instance, there is no organised rescue service and, if you need emergency help, you'll need to contact one of the local guides directly.

Information is provided in the relevant chapters about rescue services. For up-to-date information and phone numbers etc contact local tourist offices or guides groups before setting out.

HELICOPTER RESCUE

If a rescue helicopter arrives on the scene, you must give an appropriate signal to indicate whether you need help and want them to land, or not.

In order for the helicopter to land, there must be a cleared space of 25m x 25m, with a flat landing pad area of 6m x 6m. The helicopter will fly into the wind when landing. In cases of extreme emergency, where no landing area is available, a person or harness might be lowered. Take extreme care to avoid the rotors when approaching a landed helicopter.

Getting There & Away

Information on how to reach Italy is well covered in other guidebooks, including Lonely Planet's *Italy* guide. Therefore, only basic details are provided here.

AIR

Italy's main international gateway is Roma's (Rome's) Leonardo da Vinci (Fiumicino) airport, but regular international flights also serve Roma's Ciampino airport and Milano's (Milan's) Malpensa and Linate airports. Plenty of flights from other European cities are available direct to most regional capitals.

The plane ticket will probably be the single most expensive item in your budget, and buying it can be intimidating. Start early: some of the cheapest tickets have to be bought months in advance, and some popular flights sell out quickly.

Use the fares quoted in this book as a guide only. They are approximate and based on the rates advertised by travel agents at the time of going to press and are likely to have changed by the time you read this.

Official cheap tickets include advance-purchase tickets, budget fares, Apex and super-Apex and so on. Unofficial discount tickets are released by the airlines through selected travel agents and it is worth shopping around to find them. Another option, if Italy is only one stop on your grand world tour, is a Round-the-World (RTW) ticket. There may be restrictions on how many stops you can make, and the tickets are usually valid for 90 days to one year. Prices start at about UK£900, A$1800 or US$1300, depending on the season.

If you're looking for a bargain fare, reliable firms include STA Travel, which has offices worldwide, Council Travel in the USA, Travel CUTS in Canada, Flight Centres International in Australia and New Zealand, and Campus Travel and Trailfinders in Britain. All offer competitive prices to most destinations.

If you are a vegetarian or require a special diet (such as kosher food), are travelling with a baby or child, are terrified of flying or have some other special need, let the airline know as soon as possible so that they can make arrangements accordingly.

Always reconfirm your onward or return bookings by the specified time – at least 72 hours before departure on international flights. Otherwise, you risk turning up at the airport only to find you've missed your flight because it was rescheduled, or that you've been classified as a 'no show'.

The UK

London is one of the best centres in the world for discounted air tickets. The price of RTW tickets, especially, is about the best available anywhere and tickets can be bought for less than UK£1000.

The best source for the latest fares is the free newspaper *TNT*. Also check out the travel page ads of the Sunday newspapers, *Time Out* and *Exchange & Mart*. All are available from most London news stands or outside some train stations. Another good source of information on cheap fares is the magazine *Business Traveller*.

One of the more reliable, but not necessarily cheapest, agencies is STA Travel (☎ (0171) 361 61 61 for European flights). A similar agency is Trailfinders (☎ (0171) 937 54 00 for European flights). Campus Travel is in much the same league (☎ (0171) 730 34 02 for European flights).

Normal fares on a scheduled flight to Roma are around UK£255 one way and UK£510 return on the major airlines. However, Apex and other special fares are a better option and can cost as little as UK£259 return plus departure tax.

Direct charter flights from London to Roma or Milano are another option. An open return in August (high season) from London to Milano was UK£230, while a similar ticket to Roma cost UK£240. Contact Italy Sky Shuttle (☎ (0181) 748 13 33).

Still cheaper fares can be found, and it is well worth shopping around.

The Rest of Europe

France Voyages et Découvertes (☎ 01 42 61 00 01), 21 rue Cambon, is a good place to start hunting down the best air fares in Paris. There are plenty of regular flights between Paris and Roma or Milano. From Roma the CTS agency has one-way fares to Paris for students starting from L270,000.

Germany In Munich, a great source of travel information and equipment is the Därr Travel Shop (☎ (89) 28 20 32) at Theresienstr 66. In Berlin, Kilroy Travel-ARTU Reisen (☎ (30) 310 00 40), at Hardenbergstr 9 near Berlin Zoo (with five branches around the city), is a good travel agent. In Frankfurt, you might try SRID Reisen (☎ (69) 70 30 35), Bergerstr 118. A one-way fare from Roma to Berlin will cost from L290,000.

Greece Shop around the travel agents in the backstreets of Athens between Syntagma Square and Omonia Square.

Netherlands Amsterdam is a popular departure point. Some of the best fares are offered by the student travel agency NBBS Reiswinkels (☎ (20) 620 5071). Its fares are comparable to the London bucket shops, and return flights between Amsterdam and Roma start at about UK£170 for students. NBBS Reiswinkels also has branches in Brussels and Belgium.

Spain In Madrid one of the most reliable budget travel agents is Viajes Zeppelin (☎ (91) 547 79 03; fax (91) 542 65 46), Plaza de Santo Domingo 2. Return flights to Roma in low season start at about 30,000 ptas.

The USA & Canada

The *New York Times*, the *LA Times*, the *Chicago Tribune* and the *San Francisco Examiner* produce weekly travel sections in which you'll find any number of travel agents' ads. Council Travel and STA Travel have offices in major cities nationwide. The

magazine *Travel Unlimited* (PO Box 1058, Allston, Mass 02134) publishes details of cheap air fares.

Low season, open return tickets from New York to Roma or Milano can be found for as little as US$500. A one-way fare from Roma to New York will cost from around L370,000.

Both Alitalia and Air Canada have direct flights to Roma and Milano from Toronto and Montreal. Travel CUTS, specialising in discount fares for students, has offices in all major Canadian cities. Otherwise scan the budget travel agents' ads in the Toronto *Globe & Mail*, the *Toronto Star* and the *Vancouver Province*.

Australia & New Zealand

STA Travel and Flight Centres International are major dealers in cheap air fares in both countries, although heavily discounted fares can often be found at your local travel agent. Scan the ads in the Saturday travel sections of the Melbourne *Age* and the *Sydney Morning Herald*.

Discounted return air fares on mainstream airlines through reputable agents can be surprisingly cheap. Low season fares to Italy average around A$1800 return, but can go as low as A$1400 with airlines like Garuda Indonesia. High season return fares range from A$1700 with Garuda Indonesia to A$2600 with Qantas.

Qantas and Alitalia fly from Melbourne and Sydney to Roma three times a week. Flights from Perth are generally a few hundred dollars cheaper.

From New Zealand, the cheapest fares to Europe are routed through the USA, and a RTW ticket may be cheaper than a return. Otherwise, you can fly from Auckland to a connecting flight in Melbourne or Sydney.

LAND

The UK

Bus You can travel from Britain to Italy by long-distance bus. The bus either drives onto a train which carries it through the Channel Tunnel, or it uses a ferry (the fare for which is included in the ticket price). Eurolines (☎ (0171) 730 8235), 52 Grosvenor Gardens,

Victoria, London SW1, in conjunction with local bus companies across Europe, is the main international carrier. There are Eurolines offices throughout Italy. A youth/under 26 fare from London to Roma is UK£159 return (valid 30 days). The full adult fare is UK£199 return (valid 30 days).

Train Travelling from the UK, you have a choice of train tickets covering the channel crossing either by ferry, the faster Seacat, or the Eurostar train through the Channel Tunnel, the latter of which speeds up the initial part of the journey.

The cheapest standard one way/return fares to Roma, on offer at the time of research, were UK£93/£157 for students and those under 26, while the full adult fares were UK£108/£176. To Milano the respective fares were UK£79/£130 and UK£90/£140.

Discount Tickets Discount tickets are available for under 26s (Wasteels or Billet International de Jeunesse) and for children. There is a range of rail passes, most of which won't be much value to you if you're planning to spend most of your time walking. Many are also unsuitable if you plan to travel only within Italy. Eurail passes (for non-European residents), for instance, require you to travel about 2400km in two weeks to get your money's worth, while InterRail (available to European residents) also requires extensive travelling to get value for money. Other Eurail options are Flexipasses, with which the traveller is entitled to 10 or 15 days' train travel over a two-month period, and the Saverpass, which is for two or more people travelling together and is available for 15 or 21 days or one month.

Both the Europass and the InterRail pass are worthwhile only if you plan to travel to other countries in the region. Others require you to complete all of your train travel within a certain period. The Euro-Domino Pass (known as Freedom in the UK) covers travel in any one of 25 European countries, and is valid for three, five or 10 days' travel over a period of one month. For Italy, a 1st class, 10-day pass costs UK£329. Second class is

UK£239 and a youth version (under 26) costs UK£179. But again, you would need to be on trains a good amount of the time to get full value out of the pass.

A couple of Italian rail passes can be purchased in the UK. The Italy Railcard allows eight, 15, 21 or 30 days' unlimited travel on the country's network. Fares in 2nd class range from UK£110 for eight days to UK£190 for 30 days. Alternatively, you could buy a Kilometric Card. With this pass you can travel up to 3000km or make up to 20 trips, whichever comes first. The pass can be shared by up to five people and is valid for two months from the first trip. You have to pay supplements for high speed trains and the pass costs UK£88 in 2nd class.

Car & Motorcycle Coming from the UK, you can take your car across to France either by ferry or the Channel Tunnel car train, Le Shuttle. The latter runs round the clock, with up to four crossings (35 minutes) an hour in high season. You pay for the vehicle only and fares vary according to time of day and season. A normal fare is UK£149 return for a car and its passengers (valid for one year) and UK£75 for a motorcycle and rider/s (valid for one year). You can book in advance (☎ (0990) 35 35 33), but the service is designed to let you just roll up and get on the next train.

It is worth noting that motorcyclists rarely have to book ahead for ferries. Wearing crash helmets is compulsory in Italy and throughout Europe.

Proof of ownership of a private vehicle should always be carried (Vehicle Registration Document for UK-registered cars) when driving through Europe. All EU member states' driving licences are fully recognised throughout the Union, regardless of your length of stay. Third party motor insurance is a minimum requirement in Italy and throughout Europe, and it is compulsory to have a Green Card, an internationally recognised proof of insurance, which can be obtained from your insurer. In the UK, further information, as well as maps and guides, can be obtained from the RAC (☎ (01304) 20 41 53) or the AA (☎ (0990) 44 88 66).

The Rest of Europe

Bus Eurolines is the main long distance bus service in Europe, also serving Britain (see under The UK earlier in this section). The service links up numerous national bus companies and has offices throughout the continent, including Italy's major cities. In Roma, contact Lazzi Express, Via Tagliamento 27r (☎ (06) 884 08 40) or Agenzia Elios, Circonvallazione Nomentana 574, Lato Stazione Tiburtina (☎ (06) 44 23 39 28).

Train EuroCity (EC) trains run from major destinations throughout Europe – including Paris, Geneva, Zürich, Frankfurt, Vienna and Barcelona – direct to major Italian cities. On overnight hauls you can book a *cuccetta* (known outside Italy as a *couchette* or sleeping berth) for around UK£15 for most international train services. See under The UK earlier in this section for details about rail passes.

SEA

Ferries connect Italy to Greece, Turkey, Tunisia and Malta. There are also services to Corsica, Toulon and Marseille (France), Durrës and Vlora (Albania) and Barcelona (Spain). Ticket prices vary according to the time of year and are at their most expensive during summer. Prices for cars, camper vans and motorcycles vary according to the size of the vehicle, and bicycles can sometimes be taken free of charge.

Ticket prices are competitive on the heavily serviced Brindisi-Greece route, and travellers wanting to pick up the best deals can shop around in Brindisi. The main companies include Adriatica (☎ (0831) 52 38 25) and Hellenic Mediterranean Lines (☎ (0831) 52 85 31) and one-way fares are around L100,000 for deck class, L120,000 for an airline-type chair, and L165,000 for a bed in a shared cabin.

DEPARTURE TAXES

The departure tax, payable when you leave Italy by air, is included in your airline ticket. There is a port tax payable when you leave the country by ferry. This must be paid when you check in.

Warning
The information in this chapter is particularly vulnerable to change: prices for international travel are volatile, routes are introduced and cancelled, schedules change, special deals come and go, and rules and visa requirements are amended. Airlines and governments seem to take a perverse pleasure in making price structures and regulations as complicated as possible. You should check directly with the airline or a travel agent to make sure you understand how a fare (and ticket you may buy) works. In addition, the travel industry is highly competitive and there are many lurks and perks.

The upshot of this is that you should get opinions, quotes and advice from as many airlines and travel agents as possible before parting with your hard-earned cash. The details given in this chapter should be regarded as pointers and are not a subsitute for your own careful, up-to-date research.

Getting Around

Public transport is well organised and not too expensive in Italy. In this guide, there has been an effort to ensure that bus or train services are accessible to the beginning and end of the walks. However, before setting out on your walk, check up-to-date bus and train timetables (they change seasonally), as well as chair lift and cable car timetables (if you're walking in the Alps) and plan the walk ac-cordingly. You don't want to arrive at the end of the route only to find that the last bus or cablecar has just left!

AIR
Domestic Air Services

Travelling by plane is expensive within Italy and it makes much better sense to use the efficient and considerably cheaper train and bus services. The domestic lines are Alitalia, Meridiana and Air One, and all offer roughly the same fares. The main airports are in Roma (Rome), Pisa, Milano (Milan), Napoli (Naples), Catania and Cagliari, but there are other, smaller airports throughout Italy. Domestic flights can be booked through agencies such as Sestante CIT, CTS and normal travel agencies.

Discount Fares

Alitalia offers a range of discounts for young people, families, the elderly and weekend travel, as well as occasional special promotional fares. It should be noted that airline fares fluctuate, and that special deals sometimes only apply when tickets are bought in Italy, or for return fares only. The air fares map on this page will give you an idea of return fares at the time of writing. Barring special deals, a one-way fare is generally half the cost of the return fare.

Prices shown are for economy north-south direct return fares, which must pass through either Roma or Milano.

BUS

Bus travel within Italy is provided by numerous companies, and services vary from local

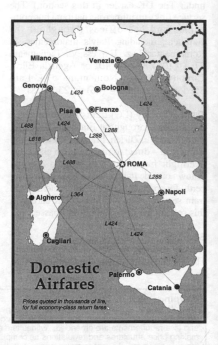

Domestic Airfares

Prices quoted in thousands of lire, for full economy-class return fares

routes linking small villages, to those making major intercity connections, which are fast and reliable. By utilising the local services, it is possible to arrive in just about any location throughout the entire country. Buses can be a cheaper and faster way to get around if your destination is not on major train lines.

There are long-haul services from the major cities to various parts of the Alps, known as Alpi buses, provided by companies including SITA and Lazzi. The service operates from Firenze and Bologna to destinations including Cortina and the Val Gardena. Other long-haul services will get you from Roma to Sicilia (Sicily) (SAIS and Segesta), or from Roma to the Amalfi Coast (Marozzi, which also runs a Roma-Brindisi service).

Useful bus companies in Roma (06 area code) are as follows:

Lazzi
(☎ 884 08 40) Via Tagliamento 27r. Services to other European cities and the Alps (departing from Firenze or Bologna for Cortina, the Val Gardena and other destinations in the Dolomiti).

Marozzi
(☎ 474 28 01) Information at Eurojet Travel Agency, Piazza della Repubblica. Services to Bari and Brindisi, via towns including Alberobello and Matera. Also services to Sorrento, the Amalfi Coast and Pompeii.

SAIS & Segesta
(☎ 481 96 76) Information at Piazza della Repubblica, or Piazzale Tiburtina bus terminal. Services to Sicilia.

Sena
(☎ 474 28 01) Information at Eurojet. Services to Siena.

It is usually possible to get bus timetables for the provinces and for intercity services from local tourist offices. In larger cities most of the main intercity bus companies have ticket offices or operate through agencies, and buses leave from either a bus station (*autostazione*) or from a particular piazza or street. In some smaller towns and villages tickets are sold in bars – just ask for *biglietti per il pullman* – or on the bus. Note that buses almost always leave on time.

Major companies which provide long-haul services include Marozzi (Roma to Brindisi); SAIS and Segesta (Roma to Sicilia); Lazzi and SITA (from Toscana (Tuscany) and other regions to the Alps) Lazzi also runs international services.

Reservations & Costs

It is usually not necessary to make reservations on buses, although it is advisable in the high season for overnight or long-haul trips. A ticket from Roma to Palermo costs L50,000 and Roma to Siena is L22,000.

TRAIN

Travelling by train in Italy is simple, cheap and generally efficient. The Ferrovie dello Stato (FS) is the partially privatised state train system and there are several private train services throughout the country. There are several types of trains. A new express service known as Eurostar operates between all of the major cities, offering a higher standard of service. The very fast train, known as the ETR450 or Pendolino, between Roma, Firenze, Bologna and Milano is part of the Eurostar network. (The Pendolino is supposed to be extended to Napoli by 2001). Other services include the fast Intercity (IC), or EuroCity (EC) trains, which stop only at major cities and you must pay a supplement to the normal fare. Other trains, a *regionale* or *interregionale*, stop at all or most stations and you don't pay a supplement.

Travellers should note that a new ticket validation system has been introduced by the FS, whereby tickets must be punched by machines installed at the entrance to all train platforms. The machines are yellow and easy to find. The rule does not apply to tickets purchased outside Italy.

There are also left-luggage facilities at all train stations. They are often open 24 hours, but if not, they usually close only for a couple of hours after midnight. They open seven days a week and charge from L1500 for each piece of luggage.

Train Passes

It is not worth buying a Eurail pass or Inter-Rail pass if you are going to travel only in Italy, since train fares are reasonably cheap (see under Discount Tickets in the Land section in the Getting There & Away chapter). The FS offers its own discount passes for travel within the country. These include the Carta Verde for young people aged 12 to 26 years. It costs L40,000, is valid for one year and entitles you to a 20% discount on all train travel, but you'll need to do a fair bit of travelling to get your money's worth. Children aged between four and 12 years are automatically entitled to a 50% discount, and under four years they can travel for free. You can buy a kilometric ticket (*biglietto kilometrico*), which is valid for two months and allows you to cover 3000km, with a maximum of 20 trips. It costs L206,000 (2nd class) and you must pay the supplement if you catch an Intercity train. Its main attraction is that it can be used by up to five people, either singly or together.

Classes

There are 1st and 2nd classes on all Italian trains, with a 1st class ticket costing a bit less than double the price of 2nd class. On the Pendolino 2nd class is much like 1st class on other trains.

Reservations

It is recommended that you book train tickets for long trips, particularly if you're travelling on weekends or during holiday periods, otherwise you could find yourself standing in the corridor for the entire journey. Reservations are obligatory for the Eurostar trains. You can get timetable information and make train bookings at most travel agents, including CTS and Sestante CIT, or you can simply buy your ticket on arrival at the station. There are special booking offices for the Eurostar trains at the relevant train stations. If you are doing a reasonable amount of travelling, it is worth buying a train timetable. There are several available, including the official FS timetables, which are available at newspaper stands in or near train stations for around L5000.

Costs

To travel on the Intercity and EuroCity trains, you are required to pay a *supplemento*, an additional charge determined by the distance you are travelling. For instance, on the Intercity train between Roma and Firenze you will pay an extra L13,500. On the Eurostar trains, it is obligatory to make a booking, since they don't carry standing room passengers. The cost of the ticket includes the supplement and booking fee. The one-way fare from Roma to Firenze on the Eurostar Pendolino is L48,000 in 2nd class and L74,500 in 1st class. The difference in price between the Pendolino (1½ hours) and the cheaper Intercity (around 2 hours) is only L8000. For the extra money you get a faster, much more comfortable service, with an airline-type snack thrown in. The Pendolino

takes priority over other trains, so there's no risk of long delays in the middle of nowhere.

Always check whether the train you are about to catch is an Intercity, and pay the supplement before you get on, otherwise you will pay extra on the train.

On overnight trips within Italy it can be worth paying extra for a *cuccetta* (sleeping berth) (L18,500).

Some price examples for one-way 2nd class train fares (including supplements) are: Roma-Firenze L39,000 (Intercity) and L48,000 (Eurostar); Roma-Torino L73,000 (Intercity) and L84,500 (Eurostar); Roma-Milano L70,000 (Intercity) and L79,500 (Eurostar).

CAR & MOTORCYCLE

Since many walks in this book start and end at geographically distant points, you'll need to plan before setting out how to get back to the car. This can be a tricky business if, for instance, you are in the Dolomiti, where a walk might start in one valley and end in another. Information about public transport is provided throughout this book, however you should check with local tourist offices to get updated timetables and more detailed information about bus or train connections. Normal precautions should be taken to avoid theft of your car or motorcycle. For instance, never leave anything in the car. Car theft is a big problem in Italy, particularly in areas such as Napoli and in Sicilia. See Dangers & Annoyances in the Facts for the Walker chapter.

Road Rules

In Italy, as throughout Continental Europe, people drive on the right side of the road and overtake on the left. Unless otherwise indicated, you must give way to cars coming from the right. It is compulsory to wear seat belts if fitted to the car (front seat belts on all cars, rear seat belts on cars produced after 26 April 1990).

Speed limits, unless otherwise indicated by local signs, are: on autostradas 130km/h for cars of 1100cc or more, 110km/h for smaller cars and for motorcycles under 350cc;

on all main, non-urban highways 110km/h; on secondary, non-urban highways 90km/h; and in built-up areas 50km/h.

You don't need a licence to ride a moped under 50cc, but you should be aged 14 years or more and a helmet is compulsory up to age 18; you can't carry passengers or ride on autostradas. The speed limit for a moped is 40 km/h. To ride a motorcycle or scooter up to 125cc, you must be at least 16 years old and have a licence (a car licence will do). Helmets are compulsory for everyone riding a motorcycle bigger than 50cc. For more than 125cc you need a motorcycle licence. There is no lights-on requirement for motorcycles during the day.

Rental

Car It is cheaper to arrange car rental before leaving your own country, for instance through some sort of fly/drive deal. Most major firms, including Hertz, Avis and Budget, will arrange this, and you simply pick up the vehicle at a nominated point when you arrive in Italy. Foreign offices of CIT, can also help to organise car or camper van rental before you leave home (see the section on Rental in the Getting There & Away chapter).

You will need to be aged 21 years or more (23 years or more for some companies) to rent a car in Italy, and you will find the deal far easier to organise if you have a credit card. Most firms will accept your standard licence, sometimes with an Italian translation (which can usually be provided by the agencies themselves) or International Driving Permit.

Motorcycle You'll have no trouble renting a small motorcycle such as a scooter (Vespa) or moped. There are numerous rental agencies in cities, where you'll also usually be able to rent larger motorcycles for touring, and at tourist destinations such as seaside resorts. Most agencies won't rent motorcycles to people under the age of 18 years.

Petrol

The cost of petrol in Italy is very high, at

around L1900 per litre (slightly less for unleaded petrol). Petrol is called *benzina*, unleaded petrol is *benzina senza piombo* and diesel is *gasolio*. If you are driving a car which uses LPG (liquid petroleum gas, known as *gasauto* or GPL in Italy), you will need to buy a special guide to service stations which have gasauto or GPL. By law these must be located in nonresidential areas and are usually in the country or on city outskirts, although you'll find plenty on the autostradas. GPL costs around L900 per litre.

Useful Organisations

The Automobile Club Italiano (ACI) no longer offers free roadside assistance to tourists. Residents of the UK and Germany should be able to organise overseas assistance through their home-country organisations, which entitles them to use ACI's emergency assistance number (☎ 116) for a small fee. Without it, you'll pay a minimum fee of L150,000 if you call ☎ 116. ACI has offices at Via Marsala 8, Roma (☎ (06) 49981); and Corso Venezia 43, Milano (☎ (02) 77451).

BICYCLE
Rental

Bikes are available for rent in most Italian towns and many places have both city and mountain bikes. Rental costs for a city bike range from L15,000 a day to around L100,000 per week. A good mountain bike will cost more.

Purchase

If you shop around, bargain prices range from L190,000 for a woman's bike without gears to L400,000 for a mountain bike with 16 gears, but you will need to pay a lot more for a very good bike. A good place to shop for bargains is Tacconi Sport, which has large outlets near Perugia, Arezzo, Trento (Trent) and in the Republic of San Marino. It buys in bulk and has some great bargains.

Planning

If you plan to bring your own bike, check with your airline for any additional costs.

The bike will need to be disassembled and packed for the journey.

A primary consideration on a cycling tour is to travel light, but you should take a few tools and spare parts, including a puncture repair kit and a spare inner tube. Panniers are essential to balance your possessions on either side of the bike frame. A bike helmet is a very good idea, as is a very solid bike lock and chain, although even that might not prevent your bike from being stolen if you leave it unattended.

Travelling with a Bicycle

Bikes can be taken very cheaply on trains (L10,000), although only some trains will actually carry them. Fast trains (IC, EC etc) will generally not accommodate bikes and they must be sent as registered luggage. This can take a few days and will probably mean that your bike won't be on the same train that you travel on. It might be an idea to send your bike in advance, if possible. Check with the FS or a travel agent for more information.

HITCHING

Hitching is never safe in any country, and we don't recommend it. Travellers who decide to hitch should understand they are taking a small but potentially serious risk. People who hitch will be safer if they travel in pairs and let someone know where they are going.

It is illegal to hitch on Italy's autostradas, but quite acceptable to stand near the entrance to the toll booths. A man and a woman travelling together is probably the best combination. Women travelling alone should be extremely cautious about hitching anywhere in Italy. In areas where walkers are common but public transport is not, you might find that drivers are even willing to go out of their way to take you back to your car or hotel. It is sometimes possible to arrange lifts in advance – ask around at youth hostels. The International Lift Centre in Firenze (☎ (055) 28 06 26) and Enjoy Roma (☎ (06) 445 18 43) may be able to help.

BOAT

Ferry & Hydrofoil

Large ferries (navi) service the islands of Sicilia and Sardegna (Sardinia), and smaller ferries (traghetti) and hydrofoils (aliscafi) service the Aeolian Islands, as well as other islands such as Elba, the Tremiti, Ischia and Capri. The main embarkation points for Sardegna are Genova, Livorno, Civitavecchia and Napoli; for Sicilia the main points are Napoli and Villa San Giovanni in Calabria. The main points of arrival in Sicilia are Palermo and Messina; in Sardegna they are Cagliari, Arbatax, Olbia and Porto Torres.

Tirrenia Navigazione is the major company servicing the Mediterranean and it has offices throughout Italy. The FS also operates ferries to Sicilia and Sardegna. Travellers can choose between cabin accommodation (men and women are usually segregated in 2nd class, although families will be kept together) or a poltrona, an airline-type armchair. Deck class is available only in summer and only on some ferries, so ask when making your booking.

Details about ferry and hydrofoil services are provided in the relevant sections.

LOCAL TRANSPORT

See individual chapters for information about getting to and from walks.

Western Alps

Italy's highest mountain and oldest national park, a great variety of flora and fauna, footpaths to high passes, tarns and alpine meadows, welcoming mountain *rifugi* (refuges), an embarrassment of riches for walkers in Parco Nazionale del Gran Paradiso (Gran Paradiso National Park) and Valle d'Aosta are all in the heart of the Western Alps. Added to this portfolio of assets are the relatively rare combination of accessible but remote areas, scarcely touched by modern civilisation.

From the huge range of walks available, a small selection is described here. They are centred on the national park, and range beyond its borders towards the head of Valle d'Aosta (north of Val di Rhêmes) and the French border in the shadow of Monte Bianco (the highest mountain in Europe) along the linking thread of a high-level, long-distance route, the Alta Via 2 (AV2).

HISTORY

Archaeological research has shown that Valle d'Aosta has been settled since about 4000 BC, but the first identifiable inhabitants were the Iron Age Salass people. They fought successfully against the Romans, but were forced to assimilate in 25 BC. Aosta was a strategically important outpost in the Roman Empire, and takes its name from Augusta Praetoria, at one time a military commander in the valley. The Romans improved roads and, using the Colle del Piccolo San Bernardo, extended into France and opened up transalpine communications.

The fall of the Roman Empire initiated a period of instability beginning with an invasion by the Burgundians and coming to an end in 576 when the Franks established their domination which endured for some 300 years. Valle d'Aosta became part of the county (later Duchy) of Savoy, French in origin, in the 11th century. Thereafter the valley's fortunes waxed and waned. Although within what became the kingdom of Savoy in 1713, the Valle enjoyed a measure of indepen-

HIGHLIGHTS

SANDRA BARDWELL

- Hearing the piercing whistles of marmots echoing through the Vallone del Grand Nomenon
- Exploring Colonna mine, north-east of Cogne
- The breathtaking view of the awesome Gran Paradiso massif and its glaciers
- Tackling the Alta Via 2, a challenging but rewarding six-day walk

dence. In 1561, French was adopted as the official language; most Valdostane people still speak a French-Provençale dialect, and Italian is used, somewhat grudgingly, when necessary.

A disastrous plague in 1630 reduced the population from about 105,000 to 35,000. Valle d'Aosta did not escape the upheavals of the French Revolution and was occupied by the French in 1789 and only returned to the kingdom of Savoy in 1815. During the 19th century, industrial development beyond the valley stimulated mass emigration.

Victor Emmanuel II, as ruler of Piemonte (Piedmont) and later a united Italy, brought some economic benefits to the eastern reaches of the area during the mid-19th century through his predeliction for hunting. His royal hunting reserve later became, ironically, the core of Italy's first national park, Gran Paradiso, embracing the larger part of southern Valle d'Aosta. It was also during the 19th century that attention began to be focussed on the Gran Paradiso area for tourism and mountaineering. Tourism did not really develop beyond catering for a wealthy, leisured elite until after WWI. However, the first ascent of Gran Paradiso by two British climbers and two Italians in 1860 awakened interest among climbers and many first ascents,

mainly by Italians, followed during the 1870s and, much later, the 1920s.

Today, attention is focused on free climbing (ie without artificial aids), and on opening routes across the many glaciers and up waterfalls. Tourism has also attracted many people away from the side valleys, and a precarious dependence on marginal agriculture, to the larger centres and more lucrative employment. However, leaving the valley in search of work has long been a matter of necessity in the area, except (for example) in Cogne where the mine, for many years, provided permanent employment.

WESTERN ALPS - MAPS	
Map 1 Valle d'Aosta	p 111
Map 2 Parco Nazionale del Gran Paradiso	p 117
Map 3 Valgrisenche La Thuile Walk	p 128

Mining in the Alps

The mineral richness of Val de Cogne has been recognised and tapped since Roman times. The earliest recorded mine was operating in 1679, but full scale exploitation came much later and then lasted for barely a century, until 1979.

There were three mines: Colonna, at 2400m, directly above Lillaz (5km east of Cogne), the centre of the underground operations; Costa del Pino, closer to Cogne; and Larcinaz, in Vallon de Grauson (north from Cogne). The main output was magnetite, a source of iron ore; serpentine, limestone and marble were also extracted.

Colonna was more than just a mine – a small village including a chapel, grew up to house the miners. Innovations in transport, especially a *funivia* (cablecar), overcame most of the problems of working high above the valley. After WWII, the industry underwent great changes, and Colonna was finally forced to close in 1979. However, recent developments at Aosta in the production of stainless steel have revitalised the iron and steel industry in Valle d'Aosta, providing a valuable boost to the economy.

SANDRA BARDWELL
Mine buildings at Colonna

The mining museum at Cogne is worth a visit. It is just 1km up the road to Gilmillan and is signposted from the main Cogne-Lillaz road. It is open from 10 am to 8 pm from May to September; entry is L4000 for adults and L2000 for students. The museum stands at the end of the now-defunct funivia up to Colonna – a red cabin is still in place. The excellent displays inside the museum, with captions in French and Italian, include photographs, geological maps, mine plans and diagrams, mineral samples and artefacts. There is also a sizeable section devoted to other aspects of local history. Fascinating photos from the end of the 19th century onwards portray Cogne's gradual growth from a small rural village to a modern tourist resort – though with few, if any of the negative aspects of such developments. Other displays focus on skiing, hunting and mountaineering, including photos of members of the Club Alpino Italiano celebrating the club's 50th anniversary in 1913 with an ascent of Gran Paradiso.

During summer the programme of guided walks from Cogne includes visits to Colonna mine (see Guided Walks under Planning later). Or you can make your own way up there. The start of the path, just east of the hamlet of Molinaz on the Lillaz road, is clearly signposted, and the path from there is easy to follow. It is a steep, but extremely scenic climb, with spectacular views of Val de Cogne. The mine buildings are still intact, but closed to the public for safety reasons.

For more information on the history of mining in Cogne and Valle d'Aosta, try the Regional Mining Museum (☎ (0165) 30 26 83) in Aosta at Via Paravera, just west of the train station and across the railway. It is open from 9 am to 7 pm every day during July and August and from 10 am to 7 pm from Tuesday to Sunday in June and from September to December. ∎

At the end of WWII General de Gaulle attempted to annex Valle d'Aosta to France, but was forced to withdraw. In February 1948 Valle d'Aosta was granted autonomy within the Italian state, becoming the smallest and most sparsely populated of the regions.

Apart from wine production, agriculture is now of minor significance to the valley's economy, which is now based on tourism, steel production, and service industries.

Even so, there are disparities between the seemingly prosperous main valley and the side valleys – much of the area within the park qualifies for funding from the European Union as a depressed area. However, visitors to the national park can still discover some of the traditional ways in the remotest reaches of the high valleys.

NATURAL HISTORY

Within the vast chain of the Western Alps, stretching from the far south-western corner of mountainous Italy, in an arc to Lago Maggiore, Valle d'Aosta divides the Pennine Alps from the Graian Alps to the south. Parco Nazionale del Gran Paradiso consists essentially of deep lateral valleys and their separating ridges, extending south from the main valley. These valleys were cut by glaciers pushing north towards Valle d'Aosta where they dumped huge moraine deposits. The Gran Paradiso massif is the most significant formation in the whole Graian Alps, with 15 glaciers, innumerable tarns and 10 major summits, topped by Gran Paradiso – at 4061m is the highest peak entirely within Italy.

Granitic gneiss is the most common rock type in the Gran Paradiso massif and greenstone also occurs widely; diorites occur in the eastern side of Valsavarenche and mica schists in Val di Rhêmes. The distinctive greenish colour of the cliffs of La Grivola above Valsavarenche, and of the peaks around Lago Djouen across that valley is, in part, explained by the occurrence of greenstone. There are magnetite outcrops around Cogne, while anthracite is found in the La Thuile area.

Valle d'Aosta's river system is essentially the catchment of the Dora Baltea River, a tributary of the River Po. Two of the major tributaries of the Dora Baltea flow through the national park: the Savara and Grand Eyvia in Val di Cogne. The Dora di Rhêmes and Dora di Valgrisenche, further to the west, also feed the Dora Baltea.

Flora

There is a wide range of vegetation within the park. Fields, potentially suitable for crops, and mixed woodlands are found in the valleys; oak woodlands and meadows grow in the lower reaches of the mountainsides. Further up, between 800m and 1000m, the woodland comprises beech, larch and spruce. In the subalpine zone, between 1600m and 2000m, up to the limit of tree growth, are spruce, larch and Arolla pine, and further up, clumps of mountain pine. Above the tree line the alpine plant communities are commonly dominated by alpenrose, usually associated with dwarf juniper and bilberry, among others. In the grasslands up to 2400m, gentians, arnica, alpine avens, tormentil, and primulas are among the species to be seen. On the cliffs and screes, where growing conditions are extreme, with frost and harsh winds, many of the species are dwarf, cushion-forming perennials. In the high alpine zones, yellow genipi, alpine rock jasmine, saxifrages, and moss campion survive; lichens, algae and mosses occur right on the snow line.

Among the endemic plants to be found in the park are Central Alps milk-vetch *Astragalus centralpinus*, and one of the cinquefoils,

Larch, Fir & Pine

Although the image of Parco Nazionale del Gran Paradiso is distinctly alpine – glaciers, snow-covered peaks and miniature plants among the screes – there are also large forested areas in the park. In Val di Cogne, below the mighty peak of La Grivola on the eastern slopes of Valsavarenche, conifers, birch, beech and maples thrive at altitudes up to 2500m.

Gran Paradiso harbours magnificent specimens of the larch (*Larix decidua*), Europe's only deciduous conifer. It grows up to 40m tall, with huge boles and enormous canopies of thick branches, the lower ones upturned at the end. Its wood is highly prized by boat builders.

Larch grows here in association with Norway spruce (*Picea abies*) and silver fir (*Abies alba*). The fir is not as widespread as the larch or the spruce and is identified by its bark which splits into platelets and the thick leaves with notched tips.

More common is the Arolla pine (*Pinus cembra*). Its dark green, stiff and dense needles are bunched in fives, and it has a small bulbous cone (the larch cone is more elongated). The branches of the Arolla pine turn up at the ends, similar to the habit of the larch, but are shorter. Overexploitation for furniture making and many other uses has decimated stocks of this tree, and despite new plantings, demand continues to exceed supply. ■

the yellow-flowering *Potentilla pennsylvanica sanguisorbilfolia*, while the twin flower *Linnaea borealis* reaches its southern limits in Val di Cogne and Valsavarenche.

Fauna

Gran Paradiso is home to several species of birds rarely seen elsewhere in Europe: bearded vulture, alpine chaffinch, spotted woodpecker, white partridge, together with the more common ptarmigan, various owl and jackdaw. The royal eagle is also present, although it is not indigenous to the park.

Ibex, chamois and marmots are the most numerous and readily observed mammals. White hare (in limited numbers), wolf, ermine, weasel, badger and vole (at very high altitudes) are also found in the park. Although the population of lynx is small, it has in-

creased since reaching near-extinction in the 19th century. Lynx inhabit high rocky areas during the summer and come down to the valleys in winter. Chamois are plentiful and enjoy cavorting about on the snow. They range far and wide during summer, but retreat during winter to the shelter of the woodlands.

CLIMATE

While the climate in Valle d'Aosta proper is suitable for cultivation of grapevines, conditions in the valleys several hundred metres above it are markedly cooler, although in settled summer weather, temperatures well into the 20°Cs are common. Even so, the mean annual temperature at Aosta is just 10°C and 8°C at Courmayeur, at the western end of the valley. Overnight frost is likely above 1800m at any time. The warmer conditions in the valley seem to bring a greater propensity for thunderstorms – dark clouds can gather over Aosta while the higher valleys are basking in sunshine. This is the wettest time of the year. The valleys experience their own local pattern of prevailing winds, which blow up Valle d'Aosta during the day and down at night. The area generally is snowbound from December until springtime, and the remotest reaches of some of the valleys are then inaccessible.

INFORMATION

Maps

For general access to the area, the Touring Club Italiana's *Piemonte, Valle d'Aosta* sheet in the 1:200,000 series is very good. At a more detailed level, the area is covered by several series of maps.

Kompass map No 85 *Monte Bianco, Mont Blanc* and No 86 *Gran Paradiso, Valle d'Aosta* (1:50,000, 100m contours) are useful for general orientation, but the numbering of footpaths is misleading as many paths are incorrectly located and badly drawn (suggesting that they are in fact 50m wide); the accompanying booklets, in Italian, French and German contain a great deal of background information. They are widely available at about L9500.

Gipeto – The Bearded Vulture

Known in Italian as the gipeto, the bearded vulture (*Gipaetus barbatus*) became extinct in the park by 1912. It had been hunted relentlessly for centuries in the belief that it preyed on domestic animals. However, about 85% of gipeto's diet consists of bones, preferably sheep, goat and chamois – it does not take live prey. The last survivor in the Italian Alps was slain in Val di Rhêmes in 1913. A major European project to reintroduce the bird was launched in 1978, under the protection of the World Wide Fund for Nature (WWF), IUCN and the Frankfurt Zoological Society. Between that year and 1995, 60 were released, after having been bred in captivity – 45 were still alive in 1995. The gipeto was first spotted in Gran Paradiso in 1989.

With its narrow dark wings spanning up to 280cm and long, wedge-shaped tail, it is easily identified in flight. On the ground, it is particularly distinguished by the feathery beard under its beak. The gipeto ranges over a huge territory and its low rate of reproduction means that the reintroduction programme is proceeding slowly. Breeding begins when it reaches 10 to 12 years of age – a single egg at a time; the young do not become self-sufficient until they are about 18 months old.

The return of the gipeto to the Gran Paradiso is the subject of an excellent display in the national park visitor centre at Chanavey, Val di Rhêmes. ■

Four sheets by the Istituto Geografico Centrale (IGC) (1:50,000 series, 100m contours) cover the area. On the periphery are sheets No 2, *Valli di Lanzo e Moncenisio* for the southern fringes, and No 9, *Ivrea-Biella e Bassa Valle d'Aosta*, for the eastern side. Centrally, sheet No 3, *Il Parco Nazionale del Gran Paradiso*, and No 4, *Massiccio del Monte Bianco*, cover the scope of this chapter. They are easy to read, and show the Alta Via 2 (AV2) and many other paths, and on the whole are reliable enough.

Studio FMB Bologna's *Gran Paradiso* map (1:50,000, 100m contours) is also clearly legible, but has many errors in the location of features and routes of paths. The information on the reverse side, in Italian, about flora, fauna, geology, and especially local mountaineering history and the long distance walks, makes the map, at L9500, worthwhile.

French and Italian versions of place names are used throughout the area, with a tendency for French to be favoured the further west you go. Thus, for example, Colle della Finestra and Col Fenêtre are the same place (between Val di Rhêmes and Valgrisenche).

Information Sources

The APT office (☎ (0165) 33352; fax 40532), Piazza Chanoux 8, 11100 Aosta, is open daily from 9 am to 8 pm; it is in the north-west corner of Piazza Chanoux. The helpful staff (some speak English) can provide information about accommodation, buses and points of interest. Basic information in French, Italian and English about Valle d'Aosta (history, useful phone numbers, transport) is available in the Valle's official Web site: http://www.aostavalley.com/index/htm.

The local branch of Club Alpino Italiano (☎ (0165) 40194; fax 34657) has an office at the same address as the Aosta APT. It is open Monday and Thursday from 5 to 7 pm, Wednesday from 5 to 8 pm and Friday from 8 to 10 pm. It may be able to advise about local walking conditions. Inquiries about accommodation at rifugi should be made direct to the rifugi.

For information about the national park, its valleys and villages, contact the Gran Paradiso APT (☎ (0165) 95055; fax 95975), Loc Champagne 18, 11018 Villeneuve. The office is on the main road (SS26) just west of Villeneuve. Details of the park visitor centres at Degioz in Valsavarenche and at Chanavey in Val di Rhêmes are given in the sections covering Valsavarenche, and Val di Rhêmes (day three of Best of the Alta Via 2 walk). The head office of the national park (☎ (011) 81 71 87) is at Via della Rocca 47, 10123 Torino. An online service, Parks in Italy, is available on the Internet at http://www.communic.it/parks.html.

One of a series of cooperative programmes run by the national park is *Solo per stranieri* (for foreigners only) a week-long course which combines walks in the park with the chance to improve your Italian in day-to-day situations. Ring ☎ (0125) 44903 for more information.

Weather forecasts may be obtained from the meteorological office (☎ (0165) 44113) based at Aosta airport. The local mountain rescue contact is Soccorso Alpino Valdostano (☎ (0165) 34983), Delegazione Regionale, Aosta, Via M Emilius 13, or Stazione di Soccorso Alpino (☎ (0165) 74335 or 74204).

Books

A generous range of guides to walks and climbs in Valle d'Aosta and the national park are available, in Italian, from well-established publishers and/or authors. *A Piedi in Valle d'Aosta* by Stefano Ardito (a prolific author) comes in two volumes, each describing more than 90 walks and priced at L22,000 each. This is the least expensive in the range with other titles starting at L30,000. Among them, *I Laghi della Valle d'Aosta* (L30,000) by Sergio Piotti includes a good map and descriptions of 185 walks, highlighting the fact that there is much more to the area than mountains. This is emphasised by *Valle d'Aosta Gastronomica* by Bovo, Sanguinetti and Vola, an excellent guide (in Italian) to the history and traditions of local wines and other delights including about 100 recipes.

The Kompass series of *Guide Naturalistiche* includes *Animali delle Alpi, Fiori*

Alpini and *Fiori di Prato*. These compact guides each include 70 colour photos with brief descriptions of the most commonly observed species; at about L9500 they are well worth having.

In Aosta, you will find bookshops along Via de Tillier, just west of Piazza Chanoux, and in Cogne, there is a good bookshop on Via Mines de Cogne.

ACCOMMODATION & SUPPLIES

There are no youth hostels in Valle d'Aosta. There are several not-too-exorbitantly priced small hotels in and around Aosta; contact the APT office (see Information Sources earlier) for a detailed guide. A similar publication is available for camping areas, of which there are two on the eastern outskirts of Aosta: *Milleluci* (☎ (0165) 23 52 78) and *Valle d'Aosta* (☎ (0165) 36 13 60). There are also three at Sarre, a suburb of Aosta, about 5km to the south-west and right beside the main road.

In Aosta, the *Standa* supermarket in Corso Battaglione, just west of Piazza della Repubblica, may not be typically Italian, but it is inexpensive, well stocked (though not with local wines) and is open on Sundays. Several shops in Via S Anselmo, which leads east from Piazza Chanoux have a good range of local specialities, though at a price. There is an excellent *gelateria* in Via Trottechien (west of Piazza Chanoux) – a fig gelato is a memorable experience. English (and several other) language newspapers are sold by the newsagent in the south-west corner of Piazza Chanoux.

Meinardi Sport, 25 Rue Edouard Albert, about five minutes walk west from Piazza Chanoux, sells Coleman and Camping Gaz and a wide range of walking and mountaineering equipment.

In Cogne there are several walking and mountaineering equipment outlets. The hardware shop at the eastern end of Via Mines de Cogne sells Camping Gaz.

GETTING THERE & AWAY

Bus

There is a twice daily SAVDA (☎ (0165) 36 12 44; fax 36 12 46) bus service from Torino (Turin) and Milano (Milan) to Aosta, several from France (Chamonix, Val d'Isère and Annency) and from Switzerland (Martigny). A comprehensive timetable is available from the APT office in Aosta (see Information Sources earlier), or from the Aosta bus station (☎ (0165) 26 20 27), Via G Carrel diagonally opposite the train station (see Train following). Tickets should be purchased in advance at the station, but can also be bought on board. The single fare from Milano to Aosta is about L21,000.

Train

Regional and direct trains link Torino, Milano and Aosta via Chivasso, where it is usually necessary to change to one of the dozen or more trains each day. The Aosta-Torino fare is L12,100; the Aosta station (☎ (0165) 42193) is at Piazza Manzetti 1.

Car

The A5 from Torino (and Milano) extends west through Valle d'Aosta as far as Morgex (about 30km from Aosta), on the way passing to the south of Aosta. (At the time of research it was being extended west towards Courmayeur.) From Morgex, SS26 and SS26D lead to Courmayeur at the western end of the Valle, the Monte Bianco tunnel and Chamonix in France. From the northern side of Aosta, SS27 heads to the Great St Bernard pass tunnel and Switzerland.

VAL DI COGNE & VALNONTEY

Val di Cogne and Valnontey are at the gateway to Parco Nazionale del Gran Paradiso. For walkers they offer the very attractive combination of a generous variety of walks, relatively easy and direct access and a range of places to stay. There are high level walks to mountain passes, treks into remote valleys past traditional summer grazing settlements and a popular rifugio within easy reach.

Among the valleys from the southern side of Valle d'Aosta, Val di Cogne, cradling Torrente Grand Eyvia, is the only one which trends south-eastwards. Valnontey is characteristically oriented north-south. Between the south-western flank of Val di Cogne and Valnontey, the Gran Paradiso-Grivola massif rises majestically, with glaciers and summits above 3500m.

Val di Cogne is the most populous and developed of the valleys, but even so, its population scarcely touches 2000. Cogne, the only town in the valley, is geared to tourism, but developments are still modest in comparison with, for example, Courmayeur at the western end of Valle d'Aosta.

Being more accessible than the other deep mountain valleys, Cogne has the longest recorded history, mainly related to mining its mineral rich rocks (see 'Mining in the Alps' boxed text earlier in this chapter). Its potential for tourism was recognised early; in 1790, M Le Chevalier de Robilant wrote glowingly of its attractions, as did Carrel in 1855. Valnontey in particular shared in the benefits deriving from the creation of the royal hunting reserve in the 1850s, being on the route of the path up to the lodge which is

Italy's First National Park

The fate of the ibex – Europe's largest Alpine wild animal – is at the heart of the history of the park; it motivated its creation, and has been the focus of a long-term conservation project in the park.

The ibex has moved into mountainous areas as the climate has changed since prehistoric times, and ibex hunting was an age old practice. The first attempt to protect it from extinction was made in the early 19th century, when hunting was forbidden, but with the caveat that the ruling House of Savoy was exempt.

King Victor Emmanuel II of Piedmont (later the first king of Italy) was a regular visitor to the Gran Paradiso area. On his initiative, a royal hunting reserve for his exclusive use was set up in 1856, covering an area of about 2200 hectares, though only a small part of it was actually in royal ownership. Opinions differ about his motives: either for protection of the ibex, or out of pure selfishness. The creation of the reserve came about mainly because local communes and land owners forfeited their hunting rights to the sovereign, in the hope of some reward. They were not disappointed. The king set up special corps of wardens who managed to curtail poaching, and used locals as beaters and porters; gamekeepers were paid to get rid of what were then regarded as predators – the bearded vulture and the lynx.

Paths (or *mulattiere*) to hunting lodges were built in Valle d'Aosta and Valle dell'Orso, and later, to new lodges high above the valleys, and across passes between valleys. Ironically perhaps, the paths are now used to protect the once-hunted fauna, and by walkers and mountaineers. Of the former hunting lodges, Lauson is now Rifugio Vittoria Sella (above Valnontey); Orveille, above Eaux Rousses in Valsavarenche, is a park office and research centre; and Nivolet is Rifugio Alberto Savoia. Orveille was Victor Emmanuel's particular favourite and he had a telegraph line built from Orveille to Degioz so that he could keep in touch; parts of it are still intact.

In 1919, his successor Victor Emmanuel III, faced with rising maintenance costs, the revival of poaching during WWI and the consequent decline in the ibex population, surrendered his hunting rights and gave the property to the state, so that a national park could be established. Subsequent parliamentary debates revealed an awareness of the importance of setting up the park for nature conservation (by then the world's first national park, Yellowstone, had existed for 50 years). The park, Italy's first, was eventually established on 3 December 1922 to preserve flora, fauna and natural beauty.

Its area is currently 70,000 hectares, of which about 90% belongs to small land owners and communes. The park is run from headquarters in Torino (Turin), and its administrative council must approve all building work and land use changes within the park – which may help to explain why most, if not all, recent building development largely conforms to traditional styles. Conflicts arise, as tourism becomes more important to the local economy, and the perceived need to develop facilities runs counter to national park policy, which aims to protect the cultural heritage of the mountains and to encourage environmentally friendly development. Park managers seek to instil an understanding of how people, wildlife and the landscape are all interrelated, through school programmes and summer activities in the park.

In 1972 Gran Paradiso was twinned with its neighbour Parc Nationale de la Vanoise in France, making a truly European park of 123,000 hectares. As much as possible, the two are managed as one – a *parco senza frontiere*.

Sandra Bardwell

now Rifugio Vittorio Sella. In several villages, including Vieyes and Valnontey, there are examples of the distinctive traditional architecture: elegant ironwork, plasterwork and skilful use of stone and timber.

INFORMATION

The APT office (☎ (0165) 74040; fax 74 91 25), Piazza Chanoux 36, 11012 Cogne, is open on weekdays from 9 am to 12.30 pm and 3 to 6 pm, and from 9 am to 12.30 pm on weekends. It's in the building next to the post office and main bus stop. Here you can get a map and guide to local walks (see Maps following), an accommodation list and information about the wide variety of local attractions, including the programme of guided walks (see also Guided Walks in the following section).

PLANNING
When to Walk

Although some walks in this area require ice axe and crampons at times, lower level walks (for which such equipment is not essential) should be accessible from late May until late September, but conditions vary from year to year. Certainly, snow lies in the higher passes well into summer. September has a good reputation as a settled month, enriched by colourful deciduous woodlands. From about mid-July the area becomes very busy until the end of August, and accommodation is at a premium. Bus services during summer are more frequent than during the rest of the year; they start in mid-June or at the beginning of July and continue through to early September. Camping areas generally open during the second half of May and close in late September.

Maps

General coverage of the area is provided by maps in the Kompass and IGC series, and the Studio FMB sheet (see Maps under Information near the start of this chapter). In

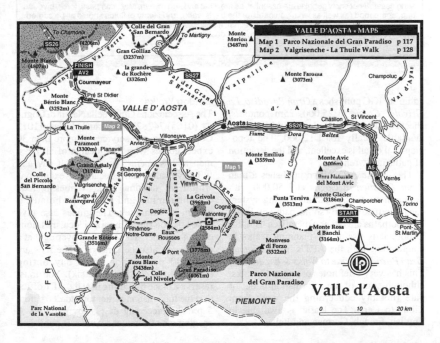

Safety in the Mountains

A perfect day: the black and white mountains are sharply etched on the saxe blue sky which darkens to ultramarine on the horizon – there's scarcely a breath of wind. On such a day, it is difficult to take seriously the warnings about the need to be prepared for the worst, at any time. But it isn't always like this and even a good day in the mountains has its hazards.

Many walkers from outside the mountainous countries of Europe may have had little experience of walking at altitudes above about 2000m. Yet it is difficult to avoid going above such heights in Parco Nazionale del Gran Paradiso: all the passes on the AV2 and all the rifugi are above 2400m. It is essential to give yourself at least three days, preferably longer (especially if you are older!), to become acclimatised so that you can really enjoy the walks properly. During high-level walks, moderate your normal walking speed, listen to your body as you climb, and slow down.

In planning your walk, a useful guide is to climb between 250m and 300m or descend 450m each hour. The times to destinations quoted on signs at the start of and at intervals along the paths are based on the vertical distances involved and on the capabilities of reasonably fit walkers, with no allowance for stops. There is no indication of the horizontal distance covered; it is very difficult to measure distance along most of the paths, where twists and turns are the norm. If you are fit, and once you become acclimatised, a day's walk involving 1200m to 1500m ascent should be surprisingly easy.

Start walking as early as possible in the morning, and aim to reach the highest point by about noon. Any snow fields en route could become soft and unstable after being exposed to the sun for a while, and the risk of afternoon thunderstorms can never be ignored. Take special care crossing areas where there are signs of recent rockfalls, which are not uncommon in late spring, after the thaw.

Wear strong walking boots with good ankle support. Boots which take crampons are essential for walks involving glacier crossings and any more than a very short distance across snow, as is an ice axe. A pair of good walking poles are good for support on steep descents, and crossing scree slopes, streams and small snow fields. Carry spare warm clothes including gloves and headgear. A waterproof jacket and overpants are absolutely essential. Umbrellas are commonly carried in the mountains in Italy. To this walker used to the windy Highlands of Scotland, this practice seemed daft, but the humble umbrella equipment does have its place if conditions are wet but still. At the other end of the spectrum, sunglasses, if not snow goggles are essential, as are a hat and sun screen. Map, compass, torch, bivouac bag, spare food (as well as what you need for the day's walk), and plenty of fluids should all be carried.

Before setting out, check the weather forecast; if possible, leave details of where you are going and when you expect to return to base or reach your destination.

Sandra Bardwell

---

addition, IGC publishes a *Gran Paradiso, La Grivola. Cogne* (1:25,000, 25m contours, sheet No 101) which is ideal for this area; it's available locally for L12,000. The topographical detail is excellent, and the depiction of paths fairly reliable.

The Cogne APT office publishes a map *Zona Turistica di Cogne* at 1:50,000 with 50m contours. The path numbering system can be confusing; only some roads are shown and footpaths are rather generalised. But, for L1500, it is useful for planning walks in conjunction with the APT's leaflet *Cogne. Gran Paradis. Guide to Walks & Excursions.* This has very brief notes of about 42 walks, although some of the information is out of date (notably concerning the walk from Lillaz to Cert). The leaflet is available in English, French, German and Italian.

Guided Walks

The Associazione Guide della Natura di Cogne (☎ (0165) 74282), Hameau de Lillaz, 11012 Cogne, offers the services of more than 30 expert guides who live locally, of all ages, men and women. They hold half-day and full-day walks and educational excursions within the national park. Venues include Colonna mine and Paradisia botanical garden at Valnontey. The guides also give slide talks on flora, fauna and local traditions during summer. Treks staying overnight at a rifugio can also be arranged. The fees are L15,000 per person for a day outing (L10,000 for children over six). You must reserve a place by calling in at the APT office (see the Information earlier for address) before 5 pm the preceding day, or by phoning. A programme of summer activities is published regularly. The Associazione Guide della Natura di Cogne office is next to the post office in Cogne and is open daily from 9 to 11.45 am; at other times inquire at the APT office nearby.

PLACES TO STAY & EAT
Valnontey

There is little to choose between the two camp sites in the village. *Lo Stambecco* (☎ (0165) 74152), at the north-eastern edge of the village, has 140 pitches on grassed terraces, some shaded by tall larches. The tariff per person and small tent is L13,000; the showers in the just-adequate facilities need L1000 tokens. There is a small shop and bar on the site, which is open from late May to late September. *Gran Paradiso* (☎ (0165) 74 92 04), a short distance beyond the southern end of the village, has 120 pitches also on grassed terraces. For one person and a small tent you will pay L16,200; a L1000 token is needed for a shower – the facilities are adequate. The well-stocked shop, next to the bar, has many local specialities. The site is open from late May until late September.

Of the hotels in the village, *Hotel Herbetet* (☎ (0165) 74180) offers full board (bed and three meals) from L63,000; singles start at L43,000. The restaurant presents a variety of set menus, featuring local specialities, from L21,000 to L27,000. The smaller *La Barme Hotel* (☎ (0165) 74 91 77), in the old heart of the village, does full board from L72,000, with singles from L55,000; a set menu is priced at L29,000.

Bar La Clicca (☎ (0165) 74157) has smallish, bright and clean rooms with a double bunk for L40,000 per person, which includes breakfast and shared facilities. The bar has a vast range of drinks (try their caffe alla valdostana); torte and snacks are also available. Worth considering is the spacious *Valnontey Ristorante*, just across the bridge from the village, offers a *menu turistico* (tourist menu) for L28,000, featuring camosco (chamois). *Bar Lauson*, right in the village, serves a good range of snacks, torte and gelati. There is also a small *alimentari* (grocery store/delicatessen) and a couple of souvenir shops/stalls.

Cogne

There is a wide range of hotels in this small town; pick up an accommodation guide from the APT office (see Information earlier). The Valleé de Cogne *camp site* (☎ (0165) 74079) is small, not particularly well positioned at the western end of the town, and virtually monopolised by caravans and mobile homes. There are also two camp sites near the village of Lillaz, 3km east of Cogne. However, both *Al Sole* (☎ (0165) 74237) and *Les Salasses* (☎ (0165) 74252) are also the preserve of caravans, though Al Sole has some small cabins for rent.

In Cogne there are numerous bars, several excellent *alimentari* and a specialist wine shop, all generously stocked with Valdostane specialities; there are also two small *supermarkets*, a couple of good *fruit and vegetable shops*.

GETTING TO/FROM THE WALKS
Bus

During summer there are six SAVDA buses (☎ (0165) 36 12 44) daily between Cogne and Aosta, via Aymavilles. The fare is L4200. In Cogne, buses arrive at and depart from a stop outside the building housing the post office and IAT office, close to the corner of the turn-off to Valnontey. Tickets can be purchased on board. There are useful local bus services between Cogne and Valnontey, Lillaz and Gilmillan, departing from near the main bus stop. During summer there are nine buses daily to and from Valnontey, although the last one does not, unfortunately, wait for the arrival of the bus from Aosta.

Car

In Valle d'Aosta, take the Aymavilles exit from the A5, and continue from that old village on the SS507; Cogne is about 21km further on. If you are planning to spend some time in Cogne, remember that cars must be parked outside the centre of the town, in one of the spacious, well signposted car parks. There is a large car park in Valnontey, close to the shops, bars and starting points for local walks.

Valdostane Gastronomy

Valdostane wines, spirits, cheese, fruit, honey, breads and biscuits are sufficient reasons for an extended visit to Parco Nazionale del Gran Paradiso and Valle d'Aosta; indeed, full appreciation of these delights is enhanced – or justified – by the energy-burning walks in the park.

Valdostane wines enjoy Italy's first *denominazione di origine controllata* authentication system; labels bear the letters DOC, which can be used for about 20 different wines. Most of the vineyards are in the main valley and the principal varieties of white grown are Chardonnay and Muller Thurgau; the reds include Pinot Noir, Torrette, Chambave Muscat and Pinot Gris. Enfer d'Arvier is a particularly fine wine, which should appeal to anyone accustomed to robust, full-flavoured Australian reds. A very drinkable wine costs L8000 to L9000, but you can pay up to L45,000 for a well-aged bottle.

Genepy (or genepi) is a Valdostane speciality and once sampled, becomes an indispensable conclusion (with a cup of strong bitter coffee) to a good day in the mountains. This herb-flavoured nectar is, strictly speaking, an infusion of an alpine plant, one of the wormwoods (*Artemesia glacialis*), which grows on the edge of moraines. A licence is needed to harvest the plant as supplies have become very scarce; fortunately, experiments with commercial cropping are proving successful. Not surprisingly, genepy is more difficult to obtain outside Valle d'Aosta (though most rifugi in the Alpi Marittime keep a bottle behind the bar). For L3000 you can enjoy a generous nip in the bar; small bottles start at L8000.

Fontina cheese is also protected against imitations by the denominazione system, using the distinctive motif of the outline of Cervino (Matterhorn) and the words Consorzio Produttori Fontina. The cheese is still made using centuries-old methods, unpasteurised milk and no colouring agents. It undergoes a long maturation and slow fermentation processes, and the result is a full fat cheese, high in calcium, which must owe something of its unique flavour and texture to the diet of the local cows – wild flower-rich alpine meadows, where artificial fertilisers seem to be unknown.

Fontina is ideal for sauces, and is used in two extremely filling local specialities: *zuppa Valdostane* (slices of bread soaked in stock and thick Fontina sauce) and *polenta Valdostane*, which unless you happen to have taken to polenta, resembles nothing so much as cheesey porridge.

For carnivores, two common items on local restaurant menus are not to be missed: *camoscio* (chamois) and *cervo* (deer or venison).

Apples and pears are grown locally, and a wide variety of mushrooms are harvested.

Honey is another speciality, derived from various flowers, including rhododendron (worth trying), clover, acacia, thyme, eucalyptus and mixtures of whatever the bees could find – millefiori, bosco and montagna.

Take a bag of *tegoleria* with you on a walk. These wafer thin, crisp biscuits made with honey and a dash of ginger, are irresistible, so they won't have to be carried far.

Caffè alla valdostane is a trap for the unwary. Seeing it advertised at a cafe in Valnontey, I thought it would be worth a try before setting out to walk up to Rifugio Vittorio Sella (a couple of hours and 1000m up). The heady concoction of strong, sweet black coffee, orange curacao and local grappa, gave a flying start up the first 500m.

Sandra Bardwell

Alp Money

Duration 5½ to 6 hours
Ascent 635m
Standard Medium
Start & Finish Valnontey
Closest Town Aosta
Permits Required No
Public Transport Access Yes
Summary An outstandingly scenic walk to traditional alpine grazing huts, near the edge of a glacier, and past ibex grazing areas.

On good paths almost all the way, this is a dramatic and extremely scenic introduction to Valnontey and the Gran Paradiso range. It is best done in the direction described so that you are walking towards the best views. The climb from Valnontey is steep, but the path is well graded. Several stream crossings along the way would make the walk extremely hazardous, if not impossible, during the spring thaw and after heavy rain. This is a comfortable day walk for reasonably fit walkers, which allows the walker plenty of time for ibex watching and, if you're interested, wild flower identification.

From Alp Money (at 2325m), the view across the valley includes Casolari dell' Herbetet (Herbetet cottages, a national park outstation) at 2435m. The climb (420m) to there from near the head of Valnontey, on an excellent zigzag path, takes about two hours return, and could provide another day's outing from Valnontey.

THE WALK

From the bridge in the village of Valnontey, where there is a cluster of signposts, set out up the broad track on the eastern side of the valley, past Camping Gran Paradiso, and through very attractive open pine woodland. After about 15 minutes, pass a bridge on the right (just across it, in the meadow, is a fine example of a typical stone cottage). Valmianaz, a small group of stone buildings further on, has

some fine examples of local woodwork in a recently renovated cottage.

After about 45 minutes (about 2.7km), the broad track ends and, a little further on along a path, go left up some steps to another path, marked as 23. Just under 10 minutes further on the turn-off for route No 20 (to Alp Money) is indicated by a marker on a rock at the edge of an open grassy area. The narrow path climbs steeply through pine woodland to the first line of cliffs, with magnificent views of Valnontey and its surrounding mountains.

The path then finds an ingenious route up the extremely steep, open mountainside, through a line of bluffs, and on across moraine and scree, with the leading edges of glaciers seemingly overhead. As you approach Alp Money, the path crosses rock formations in the shape of huge natural steps and stairs, which must have made the work of collecting building stone relatively straightforward. There are at least five buildings at the Alp, one with a roof and in good condition, the others in various stages of deterioration, sitting on a shelf high above the valley.

The path continues across the steep, rocky mountainside, pursuing an undulating route across streams and boulder fields. The yellow markers are sparse; stone cairns provide more prominent guides to the way ahead. The route becomes rough as you descend spurs composed entirely of moraine debris, where the crimson flowers of alpenrose *(Rhododendron ferrugineum)* enliven the otherwise monochrome landscape.

After about two hours from Alp Money you reach the footbridge over Torrente Valnontey – this is where you are most likely to see ibex grazing. National park officers say that ibex will stop grazing if people come closer than 70m; summer grazing is all important to the ibex, as they strive to regain weight lost during the long winter and build up for the next. The rough path continues through boulders and moraine, parallel to the river, to the junction with the path up to Casolari dell' Herbetet, liberally advertised with many markers.

Continue down the valley path and back to Valnontey.

Rules of the Park

Within Parco Nazionale del Gran Paradiso, the rules of the park are prominently displayed (in four languages) on large boards bearing the distinctive ibex logo and lively graphics to emphasise the message, along many of the walking routes and in car parks. The rules, which are really common sense guidelines for behaviour in the countryside are:

• Leave wild animals in peace.
• No dogs are allowed, at all, under any circumstances.
• Leave flowers, insects and minerals where you find them.
• Take your rubbish with you.
• Light fires and pitch tents only at authorised sites.
• Keep to the paths and tracks.
• Noise, shouting and loud music do not belong in the park.

People persist in bringing their dogs into the park. Don't follow their bad example. Picking wild flowers is a temptation some are unable to resist, as is taking short cuts between the long zigzags on the steep mountain paths. Worst of all is the unsavoury habit of leaving streamers of toilet paper in the bushes beside the path. During my three weeks in the park, despite passing several national park outstations and inspecting the two visitor centres, rangers were notable by their invisibility.

Sandra Bardwell

Vallone del Grand Nomenon

Duration 8 to 8½ hours
Ascent 800m
Standard Hard
Start Cogne
Finish Vieyes
Closest Town Aosta
Permits Required No
Public Transport Access Yes
Summary An exceptionally scenic walk, in part across wild and rugged mountainside, and through tall conifer woodlands.

The central part of this walk, where there are few, if any signs of human intrusion, has a real wilderness feeling. The paths include long stretches specially constructed by national park staff, across extremely steep and exposed mountainsides; one short section is protected by a fixed rope. The descent route described is the longer, but less steep, of two possibilities. With an early start, fit walkers should be able to catch the late afternoon bus back to Cogne from the village of Vieyes. Alternatively, you could

arrange to stay overnight at Bivacco M Gontier. This small, attractively restored timber cottage is not a rifugio so you would have to be completely self-contained to stay here. The key may be obtained from Elio Gontier (☎ (0165) 90 22 59) or Fulvio Gorrex (☎ (0165) 90 27 38), both of whom live near Aymavilles. The walk should not be attempted in poor weather – good visibility and dry rock are crucial. None of the available maps shows the route of the walk accurately, but it is adequately marked and not difficult to follow. Carry some water with you and remember that no refreshments are available at Bivacco M Gontier.

THE WALK

The walk starts at the bridge over Torrente Valnontey, just south-west of Cogne across the meadows. Follow route No 25 along the wide riverbank track beside the turbulent Torrente Grand Eyvia; after about 20 minutes pass the bridge leading to the village of Crêtaz, the huddle of old stone buildings across the river. Continue downstream mainly through conifer woodland; the track climbs slightly to negotiate a small gorge on the river. Half an hour from Cogne, at a bridge near the village of Epinel, follow the path signposted

to Alpe Grand Nomenon (which is in Vallone del Grand Nomenon, with the Bivacco M Gontier alongside it); the route numbers to keep in mind from here are 27 and 28.

The path climbs steeply through conifers; soon you may hear the shrill whistle of marmots echoing across the valley – always a friendly sound. Pass the turn-off for route No 26 and climb steeply beside a stream for a while then cross it (there may be snow here, even in mid-July) and continue up through meadows and again into conifer woodland. Ignore red and white markers; keep to the path which leads up a spur between two

streams, below the vast, towering walls of Punta Pousset.

About 1¼ hours after starting the climb you come to two wooden footbridges, the Trajo crossings referred to in the local walks brochure. The path bypasses Trajo cottages, which can be seen through the trees as a tight cluster of low old stone buildings. Another 15 minutes brings you to a clearing and the national park wardens' cottage, a typical stone building with beautiful decorative woodwork. Here route No 27 heads off to Colle del Trajo; continue with route No 28 to Alpe Grand Nomenon.

Beyond a stream the path negotiates a minor bluff, crosses meadows, then finds a way across the steep mountainside and up through cliffs – a slightly exposed section. A few yellow arrows and small cairns show the way. The breathtaking views come in quick succession: Val di Cogne and its neighbours, then north to the peaks on the French border. The narrow path leads into a wide, scree-filled valley. On the far side of the valley a fixed rope protects the ascent of an unstable slope. Conifers and alpenrose serve to stabilise the scree in the next valley. The traverse around the spur enclosing the far (northern) side of this valley, on a very narrow ledge is exhila-rating – the drop to the right is best not studied too closely. An easy traverse leads to the next, shallow, valley (about two hours from the wardens' cottage), above which the elegant spire of Grand Nomenon soars skyward.

On the far side, a relatively easy section of the path passes through conifers and alpenrose, with a fine view of high peaks to the north in full view ahead. Around the next corner you are confronted with a fine view of the wide, grassy expanses of **Vallone del Grand Nomenon** framed by Gran Nomenon and the towering crags of La Grivola. The narrow path leads up the side of the valley and across scree to Bivacco M Gontier, a park wardens' cottage and some old stone buildings, three hours in all from the first wardens' cottage. This is definitely a place at which to linger in the idyllic setting of an alpine meadow surrounded by superb moun-tain peaks.

To continue, walk past some old build-ings, keeping them on your left, and make for a yellow No 3 on a boulder ahead. A path works its way through boulders and into a small valley, across a stream and around a lightly wooded spur into the next valley, spilling down from the heights of Monte Favre. After about 1¼ hours from Bivacco M Gontier you come to a sharp bend, just below the settlement of **Arpissonet** (two old stone cottages) from where the village of Vieyes is visible far below. The path, marked intermittently as No 4, winds steeply down through conifer forest; after about an hour,

ignore a junction with route No 5. Continue downhill to the left and soon, at a Y-junction, bear left. This leads directly down to the main road and Vieyes; the bus stop is about 30m to the right.

OTHER WALKS

Colonna mine at 2400m, north-east of Cogne is a good half-day walk, or can be part of a full day, exploring Vallone di Urtier, which extends east from Cogne. The path up to Colonna starts from the eastern end of the Molinaz village where it is signposted; it climbs steeply through conifer woodland and across open mountainside, offering fine views of Val di Cogne and the surrounding mountains. Allow about two hours for the climb (900m). Even though the buildings are in a fragile condition and closed to public access, it is possible to appreciate the scale of the enterprise and the difficulties of working in an isolated alpine mine.

From near Colonna mine, paths lead east up the valley, past a few summer grazing settlements, to the road which climbs to the high meadows at the head of Vallone di Urtier. Framed by rugged peaks and dotted with tarns, the valley is crossed by an ugly power transmission line. The network of paths and tracks in this area is not accurately mapped, but in good weather it isn't difficult to pick up the well-made path on the south side of the upper reaches of the Vallone. The path winds around and into the lower reaches of Vallone de Bardonney before descending to Bouc.

The best access to this area is from Lillaz, 3km east of Cogne, by the local bus service (see Getting To/From the Walks earlier) or on foot from the eastern edge of Cogne. From the north-eastern edge of Lillaz a well-used path (No 2) climbs up, close to a picturesque waterfall, to the hamlet of Gollie. It then joins the road which leads past Cret, possibly the site of the oldest settlement in the area; a lovely chapel in Cret outside has seats in the porch made of old alpine skis. A full day can easily be spent in this area; about 1000m of climbing is required to in reach the upper valley.

VALSAVARENCHE

In the heart of Parco Nazionale del Gran Paradiso, Valsavarenche is where walkers and mountaineers feel most at home, in the presence of Italy's highest mountain (Gran Paradiso, 4061m), and on the threshold of a remarkably diverse array of walks and climbs. Though many of the peaks demand technical skills, the high passes and some of the adjacent summits provide the opportunity to climb above 3000m. There are also several beautiful and easily accessible tarns and alpine meadows, and two high mountain rifugi offer some comforts of civilisation.

The long, deep valley of Torrente Savara is flanked in the east by the glaciers and peaks of the Gran Paradiso-Grivola massif, while in the west, a long glacier-free ridge is interspersed by meadows and the wide high valley of Piano del Nivolet.

The recorded history of Valsavarenche dates back to the 15th century when the parish was founded, but Valsavarenche was virtually unknown to the outside world until the 1830s when an Englishman crossed Col du Nivolet and reached the valley. His account of the journey in *Blackwood's Magazine* aroused interest, and intrepid travellers began to visit the area. However, Vittorio Emanuele II had a more direct impact on the valley's fortunes through his hunting activities: the building of paths and the lodge at Orveille (see 'Italy's First National Park' boxed text earlier in this chapter). These were later incorporated in the park and served quite different interests. Today, Valsavarenche is the least developed of the valleys, with few concessions to modern tourism which, for many, is one of its attractions.

Valsavarenche is the birthplace of two men who played crucial roles in the modern history of Valle d'Aosta. Emile Chanoux, born at Rovenaud, was a leading campaigner for Aostan independence and head of the Aostan Liberation Committee, which was at the forefront of guerilla warfare against the Nazis during WWII. Frederico Chabod, an eminent historian, was the first president of the independent government of Valle d'Aosta in 1948.

Apart from Degioz, the 'capital' of the valley, there is only a handful of small settlements scattered along the lower slopes. Eaux Rousses (so-named for the iron-rich waters of the stream which cascades down the mountainside nearby) and Tignet, in particular, contain some fine examples of local architecture, using stone and timber (mainly larch). The ground floor of these two-storey buildings was used for housing animals and people, the upper storey, largely of timber, for storage. Many of these buildings have been carefully restored with faithful attention to the original style, although traditional uses in farming have virtually disappeared.

INFORMATION

A visit to the Parco Nazionale del Gran Paradiso visitor centre (☎ (0165) 90 57 12) at Degioz is strongly recommended. It is close to the church in the village, above the main road, and is open from 9.30 am to 12.30 pm and 3.30 to 7.15 pm daily between 14 June and 14 September; the entrance fee is L2000 for adults and L1000 for children. Numerous books on the flora and fauna of the park, collections of 35mm transparencies, coffee table books, maps and souvenirs are all available. The main purpose of the centre however is a fascinating display (captioned in French and Italian) on predators, notably the lynx. There is also a reconstruction of a marmot burrow with sound effects.

PLANNING

When to Walk

See When to Walk in the Planning section under Val di Cogne & Valnontey earlier.

Maps & Books

In addition to the IGC 1:50,000, Kompass and FMB maps (see under Maps in the Information section at the beginning of this chapter), Valsavarenche is also covered by IGC sheet No 102, *Valsavarenche, Val di Rhêmes, Valgrisenche* (1:25,000) with plenty of reasonably accurate detail. Of the books relating to Valle d'Aosta generally, Sergio Piotti's *I Laghi della Valle d'Aosta* is relevant for a visit to Valsavarenche.

What to Bring
Everything that you will need is described in the 'Safety in the Mountains' boxed text earlier in this chapter.

Guided Walks
During summer guided walks and slide talks are provided by staff at the national park visitor centre at Degioz, where you can obtain a programme (see Information on the previous page for details).

The Società delle Guide del Gran Paradiso conducts guided walks and climbs for which an ice axe, crampons, harness (and experience in using them) and clothing appropriate for high altitudes under full snow cover are required. Contact Ilvo Martin (☎ (0165) 90 57 18), at Degioz 101, 11010 Valsavarenche, or Paolo Pellisser (☎ (0165) 90 76 03) at Fraz Vieux 8, 11010 Rhêmes-Saint-Georges.

PLACES TO STAY & EAT
Of the three camping areas in Valsavarenche, *Pont Breuil* (☎ (0165) 95458; fax 95074) enjoys the best setting, just beyond the end of the valley road near the hamlet of Pont. The open, grassy and flat pitches (some with the luxury of picnic tables and fire places) are priced at L12,000 to L15,000; the tariff per person is L7000. Facilities are very good; the on site shop is a bit pricey but convenient, the nearest alternative being at Degioz, about 8km away; the availability of mosquito coils (as well as Camping Gaz) speaks for itself. The site is open from 1 June until the end of September. Of the other two areas, *Gran Paradiso* (☎ (0165) 95433), just south of Pravieux, is in the narrowest part of the valley and has a limited outlook and exposure to direct sun; *Grivola* (☎ (0165) 70 57 43), 15km south of Degioz, is set in more open surroundings but the view is dominated by a major power transmission line. Both are open from mid-June until mid-September.

At Pont, *Gran Paradiso Hotel* (☎ (0165) 95454; fax 95074) has a self-service cafete-ria in the large bar and an informal restaurant next door. Try one of the many Valdostane specialities, including zuppa and polenta valdostane or camoscio (chamois), and of course the local wines. A hearty dinner comes to about L30,000. The hotel has single rooms for L60,000. The restaurant in the *Genzianella Hotel* (☎ (0165) 95393) a little way down the road to the north, offers a menu of the day for L26,000, or a more extensive menu, including grills. Accommodation prices are similar to Hotel Gran Paradiso.

At Eaux Rousses, where the AV2 crosses the road, *Hotel du Paradis* (☎ (0165) 90 59 72) offers full board for a minimum of L95,000, as does *Parco Nationale Hotel* (☎ (0165) 905706) beside the main road at Degioz. Yet another, and attractive possibility is *Lo Mayen* (☎ (0165) 90 57 35), an agriturismo establishment at Bien. There you can enjoy staying in a traditional stone farmhouse and sample the farm's produce. Full board is around L65,000.

Rifugio Frederico Chabod (☎ (0165) 95574) (see The Rifugio Walk section later), is open from 1 July until mid-September. B&B is L34,500; for dinner, starters begin at L8000 and main courses (generous servings) are around L18,000, plus about L7000 for dessert and coffee. *Rifugio Vittorio Emanuele II* (☎ (0165) 95920) is extremely popular, so it is absolutely essential to book ahead. B&B is L33,000, plus there's a heating supplement of L5000; half board comes to L62,000. Both rifugi are open during the day for lunch, snacks and drinks, and both make an excellent torte. Rifugio Vittorio Emanuele II is open in summer.

GETTING TO/FROM THE WALKS
During summer there are three buses daily between Aosta, Villeneuve and Pont. The fare is L3800.

If you are travelling by car, leave the A5 by the Aymavilles exit and follow SS26 to Villeneuve; continue to Introd and up through a series of hairpin bends to a junction where Valsavarenche is to the left (and Val di Rhêmes to the right).

Piano del Nivolet

Duration 7½ to 8 hours
Ascent 750m
Standard Medium
Start & Finish Pont
Closest Town Aosta
Permits Required No
Public Transport Access Yes
Summary Superb walk across alpine meadows with wild flowers and classic tarns.

Piano del Nivolet is a beautiful, wide alpine valley, extending south-west from Pont. It has the precious asset of being more or less flat for a few kilometres, once you have negotiated the steep climb from Pont. Dora del Nivolet meanders across the high plain, overlooked by spiky, rugged peaks in the north-west, and more benign slopes on the other side. The well-used path is clearly defined, though it can be boggy in places; nearly all of the several stream crossings are bridged and should be safe. Lago di Rosset and several smaller tarns are not to be missed. As a day outing from Pont, this should be within the range of moderately fit walkers, since it doesn't involve a big climb. Alternatively there's always the option staying overnight at Rifugio Alberto Savoia (☎ (0165) 94141).

THE WALK
The path, route No 3, starts behind the Gran Paradiso Hotel in Pont and climbs steeply in conifer forest, beside the thundering waterfalls of Dora del Nivolet, and up through cliffs. After nearly an hour (a 350m climb), you come to a crucifix erected by a local youth group, from where there is a fine view of the Gran Paradiso range. With most of the height gained, the path then winds between large boulders and leads out into the wide, open meadow. No more than 1km further on, the path passes close to the deserted Montagna Gran Collet, sheltering against a high bluff; after about another 500m, you come to

Montagna del Nivolet, a tight cluster of ruinous stone buildings ingeniously built in and around a group of massive boulders. Here the path joins a rough road and climbs gently though grassy ground. The marmot population around here is large; their shrill whistles echo frequently around the valley.

About 100m beyond a shallow stream crossing, the path leaves the road temporarily to rejoin it higher up near the outlet from the northernmost of the Laghi del Nivolet; the road has a bitumen surface from here. Rifugio Savoia, a former royal hunting lodge (see 'Italy's First National Park' boxed text earlier in this chapter), is 1km further, 1½ hours from Montagna del Nivolet.

The popular path up to **Lago di Rosset** starts just north of the rifugio and rises steadily up the open, grassy slope; keep a group of stone buildings on your left and wind up to the broad shelf cradling the lake and its satellites, set against the spectacular backdrop of several craggy peaks of more than 3000m to the west. The path leads along the eastern side of the lake, with its tiny island near the northern shore. It is worth continuing generally northwards up the path until you have a good outlook over the Laghi Trebecchi.

The return to the rifugio and then to Pont, is simply a matter of retracing your.

The Rifugio Walk

Duration 6½ to 7 hours
Ascent 1250m
Standard Hard
Start Pravieux
Finish Pont
Closest Town Aosta
Permits Required No
Public Transport Access Yes
Summary A classic high-level route in the shadow of Italy's highest mountain.

Rifugio Frederico Chabod and Rifugio Vittorio Emanuele II are perched high above Valsavarenche in the shadow of Gran Paradiso and serve as popular bases for ascents of this superb peak. However, it is, of course, possible to visit them, without any aspirations for the big climb, on a fine high level walk. It can fit into a fairly strenuous day, or be spread over two days by staying at one of the rifugi. Booking is essential during summer and advisable at other times (see the earlier Places to Stay & Eat section for details).

Frederico Chabod was the first president of Valle d'Aosta after the area was granted autonomy in the late 1940s. Vittorio Emanuele, or Victor Emmanuel, was king of Italy from 1861 until 1878 (see 'Italy's First National Park' boxed text earlier in this chapter).

The paths throughout are well made, marked and easy to follow. The walk can be done in either direction, the choice depending perhaps on where you are staying and whether you are making use of the local bus service. The morning bus from Pont will drop you at the start of the path to Rifugio Frederico Chabod, about 3km north, in good time to complete the walk in a day. A bus also leaves Pont early in the evening. There is ample car parking at either end of the walk.

THE WALK
From the bridge over Torrente Savara at the settlement of Pravieux, the clear, well made path (route No 5) winds up through conifer woodland. The best part of an hour's climbing brings you to Montagna Lavassey (2195m), a national park outstation, next to two traditional, domed, stone buildings used for housing cattle during summer grazing. Further on, at about 2300m, the conifers dwindle and give way to grassland and alpenrose, then mountain pine takes over and wild flowers are abundant, even when the grass yields to rock and moraine debris.

As the glaciers of the Gran Paradiso massif come into awesome view, you reach a wooden footbridge; continue ahead for another 10 minutes to reach Rifugio Frederico Chabod, a relatively modern building, with solar panels. From the wide piazza in front, on a good day, eyes are drawn to climbers making their way

up the glacier to the south-east, towards Gran Paradiso's summit.

To continue, walk back down the path to the marked junction where route No 1a leads to the left (south-west). The clearly defined path winds across spurs composed entirely of slate-grey moraine, around the intervening shallow, grassy valleys and across boulder fields. You may come across small herds of chamois – they are rather shy. As you round the head of the prominent rocky spur extending west from Gran Paradiso, a stunning vista opens up: the head of Valsavarenche, ringed by snowy peaks, some sharp and pointed, others gracefully curved.

The path leads up, across a small stream and over rocky ground to the extraordinary Rifugio Vittorio Emanuele II, about two hours from Chabod. The somewhat incongruous stone-and-aluminium, three-storeyed building resembles a large scale version of the indigenous domed barns, but with rows of windows. The older stone building nearby is the former royal hunting lodge.

The path down to Pont starts about 200m below. It is wide and well used, descending in a series of fine zigzags, through the transitions from glacial landscape to grassland, then conifer woodland, down to the banks of Torrente Savara and back to the wide bridge leading to the car park at Pont.

OTHER WALKS
The AV2 route between Valsavarenche and Val di Rhêmes passes the beautiful Lago Djouen (see Day 3 of Best of the Alta Via 2 walk), the objective for a very fine day walk in its own right. As an alternative to returning to Valsavarenche the same way, a route to Pont via the wilds of Vallone delle Meyes (the next valley south from Lago Djouen), and the lower reaches of **Piano de Nivolet**, is highly recommended. On top of the 2½ to three hours and 850m up to Lago Djouen (see Day 3 of the Best of the Alta Via 2 walk), allow at least 4½ hours (330m ascent) for this alternative.

The path from the lake starts where the small stream flows into it, and leads southwards to Colle della Manteau, on the rocky ridge separating the two valleys. It is well defined in the lower sections, but has suffered from landslides in the middle reaches. With considerable care, the line of the path can be followed; do not be tempted to go very far east where the rocks are unstable. From the crest of the ridge, the path down into Valle delle Meyes, around the point of the next ridge, and into Piano de Nivolet is clear. Continue up that valley for about 2km to a junction with a steep path (route No 3a), which leads right down into the valley and the main path back to Pont.

Best of the Alta Via 2

Duration 6 days
Distance About 130km
Ascent 6840m
Standard Hard
Start Cogne
Finish Val Veny/Courmayeur
Permits Required No
Public Transport Access Yes
Summary A challenging, very rewarding traverse across high ridges and deep valleys in Praco Nazionale del Gran Paradiso and western Valle d'Aosta.

The Alta Via 2 (AV2) is a well established, high-level, long-distance route, the central sections of which traverse Parco Nazionale del Gran Paradiso. It starts at Champorcher, on the eastern fringes of Valle d'Aosta, and leads westwards over Finestra di Champorcher, through Vallone di Urtier, to Cogne where it enters the national park. From there, it continues up Valnontey and climbs to Rifugio Vittorio Sella, crosses Col Lauson and descends to Valsavarenche. From there it goes up to Lago Djouen and across Col di Entrelor and down again to Rhêmes-Notre-Dame in Val di Rhêmes on the western edge of the national park.

The next stage takes you straight up and over Col Fenêtre to Valgrisenche, where it is necessary to descend the valley for a few

kilometres to Planaval and the start of the route up to Col di Planaval on the Rutor Glacier, and on to Rifugio Albert Deffeyes. From there, the AV2 descends to the Rutor valley and the small town of La Thuile, before the final stage up to Col di Chavannes, almost opposite Monte Bianco, and down into Val Veny, and on to Courmayeur.

This route is, to some extent, a grand idea which is not entirely compatible with the topography it encounters. A continuous natural line does not exist, so some of the mountainous sections are linked by stretches of public road to define an unbroken route. These compromises detract from the integrity of the route overall, but can easily be overlooked by making use of buses, and by regarding it as a chain of shorter walks.

Detailed descriptions of the route in English are not readily available. The following outline concentrates on the section between Cogne and La Thuile, thus omitting the easternmost leg from Champorcher, and covering the section from La Thuile to Val Veny briefly. While the views of the Monte Bianco range from Col di Chavannes are quite outstanding, the walk itself, largely along roads and tracks, is very much an anticlimax after the mountain paths of preceding days.

Each of the daily stages should be well within the capabilities of fit walkers. The AV2 follows well defined and, in places, superbly built paths adequately marked with the distinctive yellow triangle, within which is a black triangle outline around the figure 2. Signposts at staging points and junctions indicate the distance to and the elevation of destinations.

There is ample scope from each of the overnight stops to further explore in the surrounding area before continuing the long walk; some suggestions are given below. Two weeks could easily be spent in the area, using the AV2 as the linking thread or theme for the visit.

Although the walk is described here from east to west, there is much to be said for doing it in the opposite direction, putting the less mountainous sections behind you, and finishing on a high note in Valnontey or nearby Cogne.

INFORMATION

The larger part of the AV2 route is covered by publications issued by the national park. The most central source is the information centre at Villeneuve (see Information Sources at the beginning of this chapter).

The national park visitor centre at Chanavey, just north of Bruil is open from 9.30 am to 12.30 pm and 3.30 to 7.15 pm daily from 14 June to 14 September; entry is L3000 for adults, L2000 for people aged from 10 to 15 while children under 10 enter free. Here you can obtain information about local accommodation, including agriturismo establishments. The centre's main function is to promote the national park, which it does effectively. A range of souvenirs (including attractive T-shirts for L15,000 to L20,000), books, videos and posters are on sale, and guided walks and slide shows are organised during summer. The permanent display focuses on the gipeto, or bearded vulture, whose reintroduction is one of the success stories of national park management; a guide to the display in English is available. There is a feature on rare and protected species of flora (including edelweiss), an interesting video including shots of ibex and chamois, and a thought-provoking display on environmental issues and the role of national parks.

The Aosta APT office provides detailed accommodation guides (see Information Sources near the beginning of this chapter). The staff at the rifugi should be able to advise about local conditions – contact numbers are given with the walk description. Local weather forecasts are available from the meteorological office based at Aosta airport (see Information Sources at the beginning of this chapter).

PLANNING
When to Walk

The season for high level walking is defined by two crucial factors. Most, if not all, of the passes between the valleys and the paths leading up to them above about 2700m, will carry snow until at least early July. The rifugi, virtually essential for a continuous walk, are generally open from spring until about mid-September.

Maps

All maps covering the AV2 have their shortcomings but given that the route is very well marked the main (but not only) reason for carrying maps is to identify features. For this purpose, the IGC 1:50,000 series, sheet Nos 3 and 4 are the easiest to read; alternatively, the 1:25,000 series from the same publisher has more topographical detail, but you will need sheet Nos 101, 102 and 107.

Valle d'Aosta, Alte Via 1 and 2, a brochure published by the Valle d'Aosta Regional Tourist Office and available from the APT office in Aosta (see Information Sources near the start of this chapter), contains basic information (in English, Italian, French and German) including tables showing the elevation of significant features, time taken between each feature, facilities and strip maps of the route.

What to Bring

All the requirements for a full-scale, high level mountain walk are essential (see 'Safety in the Mountains' boxed text earlier in this chapter). In addition, a change of clothes for the overnight stays in the rifugi is no less important; the optional extras include camera, binoculars and flora and fauna guidebooks (see Maps & Books near the start of this chapter). Throughout the walk you will never be far from a shop of some sort or another, so it won't be necessary to bring much if any food. English is scarcely spoken from the large towns; French is, for many Valdostans, the language of choice, so Lonely Planet's *French phrasebook* may be useful.

Warnings

An ice axe and crampons are mandatory for the crossing of Col di Planaval on the Rutor Glacier, which should not be tackled without up to date local advice about conditions (see Information on the previous page). Crossing the Col Lauson is less technical, but still a relatively serious task. The final section of the path up from Rifugio Vittorio Sella is exposed in places, and late-lying snow on unstable rock can be hazardous; a fixed rope offers some security. The uppermost section of the descent towards Val di Rhêmes is a little less steep and the path not particularly well defined across loose rocks and scree.

PLACES TO STAY & EAT
Accommodation and sustenance for days one and two of this walk are covered in the sections devoted to short walks from Cogne and in Valsavarenche. Details of what's available for the rest of the walk are given with the route description for each day. Apart from the two stages where an overnight stay in a rifugio is virtually essential, there is plenty of choice in the intervening valleys, from camp sites to agriturismo establishments to three or four-star hotels.

GETTING TO/FROM THE WALK
Bus
There is a SAVDA service (☎ (0165) 36 12 44) three times per day between Aosta, Villeneuve and Rhêmes-Notre-Dame in Val di Rhêmes; the fare is L3500. G Benvenuto (☎ (0165) 34507) provides a similar service from the Aosta bus station to Valgrisenche for L4000.

To reach (or escape) from La Thuile, you need to travel via Pre St Didier, changing from the Courmayeur bus to a local service. Courmayeur is well served by buses; there are at least eight local departures daily for L2000. During mid summer only a local bus service operates between the hamlet of La Joux (where the AV2 meets the road about 4km south of La Thuile) and La Thuile.

In Val Veny, a frequent summer service runs from La Visaille, about 6km north-east from where the AV2 meets the valley road, right into Courmayeur.

Train
Don't overlook the frequent local service between Aosta and Pre St Didier. The journey time is comparable with that by bus

– without traffic hold-ups and the fare is almost the same at L3500. Courmayeur and La Thuile buses stop at Pre St Didier station.

Car
Although a car isn't much use for the full through walk, it would come in handy should you decide to make a base in Val di Rhêmes, Valgrisenche or around La Thuile. For Val di Rhêmes, take the Aymavilles exit from the A5, then the SS26 to Villeneuve; continue to Introd and bear right for Val di Rhêmes. To reach Valgrisenche, follow the SS26 as far as Arvier, from where a very narrow road leads up to Valgrisenche, 29km from Aosta. For La Thuile, drive to the end of the A5 and continue on the SS26 (to Colle del Piccolo San Bernardo) to the town.

THE WALK
Note: See the Parco Nazionale del Gran Paradiso map on page 117 for Days 1, 2 and 3 of this walk.
Day 1: Cogne to Rifugio Vittorio Sella
3 to 3½ hours, 1040m ascent;
This is an easy day walk and there are plenty of ways of occupying any spare time that is left over if you complete the walk early. These include a half-day stroll from the village of Valnontey up towards the head of Valnontey and back before starting the climb to the rifugio, or a wander along the path towards Casolari dell'Herbetet from Rifugio Vittorio Sella. Some walkers may prefer to treat this as merely the first leg of a long day, right over to Valsavarenche – but this would take about nine hours, not the best start to a long walk.

From Cogne, walk up the Valnontey road for a short distance and follow the path across the meadows from the southern side of Hotel Belvedere, to the bridge over Torrente Valnontey. The broad, well-used path to Valnontey leads left from here and rises steadily, never very far from the tumbling river. After about 40 minutes you reach the bridge which leads across to the village of Valnontey.

The path, signposted as both route No 18 (to the rifugio and Col Lauson) and the AV2, leads south-west up past Paradisia botanical

Paradisia Giardino Alpino

Named after St Bruno's lily (*Paradisea liliastrum*), Paradisia alpine botanical garden, overlooking the village of Valnontey, was established in 1955. Open to visitors, it contains 1000 species of plants. Most of the species are found in the national park, but there are also many from throughout the Western Alps. In the spacious grounds, the most important and readily identified alpine habitats have been recreated: grassland, peat bog, moraine and river bank areas. Each plant species is labelled, indicating its occurrence and whether or not it is indigenous, and the various components of each habitat are described. As well as introducing visitors to alpine flora, the garden is researching improving cultivation methods, and the pastures in mountainous areas. It's also researching the cultivation of the threatened species of artemesia from which the precious genepy (see the 'Valdostane Gastronomy' boxed text earlier in this chapter) is made.

The garden is open from 9.30 am to 12.30 pm and from 2.30 to 6.30 pm daily between 15 June and 15 September. The entry fee for adults is L3000 with reductions for children and groups. An audio tape for a guided walk (L5000) and several books about alpine flora and the garden are available there.

Sandra Bardwell

garden and into conifer woodland. The superbly constructed zigzags make climbing relatively easy; the continually changing and widening views of Valnontey, the Torrente Gran Loson cascading through small gorges, and higher up, the deserted stone cottages at summer grazing settlements, provide plenty of diversions. The chances of seeing ibex and chamois are good – the local population seems to be used to humans; the processions of walkers going up in the morning and down in the afternoon are constant during summer. After an hour or more the path comes out of the conifers and into open country, with towering cliffs to the north and south and the valley rising steadily ahead. The last few hundred metres of the path up to the rifugio are suffering under the impact of cattle, brought up for summer grazing, and people taking short cuts down the zigzags.

However, the rifugio – which actually comprises four substantial stone buildings: two for accommodation, the bar and another (which was being restored at the time of research) – is a welcome sight, superbly located within a wide grassy amphitheatre, surrounded by spikey peaks.

Rifugio Vittorio Sella (☎ (0165 74310) has 150 beds and is open from Easter until the end of September. It is named after an Italian banker and adventurer who visited many remote and mountainous areas at the

end of the 19th century. The nonmember tariff for B&B (mattress and blankets) is L34,500; first course items (soup, pasta, polenta) at dinner start at L9000 and main course dishes (including more polenta and roasts) L17,000; 1L of wine costs L12,000. If you bring your own supplies, a table setting levy of L2000 is charged. At the bar, furnished with fine examples of local timber craftwork, you can buy hot and cold drinks, torte, gelati, badges and postcards.

Day 2: Rifugio Vittorio Sella to Eaux Rosses

6 to 6½ hours, 710m ascent,
1630m descent

Col Lauson is the most difficult of the passes on the AV2, apart from the Rutor Glacier. An early start needs to be made to reach the snow that almost invariably lies up there before it begins to soften and become unstable.

From the rifugio the path rises relatively easily up the valley of Torrente Gran Lauson with fine views across to the leading edges of a line of glaciers. Beyond the junction of a path (No 26a leading north to Col de la Rousse), the gradient steepens markedly as the path turns south-west and leads up to the narrow, cliff-flanked pass. Great care needs to be taken up the final stretch to the col, across snow and loose rock, about 1½ hours from the rifugio.

The first stage of the descent is little less hazardous; the path descends a short distance then swings to the right (north-west) at the foot of the cliffs; a direct descent on snow and scree carries a risk of dislodging stones which, once disturbed, can keep falling for hundreds of metres. A couple of hundred metres below the col the path becomes a little less steep and more clearly defined, as it loses height in a magnificent sequence of zigzags down the rocky, scree-covered mountain side. This is an eerily quiet place with only the occasional clatter of falling stones to disturb the silence. About 900m below the col, the path swings north-west into a more open, almost level valley and leads down to Levionaz, a group of traditional stone buildings used as a national park outstation; a tiny shrine nearby overlooks Valsavarenche far below.

The path changes direction here and leads south then west, down into conifer woodland, descending in wide zigzags and eventually out into meadows and down to the valley road at Eaux Rousses. The bus stop is almost opposite.

Day 3: Eaux Rousses to Val di Rhêmes
6½ to 7 hours; 1340m ascent

This section starts almost directly opposite the point at which the AV2 reaches the road after the descent from Col Lauson. Following the now familiar AV2 logo, walk up towards Hotel du Paradis and turn right along a lane between houses. Turn left up a steep, narrow path which leads through some old terraces and into conifer forest. Beyond a short open section, above steep grazing meadows, the path leaves the forest behind and leads into a beautiful wide alpine meadow sweeping down from the cliffs above, about 1½ hours from Eaux Rousses.

Ahead are the buildings of Orvieille, one of the old royal hunting lodges (see 'Italy's First National Park' boxed text earlier in this chapter), now used as a centre for the study of the national park's alpine flora. Continue along the path around the fenced buildings and up to Montagna Djouen, a summer grazing settlement still in use. Seeing the

cows grazing peacefully here, each wearing a bell, it's easy to appreciate why the local butter tastes so good. The views of the Gran Paradiso range from here are truly breathtaking. The path climbs around a grassy spur, into a wide valley and leads up to the shallow basin cradling Lago Djouen and its satellites (1½ hours from Orvieille). This is a delightful stretch – a gentle climb past the tarns, below the cliffs of Monte Roletta. Beyond Lago Nero the path steepens and leads into bare, rocky, moraine-strewn ground (where snow can still lie in late June) and finally up to Col di Entrelor (3007m). If the conditions are suitable, it's worth taking an extra hour to climb south from the pass to flat-topped Cima Percia (3227m) for an even better panoramic view – to Monte Bianco on the western skyline, Grand Combin to the north and the Gran Paradiso range in the east.

Some care is needed as you start to descend from the col to follow the line of markers through the boulders and scree below the near-vertical cliffs. Once clear of the boulder field, the well-made path winds down across muddy scree and steep rocky slopes into the relatively wide expanses of Vallone di Entrelor. About 1½ hours from the pass you reach the deserted Alpage Plan de la Feya, skilfully built into a small cliff. Though it has seen better days, this is still a good example of the traditional domed stone buildings used to house stock overnight. The steady descent continues, down across grassy meadows to a crucifix near the edge of fine larch woodland, and on down to a track; bear right to the bridge which leads into the village of Bruil.

Side Trip Among the many possibilities for day walks in Val di Rhêmes, a visit to the alpine grazing settlement of Vaudalettaz (at 2443m) which the national park management plans to restore, is well worthwhile. Start from the hamlet of Thumel, a few kilometres south along the road from Bruil and walk down to the river, cross over and follow route No 11 (to Col Leynir). The narrow path climbs steeply up through mixed woodland and into a superbly secluded wild

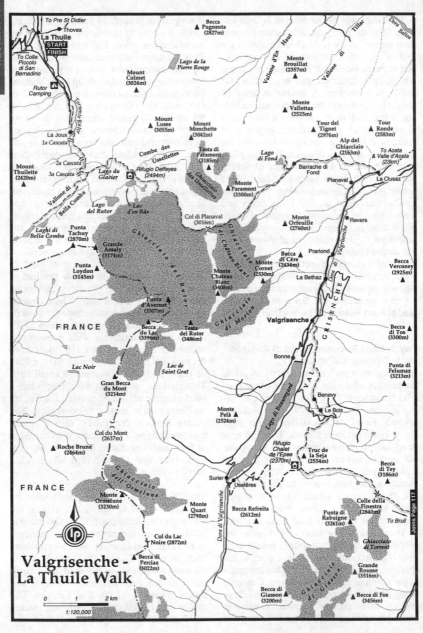

To Pre St Didier
Thovex
La Thuile
START
FINISH
To Colle
Piccolo
di San
Bernadino
Rutor
Camping
La Joux
1a Cascata
2a Cascata
3a Cascata
Mount
Thuilette
(2420m)
La Jaux
Torrente Rutor
Combe des Usselletes
Rifugio Deffeyes
(2494m)
Lago du
Glacier
Lago
del Rutor
Lac
d'en Bàs
Vallone di
Bella Comba
Laghi di
Bella Comba
Punta
Tachuy
(2870m)
Grande
Assaly
(3174m)
Punta
Loydon
(3145m)
Ghiacciaio del Rutor
Punta
d'Avernet
(3307m)
FRANCE
Becca
du Lac
(3396m)
Testa
del Rutor
(3486m)
Lac Noir
Lac de
Saint Grat
Gran Becca
du Mont
(3214m)
Col du Mont
(2637m)
Roche Brune
(2464m)
FRANCE
Chiacciaio
dell' Ormelune
Monte
Ormelune
(3230m)
Monte
Quart
(2790m)
Col du Lac
Noire
(2872m)
Becca di
Perciaz
(3022m)

**Valgrisenche -
La Thuile Walk**

Becca di
Giasson
(3200m)

Becca
Pugnenta
(2827m)
Lago de la
Pierre Rouge
Mount
Colmet
(3024m)
Mount
Lusse
(3055m)
Mount
Monchette
(3042m)
Testa di
Paramont
(3185m)
Chiacciaio
des Usselletes
Col di Planaval
(3016m)
Monte
Paramont
(3300m)
Ghiacciaio di Chateau Blanc
Monte
Chateau
Blanc
(3408m)
Monte
Cornet
(2530m)
Ghiacciaio
di Morion
Bonne
Benevy
Le Bois
Lago di Beauregard
Monte
Pelà
(2524m)
Surier
Uselères
Rifugio Chalet
de l'Epee
(2370m)
Truc de
la Seja
(2554m)
Becca
Refreita
(2612m)
Punta di
Rabuigne
(3261m)
Colle della
Finestra
(2840m)
To Bruil
Ghiacciaio
di Torrent
Grande
Rousse
(3516m)
Becca di
Fos
(3456m)
Ghiacciaio di Giasson

Monte
Brouillat
(2357m)
Vallone d'En Haut
Vallone di Tillac
Dora Baltea
Monte
Vallettaz
(2525m)
Tour del
Tignet
(2976m)
Tour
Ronde
(2583m)
Alp del
Ghiacciaio
(2163m)
To Aosta
& Valle d'Aosta
(23km)
Lago
di Fond
Barrache di
Fond
Planaval
La Clusaz
Monte
Orfeuille
(2760m)
Revers
Becca
di Cére
(2434m)
Prariond
La Bethaz
Valgrisenche
Becca
Verconey
(2925m)
Becca
di Tos
(3300m)
Punta di
Felumaz
(3213m)
VAL GRISENCHE
Dora di Valgrisenche
VAL DI RHEMES
Becca
di Tey
(3186m)

Dora di Valgrisenche

Joins Page 117

0   1   2 km
1:120,000

Val di Rhêmes

Until late July 1996 there was a camping area in Rhêmes-Notre-Dame, but after two days of torrential rain a landslide destroyed La Marmotta (fortunately without loss of life); the bar has survived, and the owner hopes to rebuild some day.

In the meantime, *Camping Val di Rhêmes Louvin* (☎(0165) 90 76 48) near Rhêmes-Saint-Georges provides a more than acceptable alternative. The tariff is L7500 per person plus L4800 to L7000 for a flat grassy pitch. The facilities are of a high standard and in the bar/gathering place several books are available for browsing, and there is a small shop where you can buy supplies, camping gas and maps. The site is open from 1 June until mid-September. There is only one *alimentari* and a post office at Rhêmes-Saint-Georges, but about 10km up the valley, there are several hotels around Rhêmes-Notre-Dame. *Hotel Granta Parey* (☎(0165) 93 61 04), at Chanavey, offers singles from L50,000 and has a self-service bar and a ristorante serving a range of set menus (L16,000 to L40,000), featuring fondues in particular. For more information, consult the Valle d'Aosta accommodation guide (see Information Sources near the start of this chapter). There are at least four *agriturismo* establishments in the valley; up to date details may be available from the national park information centre at Chanavey (see Information earlier). At Bruil, the largest of the valley villages, there are three bars, *Bazar Berard* (a good alimentari with local products) and a post office.

If you happen to be in the area in late July try to visit Rhêmes-Notre-Dame on the third weekend, when the annual convocation of valley craft workers is held. Their work is displayed for sale: woodwork (from flowers to large items of furniture), metalwork, embroidery and lacework, pottery and woollen goods. ∎

---

valley and winds up through grassy meadows to the alpage, tucked into the side of a small bluff.

Day 4: Val di Rhêmes to Valgrisenche
6½ to 7 hours; 1120m ascent

The crossing of Col Fenêtre is the most direct on the whole walk. It goes straight up from Rhêmes-Notre-Dame. The clearly signposted path starts a short distance down the road from Bruil, almost opposite La Marmotta bar, and leads up beside, then across the stream which caused the landslide in 1996. It then climbs very steeply across the flank of the valley towards a line of cliffs, and finds an ingenious route through the crags, into the aptly named Vallone di Torrent. Once clear of the cliffs the path contours the steep mountainside to the stone buildings of now-deserted Alpage Torrent (about an hour from the road). A little further on, the deeply scoured stream and rock debris along its banks testify to the power of the torrents of water that wiped out La Marmotta camp site.

The path follows the northern side of the valley to the base of the near-vertical ascent to the col, a miraculous opening in the otherwise almost impregnable ridge separating

Val di Rhêmes and Valgrisenche (about 1½ hours from the alpage). The very narrow path reaches the col via a series of zigzags one above the other – a fear of heights is certainly not cured here.

Predictably, the start of the descent is steep and rocky and likely to hold snow until well into summer. However, about 100m below the col, it becomes clear and a little less steep as it descends into the relatively broad expanses of Vallone del Douc. Near a large bluff the path becomes more of a track, swinging north and down to Rifugio Chalet de l'Epee (about 1¼ hours from the col).

The path continues by dipping slightly, then rounding a long cliff-lined spur to a very pleasant, undulating traverse of the open rocky hillside which is dotted with clumps of alpenrose. About an hour's walk from the rifugio, at a minor road, turn left and walk down to a modern bridge over the stream. Continue ahead past a group of stone buildings (Le Bois) and down across the grassy slopes to some largely ruinous buildings (Benevy) and into tall conifer woodland. The path contours, then descends, eventually reaching a road; turn right and walk down to a sharp bend where a path goes on down through trees and emerges near a tennis

Valgrisenche

Rifugio Chalet de l'Epee (☎(0165) 97215), a privately run establishment in Valgrisenche with 60 beds, is open from March to September. Full board costs L65,000; B&B costs L30,000. During the day drinks and snacks are available, or a hot lunch from about L15,000.

Unfortunately there are no public camp sites in Valgrisenche. Of the hotels, *Paramont* (☎(0165) 97106), at Planaval, about 5km down the road and north from Valgrisenche village, has clean, comfortable rooms with fine views. Half board in a single room with private facilities comes to L75,000, including a three course dinner in the excellent restaurant, where you are sure to have local specialities such as game stew and dishes featuring Fontina cheese. Snacks are available in the bar. There is also *Maison des Myrtilles* (☎(0165) 97118) further up the valley at Loc Chez Carral 7, Gerbelle. Singles start at L35,000 and full board is available from L75,000. *Albergo Perret* (☎(0165) 97107) at the hamlet of Bonne, would also be worth investigating. It's closed in June and November and the hosts speak English, French and German (and Italian).

The Pro Loco Syndicat d'Initiative (☎(0165) 97173) in Valgrisenche has maps, information about local walks and events and souvenirs; the office is open daily (except Monday and Thursday afternoons) from 9 am to 12.30 pm and from 3 to 6 pm. In the same building is a well-stocked *alimentari*, and the tempting Co-op Les Tisserands – a local cooperative for weavers, specialising in the traditional *draps* in soft, multi-coloured wools; it is open daily. There's also a bar, tabacchi and post office nearby. Between Valgrisenche and Planaval is the hamlet of La Bethaz where you will find the local agricultural cooperative which sells Fontina and local butter.

For guidance in crossing Planaval Pass via Rutor Glacier contact the Società Guide di Valgrisenche (☎(0165) 36 40 61), Bruno Bethaz or Ernesto Bethaz (☎ (0165) 99069). ∎

court. Continue to the bridge and up to Valgrisenche (about two hours from the Chalet). The bus stop is at the northern end of the village.

Day 5: Valgrisenche/Planaval to Rifugio Albert Deffeyes

6½ to 7 hours; 1460m ascent

This is the section with the crossing of the Rutor Glacier, for which an ice axe, cram-

pons and a rope are essential and, for visitors, the advice, if not services, of a local guide.

However, the walk from Planaval up to Lago di Fond and perhaps as far as the edge of the glacier is worth doing, as a moderately strenuous day's outing from Planaval; the ascent involved is 1000m.

From Valgrisenche it is best to catch the bus down to Planaval (about 5km); there are two tunnels on this stretch of road which can be circumvented if you are determined to complete the whole walk on foot. Alight from the bus at the Planaval turn-off and follow the road up through the village and on for about 1km. Just around a sharp left bend below the hamlet of La Clusaz turn off along the path signposted La Thuile and Col di Planaval (route No 21).

It climbs steeply through open woodland and finds a devious route up through lines of cliffs, out onto open rocky mountainside, and on to a succession of beautiful hanging valleys with a meandering stream which becomes the mighty waterfall near Planaval. About 15 minutes after passing an interesting stone structure built into a low cliff across the stream (marked on the map as Alp del Ghiacciaio), the path crosses the stream on a narrow log, and does so again a little further on. About 150m beyond the low ruinous stone buildings of Baracche di Fond is a group of signs. Route No 21a leads west from here up to Lago di Fond, a steepish climb on a narrow rocky path. For the best view, continue up to a bluff overlooking the lake, spectacularly framed by near-vertical cliffs on three sides.

For Col di Planaval, the path leads southwest from the turn-off to Lago di Fond, past the foot of the cliffs of Monte Paramont and through a narrow valley to the edge of Rutor Glacier. Allow a good three hours from Baracche di Fond for the crossing of Col di Planaval and the descent to Rifugio Albert Deffeyes (2494m).

Rifugio Albert Deffeyes (☎ (0165) 88 42 39) is open from mid-May to September. In a spectacular setting overlooking the tarns, the glacier and the towering peak of Grande Assaly, this rifugio has 70 beds. Nonmembers pay L36,000 for B&B, plus (perhaps) a heating supplement of L5000. A two course dinner costs L30,000, plus drinks. During the day, a set lunch is served (L25,000); drinks and snacks (especially torte) are also available. A plaque on one wall indicates that the rifugio was dedicated to Albert Deffeyes in 1964.

Day 6: Rifugio Albert Deffeyes to Val Veny
9 to 9½ hours; 1170m ascent

Rather than finish the walk with one extremely long and, in part, rather tedious day, you have the choice of spreading it over two days by staying around La Thuile, or finishing the walk there on a high note. In either case, a side trip to Laghi di Bella Comba, below and south-west of the rifugio, is highly recommended. See the following Side Trip to Laghi di Bella Comba section for details. The IGC maps do not show the defined AV2 route correctly on this stretch, notably approaching La Joux; the more northerly path to Laghi di Bella Comba is shown only on the 1:50,000 sheet.

The path from the rifugio leads north to the edge of the valley sheltering the rifugio, then descends the steep rocky mountainside to a modernised stone building overlooking Lago du Glacier, in a wide flat valley with the precipitous crags of Grande Assaly towering above. Cross the outlet stream and follow the path steeply down into the valley of Torrente Rutor. The short side paths to the three waterfalls (*cascate*) on the river are worth the extra time, especially the top (third) one – an incredible volume of water thundering down in a thick cloud of spray. The path becomes wider and more obviously used as you descend, mainly through tall mixed forest, into the valley. It crosses the river on a footbridge and winds around to the road near the hamlet of La Joux, near a bar and ristorante.

If you decide to walk down the road to La Thuile look out for the turn-offs to two paths which provide short cuts between tight bends on the road, down to the bridge over the river.

In La Thuile, on the main road less than 50m north of the junction with the road to La Joux, cross the river on a footbridge, where there are signs for the AV2 and three destinations including Col Chavennes (on route No 11). A series of short cuts between bends in the modern road to Colle del Piccolo San Bernardo, seemingly following an old line of road, bring you up to a point on the road where there is no choice but to turn left.

Continue for 50m to a junction on the right to Chavanne (as signposted). It takes about an hour to walk up this road to the end of the sealed surface, and another two to 2½ hours from there, on the broad, earth-surface road up Vallone di Chavannes to the spacious col.

The prospect of Monte Bianco and the towers and spires of the Grandes Jorasses takes a while to assimilate, but at this viewpoint you are, perhaps, just a bit too close to these mighty peaks to fully appreciate their magnificence. In any event, it really is an experience worth the effort. Either continue on a path generally northwards and down into Val Veny and the road to Courmayeur (along which there is a bus service), or return to La Thuile.

La Thuile
Rutor Camping (☎ (0165) 88 41 65; fax 88 43 73), Fraz Villaret 75, 11016, about 2km south of La Thuile, close to the road to La Joux, has about 70 flat, grassy pitches. The fee for a tent plus one person is L17,400, plus L1000 for an excellent shower; there is also a laundry and a small bar. It's open all year.

The APT office (☎ (0165) 88 41 79) in La Thuile is at Via M Collomb 4. Apart from a preponderance of fairly unattractive souvenir shops, La Thuile has a couple of *alimentari*. There is a *minimarket* with an excellent gelateria and pasticcera next door on the road to Passo Piccolo San Bernadino, just across the bridge over Torrente Rutor. The modern Planibel complex, with flats, a hotel, bookshop, alimentari and a good supermarket is on the La Joux road. The choice of places to eat is not great; *Hotel Piccolo San Bernadino* on the main road does local specialities – at a price – one of the set menus is L38,000; there is also *La Grotta* bar-pizzeria-ristorante almost opposite the junction of the road to La Joux. ∎

Side Trip: Laghi di Bella Comba
2 hours; 350m ascent

From Lago du Glacier, on the way down from Rifugio Albert Deffeyes, follow a rather faint path south-west beside a low cliff, along a spur and down to a footbridge. From here the path is much more clearly defined, as it makes its way up and along an elongated rocky spur with scattered trees and grassy areas. The views to the west to Monte Bianco and Grandes Jorasses, across the

valley of La Thuile, are very fine indeed. The path comes to an end at the middle lake with a tiny island, the blue-green waters reflecting the black and white patchwork of the surrounding crags and bluffs. Return to the footbridge and bear left to cross the spur and soon you rejoin the main path. If you are approaching Laghi di Bella Comba from La Thuile, bear in mind that this junction is about 1½ hours up from La Joux and that it is marked with the number '8'.

Lake District

It is all too easy to think of Italy's Lake District as an area which has sacrificed its soul on the altar of mass tourism and is therefore merely an exotic outpost of England, Germany or wherever, and where the mountains lack the grandeur of the Alps and the spectacular ruggedness of the Dolomiti (Dolomites). Yet it is not difficult to distance yourself from the excesses of the tourist industry and to find small unspoiled towns, and timeless villages in the remote valleys. For walkers, there is enough scope around the lakes for half a lifetime's exploration. The variety of venues for walks of all standards embraces mountain summits both benign and dramatic, ridges and valleys, forests, meadows, alpine uplands, cultivated terraces and farmlands. In most there are constant reminders of a long history and of the importance of religious belief in people's lives.

HISTORY

Evidence of prehistoric settlements have been found and reminders of the Roman empire's influence are pervasive. Subsequent historic trends were shared: the flourishing of independent city states, domination by wealthy dynasties – notably those from Milano (Milan); development as retreats for European nobility, and havens for trans-alpine travellers; fluctuating fortunes of the local economic mainstays – small industries based on local natural resources; the upheavals of the mid-19th century campaign for independence; devastation during WWI, especially around Lago di Garda in the north; and the awful conflicts of WWII and the growth of the Partisan movement.

Each lake's distinctive natural setting is emphasised by the location of regional boundaries which share Garda between Veneto, Lombardia (Lombardy) and Trento (Trent), anchor Como entirely in Lombardia, but divide Maggiore between Lombardia and Piemonte (Piedmont). On top of this, the numerous provinces within the regions and

HIGHLIGHTS

GANDRA BARDWELL

- Rambling through olive groves, tall forests, alpine pastures and towering summits
- Exploring the richness of wild flowers on Monte Baldo during spring and early summer
- The northern end of Lago Maggiore, where villages preserve a wealth of traditional stone buildings
- Limone sul Garda, a perfect base for walks which convey the feeling of being in the heart of the mountains

the *comunes* within these provinces, serve to promote a strong sense of being different from, if not better than, their neighbours.

NATURAL HISTORY

The three lakes – Garda, Como and Maggiore – and their several smaller satellites share their origins in the southward thrust of glaciers in the Quaternary era about three million years ago. However, they differ strikingly in the configurations of mountain ranges, ridges and valleys. Each individual lake is itself surrounded by an array of contrasting landscapes. In geological make-up, too, there are differences, as the predominant limestone of Garda gives way to the crystalline rocks around Maggiore.

Wherever you go, there is an abundance and diversity of wild flowers, especially in limestone country, and magnificent chestnut, beech and oak woodlands. The dearth of readily observed fauna is perhaps due in part to the long history of relatively intensive settlement.

CLIMATE

The term commonly used to describe the climate of the lakes is Mediterranean which,

strictly speaking, indicates hot, dry summers and damp, cool winters. While it is true that the lakes generally enjoy the warm and sunny summers important to the tourist industry, the few detailed statistics available suggest that the driest months are actually during winter. Precise figures for average maximum and minimum temperatures and for annual rainfall do not seem to be published for any of the lakeside towns.

However, figures are available for Monte Bisbino (1319m), about 8km north of the city of Como. These clearly show that the wettest months are May, June and August

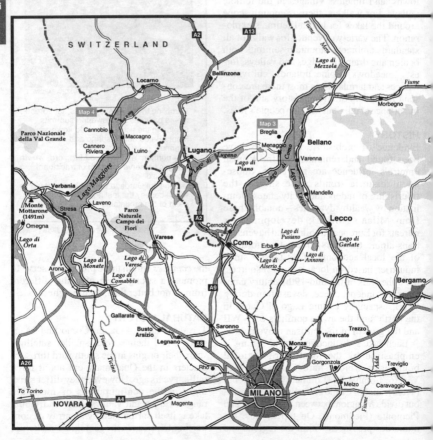

(accounting for about one-third of the annual rainfall). Average winter minimum temperatures are surprisingly mild – no lower than -3°C in January. The warmest month is July, with an average maximum of 20°C.

Of greater importance for walkers are two characteristics, one of which applies to mountainous country anywhere, and no less to the lakes – local variability: it can be clear and sunny on one side of the lake (usually the side where you aren't) and damp and overcast only 5km away across the water (where you are). Second, and peculiar to the lakes, is the phenomenon of the winds which generally blow from the north during the morning, mainly around dawn, and from the south, during the late morning and early afternoon. While of great interest to windsurfers and sailors, these breezes can bring fog which obliterates views.

The lakeside towns enjoy a relatively mild climate, to varying extents sheltered from the harsh effects of cold northerly winds, and nowhere at an elevation of more than 250m. Proximity to the large bodies of water also has a beneficial warming effect.

Snow is a factor to be taken into account only in the Monte Baldo area of Lago di

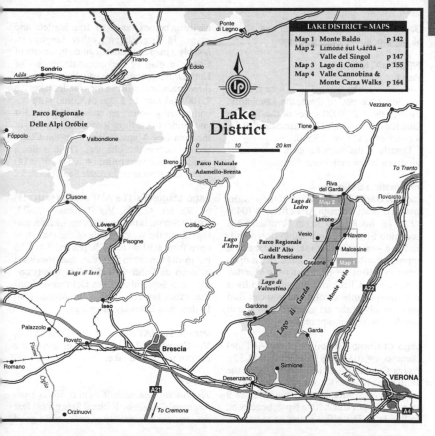

The Partisan Movement

During the latter stages of WWII, the Lake District generally was the theatre for many of the activities of the Partisan movement. Beginning in Piemonte (Piedmont) soon after Il Duce was ejected in September 1943, troops from disbanded regiments joined civilians to form groups to fight for the final overthrow of the German army and of Fascism. Political allegiances were less important than this common aim; partisans might otherwise have been communists, socialists, Christian democrats or members of the Party of Action (nonsocialist and republican).

Despite the daunting odds against taking on the professional army of a ruthless state, the partisans held many successful guerilla operations and supplied the allies with a great deal of strategic information. Partisans clashed with Fascist forces around Lago di Como near the Swiss border and memorials above Valle Cannobina suggest similar action in that area. The short-lived Free Republic of Domodossola, reaching eastwards to the edge of Valle Cannobina, was set up by the partisans during 1944. It was entirely fitting that Mussolini was finally captured at Dongo beside Lago di Como.

Sandra Bardwell

Garda and also in the mountains above Menaggio, above Lago di Como.

INFORMATION
Maps

For access to the whole Lakes area and orientation once you're there, the Lombardia sheet in the 1:200,000 series of the Touring Club Italiano's Grande Carta Stradale d'Italia, is excellent and costs L9500.

Details of the maps for each of the lakes are given in the individual sections.

Information Sources

Lago di Garda For regional and local information contact the main APT office (☎ (045) 59 28 28; fax 800 36 38) in Verona, at Via Leoncino 61 – in the *municipio* (town hall) building – on the western side of Piazza Bra, opposite the Roman arena. The office is open between 8.30 am and 7.30 pm from Monday to Saturday. Check out the email address at veronapt@mbox.vol.it and you can find out more about the area on the Web site at http://www.verona-apt.net.

Lago di Como The office of the APT del Comasco (☎ (031) 330 01 11; fax 26 11 52), Piazza Cavour 17, 22100, Como, is on the south side of Piazza Cavour, overlooking the port. It is open Monday to Saturday from 9 am to 12.30 pm and 2.30 to 6 pm, but closed on Sundays. The office issues an extraordi-

narily generous range of free leaflets and maps, in English and other languages, notably a map and detailed guide to the city of Como; a map of the mountain resorts of Lombardia (covering virtually all of the three main, and most of the smaller lakes); a 1:100,000 map of Lago di Como with accompanying notes; an accommodation list and guides to the three long distance paths in the area (see Maps & Books in the Como section later in this chapter). There is also a smaller information office (☎ (031) 26 72 14) at the train station, on Piazzale Sant' Gottardo.

Lago Maggiore The APT office (☎ (0323) 30150; fax 32561), Via P Tomaso 70-72, 28049 Stresa, is the main source of information about the western side of the lake. It is open from 8.30 am to 12.30 pm and 3 to 6.15 pm from Monday to Saturday, and from 9 am to noon on Sundays and holidays between May and September; from October to April the same hours apply from Monday to Friday, plus Saturday mornings.

Varese The IAT office (☎ (0332) 28 36 04), Via Carrobbio 2, 21100 Varese, serves the eastern side of the lake.

Books

The Italian Lakes: 30 Circular Walks from Regional Centres by Richard Sale gives clear descriptions of a variety of walks and a good introduction to history and topography, but only thumbnail sketch maps.

There are some tempting bookshops in Verona, especially Liberia Comboniana, in the arcade which is a continuation of Vicolo Regina d'Ungheria. It has a splendid array of mountaineering books – in Italian. The best source of maps and guidebooks in the city is Gulliver Liberie, in Via Mazzini, between Via Scala and Via Valerio Catullo. It is open all day from Monday to Saturday until late and on Sundays from 11 am to 1 pm and from 3 to 10 pm.

ACCOMMODATION & SUPPLIES

Both Lago di Garda and Lago di Como are well served by gateway cities – convenient and congenial bases from which to launch explorations of their nearby lakes. Lago Maggiore is less well served, though Stresa, despite – or because of – the overwhelming number of huge hotels, could fill this role (see Places to Stay & Eat in the Lago Maggiore section later in this chapter).

Lago di Garda

The *Verona Youth Hostel* (☎ (045) 59 03 60; fax 800 91 27) is in the handsome old Villa Francescatti, Salita Fontana del Ferro 15, 37121 Verona. The tariff is L20,000 per night, including sheets and breakfast; a three course evening meal is good value at L12,000. Alternatively, you can camp in the grounds for L8000. The 30-minute walk from the city centre gives a good introduction to this fine city. Otherwise, bus No 32 lands you at the bottom of the hill near Ponte Pietra; walk up Vicolo Borso Taschero to the hostel, following the signs.

An alternative, for women only, is *Casa della Giovane* (☎ (045) 59 68 80), at Via Pigna 7, north-east of Via Garibaldi. *Sport Gemmo*, on the corner of Via Cairoli and Piazza Viviani, is a handy source of Camping Gaz, walking/mountaineering clothing and equipment.

Lago di Como

In Como the *Ostello Villa Olmo* youth hostel (☎ (031) 57 38 00) is at Via Bellinzona 2, at the north-western end of the city, close to the junction of Via Bellinzona and the SS340 which runs along the western lakeshore. The tariff is L15,000 per night and the hostel is open from March to November. *International* camp site (☎ (031) 52 14 35) is on the south-western fringe of the city, near the Como Sud exit from the A2. Anticipate paying about L6000 per person and L15,000 for a tent space. Bungalows are also available.

LAGO DI GARDA

Lago di Garda lies apart from the other two main lakes to the west – Lago di Como and Lago Maggiore – and its cultural, geological and geographical affinities are closer to southern Austria and the Dolomiti, than to the Swiss Alps. Around Lago di Garda, walkers are treated to a generous and diverse menu of walks, on the Monte Baldo range above the eastern shore, and in the rugged mountains forming the backdrop to the larger part of the western shore. There are easy rambles through olive groves and tall forests, moderate excursions to alpine pastures, while several of the high summits are well within the reach of reasonably fit walkers. The walks described here are focused on two separate areas: Malcesine and the Monte Baldo range which rises well above 2000m, and Limone sul Garda and the Valle del Singol. These represent only a small selection of the possibilities: the Parco Regionale dell' Alto Garda Bresciano alone (on the western side) has many peaks between 1000m and 2000m. Then there are Garda's two satellites: Lago di Ledro in the north, and Lago d'Idro to the west – the choice is huge.

HISTORY

That the Lago di Garda area was settled in prehistoric times has been revealed in the remains of timber houses in Lago di Ledro which, together with a varied collection of artefacts, have been dated to the Bronze Age (2000 BC to 1200 BC). Possible proof of an

Etruscan settlement has been found near Tremosine (on the plateau south-west of Limone). In the 4th century BC the Etruscans were supplanted by the Gauls who in turn yielded to the Romans in 200 BC (Limone sul Garda, incidentally, derives its name from the Latin word for border). Much later, the Longobards, and then Charlemagne's Franks held sway over the area. During the Middle Ages, Lago di Garda's towns enjoyed self-government and independence, in common with towns around the other lakes. The Venetian republic, emerging victorious from struggles with the Viscontis, controlled much of the area from the 15th century; Malcesine was the headquarters of the Captain of the Lake, the supreme local authority.

Following the extinction of the Napoleonic empire, Austria-Hungary held onto the area until 1918, despite the heroic attempts of Garibaldi in particular to take it for Italy in the 1850s and 1860s. Indeed, the return of Trentino to Italy was one of the country's aims in participating in WWII. Much less gloriously, Salo, on the south-western shore, was the headquarters of Mussolini's ill-fated puppet republic between late 1943 and April 1945.

To attribute the origins of tourism in Lago di Garda to the work of a famous poet may seem pretentious, but Germany's Johann von Goethe (1749-1832) brought Garda to the attention of northern and central Europe. He visited Malcesine in September 1786 and although he fell foul of zealous Venetian authorities, his *Italian Journey* includes a beguiling account of this experience. The opening lines of his poem *Wilhelm Meisters Lehrjahre* (Willhelm Meister's Apprenticeship) were, perhaps, even more evocative:

Kennst du das Land, wo die Zitronen bluhn?
In dunkeln Laub die Gold-Orangen gluhn ...

Do you know the land where the lemon trees bloom?
Among the dark leaves the gold oranges glow...

Nevertheless, unlike Lago di Como and Lago Maggiore, Garda did not experience a surge of resort development during the 19th century. Modern tourism did not take off until comfortable and convenient travel around the lake was made possible by the building of the lakeshore roads, on the eastern side in 1929 and on the west three years later, replacing mule tracks and boats. Today, Lago di Garda is one of Europe's leading windsurfing centres, due mainly to its wide expanses and the reliable breezes which blow along its length during the summer months. Monte Baldo has been developed on a limited scale for downhill skiing.

Lago di Garda is divided between three regions: Lombardia in the west, Veneto in the east and Trentino-South Tyrol in the north, although the three provinces, Brescia, Verona and Trento, are equally important in local affairs.

NATURAL HISTORY

With an area of 370 sq km, Garda is the largest of the three lakes. About two-fifths of its depth is made up of moraine deposits, the legacy of its formation by the Garda glacier (a branch of the larger Adige glacier to the east). This extensive deposit pushed the lake south, out into the plain of the Po valley, well away from its confining valley, giving it a less mountainous appearance overall than Como and Maggiore. Garda's principal tributary is Fiume Sarca (River Sarca) flowing into the north-eastern corner; the sole outflow, Fiume Mincio (River Mincio), exits at Peschiera.

Geologically, Garda is dominated by limestone formations. Monte Carone (1621m) in the north-west, is the culmination of the Dolomiti Brescian Alps, and is prominent in the quite complex topography of ridges and valleys on the western side. Monte Baldo's elegantly simple long sweep, with steep western slopes and more gentle gradients in the east, stands in fascinating contrast.

Garda's spacious proportions (it is up to 17km wide in the south), its low elevation, lack of chilly tributaries, considerable depth (more than 300m), and the presence of mountains which deflect rain and cold winds, combine to ensure that the lake retains warmth very efficiently, yielding in turn a mild climate. Winter shoreline temperatures range from 5°C to 15°C, while summer can be hot with temperatures in the low 30°Cs.

Cypresses, bougainvilleas, oleanders and magnolias thrive, and these, together with olive, fig and citrus groves and vineyards, give the lake a distinctly Mediterranean atmosphere. Monte Baldo's renowned flora is protected in two reserves; in the west, Parco Alto Garda Bresciano (38,000 hectares) was declared in 1989 to protect a valuable diversity of environmental features and the area's historical and cultural heritage.

GETTING THERE & AWAY
Lago di Garda eastern shore – Malcesine
Bus APT (☎ (045) 800 41 29) buses on route Nos 62 and 64 depart from stop 11 opposite Verona train station to towns on the eastern shore as far as Riva. The fare to Malcesine is L9300. Buy tickets before boarding. The timetable is available from the main APT office in Verona (for full details see Lago di Garda under Information Sources near the start of this chapter).

Train Catch a train on the Milano-Venezia (Venice) line to Peschiera to link with the APT bus or water transport (see Ferry following) to Malcesine; alternatively, alight at Desenzano for similar connections. From the Brennero-Verona line there is a straightforward connection with the bus from near the Verona train station.

Car The A4 and SS11, Milano-Venezia, run along the southern shore and intersect with the A22, Verona-Trento, which parallels the eastern shore; take either the Lago di Garda Nord or Sud exit, then follow the signs to Malcesine.

Lago di Garda western shore – Limone sul Garda
Bus SIA (☎ (030) 377 42 37) provides a service between Piazza Castello, Milano (near Cairoli on the metro), Brescia (the bus station is adjacent to Viale della Stazione, near the train station) and the western side of Lago di Garda through to Riva. The fare to

---

Monte Baldo
The cablecar between Malcesine (on the eastern shore of Lago di Garda) and Monte Baldo not only enables walkers to conserve their energy for the serious business of reaching the summit, it also provides a bird's eye view of the changes in vegetation on the slopes of the Monte Baldo range, from the lakeshore at 90m elevation to 1800m at the top station.

The range is composed of a layer of limestone deposited in the Mesozoic era (135 to 220 million years ago), which was later subjected to folding. Although Lago di Garda was formed by glacial action, the Monte Baldo range escaped any direct impact of the Ice Age, a fact which has helped to determine its ecological importance.

Up to the 350m level, the cultivated groves of olives and citrus, and oak woods are widespread. Sweet chestnuts (*Castanea sativa*) take over between that elevation and 900m; next come beech (*Fagus sylvatica*) and conifers in a more open woodland. This gives way, at more than 1400m, to grassy alpine meadows, thickets of mountain pine (*Pinus mugo*) which spreads as widely as it grows high (though no more than a couple of metres here), and alpenrose (*Rhododendron ferrugineum*) with its small, deep pink to red bell-shaped clusters of flowers. Monte Baldo has long been renowned for its marvellous array of wild flowers and is popularly known as Italy's botanic garden. Three of the most striking species are the deep blue trumpet gentian (*Gentiana acaulis*), its more delicate relative, spring gentian (*Gentiana verna*), and the bright yellow globeflower (*Trollis europaeus*). Two Riserve Naturale, Gardesana Orientale on the lower slopes immediately above Navene, and Lastoni Selva Pezzi extending right along the ridge crest, have been set aside for the protection of fauna and flora, including some endemic species.
Sandra Bardwell

Limone is L18,400. In addition APT buses on route No 80 link Desenzano and Riva from Monday to Saturday.

Train From Brescia, on the Milano-Venezia line there are better onward connections than from Desenzano on the same line.

Car From the south, leave the A4 Milano-Venezia by the Brescia East exit and follow signs to Salo and Limone along SS45 bis,

with its many tunnels north of Gargagno. From the north, leave the A22 Modena-Brennero at Roverto Sud/Lago di Garda Nord exit and continue through Riva to Limone and the SS45 bis.

Ferry You can arrive in style at the lakeside towns with Navigazione sul Lago di Garda (☎ (030) 914 13 21; fax 914 46 40), Piazza Matteotti, 25015 Desenzano (BS).

Ferries and hydrofoils operate from Desenzano or Peschiera, where there are rail links, or from Salo or Gardone, on the Milano-Riva bus route. The adult fare from Desenzano to Malcesine is L12,900; fares for the western side ports range from L11,300 to L18,200.

Monte Baldo

> **Duration** 6½ to 7 hours
> **Ascent** 490m
> **Standard** Medium
> **Start & Finish** Tredespin
> **Closest Towns** Verona, Brescia
> **Permits Required** No
> **Public Transport Access** Yes
> **Summary** An outstanding mountain ridge walk with far ranging lake and alpine views and abundant wild flowers.

Monte Baldo is the name given to the long, rugged ridge paralleling the central section of Lago di Garda's eastern shore. From its broad extremities, the ridge narrows dramatically to a knife edge crest, punctuated by several precipitous peaks, the highest of which is Cima Valdritta (2218m). Popular with skiers in winter, and mountain bike riders during summer, Monte Baldo is also a magnet for walkers, and a well used path traverses the length of the ridge crest. Contrasts are of the essence on Monte Baldo, from the lakeshore to the summit ridge, and the extensive network of marked paths, in conjunction with the cablecar and local buses, provide a generous range of opportunities to explore these features.

The lower slopes are still extensively cultivated with olive groves and you can find some of the traditional villages and isolated farms which, as the many ruins testify, were once far more numerous. During spring and early summer, the meadows and the summit ridge are richly carpeted with wild flowers – take a pocket guide such as the Kompass *Guide Naturalistiche* series (written in Italian) of which *Fiori Alpini* and *Fiori di Prato* are recommended at about L9500 each.

Monte Baldo is not a walk to be taken lightly; south from Cima Pozzette the path to Cima Valdritta is narrow and quite exposed in places and includes a short scramble with a fixed cable. Beyond Valdritta, southwards to Punta Telegrafo (Monte Maggiore) the ridge is the preserve of properly equipped climbers. Choose the day prudently – Monte Baldo is not a place to be caught in bad weather. It is very exposed, and wet limestone is like a skating rink.

From the lake, several paths lead up to various points on the summit ridge, all entailing climbs of three to four hours. While this approach yields the satisfaction of a completely independent ascent, the outcome is a long, tiring day. From Navene, allow five hours (with 1620m ascent) to Tredespin (see The Walk following). Instead, a 20 minute ride in the cablecar from Malcesine to Tredespin, towards the northern end of the ridge proper (see Getting To/From the Walk following), should enable most reasonably fit walkers to complete the tour comfortably in a day. A car is not necessarily an advantage for access to this walk. It is a longish drive, from Torri on the lakeside, via Caprino and Ferrara to Bocca di Navene, or to a car park a few kilometres further south.

There are bars and restaurants in the vicinity of the cablecar station (see Places to Stay & Eat section); carry water for the duration of the walk.

INFORMATION

The main APT office (☎ (045) 725 51 94; fax 725 67 20) for Riviera degli Olivi, eastern Lago di Garda, is in the town of Garda, at

Lungolago Regina Adelaide 3. In Malcesine, the APT office (☎ (045) 740 04 44; fax 740 16 33) is in Via Capitanato (which leads north from the port along the shore) and is open daily from 9 am to 1 pm and 3 to 6 pm. It's here that you can obtain a comprehensive accommodation guide, and a useful walks map for the local area (see Maps & Books following).

PLANNING
When to Walk
Spring and autumn are the best times, when the weather is mild to warm, and most likely to be settled. July and August are the hottest months, when the maximum temperature at lakeside level and can reach the low 30°Cs, and also the busiest, when the area is very crowded and the choice of accommodation could be limited.

Maps & Books
Lago di Garda, Monte Baldo (1:50,000, 100m contours, sheet No 102 in Kompass series) comes with notes in English on the reverse side and a booklet in Italian and German outlining the history, topography, flora and fauna of the area and with detailed information about individual towns. It costs L9000 and is widely available. This map is of greatest use for walks planning, car touring and identification of features, but only use it as the last resort on a walk.

Lago di Garda, Monte Baldo-Lago d'Idro-Lago di Ledro (1:50,000, 25m contours, map No 1/5, Casa Editrice Lagiralpine) is excellent value at L8000 and is available locally. It is clear and easy to read but contains several inaccuracies, including swapping the names of the two reserves on the Monte Baldo range.

Carta dei Sentieri Monte Baldo (1:25,000 with 25m contours, published by Gruppi Alpinistici) is excellent value at L13,000. It comprises two maps, and a booklet in Italian with notes about more than 50 walks, contact phone numbers for rifugi, an explanation of the walks grading system, and mention of the Alta Via del Monte Baldo and Sentiero della Pace. It provides a wealth of accurate detail, although unwieldy to use outdoors.

The *Walks Map, Monte Baldo, Malcesine* (1:20,000, 100m contours) is published by and available from the APT office in Malcesine. The notes in English, German and Italian outline seven walks and 10 other itineraries. It is quite adequate for the area covered.

Richard Sale's book *The Italian Lakes: 30 Circular Walks from Regional Centres* (see Books near the beginning of this chapter) has descriptions of two local walks.

What to Bring
You will not need any special equipment for the walks described here, but walking poles are helpful for the longer descents. Walking boots are preferable, though good walking shoes should be adequate for shorter walks. If you don't speak much or any German, it would be worth getting Lonely Planet's *German phrasebook*. German is almost as widely spoken as Italian around the lake.

PLACES TO STAY & EAT
Malcesine
This would be the most convenient place to stay for walks on the eastern side of the lake, but the camp site in the town itself is miniscule. Inquire at the Verona Youth Hostel (see Accommodation & Supplies at the beginning of this chapter) about reserving a place at *Villa Pariani Hostel* (☎ (045) 740 04 00; fax 800 91 27), Val di Sogno, in Malcesine. It is run by the Centro Cooperazione Giovanile Internazionale to encourage contacts between young people of diverse nationalities, cultures and faiths, and is open to single young people and organised groups for short stays.

Malcesine has two *supermarkets*, one near the Municipio on the way to the port, the other just off the main road west of the bus station; there are also several good *alimentari* (delicatessen/grocery stores). The Malcesine APT (see Information earlier in this section) can provide a list of accommodation around Lago di Garda – there is a huge range of two, three and four-star hotels locally, plus self-catering establishments.

LAKE DISTRICT

Navene

This is a small, relatively quiet village about 5km north of Malcesine. Of the camping areas in the vicinity, *Camping Alpine* (☎/fax (045) 740 04 72), Lo. Baitone, 37018 Malcesine, about 1.5km north-east of the village has level pitches on terraces, looking across the road and the lake to the hills above Limone. The tariff is L15,000 for one person and a small tent, plus L500 for a shower. Alternatively, you could hire a compact bungalow for four or six people for L70,000/L80,000. There is a small shop on site, and a roadside restaurant where pizzas cost from L7500 to L16,000, pasta dishes from L9500 to L13,000 and fish is L17,000. It also sells gelati and coffee. If you arrive by the Verona-Riva bus (see Getting There & Away earlier), the nearest stop is No 41.

Camping Navene (☎/fax (045) 657 00 09), just south of the village, has several tiers of pitches, the upper ones well back from the busy road. For a tent and one person expect to pay L20,000.

Monte Baldo

The ideal way to explore the range is to stay at Monte Baldo overnight. The choice of

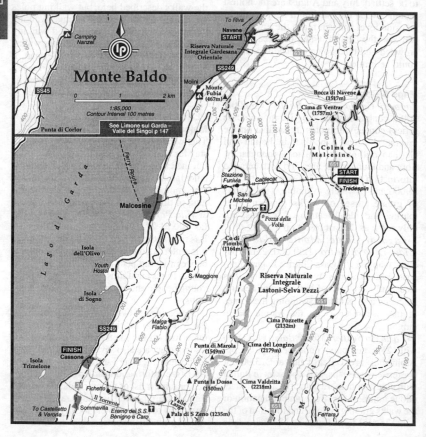

accommodation is between *Rifugio Bocca di Navene* (☎ (045) 740 17 94), directly accessible by road and also open during the day for lunch, drinks and snacks, and *La Capannina* (☎ (045) 657 00 81), closer to the cablecar station. The trattoria here does a set lunch for L20,000. There is a fairly basic restaurant in the cablecar station, and *La Baita dei Forti* restaurant nearby offers a full menu, including pasta for around L8000.

GETTING TO/FROM THE WALK
Bus
APT buses on the Verona-Riva service (see Getting There & Away earlier) link the towns along the lakeside road SS249. In Malcesine, the bus station is in the main street towards the northern end of town. It is necessary to buy tickets here before boarding the bus and it is worth making some advance purchases to save time later. There is also an automated accommodation information service, a bar and newspaper shop in the same building.

Funivia (Cablecar)
The Malcesine to Monte Baldo cablecar (☎ (045) 740 02 06) runs a half-hourly service from Malcesine between 8 am and 6 pm and from Monte Baldo between 8.45 am and 6.45 pm (stopping at San Michele on the way). The single fare for the whole trip is L12,000; returns are cheaper pro rata; reductions apply for children and groups. Tickets can be purchased at all three stations. Access to the Malcesine station is clearly signposted from the SS249, 100m north from the bus station; there is ample parking nearby.

Ferry
Ferry or hydrofoil is the best way to travel between the towns on either side of the lake. The ferry between Malcesine and Limone takes 20 minutes for L6200; the hydrofoil is slightly faster and more expensive.

THE WALK
The area around the cablecar station has all the bare unloveliness of a ski resort in summer and is not a place to linger. The route is well marked (path No 651); walk down a rough track, past a decrepit chalet and, keeping right of a small ski tow, climb up and around the western side of a small rocky knoll. From the boundary of the Riserva Naturale Integrale Lastoni-Selva Pezzi the well used path gains height through a jumble of limestone outcrops interspersed with clusters of wild flowers and low shrubs. About 10 minutes beyond a wooden sign to **Cima Pozzette** and then a steep scramble, you are on the flat summit of the Cima. From here it is clear that the peak marks the divide between the gentler landscape to the north and the jagged narrow spine southwards.

The narrow path descends from Pozzette, through low mountain pines, to traverse the eastern flank of Cima del Longino, above a vast scree slope. Back on the ridge, the **Cima Valdritta** summit massif materialises encouragingly ahead, as you cross an arete. Then, a chain provides security for the initial scramble up a massive bluff. The route switches to the eastern side of the ridge, at first a rather terrifying prospect – the narrowest of paths snaking up across the steepest of scree and rock slopes, but the reality is much less alarming. Further on, from a prominent junction, a final exhilarating climb up a crumbly rock tower yields the summit and its metal crucifix. The nearby peaks, Pettorina and Telegrafo – huge walls of grey-white limestone soaring to slender crests, make an awesome view nearby, and with luck the lake and alpine views will not be hidden by clouds. Retrace your steps to the cablecar station.

Alternative Approach
One straightforward, if somewhat tedious approach to the range on foot, is to follow path No 634 up through mainly deciduous forest from Navene to Bocca di Navene. From the rifugio, you then walk up the road for a short distance to an unmarked path on the right which in turn leads up to a wide gravel road. Follow this to a point about 40m past a large sign board and join path No 651, which climbs up a steep grassy slope to Cime di Ventrar (1757m). Continue eastwards on a broad path, across open La Colma di

Riviera degli Ulivi

The eastern shore of Lago di Garda is promoted as the Riviera degli Ulivi, a Mediterranean-style label to demonstrate the long-established cultivation of the trees there.

Some of the paths on the lower slopes of Monte Baldo pass through olive groves, some still in cultivation, others derelict. The terraces which they occupy have obviously been very carefully designed and built and the long walls of drystone construction are remarkably stable.

Under cultivation, the well spaced trees, which may be very old, are regularly pruned. The grass beneath is cut during late spring and early summer. Scythes are still used (as I saw near the village of Cassone), but mechanical cutters (strimmers) are increasingly popular – incongruously, near Campo, one of the oldest villages in the area. The trees flower in June, and the harvest takes place in November. The inaccessibility of the terraces to modern machinery ensures that this is still a manual task. Olive pickers balance on their ladders, made from single poles to which rungs are fixed, holding a branch in one hand and picking with the other. The olives are put in a leather bag tied to the belt. Any that are dropped fall into large nets strung between the trees.

The olives are then taken to the local mill and dried carefully on large wooden shelves. Pressing is the next stage – between two large granite stones, the movement of which is driven by a water wheel. The pulp is then separated from the fibrous material, chopped up and pressed again. The oil and water are separated, the oil filtered and finally bottled.

In Limone, the local cooperative society runs tours of the mill, including tastings, to encourage visitors to buy a bottle or two afterwards.

Sandra Bardwell

Malcesine, passing La Capannina, and a clutter of ski lifts and buildings, before reaching the cablecar station.

OTHER WALKS

The small lakeside towns of **Cassone** and **Castelletto** can be linked in an easy half day's walk, which need involve only 340m ascent. Carry water on this walk; there are no bars or cafes en route. The marked paths are occasionally somewhat elusive.

From Cassone, follow signs for Sommavilla, and then San Antonio, along paths (mainly No 33) through olive groves, up to the simple chapel of Sant' Antonio delle Pontare and continue to Campo, a very old village, along path No 31 and on to Biasa. The route contours through olive groves to a road; continue to an intersection, then right downhill through an arch and finally, along a path to the left to the main road in Castelletto. Bus tickets are available in the bar about 100m south of the church, outside which is the bus stop.

Here and there in the tall forests reaching high up the mountain slopes, are vantage points for wide views over the lake and more reminders of the importance of religious belief in local communities. Among the many combinations of paths on the middle reaches of the slopes of Monte Baldo, it is possible to link Navene and Cassone via **Co di Piombi** and **Malga Fiabio**, (5½ to six hours; 1100m ascent), with an optional extension to an old hermitage and spectacular gorge (seven to 7½ hours; 1200m ascent). Carry water; no refreshments are available on the way.

From Navene, path No 4 climbs around Monte Fubia, passing partly overgrown remains of WWI trenches and other defences, and the traditional settlement of Faigolo, and on to near San Michele (on the Monte Baldo cablecar route). From there climb through conifer forest to Il Signor, a large timber-roofed structure spanning the track, originally a shrine, but not now treated with much respect. Follow path No 2 to Co di Piombi; a lookout is just to the right of the track.

Continue, now on path No 7, which winds down steeply, affording good views of the dramatic peak of Punta della Marola, to Malga Fiabio, in a wide grassy meadow. Next, either follow path No 9, signposted to Cassone, or continue on No 7 for Eremo dei SS Benigno e Caro, passing the spectacular limestone tiers of Pala di Sant' Zeno. The hermitage, restored by Malcesine Comune, is a substantial stone building, part of which may date from the 8th century. Continue down a well used path, with marvellous views of the depths of Valle Larga and Il Torrente, through Fichetto to a road, and left into Cassone.

Limone sul Garda & Valle del Singol

Duration 6½ to 7 hours
Ascent 700m
Standard Medium-Hard
Start Vesio
Finish Limone sul Garda
Closest Towns Verona, Brescia
Permits Required No
Public Transport Access Yes
Summary A scenic and challenging walk, passing many sites associated with WWI.

Limone sul Garda is an ideal base for walks which portray the feeling of being in the heart of the mountains, yet in an area dominated by the vast expanses of Lago di Garda. Paths and roads built during WWI provide an extensive network of walking routes from Limone (as it is more commonly known), nearly all of which are well marked and easy to follow. Outstandingly, they centre on an ideal type of mountain walk: one which follows the rim of a valley, right around its watershed. Valle del Singol is tailor-made for this, reaching north-west into the mountains, a vast amphitheatre of limestone crags, towers, grassed ledges and precariously perched trees.

The walk described here can be adapted to suit your own interests and capability. In its entirety it would take a very long day, but can be spread over two days, by descending from either of two points on the north-western or northern arc of the ridge, to Valle del Singol, and returning another day to complete the tour; possible ways of doing this are described here. Alternatively, you could stay

overnight in Baita Bonaventura Segala (see the earlier Places to Stay & Eat section). Two optional extras, to the summits of peaks fairly close to the main path are outlined; try to do at least one for the exceptional views.

The whole walk is along excellent tracks and paths, which are clearly signposted. It is more convenient to do the walk in a clockwise direction, by starting the day with a bus journey, rather than having to chase it at the end. It's a good idea to carry water; some refreshments may be available at Baita Bonaventura Segala. The area is very popular with mountain bike riders who sometimes surprise walkers by swooping around corners at alarming speeds, in large groups, and with little warning.

INFORMATION

The Limone sul Garda Comune information office (☎ (0365) 95 47 20; fax 95 43 66) is at Piazzetta Erminia 2, off the Lungolago near the port (postal address: 25010, Limone sul Garda). Here you can obtain an accommodation list, a booklet with everything you need to know about Limone (including a busy programme of concerts for all tastes from spring to autumn), town map, bus timetables, walks leaflet with outlines of short walks near the town and details of guided walks (see Guided Walks later). There is also a small office at the main bus stop on the SS45; which is open from 8 am to 2 pm and 2.30 to 6 pm. Nearby is a rarity: clean public toilets. There is also the Limone IAT office (☎ (0365) 95 40 70), Via Comboni 15. Their Web site (http://www.limone.com/) provides a brief introduction to the town.

PLANNING
When to Walk

The best times of the year are spring and autumn, when the weather is mild to warm and most likely to be settled. July and August are the warmest months (possible maximum temperatures in the high 20°Cs) and the busiest, when the town is very crowded and accommodation is scarce.

Europe's First Lemons

Looking straight down to Limone sul Garda from the heights of Cima di Mughera, or approaching by boat, you can't help but notice rows of tall spikes sticking up from narrow terraces of flattish ground on the northern side of the town, at the base of the towering cliffs. It turns out that they are not the ruins of medieval torture chambers nor elaborate defences against rocks falling from the cliffs, but are dedicated to the entirely peaceful pursuit of citrus cultivation.

When Limone was part of the Venetian republic, a great deal of innovative effort was expended early in the 15th century to bring greater prosperity than that derived from fishing and growing olives, by making Limone the first, and most northern citrus growing area in Europe. Soil was imported from the southern reaches of the lake to be spread over the unproductive soil, an irrigation system was devised, and the huge protective structures built, with lines of walls sprouting rows of columns, to support the timber roof beams. All this was to protect the trees from the cold blasts of north-easterly winds, which they have done very successfully – the lemon trees usually flower three or four times each year. Cultivation continues, though not on the same scale as in earlier days. ■

Maps

Lago di Garda. Monte Baldo (1:50,000, 100m contours, sheet No 102 in the Kompass series) comes with a booklet in Italian and German outlining the history, topography, flora and fauna of the area and with more detailed information about individual towns. It costs L9000 and is widely available. This map is of best use for planning walks, car touring and identification of features, but only as the last resort for use on a walk.

Lago di Garda, Monte Baldo, Lago d'Idro, Lago di Ledro (1:50,000, 25m contours, map No 1/5, Casa Editrice Lagiralpine) costs L8000 and is available locally. It is clear and easy to read but alarmingly inaccurate: both the cemetery above Valle del Singol and the summit of Punta di Mois are misplaced. The *Carta Turistica* (1:12,500 with 100m contours) has notes in English, French, German and Italian, outlining walks along 20 marked footpaths, and information about the hut and chapel near Monte Carone. Published by the local Association of the Mountain Troops Corps (ANA), it is priced at about L5000 from local newsagents. It is reliable for the walks described here.

What to Bring

No special equipment is needed for any of the walks, other than, perhaps walking poles for the longer descents. Walking boots are preferable, though good walking shoes would be adequate for the shorter walks. German is widely spoken, so Lonely Planet's *German phrasebook* may be helpful.

Guided Walks

Every Sunday from June to September, the Alpine Group of Limone sul Garda conducts a free guided walk from Limone to Baita Bonaventura Segala (a mountain refuge), a distance of 8km with 1100m ascent, on good paths all the way. Contact the Limone sul Garda Comune information office (see Information earlier in this section) to book a place and to pick up the leaflet in English describing this and other walks on marked paths. Every Thursday morning during July and August the same group runs a shorter, low-level, free guided walk along the Sunpath, closer to Limone.

PLACES TO STAY & EAT

Camping Garda (☎ (0365) 95 45 50) is about 15 minutes walk south along the roadside footpath from the town centre. Some of the pitches on shady, grassed terraces have lake views. The on-site shop is expensive;

the restaurant is only open during the peak summer season. Prices per pitch and person start at L7500/L15,500; add L500 for a shower. Four person bungalows can be hired for L70,000/L110,000 in the low/high season. The address is 10 Via 14 Novembre, 25010 Limone sul Garda.

Expect to pay comparable prices at the other two sites south of town. *Camping Nanzel* (☎ (0365) 95 41 55; fax 95 44 68), further south beside the main road, does not enjoy access by the roadside footpath and is less spacious than Camping Garda. *Camping Miralago* (☎ (0365) 95 44 38; fax 95 46 59)

is close to the corner of Lungolago Marconi and the SS45.

Baita Bonaventura Segala, built by the local ANA group in the shadow of Monte Carone, is a hut or bivouac (*bivacco*), open to all walkers on a first come, first served basis. Visitors are asked to stay for one night only, and to leave a donation in an honesty box. The simple, but spacious timber building has a gas cooker, lighting, water and a bunk room beneath the main room; the toilet is a short distance south-east down the road, opposite the path to a small chapel; contact the APT office for further information.

LAKE DISTRICT

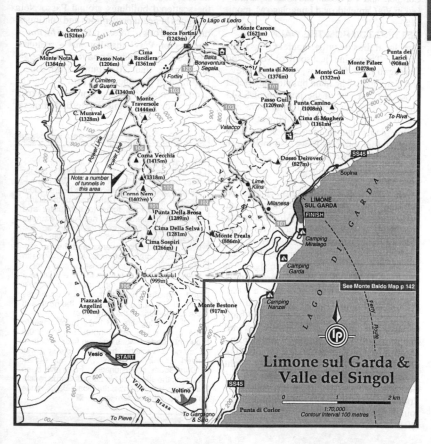

The accommodation list from the APT office provides full details of a wide range of hotels in Limone, starting from L27,000 per person in a double room. It also lists residences and apartments.

The choice of restaurants, trattorias, pizzerias and bars is excellent. *Al Torcol Pizzeria and Grill* (☎ (0365) 95 41 69), on the corner of SS45 and Lungolago Marconi, has as good a view as any of the lake from outdoor tables, a friendly atmosphere and slightly better than average pasta dishes. You can eat well: pasta, pizza, dessert and beer or wine for L22,000.

There are good *fruit and veg shops* on Via Comboni and Via Corda, and small *supermarkets* in Via Campaldo and Lungolago Marconi.

GETTING TO/FROM THE WALK

The local bus service, route G13, links Limone, Tremosine (just south of Vesio) and Gargagno three times day, via Vesio, Pieve and Campione. The main bus stop and ticket office are just east of the junction of SS45 and Via Milanesa. From Limone there is a bus to the village of Vesio (leaving at 9 am), 650m higher than Limone; there are few stops on this route (to Pieve), so make sure you get off at Vesio.

THE WALK

From Vesio walk north-west to a T-junction and right to a crossroads where there is a car park, picnic area and Parco Alto Gardesina sign board. Follow Via G Angelini for 100m to a bend and continue on a gravel road, past a sign for Sentiero Angelini and left between stables and fields, a red and white sign soon reassuringly indicating that you are on path No 106 to **Passo Nota**; it is now a wide, gravel road through forest. Shortly you will pass a boulder bearing a plaque which explains the naming of the nearby Via and Sentiero: Giulo Angelini was a forester and responsible for reafforesting the surrounding area. The road gains height in a stack of tight bends; once it levels out (below Bocca Sospiri), you can begin to appreciate the dramatic vistas of the rugged mountains surrounding the well wooded Valle di Bondo. After about two hours, the road burrows

through six tunnels in quick succession, all around 20m to 30m long.

A further 30 minutes walk from the last of the tunnels brings you to a junction. Bear left (west) downhill; 700m from the junction, and opposite some ruined stone buildings, a path to a WWI cemetery (Cimitero di Guerra) is discreetly marked on the right. It stands to one side of a peaceful meadow and contains graves and memorials of officers and men who died during the war.

Back on the main track and a few hundred metres further on, you come to a major junction; bear right (on path No 421) towards Bocca Fortini. The wide gravel road passes the scattered buildings around Passo Nota and goes beneath power lines and continues, mainly through trees, past the *fortini* – remains of WWI installations – scattered along the road. **Baita Bonaventura Segala** is no more than 10 minutes from Bocca Fortini, past the junction of path No 105 (an exciting route to Monte Carone with rock steps and fixed cables). Bottled mineral

---

Optional Extras

Monte Carone (1621m) is well worth a detour from the main path, not far from Baita Bonaventura Segala. Allow two to 2½ hours (300m ascent). About 400m south-east of the Baita, there is a plaque fixed to a boulder and inscribed 'Sentiero Alpino', next to three stripes representing the colours of the Italian flag. The superbly built path winds up to a gap. From there, continue up towards, and then across the grassy south-eastern flanks of Carone to the summit, a cluster of limestone crags, interspersed with small trees. Near the ruins of a WWI defensive encampment are a flagpole and a crucifix. The panoramic view embraces Lago di Garda, Lago di Ledro to the north and the Orobie Alps to the north-west.

Cima di Mughera (1161m) is much closer to the main route (20 minutes return, 100m ascent), and provides an even finer view than Carone. It is reached by an unmarked but well used turn-off from path 101, no more than 100m south of its junction. From the open summit the view takes in Lago di Garda reaching away into the haze, the Monte Baldo range rises from the eastern shore. ■

water and wine (if you are lucky) may be available at the Baita (please leave a donation in the honesty box). From there the solidly built road passes beneath the towering cliffs of Punta di Mois and continues south and south-east, to join path No 101 to **Valle del Singol**. The path winds down through cliffs and woodland badly burnt early in 1997, and soon recolonised by scrubby, weedy vegetation. The broad path leads down the valley, past ruins of old lime kilns, to Milanesia on the edge of Limone.

Variations

Descend from Traversole, via path No 102 to Valle del Singol and back to Limone; allow about two hours. About 15 minutes north of the last of the six tunnels, there is a clearly signposted turn-off near Traversole. On path No 102 (known as the Alpine Regiment path) climb to the ridge and continue right on a narrow path across the steep slope to a saddle and junction with path No 107. However, stay with path No 102 and angle

down fairly steeply to the next junction (with No 109); continue down left and into Valle del Singol and back to Limone.

Another possibility is to descend from Bocca Fortini on path No 120, via Valacco, to Valle del Singol (two to 2½ hours). Just before you reach Bocca Fortini (where there is a picnic table and the junction of a path leading north to Lago di Ledro), route No 120 branches off to the right. The path descends through trees, then narrows to traverse a grassy slope, with a steep drop to the left. After about 40 minutes, join path No 103 near a stream, but continue for another 10 minutes (past a shrine) to a picnic table with water nearby, at Valacco. Join path No 101 to Valle del Singol, and back to Limone.

OTHER WALKS

Of the other routes near Limone, it is worth noting that path No 111, from Valle del Singol to Monte Preals, is badly eroded.

Although Sentiero Antoniolo is marked on the Kompass map No 102 (see Maps

---

War in the Mountains

Italy entered WWI in 1915 on the Allied side, in anticipation of extending its northern borders, to liberate from Austro-Hungarian rule the lands of the Alto Adige, and the Trentino, not very far north of Lago di Garda. Limone sul Garda was evacuated for the duration since the border at that time generally followed the line of the rim of Valle del Singol. Many battles, including the Trentino offensive of summer 1916 and the Piave offensive two years later, were fought in the area. Remains of the *fortini* – barracks, gun emplacements and other wartime paraphernalia – are still evident, along the road followed by the walk described, from **Passo Nota** to **Baita Bonaventura Segala**, and on Monte Carone.

Baita Bonaventura Segala and the nearby chapel were built in recent years by members and friends of the local Associazione Nazionale Alpini (ANA – Veterans Association of the Corps of Mountain Troops) on the ruins of wartime buildings. The purpose is to provide a base, or shelter, for people who want to appreciate the beauty of the mountains by spending some time quietly in more or less natural surroundings. The chapel is dedicated to San Giovanni Nepomuceno; it is tiny (barely 5m square), stone-built, and with a timber and tin roof. Inside are four small seats and the simplest of altars, with just a crucifix and some fresh flowers. Mass is held here from time to time, and advertised locally in Limone. A major tree planting programme is part of the project, to restore the habitat of indigenous fauna.

The ANA has also constructed a path up towards Monte Carone, and another, more difficult route right to the summit, and rebuilt the large crucifix there. It is surrounded by the starkly white stones of the remains of a fortified village, which even had a hospital. The crucifix is made of long metal spikes and barbed wire with a soldier's helmet resting on each end of the horizontal arm. The wording of the plaque on the stone base of the cross is simple: it was erected as a sign of peace and fraternity.

The war cemetery near Passo Nota – perhaps the most poignant place of all – was also restored by a local ANA group. A low stone wall, surmounted by a seemingly incongruous but fittingly harsh fence of barbed wire and twisted metal spikes, encloses a grove of tall pines. Within are several anonymous headstones, a memorial, and two large headstones, one for soldiers and officers who died in a fire just before the end of the war and another, more general one for soldiers who died between 1915 and 1918.

Sandra Bardwell

earlier in this section), no information is available locally. However, the cluster of signposts for the main Valle del Singol path, just beyond the bridge near Bar Milanesia, include one indicating that it is a seven-stage history-nature path, established by the Province of Brescia to commemorate Mons G Antoniolo. Look for intermittent yellow and white marks up the Valle, and north from Passo Nota.

LAGO DI COMO

Lago di Como's renowned scenic beauty and crystal clear air have inspired volumes of often extravagant praise, which can equally apply to the lake's attractions for walkers. From the shores rise an extraordinary array of mountains, many topping 2000m; deep, steep-sided valleys extend far inland. On the lake's eastern side the highest peaks tower above Val Varrone and Valsasina: Monte Legnone (2609m) in the north and Grigna Settentrionale (2410m) in the south-east.

The Triangolo, as the peninsula between the two arms of the lake is known, seems dwarfed by these peaks, but it is nevertheless a rugged area with Corni di Canzo (1373m) yielding little to Grigna in the steepness of its crags. The western side of the lake is in fact two distinct areas, separated by the shallow Val Menaggio between the head of Lago di Lugano (Lake Lugano) (partly in Switzerland) and the shore of Lago di Como at Menaggio. South of this valley many streams dissect the main ridge, making the topography quite complex, while to the north, a mighty horseshoe ridge rising from Menaggio sweeps north along the Swiss border, over Monte Cardinello (2521m) and eastwards, down to the head of the lake.

The small town of Menaggio is the base for the walks described in this section. Its accessible hinterland offers perhaps the widest variety of walks in any one compact area around Lago di Como. All the walks, whether it be a leisurely afternoon stroll along the Torrente Senagra (River Senagra),

or a strenuous mountain expedition, share the setting of scenic landscapes replete with evidence of a long history of settlement and of striking, but mostly harmonious contrasts between the old and the new.

Menaggio owes its origins to its location at the junction of two important Roman roads, the shoreline Via Regina, and the road through Val Menaggio to Lago di Lugano and then to Lugano in Switzerland. In the town, the churches testify to a lively community dating back to before the 15th century. The fine 18th and 19th-century villas were built for Italian nobility and early travellers seeking a haven after crossing the Alps, developments which in turn paved the way for modern tourism.

Menaggio and the surrounding area has supported many small industries, including silk weaving and grain milling. Farming, long organised around high-level summer grazing in *monti*, is now a rarity rather than common practice, as the numerous deserted and ruinous stone buildings in the wooded valleys reveal. The paths and mule tracks between them have survived and are ideal for walking – for pleasure rather than necessity.

HISTORY

The area around Lago di Como has a long and often turbulent history. Evidence of Iron Age settlement was uncovered near Como itself; the Roman occupation, which began in 196 BC, was followed by invasions of Ostrogoths and Lombards. At the end of the 12th century, Como was destroyed in a war with Milano, then rebuilt, the Milanese Visconti and Sforza dynasties becoming all-powerful. After two centuries of Spanish domination ending in the 1720s, Austria took over, but at the end of the 18th century, the area was embraced by the Napoleonic empire. Under the treaty forged at the Congress of Vienna in 1815, Lombardia (including Lago di Como) came under Austrian domination again, until Austria's defeat in the struggles of the late 1850s, and the annexation of Lombardia by Piemonte in 1859, shortly before Italian unification.

During WWII, the Partisan movement

was born in the mountains north of Lecco in 1944. In April 1945, Mussolini decamped to Como from Salo on Lago di Garda, the seat of his short-lived puppet republic. At the end of the month he moved to Menaggio, then joined German soldiers fleeing to Austria, but was captured at Dongo and executed in Milano the next day.

Today, Lago di Como is within the region of Lombardia; and many of the westernmost comunes share a boundary with Switzerland.

NATURAL HISTORY

Lago di Como's origins are glacial; in the Pleistocene era, a few million years ago, the Adda glacier carved out the upper lake basin, then split on either side of a promontory to cut the two arms which give the lake its distinctive, inverted-Y shape. Two rivers flow into the lake in the north – the Mera and the Adda. The latter is the sole outlet flowing from Lago di Lecco, the eastern arm, via Lago di Garlate and Lago di Olginate. The stem of the Y is sometimes called Lago di Colico; the name Como commonly applies to the western arm, and to the lake as a whole, though Lario, the older, more traditional title (from the Roman *Lacus Larionus*) is also used.

Though smaller in area than Lago di Garda and Lago Maggiore, at 148 sq km, Como has the longest shoreline – more than 170km. It also enters the record book as the deepest lake in Italy: 410m near Aregno on the western arm.

Lago di Como lies within the southern pre-Alps, which are divided from the Alps proper by an east-west line through the Valltellina, the mountain range immediately north of the lake. Geologically, the Como basin is an area of both limestone and crystalline (gneiss) rocks. The distinctive Grigne and Resegone massifs in the south-east are similar to the Dolomiti in structure and form, and Monte Grona, above Menaggio, is the northernmost of the dolomitic peaks in the southern pre-Alps.

The Como basin's mild climate provides an ideal environment for the cultivation of olives and vines around the shores, while colourful flowering shrubs brighten many

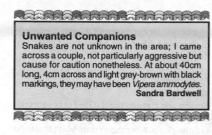

Unwanted Companions
Snakes are not unknown in the area; I came across a couple, not particularly aggressive but cause for caution nonetheless. At about 40cm long, 4cm across and light grey-brown with black markings, they may have been *Vipera ammodytes*.
Sandra Bardwell

towns and private homes. In the deciduous woodlands covering extensive tracts of the steep mountainsides, sweet chestnut *(Castanea sativa)* and oaks are prominent, many mature trees attaining massive proportions; there are also hazel, with its long yellow catkins (probably introduced by the Romans), silver birch and beech.

The limestone country supports a colourful variety of flora. Christmas rose *(Helleborus niger)* is a hardy species, its white flowers emerging at the beginning of the year. During early spring the unusually deep blue trumpet gentian *(Gentiana acaulis)*, pink spring heath *(Erica carnea)* and purplish mezereon *(Daphne mezereum)* bring early colour to the rocky ground. In summer, clusters of the well-named yellow globeflower *(Trollis europaeus)*, the orange lily *(Lilium bulbiferum)* and the violet-blue commonly seen columbine *(Aquilegia vulgaris)* are among the dozens of species to be found, many of which are protected.

INFORMATION

The IAT office (☎ (0344) 32924) in Menaggio is at Piazza Garibaldi 8 and is open from 9 am to noon and 3 to 6 pm and is closed on Sundays. At least one member of the staff is extremely knowledgeable and helpful and speaks English (and three other languages). Here you can obtain information about accommodation, local walks and three long distance paths (see Other Walks around Lago di Como later) and a useful town map and a topographical map (see Maps & Books later). The local post code is 22017.

Local mountain weather forecasts can be heard by phoning the Swiss Meteorological

Service (☎ (0041) 91162). The emergency number for mountain rescue (Corpo Nazionale di Soccorso Alpino) at Menaggio (or Dongo further north) is ☎ 118.

PLANNING
When to Walk
Spring and autumn are the best times to visit Lago di Como; snow lingers only on the Grigna peaks after the end of May; the wild flowers then are most abundant and crowds least so. During July and August, the warmest months, the lakeside towns are packed so finding accommodation without reservations made well ahead, could be difficult. Thunderstorms and heavy rain are not unknown in June, but rarely last for 24 hours.

Maps & Books
Lago di Como, Lago di Lugano (1:50,000, 100m contours, map No 91 in the Kompass series) comes with an informative booklet in Italian and German; it costs L9000 and is widely available. It is useful for walks, planning and identification of features, but unreliable for location of paths; some of those are at best very faint, at worst nonexistent. *Carta dei Sentieri* (1:35,000) is a fairly reliable adaptation of the Kompass No 91 map and adequate for local walks. It is available from the Menaggio IAT office for L1500. *Roveredo* and *Menaggio* (1:50,000, Nos 277 and 287, in the Carta Nazionale Svizzera series) are superb, but lack the numbered footpaths and are not easily available.

Hiking in the Mountains around Lago di Como is a set of booklets, free from the Menaggio IAT office, describing three long distance paths. Each booklet has maps of the main route and linking paths and notes about features along the way. Descriptions of the routes leave much to the imagination, so it is necessary to be vigilant when following the distinctive markers. Via dei Monti Lariani, from Cernobbio (north of Como) to Sorico, at the northern end of the lake, is the only one which passes close to Menaggio (see Other Walks later in this section).

Alta Via del Lario by Bruno Mazzoleni, published in Italian by CAI (Dongo),

describes a high-level walk along the watershed of Lago di Como between Menaggio and Sorico. It also has numerous variations, with planimetric maps and details of the rifugi (refuges) used. It is available from Rifugio Menaggio (see Places to Stay & Eat later in this section) for L24,000; check that your copy has pages 37 to 52. Also on sale at the rifugio for L12,000 each are *Rifugio Menaggio e Dintorni*, a guide to the area around the rifugio, and *Dal Ceresio al Lario*, from Lago di Lugano to Lago di Como.

Il Ritrovo bookshop, via Calvi 10, Menaggio, is a good source of maps and guidebooks, in Italian and German.

Richard Sale's book *The Italian Lakes: 30 Circular Walks from Regional Centres* (see Books at the beginning of this chapter) features 11 walks around Lago di Como.

What to Bring
For the shorter walks described, strong shoes or trainers are suitable, though walking boots are always preferable. A pair of walking poles will lessen the impact of the steep descents. If the prospect of having a go at a *via ferrata* route is irresistible, remember that you must wear a helmet and harness, and carry UAII No 1 rope, an energy absorber and two self-locking karabiners with rope fastening devices – and know how to use them. Camping Gaz is elusive, so stock up.

Warning
The marking of paths can be infuriatingly inconsistent. You can find markers lavishly and unnecessarily painted on trees, rocks and walls. But then they can be entirely lacking, obscurely placed or overgrown at crucial junctions, in a maze of village alleys or in flat, featureless meadows. Nevertheless, it is better to stick to the marked paths, rather than hope that a beguiling line on a map will lead to where you want to go.

PLACES TO STAY & EAT
In Menaggio *La Primula* youth hostel (☎/fax (0344) 32356), at Via 4 Novembre 38, offers a fine view of the lake. Prices are L15,000 for B&B, and L14,000 for a three course

evening meal. To reach the hostel from the centre of town, walk back towards Como along the main road and follow a path up from a service station. It is by far the cheapest place to stay in Menaggio.

Of the two camping grounds, *Europa* is best avoided. *Lido* (☎ (0344) 31150), at Via Roma 4, towards the northern end of town close to the junction with SS340D, occupies a former soccer pitch, so is level and well grassed. It costs L12,000 per place and L6000 per adult; the on site bar also serves snacks. The site has a good view of the nearby mountains and is next to the bus depot. The noise of buses departing before 6 am can be very annoying.

In the lane on the lake side of the camping ground (Via Roma 22) is *La Giara Pizzeria* a friendly, informal place, popular with locals. It offers a huge range of excellent pizzas from a genuine *forno a legna* (wood fired oven), from L6000 to L15,000, as well as a good selection of pasta (up to L15,000) meat and fish dishes, gelati, an extensive wine list and the local mineral water Chiarella, from Plésio. There are also several bars in the centre of the town. The small *Rock n' Roll* next to the bakery in Via Lusardi, the main through road, serves pizza and pasta for around L7000 and meat dishes for L10,000.

There is an excellent fruit and vegetable shop on the corner of Via Lusardi and Via Loveno. *Il Fornato*, the bakery on the other side of Via Lusardi, and closer to the town centre, is well patronised by locals. Of the two supermarkets, *Consorso Agrario*, in Via Lusardi near the ferry port, is cheaper than *Compra Bono* off Via Roma near Lido camping ground. For local cheeses, try *Casa del Formaggio* in Via Al Lago off Via Lusardi near the town centre.

The IAT office can provide a list of hotels, ranging from the four star, aptly named *Grand Hotel Victoria*, majestically overlooking the lake (with singles from L150,000), to a few one-star establishments with rooms from L30,000.

Rifugio Menaggio (☎ (0344) 37282; fax (0161) 21 37 51) is open from 20 June to 15 September, and on holidays throughout the year. Built in 1960 and later extended by the local branch of the CAI , it has 30 beds, a bar and restaurant. The B&B tariff for non-CAI members is L30,000 (members: L18,000). Lunch, snacks and drinks are available during the day; items on the menu for dinner range from L8000 to L12,000 (L500 per item less for members) and a beer is L4000. As well as the local guidebooks (see Maps & Books earlier in this section) you can buy postcards, a souvenir cap or a T-shirt.

GETTING THERE & AWAY
Bus & Train
Como is on the train line between Milano and many western European stations; plenty of Intercity, but not regional or direct services, stop at Como Sant' Giovanni. The station (☎ (0131) 26 14 94) at Piazzale San Gottardo, is about 15 minutes walk from the city centre. A reasonably frequent private service from Milano (Stazione Nord) runs to Como's Stazione Nord (☎ (0131) 30 42 00) close to the bus station and port; the fare from Milano to Como is L5000. Trains on the Milano (Stazione Centrale) to Sondrio line stop at Lecco from where SPT buses go to Como, and at Varenna from where there is a ferry/hydrofoil service to Menaggio. There are also trains from Milano Central to Bergamo from where SPT buses go to Como.

SIA buses (☎ (030) 377 42 37) on route No C10 run from Como through the towns on the western shore; there are at least eight buses daily. The fare to Menaggio is L4500. Purchase tickets in advance from the bus station in Piazza Matteotti, Como, where an information office is open from 8 am to noon, 2 to 6 pm; at other times, departures are displayed outside.

Car
Leave the A9 (Milano-Passo Sant' Gottardo) at the Como Sud exit. From there the SS35 passes through Como and links with the SS340 along the western shore of the lake. The SS36 from Milano via Monza, goes through Lecco and along the eastern shore of the lake.

LAKE DISTRICT

Monte Grona

Duration 5 to 5½ hours
Ascent 990m
Standard Medium-Hard
Start & Finish Breglia
Closest Towns Como, Bergamo
Permits Required No
Public Transport Access Yes
Summary A fairly straightforward climb that gives magnificent panoramic views of the lake and peaks.

This dramatic cluster of dolomite crags, overlooking Menaggio from the west, is surprisingly easy to climb. You can walk all the way from Menaggio, or catch the local C13 Menaggio-Breglia bus and start from there. If you are driving, there is parking space near the cemetery in Breglia. However, the walk up to Breglia via Barna is well worth doing in its own right, and is described here as a variation.

It is also worth noting that you can approach Monte Grona via the low level (basso) route from the Sentiero dei 4 Valli (see the Sass Corbee walk later). Perhaps the ideal plan is to stay overnight at Rifugio Menaggio (see Places to Stay & Eat earlier), to enjoy a leisurely wander, further up to Monte Bregagno (2107m), a superb rolling, grassy mountain, contrasting markedly with the precipitous peaks elsewhere around the lake. It is advisable to carry some water for the walk to the rifugio.

GETTING TO/FROM THE WALK
Bus
From Menaggio, opposite Piazza Garibaldi by the lakeshore, line C13 goes to Plésio and Breglia (L2100). Buy tickets in advance from La Provincia newsagent in Piazza Garibaldi. A timetable is available from the IAT office.

THE WALK
From the piazza by the cemetery and war memorial, just follow signs to Rifugio

Menaggio, up the road ahead. After about 10 minutes, turn left; after 50m follow the distinctive red and yellow markers, here and at subsequent junctions. The path leads up through woodland burnt in spring 1997 after a winter drought. Pass the junction with the 'Basso' (low level) route, and another one to Sant' Amate and Monte Bregagno. Note the change around here in the local geology, from crystalline rocks to smooth, grey-white limestone. The path makes a fine rising traverse of a small valley to reach the rifugio, on a wide promontory below Monte Grona.

Having enjoyed the excellent torte and a drink, head for **Monte Grona** (about an hour) – the red and yellow signs are in sight above the rifugio. The Via Direttissima (to the left) is very steep, and even the Via Normale has its moments. The very well used path for the latter climbs to La Forcoletta (a small saddle/col) then swings westwards (where the path to Monte Bregagno leads northwards) to cross Grona's wooded northern flank, a striking contrast to the rugged south face. The steep drop to the right of this path calls for sure-footedness; up on the summit ridge there is a fixed wire beside the final scramble to the grassy top – where it's all too noticeable that the feral goats enjoy browsing among the rocks. A handy topograph identifies the myriad of peaks in the panoramic view. Return to the rifugio by your preferred route.

Alternative Start
2½ hours; 550m ascent
Follow the route described for the Sass Corbee walk to the trout farm. Continue past the farm for about 30m and go up a flight of steps on the right (on Via dei Monti Lariani) and through woodland to the village of Barna. From the piazza keep the church on the left and go up a cobbled alley and right just past a drinking fountain.

Be on the lookout for markers up through woodland to a small building set into the slope; bear right here on a minor path and go on, in fine mixed woodland; pass between and then left of a group of farm buildings, to a track and bear right to a road at Piazza (see the Via guide) near a restored chapel.

Further up the road, turn off right along a track near a large building on the right. Then fork left just past two small buildings on the right, among beautiful mature birch and chestnut trees. Go down to the right to a junction where Plésio is to the right and Breglia to the left. Through the woods, keep to the higher path, though still heading downwards to cross a stream. Soon you will find yourself between houses on a lane which leads to the piazza by the cemetery at Breglia.

Side Trip: Rifugio Menaggio to Monte Bregagno
2 hours; 700m ascent

Monte Bregagno needs a clear day, not only for the views, but also because in poor visibility it would be easy to stray from the path on the broad ridge. The route from the rifugio is straightforward, up to La Forcoletta then generally north along the ridge, past Sant' Amate (a chapel which, according to a plaque on the wall, could date from 1500 and have been named Sant' Mamete). Then, following red and white marks, it heads up the grassy ridge to the crucifix-topped summit.

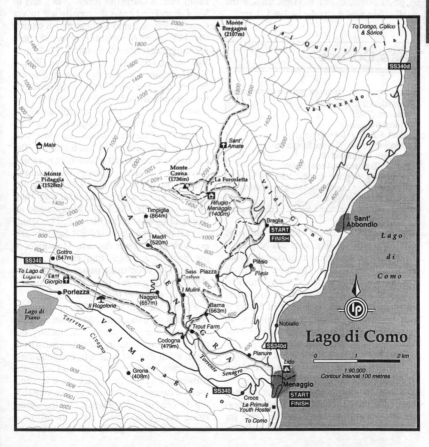

The highlights of the view are nearly all Lago di Como almost at your feet, the Valtellina at the head of Lago di Como, and (with luck) Monte Rosa on the Italian-Swiss border to the west. It was on this ridge that a herd of grazing cows, all typically wearing a bell, reminded me of an anarchic mirimbah band, with some nearby sheep adding a chimes accompaniment.

From Breglia, the most direct approach is to follow the route already described towards the rifugio, and after an hour, at a clearly marked junction (before the rifugio) bear right (north-east) for Sant' Amate, and continue up, past a communications installation, to the small col in which sits the isolated chapel.

Sass Corbee

Duration 3 to 3½ hours
Ascent 300m
Standard Easy
Start & Finish Menaggio
Closest Towns Como, Bergamo
Permits Required No
Public Transport Access Yes
Summary A good family walk to Sass Corbee with a huge rock sitting in a canyon on Torrente Senagra.

To eliminate most of the climbing and road walking for this outing, cars can be parked at the start of the fitness trail (see the walk description following). The route described is along narrow town lanes, quiet roads and a marked path. An extension of this walk, upstream to the old settlement of Madri is well worthwhile. A further continuation, up to another old settlement, Timpiglia, on the Sentiero dei 4 Valli and on to Breglia, is marked but difficult to follow. Check with the IAT office in Menaggio about an English language edition of the leaflet describing the walk, and the condition of the latter section. Water is readily available to Madri. The restaurant at the trout farm may be open for refreshments in summer. The basic walk can

be combined with the Il Rogolone outing (on the next page) to make a full day, by walking up the road to Codogna from the trout farm. The local spelling of the name Senagra (river and valley) has been adopted; it is spelt Sanagra on the Kompass map.

GETTING TO/FROM THE WALK
Bus
See the Getting There & Away section earlier for details on how to get from Como to Menaggio, the base for this walk.

THE WALK
From Piazza Garibaldi follow Via Calvi to Via Lusardi and cross diagonally left to Via Caronti, left of Santo Stefano parish church (the IAT leaflet *Historical Itinerary through Menaggio* describes its features). Walk up to Via Como, turn right, then left after 30m to Via Castelino which rises between fine old houses, past the outer walls of the castle on the right (destroyed in the 15th century) and around to Via N Sauro. Bear right along the road, over **Torrente Senagra** to a path up beside Hotel Loveno, to cut out some road walking. Continue along Via Sauro for 30m to a junction on the left where there is a small shrine and a sign, 'Passeggiate Pianure', which you follow past Piazza Wachs Mylius (named after a local benefactor) then swing right into Via XXIV Maggio and up to a road signposted to 'Pianure'. This winds up past the large church of San Lorenzo and on, with good views down to Menaggio, to the start of a fitness trail *Percorso della Salute*. The wide track passes beside a flat meadow (Pianure) then through mixed forest, up and over to Torrente Senagra.

Follow the sign to Sass Corbee along the riverbank path to a road and cluster of stone buildings, once the site of a nail factory, but now a restaurant (during summer) and a trout farm. With this on your left, continue on a wide track up the leafy valley to I Mulini, a former grain mill. From here there is a fine view of the crags of Monte Grona commanding the head of Val Senagra. Cross the arched stone bridge and bear right to follow a narrow woodland path, with the limestone cliffs closing in as the river steepens. Cross a metal footbridge and go left to climb the steps (with handrail) cut in a massive, displaced slice of the cliff.

At the top, walk across the massive boulders in the middle of the gorge to come breathtakingly close to the river thundering down in cascades and turbulent torrents beneath your feet. **Sass Corbee**, partly resting against the cliff, measures at least 25m across and is host to several small trees and shrubs. The mind boggles at the force which landed it there originally. Return to your starting point, or continue to Madri.

Extension

Allow an hour up the river; the gain in height is only 20m. From Sass Corbee the path to Madri is fairly clear and marked (although sparsely) with red paint blobs. It passes through woodland and deserted farm buildings, then crosses a clearing. Further on, keep to the left of a stone building with a fresco and modern roof, and on to the wide grassy clearing, in the shadow of Monte Grona where lie the deserted stone buildings of Madri.

Il Rogolone

> **Duration** 4 to 4½ hours
> **Ascent** 460m
> **Standard** Easy
> **Start & Finish** Menaggio
> **Closest Towns** Como, Bergamo
> **Permits Required** No
> **Public Transport Access** Yes
> **Summary** An easy walk on well marked paths and quiet roads to a huge old oak tree.

This is a very adaptable walk; which can be shortened by using the bus from Menaggio, or by driving to Codogna, where you can park your car near the piazza. Or, it can be extended, by combining with the excursion to Sass Corbee (see above). Carry some

> **Il Rogolone**
>
> Oaks, or at least English oaks (*Quercus robur*), can live to a great age, 400 years not being unusual.
>
> A few kilometres west of the village of Codogna in Val Menaggio stands a fine old oak known as Il Rugulon (meaning big oak in the local dialect; the Italian is Grande Rovere). Its birth date has been established with certainty as before 1730, and documentary sources suggest that it may even date from medieval times (about the 14th century). It is believed to have been the place where local rulers (perhaps members of the commune) went to make important decisions. Today it is classed as a natural monument. Young Il Rugulini, a mere 100 years old, stands nearby in the same clearing.
>
> **Sandra Bardwell**

water on the walk. There is a bar and cafe in Codogna near the piazza.

THE WALK

From Menaggio, follow the Sass Corbee walk to the trout farm (described earlier in this chapter), bear left across the bridge and walk up to **Codogna** (on Via dei Monti Lariani) and through to the piazza. Here a sign points to Il Rogolone, and a small notice outlines the tree's importance. It is more than 260 years old, and may even date from Medieval times (see the 'Il Rogolone' boxed text for more information).

Via alla Santa, the road on which you continue (or set out) soon becomes a lane between houses and terraced fields, then mostly through woodland; Lago di Piano and Lago di Lugana can be seen from breaks in the trees. A short climb brings you to **Il Rogolone**, dominating a grassy meadow. The tree's trunk is a healthy 3m wide and the canopy shades an area 25m across. Continue on the path wide of the clearing, through a gate and into woodland; after about 15 minutes the path merges with a mule track and soon you reach the church of San Giorgio, its bell tower and frescoes suggesting medieval origin according to a sign, in Italian, on the gate. Cross the bridge here and walk up the road to the hamlet of Gottro, a harmonious blend of the old and new.

Turn right and follow the road, which climbs gently, affording splendid lake and valley views all the way to **Naggio**, with its late 17th-century church. It's worth diverging briefly here to wander along Via alla Piazza, the narrowest of lanes, between old houses, to the oddly beautiful Piazza Maggiore. Back at the church, turn right along the road to a bend and continue ahead. Follow the grassy path, the old mule track, pursuing its direct downhill route across the bends of the modern road, then between a cemetery and large church, to the piazza in Codogna. From here, return to Menaggio by bus or by retracing your steps down to the trout farm, along the river, past Pianure, and back to the town.

Other Walks around Lago di Como

WESTERN SHORE

The **Alta Via del Lario** is mainly between 2000m and 2450m along Lago di Como between Menaggio and Sorico. Allow at least three days for this challenging walk, involving about 4100m ascent. Rifugi are used throughout, so it is only practicable between mid-June and mid-September; treacherous snow drifts usually linger until June, and conditions can become icy in October. The area is subject to poor weather. A rope should be carried to provide security on exposed sections. The Carta Nazionale Svizzera (1:50,000) map (see Maps & Books earlier) Nos 277 and 287 are recommended. You'll need to be completely self-sufficient; there are no villages along the high-level route. The Alta Via was devised, and a guide first published, by the Dongo branch of the CAI during the 1980s. The more recent edition of the guide has been updated (see Maps & Books earlier).

The Sentiero delle 4 Valli, from Breglia to Dasio above Lago di Lugano, takes an easy three days with only 1410m ascent. The four

valleys are: Senagra, Cavargna (passing the highest point on the walk, Alpe Colone, 1400m), Rezzo and Valsolda. The Sentiero follows cart and mule tracks through chestnut and beech woods, across meadows, through hamlets, past isolated farms and historical features including an abandoned iron mine and remains of WWI fortifications. The Kompass map No 91 and *Hiking in the Mountains around Lago di Como* (see Maps & Books earlier) are useful. Accommodation is available at Male, Cavargna and Monti Colone (where the rifugio is open only in July and August); there is a camp site at Ranco, near Dasio. The Menaggio IAT office (see Information earlier) can help with reservations (strongly advised).

The **Via dei Monti Lariani** is a fairly strenuous seven-day walk from Cernobbio (just north of Como) to Sorico at the northern extremity of the lake, via San Fedele, Croce (near Menaggio) and Garzeno, with about 4660m ascent. It follows paths and tracks, some still used by local people to reach *monti* – alpine pastures used for summer grazing, and so affords insights into local rural life. The Via (the full name of which is derived from Lario, the traditional name for Lago di Como), is marked with distinctive red and white signs; near Menaggio walking requires vigilance and intuition to avoid going astray. The Via is covered by Kompass map Nos 91 and 92 and also *Hiking in the Mountains around Lago di Como*, and is part of the north Lombardia section of the Sentiero Italia (see The Route in the Long-Distance Walks chapter). Menaggio IAT office has advice about accommodation.

TRIANGOLO LARIANO

The **Dorsale del Triangolo Lariano** trail follows mule tracks for much of its distance along a high ridge across the peninsula between the two arms of Lago di Como. It links Brunate above Como and Bellagio at the northern tip of the peninsula, and can be completed in two days. The highest point reached is Monte Bolettone (1310m). There are plenty of restaurants and accommodation along the way. For more details contact the tourist offices at Menaggio (see Information earlier), or Canzo (☎ (031) 68 24 57), only in summer, or Bellagio (☎ (031) 95 02 04).

The **Corni di Canzo** is a compact group of spiky peaks of 1200m and more, in the south-eastern corner of the Triangolo, east of Canzo. It has an extensive network of paths, including a via ferrata as one of the approaches to the highest point (1378m); rifugi and other accommodation are available. Contact Pro Loco, Canzo (☎ (031) 68 24 57) for more information.

The Costiera degli Olivi extends along the north-eastern fringe of Triangolo between Onno and Limonta, where marked paths offer easy and medium walks through wooded mountain slopes and olive groves. For more information contact the IAT office (☎ (0341) 36 23 60; fax 28 62 31), Via Nazario Sauro 6, 22053 Lecco, or try the Comune Oliveto Lario (☎ (031) 95 17 97) in Limonta (see also Maps & Books earlier).

EASTERN SHORE
The **Wayfarer's Trail** is a route of about 37km between Borbino and Colico, following old lines of communication between villages and small towns. The **Grigna Mountains**, north of Lecco, are the most rugged and formidable in the whole area, rising precipitously to 2409m at Grigna Settentrionale, and are well endowed with several vie ferrate (see What to Bring earlier) and few, if any, easy walks. The **Resegone**, and the **Piani d'Erna** group, of similar character to the Grigna, lie east and south-east of Lecco. For more information on these areas, contact the Lecco IAT office.

LAGO MAGGIORE

Lago Maggiore may not be dominated by dramatic peaks, as are Lago di Garda and Lago di Como, but at its northern end, close to the Swiss border, not only are there some fine mountains offering surprisingly wide views, but also secluded valleys where tightly clustered villages preserve a wealth of traditional stone buildings. The walks described in this section centre on the fine old town of Cannobio, which is the main town in Valle Cannobina, and the nearby smaller town of Cannero. Cannero's full (but little used) name of Cannero Riviera reflects earlier local zeal to promote its attractions. The network of paths through Valle Cannobina offers many wonderful opportunities for a wide range of walks. And whatever you do, make sure you have a ferry ride on the lake, to fully appreciate the town's setting, at the end of its long wooded valley.

HISTORY
The Romans were early occupants of the area around the lake, and gave it the name of Verbano, an alternative still in use. The decline of feudalism was followed by a long period of independence and commercial prosperity, which gave way to Milanese domination on the western shore mainly by the despotic Visconti dynasty. Much later, the people of Luino rallied to support Garibaldi in his struggles against the Austrians in the mid-19th century, as Italy moved towards unification.

Modern tourism has its origins in the trans-Alps travellers of the 19th century who found a haven by the restful shores of the lake. Their successors sought the even greater comforts of the lakeside resorts, epitomised in the sprawling hotels along Stresa's waterfront. The centuries-long importance of vineyards and milling was all but extinguished by the late 19th century, leaving only the evidence in names – Molineggi (milling centre), between Cannobio and Cannero; carefully preserved artefacts – at Oggebbio near Cannero; and many silent ruins. During WWI, General Luigi Cadorna, fearing attack from the north, masterminded the construction of a network of military roads inland from Cannero, but his fears proved groundless; the same area is also honeycombed with wartime trenches. Late in WWII, the southern boundary of the Partisans' short-lived Free Republic of Domodossola passed through Cannobio.

Today, Lago Maggiore is divided between two Italian provinces and a Swiss Canton:

the western side is in Piemonte, Lombardia has the opposite shore, and the northern reaches are in Ticino, Switzerland.

Cannobio, the centre for the walks in this section, was an independent city state-commune in the 12th century, but the valley's churches testify to earlier settlement: there is a 5th-century church at Orasso, the oldest in the valley, while those in Cavaglio and at Sant' Anna near Traffiume date from the 15th and 16th centuries respectively. The woods and waters of the valley of the Torrente Cannobino and exploitation of the lake as a trade route, were the foundation for Cannobio's past affluence. This is still evident in many fine 16th and 17th-century buildings, notably in the shorefront arcade, and now serving tourism as restaurants and shops.

NATURAL HISTORY
Each of the three lakes has a claim to primacy – Maggiore's is its length (65km) although it is generally on the slender side (no more than 4km at its widest point). With an area of 215 sq km it is smaller than Garda but more extensive than Como.

Glacial in origin, its main feeders are the Ticino, coming in from the north, and which carries right through to become the only outflow, at Sesto Callende; the Toce flowing from the west along Val d'Ossola to a bay between Verbania and Stresa; and to the east, the Tresa which arrives at Luino via Lago di Lugano. The highest and most rugged peaks are in the north and north-west, and generally set well back from the lake: Limidario (2187m) on the Swiss border and flanked by the towering rock walls of the Gridone; and Monte Zeda (2156m) and a brace of craggy peaks around 2000m in Parco Nazionale della Val Grande, well west of Cannero. Elsewhere, elevations are much more modest, giving much of the lake's environs a relatively gentle, even tame appearance. The main mountain masses are built of crystalline schists and gneisses, though there are limestone outcrops on the plateau of Campo dei Fiori in the south.

Chestnuts predominate in the extensive woodlands on the steep slopes, together with various oaks, beech, European larch and rhododendrons. Around the shores, the mild climate, free of extreme cold, fosters the cultivation of citrus groves, and the widespread use of palms and oleanders in public gardens and along promenades.

Two valuable reserves have been set aside around the lake. Parco Nazionale della Val Grande (11,700 hectares) embraces Italy's largest wild area, with luxuriant beech and oak forests, a rich variety of fauna and deep rocky valleys. Parco Naturale Campo dei Fiori (5400 hectares) protects an extraordinary range of limestone features. Its upper reaches support beech forest, with conifers, ash, chestnut and oaks lower down. There is also an important centre for natural science field studies.

INFORMATION
Cannobio
The APT office (☎ (0323) 71212) is in Viale V Veneto 4, 28052, Cannobio. It is open between 9 am and noon and 4.30 to 7 pm from Monday to Friday and between 9 am and noon on weekends. Here you can obtain accommodation lists and a guide to local walks; the office has a currency exchange service.

Cannero
The small, helpful Pro Loco office in Via Lazzaro, is open on weekdays (except Wednesdays) from 10 am to noon and from 3.30 to 6 pm and from 9.30 am to noon on weekends. Pick up the splendid map folder *Alto Verbano Guide to Hiking Trails* describing local walks (see Maps & Books following).

PLANNING
When to Walk
Since none of the walks described here is above 1800m, they should be free of snow from mid-May to early October. The busiest months are July and August.

Maps & Books
Lago Maggiore, Lago di Varese (1:50,000, 100m contours, map No 90 in the Kompass

Top: Graziers' summer dwelling at Montagna Djouen, and beyond, the former royal hunting lodge of Orvieille, in Valsavarenche, Parco Nazionale del Gran Paradiso

Bottom: On the way to Laghi di Bella Comba, south of La Thuile in the Western Alps, where blue-green waters and views of the surrounding peaks await

SANDRA BARDWELL

SANDRA BARDWELL

SANDRA BARDWELL

Top: Traditional lakeside houses at Cannero Riviera, on Lago Maggiore's western shore.
Bottom Left: The Baita Bonaventura Segala is handy for an overnight stay when attempting the Limone sul Garda & Valle del Singol walk.
Bottom Right: The tranquil little ferry port of Malcesine, on Lago di Garda's eastern shore.

series) is priced at L9000 and is widely available. The accompanying booklet in Italian and German describes topography, reserves, the Via Verde Varesina (see Other Walks later in this section) and features of several towns. It is ideal for identifying landmarks and planning walks; the depiction of paths is more accurate than many other Kompass maps. *Laghi Maggiore d'Orta e di Varese* (1:50,000, 50m contours, map No 12 in the IGC series) is easy to read and accurate, and although the paths do not have the local numbering system, it is the best map for the area.

Brissago (1:25,000, 20m contours, sheet 1332, Carta Nazionale della Svizzera) costs L14,500 and is a cartographic masterpiece but contains almost too much information. Although the series lacks the numbered paths in Valle Cannobina, it is useful for identifying small geographical and cultural features. The *Luino* sheet in the same series covers walks from Cannero. You can find them in the newsagent-bookshop at the southern end of Via Marconi, Cannobio. *Lago Maggiore, Lago di Varese, Lago di Lugano* (1:50,000), produced by Studio Cartografico Italiano, and priced at L15,000, is available locally. It covers the area between Varese in the south, and Luino and Lugano in the north, showing the route of the long distance paths E/1 (see the Long-Distance Walks chapter) and Via Verde Varesina (see Other Walks around Lago Maggiore later in this section). The accompanying booklet includes walks in Parco Naturale Campo dei Fiori near Varese and general information about Parco Naturale della Valle del Ticino at the southern end of the lake, and Parco Nazionale della Val Grande to the northwest.

The descriptive notes with the next three maps are in English, French, German and of course Italian. *Valle Cannobina, Itinerari Escursionistici* is a superbly produced folder of panorama maps of the valley showing marked walks, plus notes about historical and cultural features, and a town map of Cannobio. It is ideal for trip planning but not for navigation, and is available from the APT office (see the Information section earlier in

this chapter) for L3000. Note that the 1:25,000 map of footpaths referred to no longer exists.

Alto Verbano: Guide to Hiking Trails (1:25,000, 20m contours) is published by the Comunità Montana Alto Verbana, Ghiffa, and available free from the Pro Loco office in Cannero (see Information section earlier). Superimposed on the map are routes of 18 walks in the area between Cannero and Ghiffa and extending inland to Monte Zeda (2156m). *Lago Maggiore, Trekking per Tutti* is a booklet describing the opportunities for walks on the Piemonte side of the lake. It is available free from Stresa APT office (see Information Sources at the start of this chapter).

Richard Sale's book covering the entire Lakes District includes eight walks around Lago Maggiore (see Books near the start of this chapter).

What to Bring
Other than the usual walking boots and poles, no special equipment is needed for the walks in this section.

PLACES TO STAY & EAT
Of the several sites in and near Cannobio, *Camping Riviera* (☎/fax (0323) 71360), Via Darbedo, 28052 Cannobio (NO), has the best location, on the peninsula between the north side of Torrente Cannobino and the lakeshore. It is open from mid-March to mid-October. The shady, grassed pitches are L5000 each, plus L11,000 per adult. Bungalows for four people are available for L70,000 to L140,000 per day. Facilities are excellent; the *restaurant* has a German flavour, and the shop is pricey. Alternatively, there are a few one-star and several two and three-star hotels in town; single rooms start at about L45,000.

Many of the pizzerias and restaurants have clear views over the lake. Four *pizzerias* sit shoulder to shoulder in Piazza Indipendenza on the lakeside, and there are more elaborate restaurants nearby. The choice is more according to style than price. North from the piazza in Via Magistri, the establishments are more down to earth and prices lower.

Speedy Pizza does its speciality quite adequately, as well as pasta (especially with pesto), but the wine list is brief. You can eat and drink well here for about L32,000.

If you are shopping, remember that many shops are closed all or part of Monday. There is a good *supermarket* in Via al Lago at the northern end of town near a large car park. Camping Gaz is available from two shops in Via A Giavanola, near the collegiate church of San Vittore, where there are also some tempting *alimentari* (delicatessen/grocery stores). If the Friday morning market in Cannero is any guide, the Sunday morning market in Cannobio shouldn't be missed for bargains in fruit, vegetables and local cheese.

GETTING THERE & AWAY
Lago Maggiore western shore – Valle Cannobina
Bus ASPAN (☎ (0323) 55 66 33; fax 55 63 47), at Via Olanda 55, Verbania, and COMAZZI both provide a thrice-daily service between Domodossola train station and Verbania Intra, where you can connect with local buses and ferries.

Train Stresa is on the busy Milano (Stazione Centrale)-Domodossola-Bern (Switzerland) line.

Car The A8/26 skirts the southern end of the lake and the A8 towards Domodossola leads across its south-western fringe. Exit at Gravellona to the SS34 which follows the north-western shore; exit for Arona to also reach Stresa, on SS33.

Ferry From Arona it is possible to reach Stresa, Intra and the lakeside towns further north, changing at Stresa; the journey from Arona takes 2½ hours and costs L11,300. Contact Navigazione sul Lago Maggiore (☎ (0322) 46651/23 32 00; fax 24 95 30), or at 28041 Arona, Viale Baracca 1. Timetables are available at all lakeside ports.

Lago Maggiore eastern shore – Maccagno
Bus Attilio Baldioli (☎ (0332) 53 02 71; fax

51 08 07), or at 21016 Luino, Via Dante, 9, provides a twice daily service between Piazza Castello, Milano, Luino, Maccagno and Val Veddasca. The fare is L10,000 to Maccagno.

Train There is a reasonably frequent service between Milano Central and Luino, from where a local train more or less connects to the lakeside towns further north, including Maccagno.

Car From the A8, take the Sesto Vergiate exit to SS394 which leads to Laveno and the eastern shore. From the A2 Milano-Lugano, exit near Lugano in Switzerland to the Locarno road and turn off to Lago Maggiore at the head of the lake.

Valle Cannobina

Duration 7½ to 8 hours
Ascent 1230m
Standard Hard
Start Cannobio (or Traffiume)
Finish Cavaglio
Closest Towns Varese, Novara
Permits Required No
Public Transport Access Yes
Summary Follow an ancient network of paths in Valle Cannobina through magnificent woodlands and around precipitous gorges. Enjoy fine views of valley, gorge and lake.

The paths in Valle Cannobina are generally well marked, with red and white (low-level) or red and yellow (high-level) markers, and signposts. A medium walk to either Spoccia or Orasso, further upstream, is possible by making use of the local bus service to return to Cannobio (see Getting To/From the Walk following). It would be worth considering doing the walk in reverse, to free yourself from the tyranny of the bus timetable – there's only a late afternoon bus back to Cannobio. If you are driving, cars can be parked in Traffiume (saving about 30 minutes walk from Cannobio), or in Cavaglio.

GETTING TO/FROM THE WALK

The western shore of Lago Maggiore is well served by bus. The Verbania-Brissago ASPAN line passes through Cannero and Cannobio; there are several buses daily, and the fare from Verbania to Cannobio is L2700. There is also a daily bus each way on the Pallanza-Verbania-Locarno run.

Ferry Cannobio is linked to Cannero and towns on the eastern side of the lake by ferry (see Getting There & Away at the beginning of this chapter).

THE WALK

Start from the bridge over Torrente Cannobino by going down some steps on the south-western side to Via Sotti di Chiosi and follow it to Via Ponte Ballerino, then cross the river on a footbridge. Keep left at junctions to reach Traffiume and the start of the marked route at the intersection of Via Torri and Via Sant' Anna (where there is a car park; see the Cannobio town map in the *Valle Cannobina: Itinerari Escursionistici* map, or the *Luino* 1:25,000 sheet – Maps & Books section). There is also a shrine and signposts to several destinations here. The best view of the spectacular Santa Anna gorge nearby is to be seen by following the road downhill from the shrine to a bridge near a former church. From the shrine, the wide path leads up and soon settles down to contour above the depths of the Torrente Cannobino. Past the typical stone buildings of Al Campo, the path dips to cross Rio di Cavaglio. Regaining height, the path meets a road; follow this into Cavaglio where there is a *tabacchi* (tobacconist) near the war memorial.

Continue ahead, as indicated by signposts, along a narrow lane and fork right towards Gurrone, which you reach after about half an hour up the quiet road. In this small compact village of old stone houses, bear left (almost opposite the church) towards **Spoccia**; shortly, go left again and right at the next junction into woodland. The narrow,

superbly built path, with some fine stone bridges, winds around the valley of Rio Ponte Secco. Then, cross a road and continue up to a junction by a shrine and climb some steps to Spoccia's war memorial. Turn to the right here towards Bronte. Climb more steps

Wayside Shrines

Throughout the mountains, in villages and at roadsides, wayside shrines testify to the importance of religious belief in people's lives. Some are simple – just a crucifix on a stone base; some are elaborate – extending to structures the size of a small room, with altar and cloth, frescoes, statues, flowers and candles.

There are contradictions: neglected shrines used as rubbish bins, spent candles strewn on the ground nearby. Nevertheless, they are a distinctive and fascinating aspect of walking in Italy.

Near the old settlement of Bronte, high above Valle Cannobina, is a particularly intriguing shrine. It has a timber roof and spans the path. Beneath the roof, a weatherbeaten old wooden crucifix is fixed to one wall. A sign explains that this cross was once carried in processions conducted in the area between the Monday and Wednesday before Pentecost. On the Tuesday, the route followed was from the church in Niv, high in the valley of Rio di Orasso – a tributary of Torrente Cannobina, and a few km to the west. The procession then continued along the path towards La Piazza (east of Olzeno), to two other localities (not shown on any of the available maps), and back to the shrine, after which celebrations began.

Sandra Bardwell

SANDRA BARDWELL

between houses to the next junction where you go to the right, now following red and yellow markers, along a narrow lane which becomes a cobbled path.

Beyond a stream crossing, you will pass a substantial shrine and continue along a well-graded path to the settlement of Bronte, where there are magnificent views of upper Valle Cannobino. Bear left across the hillside just above some trees; from a pair of stone buildings a narrow grassy path leads towards a wooden stake with the red and yellow marker, then up to stone buildings on the edge of woodland. Climb steadily for about

half an hour to a wide track at Tre Confini; continue southwards and soon Monte Faierone and the ridge leading up to Monte Limidario (2187m) on the Swiss border, come into view to the north-east. Soon you reach the first of the stone houses (several with modern roofing, strung out along the track, that constitute **Le Biuse**. On one wall and in a small chapel are memorials to two young men who died in 1945 fighting the Fascists.

Continue along the track then follow another, rougher track down to the tight cluster of buildings that is Olzeno. Nearly all have been beautifully restored, and most

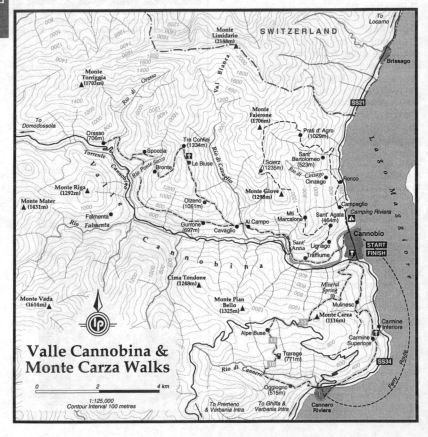

Valle Cannobina & Monte Carza Walks

0   2   4 km

1:125,000
Contour Interval 100 metres

sport solar heating panels. Despite the neatly cut grass and colourful flower tubs, the village was completely deserted on a sunny afternoon in mid-June. A sign points the way between the houses, past a flying fox (aerial cableway), then the path descends through grassland, with fine views of the lake and the mountains to the east. Then, cross a vehicle track and continue to a junction; go left towards **Cavaglio**. In the village, markers guide you between the houses and down to the road; turn left for Traffiume. Return by the same route as for the outward journey, or by bus to Cannobio.

Alternative Route It should take no more than 2½ hours (with 100m ascent) from Spoccia to Orasso. In Spoccia, turn left at the junction mentioned earlier, by a shrine, and follow the marked path to Orasso.

Monte Carza

Duration 7½ to 8 hours	
Ascent 1015m	
Standard Hard	
Start & Finish Cannobio	
Closest Towns Varese, Novara	
Permits Required No	
Public Transport Access Yes	
Summary A walk full of variety: age-old villages, lake and mountain views.	

The majority of this walk is along paths, plus a few short sections on quiet roads. It could be modified by taking the afternoon bus from Cannobio or Cannero to Trarego, saving about 1½ hours and 500m ascent. Carry water, whichever you do; there are bars and cafes in Cannobio, and an inn at Trarego. The walk to Cannero alone would make an easy half-day outing, or could be spread over a whole day, by lingering there and returning to Cannobio or foot, by bus or ferry (see Getting To/From the Walk in the preceding section).

THE WALK
At the southern end of Cannobio, turn right from the main road along Strada Provinciale della Valle Cannobina for about 50m to Via Cuserina where a clutch of signposts includes some for the route to Cannero. Shortly, keep left at a parting of the ways, on a cobbled woodland path. After about half an hour, turn right up a road for about 250m, with fine lake and hill views, then bear left onto a cobbled path.

Mulinesc, a deserted village surrounded by magnificent chestnut woodland, is the highest point (454m) reached on the way to Cannero. It isn't shown as such on any of the maps, but is probably 'Mulineggi' on the *Alto Verbano: Guide to Hiking Trails* map (see Maps & Books section earlier). Five minutes further on, bear left at a junction and continue to Carmine Superiore, a tranquil old village, centered on the large church of San Gottardo (just left of the path) from which there is a fine view of the northern reaches of the lake. The marked route then passes through woodland to the main road east of Cannero; cross diagonally and descend steps to a lane and on to the lakeside.

The walk to Trarego and Monte Carza starts on the main road, just west of the bridge over Rio di Cannero. There is a bus stop, with a car park opposite, a little further along the road from Cannero. Following signs to route Nos 10 and 15, walk up a cobbled lane then a wide stepped path, keeping on route No 10. After about half an hour, in the village of Oggiogno, bear right, still on route No 10, towards Trarego (the other signs temptingly displaying the wealth of walks in this area). Pass a low stone building with a sign 'Torchio Secolare dei Terrieri' – a centuries-old wine press, restored in 1963, among an amazing collection of timber implements.

Continue down through shady chestnuts to a substantial stone bridge over Rio di Cannero, far below in a small gorge. The path leads on through intensively terraced hillsides, dotted with deserted buildings, up to Trarego with its colourful houses sitting on a ledge on the steep mountain slope.

LAKE DISTRICT

Carmine Superiore – a Pilgrims' Village

Carmine Superiore, overlooking Lago Maggiore from an unrivalled perch between Cannobio and Cannero, is typical of the old villages around the lake (and the other lakes as well). Solidly built houses, separated by very narrow passage ways, cluster intimately around a large church; some of the houses are empty and decaying, but many more have been restored in the traditional style. This renaissance has helped to reverse what seemed to be the terminal decline of the village after many of its people left during the interwar years. Superiore, incidentally, is not an elitist term, but is used to distinguish the two Carmines: Inferiore on the lakeshore and Superiore about 300m above.

Carmine, and its church of San Gottardo stand on a site first occupied more than 1000 years ago by the fortified house of a prominent Cannobio family. Construction of the church began in 1330 and was completed a century or more later. The church formed the nucleus of the village and was a haven for the inhabitants in times of strife. Frescoes, the work of Lombard artisans and dating from the late 14th century, still adorn the outside and the interior of the church. They are now very faded, but the faint colours of the images on the cream walls still convey much of their beauty and artistry. The forecourt (the best place for views of the lake), was actually the village cemetery until 1875.

The Visconti family dedicated the church to San Gottardo, the patron saint of sufferers from gout/paralysis, and ever since it has been a place of pilgrimage from people in poor health seeking comfort and blessing.

Sandra Bardwell

Finding route No 14 – the continuation of the walk – is a challenge in the maze of narrow lanes. You shouldn't go astray by walking left up Via Dell' Unione, then right, first left, and left again at a T-junction. Follow Via Principale uphill and turn right along Via Passo Piazza (ignoring signs for the western leg of route No 14).

Just before *Albergo La Perla* (or after you emerge from the bar), go left along Via Strada Cavalli and very soon right. Pass between some stone houses to a rough track and bear right along a narrow path, which soon meets a stream. Cross it a little further on and continue to Alpe Buse in a clearing. Again, go between the buildings and, keeping to a stone wall on the right, follow a narrow path uphill through scattered trees to a road, where there is a prominent route No 14 sign pointing uphill. However, it is easier to approach Monte Carza by walking along the road for about 10 minutes until you meet route No 13, on either hand. Climb up to the ridge and go along the crest to the open, grassy summit of **Monte Carza** (1116m). The superb panorama makes the tricky route worthwhile: Valle Cannobina and some Alpine peaks to the west, and nearly all Lago Maggiore and its mountains. Return to the saddle just west of the top

and follow red and yellow markers down through partly cleared woodland, over a stile and to signs pointing to Cannobio. Further on, keep right below a large house and stables. The mineral spring, indicated at the next signposted junction, isn't enticing. The descent to Cannobio is direct, though the markers can be obscure. Rejoin the morning's outward route near Strada Provinciale.

Other Walks around Lago Maggiore

CANNOBIO

Rising sharply above Cannobio, **Monte Faierone** (1706m) affords excellent views of the lake, Valle Cannobino and the mountains beyond. It entails a full, fairly strenuous day: allow at least eight hours for the ascent; the bus from Cannobio to Sant' Agata would save about an hour. From Lignago on the Traffiume road, a marked path leads up to Sant' Agata, from where the route onwards is well signed, to the small church of Sant' Luca, then past the terraces and vines of Monti Marcalone. Markers lead up, into conifer then birch forest, and around the eastern and northern slopes of Monte Giove (1298m) to a saddle. The peak can be climbed from here – the view is superb.

Continue to the strangely lifeless but not entirely ruinous hamlet of Scierz, accessible only on foot. Follow markers up to the undulating open ridge and Monte Faierone's commanding summit. The descent eastwards is, at first, extremely steep, on a narrow, well marked (but not well used) path, through birch and alpenrose, past Prati d'Agro and, following the signposts, to Sant' Bartolomeo and on through Ronco to Campeglio. From there you go left down a path, near a two-storey house with two birches in front, and finally down to the Traffiume road not too far from Cannobio.

MACCAGNO

The main walking area on the eastern side of Lago Maggiore is around Val Veddasca, inland from the small town of Maccagno. The Pro Loco office (☎ (0332) 56 12 00) can provide a guide to local accommodation, advice about local walks and a bus timetable. The IAT office (☎ (0332) 53 00 19) in Luino, a few kilometres to the south, issues a free beautiful panorama map *Carta dei Sentieri e Delle Escursioni* covering a sizeable area to the north-east of the lake, including some Swiss territory, and showing routes of more than 25 walks. *Lago Maggiore, Lago di Varese*, Kompass map No 90 (see Maps & Books earlier in this chapter) covers the area.

Camping Lido (☎/fax (0332) 56 02 50) is likely to be the less crowded and quieter of the two camp sites; it is certainly the cheaper one. A pitch costs around L13,000, plus L8000 per adult. *La Guabella* (☎ (0332) 56 03 27), about a seven-minute walk north along the shore from Camping Lido, makes better than average al forno lega pizzas from L7000 to L14,000; for fish, the house speciality, expect to fork out up to L18,000.

Buses link Luino, Maccagno and all the villages in Val Veddasca, although infrequently. There is a ferry and hydrofoil service between Cannobio, Maccagno and Luino.

Lago d'Elio is a popular destination from Maccagno. Allow about three hours return;

the ascent is 730m. The route starts almost opposite the bus and train station, and is well marked as it climbs steeply, mainly through forest, to Musignano (also accessible by bus from Maccagno). There is a bar here. From there, a shortish path leads to the road near the defunct *Albergo Monte Borga*; the artificial lake is a few hundred metres further on. You can continue from its northern end up to Passo Forcolo (the one-way walk takes one hour, with 250m ascent) on a good path, to a bar and restaurant, open daily, and also accessible by car. *Rifugio Passo Forcora* (☎ (0332) 55 81 32) nearby could serve as a base for exploring Val Veddasca and the surrounding mountains.

The **Via Verde Varesina** is a long distance route from Porto Ceresio (on Lago di Lugano, north-east of Varese) to Maccagno, via Campo dei Fiori, Vararo (north-east of Loveno), Luino and Val Veddasca. It follows paths and rural roads through the foothills of the ranges rising above Lago Maggiore; accommodation is in rifugi and small inns. Known as the '3V' route, it is shown on Kompass map No 90 and outlined in the accompanying booklet, and is also featured on the *Lago Maggiore, Lago di Varese, Lago di Lugano* map from Studio Cartografico Italiano (see Maps & Books earlier). The route is well marked around Maccagno.

The Maccagno Pro Loco office issues a simple map showing details of the route of a pleasant half-day round walk (430m ascent) to the small town of Agra, on the southern side of Val Veddasca.

STRESA

Il Mottarone (1491m) is a prominent peak above Stresa, on the south-western shore of the lake. While the summit views are very fine, encompassing Monte Rosa in the Alps to the west, its attraction as a destination for walkers is compromised by the presence of a road and funicular to the top. However, there is a marked path from the village of Levo, 5km west of Stresa, through woodlands to the summit; allow a whole day for this pleasant walk. The Stresa Pro Loco office (☎ (0323) 31308), near the corner of

LAKE DISTRICT

Via Roma and Via di Amicis, provides an accommodation list and a leaflet describing the walk. *Omegna-Varallo, Lago d'Orta* (1:50,000, 100m contours, map No 97, Kompass series) covers the area. This walk is also described in Richard Sale's book *The Italian Lakes: 30 Circular Walks from Regional Centres* (see Books near the beginning of this chapter).

PARCO NATURALE CAMPO DEI FIORI

Several walks in this reserve, north-west of Varese, are outlined in the booklet with the Studio Cartografico map of Lago Maggiore (see Maps & Books earlier); Richard Sale's book (see Books near the start of this chapter) includes a walk to this area. It is worth noting that the summit plateau (1227m) is accessible by road.

This Way

Dolomiti

Rich in ancient culture and tradition, the mountains and valleys of the Dolomiti (Dolomites) are largely protected as regional parks and are crisscrossed by a vast network of well-marked trails.

Tourism is one of the principal resources of the region and there are excellent accommodation, restaurant and public transport facilities in the valleys. A network of high-altitude *rifugi* (refuges) offer food, lodging and assistance to walkers from around mid-June to the end of September, and sometimes until as late as the beginning of October (depending on the weather).

The northern section of the Dolomiti is largely part of the bilingual German/Italian-speaking region of Alto Adige-Südtirol (South Tyrol). Geographically, it forms an 80km-long rocky strip that extends east-west between Val d'Isarco (north-east of Bolzano) and Val di Sesto (south-east of Candido) and is defined to the north by Val Pusteria. The entire geological area of the Dolomiti extends well to the south into the regions of Trentino and Veneto. It contains spectacular mountains, such as the Tofane, Marmolada, Civetta, Pale di San Martino and the Brenta group, which all reach heights of more than 3000m and are separated by numerous valleys that are mostly oriented north/south.

The main walk described in this chapter is a panoramic, six-day, high-altitude excursion across the northern Dolomiti, which can be divided up into a number of shorter sections. While it is only one of an incredible number of possibilities, it does provides an excellent introduction to these spectacular mountains. This chapter also outlines a number of shorter walks and one-day loops.

Many places in the Dolomiti, particularly in the Fanes area and around Val Gardena and Val Badia, are referred to in the Ladin language (see 'The Ladin Tradition' boxed text later in this chapter) as well as Italian and German. Some maps use all three, some use two, others only use one. In this chapter,

HIGHLIGHTS

STEFANO CAVEDONI

- Spectacular views of 3000m-high mountains on the Northern Dolomiti trek
- Watching the magnificent silhouette of the Marmolada, with its imposing glacier, materialise before your eyes at sunrise
- Descending into the natural karstic amphitheatre of Alpe di Fanes, unmatched in the Dolomiti for its magical atmosphere
- A cup of delicious hot chocolate served with fresh cream at the Malga Ra Stua

where appropiate, we have used the Ladin spelling for place names on the maps.

HISTORY

That the Alpine valleys were frequented by humans in prehistoric times, even at high altitudes, has been well-documented by archaeological finds dating back to the 8th millennium BC (the Mesolithic period). It seems that these first explorers and hunters followed their prey up to high altitudes in the warmer seasons.

The skeleton of the so-called Mondeval man (7000 BC) was found reclining alongside ritual funeral objects in a grave under dolomitic rock at 2100m near the Mondeval Malga di Sopra in the area of Cortina. In September 1991, the body of 'Otzi' (as he is known to scholars) was discovered in Val Senales, north-east of Merano (Meran), just outside the territory of the Dolomiti. Yielded up by the Similaun glacier, the body was perfectly preserved along with his clothes and tools – a waterproof cloak made of woven grass, a leather belt, shoes sewn together with grass fibres, an ingenious rudimentary rucksack, arrows and a copper hatchet. Otzi was probably a hunter or merchant who lived around 5300 BC (the Neolithic period) and died trying to cross over the ridge.

By the time this region was absorbed into the ancient Roman Empire it already had developed a long history of intense intercultural and commercial exchange. Then, as today, this area was a slice of Italy where the cultural diversity of the different minorities that inhabited it created an unusual backdrop. The Ladin ethnic group, which developed over the centuries in the Badia, Gardena and Fassa valleys, and in the Ampezzo basin, are descendants of the Celts. Romanised under the Emperors Augustus and Claudius in the first decades after Christ, they still maintain their own romance language as well as a social system founded on the model of the *viles* – clusters of family houses where several agricultural activities were carried out in common.

In the northernmost valleys, the original Südtirol populations, Germanic in language and culture, preserve to this day the system of *maso chiuso* – single-family farms and land that, each generation, are passed down to the first-born son. These territories, which today make up the region of Alto Adige-Südtirol, were administered in the Middle Ages by Germanic bishops or feudal lords. They were subsequently made part of the Kingdom of Bavaria and finally of the Austro-Hungarian Empire of the Hapsburgs. In 1919, with the defeat of the Hapsburgs at the end of WWI, Südtirol was annexed by Italy. The population, after suffering a forced attempt at integration under

Mussolini, today enjoys an autonomous government status; however, there are still some who would prefer a greater degree of independence from central control.

At the beginning of the 19th century, the Dolomiti figured as one of the principal sites in the first explorations and early triumphs in Alpine mountaineering. They were considered to be 'the most beautiful mountains in the world' by the first English and Austrian gentlemen who set out to 'discover' and 'conquer' them. The explorations of these early mountaineers laid the foundations of the region's current tourism, which has been

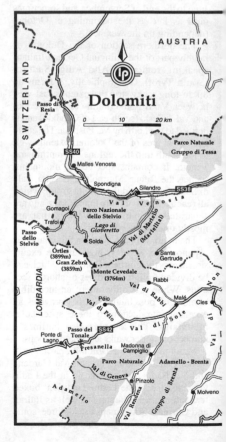

comfortably absorbed into the simple mountain economies without compromising them.

NATURAL HISTORY

To the explorers of the 19th century, influenced by a romantic and heroic vision, these mountains were especially atmospheric. The bizarre vertical shapes – steeples, pinnacles and towers of white rock – standing out among brilliant green forests and grassy slopes dotted here and there with cows and tidy farms captured their imaginations. The landscape of today is no different. The meadows are still gentle and hospitable, flora

and fauna are rich and varied, and the mountains are just as impressive.

Geology

The Dolomiti owe their name to the French geologist, Deodat de Dolomieu, who first described their composition in 1788. De Dolomieu found that the Dolomiti are largely made up of extensive stratifications of calcium and magnesium rock – all that remains of millions of sponges and coral.

Flora & Fauna

One of the most obvious qualities of the

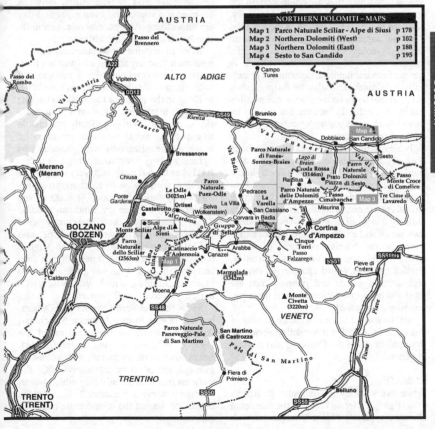

NORTHERN DOLOMITI – MAPS	
Map 1 Parco Naturale Sciliar - Alpe di Siusi	p 178
Map 2 Northern Dolomiti (West)	p 182
Map 3 Northern Dolomiti (East)	p 188
Map 4 Sesto to San Candido	p 195

Coral Reefs at 3000m

The Dolomiti are incredibly rich in marine fossils and owe much of their charm to the fact that they were born out of an ancient tropical sea that existed some 250 million years ago. The bed of this sea, known as the Tethys to scholars, consisted of layers of organic sediments, in some areas 1000m thick, that accumulated over a period of 120 million years. At the start of the Tertiary period (70 million years ago), the pressure of the African plate on the European plate compressed and pushed up what remained of the coral reefs and sediment to form a magnificent mountain range. Today, the Dolomiti continue to be reshaped by atmospheric elements and the movement of glaciers (at the height of the last Ice Age the glaciers extended as low as 400m above sea level). ■

Dolomiti is their colour. The great vertical peaks are softened by the pale shades of the minerals of which they are composed. In the sunlight they go from whitish to blue-grey, and then turn rose and purple as the sun sets. This luminescence is elegantly paired with the lively colours of the flowers and the various shades of green in the valleys. A series of natural habitats, determined principally by altitude, can also be distinguished in horizontal strips on the slopes. Each valley has its own natural character determined by factors such as exposure, quantity of water and soil composition.

Typical Alpine carnivores like the bear, lynx, wolf and bearded vulture (known in Italy as the *gipeto*) have been extinct in the area since the beginning of this century. Projects are now underway to reintroduce these animals to their natural habitats, but it is very unlikely that you'll manage to spot one since they are all still extremely rare. Minor carnivores, hoofed herbivores (some of which have been reintroduced) rodents, mustelids, reptiles and many bird species inhabit the high-altitude woods and prairies. You are most likely to encounter them in the early morning or at sunset.

See the special section at the beginning of this book for detailed information about the flora and fauna of the Dolomiti and of Italy in general.

CLIMATE

While every valley in the Dolomiti has its own slightly different climate, the dominant climate is typically Alpine/Continental, with long, harsh winters and short, temperate summers. However, the range of different temperatures you can encounter between summer and winter and even night and day are astonishing. As a general rule, precipitation levels increase with altitude.

In the mountains the weather can truly be your enemy, so pay attention to weather forecasts before you set out, take clothing to deal with extreme weather conditions (see What to Bring in the Facts for the Walker chapter) and don't tempt fate. Even on a clear blue-sky summer's day it is perfectly reasonable to expect a violent localised storm to let loose in the afternoon with thunder and lightning – very dangerous at high altitudes. It is better to start your walk very early in the morning, with a view to reaching your destination by early afternoon. At 3000m even a brief flurry with an icy wind can become deadly, and more than one unprepared walker has died in the wake of a sudden and radical drop in temperature. Even in August, it is surprising how the temperature can drop and the wind pick up as you gradually climb higher and higher, which will cause problems if you aren't well prepared.

Snow falls between October and December and begins to melt between March and April; depending on the exposure of the slope it could last as long as July/August. January is the coldest month, with a constant average temperature of below 0°C; the warmest month is usually July which has an average temperature around 20°C. After the middle of August the temperature can drop suddenly.

INFORMATION

The Dolomiti are largely contained in the autonomous Italian Alpine region of Trentino-Alto Adige (Südtirol). This region is best thought of as two distinct areas, since the two autonomous provinces of Alto Adige (South Tyrol, known in German as Südtirol) and Trentino are culturally, linguistically and historically separate. Südtirol in the north was part of the Tyrol area of Austria until it was ceded to Italy in 1918. The people are mostly of German descent and favour the German language (68%) over Italian (28%). Ladin, an ancient Latin-based language, is also spoken in some areas (4%). The South Tyrol Autonomous Charter has special provisions regarding the speaking of the mother tongue, bilingualism and ethnic proportions in employment. All signs are bilingual. About 17% of the province of Alto Adige-Südtirol (a total area of 123,970 hectares) is protected in a national park, the Parco Nazionale dello Stelvio, and seven parchi naturali (nature parks).

Maps

Road maps for Alto Adige-Südtirol scaled at 1:200,000 and a wide range of walking maps scaled at 1:25,000, with marked trails, are available in bookshops and newsstands throughout the Dolomiti. The province of Bolzano (Bozen) offers its own, free provincial map, distributed by the Istituto Geografico De Agostini. All the nature parks and principal local mapping firms produce and distribute their own versions of maps scaled at 1:25,000, with marked trails.

Kompass, Multigraphic and Tabacco all publish a wide range of maps that cover the entire area of the Dolomiti. To cover the whole route of the Northern Dolomiti Trek that we suggest, the following Tabacco maps scaled at 1:25,000 are, in our opinion, the clearest: No 05 (Val Gardena), No 07 (Val Badia), No 03 (Cortina), No 010 (Val di Sesto). They cost L10,000 each. Tabacco also publishes a series scaled at 1:50,000 in which No 1 (Cadore-Cortina-Dolomiti di Sesto) and No 2 (Val di Fassa-Alta Badia-Val Gardena) cover the entire Northern Dolomiti

Trek and the other alternative routes, but these are older editions and some altitudes and names of peaks do not correspond with the newer editions.

Information Sources

All the routes proposed in this chapter pass through nature parks. Detailed information, brochures and pocket guides (some in English), regional maps scaled at 1:200,000 and maps of the parks scaled at 1:25,000 with marked trails, are available at the Ufficio Parchi Naturali (Provincial Parks Office; ☎ (0471) 99 43 00), Via Cesare Battisti 21, 39100 Bolzano. Some of these are also available at the Azienda Promozione Turistica for Alto Adige (APT) (☎ (0471) 99 38 08; fax 99 38 99), Piazza Parrocchia 11, 39100 Bolzano. This is open Monday to Friday from 9 am to noon and 3 to 5.30 pm (5 pm in winter). Here you can also pick up regional information about accommodation, activities and transport, as well as walking and trekking possibilities, including a free regional map scaled at 1:200,000. The office's Alpine information desk can help with planning treks and climbs.

Permits

No permits are required for excursions. A daily permit is required if you want to pick mushrooms. The permit limits the amount you can pick and you must pay for a new one (L5000) each day. Within the protected park territory it is prohibited to remove certain plant and animal species (eg flowers, seeds, trees, leaves, insects, butterflies, reptiles, amphibians, larvae, chrysalises, ants, nests and eggs of any species), as well as fossils and minerals. It is also forbidden to camp out with tents, trailers or the like (with the exception of an Alpine bivouac), to light fires, except in the case of emergency, to circulate with motor vehicles or leave rubbish of any kind.

Books

A large variety of books and guides, can be found in almost all the bookshops and better newsstands both in the cities and in the valley

DOLOMITI

towns. For more information see Books in the Facts for the Walker chapter.

Place Names

It is very likely that you might get confused while trying to follow signs and maps in the Dolomiti. As mentioned earlier, there are three languages spoken in the region: Italian, German and Ladin. In Alto Adige, all place names must by law be referred to in both Italian and German. This means that you'll find both the German and Italian names for geographical features on maps. In the areas where Ladin is spoken (in and around the Gardena, Badia and Fassa valleys), you might find that places and geographical features are also referred by the Ladin names. You will also come across lots of Ladin names while walking in the Fanes high plain. In this guide we have generally used both Italian and German place names, and only used the Ladin names when they are the ones in common use.

Guided Walks

Scuola Alpina Dolomiten walking (☎ (0471) 70 53 43; fax 70 73 89; email dolomit@cenida.it), Via Vogelweidergasse 6, 39040 Castelrotto, is a ski and climbing school which also runs a programme of organised treks and other activities. It is one of the most efficient and reliable organisations in the Alps. Its programme includes a seven-day trek in the Dolomiti and a trek around Monte Bianco, as well as winter activities. In every valley in the Dolomiti there is an organisation of local guides which arranges guided walks and climbs for both groups and individuals. Information about these groups is always available at local tourist offices.

Emergency

Throughout Italy, in an emergency, call ☎ 118 to be placed in contact with the national system of emergency services, including ambulance, hospitals and helicopter rescue services where available.

The Aiut Alpin Dolomites (☎ (0471) 79 71 71), is a helicopter rescue service operating throughout the Alps. Italy's finance police, the Guardia di Finanza, also operate a special Alpine helicopter rescue service. There is generally a service in every valley (Sesto ☎ (0474) 71 03 25; Cortina ☎ (0436) 2943). Otherwise, local guides groups offer volunteer rescue services – check with the local tourist office for information.

ACCOMMODATION & SUPPLIES

Bolzano is the provincial capital of Alto Adige-Südtirol. The town is well served by the main national railways and by the A22 (the Brennero autostrada) which leads to Brennero and northern Europe. Along the A22, 22km north of Bolzano, is Ponte Gardena, the beginning of the Dolomiti valley of Val Gardena (Grödnertal). (The Northern Dolomiti Trek described later in this chapter begins at Ortisei (St Ulrich) in Val Gardena). While you'll be able to find everything you need in the main towns of the Dolomiti valleys, Bolzano has a pleasant historic centre, efficient services and well-supplied shops for equipment, maps and technical foods (specially packaged food for hikers). There is also a baggage deposit, L5000 per bag per day, at the train station. There are also car parks near the station, but they charge a fee.

In Bolzano, *Moosbauer* camping ground (☎ (0471) 91 84 92), Via San Maurizio 83, is on the way out of town towards Merano. *Albergo Croce Bianca/Gasthof Weisses Kreuz* (☎ (0471) 97 75 52), Piazza del Grano 3, off Via dei Portici, charges up to L46,000 per person for B&B. *Albergo/Gasthof Figl* (☎ (0471) 97 84 12), Piazza del Grano 9, has good rooms for L67,500/L120,000 a single/double. *Hotel Feichter* (☎ (0471) 97 87 68), Via Grappoli 15, charges similar rates to the Albergo.

Out of town at Colle (Kohlern), accessible by road or the Funivia del Colle (*funivia* is Italian for cablecar) is *Klaushof* (☎ (0471) 97 12 94) which offers B&B for a more affordable L40,000 per person.

You can pick up supplies of fresh fruit, vegetables, bread and cheese etc from the open market held every morning from Monday to Saturday at the Piazza delle Erbe in Bolzano. In the same area there are numerous bakeries, pastry shops and cafes, as well as a small supermarket. While you can eat pizza and pasta if you wish, Bolzano's best restaurants specialise in Tyrolean food (see Food in the Facts for the Walker chapter for information on Tyrolean food). *Cavallino Bianco (Das Weiss Rossl)*, Via Bottai, is extremely popular and reasonably priced at around L30,000 for a full meal.

Sportler, Via Portici 37, is the best equipped of Bolzano's sports supplies shops. It specialises in technical gear for mountain walking and climbing, including a good range of clothing. The many shops in Bolzano that specialise in mountain clothing and equipment sometimes also have maps and food for trekkers, such as muesli bars, mineral salts etc, but these types of provisions are less expensive in supermarkets.

GETTING THERE & AWAY
Air
The nearest airports are in Verona (one hour) and in the Austrian town of Innsbruck (two hours); both are served by a shuttle bus from the Bolzano train station.

Bus
Bolzano is a major transport hub for Alto Adige. SAD buses leave from the bus terminal in Via Perathoner near Piazza Walther, for destinations throughout the province, including Val Gardena, Alpe di Siusi (Seiser Alm), Val Badia (Gadertal), Brunico and Val Pusteria. SAD buses also head for resort towns outside the province, such as Canazei and Cortina d'Ampezzo (more commonly known as Cortina) (for the latter you have to change at Dobbiaco). Timetables are available from the bus station or the APT office (see Information Sources in the Information section earlier in this chapter for the address and telephone number of the APT office). You can call toll free for bus information (in Italian and German) on ☎ (1678) 4 60 47.

Train
Regular trains connect Bolzano with Merano, Trento (Trent), Verona, Milano (Milan), Innsbruck (Austria) and Munich (Germany). You can also catch a train from Bolzano to Brunico and San Candido in Val Pusteria.

Car & Motorcycle
Bolzano is easily accessible from the north and south on the A22 autostrada.

Parco Naturale Sciliar & Alpe di Siusi

Duration 3-day loop
Standard Medium
Start/Finish Compaccio (Compatsch)
Closest Towns Siusi (Seis), Castelrotto (Kastelruth), Bolzano (Bozen)
Permits Required No
Public Transport Access Yes
Summary This is a three-day trek through the Alpe di Siusi, up to Monte Sciliar (Schlern) and across to the Catinaccio d'Antermoia (Kessel-Kgl) and the famous Torri del Vajolet (Vajoletturme) and Il Catinaccio (Rosengarten). The departure point for the walk is easily accessible by car or bus from the town of Siusi.

There's something magical about the view across the Alpe di Siusi to Monte Sciliar (2563m), where undulating green pastures end dramatically at the foot of towering peaks. The Alpe di Siusi (1700m-2200m), the largest plateau in Europe, forms part of what is known as the Altipiano dello Sciliar which, lower down at about 1000m, also incorporates the villages of Castelrotto and Siusi. This area holds something for walkers of all ages and expertise. The gentle slopes of the Alpe di Siusi are perfect for families with young kids, and you won't need much more than average stamina to make it to the Rifugio Bolzano (Schlernhaus) (2450m), just under Monte Pez, Monte Sciliar's summit. If you're after more challenging walks, then the jagged peaks of the Il Catinaccio group and the Sasso Lungo (Langkofel; 3181m) are nearby. These mountains are famous among

---

Legend of the Red Roses

Over the centuries many popular legends were set in the Catinaccio group. One of the most famous is the *Legend of the Roses*, which explains why the Rosengarten turns red at dusk, a common phenomenon in the Dolomiti. It tells the story of the dwarf King Laurens, whose kingdom is a virtual garden of red roses, the *Rosengarten*. Peace-loving and wealthy, Laurens wants for nothing but the hand in marriage of Similda, a beautiful princess from a neighbouring kingdom. His request refused, Laurens uses magic to kidnap the princess and holds her prisoner for seven years – until her brother discovers her whereabouts and sets off with his men to rescue her. In the ensuing battles, Laurens is eventually defeated and taken prisoner. Only after many years does he manage to escape and return to his kingdom in the mountains where, on his arrival, he sees the beautiful rose garden. Realising that the roses had led his enemies into his kingdom, Laurens casts a spell to turn the rose garden into stone: saying that the roses must not show themselves day or night. But Laurens forgot to include dusk in his spell, so every evening at sunset the enchanted garden becomes visible, casting a beautiful red glow over the Dolomiti. 'And when the Rosengarten disappears and the roses again turn to stone, clear and cold, men are gripped by an inexplicable sadness as they return to their smoky huts.' If you're lucky, perhaps you will meet some elves, fairies or witches during the walk – at the very least you will have no trouble imagining them!

Helen Gillman & Stefano Cavedoni

---

climbers worldwide and the views are spectacular – the gentle green slopes of the Alpe di Siusi and the Gothic pinnacles and rocky towers of the Il Catinaccio group give you the impression that you're looking at a fairytale castle. You must book in advance if you want to sleep at the small Rifugio Passo Santner under the summit of Il Catinaccio.

PLANNING
Tourist Offices

The area is popular in both summer and winter and its tourist offices are highly organised. All local offices will send out information, hotel lists and prices. There are three offices of the Associazione Turistica Sciliar: Castelrotto (☎ (0471) 70 63 33), Piazza Kraus 1; Siusi (☎ (0471) 70 70 24), Via Sciliar 8; and Compaccio in the Alpe di Suisi (☎ (0471) 72 79 04).

When to Walk

The walking season is from late June to late September. However, this area is extremely crowded in August, so July and September are the best times to walk here. No matter when you visit, the crowds start to thin out as soon as you get to higher altitudes. Using a good map and following the tourist office recommendations, you could spend days

taking leisurely walks in the Alpe di Siusi, stopping for picnics or planning your walks to ensure that you reach a *malga* (an Alpine hut where graziers make butter and cheese in summer) for a lunch break.

The climate in the Dolomiti can be unpredictable, with sunny mornings giving way to sudden, violent thunderstorms in the afternoon (see under Climate earlier in this chapter). The end of June to the end of September, when the rifugi are open, is the best time for low-risk walking, even at high altitudes. August is more stable than June weather-wise, but the rifugi are usually full, while September is more tranquil (fewer walkers), but the days begin to be shorter.

Maps

The Tabacco 1:25.000 No 05 *Val Gardena-Alpe di Siusi* is recommended for the area.

What to Bring

This walk will take you into an area of world-famous rock climbs. There are also some challenging *vie ferrate* (cord trails) along the way (which can be tackled as deviations to the main walk). If you plan to climb or go on a via ferrata, be sure that you carry the necessary equipment: helmet, ropes, harness etc.

Guided Walks

See Guided Walks under Information earlier in this chapter for details about Scuola Alpina Dolomiten. The Scuola d'Alpinismo Sciliar (☎ (0471) 70 62 85) at Siusi also organises walks in the area.

Medical & Emergency Services

In a medical emergency phone ☎ 118 or ☎ (0471) 70 65 55. The Guardia Medica Turistica (☎ (0471) 70 54 44) is based at Telfen, between Castelrotto and Siusi.

The Soccorso Alpino (Alpine Rescue) for Siusi-Sciliar (☎ (0471) 70 52 22) and for Val Gardena (☎ (0471) 79 72 22) should be contacted in the event of an emergency in the mountains. Aiut Alpin (☎ (0471) 79 71 71) is the emergency helicopter rescue service.

PLACES TO STAY & EAT

There are plenty of hotels and pensioni in all of the local towns, but bookings are recommended. If you're travelling with kids, ask the tourist office for information on hotels equipped for, or offering special deals for children. You can choose to stay in the villages (Castelrotto, Siusi etc) or up on the Alpe di Siusi. If you decide to stay in the Alpe di Siusi, there is a regular bus service. In summer, normal traffic is banned from the plateau (see the following Getting To/From the Walk section).

Try *Albergo Zallinger* (☎ (0471) 72 79 47), Saltria 74, at the foot of the Sasso Piatto (Plattkofel). Half board per person per day costs up to L68,000. In Castelrotto, *Garni Villa Rosa* (☎ (0471) 70 63 27), St Annaweg 3, offers B&B in double rooms for L33,000 to L50,000 per person. The rifugi on the trek are:

Bolzano	(☎ (0471) 61 20 24)
Alpe di Tires	(☎ (0471) 72 79 58)
Passo Principe	(☎ (0462) 64244)
Vajolet	(☎ (0471) 76 32 92)
Preuss	(no telephone)
Re Alberto	(no telephone)
Passo Santner	(☎ (0471) 64 22 30)
Antermoia	(☎ (0462) 60 22 72)
Molignon	(☎ (0471) 72 79 12)

Remember that is always better to book. The average price per person for an overnight stay plus breakfast is L18,000 to around L40,000.

GETTING TO/FROM THE WALK

The Altipiano dello Sciliar is accessible by SAD bus from Bolzano, Val Gardena and Bressanone (Brixen). By car, you can exit the A22 at Bolzano Nord or Chiusa.

From May to October the roads of the Alpe di Siusi are closed to normal traffic. Tourists who have a booking at a hotel in the zone and who are staying for five days or more, can obtain a special permit from the tourist office at Compaccio to drive between 6 pm and 9 am. It is best to organise your pass before arriving in the area; ask the hotel owner for assistance.

A regular bus service operates from Castelrotto and Siusi to Compaccio and from there on to the Alpe di Siusi. Tourists staying in hotels in the area will be given a special *Favorit* card which entitles them to free bus travel.

THE WALK
Day 1: Compaccio to Rifugio Bolzano
3 to 4 hours

From the big car park at Compaccio, take the trail to the south marked No 10 until it intersects with trail No 5 and then you head left (south-east) along trail No 5 for Malga Saltner (Saltnerhütte). You will be walking through the western part of the Alpe di Siusi, a vast and beautiful area of undulating green pastures, packed full of tourists in summer. Make sure you stop at the Saltnerhütte (1832m) for a drink before tackling the next part of the walk – the ascent to Monte Sciliar.

From the Saltnerhutte continue along trail No 5 (known as the Sentiero dei Turisti) which later becomes trail No 1. This snakes its way up to the Monte Sciliar high plain and the Rifugio Bolzano (2450m). The ascent is tiring, but by no means difficult, although you should watch out for falling rocks dislodged by chamois. There is a great view across the Alpe di Siusi to the Sasso Lungo, the Sella group (3152m) and Le Odle (3025m at Sass Rigais, the highest peak).

Once you arrive at Rifugio Bolzano, if you

have the energy, climb the nearby Monte Pez (2563m). From its summit you have a 360° view: to the north you can see the Alps stretching into Austria; to the north-east you see Le Odle, Puez (2913m), and Sassongher (2665m); to the east is the Sella group, Sasso Lungo and Sasso Piatto (2964m); south-east you can see the Il Catinaccio group, where you'll be heading tomorrow.

Day 2: Rifugio Bolzano to Rifugio Passo Santner
5 to 6 hours

This part of the walk will take you to the Rifugio Passo Santner under the summit of Il Catinaccio. Starting from Rifugio Bolzano, head back along trail No 1 (towards the Alpe di Siusi), then turn right (south-east) onto trail No 3-4. This crosses the Monte Sciliar high plain towards the Il Catinaccio group and you will pass the Cima di Terrarossa and the spectacular, jagged peaks of the Denti di Terrarossa. Make sure you stick to trail No 3-4 – don't take No 3 – until you reach the Rifugio Alpe di Tires (2440m). From the rifugio head south along trail No 3a-554, ascend to the Passo Alpe di Tires and continue for the nearby Passo Molignon (2598m).

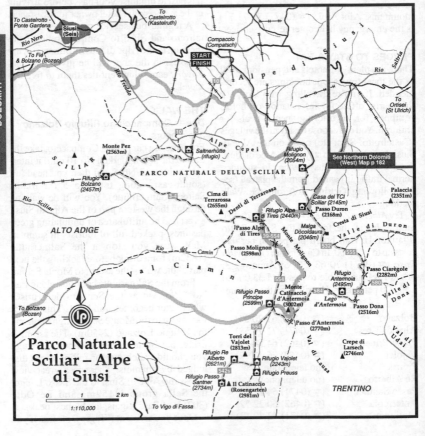

From Passo Molignon you start the very steep descent down a *ghiaione* (scree slope) into the lunar landscape of a *canalone*, a typical Alpine rocky valley. Before reaching the valley floor, the trail forks. Keep to the left and stay on trail No 554, which will take you up to Rifugio Passo Principe (2599m), under Monte Catinaccio d'Antermoia (3002m). You can take a break at this tiny rifugio. From here, descend into the valley along the comfortable trail No 584. You'll arrive at the Vajolet and Preuss rifugi (both at 2243m), from where you take trail No 542s up to the Rifugio Re Alberto (2621m).

This part of the walk between Vajolet and Re Alberto is better described as a climb, and inexperienced mountaineers will find it quite challenging. There are plans to install an iron cord for safety reasons, which would significantly reduce the excitement of the ascent for many. Once at the top you will be in a wide valley with the Torri del Vajolet, famous among climbers, to your right and the peak of Il Catinaccio to your left. Follow trail No 542s up to Rifugio Passo Santner (2734m), one of the most spectacularly located rifugi in the Alps. It is perched on a precipice under Il Catinaccio and on the edge of an almost sheer drop down into the Val di Tires. The rifugio itself is tiny, with only two rooms, each containing four beds. Climbers flock here in summer to tackle the Torri del Vajolet and Il Catinaccio.

Trail No 542s becomes a steep via ferrata where it descends to the south-west from the rifugio. If you intend to tackle either the ferrata or a climb, make sure you are properly equipped.

Day 3: Rifugio Passo Santner to Compaccio
6 to 7 hours
Return down trail No 542s to Rifugio Vajolet and then return up to Passo Principe along trail No 584. However, instead of continuing for Passo Molignon along trail No 554, remain on trail No 584, which veers to the right (east) to reach Passo d'Antermoia (2770m) and then descends to Lago d'Antermoia (2495m). Shortly afterwards you will reach Rifugio Antermoia. Here the trail becomes No 580, which heads east to Passo Dona (2516m) and then descends towards Alpe di Siusi.

After a relatively short distance trail No 580 veers to the right (east), but you continue straight ahead. At the next fork, take trail No 555, which will take you in a north-westerly direction along the northern slopes of the Molignon group. At the base of the Molignon, the trail joins a dirt road (trail No 532) near the group of herders' shelters known as Malga Dòcoldaura (2046m). Follow No 532 to the Casa del TCI Sciliar, then go straight head along trail No 7, which will take you all the way down to Compaccio. (At Rifugio Molignon, the trail becomes a small road and some distance ahead it becomes trail No 7-12.)

Northern Dolomiti

Distance About 70km
Duration 5 or 6 days
Standard Easy-Medium
Start Ortisei in Val Gardena
Finish Sesto in Val di Sesto
Closest Towns Bolzano, Cortina, Dobbiaco
Permits Required No
Public Transport Access Yes
Summary High-altitude route (approximately 2000m) on marked trails, walking from rifugio to rifugio (you'll need to book ahead). Daily elevation changes from 400m up to 1000m per each five to eight-hour leg. Has unforgettable views and magnificent Alpine environment rich in fauna and flora.

This beautiful route runs at high altitude along the northernmost borders of the Dolomiti system, and offers extraordinary views over spectacular 3000m-high mountains such as the Sella, Marmolada, Le Tofane and the Tre Cime di Lavaredo. The highest points have magnificent views of deep valleys and imposing mountain ranges. The trek crosses through territory protected by a series of natural parks – Puez-Odle,

DOLOMITI

Fanes-Sennes-Braies, Dolomiti d'Ampezzo and Dolomiti di Sesto – which are regulated by strict rules and are very well organised.

The trails are well marked and easy to follow. The numerous, comfortable rifugi offer good cooking and comfortable beds. This route reduces the problem of ascending and descending to a minimum, but where it must cross over the valley floor on two occasions, it requires an elevation change of 1000m. The environment ranges from elegant fir woods containing a variety of birds to the haunting rocky architecture of the higher elevations, inhabited by acrobatic herbivores. You'll need strong legs and a willingness to walk for a minimum of five to six hours to a maximum of eight to nine hours a day.

In some places the trek is presented in two versions – Days A and B – in order to offer different grades of difficulty and walking times. In addition, we have listed all the possible entrances and exits from the valleys that are crossed in the course of the trek, along with a brief profile of the valleys and of other possible routes.

The enchanting Alpine valley of Val Gardena is hemmed in by the towering peaks of the Parco Naturale Puez-Odle, the imposing Sella group and the Sasso Lungo, and the gentle slopes and pastures of the Alpe di Siusi, the largest high plain in the Alps. While Val Gardena is the starting point of our Northern Dolomiti walk, it also contains many pleasant one-day walks.

The valley's main towns, Ortisei (St Ulrich), Santa Cristina (St Christina) and Selva (Wolkenstein), all offer abundant accommodation. Along with Val Badia, Val Gardena is an enclave that has managed to preserve the ancient Ladin language and culture, and a rich tradition in colourful legends (see the boxed text 'The Ladin Tradition' on this page). The ancient tradition of woodcarving has also been maintained and the valley's artisans are famed for their statues, figurines, altars and toys. Beware of mass-produced imitations!

PLANNING
When to Walk

As mentioned earlier in this chapter, the walking season in the Dolomiti is from the end of June to the end of September, when the rifugi are open. On a long walk like this, it is impossible to be sure of good weather for the entire time, since the climate in the mountains is so unpredictable. However, generally speaking, the weather is more stable in August – the month in which the

---

The Ladin Tradition

The Ladin language and culture trace their ancestry to around 15 BC, when the people of the Central Alps were forcibly united into the Roman province of Rhaetia. The Romans, of course, introduced Latin to the province, but the original inhabitants of the area, with their diverse linguistic and cultural backgrounds, modified the language to such an extent that, by around 450 AD, it had evolved into an independent Romance language, known as Raeto-Romanic. At one point the entire Tyrol was Ladin, but today the language and culture are confined mainly to the Val Gardena and the Val Badia, where about 90% of the locals declared in the 1981 census that they belonged to the Ladin language group. Along with German and Italian, Ladin is taught in schools and the survival of the Ladin cultural and linguistic identity is protected by law.

The Ladin culture is rich in vibrant poetry and legends, set amid the jagged peaks of the Dolomiti and peopled by fairies, gnomes, elves, giants, princesses and heroes. Passed on by word of mouth for centuries and often heavily influenced by Germanic myths, many of these legends were in danger of being lost. In the first decade of this century, journalist Carlo Felice Wolff, who had lived most of his life at Bolzano, undertook a major project: he spent 10 years gathering and researching the local legends, listening as the old folk, farmers and shepherds recounted the legends and fairytales. The originality of the legends he eventually published is that, instead of simply writing down what he was told, Wolff reconstructed the tales from the many different versions and recollections he gathered.

Helen Gillman & Stefano Cavedoni

mountains are jam-packed with walkers. If you plan to set out very early each day, you might manage to avoid frequent afternoon thunderstorms which batter the Dolomiti in summer. We have walked in these mountains at various times during the walking season: sometimes the weather has been good, other times it has rained incessantly – you just have to be lucky!

Information Sources
There are tourist offices in each of the towns: Ortisei (☎ (0471) 79 63 28), Santa Cristina (☎ (0471) 79 30 46) and Selva (☎ (0471) 79 51 22). All have extensive information on accommodation and walking trails. An English-language guidebook is available for each town, along with information on guided treks and rock-climbing schools.

Maps
Make sure you carry good maps – the Tabacco 1:25,000 Nos 05, 07, 03 and 010 are recommended. Tabacco also produces maps at a 1:50,000 scale – Nos 1 and 2 cover the entire trek, but they are outdated editions and contain some wrong information.

What to Bring
You don't need any special equipment unless you choose Route B on Day 2 of the trek, which involves climbing a via ferrata up Sasso della Croce to the Alpe di Fanes. The trail is not difficult, but it is advisable to have the correct equipment (cords, harness and helmet).

On a long walk it is essential that you think carefully about what to carry in your pack. Ensure that you have clothing for extreme weather conditions, such as a pile jacket, a wind jacket, a pile hat and gloves, as well as good quality, worn-in trekking boots and emergency gear (torch, bivouac bag etc). See the list of essential items that are recommended under What to Bring in the Planning section in the Facts for the Walker chapter for a detailed guide to what you'll need on this trek. You'll be able to get water and food at each of the rifugi, but ensure that you carry at least 1L per person during the day.

Emergency
Soccorso Alpino (Alpine Rescue) is efficient (☎ (0471) 79 72 22 or 79 71 71). Notify your hotels or rifugi of your planned routes.

ACCOMMODATION & SUPPLIES
Rifugi
It's a good idea to book all the rifugi in your planned itinerary in advance. This is especially important in August and on weekends, as they are often fully booked. The rifugi are as follows:

Puez	(☎ (0471) 79 53 65)
Gardenaccia	(☎ (0471) 84 92 82)
Ospizio La Crusc Sasso della Croce	
	(☎ (0471) 83 96 32)
Fanes	(☎ (0474) 50 10 97)
Lavarela	(☎ (0474) 50 10 79)
Pederù	(☎ (0474) 50 10 86)
Fodara Vedla	(☎ (0474) 50 10 93)
Sennes	(☎ (0474) 50 10 92)
Biella	(☎ (0436) 86 69 91)
Pratopiazza	(☎ (0474) 74 86 50)
Hotel Croda Rossa	(☎ (0474) 55 58 08) or
	(☎ (0474) 74 86 06)
Vallandro	(☎ (0474) 97 25 05)
Hotel Tre Cime di Lavaredo	
	(☎ (0474) 97 26 33)
Locatelli	(☎ (0474) 97 20 02) or
	(☎ (0474) 71 03 47)
Fondo Valle	(☎ (0474) 71 06 06)

For the one-day loop from Val Fiscalina: Rifugio Comici (☎ (0474) 71 03 58) and Rifugio Pian di Cengia (☎ (0337) 45 15 17).

GETTING TO/FROM THE WALK
Daily SAD bus services from Bolzano connect all the villages of the valley. If you're driving, take the Α22 from Bolzano – the turn-off into Val Gardena is 25km to the north. Access to the start of the walk is by cablecar from Ortisei to Seceda.

THE WALK
Day 1: Seceda to Rifugio Gardenaccia
6 to 8 hours
This is a full-day high-altitude walk through the Alpe di Cisles, an exceptionally beautiful

landscape, dominated by the Odle and Puez groups.

From the northern part of Ortisei (about 1250m), take the cablecar up to Seceda (2453m). This is the highest point you will reach during the day and the view is memorable: behind you is the Odle group, a series of spiky pinnacles with the Sass Rigais at the north-east, the highest of which is crowned with a cross (3025m); to the south-east, are the massive Sella group (3152m) and the Sasso Lungo; to the south-west, you can see the green high plain of the Alpe di Siusi at the foot of Monte Sciliar; to the west you can see all the way to the Adamello and Ortles glaciers on the border with the Lombardia (Lombardy) region.

Take trail No 2a (watch that you don't accidentally deviate on to trail No 6), which heads east at mid-slope through what most people would consider to be a typical Alpine environment – lush green, sloping pastures dotted with wooden *malghe*, which herders use as summer shelters. (This type of environment is in fact unusual at such high altitudes.) Following trail No 2a through the scenic Alpe di Cisles you will descend to an area known as Prera Longia, where huge

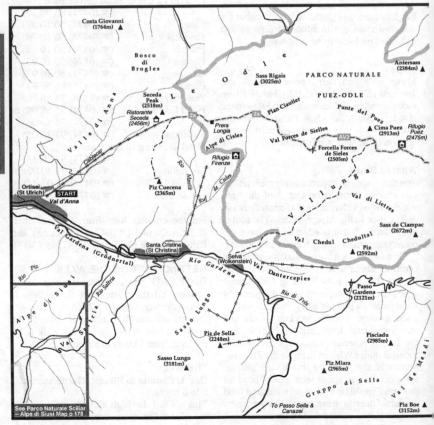

See Parco Naturale Sciliar – Alpe di Siusi Map p 178

surreal boulders dot the landscape. Be careful here as when it rains this trail is very slippery. In the early morning it is likely that you'll see marmots, roe deer and lots of small birds, such as the Alpine finch.

Stay on trail No 2a until you arrive at Plan Ciautier, a green natural terrace marked by strips of white pebbles. Here many trails ascend north towards canyons where there are via ferratas. From Plan Ciautier, trail No 2a becomes less clear, but you continue to follow it south-east along the inner edge of the terrace. The trail descends to the convergence of Val Mont da l'Ega and Val Forces

de Sieles, about 200m below. This convergence forms the beginning of the dry riverbed of the Ruf de Cisles, where water flows only when it rains. Cross the riverbed and climb up Val Forces de Sieles (don't go off for the Rifugio Firenze to the southwest), following the signs for the Forcella Forces de Sielles (2505m).

On the way up to the saddle the trail changes from No 2a to No 2. At the saddle you will see a section of the picturesque Vallunga downhill to the south-east, and there is a spectacular view over the Odle group to the north-west. By this time you will

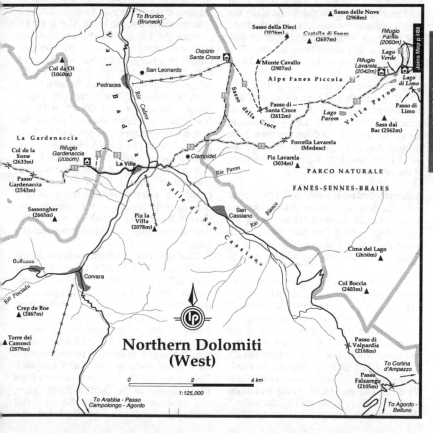

Northern Dolomiti
(West)

1:125,000

DOLOMITI

probably be ready for a rest, so save your snacks and drinks for this scenic spot!

After your break get back on trail No 2 and follow it to the left (north). You will come to a section of via ferrata, but don't panic – you don't need any equipment. Just hold on to the cord if you need help in crossing this short, exposed tract. Turning east with the trail, you'll pass a crest and then descend to a small green terrace, almost like a rocky balcony, above Vallunga. You are directly beneath the Puez group at this point, of which the highest peak is the Cima Puez at 2913m. Here the trail joins the main path of the Alta Via No 2 (marked with the number 2 enclosed in a triangle) coming down from the Forcella Nives. Continue east along the trail, heading towards the Rifugio Puez (Puezhütte; 1½ hours from the Forcella Forces de Sielles – 4½ hours from Seceda). This rifugio is a good spot for a meal and a well earned rest.

To continue the trek, take trail No 15 which crosses an arid high plain, inhabited by white partridges, and leads to Passo Gardenaccia (2543m) and then descends to Rifugio Gardenaccia (2050m; two hours from Rifugio Puez, 6½ hours from Seceda), which is the most logical place to end this leg of the first day of the walk.

Return to Ortisei If you'd prefer to go back to Val Gardena to complete this as a one-day loop, about 20 minutes (1km) before the Puez rifugio you'll find trail No 4, which descends into a broad valley, eventually reaching the Vallunga and trail No 4-14 to Selva.

At the bottom of the valley the trail becomes a small dirt road. Follow it to the right and meander down the pretty Vallunga with its Alpine vegetation. If you walk quietly you should come across quite a few small animals such as fawns, squirrels, Roe deer and many birds. The contrast between the majesty of the high mountains and the gentle environment of the valley creates a memorable effect and provides a fitting end to the walk (2½ hours to the end of the valley). Once at the end of the Vallunga, it takes about

15 minutes to reach the town of Selva, from where you can catch a bus back to Ortisei.

Day 2A: Rifugio Gardenaccia to Rifugio Lavarela or Rifugio Fanes via Passo Lavarela
6 to 8 hours
By either route, Day 2 is a challenging all-day walk that crosses Val Badia. We suggest that you choose your route before setting off from the rifugio – Days 2A and 2B coincide up until La Ville in the Val Badia, from where Day 2B heads to the south. Shorter and less demanding, Day 2A will take a total of six to eight hours to walk. From the town of La Villa, ascend on trail No 12 to Passo Lavarela (Medesc), also known as Forcella Lavarela (Medesc), and descend to the Alpe di Fanes.

From the Rifugio Gardenaccia descend south-east along trail No 11 into the Gardenaccia valley (trail No 5-15, which branches off to the left shortly after the refuge, also descends to La Villa but takes an extra 30 minutes). You'll cross through a forest, coming out near the Maso Ploten, from where you descend to a church which is at the beginning of the town of La Villa (1420m; 1½ to two hours). From the church take the paved road downhill to reach provincial road No 244 and the tourist information office. If you want to continue on the trek, you should take a rest break here of no more than one hour (but remember that this rest break is not included in our calculation of the time needed to complete the walks).

Take trail No 12 which starts across the road from the La Villa information office and to the left of Hotel Aurora. Go downhill and cross a bridge over a stream. When you reach the asphalt road, turn right and follow it up the slope for a few metres until you find the sign indicating where trail No 12 recommences to the left. Pass the Cianins resort area and ascend to the east, passing through the pastures of the nearby Maso Ciampidel. Cross over trail No 15, which ascends from San Cassiano to the Ospizio Santa Croce, and continue east on trail No 12 (well marked), through an enchanting forest, rich in birdlife, until you reach the mountain pines. Here, avoid the deviation off to the left (it connects to the north with trail No 15) and continue your ascent on trail No 12, which becomes increasingly steep over a section of scree. After a zigzagging stretch, it is advisable to avoid the trail to the right and instead take the steeper trail to the left for the Forcella Lavarela – called Medesc on the Tabacco map (2533m, 2½ to three hours). Take a break here and enjoy the incredible view, then descend north-east on trail No 12. Shortly afterwards, this trail merges with trail No 7 (on our Day 2B from the Passo di Santa Croce).

It is at this point where Days 2A and 2B again merge. Take trail No 7, descending through a strange, silent landscape of plume-shaped rocks that, when tapped, emit glassy sounds. This recalls the remote time when they were part of the coral reef of a tropical sea (see the boxed text 'A Magical World' on this page). Pass alongside Lago Parom (which is sometimes there and sometimes not), and some sparse arolla pines that are growing high up among the rocks in a kind of twisted and inhospitable surreal garden. You are also likely to see carpets of edelweiss (*Leontopodium alpinum*) along here.

When you can hear the roar of water surging from the numerous springs that feed the Lago Verde (Green Lake) you will be just above Rifugio Lavarela (☎ (0474) 50 10 79; 2042m) (two to three hours from Passo di Santa Croce). A short distance away, on the other side of the stream, is Rifugio Fanes (☎ (0474) 50 10 97).

Alternative Finish Options If you wish to finish the trek at the end of Day 2 you have two options. The first is to head south-east from the Lavarela or Fanes rifugi, taking trail No 10 up to Passo di Limo and then down into the gorgeous Valle di Fanes. You continue along this trail, passing Ponte Alto, until you reach the Pian di Loa (two hours). Here you are only a few hundred metres from the SS51, where you can catch a bus south to Cortina (9km) or north to Dobbiaco (10km).

A Magical World

You are now in the magical world of the Fanes, an imaginary people of ancient folk legend. Hidden among these dry, windswept rocks, the Fanes people are waiting to rebuild their kingdom. Eologically speaking, this is very special indeed – it is a great Karst amphitheatre where *anidride carbonica* (carbon dioxide) dissolved in rainwater has split the limestone rock to form fissures, wells, depressions that periodically become ponds, and curious formations of flat rock plains on almost level ground furrowed by numerous channels. Each step brings you to yet another bizarre formation. While walking through the Alpe di Fanes, you will be struck not only by the unusual, in fact quite unique beauty of the place, but also by the silence. It is as though this great high plain absorbs not only water, but also sound.

Helen Gillman & Stefano Cavedoni

The alternative for those with a bit more energy is to continue along the trek route for another 3½ to four hours until you reach the Rifugio Sennes (see Day 3 for details of this route). From here you take trail No 6 south-east through the beautiful Val Salata and down to the Malga Ra Stua (two hours – see the discussion of this walk earlier in this chapter). It is not possible to stay at Malga Ra Stua, but they do serve a marvellous hot chocolate topped with fresh whipped cream. From Malga Ra Stua descend along the asphalt road to reach the state road SS51 (one hour), or catch the shuttle bus to the Cortina bus stop on the state road.

An appealing variation would be to stop off at the Rifugio Fodara Vedla on the way to the Rifugio Sennes, then take trail No 9 down into Val Salata and on to Malga Ra Stua (one hour). This trail follows an old WWI military road.

Day 2B: Rifugio Gardenaccia to Rifugio Lavarela or Rifugio Fanes via Passo di Santa Croce
7 to 9 hours
This alternative is recommended as an interesting mountaineering experience. You'll need 1½ to two hours to tackle the via ferrata

which ascends diagonally from Ospizio di Santa Croce (2045m) across a steep face to Passo di Santa Croce (2612m). This very popular route will make experts laugh but could cause novices to weep, so it is very important to evaluate your true level of expertise before setting out (if you're prone to vertigo, for instance, take the other route). It is worth noting that children often tackle this route.

Good weather conditions are absolutely essential and you'll need the correct equipment (see What to Bring earlier in this chapter and also in the Facts for the Walker chapter). Remember the entire route takes about eight to nine hours.

We also strongly advise you to set off very early in the morning. Luckily dawn at the Rifugio Gardenaccia is something special. Slowly, in the clear amber light of a good day, the magnificent silhouette of the Marmolada, with its imposing glacier, begins to materialise in the south. In the foreground is the Sella group, and if you shift your gaze to the east you can see the Civetta behind the Col di Lana, Pelmo, L'Averau, Le Tofane and, beyond Val Badia, the Conturines and Lavarela. To the north-east is the Sasso della Croce. From this standpoint a crossing of its west face will seem totally impossible, nevertheless you'll be up there within a few hours.

Follow the description of Day 2A as far as La Villa, then take the bus to Pedraces (about 15 minutes away). At the time of writing, the summer schedule for buses to Pedraces was 7.50, 8.50 and 10.40 am (plus afternoon buses at 1.10, 3, 4.55 and 6.05 pm). The cablecar (on Route B) operates from 8.30 am to 12.30 pm and 2 to 6 pm (it will save you 1½ hours of walking time and a 500m climb). To check these schedules, contact the information office at La Villa on ☎ (0471) 84 70 37.

From the bus stop of Pedraces you follow the signs for San Leonardo to the east. Just before San Leonardo, you will find the cablecar for Santa Croce. The 10-minute ride will take you up to a height of 1840m, where you continue the climb east on trail No 7 and eventually reach the Ospizio Santa Croce

(2045m; 30 minutes). The little church was built in 1511 on the site where, according to local legend, a cruel dragon was killed by a feudal knight. There is a private rifugio here (☎ (0471) 83 96 32) that should be open year-round. From the Ospizio, trail No 7 heads west and after a short distance turns right to ascend south-east through the mountain pines, traversing a scree until it meets the rocky base of the mountain.

This is the beginning of the difficult part of the ascent. It follows a series of ledges south-east across the steep natural stairway that forms the western face of Sasso della Croce (known as Sass dla Crusc in the Ladin language). Fixed metal cables have been placed to help the less sure-footed, although this is not a true via ferrata.

Experienced mountaineers will find this trail a breeze, but if you suffer from vertigo, or have never tackled a via ferrata before, then think twice before choosing this route. As the metal cables attract lightning, be sure that weather conditions are suitable before you set out – you don't want to have to turn back and try to descend on slippery rock in the middle of a storm.

Once at Passo di Santa Croce (2612m, 2½ to three hours from the Ospizio), you'll see a trail that goes north up the crest to the summit of the Sass dla Crusc (2907m; one hour; called Monte Cavallo on the Tabacco maps) and then continues on for the Sasso delle Dieci (3026m; another hour; also known as Cima Dieci or Sas dales Diesc in the Ladin language). This is a steep and tricky route which can pose a problem if you're tired, and it is not advisable to undertake it at this point as you'd be adding an extra four hours to an already long day!

Instead, continue east along trail No 7, descending into the evocative Alpe di Fanes, a type of natural karstic amphitheatre, unmatched in the Dolomiti for its magical atmosphere. It is no coincidence that it has inspired so many myths, folk legends and fairytales over the centuries. In about 45 minutes you will meet up with trail No 12 of Day 2A. Follow that route description to Rifugio Lavarela or Rifugio Fanes.

Day 3: Rifugio Lavarela or Rifugio Fanes to Rifugio Biella
5 to 7 hours

Leaving the Lavarela and Fanes rifugi, follow trail No 7 (also marked with the blue triangular Alta Via No 1 signs) down into the small valley of the San Vigilio river until you reach Lago Piciodèl on your right (avoid shortcuts and stay on the road). On your right, shortly after you pass the lake, is a trail that can be taken as an alternative to Alta Via No 1.

If you decide to stay on Alta Via No 1 (which corresponds to trail No 7), from Lago Piciodèl the trail begins its long descent to Rifugio Pederù (☎ (0474) 50 10 86) (1548m) from where you have to ascend again to 2000m on trail No 7. This trail is near, and often on, a road used by 4WD vehicles ferrying tourist groups up and down to the rifugi (Fanes to Pederù – L10,000 a head, minimum of four people; Fanes-Pederù-Sennes – L22,000).

For those who want to end their trek here, a road descends from Rifugio Pederù into Val Badia (to San Vigilio is about three hours walking time).

The unnumbered alternative trail, which heads off to the right just after Lago Piciodèl, saves at least an hour and is an atmospheric route which, although tiring at times, is not difficult. It is marked on the Tabacco map with black dots and dashes. It leaves the road near a gravel riverbed and ascends north-east into the heart of the semi-wilderness, Bancdalse, to Rifugio Fodara Vedla (☎ (0474) 50 10 93) (1966m; three to four hours). This place has a great terrace where you can relax and enjoy the magnificent scenery.

From here you rejoin the Alta Via No 1, heading north in the direction of Rifugio Sennes (☎ (0474) 50 10 92) (2116m). After a few hundred metres the road forks. We recommend you take the detour to your right, which avoids the busy dirt road and crosses a high plain. It is not uncommon to encounter chamois and marmots in this area.

Once you rejoin Alta Via No 1, follow it until you reach a crossroad then take the left fork to the Rifugio Sennes, situated by a lake of the same name and surrounded by a small village of malghe.

From Rifugio Sennes you can either follow the Alta Via No 1, now a dirt road – this trail affords great views – or take trail No 6, which crosses a beautiful high plain containing the odd bit of twisted metal left over from WWI. This area was the scene of some of the most ferocious battles along the Alpine front line and now forms the regional boundary between Alto Adige-Südtirol and Veneto. From trail No 6 you descend to rejoin the Alta Via in sight of the old wooden Rifugio Biella (☎ (0436) 86 69 91) (2327m; two to three hours), set in an unforgettable lunar landscape. Here you can eat a meal and spend the night. If you still have some energy, it's an easy climb up the Croda del Becco (two to three hours return).

On Day 4 you have a choice of routes to take. Route A takes you to Rifugio Pratopiazza where you have the option of ascending to the summit of Picco di Vallandro. It also allows for a rest stop at the foot of Tre Cime di Lavaredo. An extra day is required, however, to complete the trek. Route B is the continuation of Route A (two hours longer) and it will enable you to shorten the trek to Sesto by one day. However, you will be obliged to spend the night in the Hotel Tre Cime di Lavaredo, a two-star hotel.

Day 4A: Rifugio Biella to Rifugio Vallandro
4 to 6 hours

Leaving the Alta Via No 1, which descends to Lago di Braies (a short distance to the north), you ascend trail No 28, which follows the mountain crest south-east above the rifugio towards the Croda Rossa, a majestic mountain inhabited by golden eagles and ibex. Once you reach Forcella Cocodain, a mountain pass at 2332m, descend in a northerly direction until you pick up trail No 3. Continue the descent along trail No 3 until you reach an intersection with trail No 4 coming from the north-west. Following trail No 3 to the right, you will reach Casera Cavallo di Sopra (2164m). From here the trail starts to ascend, always towards the right, along the face of the Croda Rossa. At one point the trail narrows and there is a sheer drop to one side, but there are fixed cables to hold onto for safety. This section may be difficult for those afraid of heights, but otherwise presents no technical difficulty.

Continuing along trail No 3, descend towards the valley. When you reach a fork take the right-hand path – the left, trail No 18, descends north-west towards Ponticello. At the next fork, take trail No 3A to the left (1980m), which descends north-east, crosses over a stream and goes up to Pratopiazza. The Alternative Finish Option at the end of Day 4A outlines a further possibility at this point.

There are three options for an overnight stay. Trail No 3A brings you to the Rifugio Pratopiazza (☎ (0474) 74 86 50) (1991m), at the end of the paved road from the Valle de Braies. From 10 July to 20 September there is a half-hourly shuttle-bus for Ponticello, where you can catch a SAD bus for Villabassa, Monguelfo or Braies.

If you continue to ascend along the dirt road, you will reach the lovely Hotel Croda Rossa (☎ (0474) 74 86 06) (1992m) and after 20 minutes reach a detour to the right where the old military road begins, shortened by trail No 37, which descends in less than an hour to Carbonin (which has bus stops for

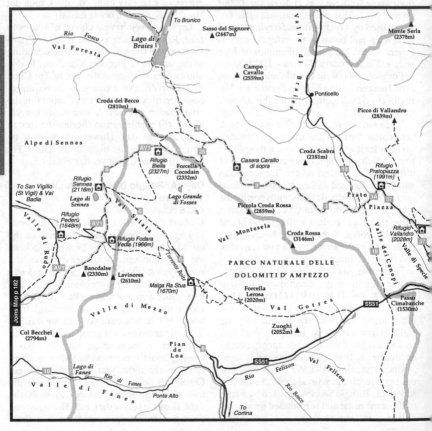

Cortina and Dobbiaco). If, instead, you continue to ascend, in 10 minutes you will be at the Rifugio Vallandro (☎ (0474) 97 25 05) (2040m) about five hours from Rifugio Biella. It has great views of the Croda Rossa to the west and Cristallo to the south.

The walk up to this point is not very strenuous, so those wishing to keep going can spend another four hours (return) making the ascent to the summit of the Picco di Vallandro (2839m) on trail No 40, which starts from the chapel next to Rifugio Pratopiazza.

Alternative Finish Option To leave the

walk and head back to Cortina, take trail No 18 to the right (south) towards the Valle dei Canopi, where a slippery descent brings you to the SS51 and Passo Cimabanche (1530m) just to your right. Here there is a bar and bus stops for Cortina (15 km) and Dobbiaco (Toblach) in Val Pusteria. Hitchhiking is also possible.

Day 4B: Rifugio Biella to Hotel Tre Cime di Lavaredo
6 to 8 hours

To reach Hotel Tre Cime di Lavaredo, take trail No 34, which ascends to the left of

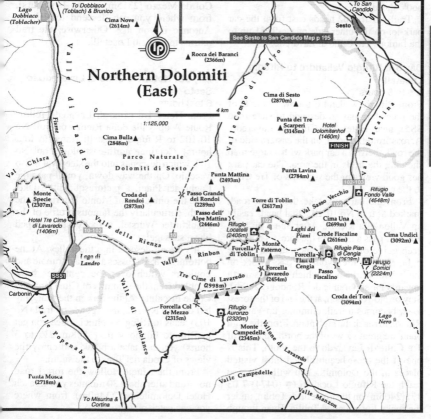

Rifugio Vallandro, up to the saddle of Monte Specie at 2200m. Avoid the trail on the right, which heads up to the summit of Monte Specie (2307m).

Make the steep descent on trail No 34 (which is marked with a triangle like the Alta Via No 3) until you reach the SS51 in Valle della Rienza, right behind Hotel Tre Cime di Lavaredo (☎ (0474) 97 26 33) (1406m; 1½ to two hours), where buses connect with Dobbiaco in Val Pusteria (10km) or with Cortina (24km).

The two-star *Hotel Tre Cime di Lavaredo* is the only lodging in the area and offers half board from L70,000 to L100,000 per person, depending on the season. It is advisable to book ahead.

Trail No 10-102 heads east from the car park lot on the other side of the SS51 up to the famous Tre Cime di Lavaredo.

Day 5A: Rifugio Vallandro to Rifugio Locatelli
4½ to 6 hours

From Rifugio Vallandro follow Route B of the preceding day to descend to state road SS51 near Hotel Tre Cime di Lavaredo. Across from the hotel, on the eastern side of the road, there is a car park with a large map showing the trails in the area. The car park has good views of the summits of Tre Cime to the east.

From the car park take the forest road, marked as trail No 10-102, that heads easily up Valle della Rienza. After about an hour you will pass a house in the forest – note the deep gorge of the Rinbianco stream on the right. Shortly after, you will pass a fork on the left for trail No 10 which ascends north towards Passo Grande dei Rondoi (2289m). Stay on No 102 which, at the end of the forest road, becomes a trail, climbing up Valle di Rinbon to reach the high plain. From the high plain are great views of the northern faces of Tre Cime di Lavaredo to the south. This is one of the most beautiful and most visited places in the Dolomiti. You will soon you reach the Rifugio Locatelli (☎ (0474) 7 03 47) (2405m) on the Forcella di Toblin, under the rocky tower called Toblin. Even though

the rifugio has 60 beds and 102 bunks, it is popular with large groups and you should book in advance.

Side Trip: Tre Cime di Lavaredo If you want to finish up the day by taking a closer look at Tre Cime, you should avoid trail No 101 for Forcella Lavaredo. Crowds of people arrive daily on this trail from Rifugio Auronzo, on the southern slope of Tre Cime, ferried up by buses on the controversial, paved toll-road from Misurina. It is better to take trail No 105, which passes by some lovely small lakes right under the north face of Tre Cime and then heads up to Forcella Col de Mezzo (2315m; one to 1½ hours), from where you can descend to Rifugio Auronzo if you like. Otherwise, the trail returns to Rifugio Locatelli.

Day 5B: Hotel Tre Cime di Lavaredo to Sesto
6 to 8 hours

From Hotel Tre Cime di Lavaredo follow Route A up Valle della Rienza on trail No 10-102 to Rifugio Locatelli (three to four hours). Continue north-east along trail No 102, which descends into the steep Val Sasso Vecchio. On the way down, you'll pass the Laghi dei Piani, a picturesque little lake. Note the pinnacles of Monte Paterno to the south, particularly the famous profile of the Frankfurter Würstel, a rocky spur shaped like a sausage!

It's a long descent into the valley. At the bottom, the trail crosses an area of rubble and boulders which over the centuries have tumbled from the summits of Cima Una and Crode Fiscaline. At the fork in the trail, stay left on trail No 102; the right-hand trail (No 103) leads to Rifugio Comici. Once you get to Rifugio Fondo Valle (1548m, 2½ to 3 hours) you can take a break and enjoy the views of Croda dei Toni to the south.

From the rifugio, follow the forest road north and after about 30 minutes you'll reach Hotel Dolomitenhof (1460m), from where you can catch a bus to Sesto.

Day 6: Rifugio Locatelli to Val Fiscalina
3 to 4 hours

This last leg is an easy finish to the trek for those who prefer not to rush. Buses run from Hotel Dolomitenhof to Sesto and San Candido where you can find either accommodation (see Places to Stay in the Parco Naturale Dolomiti di Sesto section later in this chapter for accommodation options in San Candido) or a train or bus to Bolzano.

Follow the description of Day 5B above to reach Hotel Dolomitenhof from Rifugio Locatelli.

Parco Naturale delle Dolomiti d'Ampezzo

Duration 4 hours
Standard Easy
Start/Finish Malga Ra Stua
Closest Town Cortina
Permits Required No
Public Transport Access Yes
Summary An easy return walk from Malga Ra Stua to Forcella Lerosa, with the option of continuing on to Passo Cimabanche.

One of the main attractions of this walk is the rich hot chocolate topped with fresh cream which awaits you on your return to the Malga Ra Stua. You can vary the walk considerably to make it longer or shorter, or more or less demanding. Although we present it as ideal for families, this walk through the Parco Naturale delle Dolomiti d'Ampezzo is suitable for all walkers, particularly since it provides a good introduction to some of the Dolomiti's more scenic mountains, notably the Croda Rossa.

PLANNING
Information Sources
The Cortina APT (☎ (0436) 3231), Piazzetta San Francesco 8, has extensive information on walking, transport, hotels and camping

grounds, as well as maps. The office has a Web site at http://www.sunrise.it/dolomiti. Its email address is: apt1@sunrise.it.

The Parco Naturale delle Dolomiti d'Ampezzo is operated by the Comunanza delle Regole d'Ampezzo, an ancient consortium of families dating back to the first Celtic and Roman settlements in the valley. The group manages the collective use of the pastures and forests according to tradition, and can provide information about the park. The headquarters (☎ (0436) 2206) is in Via del Parco 1. There is also a summer office (June to September: ☎ (0436) 3031 or ☎ (0336) 49 46 09) at the entrance to the park in the area of Fiames, where you can get the schedule for the shuttle to Malga Ra Stua (☎ (0436) 5753).

When to Walk
As with all walks in the Dolomiti, the season is from late June to late September, but August is best avoided if possible because of the large numbers of tourists.

Maps
The Tabacco 1:25,000 map No 03 *Cortina d'Ampezzo e Dolomiti Ampezzane* is the recommended one for this walk.

What to Bring
You won't need anything special other than suitable clothing for high-altitude walking, as outlined in the Facts for the Walker chapter.

Guided Walks
The Cortina Alpine Guides (☎ (0436) 4740) work with the park management to organise nature walks. Guides are also available for climbing and via ferrata expeditions.

Emergency
The Guardia di Finanza (☎ (0436) 2943) provides the local rescue service, including helicopter rescue.

PLACES TO STAY & EAT
International Camping Olympia (☎ (0436) 5057) is a few kilometres north of Cortina at Fiames, from where you can get transport to

Malga Ra Stua. *Pensione Fiammes* (☎ (0436) 2366), Via Fiames 13, is another option with doubles costing up to L115,000.

In Cortina, you'll struggle to find reasonably priced accommodation. Try *Albergo Cavallino* (☎ (0436) 2614), Corso Italia 142, which charges up to L95,000 per person with breakfast.

You can eat at Malga Ra Stua, if you arrive back from your walk in time. In Cortina, try *Il Ponte*, Via Franchetti 8, where you'll be able to enjoy good pizza.

GETTING TO/FROM THE WALK

Cortina's bus station is in Via Marconi. SAD buses connect Cortina and Dobbiaco (To-blach), where you can change for Brunico and Bolzano. Dolomiti Bus travels to Belluno, Pocol and Passo Falzarego from Cortina. There are also frequent bus services from Cortina to Venezia (Venice), Padova (Padua), Bologna, Milano, Firenze (Florence) and Roma (Rome).

If you are coming by car from Cortina, take the small road to the left at the first switch-back, 7km from Cortina. If you are coming from Dobbiaco it is the first switchback after Passo Cimabanche. From mid-June to mid-September the road up to Malga Ra Stua is closed to normal traffic. You can either walk the 2km or 3km from the car park (1429m) to Ra Stua (1670m) – it takes about one hour – or, in summer, take advantage of the reasonably priced minibus service that runs from Albergo Fiames, on the SS51 about 4km north of Cortina, stops at the car park and continues up to Ra Stua. If you're catching the bus then make sure you check the departure time of the last minibus from Ra Stua.

The public bus for Passo Cimabanche and Dobbiaco also stops at Albergo Fiames. It runs five times a day leaving from Cortina at 8.45 and 10 am and 12.40, 4 and 6.55 pm. Tickets can be purchased on board.

THE WALK

If you decide to walk up to Malga Ra Stua from the car park take the track that heads uphill from the eastern side of the switch-back and follow the slope of the Croda de R'Ancona. The track doesn't have a number but is marked on the Tabacco map. In about an hour you'll arrive at Malga Ra Stua (☎ (0436) 5753) at the beginning of Val Salata, a lovely Alpine valley that is perfect for a relaxing walk. More serious walkers can walk north-west to the end of Val Salata, ascend to Lago di Sennes (2116m) and pick up the walk through the Parco Naturale Fanes-Sennes-Braies which is detailed in the Northern Dolomiti section earlier in this chapter.

Otherwise, from Ra Stua, continue to ascend along Val Salata for about 150m and take the dirt road to your right which ascends for about 250m, then turn right to take trail No 8. Another 250m ahead the trail forks; take the fork which heads to the right – it's longer but much easier and far more scenic. Follow the series of switchbacks winding uphill past ancient fir trees – at certain points there are panoramic views across the Fanes high plain. Always keep to the left.

You will reach a small valley where, if you approach quietly, you might see the resident marmots, chamois and squirrels. Follow the trail around the valley, avoiding the deviations which head off to the right. In front of you now is the majestic Croda Rossa (3146m), one of the most beautiful peaks in the Dolomiti. The trail will bring you to a wide valley, near the Forcella Lerosa (2020m), that contains a little wooden house and a water fountain.

At this point you have three options. The first is to turn left at the wooden house and follow trail No 8 back down to Malga Ra Stua. This route is much shorter, but less attractive than the ascent – so, if you're in no hurry, you can take the second option and return the way you came. Once back at the Malga Ra Stua make sure you stop and sample the fantastic hot chocolate.

The third option is to turn right, still following No 8, to reach the pass. After a picturesque walk of roughly 4km (1 hour) you will reach the SS51, just 1km before Passo Cimabanche, about 13km from Cortina. At the time of writing, buses passed Passo Cimabanche for Cortina at 3.50 and 6.35 pm. It would be advisable to check with the tourist office in Cortina for exact times.

STEFANO CAVEDONI

STEFANO CAVEDONI

STEFANO CAVEDONI

STEFANO CAVEDONI

Top: The imposing Piz de Cir is typical of the scenery walkers enjoy in the Northern Dolomiti.
Middle Left: Croda dei Toni from Val Fiscalina, on the last day of the Northern Dolomiti walk.
Middle Right: The craggy peaks of the Sella group are visible from many vantage points.
Bottom: The Sella group and its even higher neighbour, Sasso Lungo.

Top: The Argentera massif looms in the distance, from just below Passo dei Ghiacciai.
Middle Left: Rifugio Pagarì (2650m), below Cima della Maledia, high in the Alpi Marittime.
Middle Right: Riomaggiore, in the Cinque Terre, at the eastern end of the Sentiero Azzurro.
Bottom: Vernazza, perhaps the most picturesque of the five villages in the Cinque Terre.

OTHER WALKS

There is an interesting walk in the Cortina area for experienced mountaineers that incorporates sections of via ferrata – for which you'll need the appropriate equipment. Take the local bus from Cortina east to Passo Tre Croci (1805m) and take the southern trail No 215 (which is a section of Alta Via No 3) up to the Rifugio Vandelli (1928m) in the heart of the Sorapiss group. From here the Alta Via No 3 continues to the south-west up to 2316m and then veers to the left (south), as trail No 242. This section incorporates a section of via ferrate, as does trail No 215, which heads off to the right (north).

The Dolomiti around Cortina offer a network of spectacular trails. In summer (only), a series of three cablecars (L84,000) will take you up to the Tofana di Mezzo (3243m), from where all the trails are difficult and incorporate via ferratas. You can link up with the Alta Via No 1 at either the Passo Falzarego, or at the evocative Passo Giau, with the spiky Croda da Lago to the east and the Cinque Torri to the north. To get to the Passo Giau, catch a bus from Cortina to Pocol and then hitch a ride.

Not far from Cortina, and accessible by Dolomiti Bus in summer, are the Tre Cime di Lavaredo, one of the most famous climbing locations in the world and also a very panoramic place to walk. The fact that you can arrive by bus from Misurina literally at the foot of the Tre Cime di Lavaredo means the area is crawling with tourists in the high season.

PARCO NATURALE DOLOMITI DI SESTO

Val Pusteria forms the northern border of the Dolomiti. Culturally, linguistically and geographically it is the Südtirol. The upper Val Pusteria takes in Dolomiti di Sesto, Tre Cime di Lavaredo, the fabled Lago di Braies and the resort towns of San Candido and Sesto.

San Candido grew from where Val di Sesto meets the Drava River. The Romanesque *Collegiata*, which is still standing, is one of the original buildings. It was built in 769 AD by Bavarian colonisers who had crushed the pre-existing, pagan Slavic populations. The present-day Austrian border is only 8km away to the east.

The Val di Sesto, south-east of San Candido, is the centre of Parco Naturale Dolomiti di Sesto. Val Fiscalina runs off Val di Sesto at Moso and is one of the most impressive approaches to Tre Cime di Lavaredo, Croda dei Toni and Tre Scarperi. Ascending Val di Sesto from the base of the valley, you reach the Passo Monte Croce di Comelico, which gives access to the province of Belluno in the Veneto region.

Lago di Braies (1490m), in the valley of the same name, lies in the shadow of the Croda del Becco (2810m). The villages of Valle di Braies and the broad panoramas of the mountain pastures of Prato Piazza make it one of the most enchanting places in the Dolomiti.

PLANNING
Information Sources
The tourist office in San Candido (☎ (0474) 91 31 49) is in Piazza Magistrato; the Sesto office (☎ (0474) 71 03 10) is in Via Dolomiti. There is also a tourist office at Brunico (☎ (0474) 55 57 22), the valley's main town, at the bus station in Piazza Europa.

Maps
Tabacco 1:25,000 No 010 *Dolomiti di Sesto* map is recommended.

Guided Walks
The Scuola d'Alpinismo Michl Innerkofler (☎ (0474) 71 00 30), Via Dolomiti 23, in Sesto, and the Ufficio Guide Alpine Strobl Luis (☎ (0474) 97 25 83), Via Dolomiti 5, in Dobbiaco, both organise guided walks and climbs.

Emergency
For Pronto Soccorso Alpino (Alpine First Aid) call the Guardia di Finanza (☎ (0474)

71 03 25). It also operates a helicopter rescue service. Dial ☎ 118 to reach national emergency services.

PLACES TO STAY
In San Candido, *Residence Obermüller-Fauster Melchior* (☎ (0474) 91 34 12), Via Castello (Burgweg) 8, has rooms and apartments for around L38,000 per person per day. *Villa Waldheim* (☎ (0474) 91 31 87), Via Pascolo (Am Erschbann) 1, offers half board for around L100,000 per person per day.

GETTING THERE & AWAY
By SAD bus you can reach Brunico and San Candido from Bolzano, Merano, Val Gardena (on the Innsbruck bus) and Cortina. Buses leave from Dobbiaco for Lago di Braies. To get to Rifugio Auronzo at Tre Cime di Lavaredo, catch the Cortina bus from San Candido or Dobbiaco; from Cortina, catch the bus for Misurina and Tre Cime di Lavaredo.

By train, you can reach Val Pusteria from Bolzano. By car, it is easily accessible from Val Badia, from Cortina via Valle di Landro, and from the A22.

Sesto to San Candido

Duration	3 to 4 hours
Standard	Easy
Start	Sesto
Finish	San Candido
Closest Town	Brunico
Permits Required	No
Public Transport Access	Yes
Summary	A pleasant stroll through forest from Sesto to San Candido in Val Pusteria with spectacular Dolomiti views.

THE WALK
From Sesto's *municipio* (town hall), take Via San Vito uphill. After about 30m you come to a wide intersection where there is a sign indicating numerous different trails. Take No 4D for Cappella nel Bosco/Waldkapelle,

also known as the Sentiero di Meditazione (Meditation Path). Follow the sign to the right on the paved road and, in a short time, you will connect with No 4D, which heads north alongside a stream. When it hits the paved road again follow the asphalt for a few metres up to the next sharp curve. Here on the left, where there are some houses just before a small bridge (1400m), is the beginning of the paved with a sign pointing towards the Cappella nel Bosco. Via Hosler ascends gently, in a westerly direction, affording magnificent views over the Dolomiti and Val di Sesto, with its gentle pastures dotted with wooden *fienili* (haystacks inside wooden shacks).

In a few minutes you come to a farm (1449m) where Via Hosler ends. Following the 4D trail signs, you'll pass under the ramp of a hay barn and find yourself facing the frescoed façade of a house. Pass along the right-hand side of the house and pick up the path that heads into the woods. Climbing a steep incline among fir trees and moss-covered boulders, you'll pass two of the numerous wooden sculptures that mark the meditation stops along the way.

After crossing a pasture with two hay barns, you'll reach a wide clearing. Instead of heading to the right for the Albergo Waldruhe, go up to the edge of the woods and take a break at the little wooden table (1470m; 40 minutes) and enjoy the spectacular panorama of Croda Rossa di Sesto, Croda dei Toni, Tre Scarperi and Croda dei Baranci in the background.

If you're not already too weary, you can make a 30-minute return deviation to visit the site of a prehistoric place of worship. To reach the prehistoric site, continue into the woods from the table. After about 20m, you'll find a path on the right marked 'Pietre Preistoriche'. Follow this path east, climbing the grassy slope and, after passing a hay barn, enter the woods where you'll find two stone slabs with strange incisions which are typical of the rock-carving in the Alps during the Neolithic period.

To continue along the walk, from the wooden table take up the trail which heads north-west through the wood, avoiding deviations along the way. After passing a fountain with a statue, the trail climbs a small, rocky valley, until it reaches the Waldkapelle (1500m; 10 minutes), a rustic log chapel built into the side of a huge boulder. It was built in 1917 during WWI, after locals had to be evacuated from the valley due to Italian bombing of what was then Austria. Inside the chapel is a simple altar with a book where visitors can record their thoughts.

From the chapel, continue up the path until you come to a fork, where you descend to the left onto a dirt road, following the sign for trail No 4 to San Candido. It's a pleasant descent down through the lush woods of the crest all the way to San Candido.

Avoiding any deviations, descend first through the firs and then, after a sharp curve to the right, some Scotch pines. If you proceed quietly, you might even surprise a squirrel or two skipping among the branches or a fawn.

Still walking along trail No 4, ignore the fork to the left for trail No 5 to Sesto. You'll come to another little table placed in just the right position for a fantastic view over Val Campo di Dentro, with the Torre dei Scarperi to the left (east) and the Croda dei Rondoi to the right (1400m). Continuing on you will come to a fork without signs – go straight ahead downhill, avoiding the dirt road that ascends to the right.

After passing under some power lines you'll come to a fork. At this point the road heads to the right, marked with the red and white indication '4+5'. You must instead go downhill on the shortcut marked with an arrow for San Candido, which will bring you to the bicycle path of Rio di Sesto at the bottom of the valley. Follow the bicycle path to the right to reach the playground, from where a short zigzagging ramp leads down to the northern side of the town (the dirt road circles around to the right and is somewhat longer).

DOLOMITI

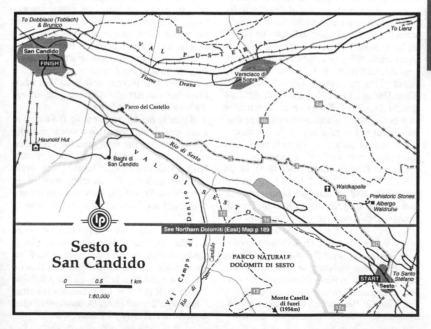

Sesto to
San Candido

0   0.5   1 km

1:60,000

Val Fiscalina to Tre Cime di Lavaredo

Duration 6½ to 8 hours
Standard Easy
Start/Finish Sesto
Closest Town Brunico
Permits Required No
Public Transport Access Yes
Summary A high-altitude loop from Sesto to Tre Cime di Lavaredo.

THE WALK

From the Park Hotel Dolomitenhof at the beginning of Val Fiscalina (1460m), take the dirt road south (trail No 102-103) towards the head of Val Fiscalina, which is dominated by the spires of Croda dei Toni. As you set out near the hotel, note the unusual fresco on the wall of a house depicting the giants Huno and Hauno, who figure in several ancient legends about the founding of San Candido.

After walking for about 30 minutes you'll reach the Rifugio Fondo Valle (☎ (0474) 71 06 06) (1548m). From here the trail starts its long ascent. When you reach a fork in the trail, head left on trail No 103. The trail takes you higher along the western side of the valley (Cima Undici is to your left and Croda dei Toni straight ahead) to Rifugio Comici. The trail is easy but, in some places, steep and exposed. Be careful not to take any of the shortcuts, which occasionally cross slippery rockfaces and should be tackled only by experts.

Once at Rifugio Comici (☎ (0474) 71 04 13); (2224m, two to 2½ hours), set in the gravelly base of the crag, you head south and then west on trail No 101 for Rifugio Pian di Cengia. Don't take the unmarked path that branches off to the north-west into a small rocky valley, shortly after Rifugio Comici. Also ignore the turn-off to the left for Croda dei Toni. When you come to a fork in the trail, take care to stay on the main trail (trail No 101) and continue climbing west up to Passo Fiscalino (2519m) which has great views of Marmarole, Cadini di Misurina and Cristallo.

Go to the right on trail No 101, which runs along a ledge among WWI trenches, to reach Rifugio Pian di Cengia (☎ (0337) 45 15 17) (2528m; one hour). This tiny rifugio has a 15-bunk dormitory on the upper floor which is accessible through a trap door at the top of a ladder. You can also get a meal here.

From the rifugio, continue west along trail No 101, passing more old military trenches, until you come to Forcella Pian di Cengia (2522m; 15 minutes). From this saddle there are great views of the basin of the Alpe dei Piani with its little lakes, Torre of Toblin, Croda dei Rondoi, Croda dei Baranci and Tre Scarperi.

At the saddle take trail No 101 to the right, and descend among loose rock towards the Rifugio Locatelli, at the base of Torre di Toblin. After a brief descent the trail passes above a lake, then ascends to a second one before reaching Forcella di Toblin and Rifugio Locatelli (☎ (0474) 97 20 02) (2405m; one hour). To the south are the Tre Cime di Lavaredo (which actually prove to be four peaks, not three, on closer inspection), dominating a vast, heavily-furrowed limestone high plain. The place is very special and its only defect is that everyone knows this. In summer, particularly in August, hundreds of tourists are bussed in daily on the paved, toll-road between Misurina and Rifugio Auronzo (2298m on the south side of Tre Cime).

If you're not fortunate enough to arrive in a moment of calm, the chaos is worth enduring for the sake of the view, and the afternoon light all but guarantees outstanding photos. Rifugio Locatelli is a large 1950s-style building with the disconcerting look of an army barracks, but the view from its terrace is marvellous. You can eat and sleep here as well.

To head back, take trail No 102 north-east for Val Fiscalina. The long, and in places steep, descent over the rocky ledges of Val Sasso Vecchio is well marked. You'll actually descend 850m before reaching Rifugio Fonda Valle (1548m; 1½ to two hours), from where you'll reach Hotel Dolomitenhof after a pleasant and easy 30-minute walk.

Alpi Marittime

The Alpi Marittime (Maritime Alps or Alpes Maritimes in French), the southernmost wag in the tail of the mighty Alps, is a range full of surprises. The range is accessible yet pleasingly wild in character, where glacial valleys sheltering high meadows, streams and tarns are separated by rugged ridges and numerous peaks of more than 3000m.

The northern limit of the Alpi Marittime is Colle della Maddalena, at the head of Valle Stura, 55km west of the provincial capital of Cuneo in southern Piemonte (Piedmont). From here the range extends south-east in a meandering arc to Colle di Cadibone, behind the Ligurian coastal city of Savona, where the Alpi Marittime (also known, between Colle di Tenda and Colle di Cadibone, as the Alpi Liguri) give way to the Appennino Ligure. For much of their length the Alpi Marittime straddle the border between Italy and France.

On the Italian side of the Alpi Marittime are a number of nature reserves of varied character. The largest two are the 258.9 sq km Parco Naturale Alpi Marittime, home of the highest peaks in the range, including the tallest, Cima Sud Argentera (3297m); and the 67.7 sq km Parco Naturale Alta Valle Pesio e Tanaro, which protects an area of rugged cliffs and limestone formations above ground and extensive karst cave systems below. This chapter describes three walks in these two parks. All three follow the Grande Traversata delle Alpi, or GTA (see the Long-Distance Walks chapter) for at least part of their length. In summer it is possible to link the two parks on a three-day walk along the GTA.

The walker from afar is likely to receive a warm if somewhat incredulous reception in the Alpi Marittime, especially outside the peak holiday season. Locals seem accustomed to the relative obscurity of their corner of the Alps, and are surprised to find visitors as enthusiastic about its many splendours as they are. Without wishing to ruin the fun – the relative isolation of the Alpi Marittime is, after all, a major ingredient of their charm –

we recommend this area as both a fine introduction to the Alps and a worthy destination in its own right.

HISTORY

Recent archaeological discoveries point to the occupation of the Vei del Bouc valley, south-east of San Giacomo, by shepherds during the Bronze Age. A better known site from the same period is Valle delle Meraviglie (Valley of the Marvels, or Vallée des Merveilles in French), south of the border in France's Parc National du Mercantour, where there is an extensive collection of rock engravings that date from about 1800 BC to 1500 BC. The practice of grazing livestock in the valleys and high meadows of the Alpi Marittime continues today, though many of the *gias*, or herders' camps, that walkers come across are now abandoned.

The profusion of walking routes across the Alpi Marittime from north to south testify to the centuries-old commerce between southern Piemonte and France. Track M11 over Colle di Finestra, for example, is sometimes referred to as the Sentiero del Sale or 'Salt Route' in reference to its former status as a trade route. People, ideas and goods for trade have crossed the Alps freely in this region since before the days of the Roman Empire. Even the dominant language on both sides of the Alps was for a long time the same – the *langue d'oc*. The division between the lands of the Savoy state, named after a dynasty which controlled varying amounts of territory in and around the Alps for several centuries, which became part of Italy in the

north and French territory in the south, was formalised in 1713 by the Treaty of Utrecht.

All the walks in this chapter have stages in common with the GTA. Some of these date from the mid-19th century when the Argentera was a huge royal hunting reserve, and follow the hunting road built for Victor Emmanuel II, king of Sardegna-Piemonte and the first king of a united Kingdom of Italy. Lodges occupied by the king's hunting parties can be seen at Terme di Valdieri, Pian del Valasco and near San Giacomo. For more information on the GTA, see the Long-Distance Walks chapter.

NATURAL HISTORY

Though the flora and fauna of the two natural parks in this chapter are related, and include many species in common with more northerly parts of the Alps, the geology of the two parks is quite different. The natural history of each park is therefore discussed in the corresponding section.

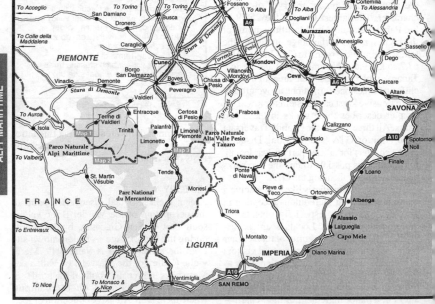

CLIMATE

The position of the Alpi Marittime exposes them to Mediterranean as well as continental weather patterns. This, combined with their somewhat lower altitude, means that the weather here is generally milder than in the mountains further north. They become free of snow somewhat earlier than more northerly parts of the Alps, but snow-covered in winter they certainly are.

INFORMATION
Maps

Although the Alpi Marittime are in southern Piemonte, the Touring Club Italiano (TCI) (1:200,000) *Liguria* map, widely sold in bookshops for L9500, is good for planning and access information; it includes the area described here and all the approaches to it from within Italy. See under Maps in the individual walks sections later in this chapter for details of walking maps.

Information Sources

The friendly staff in the APT in Cuneo (☎ (0171) 66615) at Corso Nizza 17 have local transport and accommodation information and speak English and French. They also have a selection of very useful free brochures, some of them in English, including a couple on the GTA and another on all the mountain *rifugi* (refuges) in the province. Other information sources specific to walks are given in the relevant sections later in this chapter.

Books

Wild Italy by Tim Jepson has a good section on Alpi Marittime flora and fauna. The Club Alpino Italiano (CAI) guide to the area is called *Valli Cuneesi: Pesio, Gesso e Stura*.

Place Names

Place names in Italian, French and local dialects are at times used interchangeably in this region. The local word *gias*, found on signposts and maps throughout the region, refers

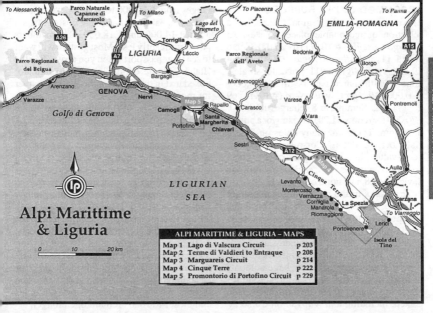

Alpi Marittime & Liguria

0   10   20 km

ALPI MARITTIME & LIGURIA – MAPS	
Map 1 Lago di Valscura Circuit	p 203
Map 2 Terme di Valdieri to Entraque	p 208
Map 3 Marguareis Circuit	p 214
Map 4 Cinque Terre	p 222
Map 5 Promontorio di Portofino Circuit	p 229

ALPI MARITTIME

to a place where a herder brought livestock to graze. A gias will usually consist of a stone building or two in varying states of repair, and perhaps a pen or corral, in a relatively flat, grassy area. There's generally water nearby, but don't rely on a gias for shelter as many are roofless, and those that are not may be occupied.

The Parco Naturale Alpi Marittime used to be known as the Parco Naturale dell' Argentera. Both names are in use on maps of the region, in other publications and on signs, including some installed by the park administration.

Emergency

A mountain rescue service can be contacted 24 hours a day on ☎ 118. Outside populated areas in the Alpi Marittime, reaching a telephone will generally mean reaching a rifugio (see Accommodation & Supplies following).

Weather Information

A regional weather report in Italian is available on ☎ (011) 318 55 55.

ACCOMMODATION & SUPPLIES

The major city in the region, Cuneo, has a selection of reasonable places to stay. At *Albergo Ciriegia* (☎ (0171) 69 27 03), Corso Nizza 11, and *Albergo Ligure* (☎ (0171) 68 19 42), Via Savigliano 11, prices for singles/doubles with shared bath begin at L40,000/L70,000. *Albergo Cavallo Nero* (☎ (0171) 69 20 17), Via Seminario 8, charges L50,000/L70,000 for rooms – L20,000 extra for a private bathroom. There are many cafes on Piazza Galimberti and along Corso Nizza. A quiet, good-value place where most of the diners appear to be locals is *Pizzeria Il Veliero*, Via Savigliano 18, just north of Piazza Galimberti.

The walks in the region allow overnight stops at rifugi, where dinner and breakfast are normally provided and a *pranzo a sacco* (packed lunch) and snacks such as chocolate, to carry with you during the day, are available for purchase. Consequently there is no need to carry a fuel stove or large amounts of food. If you wish to stock up on food for lunch and snacks, there are *supermarkets* in Cuneo, including a *Megafresh* on Corso IV

Novembre, a couple of blocks north-east of the train station, and *panetterie* dotted through the town, including *Il Forno* on Corso Nizza.

Rifugi

Rifugio accommodation is in bunk rooms which sleep anywhere from two to a dozen or more people. Half board (dinner, bed and breakfast) includes an evening meal prepared by the *gestore* (manager) and their assistants. You'll generally be given a choice between pasta and soup, followed by a set *secondo*, almost always a meat dish such as *stufato* (stew). Dessert or cheese is often, but not always, included. Drinks and coffee are extra. Food is plentiful, and the standard is good – sometimes, given the circumstances, astonishingly so. Breakfast is usually the standard cheaper hotel fare of bread, jam and coffee. A sign may announce meal times, or the gestore may ask what time suits you.

All the rifugi mentioned in this chapter are maintained by the CAI and charge for meals and accommodation according to a schedule set out by them. Half board for visitors ranges from L45,000 to L53,000 per person. A main meal during the day costs between about L14,000 and L18,000. CAI members pay significantly less. Most gestore will want to see your passport when you arrive. See the 'Italian Alpine Club/Club Alpino Italiano' boxed text in the Facts for the Walker chapter for more on the CAI.

As well as the CAI rifugi, there are some private ones and a number of *bivacchi*. A bivacco is a more basic hut without a gestore. Some bivacchi are always open; for others it is necessary to arrange to collect a key in advance, by telephone.

All the rifugi suggested in this section as overnight staging posts are open continuously from at least 15 June to 15 September. Rifugio Morelli-Buzzi, a possible lunch spot on Day 1 of the Terme di Valdieri to Entracque walk, remains open until 30 September. Some rifugi open on the weekend (overnight accommodation on Saturday night only) for an additional period before and after the main season. As a rule, those at lower altitudes and closer to roads remain open longer.

If you are counting on staying overnight in a rifugio, *always* phone ahead, or ask someone to do it for you, to make sure the place is open and has room, and to let the staff know approximately what time you'll be arriving. Rifugi fill up quickly at some times of year, and occasionally one burns down or closes for repairs. Rifugi are also the first line of inquiry if someone goes missing in the mountains, and staff are genuinely concerned for the safety of walkers.

A useful brochure, *Rifugi alpini in provincia di Cuneo*, lists and shows on a map all the rifugi mentioned in this section and many more. It gives opening periods, contact details and the services each rifugio offers. It's free from the APT in Cuneo and elsewhere.

GETTING THERE & AWAY
Cuneo is readily accessible by train, bus or car. There are regular trains to and from Saluzzo, Torino, San Remo, Ventimiglia and Nice (France). Various bus companies run services from Saluzzo, Torino, Imperia, Savona and towns in Valle Stura. If travelling by car from Torino, take either the S20 direct or the A6 as far as Fossano, then the S231 to Cuneo.

See Getting To/From the Walk under the relevant walk later in this chapter for details of how to get from Cuneo into the mountains.

PARCO NATURALE ALPI MARITTIME

The 258.9 sq km Parco Naturale Alpi Marittime, formerly known as the Parco Naturale dell'Argentera, was established in 1980. For 30km, along the French border, the park abuts the Parc National du Mercantour. Both parks have their origin in a huge hunting reserve created in 1857 for Victor Emmanuel II, who was to become the first king of modern Italy.

Two walks are described, one of just a day and the other of four days. Both give superb views of the peaks in the park, which are the highest in the Alpi Marittime.

NATURAL HISTORY
The Parco Naturale Alpi Marittime is dominated by a number of granite massifs with peaks over 3000m, in particular the Argentera group, which gave the park its old name and whose highest point is Cima Sud Argentera (3297m). To the north-west, separated from the Argentera group by Valle del Valasco and Valle Gesso della Barra, is the massif topped by Monte Matto (3097m). To the south-east, on the French border and accessible from both countries, is the Gelas group, which includes Cima dei Gelas (3143m), Cima della Maledia (3061m) and Monte Clapier (3045m).

The park also harbours the most southerly permanent snow in the Alps. The *ghiacciai* that appear on maps of the region, in the vicinity of Cima dei Gelas and Cima della Maledia, are, however, more properly termed névés or high snowfields rather than glaciers.

Flora
The dominant vegetation types above the tree line are peat bogs, grasses (some of them serving as summer pastures for flocks of sheep or cattle), abundant wild flowers and low, wiry Alpine heathland plants including the dwarf pine and bilberry. Most of the forests on the lower slopes of the park are almost pure stands of *faggio* (beech). Much of the remainder consists of conifers such as the silver fir, red spruce, arolla pine and European larch.

There are a number of smaller plants endemic, or nearly so, to the Argentera region, including a species of gentian (*Gentiana villarsii*), a violet (*Viola nummularifolia*) found only here and on Corsica, and the so-called ancient king (*Saxifraga florulenta*), a rare plant that grows slowly in cracks in the cliffs between 1800m and 3200m in altitude, takes decades to reach maturity, flowers once and then dies.

Fauna
The open higher slopes and ridges of the Alpi Marittime are home to the *stambecco* (ibex) – reintroduced earlier this century – and the

more timid *camoscio* (chamois). It is some-times possible to approach the thickset ibex, with their long, ridged horns, quite closely as they graze, whereas you are more likely to see the agile chamois bounding away across a rocky slope. The rarer mouflon crosses into the area from Parc National du Mercantour in France but is seldom seen.

In grassy valleys, Alpine marmots, or *marmotte*, are occasionally seen and often heard. Their high-pitched alarm call is star-tling at close range and carries over a great distance. Fox, badger, marten and snow hare are also found in the region.

Flocks of choughs, or *gracchi*, wheel and whistle overhead in the higher parts of the park, and the very fortunate walker may spot a golden eagle, or *aquila reale*. At lower altitudes, forest species include the black woodpecker and eagle owl.

On a smaller scale, a variety of butterfly species, of all shades from drab through to conspicuous blue, flit about on the grassy valley floors and slopes.

INFORMATION
Information Sources

The headquarters of the Parco Naturale Alpi Marittime (☎ (0171) 97397; fax 97542) is at Corso Dante Livio Bianco 5, Valdieri. More conveniently placed for walkers using public transport are the park visitor centres opposite the Albergo Turismo in Terme di Valdieri and on Piazza del Municipio in Entracque (☎ (0171) 97 86 16).

The friendly staff in the APT in Cuneo (☎ (0171) 66615) have information about local transport to, and accommodation in, Terme di Valdieri and Entracque, where the walks in this section begin and end. The APT office is at Corso Nizza 17.

PLACES TO STAY & EAT

There is still no wild camping in the park, and overnight accommodation on the walks is in rifugi. See under Accommodation & Supplies earlier in this chapter for details.

The only realistic accommodation option at the start of the walk in Terme di Valdieri is *Albergo Turismo* (☎ (0171) 97334), at the

south-western end of Terme, open between 20 May and 31 October. A single/double costs L32,000/L64,000 and full board, with a packed lunch, is L75,000 per person.

Entracque, at the other end of the walk, has two camp sites. *Campeggio Valle Gesso* (☎ (0171) 97 82 47), about 1km north-west of the town towards Valdieri, on the west side of the main road, charges L7500 to pitch your tent plus L6500 per person. *Campeggio Il Bosco* (☎ (0171) 97 83 96), 1km south-east of Entracque on the road to Trinità, has good facilities but limited space for tents; sites cost L7500 plus L5700 per person. Right in town, *Albergo Pagarì* (☎ (0171) 97 81 57), Via della Resistenza 2, is open year-round and charges L50,000 for a double (no singles) during summer; the rest of the year, a single/double costs L30,000/L45,000. *Hotel Miramonti* (☎ (0171) 97 82 22), Viale Kennedy 2, charges L70,000/L90,000 during summer and L50,000/L60,000 the rest of the year. Both hotels have restaurants.

GETTING TO/FROM THE WALKS

Terme di Valdieri and Entracque are served by Nuova Benese buses (☎ (0171) 69 29 29) from Cuneo. Buses for Terme leave Cuneo's Piazza Galimberti once or twice a day between 2 June and 16 September (the Sunday service operates during July and August only). The fare is L5000. As many as seven buses a day (only one on Sunday) travel between Piazza Galimberti and Entracque from mid-June to mid-September, and reduced numbers run the rest of the year. The fare is L3800. Terme and Entracque buses also call at the stop outside the Cuneo train station.

In addition, in June, July and August, Alpibus runs two minibus services, twice a day, from Entracque to San Giacomo and Trinità. Alpibus minibuses are also available to take chartered groups of eight people or more to other destinations in the area. Details and a timetable are available from the park visitor centre (☎ (0171) 97 86 16) on Piazza del Municipio in Entracque, where the buses leave from. This service might widen your options if you want to vary the walks described.

Lago di Valscura Circuit

Duration 5 to 6 hours
Standard Easy-Medium
Start/Finish Terme di Valdieri
Closest Town Cuneo
Permits Required No
Public Transport Access Yes (in summer)
Summary A superb day walk to a high Alpine valley and a series of glacial lakes. Great mountain views. A fine introduction to the Alps.

A fine introduction to the Argentera area, and hard to beat for those with limited time in the Alpi Marittime, this walk begins and ends near the park visitor centre in Terme di Valdieri. It follows the GTA along a former hunting road of Victor Emmanuel II to Pian del Valasco, an alpine meadow in a magnificent glacial valley, then climbs past waterfalls and

through a tunnel almost to the French border. It visits three scenic lakes and offers excellent views of the Argentera massif before returning to the valley. It is described as a day walk but could be extended over two days, with an overnight stay at Rifugio Questa, to allow more time to explore.

THE WALK

From the south-western end of Terme di Valdieri, just uphill from the Parco Naturale Alpi Marittime visitor centre, follow the rocky road south-west, then west, for 15 minutes to the point where a foot track heads off along the valley bottom while the road climbs. The foot track offers a shorter and at times steeper route, while the road makes more steady progress to the same destination, the lower end of **Pian del Valasco**, an hour from Terme.

The Reale Casa di Caccia (Royal Hunting Lodge), extensively fire-damaged, is visible

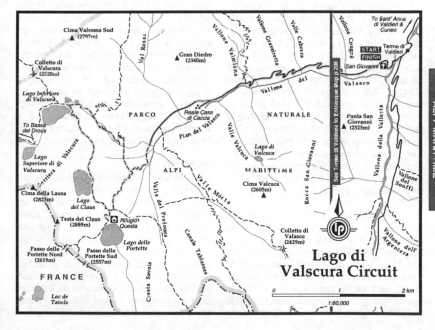

Lago di
Valscura Circuit

further up the plain, only a short detour from the main track.

From a signpost on the upper end of the Pian del Valasco (1814m), a track goes off to the left (south-east) towards Colletto di Valasco. Carry on ahead, following the signs towards Rifugio Questa. After 30 minutes (1km) the track divides and a signpost indicates two ways to reach the rifugio. Take the right fork, which leads north past some small waterfalls, swings around and through a tunnel in the rock, and winds generally north- west up a glacial valley to reach **Lago Inferiore di Valscura** (2274m), in a pretty cirque, after 50 minutes to an hour.

Ignore a signposted track which leads around the north side of the lake towards Bassa del Drous (2628m) on the French border. Follow the GTA to the left as it climbs out of the valley and heads roughly south towards Lago del Claus. A royal hunting party would fit comfortably on the wide, level track – a military road built between the world wars – as it crosses a large jumble of scree.

There are fine views of the Argentera massif away to the east and, closer at hand, back down Vallone del Valasco. Forty minutes from Lago Inferiore di Valscura the track passes behind a moraine wall and through a glacial basin where cliffs surround the deep, clear waters of **Lago del Claus** (2344m). After another 20 minutes south, a zigzagging descent leads to a track junction where a signpost points up the hill to **Rifugio Questa** (2388m), which is perched 27m above the steep-sided Lago delle Portette. The rifugio is open between 15 June and 15 September. It sleeps 45 people and serves drinks and meals, including hot lunches. To stay overnight, phone ahead on ☎ (0171) 97338.

Back at the signpost below Rifugio Questa, head down to the left (north) on the GTA, leaving the more substantial track which heads east. The GTA is mostly easy to follow, and always adequately marked with red-and-white squares, as it descends in 45 minutes (1km) back to the three-way junction you passed through earlier on the route. Go right, and in less than two hours (6km), returning by the way you came, you will be back in Terme di Valdieri.

Terme di Valdieri to Entracque

> **Duration** 4 days
> **Standard** Hard
> **Start** Terme di Valdieri
> **Finish** Entracque
> **Closest Town** Cuneo
> **Permits Required** No
> **Public Transport Access** Yes (in summer)
> **Summary** Three pass crossings and a visit to a fourth pass on the French border, in wild terrain among 3000m-plus peaks. Technically challenging crossing of Passo dei Ghiacciai requires experience and caution.

Because of the rugged nature of the ridges in the Argentera region, most walking routes follow valleys, or link valleys by means of pass crossings. This four-day walk could be dubbed 'the four passes route'. It crosses three passes and makes a side trip to a fourth, the Colle di Finestra, on the border with France. Of the four passes the walk visits, only Passo dei Ghiacciai is technically challenging, and we describe an alternative route that avoids the pass should weather or snow conditions dictate it necessary.

The walk begins in the tiny spa village of Terme di Valdieri and ends in the somewhat larger centre of Entracque.

WARNING
Speak to other walkers and rifugio staff before attempting to cross Passo dei Ghiacciai. The crossing should not be attempted in poor visibility. Until late in the summer, snow conditions may make it extremely hazardous unless you are equipped with crampons and an ice axe and are familiar with their use. If in doubt, take the alternative route described from Rifugio Ellena-Soria to Rifugio Pagarì via San Giacomo, or complete the walk in three days by descending from Rifugio Ellena-Soria through San Giacomo to Entracque.

ALPI MARITTIME

PLANNING
When to Walk
The best period in which to do this walk is from mid-June until mid-September, when all rifugi (see Accommodation & Supplies earlier in this chapter) are open and public transport reaches the more remote destinations in the area, such as Terme di Valdieri. At the risk of stating the obvious, these months also have the best weather. Larger bus companies operate to a restricted timetable outside this period, and many places to stay close down. Note that the Alpibus service to San Giacomo and Trinità (see Getting To/From the Walks earlier in the chapter) only runs during June, July and August.

Until late summer – say, the end of August or sometimes even later – firm snow slopes may make the Passo dei Ghiacciai crossing, as they say, *una cosa alpinistica* (a serious undertaking) requiring crampons and an ice axe (see Warning on the previous page). The slopes in question are, however, not extensive, and a few days of warm weather can all but eliminate the difficulties.

Maps
The best map for the walk is the Istituto Geografico Centrale (IGC) (1:25,000) *Parco Naturale Alpi Marittime*, No 113, available in bigger bookshops in the region for L12,000. Though not faultless, it is the most detailed and accurate, notably in the area of Passo dei Ghiacciai (labelled 'Passo dei Ghiacciai del Gelas'), of all the maps listed here.

The IGC (1:50,000) *Alpi Marittime e Liguri* is more widely available, covers a larger area including the Marguareis group, and costs L9000. The Edizioni Multigraphic (1:25,000) *Alpi Marittime e Liguri – Gruppi Argentera e Marguareis*, sold in many bookshops for L10,000, lists telephone numbers and other details for rifugi, but does not show Passo dei Ghiacciai or Rifugio Pagarì.

The area of the walk appears on map No Il of a set of four Geocart (1:50,000) maps, *Montagnes sans Frontière*/Montagne senza Frontiere, sold in Parco Naturale Alpi Marittime visitor centres for L20,000. Of all the maps of the Argentera group, this is the most

attractive to look at but contains the least information for walkers despite extensive notes printed on the back.

What to Bring
All the warm and waterproof clothing and other personal equipment (see the Equipment & Clothing section in the Facts for the Walker chapter) required elsewhere in the mountains is just as vital here. Wild camping is not permitted within Parco Naturale Alpi Marittime, however, each day's walk ends at a rifugio, where prepared meals and a bed, pillow and blankets are available at a moderate price. Hence you can leave behind some of the equipment usually necessary on a walk of this length through mountainous terrain. Provided you phone ahead and ensure that there will be room for you at the next night's rifugio, there's no need to carry a tent, sleeping bag, stove, fuel, or food other than snacks to eat during the day and perhaps some lunches. A bivouac bag for emergency shelter is a sensible item of group equipment. You should bring a sleeping sheet and light footwear to put on when you remove your boots at the rifugio (though most rifugi have a supply of 'hut slippers').

Bring enough lire in cash to cover accommodation and meals. At most rifugi, staff will ask to see your passport (or CAI membership card should you decide to join) when you arrive, and may keep it overnight.

See the Warning earlier in this section

ALPI MARITTIME

regarding Passo dei Ghiacciai. Bring crampons and an ice axe – and make sure you know how to use them – if you intend to cross the pass early in the summer.

THE WALK
Day 1: Terme di Valdieri to Rifugio Genova-Figari
5½ to 6½ hours, 1160m ascent, 510m descent

The start of the track is well signposted where it leaves the main road on the southeast (true right) bank of the Torrente Gesso della Valletta about 50m downhill from the expensive Grande Albergo Royal in Terme di Valdieri. Within a few minutes the track crosses the stream, that enters from the south-east, on a footbridge, turns up the north-east (true right) bank of the stream and begins to climb on switchbacks. Deciduous forest, with occasional clearings that offer views back to Terme, gives way to pines. After about an hour, there are views across the valley to Monte Stella (3262m) and to the dramatic couloir of **Canalone di Lourousa**.

Another 25 minutes of straightforward walking leads to Gias Lagarot, a stone-walled, tin-roofed hut and a stockyard. After a further 10 minutes, near a memorial cross beside a beautiful stream, a track branches off to the right, across the valley and up to

Bivacco Varrone, now visible near the foot of the couloir. Ignore this and continue up the valley to surmount a big moraine wall which brings first Colle del Chiapous, then **Rifugio Morelli-Buzzi** (2381m), into view. Open from 15 June to 30 September, the rifugio serves hot meals and drinks – including coffee, of course – and makes a good spot for lunch. To stay overnight, phone ahead on ☎ (0171) 97394.

Twenty minutes beyond Rifugio Morelli-Buzzi a set of switchbacks up a moraine wall comes into view. The ascent is less strenuous than it looks, and from the top it's only a short distance to the signpost that marks the top of the grassy **Colle del Chiapous** (2526m). From the pass the track crosses a mass of moraine, then zigzags down below cliffs, first on the west side of the valley, then on the east. **Lago del Chiotas**, nearly 550m below the pass, is artificial but still spectacular, especially if cloud is billowing up over the dam wall. The track drops down the valley almost level with the top of the wall, makes its way eastwards around to the wall and crosses it.

Once across, follow the occasional red-and-white GTA markers down a short stretch of road, through a tunnel, then up and around the south-eastern end of Lago del Chiotas on a rough road, to **Rifugio Genova-Figari**

After-Dinner Drinks
An evening spent in an alpine rifugio can be quite a gastronomic and cultural adventure, and a significant centre of attention in many rifugi is the bar. This is not to say that a walk in this region is merely an excuse for alcoholic excesses; rather, local walkers feel they've earned the right to relax when they reach a rifugio, and there's no reason a visitor should think otherwise.

Grappa, a strong, clear grape spirit, is a perennial after-dinner favourite. Other popular drops are *genepè* and a number of varieties of bitter *amaro*, all flavoured with herbs. In some rifugi the *gestore* or caretaker may favour you with a herbal concoction of their own making, such as the cloudy, exceedingly bitter *genzianella* I sampled at Rifugio Pagarì. Go on, take the risk.

Coffee is an important part of the evening's proceedings, sometimes taken as *caffè corretto* – with a dash of grappa. A variation on this theme is *grolla valdostana*, whose name betrays its origins in the villages of Valle d'Aosta. Grolla is a dark brew of black coffee, grappa and sugar, sometimes with lemon zest or cloves added, which generally comes to the table flaming, in a carved wooden tub with a number of spouts – one for each person partaking. After the tub has been round the group a few times, you may not know whether to subside under the table or dance on top of it. If you can't decide, never mind: the after-dinner conversation will almost certainly be wide-ranging and animated.

Nick Tapp

(2015m) between Lago del Chiotas and Lago Brocan. (Note the junction and signpost, 10 minutes before the rifugio, indicating the start of the following day's route over Colle di Fenestrelle.) The rifugio sleeps 70 people and is open from 15 June to 15 September. You're in luck if you find polenta or panna cotta con mirtilli on the menu, and the grolla valdostana (see the boxed text) is worth a try on a chilly night. Phone ahead (☎ (0171) 97 81 38) to be sure of a place at the table.

Day 2: Rifugio Genova-Figari to Rifugio Ellena-Soria

3 to 3½ hours, 490m ascent, 660m descent

From the rifugio return to the signpost that points towards Colle di Fenestrelle, and follow that track as it climbs gently, then somewhat more steeply, to the east. After about 90 minutes of zigzagging ascent around the north and east sides of the Vallone di Fenestrelle, the track crosses a false pass over a spur, descends to cross a gully where there may be some snow, then climbs for another 20 minutes to the signposted **Colle di Fenestrelle** (2463m).

The descent from the pass is well defined and adequately marked. Ibex and the more timid chamois often graze higher up in this open, grassy valley. Lower down towards the Pian del Praiet you may hear the piercing alarm cry of the marmot, but these watchful creatures are likely to spot you and scamper for cover long before you get close enough to see them. Cowbells are another common sound in this valley. On the valley bottom a signpost points the way to **Rifugio Ellena-Soria** (1840m), which looms atop a knoll on the east side of the stream. The 40m climb from the river bank to the rifugio is the steepest ascent of the day. Rifugio Ellena-Soria sleeps 80 people and is open from 15 June to 15 September. Phone ahead (☎ (0171) 97 83 82) if you plan to stay here.

Side Trip: Colle di Finestra

2½ to 3 hours, 690m ascent & descent

On a clear day it's well worth following the track that leads south, up the valley beyond Rifugio Ellena-Soria, to Colle di Finestra

(2471m) on the French border. From the rifugio, return to the valley floor and follow the well-defined track south, which soon begins to climb and, after a couple of switchbacks, reaches a signposted junction where track M18 goes left towards Pera de Fener. This is the route to Passo dei Ghiacciai and Rifugio Pagarì described under Day 3A below. Take the right fork (M11) and ascend gradually south for 20 minutes to the remains of a building on the east side of the track, then it's another 40 minutes to **Colle di Finestra**. Beyond lies France. The track continues south into the Parc National du Mercantour past Lac de Fenestre, visible less than 1km away, to the GR52 long-distance track and Rifugio Madone de Fenestre.

Retrace your steps to Rifugio Ellena-Soria.

Day 3A: Rifugio Ellena-Soria to Rifugio Pagarì via Passo dei Ghiacciai

4½ to 6 hours, 1160m ascent, 350m descent

From the rifugio drop to the valley floor and follow the track south towards Colle di Finestra for 15 to 20 minutes, as far as the signpost to Pera de Fener. Go left here, and follow the well-defined track M18, marked with occasional cairns, red paint stripes and arrows, as it zigzags up a spur, keeping a series of rocky cascades on its left (north) side. A steep, direct track eschews the switchbacks if you're so inclined. About an hour from the rifugio the track crosses, then recrosses, a stream tumbling from a wide, scree-filled gully below Cima dei Gelas (3143m), which dominates the skyline as you look up. Continue up scree slopes, with occasional cairns to indicate the way, into a gully with views of Lago della Maura down on the left side and, back to the north-west, the Argentera massif. After climbing steeply up a spur between two streams, cross the stream on the left to its true right side. The track becomes clear and well marked once again, then shortly recrosses the stream and continues to the remains of a stone building on a grassy area.

In good conditions the pass is visible from here, only a couple of hundred metres away to the north-east. Note that there is a lower, more precipitous notch further north on the

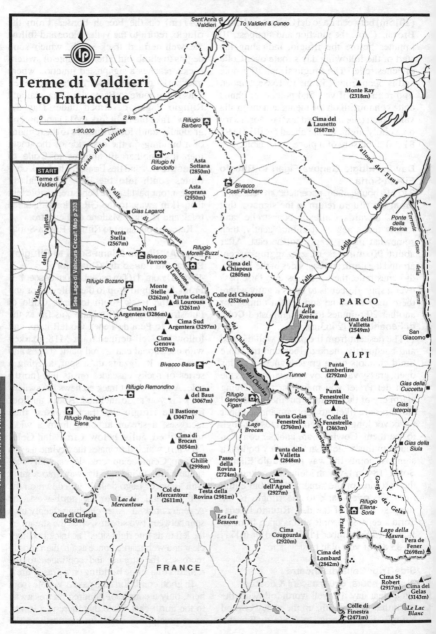

Terme di Valdieri to Entracque

0   1   2 km

1:90,000

START
Terme di
Valdieri

See Lago di Valscura Circuit Map p 203

Sant'Anna di
Valdieri

To Valdieri & Cuneo

Monte Ray
(2318m)

Cima del
Lausetto
(2687m)

Vallone del Fiaus

Rifugio
Barbero

Rifugio N
Gandolfo

Asta
Sottana
(2850m)

Asta
Soprana
(2950m)

Bivacco
Costi-Falchero

Gesso della Valletta

Valle della Valletta

Vallone della Valletta

Gias Lagarot
di

Lourousa

Rifugio
Morelli-Buzzi

Punta
Stella
(2567m)

Bivacco
Varrone

Gandalena
di Lourousa

Cima del
Chiapous
(2805m)

Rifugio Bozano

Monte
Stelle
(3262m)

Punta Gelas
di Lourousa
(3261m)

Colle del Chiapous
(2526m)

Cima Nord
Argentera
(3286m)

Cima Sud
Argentera
(3297m)

Vallone del Chiapous

Valle della Rovina

Lago
della
Rovina

Ponte
della
Rovina

Torrente Cesso della Rovina

Gesso della Barra

PARCO

Cima della
Valletta
(2549m)

San
Giacomo

Cima
Genova
(3257m)

ALPI

Bivacco Baus

Lago del Chiotas

Tunnel

Punta
Ciamberline
(2792m)

Gias della
Cuccetta

Rifugio Remondino

Cima
del Baus
(3067m)

Rifugio
Genova-
Figari

Punta
Fenestrelle
(2701m)

Gias
Isterpis

il Bastione
(3047m)

Lago
Brocan

Punta Gelas
Fenestrelle
(2760m)

Colle di
Fenestrelle
(2463m)

Gias della
Siula

Cima di
Brocan
(3054m)

Punta della
Valletta
(2848m)

Vallone Fenestrelle

Cima
Ghiliè
(2998m)

Passo
della
Rovina
(2724m)

Cima
dell'Agnel
(2927m)

Gorgia dei Gelas

Rifugio
Ellena-
Soria

Col du
Mercantour
(2611m)

Testa della
Rovina (2981m)

Plan del Praiet

Lac du
Mercantour

Les Lac
Bessons

Lago della
Maura

Colle di Ciriegia
(2543m)

Cima
Cougourda
(2920m)

Pera de
Fener
(2698m)

FRANCE

Cima del
Lombard
(2842m)

Cima St
Robert
(2917m)

Cima dei
Gelas
(3143m)

Colle di
Finestra
(2471m)

Le Lac
Blanc

ALPI MARITTIME

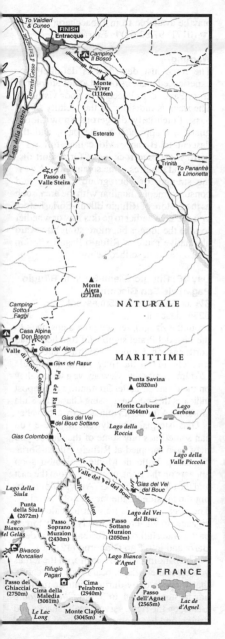

same ridge; the route does not go through it. Cairns now lead up and around unstable slopes of scree to the top of the knoll above the ruined building. From this knoll, rocky terraces lead below cliffs towards the pass. Depending on the season, the cairned and marked route may be interrupted by several quite steep tongues of snow. These remain in shade for much of the day and consequently may be too firm to cross safely unless you are equipped with crampons and/or an ice axe. Late in the summer, a safe route can be found by descending on rocky ground, skirting below the tongues of steep snow and scrambling up below the pass to rejoin the marked route. Cairns and red paint markers lead around to the left and finally up to **Passo dei Ghiacciai** (2750m), a dip in the narrow, rocky ridge top. Below and to the left (north) is Bivacco Moncalieri, and below it are two lakes, Lago Bianco del Gelas and a smaller, unnamed one that does not appear on the survey maps. Far below to the north-east, beyond the lakes, a walking track can be seen snaking up the side of Valle del Vei del Bouc.

The descent from the pass begins with a short traverse to the right (south) along a rather narrow, exposed ledge. Easier ground then leads back below the pass, across a stretch of moraine and down a gully which

NICK TAPP

Passo dei Ghiacciai from the knoll above the ruined building (see text). The cairned route leads across the sunlit rocky terrace on the right, but it may be necessary to follow a lower route in the shade on the left.

ALPI MARITTIME

may contain snow, to **Bivacco Moncalieri** (2710m). This 11-bed private hut will be locked unless someone with a key is in residence, but the surrounds make a pleasant place to stop for lunch. Ibex graze nearby.

From here the track is indistinct at times, though it's marked with cairns and faded splashes of red paint, as it winds across the loose slope (which is optimistically labelled 'Ghiacciaio' on the IGC (1:25,000) map) above Lago Bianco del Gelas, then down to cross the outlet from the lake. Painted arrows on the rocks here indicate a parting of ways. Take the right fork towards Rifugio Pagarì. This leads between the two lakes and passes on the downhill side of the smaller, unnamed one and along the moraine wall which dams it. Follow cairns and paint markers left (north), over the lip of the moraine and across the outlet stream from the unnamed lake, which vanishes under rocks here for a short distance. Alternating patches of grass and rocky ground lead generally east across a couple of stream gullies and around the base of a big rock bluff. At a prominent red paint marker, the track veers north-west for a short way, down the toe of a spur through scrubby alpine vegetation. It then doubles back to the east at more markers and traverses into a big, scree-filled basin, where it stays high below cliffs, avoiding the worst of the scree. A climb of 15 to 20 minutes leads to a ridge top and **Passo Soprano Muraion** (2430m). The Valle Muraion and the track from Rifugio Pagarì down the valley to San Giacomo now appear below, and across to the east is Lago Bianco d'Agnel.

A winding, ascending traverse leads across a broad gully to another ridge, where the rifugio comes into view. Ten minutes later the main track down the valley goes off to the left. Go right and just over the brow of the hill, with the impressive north-east face of Cima della Maledia (3061m) behind it, is **Rifugio Pagarì** (also known as Rifugio Federici-Marchesini). Open from mid-June to mid September, this rifugio is the highest in the Alpi Marittime at 2650m and sleeps 30. To stay, phone ahead on ☎ (0171) 97 83 98. Outside the normal opening period, keys

may be available from Tabaccheria Fantino (☎ (0171) 97 82 62) in Entracque.

Warning
The route just described is definitely for experienced walkers only. Do not attempt to cross Passo dei Ghiacciai in poor visibility. The track is indistinct in the vicinity of the pass. Potentially dangerous snow slopes guard the approach to the pass, and the descent to Bivacco Moncalieri follows a narrow, exposed rock ledge for a short distance and requires some scrambling. Assess the strength of your group carefully and consult someone familiar with the area, such as the gestore of Rifugio Ellena-Soria, before you decide whether to go this way or whether to take the longer but more straightforward alternative route to Rifugio Pagarì via San Giacomo, as described below.

Day 3B: Rifugio Ellena-Soria to Rifugio Pagarì via San Giacomo
6½ to 7½ hours, 1435m ascent,
625m descent
From the rifugio, retrace your steps back to the Pian del Praiet signpost. From here head north-east on a wide, rocky track above the true left side of the river. Punta della Siula (2672m) comes into view above a wide valley on the right, and after 30 minutes a signpost indicates that you are passing Gias della Siula (1480m). A further 15 minutes down the valley is Gias Isterpis, recently rebuilt, where you can sometimes buy some of the cheese you may have sampled at Rifugio Ellena-Soria. The deep Valle di Monte Colombo soon appears on the right, coming in from the east and the old route of the GTA is visible climbing the hillside on the far side of the valley. The track, which is now an unsealed road, zigzags down through lovely beech forest, past a waterfall on the Torrente Gesso della Barra and into **San Giacomo** (1213m).

The park information centre, on the left as you enter the village, bears signs indicating that it opens daily during summer from 10 am to noon and 4 to 7 pm. *Baita Monte Gelas*, on the right, serves meals, snacks and drinks, and has rooms during June, July and

Track Rage

It looked good on the map. A nice thick red line labelled 'GTA' ran along the east bank of the river and avoided a parallel 3km 'road bash' on the opposite bank. On the ground, the red-and-white markers painted on the rocks began where the map indicated they ought to, and the track led off through a pretty patch of cool, green forest.

The markers continued, but the track soon dwindled. Still in the late morning shade, its leafy surface was damp and slippery. Lush, green stinging nettles quivered with anticipation at every step. I began to wonder whether anyone (apart from a zealot with two cans of paint) had ever walked this way. When a trivial rocky spur interrupted progress along the river bank, even the markers vanished, and it took precious minutes to find them winding tortuously up the spur and back down on the other side. All in all, this track was costing me more than its fair share of time and energy. Still, I was on a mission, and I persevered.

I can't remember what finally snapped, but suddenly I'd had enough. Seeing red amidst all the greenery, I thrashed knee deep through the snagging, stinging undergrowth to the river, scrambled along the slippery bank to a spot where it seemed conceivable I might not drown, crossed the raging *torrente* and clambered up the other side to the road.

As I emptied my boots and wrung out my socks, it occurred to me that there was a lesson in this minor misadventure. At the risk of stating the obvious, a red line on a map and a label such as 'Grande Traversata' or 'Alta Via' may sometimes have more to do with a splendid vision than with reality on the ground. Not always, but sometimes.

And the road bash? It was lovely, thanks.

Nick Tapp

August from L18,000 to L23,000 per person. At *Camping Sotto i Faggi*, across the bridge just below the village, a tent site costs L7000 plus L5000 per person.

At the bridge, turn east across the river, past the camping ground, and follow the route description given below for Day 4, in reverse, for 4½ to 5½ hours to reach **Rifugio Pagarì** (see Day 3A earlier for details).

Day 4: Rifugio Pagarì to Entracque

5 to 6 hours, 1750m descent

From the rifugio the well-marked track M13 zigzags in a north-easterly direction at first, down a rocky spur with good views towards Passo dell'Agnel and the peaks that surround it, away to the east. The track then swings west of north and follows the side of Valle Muraion for a couple of kilometres, finally dropping to the valley floor, and a signpost, about 1½ hours walk from the rifugio. Later in the summer, the time it takes you to reach this point may be influenced by the quantity of *mirtilli* (blueberries or bilberries) and, lower down, of *lamponi* (raspberries) on offer beside the track. A couple of minutes on from the signpost is a lovely pool where a stream cascades across the track from the south-west.

Proceed roughly north down the valley, which maps refer to here as Valle (or Vallone) di Monte Colombo, and cross to the east side and Gias del Vei del Bouc Sottano. Here a signpost indicates the start of the track up Valle del Vei del Bouc that is visible from Passo dei Ghiacciai. Continue north along a grassy plain, Prà del Rasur, which extends for a kilometre or more. The track enters the first patches of beech forest and soon passes Gias dell'Aiera, an old building with a new roof. Near here is the start of a track which older maps show as part of the GTA. It climbs to about 2250m on the west side of Monte Aiera (2713m) and might make a scenic alternative route to Esterate and Entracque on a good day. It can be seen from various vantage points zigzagging up the hillside, but the start is not obvious and you might need to ask for help in finding it.

The main track, which has become a little-used road, now winds along the north bank of the river as it twists and cascades below. Several pedestrian short cuts avoid bends, but the distance saved is not great. The road passes a former Reale Casa di Caccia (Royal Hunting Lodge), now the Casa Alpina Don Bosco, among tall pines and beeches, and

ALPI MARITTIME

five minutes later crosses a bridge over the Torrente Gesso della Barra just below **San Giacomo** (see Day 3B earlier for details).

The IGC 1:50,000 and 1:25,000 maps both show the GTA following the east bank of Torrente Gesso della Barra downstream from here to Ponte della Rovina, then climbing to Passo di Valle Steira (1515m; the unnamed pass just south of Caire Cabanàs on the 1:50,000 sheet) and descending to Esterate. From Esterate it is just 2km by back roads to Entracque. The start of the track can be found, marked with the usual red-and-white GTA markers, heading into the woods beside the office of Camping Sotto i Faggi on the east bank of the river in San Giacomo. At the time of writing, though, the track downstream of this point was indistinct and overgrown and evidently received very little foot traffic. The road down the west side of the river makes a better alternative. It's 4km by road from San Giacomo to Ponte della Rovina, where there's a trough and running water. A further 3km takes you the length of Lago della Piastra and brings you to a signposted turn-off down to the right towards Entracque. Follow this road back towards the base of the dam that holds back the lake, then north through a peaceful rural setting to **Entracque**, which should take another 30 minutes or so.

PARCO NATURALE ALTA VALLE PESIO E TANARO

This park, only 10km east of Parco Naturale Alpi Marittime, might almost be in another mountain range, so different is the landscape – thanks mainly to its distinct underlying geology. The peaks of the Argentera and Gelas massifs are clearly visible from the summit of Punta Marguareis (2651m), the highest point in the park and the highlight of the two-day walk described here, which begins and ends in the popular winter resort of Limone Piemonte.

The 67.7 sq km park was founded in 1978, but the valley's environment has been carefully managed since the 12th century, when Carthusian monks founded the Certosa di Santa Maria charterhouse, now near the northern edge of the park.

NATURAL HISTORY

Whereas the Argentera and Gelas are granite formations, the Alta Valle Pesio is limestone country. The north-facing ramparts of Punta Marguareis and its satellite peaks are the most impressive of many cliffs in the area, and the surrounding valleys and plateaus are riddled with caves. Some of these, below the Conca delle Carsene karstic basin to the west of Punta Marguareis, have been plumbed to depths in excess of 600m. In all, more than 150km of caves have been explored in the region. Rainfall is abundant but, instead of forming streams and clear, deep lakes, surface water here tends to disappear underground. Sometimes it reappears later in spectacular fashion, as in the Piscio del Pesio waterfall, where an underground river gushes from a cliff.

Though robbed of much of the rain that falls by the porous terrain, the upper slopes of the park harbour a wide variety of plant species, including lilies, gentians and alpine pasqueflowers. By contrast, the deep valleys are well watered and densely wooded. There are extensive pure stands of silver fir, sweet chestnut, beech and European larch as well as mixed broad-leaved forests.

Some Alpine animals are found here too, in particular the Alpine marmot, the chamois and, at lower altitudes, wild boar, roe deer and red deer.

INFORMATION

The horse's mouth for information about the park is the Ente di Gestione dei Parchi e delle Riserve Cuneesi (☎ (0171) 73 40 21), Via Sant'Anna 34, Chiusa di Pesio. The APT offices in Cuneo (☎ (0171) 66615), at Corso Nizza 17, and in Limone Piemonte (☎ (0171) 92101), at Via Roma 30, should be able to help with more general information, including transport and accommodation options.

PLACES TO STAY & EAT

Conveniently close to the train station in Limone Piemonte at Viale Vallegia 23 is *Albergo La Primula* (☎ (0171) 92366), where singles/doubles with shared bathroom cost L40,000/L80,000 (breakfast included) during July and August and half board starts from L80,000 per person. Prices are lower from 1 September to 20 September. Also central, at Via San Secondo 9 on the corner of Via Genova, is the three-star *Hotel Marguareis*, which charges L90,000/L120,000 during May, June and October, rising to L115,000/L170,000 at the height of summer (from 26 July to 31 August); half board ranges from L80,000 to L110,000 for double occupancy, or L30,000 more if you're on your own. Both hotels have restaurants.

GETTING TO/FROM THE WALK

Limone Piemonte lies on the train line from Cuneo to Ventimiglia and Nice (France). Numerous trains make the 28km journey from Cuneo every day, and the fare is L2800.

Certosa di Santa Maria (Certosa di Pesio), an alternative access point at the northern end of the park, is accessible during the summer months by bus from Cuneo. Contact Autolinee Valle Pesio (☎ (0171) 73 44 96) for details.

Marguareis Circuit

Duration 2 days
Standard Medium-Hard
Start/Finish Limone Piemonte
Closest Town Cuneo
Permits Required No
Public Transport Access Yes
Summary A long climb from the valley to the karst country of the Alta Valle Pesio and a fascinating mountain *rifugio*. Grandstand views of the limestone cliffs of Punta Marguareis and sweeping views from the top.

This two-day walk begins and ends just outside the park, among the groomed slopes and condominiums of Limone Piemonte, one of the most popular downhill ski resorts in the southern Alps. It soon climbs above the lifts onto the dramatic ridge that overlooks Limone, then heads east across karstic plains and drops into Vallone del Marguareis at the foot of the Marguareis massif. Rifugio Garelli offers outstanding views of these cliffs. On the second day, the walk climbs to the summit of Punta Marguareis, then returns to Limone after making a minor incursion into French territory.

WARNING

The walk does not pass close by any of the major caves in the area. There are, however, many smaller sinkholes around, some of them very close to the track and few of them are marked or fenced off. Watch your step, stay on marked tracks and excercise due care near depressions in the ground.

PLANNING
When to Walk

In conjunction with the weather, the factor that determines the best time to do this walk is the availability of accommodation at Rifugio Garelli. The rifugio is open continuously from 15 June to 15 September and over weekends (overnight accommodation on Saturday night only) for an additional month at either end of the season, starting on 15 May and ending on 15 October. While it is possible to obtain a key to the rifugio and let yourself in at other times, the opening periods give a good indication of when the weather is likely to be good.

Maps

The best and most detailed map for the walk is the IGC (1:25,000) *Limone Piemonte – Valle delle Meraviglie – St Dalmas de Tende*, No 114, available in bigger bookshops in the region for L12,000. The area of the walk also appears on the IGC (1:50,000) *Alpi Marittime e Liguri* map, which is more widely available, covers a larger area, including the Argentera group, and costs L9000. Neither of these maps shows the route from Porta Sestrera to Lago Rataira (labelled 'Lago

ALPI MARITTIME

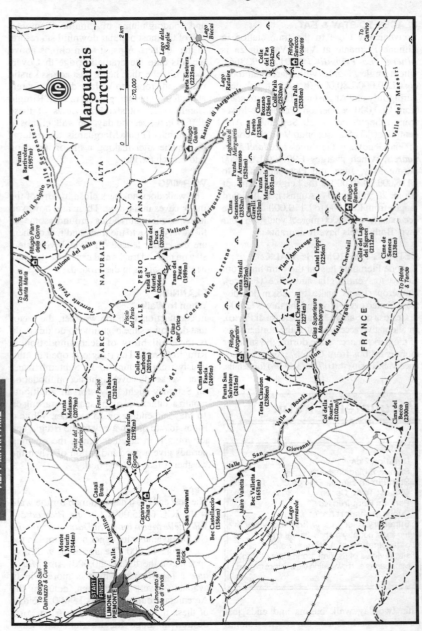

Ratavuloira' on the 1:50,000 sheet) or the track through Colle Palù to Punta Marguareis; even so, they are easier to use and more useful than the two listed below.

The Edizioni Multigraphic (1:25,000) *Alpi Marittime e Liguri – Gruppi Argentera e Marguareis*, Nos 109 and 115 (on one sheet), sold in many bookshops for L10,000, lists telephone numbers and other details for rifugi, but is somewhat difficult to read. Map No III of a set of four Geocart 1:50,000 maps, *Montagnes sans Frontière/Montagne senza Frontiere*, sold in park visitor centres in the region for L20,000, is the most attractive to look at of all the maps of the Marguareis group, but contains the least information for walkers despite the extensive notes printed on the back.

What to Bring

No special equipment is necessary for this walk besides the usual warm and waterproof clothing and other personal equipment you'd take on any walk in an alpine environment. A tent and sleeping bag are not required provided you phone ahead to Rifugio Garelli and reserve a place. You will need enough cash to pay for food and accommodation at the rifugio. You should carry your passport in case the rifugio gestore asks to see it.

French Visa If you want to cover every tiniest contingency, and are a citizen of a country whose nationals require a visa to enter France, you might obtain one for this walk. In practice, the walk traverses 4km of a remote corner of France, crossing over the border from Italy into France and back again within 90 minutes or so, at two windswept cols far from human habitation.

THE WALK
Day 1: Limone Piemonte to Rifugio Garelli

5 to 6 hours, 1585m ascent, 595m descent
From Piazza Risorgimento, in front of the train station in Limone, head under the railway bridge and uphill, steeply at times, to the east along Via Almellina. This dwindles to an unsealed road as it climbs up the Valle Almellina for 2km or so to a cluster of

buildings, some newly roofed and others without roofs, labelled Casali Braia on the IGC 1:25,000 map.

Follow the most obvious road here as it bends back to the south and, within a few minutes, passes under a ski lift next to its bottom station. After a few switchbacks up the line of the lift, the track heads south around a spur through a patch of beech forest to emerge onto open slopes near a lodge, Capanno Chiara, at the bottom of another two ski lifts. There are many tracks in this area. Take one that leads up a small spur, roughly parallel with the more northerly of the two lifts, passing the remains of Gias Gorgia, to the lift's top station, after about an hour's walking.

Continue climbing, under the top of the lift you first encountered down near Casali Braia and away from the ski resort infrastructure, on a track that snakes up grassy slopes with ever-expanding views. The track rounds a spur and becomes more easterly, passing through a lush, damp saddle, then winds its way into an eroded gully system, where the trickle emitted by Fonte di Carlaccio may be the only water. Continue to the north-west up this gully system on very faint tracks, then up grassy slopes to meet the ridge top and a prominent track just south of Punta Melasso (2079m), one hour from the top the lifts).

Turn south on this track. Despite the proximity of Limone in the valley to the west, the walk now takes on an increasingly wild feel thanks to the imposing formations of Rocce del Cros straight ahead and Roccia il Pulpito across Valle Pesio to the north-east. The track passes the cow-trodden Fonte Paciot, then skirts below the cliffs of Cima Baban (2102m) and heads for Monte Iurin (2192m) before sidling around its eastern slopes. To the south-east, through a low saddle and across the limestone plain of Conca delle Carsene, Punta Marguareis looms. The track winds easily down to the valley bottom, then climbs again for a short distance beside a last, low set of cliffs to the saddle, **Colle del Carbone** (2019m).

A fainter track now continues down through the col, in a direction slightly north

ALPI MARITTIME

Rifugio Phoenix

The original Rifugio Piero Garelli, perched above Vallone del Marguareis on Pian del Lupo (Plain of the Wolf), was totally destroyed by fire in 1987. Over the next two summers, volunteers from the Mondovì section of CAI, and others, built the present rifugio in its place.

During the 1988 season they constructed the outer shell – walls, roof and shutters – so that it would be able to weather the winter. The following year they completed and fitted out the interior of the building. In all, helicopters made about a thousand trips to transport materials for the new rifugio from the nearest roadhead to Pian del Lupo at an altitude of 2000m. At the opening ceremony, the symphony orchestra of Cuneo played from the forecourt of the rifugio to a crowd of thousands, who sat in the sun on the natural amphitheatre of the ridge to the south. If you ask nicely, the gestore will probably show you the albums of photos that document the process.

Nick Tapp

NICK TAPP

of north-east, to meet the GTA with its reassuring red-and-white markers. Follow the GTA east, passing the remains of Gias dell'Ortica on a hillock just south of the track, and a signpost where track H11 departs in a northerly direction. The GTA climbs amidst a bewildering profusion of minor tracks through a small pass to the south of Testa di Murtel (2066m), then along a scenic, pine-clad ridge top. Watch out for a scantily fenced-off sinkhole right beside the track before a final switchback leads to **Passo del Duca** (1989m) after another 50 minutes from Colle del Carbone.

The track drops into a small saddle, where track H10 heads north. Stick to the GTA as it swings around to the south below Testa del Duca, then tends gradually east and descends for half an hour to the bottom of Vallone del Marguareis and a small forest of signposts. Head up the valley for 40 minutes to the south-east to the shallow, glacial **Laghetto di Marguareis**. The level of this lakelet is lower each year as the flow of water from melting snow scours the bed of its outlet stream deeper. Here the track nearly doubles

back on itself and sidles to the north-west across the north side of the valley. Just around a ridge sits the palatial **Rifugio Garelli** (1990m), its steeply pitched roofs mirroring (in more ways than one) the shape of the limestone cliffs opposite. This modern structure sleeps up to 94 people and has excellent facilities, including hot showers. To stay during the normal opening period (see under When to Walk earlier in this section), phone ahead on ☎ (0171) 73 80 78. At other times, keys may be available from Corso Italia 20, Mondovì (☎ (0174) 44730).

Day 2: Rifugio Garelli to Limone Piemonte

6 to 7½ hours, 1120m ascent, 2110m descent

From a signpost on the edge of Pian del Lupo, the tiny plain behind the rifugio, follow red-and-white GTA markers uphill to the east. They lead up the left (north) side of a valley to **Porta Sestrera** (2225m) after 30 minutes. Proceed for a few minutes down the broad, grassy valley ahead, until a well-defined but less clearly marked track diverges to the right towards a cairn, in a saddle, on a small spur that protrudes into the valley from the ridge to the west. From this saddle a very broad col is visible to the south. This is Colle del Pas. Still invisible between here and there, however, is Lago Rataira. Cairns and occasional red paint markers persist as the track contours a little east of south. If you lose the trail here, continue south and don't lose too much height. Look out for a stone pillar which stands on the lip of the depression which hides Lago Rataira, and in clear conditions makes navigation easy from here to the lake. (In poor visibility it would be possible, and not too inconvenient a detour, to follow the GTA as far as Lago Biecai and then head back to Lago Rataira along track G5.) At Lago Rataira you join track G5, and paint markers lead south over a little spur and up the right (west) side of a valley to **Colle del Pas** (2342m), 45 minutes from Porta Sestrera.

Head through the pass and down towards a grassy plain, just west of Rifugio Saracco Volante, and the dark entrance to one of this region's many deep caves. Descend from the pass for 10 minutes, passing an indistinct fork on the left which leads to the rifugio, until the rifugio lies away to the east and signs prominently painted on two large rocks point the way to 'Marguareis'. Leave the track shown on the IGC 1:25,000 map here and follow a distinct, smaller track west, in the direction indicated by the signs, up grassy slopes, then cunningly through some bands of rock to **Colle Palù** (2520m) after 30 minutes.

The mighty whaleback of Punta Margua reis, with its prominent summit cross, is clearly visible 1km to the west. After negotiating a short section of steeper, rocky ground to the right (north) of the pass, a well-defined track leads across the rounded, grassy southern slopes of Cima Bozano and Cima Pareto. Finally it winds up and across a broad rocky spur, across a gully and up to the summit of **Punta Marguareis** (2651m), a lunch spot with a view. From here on a clear day you will see the peaks of the Argentera group to the west and solitary Monviso

(3841m), the source of the river Po, further away to the north-west.

From the summit, follow the crest of the main ridge south on a faint and sometimes steep track for 20 minutes into a saddle. Here a well-defined, marked track crosses the ridge. Follow it to the south-west, around a knoll, and down across slopes and gullies riddled with limestone formations, to reach **Colle del Lago dei Signori** (2112m) after a further 30 minutes or so. The yellow and red Rifugio Barbera, just north-east of the col, is normally locked.

The route now ducks across French territory for a few kilometres. About the only changes you'll notice are the language on the signposts (French) and the colour of the painted route markers (yellow rather than red). A road leads through Colle del Lago dei Signori and circuitously towards Col della Boaria. A few metres north of Colle del Lago dei Signori, leave the road and descend to the west on a walking track onto the grassy Plan Chevolail. The walking is easy but markers are few until the track passes through a narrowing at the western end of the plain, then up through a gap to the right of a plug of rock. The track is now more adequately marked as it continues west around the head of a succession of gullies which drain to the south. Half an hour after leaving the col, the track descends across grassy slopes to the floor of Vallon de Malabergue to meet a track that comes up the valley from Rèfrei and Tende. Follow this, still on the north side of the stream bed (which may be dry), through a grassy bowl and a narrow, rocky stretch, until a tributary gully enters from the north. Cross here to the south side of the main gully and continue slightly to the north of west, past Gias Superieure Malabergue on the opposite bank, until a signpost points back down the valley to Rèfrei and Tende.

Head west from the signpost for 50m, along a tributary gully that leads towards Col della Boaria, then follow yellow markers up through a notch onto a small rocky spur on the south side of the gully. The track leads cunningly through a maze of ramps, slots and winding gullies and emerges on top of a

ALPI MARITIME

grassy knoll within sight of the road from Colle del Lago dei Signori. Ten minutes further west, the track rejoins the road, and some ruined buildings and a signpost indicate that you have reached **Col della Boaria** (2102m).

On Italian territory once more, leave the road again and follow a marked track down into a valley which leads to the north-west from the col. This drops quite steeply at times, first on the true left side of the valley, then on the right, and eventually swings west into the broader Valle San Giovanni after 30 minutes. The track swings north again and remains above the river as it tumbles through a short gorge, then another 100m further downstream it winds down to the river and crosses to the true left (west) bank. Signs of civilisation become more frequent as the track leaves the river and winds through pastures on the north side of the craggy Bec Valletta to a T-junction above a cluster of buildings at Maire Valletta.

Go left for 50m, then right at another junction, following yellow markers down the hill to the north-west on a very rustic track. This soon joins a dirt road, which continues down Valle San Giovanni. The IGC 1:25,000 map shows a short cut to San Giovanni below Bec Castellaccio, but the start of it is not obvious. In any case it's a pleasant walk down the road, which is sealed below Casali Brick, to a tiny parish church in the somewhat tumbledown village of San Giovanni. From here it's a straightforward walk of a couple of kilometres, on down the

road through increasingly developed surroundings, back to the bright lights of **Limone**.

OTHER WALKS IN THE ALPI MARITTIME

Other walk options, both long and short, abound in the Alpi Marittime, especially from mid-July to mid-September. As long as transport services run and accommodation remains open, the GTA and its network of rifugi and other places to stay, known as *posti tappa* or staging posts, are an excellent basis for walks of almost any length. For example, three stages of the GTA connect Trinità, near Entracque at the end of the Terme di Valdieri to Entracque walk, via the villages of Palanfrè and Limonetto, to Rifugio Garelli, on the Marguareis Circuit. Further east beyond Rifugio Garelli, two more stages reach the end of the GTA at Viozene. It would thus be possible, just for example, to follow the GTA for eight days, from Viozene to Terme di Valdieri or vice versa, linking much of the territory covered by the walks in this chapter. See the Long-Distance Walks chapter for more information on the GTA. In addition, minor tracks make many variations possible. And just over the border on the French side of the range, linked via a number of passes to the Italian system, is a comparable network of French tracks and rifugi.

Liguria

The Ligurian coast was inhabited by Neanderthals about one million years ago, and many remains have been unearthed in the area. Locals say they were lured by the beaches, which still exert a hold over the hundreds of thousands of tourists who flock to this narrow coastal region each year. There is more to Liguria, however, than its beaches. Stretching from the French border in the west to La Spezia in the east (see the Alpi Marittime chapter for a regional map), the coast is dotted with resorts and medieval towns and also harbours isolated pockets of relatively undisturbed coastal vegetation; the mountainous hinterland hides several natural parks with scope for walkers and climbers, hilltop villages and the occasional piste. The walks in this chapter combine some of the most popular and picturesque parts of the coastal fringe with wilder, less-often visited stretches of the coast and immediate hinterland. Plenty more remains to tempt the adventurous – or swell a subsequent edition of this book.

HISTORY

Liguria has been ruled by the Greeks, Saracens, Romans, Venetians, Lombards and French, and strong early trade influences from as far afield as Sicilia (Sicily), North Africa and Spain are evident. Fortified buildings that dot the coast are a reminder that trade and prosperity came at a cost. Raiders from North Africa attacked frequently during the Middle Ages.

The present-day capital Genova (Genoa) was founded in the 4th century BC, and became a key Roman port. It later became a mercantile power and, although often subject to the domination of others, dominated the fortunes of the whole Ligurian coast from the 13th to the 18th century. Genova reached its peak in the 16th century under the rule of imperial admiral, Andrea Doria, and managed to benefit from Spain's American fortunes by financing Spanish

HIGHLIGHTS

NICK TAPP

- The fantastically scenic Sentiero Azzurro walk to the five villages of the Cinque Terre
- The smell of the *vendemmia* in the Cinque Terre's cool stone laneways
- The coastal plant communities, isolated farmlets, small villages and relatively undeveloped promontory of Parco Regionale di Portofino
- Exploring the full length of the Cinque Terre on the Portovenere to Levanto Combination walk

exploration. As the importance of the Mediterranean declined, so too did Genova's and Liguria's fortunes.

In 1796 Napoleon Bonaparte captured Genova, and in 1797 he created the so-called Repubblica Ligure, which was tied to France and administered by an appointee of Napoleon. In 1805 the Repubblica Ligure became part of the French Empire, and in 1815, after Napoleon's defeat at Waterloo, the Congress of Vienna gave the region to the kingdom of Sardegna-Piemonte (Sardinia-Piedmont). In 1861 Victor Emmanuel II, king of Sardegna-Piemonte, became the first king of a still incompletely united Italy. Genova was a leading participant in the Risorgimento – the process of Italian unification and independence in the 19th century – and was also the first northern city to rise against the Germans and the Italian Fascists towards the close of WWII. After the war, the city expanded rapidly along the coast and swallowed numerous villages along the way.

CLIMATE

Protected by both the Alps and the Appennini from cold northerly weather patterns, Liguria enjoys a mild, Mediterranean climate. The climate chart for Genova in the Facts about Italy chapter gives a good indication of average temperatures and rainfall all along the Ligurian coast. As a consequence, the walks in this chapter, which are all on or close to the coast, can be done at any time of year. Walkers seldom, if ever, need to take elaborate precautions against extremes of cold here. Indeed, quite the opposite: a full water bottle and protection from the sun are essential, especially in summer.

INFORMATION
When to Walk
Any time should be OK (see Climate above).

Maps
A map such as the Touring Club Italiano *Liguria* (1:200,000), widely sold in bookshops for L9500, may be helpful at the planning stage and in getting to and from the walks in this chapter. For details of larger-scale maps of the walks themselves, see the individual walks Maps sections later in the chapter.

ACCOMMODATION & SUPPLIES

There is no camping ground in La Spezia, the most convenient base for the walks in this chapter, but there are several in nearby small towns. The APT in La Spezia has details. There are a couple of decent and reasonably cheap hotels conveniently close to the train station in La Spezia. At *Albergo Parma* (☎ (0187) 74 30 10), down the steps opposite the station and across the road at Via Fiume 143, singles/doubles with shared bath start at

L40,000/L56,000 and those with a private bath L50,000/L80,000. *Albergo Terminus* (☎ (0187) 70 34 36), at Via Paleocapa 21, a few metres downhill to the left as you leave the station, is slightly cheaper.

Most of the walks described in this chapter pass through villages with *trattorie* where walkers can sit down for a cooked meal; at the very least they pass shops that sell fresh food. If you prefer to carry your own food from the start, there's no shortage of places to buy it in La Spezia, including a *produce market* held every day on Piazza Cavour.

GETTING THERE & AWAY

La Spezia is on the busy train line between Roma (Rome) and Genova and is also connected by train to Milano (Milan), Torino (Turin), Pisa and other northern Italian cities. For those with a car, La Spezia lies close to the A12 autostrada between Genova and Livorno, and the A15 links it to Parma and the main north-south autostrada, the A1. The SS1 passes through the city and connects with the SS62 for Parma and the north.

CINQUE TERRE

The region known as the Cinque Terre owes its name to five villages – Monterosso al Mare, Vernazza, Corniglia, Manarola and Riomaggiore – that perch along a precipitous stretch of the Riviera di Levante, the coast east of Genova. The steep hillsides that rise out of the Ligurian Sea are crowded with terraced vineyards and olive groves. Some villages sit high on promontories and others line deep ravines at the sea's edge with fishing boats piled in their narrow quayside streets or bobbing in tiny protected harbours.

Grapes, olives and fish are still produced here, but tourism now fuels the local economy to a significant extent. Some visitors to the Cinque Terre come to eat, drink and loll beside the sea, but many tackle at least a part of the Sentiero Azzurro (Blue Track), an often spectacular coastal walking route which connects the five villages. Fewer tackle the Sentiero Rosso (Red Track), a ridge-top track that climbs from the coast at Portovenere to a height of 800m, then returns to sea level at Levanto, and looks down on the Cinque Terre from much of its length. Both these walks are described here in full. The third walk in this section takes two days, spends a night in one of the five villages and combines the best of the Sentiero Rosso with the whole of the Sentiero Azzurro in an end-to-end exploration of the Cinque Terre.

NATURAL HISTORY

The Cinque Terre is part of the north-western extremity of the Appennini. The hillsides of the Cinque Terre have been terraced and intensively cultivated for centuries, and little remains of the original coastal vegetation except at the south-eastern extreme, towards Portovenere, and on Punta Mesco, between Monterosso and Levanto. Here there are extensive stands of Aleppo pines and patches of coastal *macchia* or scrub. A little further inland, higher up on the ridge traversed by the Sentiero Rosso, cluster pines and broad-leaved trees such as chestnuts form almost pure forests, though walkers will also see the occasional cork oak.

There's not much large terrestrial fauna about – occasional signs that warn of hunting activities may explain the lack of mammals – but a little birdlife survives and there's quite a variety of marine species along some stretches of the coast, in particular Punta Mesco and surrounds.

INFORMATION
Maps

The Cinque Terre is well mapped. The La Spezia section of the Club Alpino Italiano (CAI) produces a good map at 1:40,000 scale, *Cinque Terre e Parco di Montemarcello*, with track notes (in Italian and German) and profiles on the back for the Sentiero Azzurro and the Sentiero Rosso. The 8th edition (1997) costs L7000 and is available in bookshops in La Spezia. Occasionally more accurate, but less easy to read, is Kompass map No 644, *Cinque Terre* (1:50,000) which has inset street maps of all five villages, plus

Levanto and Portovenere, and comes with a slender illustrated guide to the region (also in Italian and German). It is widely available in bookshops for L10,000, as is the Edizioni Multigraphic *Cinque Terre, Golfo della Spezia, Montemarcello* (1:25,000) which has a guide in Italian printed on the reverse side.

Information Sources

Should you need more information, or help with booking accommodation in the Cinque Terre, try the APT (☎ (0187) 77 09 00), Viale Mazzini 47 in La Spezia facing the waterfront, or at the train station (☎ (0187) 71 89 97).

Books

Detailed descriptions in English of the Cinque Terre are hard to find, though *Wild Italy* by Tim Jepson has useful information on the natural history of the area. The guide sold with Kompass map No 644 (see Maps earlier) is helpful if you read Italian or German, and the notes in Italian on the back of the Multigraphic map are sold separately for L10,000 as a slim book, with maps and photographs, called *Su e Giù per le Cinque Terre*.

Emergency

In case of an accident on the tracks in the Cinque Terre, the best bet for assistance is the fire service, which is accessible by telephone on ☎ 113 or ☎ 116.

Leaving Luggage

You can leave excess gear at any train station while you do an overnight walk but, at L5000 for every 12 hours or part thereof, this is an expensive business. Your hotel in town may store a spare bag for a day or two.

GETTING THERE & AWAY

All five Cinque Terre villages, plus Levanto, are served several times a day by La Spezia-Genova trains. Frequent ATC buses connect La Spezia and Portovenere. The beginning and end of all walks in this section are accessible by car, though some Cinque Terre roads are rough. You cannot drive right into any of the five villages but must park at the perimeter. See individual walk descriptions for details.

LIGURIA

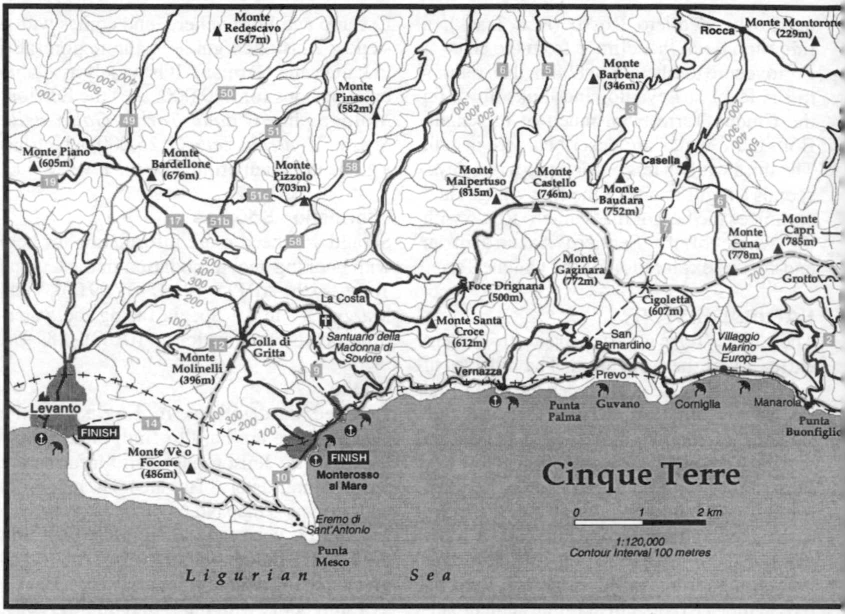

Cinque Terre

0   1   2 km

1:120,000
Contour Interval 100 metres

Sentiero Azzurro

> **Duration** 2½ to 5 hours
> **Ascent** 440m (ascent and descent)
> **Standard** Easy-Medium
> **Start** Riomaggiore
> **Finish** Monterosso al Mare
> **Closest Town** La Spezia
> **Permits Required** No
> **Public Transport Access** Yes
> **Summary** The classic way to see the extraordinary villages and cultivated hillsides of the Cinque Terre. Delightful coastal scenery. A day walk with time to relax and explore.

This short, fantastically scenic walk is the classic way to see the Cinque Terre, and is done daily by many during the region's year-round tourist season. The Sentiero Azzurro (Blue Track) is named for its proximity, throughout its length, to the blue Mediterra-

nean – or, strictly, the Ligurian Sea. It is also marked, in part, with blue paint markers easily distinguishable from the usual red ones.

The four stages of the track link the five villages of the Cinque Terre by the easiest route. Owing to the precipitous nature of the terrain, however, even the easiest route is hairy and somewhat strenuous in parts, and many of the holiday-makers who tackle the Sentiero Azzurro complete only the easier sections between Riomaggiore and Corniglia. To a seasoned walker fresh from the Alps or any of the other more challenging areas described in this book, the Sentiero Azzurro is a delightful, undemanding day's outing which offers fine coastal views.

The route is described here from south-east to north-west, from Riomaggiore to Monterosso al Mare, because that way, with a reasonably early start, you'll have the sun behind you rather than in your face. As well, the going becomes progressively harder as

LIGURIA

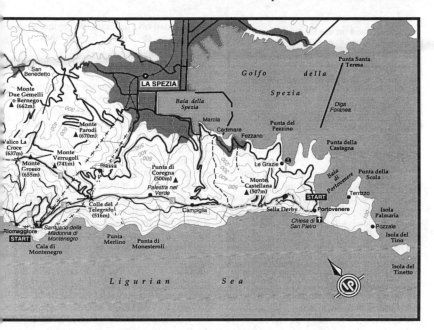

you proceed in this direction, and it's probably a better idea to start out on the easier sections. You can, however, start at either end.

From Riomaggiore to Monterosso al Mare is a distance, as the seagull flies, of a little more than 8km. The route winds and twists, but it's not a long walk. Signposts and maps give a total 'official' walking time of five hours and 10 minutes, but many reasonably fit, experienced walkers will cover the distance in half that (see the table on the next page). Take your time, relax, explore, enjoy the scenery and make a day of it.

PLANNING
What to Bring

You can get by without many of the requisites for a walk in more isolated regions. It's possible, for example, to pick up food in shops and cafes in the villages along the way, and extreme cold is not a common problem – but do bring a full water bottle and protection from the sun.

GETTING TO/FROM THE WALK

Riomaggiore is the first stop west of La Spezia Centrale station on the busy La Spezia-Genova line. The trip takes only a few minutes and costs L1500.

The trip back to La Spezia from Monterosso takes less than half an hour and costs L2000. If you're travelling by car, it would be possible also to drive to the start of the walk, park on the perimeter of Riomaggiore, and catch a train back from Monterosso for L1500 at the end of the day to retrieve the car.

THE WALK

Although it's possible to walk out of the train station at **Riomaggiore** and turn immediately up the coast towards Manarola, it's worth first exploring the most interesting part of this, the easternmost of the five villages of the Cinque Terre. To do so, turn back towards La Spezia and follow the footpath beside the railway line through a tunnel for

LIGURIA

Walking Times on the Sentiero Azzurro		
Stage	Official time	Fit walker's time
Riomaggiore-Manarola		
	30 mins	15 mins
Manarola-Corniglia		
	1 hour 10 mins	30 mins
Corniglia-Vernazza		
	1 hour 45 mins	50 mins
Vernazza-Monterosso		
	1 hour 45 mins	60 mins
Total	5 hours 10 mins	2 hours 35 mins

150m. Once you emerge into daylight again, passageways lead down to the right to the waterfront, where small fishing boats are stacked in a tiny piazza, while the pedestrian main street leads left up the steep-sided Valle di Riomaggiore.

The Sentiero Azzurro proper, also known and labelled as track No 2, begins back at the piazza outside the train station, where a staircase leads over the railway line to the beginning of the excessively famous **Via dell'Amore** (Lovers' Lane). This cliffside footway between Riomaggiore and Manarola passes through a roofed gallery, something of a shrine on the theme of *l'amore*, which serves also the more practical purpose of protecting walkers from falling rocks. At the end of Via dell'Amore a 150m tunnel leads from the train station into the village of **Manarola**. Head left, down towards the picturesque waterfront with its rocky boat landing and tiny harbour protected by a breakwater.

From here, follow the marked footpath north, up over a small headland and past the village cemetery. The way ahead to Corniglia is clear. It soon gains the route once followed by the old railway and now colonised along some of its length by a low-key holiday resort, then passes under the present-day line and alongside the platforms of the station. A brick staircase zigzags up to the ridge top where the village of **Corniglia** perches above the sea. The Sentiero Azzurro keeps the centre of Corniglia on its seaward side, passing the Chiesa di San Pietro with its grey Gothic façade and rose window, and crossing the sealed road to San Bernardino.

Two small bridges mark the beginning of the climb to Prevo. The hillside above the tiny grey sand beach of Guvano is steep and somewhat unstable. Even so, the buildings of Prevo soon come and go, and the track proceeds more gently again through olive groves. As **Vernazza** nears, the views across the village and along the coast to Monterosso al Mare are truly grand. The buildings of Vernazza cluster improbably on a headland dominated by the tower of the Castello Belforte, and a breakwater extends across the entrance of a small harbour where colourful boats are moored in rows.

Track No 2 winds down through narrow laneways and crosses the main pedestrian street, which runs from east to west, between the waterfront piazza and the train station. By now it's likely to be lunch time, and there's any number of fairly pricey cafes in Vernazza. At *Trattoria Incadasè*, beside the 'track' just before it crosses the main street, primi begin at L9000 and most secondi are between L14,000 and L25,000. Not surprisingly, there's plenty of seafood on menus in the Cinque Terre.

The Sentiero Azzurro winds through Vernazza to its north-western corner, where it leaves the village on a well-formed track beside the Chiesa di Santa Margherita d'Antiochia. This climbs away steeply and gives excellent views as far back, eventually, as Corniglia and Riomaggiore. It levels out and becomes narrower and less well maintained, but remains generally well marked and is not difficult to follow all the way to **Monterosso al Mare**. Here, after skirting around the seaward side of an upmarket hotel, it comes to a sheltered beach separated by the railway line from Piazza Garibaldi in old Monterosso, where the Sentiero Azzurro officially ends.

To reach the train station, you continue on foot around the waterfront. Follow signs that bear left towards the Torre Aurora, out on a small headland, then go through a tunnel under the headland to another, longer beach. The train station is upstairs in the buildings that face onto the sea, approximately halfway along.

Sentiero Rosso

Duration 6 to 8 hours
Ascent 1150m (ascent and descent)
Standard Medium
Start Portovenere
Finish Levanto
Closest Town La Spezia
Permits Required No
Public Transport Access Yes
Summary An *alta via* or ridge-top traverse of the Cinque Terre from end to end. Sweeping coastal views.

Few of the casual holiday-makers who step out along portions of the coastal Sentiero Azzurro, described in the previous section, complete its full length. Fewer still venture onto the Sentiero Rosso. Though its highest point is barely 800m above sea level, this ridge-top route is as close as the Cinque Terre gets to a true *alta via* and is sufficiently long (about 38km), and involves enough gain and loss of height, to deter casual strollers. As a long day walk it offers the satisfaction of a complete traverse of the highest part of the Cinque Terre. Navigational difficulties are all but nonexistent, and experienced walkers, especially those fresh from more demanding Alpine terrain, will find the 'official' walking times posted along the route excessively generous.

You may come across the suggestion that the Sentiero Rosso is better walked in two days, with an overnight stay at the Santuario della Madonna di Soviore. In our view a more rewarding alternative for those who prefer to explore the Cinque Terre on an overnight walk at a more relaxed pace is the Portovenere to Levanto Combination walk described later in this chapter.

PLANNING

All the practical information given in the Sentiero Azzurro section regarding what to bring, when to walk and where to stay before and after the walk applies equally to the Sentiero Rosso.

GETTING TO/FROM THE WALK

ATC buses run down the Golfo della Spezia from La Spezia to the beginning of the walk in Portovenere at regular intervals from early in the morning to late at night. Buy a ticket beforehand from a *tabacchi* (tobacconist), newsstand or cafe. The one-way fare is L2000.

Many trains on the busy La Spezia-Genova line stop in Levanto, where the walk ends. The trip back to La Spezia takes about half an hour and costs L2800.

THE WALK

The Sentiero Rosso, or track No 1, begins at Piazza Bastreri in **Portovenere**, where the bus from La Spezia turns around, with a brisk climb up the staircase beside the town's 16th-century castle. On days when the air above the Golfo della Spezia sheds its characteristic brown haze, there is a magnificent view from here across the gulf to the Alpi Apuane in northern Toscana (Tuscany). The 13th-century Chiesa di San Pietro, perched dramatically at the seaward end of the promontory in Portovenere, is also seen to good advantage as the track climbs past the castle. Ignore track No 1a as it goes off to the left, then returns 600m later at a hairpin bend on a sealed road. Continue on the lower arm of the hairpin, past an abandoned marble quarry, and take a marked foot track on the right which cuts off one of the road's numerous switchbacks. The road leads around to the left into Sella Derby, where signposts near a building at the extreme left of another big bend point left into the coastal vegetation and up a small spur with fine coastal views.

The track, now a foot track, touches a further hairpin bend, where the Alta Via del Golfo (AVG) heads off to the right along a road, then continues up the crest of the ridge. Yet another loop of road appears out of the pine forest and vanishes again before the track joins the road into Campiglia. At a small soccer pitch on the left on the outskirts of the village, track No 1 detours left through pines and climbs gently into the little piazza beside the Chiesa di Santa Caterina in **Campiglia**.

LIGURIA

Follow signs through the village (there's a good shop on the right for coffee, focaccia, cheese, fruit etc) then left up stairs at a junction. Track No 1 climbs quite steeply up a ridge, then levels out and proceeds along the crest, passing the exercise stations of Palestra nel Verde (Gymnasium in the Forest) and La Pineta bar, and joining, then leaving, a made road, to **Colle del Telegrafo** (516m), where several roads and tracks meet. Track No 3 heads left down the hill from here towards Riomaggiore (see the Portovenere to Levanto Combination section later in this chapter).

Cross the road and continue up the foot track labelled '1'. This soon gives characteristic Cinque Terre views all the way along the coast to Monterosso. After 10 minutes a telegraph tower appears ahead atop Monte Verrugoli, while down to the left Riomaggiore clings impressively to the sides of a canyon. The route follows a pleasantly shady vehicular track through chestnut forest, past track No 4e on the right, and into the small saddle of Valico La Croce, where track No 01 (not to be confused with No 1) crosses the ridge.

Heading to the left here, away from the vehicular track, continue along the crest of the main ridge, passing a grotto, then an intersection with track No 02 and, a few minutes later, a sign that points to the Menhir di Monte Capri. This standing stone lies, rather than stands, 50m off to the right. Some 15 minutes later the track switches back to the west side of the ridge and the first significant descent of the day begins. The track drops steadily into a saddle where track No 6 meets it, then continues more levelly into a grassy clearing that makes a pleasant spot to halt for lunch. A few minutes further on, signposts announce the saddle known as **Cigoletta**, where track No 7 comes in from the right.

Track Nos 1 and 7 merge for a short distance, then No 1 doubles back to the right and heads uphill. It swings north for a way, then west again, around the head of the drainage basin that feeds Rio Vernazza. Chestnut forests give welcome shade, and the Sentiero

Rosso reaches its highest point on the ridge of **Monte Malpertuso** (815m). Descend, on and off a vehicular track, to a three-way junction of sealed roads. Follow the markers along the road that leads west to a larger road and a sign for track No 8 on the left at Foce Drignana. Cross the road and head up a spur. The foot track rounds Monte Santa Croce on its north side, continues through a saddle and along the ridge, then descends to meet a major sealed road at a T-junction.

A sign points left down the road towards Genova, Levanto and Monterosso. This road is the route for the next 3.5km with the exception of a brief detour, after 1.5km, through the grounds of the **Santuario della Madonna di Soviore**. Here drinks, snacks and meals are sold and track No 9 heads down to Monterosso. Another 2km down the road at **Colla di Gritta**, Levanto comes into view.

Cross the road ahead, enter the car park beside Ristorante Albergo Il Bivio and go left to find track No 1 as it leaves the car park by a set of stairs. The track climbs a pine-clad ridge with occasional views back to the south-east along the coast. It rises and falls over some minor peaks, including Monte Molinelli, then descends into a saddle, 2.8km from Colla di Gritta, where track No 14 heads right. Straight ahead is Monte Vè o Focone, but the track swings left (south) around it towards **Punta Mesco**. Just short of the point, track No 1 doubles back to the right towards Levanto. It's worth continuing for five minutes along track No 10 and out to the abandoned Eremo di Sant'Antonio and an old *semaforo* (beacon), which gives an uninterrupted view back along the Cinque Terre coast.

Back at the sharp bend in track No 1, go left and make the gradual 5km descent, through pine forest and then cultivated land, briefly joining a sealed road along the way, to **Levanto**. A final staircase below the 13th century walls of a Malaspina family castle leads down to the grey-sand beach. To reach the train station, head north along the waterfront for 500m, then follow the main street, Corso Roma, away from the beach for 1km.

Portovenere to Levanto Combination

Duration 2 days
Standard Easy-Medium
Start Portovenere
Finish Levanto
Closest Town La Spezia
Permits Required No
Public Transport Access Yes
Summary Walk the Cinque Terre from end to end with time to explore and an overnight stop in one of the villages. See the cultivated side of the region and its wilder aspects in one walk.

This two-day walk combines the off-the-beaten-track scenic highlights of the Senticro Rosso – its beginning and its end – with the entire Sentiero Azzurro. It gives you time to explore the full length of the Cinque Terre, and an overnight stop places you in one of the five villages in the evening and early in the morning, when the crowds will be thinnest and the natural light (weather permitting) at its best.

All the logistics of doing this walk, including maps, equipment and access from La Spezia, are identical to those for the Sentiero Rosso, except that you need somewhere to stay overnight in Corniglia or Vernazza.

PLANNING

All the practical information given in the preceding two sections regarding what to bring, when to walk, where to stay before and after the walk, and getting to and from the walk, applies equally to this walk.

THE WALK
Day 1: Portovenere to Corniglia or Vernazza
4 to 5 hours, 790m or 900m ascent, 680m or 900m descent

Follow the Sentiero Rosso from **Portovenere** to **Colle del Telegrafo** as described in the preceding Sentiero Rosso section.

At this point the Sentiero Rosso proceeds along the main ridge and track No 3a takes a

minor road to the left towards Riomaggiore. Find track No 3, a foot track that heads left of No 3a and down the hill from just in front of Bar Trattoria da Natale. This track is well marked, and there's a good chance you'll meet walkers heading in the opposite direction, from Riomaggiore to Portovenere. At intervals as it winds about, the track overlooks the main La Spezia-Riomaggiore road, but the views also include coastal cliffs, blue water and built-up, terraced vineyards. Note the ingenious monorails that carry the locals to and from the *vendemmia* (grape harvest) and transport the picked grapes down to the villages on the coast.

Continue down the hill to emerge through a gap in a wall at a very rustic, but adequately marked, T-junction. Track No 3a heads up to the east here to meet the minor road that descends from Colle del Telegrafo. A further 500m downhill to the west, with fine views, is the Santuario della Madonna di Montenegro, a fine church that now houses an elegant restaurant. From here the roughly paved track swings back towards the east, into a gully which eventually feeds down into the canyon that becomes the main street of Riomaggiore. Head back to the west again, down the gully, and cross the La Spezia road. Continue down the left (south) side of the gully, following red-and-white markers and descending a long flight of stairs to meet the made road on the outskirts of **Riomaggiore**. Cross here and follow the Valle di Riomaggiore, which now becomes the main thoroughfare through the village, down to the entrance to the railway tunnel, just above the water.

Head through the tunnel on the footpath beside the train line to the piazza outside the station, where the Sentiero Azzurro begins. Now follow that route to **Corniglia** or **Vernazza**, as described earlier in this chapter. Vernazza can get pretty crowded so it is wise to book your accommodation in advance. If you haven't done this, then try *Del Capitano* (☎ (0187) 81 22 01), Piazza G Marconi 21, or *Da Sandro* (☎ (0187) 81 22 23), Via Roma 62, both in Vernazza, where single/double rooms in the high season go for about L50,000/L70,000. In Corniglia (and in Vernazza too if other places are full), look around town, and in bars and shops, for signs advertising 'camere' or 'affittacamere' (rooms for rent). Local wine grower Domenico Spora (☎ (0187) 81 22 93) is one person who has rooms available in this way.

Day 2: Corniglia or Vernazza to Levanto
2½ to 3½ hours, 595m or 485m ascent, 705m or 485m descent

Continue along the Sentiero Azzurro to the train station in **Monterosso al Mare**. From here track No 10 heads west along the waterfront to a huge sculpture known as *Il Gigante*, which depicts Neptune. The track begins to climb, keeping the sculpture between it and the water and following signs, towards a little tower. It passes some impressive buildings, then emerges beside a road. Walk beside the road, then on it for a couple of minutes, before heading up a set of stairs at a bend in the road. There are lovely views back along the Cinque Terre as the track continues to climb, and in little more than 30 minutes from Monterosso comes to a junction where signs point left to **Punta Mesco**. The short detour left to the abandoned Eremo di Sant'Antonio and the old semaforo is worthwhile on a good day. From there, follow the last stage of the Sentiero Rosso, as described in the preceding Sentiero Rosso walk, into **Levanto**.

PARCO REGIONALE DI PORTOFINO

Portofino is perhaps an unlikely place to find a day's walk in relatively undisturbed coastal terrain. Portofino, the town, is one of the most fashionable seaside hang-outs in Italy, where the country's rich and famous come to get away from it all – or, at least, do it in a different setting. Portofino, the natural park, on the other hand, is small (11.5 sq km) but set on a beautiful and relatively undeveloped promontory ringed by dramatic cliffs and small coves. The circuit of the promontory described here, from Camogli at the northwestern corner to the tiny, picturesque settlement of San Fruttuoso at the southern end, then across to the east side, takes in the full range of environments from coastal plant communities, isolated farmlets and small villages to the restrained luxury of Portofino.

The promontory rises to a high point of 610m at Monte di Portofino, and its limestone and conglomerate soils support a wide variety of plant species. The southern slopes of the promontory experience a predominantly Mediterranean climate, and the vegetation is dominated by pines, oaks and other species of the coastal macchia. North of the ridge of hills that cross from west to east, however, the hours of sunlight are reduced, the prevailing winds are continental ones and the plant species that thrive are those usually associated with cooler climates further north. The two air currents, one warm and humid and the other cool, collide above the ridge and frequently give rise to cloud or fog about the tops. Many bird species are found here, including a number of migratory ones that call in twice a year on their way back and forth between continental Europe and Africa. The waters off the promontory are one of the richest marine habitats in the Mediterranean, and there is a proposal to make them a marine reserve.

Promontorio di Portofino Circuit

Duration 4½ to 5½ hours
Ascent 900m ascent and 925m descent
Standard Easy-Medium
Start Camogli
Finish Santa Margherita
Closest Towns Genova, La Spezia
Permits Required No
Public Transport Access Yes
Summary Picturesque, unspoiled coastal scenery; the tiny, remote settlement of San Fruttuoso and its historic abbey; a coastal track linking luxury resorts and rustic villages.

The Parco Regionale di Portofino is laced with well-established, marked walking tracks.

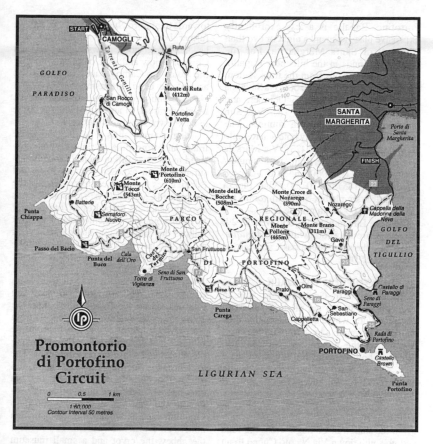

Promontorio
di Portofino
Circuit

0   0.5   1 km
1:60,000
Contour Interval 50 metres

This walk combines a series of those tracks into a full traverse of the promontory It can be done comfortably in a day, using trains for access, either from La Spezia or from somewhere closer, such as Rapallo. It can be shortened by taking a boat from San Fruttuoso back to Camogli or on to Portofino, which is connected to Santa Margherita by bus.

PLANNING
Maps
The Sagep *Guida al Monte di Portofino* (1:10,000) map, sold with a detailed guidebook in Italian to all the marked tracks in the

park, costs L20,000 from large bookshops in the region. If you can't find it, the IGM *Chiavari* (1:25,000) sheet also covers the area of the walk.

What to Bring
As for the walks in the Cinque Terre described earlier in the chapter, be sure to bring water, sunscreen and a shady hat.

PLACES TO STAY & EAT
Cheap accommodation options in La Spezia are mentioned under Accommodation & Supplies at the start of this chapter. Closer to

Portofino, Rapallo is a less exorbitantly expensive place to spend a night or two than Camogli or Santa Margherita. For the camping grounds in the hills near Rapallo, take the Savagna bus from the train station. *Miraflores* (☎ (0185) 26 30 00), Via Savagna 12, is open from April to October, and *Rapallo* (☎ (0185) 26 20 18), Via San Lazzaro 4, is open only in summer. The cheap-end pick of the many hotels in Rapallo is *Bandoni* (☎ (0185) 50423), Via Marsala 24, right on the waterfront, with singles/doubles from L35,000/L65,000. *Albergo Centro* (☎ (0185) 23 10 58), Vico Piazza Venezia 1, is simple but fine, with rooms for L35,000/L60,000 with private bath.

Vesuvio, Lungomare Vittorio Veneto 29, has pizzas from L8000, while *Da Monique*, at No 5 on the same street, has a set seafood meal for L35,000.

GETTING TO/FROM THE WALK

Not all La Spezia-Genova trains stop in Camogli, but if you get off in Santa Margherita Ligure, where most do stop, it's then possible to swap to a local train for the short hop across the promontory to Camogli. Trains of both varieties run several times a day. The fare from La Spezia to Santa Margherita is L5900, and another L1500 will get you to Camogli.

THE WALK

From the station in Camogli, cross the road and go south down Via Nicolò Cuneo to an intersection with a lane between buildings. Go left here, and within 200m the lane comes to the Torrente Gentile and crosses to its west bank. A gentle, sometimes winding ascent of just more than 1km between old houses and stone walls leads to **San Rocco di Camogli**. Around to the right of the parish church, which is decorated in the trompe l'oeil style seen in many Ligurian towns, is a *bivio* or fork in the track. Take the right branch and then, after another 200m, the left branch, and proceed along a reasonably level track, No 5, marked periodically with two dots in red paint. Ignore track No 3, marked with two red triangles, which goes off to the left

towards Semaforo Nuovo after 1km. After a further 1km No 5 comes to a grotto on a headland with good views of rocky Punta Chiappa below and, on a clear day, back up the coast to Camogli and beyond. Just around the bend, the remains of a WWII German anti-aircraft gun emplacement sit beside the track in an area which has come to be known, simply, as **Batterie**.

Conglomerate cliffs now rise above the track, and from time to time a wire cable fixed to the rock offers protection and reassurance on an exposed section. Passo del Bacio gives more fine views. Across the steep-sided Cala dell'Oro to the south-east is a rocky headland topped by a 16th-century *torre di vigilanza* (watchtower). The track follows the contours into and out of several gullies and into the valley at the head of the Cala dell'Oro, then climbs to the crest of the Costa Termine ridge.

It's a straightforward descent from here, with occasional glimpses of the Seno di San Fruttuoso and of the Torre Doria, built in the 16th century for defence against raiders from North Africa, to the tiny and very picturesque settlement of **San Fruttuoso**, nestled among olive trees and some magnificent pines. The grey beach is lined with foldout chairs, and ferries from Portofino and Camogli dock one after another at the tiny quay, bringing visitors to the Abbazia di San Fruttuoso di Capodimonte, a Benedictine abbey which houses the Doria family crypt. You can tour the abbey, the crypt and a small museum between 10 am and 6 pm in summer and for shorter periods at other times of year. Admission is L5000. A selection of more or less expensive eateries cluster around the beach.

Continue over a small promontory and through another small group of waterfront buildings, up a gully, past a helipad and around the coast, climbing to a track junction shown on the Sagep map as Base 'O'. From here go east, still on the track marked by two red dots. Pines and Mediterranean macchia dominate the headlands and broader-leaved vegetation abounds in the gullies. The coastal scenery is impressive. Just before the village of Prato comes the incongruous sight of a display of macramé, the work of a local artisan, beside the track. Street lamps line the track from Prato to Olmi, where the track branches right, past a boom gate. The red dots now accompany an alternative, paved route via San Sebastiano, while track No 21 continues around the hillside to the few houses of Cappelletta. Go left here rather than down towards the sea, and a couple of minutes later at a T-junction go right, down stone stairs, while a less distinct track goes straight ahead towards San Sebastiano. The stairs lead south-east, steeply at times, down a gully to **Portofino**.

It's a pleasant walk of just more than an hour to Santa Margherita from here, but if you're fed up with walking, there's a bus stop beside the parish church on the south side of the main road. Directly over the road from here, a walking track zigzags up towards San Sebastiano and another, marked with three dots, heads roughly east at first, among elegant residences just above the road, towards Paraggi. After a few paces to the right down a sealed road, then up to the left beside an imposing gateway, the track proceeds without fuss, staying above the road but within sight of it, until it descends to meet the road at the attractive harbour at **Paraggi**.

When you hit the road go left (north) for just one short block to Hotel Argentina. Turn left here, then right behind the hotel and up narrow stairs between stone walls, sometimes roofed over by greenery. The going is again straightforward and there is only the odd track junction to watch out for. Track marking is adequate. Follow the sign of three dots arranged in a triangle to the hillside hamlet of Gave and its restored chapel, the Oratorio di San Gerolamo. As you continue north down the hill, on a track marked with '+' signs, Santa Margherita is visible ahead. After going right at a fork, the track comes to a road, goes right and descends a ramp to the road, then follows it to the tiny chapel of the Madonna della Neve below the settlement of Nozarego. The track passes to the left of the chapel and continues down a spur through increasingly suburban surroundings

to its signposted end at the southern corner of the boat harbour in **Santa Margherita**. The train station is on the north side of the port, just a few blocks uphill from the waterfront.

OTHER WALKS IN LIGURIA

ALPI LIGURI & APPENNINO LIGURE
The mountains of the Ligurian hinterland – Colle di Cadibona, behind Savona, marks the division between the Alps to the west and the Appennini to the east – reach no great heights, but contain several natural parks and regional parks. These are crisscrossed by walking tracks and dotted with *rifugi*. Tracks and rifugi are both maintained, for the most part, by branches of the CAI. Those branches are the best sources of information on the considerable possibilities for walks in their local hills. Even so, such information is not easy to come by. Visitors are generally welcomed to CAI clubrooms and their libraries, but finding the rooms, and then finding the information you seek, can be difficult.

ALTA VIA DEL GOLFO
Beginning at Bocca di Magra, south-east of La Spezia at the mouth of the Magra River, the Alta Via del Golfo (AVG) follows ridge tops around the Golfo della Spezia only a kilometre or two from the coast, avoiding La Spezia and finally meeting the Sentiero Rosso at Campiglia and descending to Portovenere. The route is shown on the CAI *Cinque Terre e Parco di Montemarcello* (1:40,000) map but not on the Kompass *Cinque Terre* (1:50,000). The 'official' walking time of just over 15 hours, while likely to be well on the conservative side, suggests that the AVG might best be done over two days. Finding somewhere to stay in Buonviaggio or Sarbia might not be easy: check with the APT or CAI in La Spezia before you set off.

Volcanoes of Southern Italy

There are six active volcanoes in Italy, all in the south – Etna, Stromboli and Vulcano in Sicilia (Sicily); Vesuvio (Mt Vesuvius), Ischia and the Campi Flegrei (Phlegraean Fields) in Campania. Etna and Stromboli are among the world's most active volcanoes, while Vesuvio towers over an urban area which is among the world's most populous.

It is easy to underestimate the sheer awe and excitement – not to mention the raw fear – that you'll feel if you climb to the summit of a volcano. The strange, grey lunar-landscape and the tumbling masses of old lava flows will remind you of what can happen, even if the volcano seems quiet enough at the time.

Etna's eruptions are usually decades, even centuries apart, but they sometimes occur with an awesome power: in 1669 a devastating eruption lasted 122 days and a massive stream of lava partially engulfed the city of Catania. Stromboli is constantly erupting – its main crater throwing up showers of burning pumice known as *lapilli* every 10 minutes or so – in a spectacle which attracts thousands of tourists every year.

Vesuvio, of course, has the greatest claim to fame. Its most catastrophic eruption destroyed the ancient Roman resort towns of Pompeii and Ercolano (Herculaneum) in 79 AD. Today, the region around Vesuvio is densely populated and an eruption of similar proportions could cause incredible devastation.

The walks detailed in this chapter go to the summits of Etna, Stromboli, Vulcano and Vesuvio. Those on Vesuvio and Vulcano are easy to medium half-day walks; on Etna you have the choice of a one-day ascent to the craters, or a three-day circuit of the volcano, staying in mountain *rifugi* (refuges); and the Stromboli walk is a tough two or three-day trek which requires third grade Alpine skills – some climbing is involved and beginners will need a safety rope – and, officially, the use of a guide.

Apart from the excitement of walking on live volcanoes and peering into craters, these

HIGHLIGHTS

STEFANO CAVEDONI

- Ascending to the craters of Vesuvio, perhaps the world's most famous volcano
- Stromboli – big enough to inspire awe and small enough to climb in a few hours
- Conquering the smouldering heights of Etna's craters
- Immersing yourself in the history of Vesuvio and Pompeii

volcanoes will also give you the chance to explore Italy's Mediterranean flora, and on Stromboli, test your mountaineering skills.

The volcanoes are easy to reach by public transport. If you plan to tackle all four, we suggest that you start with Vesuvio, catch the overnight ferry from Napoli to Stromboli in the Isole Eolie (Aeolian Islands), just off the north coast of Sicilia, then head for Vulcano before crossing over to Sicilia and Etna.

INFORMATION

Local tourist offices and guides groups, where you can get information for each of the volcanoes and surrounding areas, are listed throughout this chapter. Probably

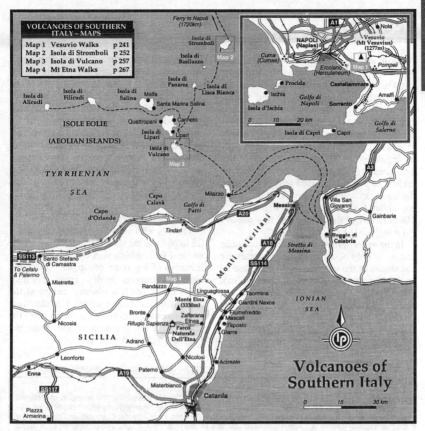

VOLCANOES OF SOUTHERN ITALY – MAPS

Map 1	Vesuvio Walks	p 241
Map 2	Isola di Stromboli	p 252
Map 3	Isola di Vulcano	p 257
Map 4	Mt Etna Walks	p 267

Volcanoes of Southern Italy

more than for any other area covered by this book, it is important that you plan your excursions with some precision, particularly if you're heading for Stromboli and Etna.

It is difficult to get good maps locally, so it is best to buy all the maps you'll need for the walks in this chapter, especially IGM maps, before leaving Roma (Rome) or Napoli. See the Facts for the Walker chapter and under Maps & Books in the Vesuvio section later in this chapter for details.

Warning

Volcanoes are dangerous and climbing one is not something to be taken lightly. While controls on ascents to the craters of Italy's volcanoes are slack to say the least, authorities have in recent years attempted to limit their liability by placing warning signs and imposing bans (which they do not then enforce). People climb to the craters of Etna and Stromboli all the time – and occasionally someone is injured or killed when hit by flying volcanic debris. The walk descriptions in this chapter show you the way, but if you decide to climb to the craters, you must be aware of the potential danger and realise that you do so at your own risk.

VOLCANOES

VESUVIO

Among all the volcanoes on the planet, Vesuvio (1277m) is probably the best known. With its natural predisposition for catastrophe, the volcano entered triumphantly into the history books when it erupted in 79 AD. In the space of two days the Roman settlements of Pompeii, Ercolano, Stabia and Oplontis were wiped out. Today its reputation as a merciless destroyer has been greatly diluted and the volcano is in the middle of a vast urbanised territory, among the most densely populated in Italy. There are about 600,000 people living within a 10km radius of the crater, and that doesn't even include the city of Napoli.

In the midst of this teeming Mediterranean chaos the only oases of nature left intact are the slopes of the volcano itself and those of the adjacent Monte Somma (1132m). Between these two peaks, at an altitude of about 800m, is the enchanting Valle del Gigante (Valley of the Giant), where the rampant pioneer vegetation has to recolonise the fertile volcanic ash after every eruption.

In 1991, the Parco Nazionale del Vesuvio was created, partly to protect against illegal building and poaching. Unfortunately, the park as yet has no infrastructure: there are no park offices or services and no locally based rangers. Access to the remotest parts of the protected area, the Riserva Tirone-Alto Vesuvio, which takes in the Valle del Gigante, is restricted and it is necessary to obtain a permit. This must be requested by fax from the Guardia Forestale (Forest Rangers) of Caserta (see Permits later in this section). However, appreciating the difficulty that a foreigner may encounter in requesting this permit, the authorities will tolerate small groups of independent walkers entering the restricted area without official permission.

Tourists who visit Vesuvio usually pay a fee to go up to the summit along a trail on the western face, which was constructed at the initiative of a private group, the Guide del Vesuvio (Vesuvius Guides). Every day hundreds easily reach a visitors' centre at the edge of the enormous crater. For the more adventurous, a trail from this point links the crater with the crossing of the Valle del Gigante in the park reserve.

Pompeii

Ever since Pliny the Younger wrote his moving letters to Tacitus describing the eruption of Vesuvio that buried the city in 79 AD, Pompeii has been the stuff of books, learned and frivolous, and equally a perfect subject for the big screen. Founded in the 7th century BC by the Campanian Oscans on a prehistoric lava flow of Vesuvio, Pompeii became a Roman colony in 80 BC and prospered as a major port and trading town, adorned with grand temples, villas and palaces, until it was devastated by an earthquake in 63 AD. The town had been largely rebuilt when Vesuvio, overshadowing the town to the north, erupted in 79 AD and buried it under a layer of lapilli (burning fragments of pumice stone). Although the town was completely covered by the shower, only about 2000 of its 20,000 inhabitants are believed to have perished. In later years, Emperor Titus briefly considered rebuilding the city, and Severus carried out a little plundering, but Pompeii gradually receded from the public eye.

The Pompeii area was completely abandoned during the period of Saracen raids and its remains were further shaken by subsequent earthquakes. In 1594, the architect Domenico Fontana stumbled across the ruins during the construction of a canal. The discovery was recorded but substantial excavation was not conducted until 1748, in the time of Charles of Bourbon, who was interested above all in retrieving items of value. Credit for most of the major discoveries belongs to Giuseppe Fiorelli, who worked under the auspices of the Italian government from 1860.

Work continues, but most of the ancient city has been uncovered. Many of the mosaics and murals have been removed to the Museo Archeologico Nazionale in Napoli and other museums around the world. The exception is the Villa dei Misteri (Villa of the Mysteries), whose frescoes remain *in situ*. They are the single most important series on the site.

Much of the site, the richest insight into the daily life of the Romans, is open to the public and requires at least three or four hours to visit. ■

While in the area, make the time to visit the remarkable archaeological sites of Pompeii and Ercolano as well as the impressive archaeological museum in Napoli.

The telephone prefix for Napoli is ☎ 081.

HISTORY

The fame of Vesuvio is inexorably linked with Europe's astonishment in the 18th century when, by chance, the first traces of the buried city of Pompeii were uncovered. In 1748, the King of Napoli, Charles of Bourbon, began the excavations which, even today, continue to yield surprises. The terrible eruption took place on 24 August 79 AD, dumping a 5m-thick layer of ash and stone on Pompeii, Ercolano, Stabia and Oplontis, in two days disappearing completely. It is believed that 2000 people died in Pompeii and Ercolano, which was the hardest hit.

The most illustrious victim was Pliny the Older, commander of the Roman fleet stationed at Porto Miseno. Pliny the Older was a passionate naturalist and it is said that, while carrying out rescue operations along the coast, his curiosity took him to observe the cataclysm from too close.

After a long period of dormancy, allowing for the extensive recultivation of grapevines, olives, apricots and citrus fruits in the very fertile soil on the volcano's slopes, another powerful eruption let loose on 16 December 1631. Massa, Somma and Bosco were destroyed. The event reverberated throughout Europe, and Vesuvio, with its smoky peak, became the hallmark of the Neapolitan landscape in prints and paintings of the era. In the second half of the 18th century, Napoli, Vesuvio and Pompeii had become obligatory destinations on the Italian Grand Tour.

From that day to this the list of illustrious visitors has grown considerably. To name a few: Montesquieu, Casanova, Mozart, Swinburne, Goethe, Shelley, Stendhal, Hans Christian Andersen, Gogol, Dickens, Melville, Mark Twain, Anton Chekhov and Walter Benjamin. At the end of the 18th century the most well-to-do visitors went up with guides and porters on mules or horseback, which they then left at the Atrio del Cavallo, where they continued on foot. The laziest were carried up on sedans to the edge of the crater. Those who found the courage climbed down inside the crater, which is no longer possible. In 1848, King Ferdinand II had the Osservatorio Vesuviano (Vesuvius Observatory), at a height of 600m, the first vulcanological observatory in the world.

NATURAL HISTORY
Geology

Vesuvio began to form about 300,000 years ago. The great crater of Monte Somma was the first to form – it ended its activity in ancient times with the collapse of its summit caldera. Inside the depression created by the collapse, Vesuvio began to grow, with its startling crater 500m in diameter and 230m deep. Vesuvio is part of a vast volcanic area that includes the Campi Flegrei (Phlegraean Fields) west of Napoli with the adjacent crater lakes of Averno, Fusaro and Miseno, and beyond, the islands of Ischia, Procida and Vivara. The Campi Flegrei, currently dormant and active only in the form of *solfatare* (volcanic vapours), last erupted in 1538. The island of Ischia is actually an active volcano, which last erupted in 1301.

Vesuvio last erupted in 1944, as Napoli struggled to recover from the devastation of WWII. It produced a relatively modest mixture of explosive and effusive activity that generated lava flow in the Atrio del Cavallo, visible from the road that comes up from Ercolano. The big, so-called Plinian eruption, a vulcanological category indicating catastrophic proportions, of 79 AD was the last in a sequence of five plinian eruptions during a period of 20,000 years, separated by centuries of dormancy and numerous sub-Plinian eruptions. The last subplinian eruption was that of 1631 and caused the devastation of an area of 500 sq km and the deaths of 4000 people.

Flora

Eruptions have exterminated the vegetation on Vesuvio more than once. Recolonisation begins immediately after the lava cools with the settling in of a silvery-grey lichen,

Stereocaulon vesuvianum, which gives a bit of bright colour to the dark, gloomy lava. After a few decades it is the turn of robust small Mediterranean plants, among them *Rumex bucephalophorus*, *Glaucium flavum*, *Vulpia ciliata* and others. Then the ginestre (broom) arrives, with its brilliant yellow June flowers. Various versions of this plant were imported at the beginning of this century, including the ginestra dei carbonai (*Sarothamnus scoparius*), the ginestra odorosa (*Spartium junceum*) and the ginestra dell'Etna (*Genista aetnensis*). Growing in the midst of the broom are *Artemesia campestre*, elicriso and red valerian, and in the late spring they all bloom together in a riotous perfumed technicolour mix.

Reforestation in this century has accelerated the comeback of the wooded areas. There are holm oaks (*Quercus ilex*), cluster pines (*Pinus pinaster*), Aleppo pines (*Pinus halepensis*) and in the Valle del Gigante there are clusters of locust trees (*Robinia pseudoacacia*) and silver birch (*Betula pendula*).

Fauna

Groups of stray dogs hang around the tourists in the parking area at 1000m, but they aren't dangerous. The wild rabbit has not been seen since the end of the 1970s. In the park there are fox, weasel and marten, which probably find food in the outskirts of the towns since only little dormouse and its relatives the topo quercino (*Eliomys quercinus*) and moscardino (*Muscardinus avellanarius*) remain. Many bird species pass through during periods of migration including buzzards, kestrels, owls, turtledoves, quails, cuckoos, whippoorwills, golden orioles and many others. A colony of ravens is stationed on Monte Somma where the red woodpecker nests as well, along with the tawny owl, the wryneck, the tomtit and the robin redbreast.

Among reptiles are two innocuous serpents: the black coluber (*Coluber viridiflavus*) on the warm slopes of Vesuvio and the robust cervone (*Elaphe quatuorlineata*) on Monte Somma. It is also possible to find poisonous vipers in the rocky areas of Valle del Gigante.

CLIMATE

The climate of the Golfo di Napoli (Gulf of Naples) is known for its mildness. The average annual temperature is around 16°C. The coldest months are January and February and the hottest July and August. Only rarely does the temperature drop below 0°C and it doesn't often exceed 30°C. Maritime winds temper the climate and humidity is very low with an average of 68%. At the crater (approximately 1200m) temperatures drop and there can be strong winds. Annually, there is an average of 170 clear days and 90 cloudy days.

INFORMATION
Maps & Books

The area of Vesuvio is covered by two maps in the new, seven-colour series 25, 1:25,000 scale, published by the Istituto Geografico Militare (IGM), updated to 1995. One is *Ercolano 448 III* and the other is *Torre del Greco 466 IV*, and each costs L19,000. The sheet of the old IGM series (1:25,000) *Vesuvio 184 II NE* is based on 1954 reliefs, but covers the whole walking area. It costs L11,000. The Kompass No 682 map of the Penisola Sorrentina (Sorrento Peninsula) in 1:50,000 scale (L9000) covers the Vesuvio area, but is insufficient for navigation.

In Napoli, Yamm bookshop (☎ (081) 552 63 99; fax (081) 552 97 82), Via G Summonte 10, on the corner of Corso Umberto I, near the Università Federico II, specialises in maps, travel books and guides. It is among the few places where you can obtain IGM maps covering Vesuvio. Staff will also order IGM maps for any other part of Italy, although the maps will take 10 days to arrive. It also has the CAI maps for the Monti Lattari (Amalfi Coast) and Picentini and a wide selection of Lonely Planet guidebooks.

Information Sources

Unfortunately, there are no useful offices where you can get information on the Vesuvio park area. The organisation of the Ente Parco del Vesuvio is still in its preparatory phase. At the time of research, the park staff were temporarily based in the *municipio* (town hall) of San Sebastiano (☎ (081) 771 75 49) and no printed information was available.

The Guardia Forestale di Caserta (☎ (0823) 36 17 12) (see Permits on this page for details) manages and protects the combined Riserva Tirone-Alto Vesuvio, through which part of the walk described in this section will pass.

The main tourist office in Napoli, the Ente Provinciale del Turismo (EPT) (☎ (081) 40 53 11) is at Piazza dei Martiri 58. It has branch offices at the Stazione Centrale (☎ (081) 26 87 79), at the Stazione Mergellina (☎ (081) 761 21 02) and at the Capodichino airport (☎ (081) 780 57 61). It offers information on transport, hotels, museums, services and a map of the city. The pleasant personnel can direct you to the shops for the maps and equipment suggested in this guidebook.

At Ercolano there is a tourist office (☎ (081) 788 12 34) at Via IV Novembre 84, but it has little to offer other than a brochure with a map of the ruined city. The *Amadeo Maiuri* guide to Ercolano sells at some tourist stands for L10,000, and is considered one of the better ones.

At Pompeii there are two tourist offices, one in modern Pompeii at Via Sacra 1 (☎ (081) 850 72 55), open Monday to Saturday from 8 am to 7.30 pm. The other office is just outside the excavations at Piazza Porta Marina Inferiore 12 (☎ (081) 861 09 13), near the Porta Marina entrance. Pick up a map and a copy of the handy *Notiziario Turistico*

Regionale (NTR). *How to visit Pompeii* (L7000) is a small book, but comprehensive. *Guide d'Agostini – Pompeii* (L12,000) is most probably the best book around.

Permits

You need a permit to go into the Riserva Tirone-Alto Vesuvio, which can be obtained from the Guardia Forestale di Caserta. The process to obtain a permit might baffle the average foreigner and the Guardia Forestale are reasonably sympathetic about this. They say they will tolerate small groups of independent walkers entering the park without permits, as long as walkers respect the environment and obey park rules.

However, if you wish to apply for a permit, you need to apply in Italian by fax (0832) 36 17 34) or by mail to the Ministero per le politiche agricole, Gestione ex ASFD, Via Tescione 125 bis, 81100 Caserta. For information you can phone ☎ (0823) 36 17 12.

It is also possible to obtain a permit on site, at the Guardia Forestale station at Trecase (☎ (081) 537 23 91). Unfortunately this is the only Guardia Forestale station on Vesuvio. It is on the access road to the crater from the south-east face of Boscotrecase, accessible only by car or after many kilometres on foot. A telephone call to the station to leave your name and inform the person in charge that you want to obtain a permit could be another solution to this rather intricate puzzle.

Danger Brewing

Vesuvio is not Europe's most active volcano, but it is potentially its most dangerous. More than 1.5 million people live around and on its slopes. A major eruption, particularly if accompanied by a cloud of burning ash and poisonous gases (as occurred during the 79 AD eruption which destroyed Pompeii and Herculaneum), could cause the loss of many lives.

An emergency plan, covering a worst case scenario, recommends the evacuation of 600,000 people in the event of an eruption. But there are many theories about what would happen in the event of a disaster in an area noted for disorganisation which verges on lawlessness. Even the authors of the plan warn of the possibility of shoot-outs and people being crushed by crowds if they panic.

The volcano last erupted in 1944, during the allied occupation of Napoli and, since then, it has remained ominously silent – a cause for concern, since the longer it remains dormant, the greater the risk of a violent eruption. Seismologists monitor Vesuvio around the clock and scientists are using computer simulations of past eruptions in an effort to predict the potential force of new ones. This close monitoring, combined with Vesuvio's tendency to give plenty of warning of impending eruptions, gives emergency planners, and local residents, at least some comfort. ■

In any case, it is very improbable you'll meet anyone checking permits in the reserve. It is strictly forbidden to enter with motor vehicles, to camp, hunt, light fires, gather plants or disturb animals.

Warning

Vesuvio is under constant monitoring by seismologists at the Osservatorio Vesuviano (Vesuvius Observatory) (see the 'Danger Brewing' boxed text on the previous page). Sooner or later there will be another memorable eruption. As with all of the volcano walks described in this guide, you climb Vesuvio at your own risk, particularly if you plan to go to the crater. Those who wish to be reassured personally by vulcanologists may phone the Osservatorio Vesuviano (☎ (081) 583 22 18). On a lighter note, watch out for vipers and illegal taxi drivers.

ACCOMMODATION & SUPPLIES
Accommodation

If you plan to stay in Napoli, the HI *Ostello Mergellina Napoli* (☎ (081) 761 23 46), Salita della Grotta 23, in Mergellina (a suburb of Napoli), is modern and safe. B&B is L22,000 and a meal is L12,000. It is open all year and imposes a minimum three night stay in summer. Take bus No 152 from Stazione Centrale or the Metropolitana to Mergellina and follow the signs.

Around Stazione Centrale, *Hotel Zara* (☎ (081) 28 71 25), Via Firenze 81, is clean and safe with singles/doubles from L35,000/ L50,000. Via Firenze is off Corso Novara, to the right as you exit the station. *Albergo Ginevra* (☎ (081) 28 32 10), Via Genova 116, the second street to the right off Corso Novara, is another reliable hotel with doubles only, starting at L50,000. Moving up the price scale, the three star *Prati* (☎ (081) 554 18 02), Via C Rosaroll 4, has singles/doubles from L90,000/ L140,000. It is one of the area's best hotels.

A popular spot tucked away in the heart of Spaccanapoli, the historical centre of Napoli, is *Bellini* (☎ (081) 45 69 96), Via San Paolo 44, with singles/doubles for L30,000/L50,000. Just down from the cathedral is *Duomo* (☎ (081) 26 59 88), Via Duomo 228, with doubles/triples for L60,000/L90,000. Don't be put off by the entrance.

Supplies

Arbiter (☎ (081) 41 64 63), Via Toledo 286, near the cable car, is an outdoor shop regularly frequented by Neapolitan mountain enthusiasts and is one of the best stocked in southern Italy.

It has backpacks, trekking shoes, sleeping bags, wind jackets, pile garments, compasses, altimeters, canteens, cooking stoves, tents and torches. Technical mountaineering rope must be ordered three or four days in advance. Saba Sport (☎ (081) 20 51 18) is on the opposite side of Piazza Garibaldi to the station, at Vico VII Duchessa 38/39. It has mostly camping equipment and trekking gear, including compasses and altimeters.

PLANNING
When to Walk

The hottest months, usually July and August, are to be avoided. In spring there is the added spectacle of the flowers. In winter, with the right equipment, Vesuvio offers lovely walks and picturesque panoramas.

What to Bring

The walks described here are fairly straightforward and have no particular requirements for technical gear, although you should bring along a compass and altimeter in case of fog. A normal season-specific outfit is enough for this walk – good, light trekking shoes, a rain poncho and a pile jacket (or similar), as well as sunglasses and sunblock. Bring your own supply of water, since there are no natural water sources on Vesuvio (although there is a soft-drink (soda) stand at the summit!).

Guided Walks

Since the infrastructure for the park is still nonexistent, there is no facility for guided visits. The groups that meet on the volcano are organised beforehand. Luigi Guido (☎ (081) 776 44 26) in San Giorgio a Cremano is a competent environmental guide who speaks English and takes bookings for small groups, charging L80,000 for a four-hour visit, or L140,000 for a seven-hour visit.

The Guide Alpine Vulcanologiche del Vesuvio (☎ (081) 777 57 20) normally limits itself to monitoring tourists along the path to the summit and in the paid tourist area (L5500) at the edge of the crater. On request they can provide information on the history and geology of the volcano.

Guided visits (in English) to the Museo Vulcanologico, inside the Osservatorio Vesuviano, can be booked in advance. Call a few days beforehand on ☎ (081) 583 22 18 or by fax on (081) 575 42 39, except in March, April and May when tours are booked out by local schools. The museum is closed on Saturday and Sunday.

PLACES TO STAY & EAT

There are various panoramic hotels along the routes from Ercolano and Torre del Greco to the volcano; many however are best avoided. Local sources say they tend to rent out their rooms on an hourly, rather than daily basis and so their clients tend not to be tourists.

The ideal place for an excursionist ascending Vesuvio is the *Centro di Accoglienza Turistico-Ambientale, Il Fiume di Pietra* (☎ (081) 47 26 37), in a panoramic position at an altitude of 540m and a few steps from the petrified lava flow of the 1944 eruption. It is on the road that the bus takes from Ercolano up to Vesuvio, shortly after the turn-off for the Osservatorio Vesuviano. There are camp sites and bunks in four, eight or 10-bed dormitories. A tent site is L8000, plus L12,000 per person and L8000 for children up to 12 years old. A bunk costs L27,000 for B&B in summer and L24,000 the low season (usually from November through to Easter excluding Christmas). Hot showers are available and use of the washing machine costs L1000. There is a communal kitchen with a wood oven, and outside there's a barbecue and a playground.

Ercolano

Albergo Belvedere (☎ (081) 739 07 44) is close to the train station and has decent singles/doubles for L45,000/L60,000. There are several bars around the entrance to the ruins where you can buy panini (sandwiches) and other snacks – the one right across the

road from the ancient site, on the right-hand corner of Via IV Novembre, is fine.

Torre del Greco

On the road from Torre del Greco to Ercolano, at Corso Vittorio Emanuele 88, is *Albergo Santa Teresa* (☎ (081) 881 30 26) set in beautiful grounds. It has decent singles/doubles with bath for L60,000/L100,000. Restaurant *da Peppino sott'o ponte* (☎(081) 881 34 45), at Cupa Cianfrone 7, offers excellent pasta and fish dishes with a range of local wines for L25,000 to L30,000.

Pompeii

Camping Zeus (☎ (081) 861 53 29) is near the Stazione Pompeii-Villa dei Misteri and has sites from L10,000, plus L6000 per person. *Camping Pompeii* (☎ (081) 862 28 82), Via Plinio, has bungalows from L50,000 a double. There are about 25 hotels around the site of ancient Pompeii and in the nearby modern town. *Pensione Minerva* (☎ (081) 863 25 86), Via Plinio 23, has simple rooms with a bath for L45,000. *Motel Villa dei Misteri* (☎ (081) 861 35 93), near the villa itself, has doubles for L80,000.

For meals you are better off making the effort to go to the modern town. *A' Do' Giardiniello*, at Via Roma 89, is a no-nonsense pizzeria with prices starting at L5000. *Ristorante Tiberius*, Villa dei Misteri 1B, near the villa, has pasta from L6000.

GETTING THERE & AWAY

The easiest way to get from central Napoli to Vesuvio is by the Circumvesuviana train (which connects Napoli and Sorrento) which leaves the Stazione Centrale every 20 minutes. You can get off at either Ercolano or Pompeii (and visit the archaeological sites). Trasporti Vesuviani buses leave from the Pompeii station of the Circumvesuviana, passing by Ercolano station, and go up as far as the Quota 1000 car park on Vesuvio. The buses run daily, leaving Pompeii at approximately 9, 10 and 11 am and 12.10, 1.20, 2.20 and 3.05 pm. The bus stops at Ercolano approximately 30 to 40 minutes after leaving Pompeii (except for the 3.05 pm bus, which does not stop at

Ercolano). In the winter the schedule is reduced. The last bus returns from the Quota 1000 car park at 6 pm in summer and at 5 pm in the winter. Check the schedule on ☎ (081) 739 28 33. The cost is L10,000 return from Pompeii and L6000 from Ercolano.

SITA buses run from Napoli to Pompeii, ATAC city buses run from Salerno to Pompeii and Marozzi runs a service between Pompeii and Roma. Buses arrive at the Stazione Pompeii-Villa dei Misteri.

Another option is a licensed taxi (beware of unlicensed taxis, which don't have the taxi sign on the roof – once they've delivered you, they might demand an exaggerated fare) from the train station at Ercolano. The licensed taxi runs from 8 am to 7 pm and charges L50,000 return for four people. If you are only going on the tourist walk to the craters, the driver will wait at the car park until you are ready to go back. This company (☎ (081) 39 36 66) also rents vans for larger groups.

By car, take the A3 from Napoli, exit at Ercolano, and follow the signs to Vesuvio, which will take you up to the Quota 1000 car park.

Vesuvio Walks

Duration 3½ hours; 2 hours; 1 hour
Distance 6km-plus; 3km-plus; 2km
Standard Easy-Medium
Start/Finish Quota 1000 car park
Permits Required Yes, but the regulations are not rigid
Public Transport Access Yes
Summary Two circular routes, a short one around the crater and a longer one on unmarked trails which crosses the exquisite and isolated Valle del Gigante. There is also a third short variation in the valley. Wide vistas, silence and undisturbed nature, just around the corner from the tourist route.

VESUVIO LONG CIRCUIT
3½ hours, 310m ascent

This is a scenic, easy route that crosses the pleasant Valle del Gigante and ascends to the crater. References have been inserted that will serve to avoid repetition in the Vesuvio Short Circuit section following, since sections of these walks overlap.

From the Quota 1000 car park (1000m), the end of the line for the bus, go back downhill to the east along the asphalt road for 400m until you reach the first curve and the ruins of an old vulcanological observatory (approximately 875m). The ruins are protected by the fencing of the park reserve and a wooden gate. Two unmarked paths leave from the sides of the ruined building. The one to the right proceeds along the hillside at a constant altitude, the other, to the left of the building, is narrower and descends into the bush.

Climb over the guard rail where the fencing is interrupted and descend on this second path, skirting an old ruined retaining wall with iron gratings. The path bypasses the ruin and curves slightly to the right. Avoid a minor deviation that goes down to the left, and continue in slight descent over massive banks of hardened lava, going basically in a south-east direction. The majestic panorama of the Valle del Gigante and the lava flow of 1944 are to your left.

Be careful of the huge webs that spiders drape across the path. Shortly, the path curves to the left towards the north-east and begins to descend sharply into the valley. Soon you will find yourself on flat ground, following the snaking trail across the peaceful, gentle environment of the valley floor, in a sparse forest of pines and tall broom. Avoid deviations and before long you will reach the base of Monte Somma on the other side of the valley – note the strange rock arch. From here the trail turns right, in an easterly direction, and skirts the rock wall for a few metres before entering into a sort of natural arena, closed off to the north by a wide scree. Here you could see some kestrels and ravens, and this is a good place to take a short rest. Note the strange blade-like rocks that sprout from the ground and the view of the dark cone of Vesuvio.

Follow the trail (which in some places divides in two to avoid obstacles) heading south-east for the scree. Pass over it and you'll see beyond, at about the same altitude

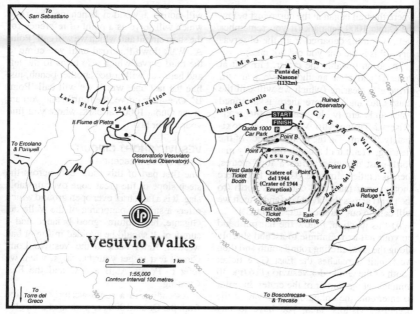

Vesuvio Walks

0   0.5   1 km

1:55,000
Contour Interval 100 metres

as you are now, a vegetation-covered pass where the crest of Monte Somma begins to drop sharply. The trail takes you up and down hills to the final short ascent that ends at the pass, where there is a paling fence. From here, to the east, there is a wide vista of the countryside of Sarno, which seems almost a carpet of greenhouse roofs. To the south, there is the sea with the Penisola Sorrentina (Sorrento Peninsula) and the island of Capri.

The trail now turns right and heads south, following the crest alongside the barbed wire. To the right, cords of lava come together in strange, but beautifully twisted formations and in the distance the ruin of an old rifugio can be seen. To the west, you have the evocative sight of the silent valley at the foot of the volcano. Keep going, up and over the pyramid-like dunes of volcanic slag that make up the crest. Finally, you'll reach a large clearing with an abandoned rifugio which burnt down shortly after it was built.

Looking towards the valley from the clearing, with your back to the refugio, you need to find a trail to your right (south-west) which, about 30m closer to the mountain, begins a slight ascent into the vegetation. (Standing at the same point, you'll notice another trail which descends from the southern corner of the clearing – use it as a point of reference only.) Follow the very clear trail up and down little hills of slag which, after an arduous 1km, turns right (north-west) and soon reaches the dirt road known as 'Matrona', that comes up from Boscotrecase.

Turn right and go up this old, winding road that, in some places, maintains some ancient polished paving stones. Before the 1944 eruption, buses used this road. Where the third hairpin bend turns left, you'll see a dirt road to the right – we are calling this turn-off 'Point D'.

If you turn off here and follow this pleasant trail, in about 15 minutes you will arrive back at the ruined observatory, the point where the trail began at the curve just below the Quota 1000 car park (if you remember well, two trails departed from the observatory – this is the one you did not take).

To go on towards the crater, turn left at Point D and after another curve you will arrive at a clearing (which we will call the 'East Clearing'), where there is a ruined shack and a crusty old green sign that reads 'Riserva Tirone-Alto Vesuvio' (approximately 1050m). On the mountain side of the clearing, a faint trail ascends diagonally in a north-west direction. After a few metres, there is a little hairpin bend on the left where another very faint trail continues north (to the right) across the lava slag (and which we will call, in our short circuit, 'Point C').

At this junction, follow the hairpin bend on your left and continue to ascend sharply along the lava, circling round south and then west until it reaches the East Gate ticket booth of the Guide del Vesuvio (1167m, 30 minutes) at the border of the crater. In order to enter onto the obligatory walkway of the organised visitors' area, you have to pay L5500. Now mingling with the tourists, you can take a look at the impressive chasm of the 230m deep and 550m wide crater with its weak fumaroles. A little road skirts the edge up to the West Gate ticket booth, which is the entrance for those who come up from the Quota 1000 car park. Halfway there is a rather surreal kiosk selling postcards, drinks and traditional fake lava souvenirs.

On clear days you can glimpse (in between the heads of the several hundred tourists) a splendid panorama of the Golfo di Napoli. From right to left you can see the islands of Ischia and Procida, Posillipo, Castel dell'Ovo and the port of Napoli, Portici, Torre del Greco, Torre Annunziata, the rocks of Rovigliano, the Penisola Sorrentina up to Punta Campanella and the island of Capri on the extreme left.

After 50 minutes of slow walking (15 minutes walking quickly), with pauses for observation and picnicking, you come to the West Gate ticket booth. Descend quickly on the first diagonal part of the tourist trail until you reach a road which turns to the left. You

will notice a wooden bench on the right which will serve as a point of reference for the short circuit and which we will call 'Point A'. Walk down this road until you come to the third curve, which also turns to the left and here you will notice another bench, just like the last one, which we will call 'Point B'. One more curve, the fourth, and you are at the Quota 1000 car park, where you find your bus or taxi.

VESUVIO SHORT CIRCUIT
2 hours, 200m ascent

The first part of this route cuts across the steep slope of the great cone over unstable slag. It is a faint trail over open ground which offers a striking panorama of the Valle del Gigante, but requires good balance and a sure foot. It should be avoided in fog or bad weather. Refer back to the Vesuvio Long Circuit text to get your bearings, when we refer to Points A, B and C and the East Clearing.

Ascending in a south-westerly direction from the Quota 1000 car park area along the tourist trail up to the fourth and last curve before the summit, you'll find a wooden bench (which we called Point A in the Vesuvio Long Circuit description), behind which there is a faint trail. Taking the trail from behind the Point A wooden bench, you'll cross the slope in an easterly direction. For those who like this sort of thing, this trail is a bit challenging since it crosses the very steep slope over unstable and loose lava slag.

As the trail turns to the south, it comes to the curve which we called Point C, above the East Clearing, where the Matrona road ends. From here, instead of going down to the clearing, keep going up (south-west) on the trail until you come to the East Gate ticket booth of the Guide del Vesuvio (30 minutes), where you must pay the L5500 to enter the visitors' area of the crater. The descent, which completes the circuit, is from the West Gate ticket booth of the visitors area.

Following the crowd of tourists it is impossible to get lost, but you could eventually lose your patience.

ANOTHER VESUVIO LOOP
1 hour, 310m ascent

If you have an extra hour to spare and you'd like to continue, the following is another walk which will take you far from the throng of tourists.

Descending from the crater along the winding tourist trail, you come to the wooden bench which we called Point B. Behind the bench take the well-marked trail through the vegetation that traverses the slope of the great volcano. Thirty metres before coming to the East Clearing, the trail breaks up into many tracks, forcing you to find your way to the clearing on your own through the thick locust plants (30 minutes). This trail leads directly to the clearing.

At the left corner of the clearing, facing the valley, there is a short cut where, digging your heels into the slag, you make a straight descent for 30m, down to a turn-off on the Matrona road, which we have called Point D. If you decide to ignore the short cut and descend on the road from the clearing, after a curve you reach Point D, where you go left. The wide dirt road leads you north to the ruined observatory in 15 minutes, from where the long circuit began, just below the Quota 1000 car park.

STROMBOLI & VULCANO

Stromboli and Vulcano are two active volcanic islands in the Isole Eolie north of Messina. The seven volcanic islands of the archipelago were known in ancient times for their deposits of obsidian. The ancient Greeks witnessed terrifying eruptions and believed that the islands were the residence of Aeolus, the god of the winds. Tourism, now a flourishing industry, has blurred the hard years from the 1930s to 1950s, when many of the islands' residents were forced to emigrate. Most went to Australia, which is often referred to as the eighth Aeolian island.

Vulcano is the island closest to the coast of Sicilia and is right next to Lipari, the main island, where the archipelago's administra-

tive offices and tourist office (the AAST) are located.

The ascent to the crater of Vulcano (391m), low and docile with its fairly innocuous geysers of sulphurous steam, is very short and interesting and presents no technical problems – a volcano for the whole family, so to speak!

Stromboli is quite a distance away to the north-east and climbing the volcano is as atmospheric as it is demanding. It is well-connected by boat with the other islands, the coast of Sicilia and with Napoli. Stromboli is 924m high and the vigorous, explosive activity of its craters, the difficulty of climbing its slopes and the luminous Mediterranean beauty of its vistas make an excursion to its summit a contender for the title of 'Mother of All Volcano Climbs'.

It is possible to climb Stromboli safely along the normal routes and in the company of guides. However, we are proposing a technically demanding excursion, requiring third grade Alpine skills and some mountaineering equipment.

HISTORY
The Isole Eolie were already inhabited in the 4th millennium BC by people who prospered from mining and selling obsidian, a sharp, black, lustrous and valuable volcanic glass that can still be found in Lipari. Before the use of metal, obsidian was in great demand for the making of arms and tools – obsidian mined on Lipari in that period has been found as far away as Dalmatia and southern France. In the Bronze Age, around the 18th century BC, the islands were populated by people of Mycenaean Greece who gave the archipelago its name, linking it with the myth of the wind god, Aeolus (Eolo). This myth is cited by Homer in the Odyssey. Thucydides, in the 5th century BC, reported a tremendous eruption on Vulcano.

With their strategic position in the Mediterranean, the Isole Eolie were coveted by the Sicilian city-states of Magna Grecia and later by Carthage and Roma. Since ancient times, the caves of Vulcano have yielded alum, a mineral salt used as a powerful caustic, and in the days of the Roman Empire, Cicero cited the excellent thermal waters of Lipari and Vulcano. In the Middle Ages, the crater of Vulcano was believed to be the mouth of Hell.

In 1083, the islands were conquered by the Normans and in 1544 Lipari was sacked by the Moslem pirate Ariadeno Barbarossa who carried the entire population away into slavery. The island was repopulated by Charles V and from that time on its history followed that of Sicilia and the Kingdom of Napoli.

NATURAL HISTORY
Geology

The volcanic archipelago of the Isole Eolie is found in the lower Tyrrhenian sea, from 20km to 40km north of the north-eastern tip of Sicilia, and is made up of seven originally volcanic islands: Alicudi, Filicudi, Salina, Lipari, Vulcano, Panarea and Stromboli. The archipelago was formed during the Pliocene Age by the movements of land plates that created the shelves of the Tyrrhenian Sea. From fissures in the sea floor up to 1000m deep, the magma that gave birth to the Aeolian volcanism gushed forth.

Around 300,000 years ago, parts of the islands of Panarea, Filicudi and Alicudi began to take shape; Salina and Lipari followed 130,000 years ago; Vulcano rose up 100,000 years ago, while Stromboli, the youngest of the islands, was born 40,000 years ago. The volcanoes of Vulcano and Stromboli are the only ones still active today. Vulcanello (123m), a small, inactive peninsula of the island of Vulcano, was created suddenly in an underwater eruption in 183 BC which is recorded in eyewitness accounts of the time. All these volcanic cones are made up of layered strips of solidified lava (which generally flows slowly down the slopes before becoming solid) and layers of material expelled by the violent thrust of eruptions: ash, stones and the so-called bombs – projectiles of various sizes generically known as ejecta.

Erosion due to atmospheric agents such as wind and rain has consumed and compacted the most ancient of the structures over thousands of years. The crater of Vulcano (391m), which maintains a slight level of activity with its *solfatare*, sulphurous geysers, is low and flattened.

Stromboli (924m), the youngest of the Aeolian volcanoes, maintains a constant explosive activity. Rising majestically from the sea, it is an imposing cone-shaped mass of heavily eroded layers of unstable material. Vulcano, Lipari and Panarea are all favoured by post-volcanic thermal phenomena. The volcanic mud of Vulcano has a high radon content and, along with the hot springs in the shallow waters along the shores behind the island's Porto di Levante, is said to cure joint pain, neuralgia, phlebitis and skin diseases.

Flora

The Isole Eolie are covered with typical Mediterranean shrubbery: oleander (*oleandro*), myrtle (*mirto*), cistus (*cisto*), heather (*erica*), broom (*ginestra*), and spiny-leafed oak (*quercia a foglia spinosa*). Among the many aromatic plants found on the islands are rosemary (*rosmarino*), thyme (*timo*) and mastic tree (*lentisco*). Before the influx of tourists, malvasia grape vines were cultivated extensively, along with olives and capers, all of which are practically abandoned today. Growing among the terraces you can find figs and almonds, plums, carob and prickly pears. Two shrubs make up the typical Aeolian land cover – the *Cytisus aeolicus* and the *Centaurea cineraria aeolica*.

Fauna

The only mammals on the islands are wild rabbits, mice and rats. Among the numerous migratory birds which pass through briefly in spring and autumn, are pelicans, herons, swans, brown kites, various species of falcons and hawks, cranes, swallows, geese, curlews, glossy ibis, scoopers, woodcocks, flamingoes, hoopoes, golden orioles, starlings and quails. Permanent species include the imperial crow (*Corvus corax*), shearwater, royal seagull, buzzard, kestrel, owl and whippoorwill. The queen hawk and swamp hawk stop only long enough on the islands to build their nests.

Reptiles, all harmless, include the coluber (a type of snake) and the common lizard, of which there is a very rare variety endemic to the tiny island of Strombolicchio. Tuna and swordfish are caught off Stromboli and Lipari in late spring (remember Ingrid Bergman in Roberto Rossellini's *Stromboli*?) and at the end of the autumn you may even see migrating sperm whales off Stromboli.

CLIMATE

Mild temperatures in winter and not-too-high temperatures in summer, combined with scarce rain, make for a very pleasant climate year-round in the Isole Eolie. Average temperatures vary from 13°C in January to 20°C in May, and from 27°C in July to 21°C in October. The average annual temperature is between 16°C and 20°C. Average precipitation is only 500mm to 600mm annually, the wettest months being January and December, with July the driest. Winds are, on an annual average, predominantly from the north-west – the *maestrale* – or from the south-east – the *scirocco* (sirocco).

INFORMATION
Stromboli

The island of Stromboli covers an area of 12.6 sq km, which is completely taken up by the slopes of the 924m volcano. There are no connecting roads between the only two towns on the island, Stromboli and Ginostra. These are separated to the north-west of the island by the *Sciara del Fuoco*, an immense expanse of volcanic waste flowing directly into the sea from the craters above. The slopes of all the other faces are forbidding and impracticable. The more convenient areas are on the north-east coast where, with tourism and the port activity, Stromboli has become very developed. You'll see few cars parked between the houses of the new and old neighbourhoods. Instead, a myriad of noisy mopeds speed up and down the narrow alleyways. The town is well organised and offers good accommodation.

Ginostra is another world. The occasional house and one church are nestled in the green of a natural hollow on the opposite side of the island. It is a tiny, silent kingdom where the atmosphere of another time has been preserved. The village is easy to reach only by sea: there are no cars and goods are brought in on mules along narrow trails that pass through vegetable gardens and back yards. There are no hotels, only houses or rooms to let; and there are only two cafe/ restaurants, an *alimentari* (small general store) and a post office. Almost all houses use rainwater gathered in tanks, oil lamps, gas refrigerators and they rarely have hot water.

Disembarking at Ginostra is on request only. Ships and hovercraft have to stop off-shore to let passengers onto a small motorboat that ferries them in, but this service is suspended in rough seas. In winter, the village can be isolated for days on end if the sea is rough. Perhaps Ginostra won't have a real pier for a little longer yet.

Stromboli has, by now, become popular and attracts a steady stream of tourists from northern Europe, spring to autumn. In the summer months, it is a very popular destination for holidaymakers, and the island's hotels, pensioni and many houses to let offer a range of prices and arrangements.

Vulcano

Vulcano extends over 21 sq km, separated from Lipari by a narrow stretch of sea. It is formed by the vast high plain of Vulcano Piano, dominated to the south by Monte Aria (500m), to the north by the promontory of Vulcanello (123m), with its three small inactive craters, and by the large active central crater called the Fossa (391m) which looms over the Porto di Levante where the hovercraft and ferries dock. A single road connects the most densely populated area of the port with Vulcano Piano and Vulcanello, where the population becomes sparser.

On the western side of the sandy isthmus linking Vulcanello to Vulcano there is a wide beach of black sand and on the east side are the famous fumarole gurgling like a jacuzzi in the waters along the shore, not far from the sulphuric mud pool known in ancient times for its therapeutic effects. The crater of the Fossa is an easy climb and can be explored in half a day. It is about 500m wide and is made up of two adjacent calderas approximately 200m deep. The volcano's activity is limited to the emission of unpleasant, but harmless, sulphuric fumes from the internal walls of the cone.

Maps

Kompass map No 693, *Isole Eolie o Lipari* (1:25,000) costs L9000 and covers Stromboli and Vulcano, and has a synoptic chart showing the position of the Isole Eolie in relation to Napoli, Sicilia and Calabria, as well as a small map of Lipari town. The map of Vulcano is good enough for navigation, but for Stromboli it would be better to get *Alla Scoperta dell'Isola di Stromboli* (1:5000, sold locally in several languages) with information on trails and maps of the two villages.

Information Sources

The post code for the Isole Eolie is 98055 and the telephone prefix is ☎ 090.

Lipari The AAST of Lipari (☎ (090) 988 00 95), the tourist office for the entire archipelago is at Corso Vittorio Emanuele 223. The office has plenty of information about accommodation, transport and more. It is open Monday to Saturday from 8 am to 2 pm and 4.30 to 7.30 pm.

Stromboli The branch tourist office on Stromboli has closed down, so all information should be requested from the office on Lipari. For up-to-date information (in English as well) on weather and sea conditions on Stromboli, and especially at Ginostra, you can call the legendary local resident Ulli (at dinner time) on ☎ (090) 981 24 23. He also gives information on accommodation in Ginostra, and speaks English (see Guided Walks later in this section for more information).

Vulcano The tourist information office in Vulcano (☎ (090) 985 20 28) opens only in summer, in front of the mud baths.

Milazzo The Milazzo AAST (☎ (090) 922 28 65) is in Piazza Caio Duilio.

Permits

The Mayor of Stromboli has recently banned people from climbing to Stromboli's active crater without the assistance of an authorised guide. The ban covers only the summit area around the crater, but nobody knows if it will, in fact, be enforced. In the meantime, many tourists continue to climb the normal route freely, without a guide and camp out near the crater. Although this is common practice, the danger in being at the crater cannot be underestimated. Stromboli is a very active volcano and you go to the crater area at your own risk (see boxed Warnings in the Stromboli Circuit section).

Books

The AAST tourist office in Lipari has a free 60-page booklet entitled *Isole Eolie*, with maps, also available in English. There is also one for Sicily called *Sicily and its islands*.

Place Names

The names of some locations change depending on the map you're using. On the small maps for sale only in Stromboli, the place names are in local dialect only. These will be cited in the walk description, followed by the standard Italian name, which is that used on the IGM map of the archipelago, in brackets.

ACCOMMODATION & SUPPLIES

To get to Stromboli and Vulcano you will most probably be coming from either Napoli, or from Sicily via Milazzo. Lipari is the main island of the archipelago and is a good place to pick up supplies. It is also worthwhile to stay there and explore the town and island. There are no technical supplies available.

Accommodation

Lipari The island's camping ground, the *Baia Unci* (☎ (090) 981 19 09), is at Canneto, about 2km out of Lipari township and accessible by bus from the Esso service station at Marina Lunga. It isn't cheap at L15,000 per person and L25,000 for a tent/caravan site.

The *HI Youth Hostel* (☎ (090) 981 15 40), Via Castello 17, is inside the walls of the castle. B&B costs L15,500 per person, plus L2000 for a hot shower, and L15,000 for a meal – or you can cook your own. It is open from March to October. *Cassarà Vittorio* (☎ (090) 981 15 23), Vico Sparviero 15, off Via Garibaldi near Marina Corta, costs L40,000 per person, or L45,000 with private bathroom. There are two terraces with views, and use of the kitchen is L5000. The owner can be found (unless he finds you first) at Via Garibaldi 78, on the way from the port to the city centre. *Enzo il Negro* (☎ (090) 981 24 73), at Via Garibaldi 29, has spotless, comfortable digs for up to L45,000 per person in the high season. All rooms have a bathroom and balcony and there is a large terrace.

Milazzo Try the *Central* (☎ (090) 928 10 43), Via del Sole 8, near the port. It has basic rooms for L35,000/L60,000.

Supplies

There are no shops specialising in outdoor equipment in the Isole Eolie or at Milazzo, although you might find camping equipment and perhaps walking shoes at sporting goods stores. The best idea is to pick up whatever you need, particularly the 10m length of mountaineering rope if you plan to do the Stromboli circuit, either in Roma or Napoli (see the Facts for the Walker chapter and under Supplies in the earlier Vesuvio section).

PLANNING
When to Walk

The warm season is from April to October. The high number of tourists and the excessive heat in midsummer make daytime walks unbearable. The best months to walk are April and May (when the wild flowers are blooming) and September and October, when it is still possible to swim in the warm sea. Prices are lower from November to March (not including Easter), but many hotels are closed and fewer people rent out private rooms. Those who go exclusively to see the eruptions prefer to climb up at dusk and then descend with a torch or stay and

sleep on or near the crater. For the crater of Vulcano you'll only need about a half a day, so it is easier to avoid the hottest hours.

What to Bring

Good walking shoes are essential for walking on Stromboli. High-top, lightweight walking shoes with heavy soles and a good tread are a good idea. The trails on Stromboli sometimes cross through prickly shrubs, so long pants are recommended. At the summit, it is like being out in the middle of the sea, there is always wind and the temperature drops considerably at night. Bring a wind jacket and something warm to put on, such as a pile jacket. There is no water along the way: bring along a minimum of 2L per person, including for the coastal section. A torch (flashlight) is also a good idea. Those who decide to spend the night at the summit will need a sleeping bag. Those who intend to walk the section of coast between Stromboli and Ginostra must have a 10m length of mountaineering rope for safety. A compass might come in handy, especially in case of poor visibility.

For walking on both volcanoes you'll need a hat and sunglasses, as well as a good sunblock. There is absolutely no shade at the crater of Vulcano and the sun is searingly hot. A cotton scarf to shield out the sulphur vapours could be useful. To climb Vulcano you need light, comfortable clothes, even shorts. Running shoes will suffice if you don't have good walking shoes.

Guided Walks

As stated in the boxed Warnings in the Stromboli Circuit section, it is forbidden to climb to the crater of Stromboli unless accompanied by an authorised guide. There are two official guide organisations on Stromboli which can each take a maximum of 20 people to the summit at sundown on the main trail via Punta d' a'Brunzu (Punta Labronzo). They stay for half an hour at the crater in the half-light of dusk, which is the best light in which to view the eruptions, then come back down by the light of their torches.

The cooler months of spring and autumn are the best times for these excursions. The guides are expert on the trails and on the specific difficulties imposed by the unstable volcanic terrain, and they are always linked via radio with the town below – so making the ascent with them means making it in greater safety. Unfortunately, as the numbers of tourists travelling to Stromboli increase, the guided tours are not always as interesting as they could be.

The Guide Ambientali Escursionistiche (GAE) in Stromboli is a group of three guides, headed by Mario Zaia (☎ (090) 98 63 15). One of the guides – Lorenzo – is particularly competent and speaks English. They will also advise people who want to plan their own excursion without a guide. The GAE will provide guides for individuals as well as small groups wanting to go on personalised walks (including the route described in this section). It is recommended that you agree on a fee in advance and be firm about what you want. Some guides are used to the profit to be made from taking large groups to the summit and, particularly in the high season, tend to discourage alternative routes – they will either push the classic route or overestimate the price of any alternative ones.

The GAE in Ginostra organises evening ascents from their side of the volcano, which some say is more beautiful and which is definitely less travelled. You can also stay the night on the volcano with a guide, who will then accompany you down the next day. The head of the group is Ulli, a resident German. He speaks English and generously offers information, even to those not wanting to use a guide (☎ (090) 981 24 23).

Antonio Aquilone's AGAI (☎ (090) 98 62 11) is another agency that offers guided group excursions to the crater. It is in a kiosk at Porto di Scari in Stromboli.

The guided evening ascent from Stromboli or Ginostra is L30,000 and takes five to six hours. Guided tours can be booked by calling the GAE in Stromboli or Ginostra, or by going directly to the AGAI kiosk.

There is no guide service on Vulcano because the ascent is so easy and short.

PLACES TO STAY & EAT
Stromboli
In the town of Stromboli, the cheapest option is to rent a room with cooking facilities. Prices listed here are for low-medium season. Many are closed from November to March. *Casa del Sole* (☎ (090) 98 60 17) is a type of hostel in Via Soldato Cincotta in the Piscità area. It has beds in dorms for around L35,000 and double rooms without bath for L70,000 to L80,000.

Tahar Badino (☎ (090) 98 60 30), near San Vincenzo, has a lovely atmosphere in a typical house with internal garden, terraces and a wide choice of rooms for L25,000 to L30,000 per day. *Umberto Palino* (☎ (090) 98 60 26), at Via Fabio Filzi 27, lets rooms near the seaside for the same prices. *Locanda Stella* (☎ (090) 98 60 20), Via Fabio Filzi 14, charges L55,000 to L70,000 for a double and L120,000 to L140,000 for half board. The pleasant *Villa Petrusa* (☎ (090) 98 60 45), in via Soldato Panettieri 3, has a big terrace for breakfast and dinner with a view over the sea. B&B costs L40,000/L80,000 and half pension L70,000/L110,000 in the low/high season.

The *Malandrino* bar, at the pier of Scari, makes good sandwiches and has a terrace. In San Vincenzo, across from the church, the *Ingrid* bar/grill has a terrace with a panoramic view of the sea. *Il Canneto*, Via Roma 64, serves dinner in the open, but without a view, from L40,000 per person.

In Ginostra you can get information on rooms and houses to rent from Ulli (☎ (090) 981 24 23). In August, the average price per person is L40,000, in July it's L30,000, in September L25,000 and in the other months L20,000. There are only two bar/restaurants in town and you'll have no trouble finding them.

Vulcano
Togo-Togo camping ground (☎ (090) 985 23 03), on the black sand beach of Porto di Ponente, is open from April to September and has bungalows for L25,000 per person. *Rosario Muscarà* (☎ (090) 985 20 66) rents rooms in his house (next to the Hotel Sabbie Nere) for L20,000 to L25,000 in the low season. The *Natoli residence* (☎ (090) 985

20 59), in Via Porto di Levante 4, lets rooms with bath, kitchen area and linen for L30,000 per day in low season, L35,000 in June and July and L50,000 in August.

Pensione La Giara (☎ (090) 985 22 29), Via Provinciale 18, is on the way to the crater. It is open from April to mid-October and offers B&B with bathroom and air-conditioning for L38,000 in April, May and October, and L42,000/L73,000 a single/double from June to August. *Residence Lanterne Blu* (☎ (090) 985 21 78), Via Lentia 58, offers one-room studios from L50,000 to L110,000, depending on the season, and two-room studios from L110,000 to L220,000.

Hotel Arcipelago (☎ (090) 985 20 02) is in an isolated area on the point north of Vulcanello and from its swimming pool there are beautiful views of Lipari's faraglioni and of Filicudi. It is open from March to mid-October and half board costs from L120,000 to L230,000 depending on the season. Prices drop if you stay for three days of more.

Il Cratere, Via Provinciale 31, has a terrace overlooking the sea, where you can eat good pasta dishes and seafood at very reasonable prices. There is a *supermarket* across the road. You will eat well, spending a little more, at *da Maurizio* and *da Vincenzino*, both in Via Porto di Levante.

GETTING THERE & AWAY

Prices and schedules change according to the season and those listed here should be checked before you set out. Boat services are sometimes disrupted to the islands due to rough seas or lack of passengers. Fares quoted here are one way.

Stromboli

The island of Stromboli is connected by boat with Napoli, Palermo, Messina, Catania, Cefalù and Milazzo, the closest Sicilian port, as well as with the other Isole Eolie. Siremar hovercrafts (*aliscafi*) make four trips a day from Stromboli to Lipari and other islands at 7.25 and 9.45 am and 3 and 5.10 pm (L19,000 one way). Siremar stops at Ginostra only twice a day. The hovercraft takes only 10 minutes

to make the trip between Ginostra and Stromboli towns. There is also an irregular private boat service between the two towns (L25,000, half-hour trip). Siremar also makes a daily ferryboat run that connects Stromboli and the other islands with Milazzo. It stops at Ginostra on Tuesdays and Saturdays at 12.10 pm. As previously mentioned, boats stop off-shore and passengers are ferried to Ginostra's small pier by motorboat. The Siremar hovercraft to Ginostra takes 10 minutes and leaves only twice a day in summer, at 7.25 am and at 3 pm from the pier at Scari. There are also small private boats that will bring you to Ginostra for L20,000 to L25,000. The trip takes 30 minutes and doesn't go every day.

SNAV operates *aliscafi* hovercraft that connect Stromboli with the other islands (Lipari L23,000; Vulcano L26,000) and with Milazzo (L28,000) six times a day, and some trips go all the way to Messina (L34,100), Catania (L64,000), Cefalù (L56,000) and Palermo (L77,000).

Travelling by hovercraft or ferry from Napoli is the easiest way to get to the Isole Eolie from Vesuvio. SNAV runs daily hovercraft from Napoli to Stromboli, Lipari followed by Vulcano from April to September. They depart from the pier at Mergellina at 2.30 pm and reach Stromboli at 6.30 pm (L98,000), Vulcano at 8.10 pm and Lipari at 8.30 pm.

For information on SNAV services call the office for the Isole Eolie on ☎ (090) 928 78 21, or the central booking office in Messina on ☎ (090) 71 79 21, where some operators speak English. For information on Siremar services call the office in Palermo on ☎ (091) 33 66 31, or look up the Siremar home page on the Internet: http://siremar.gesteinet.it.

A Tirrenia ferry makes six overnight runs a week from Napoli in the high season (reduced to five in September and three in the low season). The boat leaves in all seasons at 9 pm and arrives at Stromboli at 5 am (L65,000), Ginostra at 6 am (L66,000), Lipari at 9.35 am (L73,000) and Vulcano at 10.05 am (L74,000), ending its run at Milazzo at 12.25 pm (L82,000). It makes the

VOLCANOES

return trip the following day. From mid-April to mid-September, the Demartour bus company (☎ (06) 444 05 27), Via Solferino 28 in Roma runs a direct service from Roma's Piazza Indipendenza to Napoli's Stazione Marittima to correspond with the departure of the Tirrenia ferry (L35,000).

Tirrenia can be contacted in Napoli on ☎ (081) 780 11 11.

Vulcano

The island of Vulcano is served regularly by hovercraft and ferry, since it is practically a neighbourhood of Lipari. There are more than 15 hovercraft per day between the two islands, as well as less frequent ferries (Siremar and SNAV). There are connections for all the other islands, Milazzo, Palermo, Messina (L31,000 – useful for those going

---

Warnings

Volcanic Activity The Stromboli crater is the youngest in the Isole Eolie – it was formed only 40,000 years ago – and it is still very much awake. It is very explosive, launching periodical showers of incandescent lava accompanied by the more or less violent emission of sulphurous fumes and small overflows of lava. Technical volcano language, taking this kind of behaviour as a model, has come to include the term *attività stromboliana* (strombolian activity).

In recent years, eruptions have been of modest proportions and have occurred within the vicinity of the crater. A major eruption in 1930 was an additional cause of the emigration to Australia of many of the island's 4000 inhabitants. The last substantial eruption was in 1966.

Eruptions occur roughly every 10 to 30 minutes, although they are basically unpredictable. There could be no eruptions for hours or days, or they could occur suddenly one immediately after another. Another variable is their power. Usually the material expelled from the mouth does not manage to get up as high as the tourist observation point at the Pizzo o Sopra la Fossa, 300m away and 200m higher up. Nor does it usually reach the circular line of the so-called *fortini*, the low protective walls of piled up stones that stand above the area of the eruptions.

However, on rare occasions the volcano can throw up a light rain of incandescent lapilli (pumice) and *bombe* (larger masses of molten rock) – as far up as the Pizzo and even beyond. It is impossible to predict when this might happen: the best way to confront the arrival of these projectiles is head on. They are usually travelling slowly enough to allow you to dodge them easily, so trying to escape by turning your back and running just increases your chances of being hit. Those surprised in their sleep risk getting knocked on the head, as happened to one unlucky young man in 1996.

Use of Guides At the point where the normal climb from Punta Labronzo begins, a very visible sign (in English as well as Italian), warns walkers not to climb to the crater unless accompanied by an authorised guide. A recent mayoral ordinance has expressly forbidden it. Ignoring this, many visitors still make the climb without a guide and some even pass the night at the crater, lulled by the rumblings of the eruptions, sheltered within the primitive *fortini*.

Lonely Planet does not recommend that walkers climb to the crater without a guide. The terrain in the medium-high areas of the volcano is very steep and made up predominantly of extremely porous, lightweight and unstable volcanic debris. Walking on this type of terrain is very tiring and, especially on the steep slopes where there are often small landslides, it is easy to lose your footing.

It is possible to hire a guide to accompany you on the walk described here. See Guided Walks earlier in this chapter for details. In summer, guides take as many as 400 people up to the Pizzo every evening to witness the spectacular explosions at the crater. Before they go back down they usually leave behind enough litter to bring out the rats, which can be spotted at night around the sleeping bags of those who stay up there.

Even with a guide, the Stromboli Circuit is a difficult undertaking for people who are not adequately experienced and/or equipped, or who are travelling with children. It includes a 6km coastal walk which requires third grade alpine skills, ie some climbing is involved and beginners will need a safety rope handled by someone more proficient. If you are inexperienced, or nervous about climbing you should definitely not attempt this walk. The coastal section can be tackled only when particular weather conditions prevail and the sea is absolutely calm – otherwise you run the risk of being dragged out to sea (see the walk description). This is not a walk for the faint-hearted.

As with all the volcano walks in this chapter, you should remember that it is potentially extremely dangerous to climb to the crater and you do so at your own risk. ■

to Etna), Catania (via Lipari – L60,000) and Napoli (see the previous Stromboli Getting To/From the Walks section).

Milazzo

Regular buses connect Milazzo with Messina and Catania. Giunta bus (☎ (090) 67 37 82) runs a fast service on the autostrada from Milazzo to Messina 15 times a day from Monday to Saturday and once a day at 6 pm on Sundays and holidays. SAIS (☎ (090) 77 19 14) links Milazzo with Catania's Fontanarossa airport as well as Catania and Messina, 15 times a day.

There are also regular trains connecting Catania, Messina and Milazzo with major cities on the mainland.

If you want to leave your car at Milazzo, there are several supervised car parks including the Mylarum garage (☎ (090) 928 34 33) near the port in Via G Rizzo 58, where covered parking costs L15,000 a day, L6000 for motorcycles up to 350cc. Leaving your car or motorcycle parked in the open for several days could be risky.

Stromboli Circuit

> **Duration** 2 to 3 days
> **Standard** Hard; third Alpine grade
> **Start/Finish** Stromboli town
> **Permits Required** Visits to the crater without a guide are officially banned.
> **Summary** Demanding route on the slopes and to the summit of the Stromboli volcano, with a short section along the coast requiring third grade Alpine skills. Steep climbs, shifting terrain, and spectacular views of volcanic eruptions and the surrounding sea.

At the end of the boat trip from Napoli, through the misty light of dawn, you see Stromboli in the distance – a large, dark crater, completely isolated in the sea, its soft, symmetric profile looking just like the classic child's drawing of a volcano. Sometimes its peak gets lost in a cloud of sulphur and mist, and the

sea, with its ever shifting reflections, heightens the effect of this murky, immobile mass.

Stromboli is big enough to inspire awe and small enough to climb in just a few hours. It has a small but interesting system of excursion routes at two different levels of difficulty. These are the route used by the guides to take groups to within 200m of the volcano's active crater, and the independent routes which all include sections of unstable terrain and steep slopes and require some mountaineering skills and a good level of fitness, as well as adequate equipment (see What to Bring under Planning earlier).

This requires a grade three level of mountaineering skill. It can be done in two days, or in three if you decide to spend the second night at the crater (in a well-sheltered position at a safe distance from the explosive activity). Stromboli and Ginostra are separated by the Sciara del Fuoco, the impressive lava stream that flows down to the sea, creating a slow-moving barrier on the north-west face of the volcano.

The volcano's other slopes are too difficult to traverse, even on foot, so there are only two possibilities for crossing the island on foot, both very demanding: you can climb up to the Pizzo (918m), above the crater, and cross down to the other side, or follow a coastal south-eastern face (on the opposite side of the volcano to the Sciara). The walk described here incorporates both routes into what we have called the Stromboli Circuit.

The coastal trail can be tackled only when the sea is absolutely calm and downwind for the entire day. The dominant winds usually blow favourably from the north-west, but it is essential that you check weather forecasts and verify the situation on the same day of the walk. Local guides can be of assistance here.

The route follows the coastline from Scari to Lazzaro along cliff edges and is frequented only rarely. As previously mentioned, there are two short sections requiring third grade mountaineering expertise, and it is not recommended for those who are inexperienced or unsure. You have to be willing to jump about acrobatically between the cliffs, always just a few centimetres from the sea, for the 6km

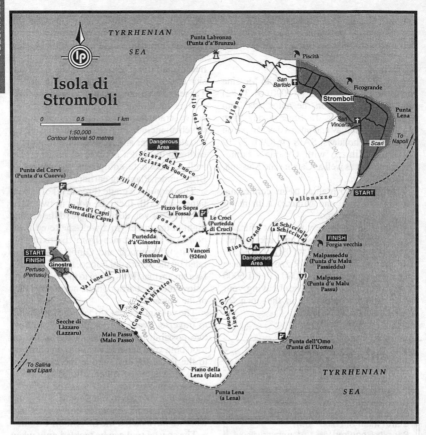

from Scari to Lazzaro. There is a danger of landslides along the final section between Punta Lena and Lazzaro, especially after rain. When the sea is rough, the very narrow corridor along the cliffs between the magnificent rocky overhanging walls and the sea, becomes unpassable in some places and there is a risk you could be dragged out to sea.

The other route between the two villages is by way of the summit – a fascinating, but exacting mountain route. Because of the steepness of some sections, the descent can be more difficult than the ascent. It is advisable, and also more interesting, to go up on the less-travelled side of the volcano, from Ginostra to the crest of the Pizzo. The descent is then on the more convenient and spectacular side to the Forgia Vecchia, one of the most beautiful beaches in Stromboli, and is off the beaten tourist track too. This climb up to 918m and then back down to sea level is on steep-to-very-steep slopes. The terrain is an accumulation of ash and stones and very unstable. This can be a serious hindrance in some places. It is a good idea, for the descent, to have become acquainted with the technique of hopping over and through the scree.

If you arrive on the boat from Napoli and find that the wind is coming from the south-east and the sea is rough, it might be a good idea to get off at Ginostra (this can be done only on request and only if the sea is not too rough. You can then avoid the first leg along the coast.

If you get to Stromboli town early in the morning and intend to do the whole circuit, it's best to book accommodation for the night on your return and ask if you can leave your bags. It takes four to five hours to reach Ginostra along the coastal trail and even in good weather, there's a chance you'll get wet. You'll need to carry 2L of water per person, per day.

THE WALK
Day 1: Stromboli Town to Ginostra
3½ to 4½ hours, 6km

From the pier at Scari, where the hovercraft arrive, go south along the black pebble beach. The going is slow and tiring. You'll pass a red and white marker for trail No 12, which goes off to the right into the blind valley, Vallonazzo, and continue on for the long, beautiful beach of the Forgia vecchia. To your right there is a spectacular sight of fine black sand cascading down from the rocky peaks of the Roccazza. In two or three days you'll be making your way down from up there, speeding all the way to the sea for a swim.

At the end of the Forgia Vecchia beach is the Punta d'u Malu Passieddu (Malpasseddu). This is a high rock, shaped like a knife blade, which you pass, walking on the sand at low tide. Otherwise, there is a little path to the right which will take you over the rock to the next pretty inlet. At the end of this next beach of black pebbles, there is the obstacle of Punta d'u Malu Passu (Malpasso) (1½ hours from the pier at Mascari). This is a high, thick lava flow, where you must climb a vertical rockface, which is only 3m to 4m high. It is, however, exposed to the sea above sharp rocks and requires third to fourth Alpine grade mountaineering skill, and is not recommended for the inexperienced. When we tackled the climb, it had been outfitted in an extremely unsafe manner with an old orange rope. The system for securing the rope to the high part of the rockface was not visible from

below and when we arrived at the top, without having used it, it was clearly unsafe and not to be trusted.

It is safer for the most expert in the group to free-climb up, using their own cord in order to ensure the safety of the others from above. Unless you are an expert, it is not a good idea to attempt this climb alone – very few people pass this way, which presents a problem if you are injured.

After Malu Passu you come to an inlet jammed with massive boulders, where a niche has been formed by the erosion of the sea on the surface of an ancient lava stream. The volcano seen from below is a very impressive sight. You have a clear view of its shifting, heavily-eroded slopes. It is a good idea to keep an eye out as you pass under towering cliffs of rock and lava mushed together in what looks like a giant nougat!

You'll soon reach the second difficult passage at Punta di l'Uomo (Punta dell'Omo) (30 minutes). Here you find a mountaineering grade two/three rockface, about 4m high. Its only drawback is that the easiest approach is from a cliff rising straight up out of the water and, if the sea is rough, it can present some difficulty.

Swimming across Punta dell'Omo is more difficult than it seems because of the currents. There is, however, a gorgeous natural swimming pool among the cliffs, full of sea urchins (so be careful!) where you can take a refreshing dip.

Once past Punta dell'Omo you can see the coast which turns south-west, with the piano della Lena beyond. Hopping among the rocks, continue on, crossing over the old telegraph line, and passing two little inlets separated by a rocky strip, to reach a Lena (Punta Lena) (30 minutes).

There is a gorge on the right, overgrown with a form of vegetation called o Cavone (i Cavoni). It is the deepest gorge on the island and it is possible to climb up (one hour return), turning right along the river bed that you meet just before arriving at the first abandoned house of La Lena. It quickly becomes a deep, narrow passage between walls of loose rock. This area is subject to

VOLCANOES

frequent landslides and is blocked at the end by an imposing rockface, which is not possible to climb.

A trail in the tall grass leads you from a first little white house to a second, set a bit higher up, which has a pergola outside with stone benches – a great place for a rest. Here you might see swamp hawks hunting and imperial crows.

To continue it's best to go back to the first house and then on to the pebble beach and you'll gradually turn north-west, from where you can see Lazzaru (Secche di Lazzaro). At the end of the beach you find your second Malu Passu (Malo Passo) (40 minutes), a crossing over the cliffs, between the rocks and the sea, that becomes problematic only when the sea is rough.

Shortly after this, you are forced to pass along the base of a very steep scree of black sand called Sciaratu (Cugno Aghiastro), that very easily releases rockslides. Here it's best to pass quickly, even if it seems peaceful enough. Soon after this little adventure, you'll reach a spring of hot, fresh water at sea level, where you can see the tracks of the many birds that stop here to drink. After a few minutes you'll reach the tiny landing of Lazzaru (30 minutes) from where a lovely mule track between stone walls covered with capers leads you, your steps echoing, to Ginostra (10 minutes).

Day 2: Ginostra to Stromboli Town
3½ to 4 hours Ginostra to the Pizzo;
1½ to 2 hours the Pizzo to Stromboli town
If you plan to climb the Pizzo to watch the colourful eruptions and then spend the night on the volcano, leave in the late afternoon in order to be at the Pizzo at sunset. This allows you to avoid the heat and means you'll be there at the best time to see the explosions and to see dawn approaching over the mountain. However, it does mean spending the night in a sleeping bag in the sand at an altitude of about 460m, on the route of the descent.

It is not advisable to attempt to descend in the dark from this point along the route to Forgia Vecchia. Even with a torch it is easy to lose your way and end up at the edge of a dangerous cliff. The only descent is on a tricky path through the vegetation and it requires concentration. If you want to reach Stromboli town in one day, you are advised to go up in the early morning and, if possible, wait until late afternoon to make the descent, which, with good visibility, is fun.

The climb up is strenuous and you'll need a minimum of 2L of water, since there is no fresh water along the route.

Stage 1: Ginostra to the Pizzo After a drink on the terrace of the bar Il Puntazzo, head up towards the mountain on the trail that skirts the terrace and after 20m turn left and go down through a ditch. Turn left again and go up to some houses surrounded by prickly pears. Here turn right and continue to ascend. At the trail junction by the post office (marked with a circular sign with a PT inside) turn right and you'll come to the garbage truck depot where you follow the little road to the right. When you get to a wall, turn left and ascend until you come to a junction with a lamppost, where you go to the right, continuing to ascend.

Avoiding deviations, continue going up until you come to a house with a big white oven outside. Skirt around it keeping to the right. You'll come to another house with some bushes, where you go right again. Continue on to a cistern fitted with solar panels, pass it and at the corner of the stone-wall turn right and descend into a pleasant valley from where there is a stupendous view of the sea. You have now left the romantic little stone-wall lined lanes of the town behind you, and the trail is almost suffocated by the exuberant vegetation that overtakes the abandoned fields.

Continue north through the thickets, in one place walking on top of the ruined stone wall of some abandoned terraces: terracing was a typical means of cultivating the steep slopes of the volcano. You'll come to an observation point at an altitude of 100m, marked on the map as Punta d'u'Cuorvu (Punta dei Corvi) (30 minutes). In the middle of the clearing, some chunks of lava have been placed in concentric circles by recent visitors but seem like the mysterious symbols of some neo-pagan sun worship. The views from here are truly breathtaking – to the south-west are the other Isole Eolie with the high twin peaks of Salina and, further off to the right Filicudi and Alicudi; to the north-east you can see the impressive Sciara d'u Fuocu (Sciara del Fuoco), the enormous mass of volcanic debris fed by Stromboli's continuous eruptions, flowing directly into the sea.

Here the real climb up to the volcano begins. Going south-east and keeping a safe distance from the edge, skirt the unstable rocky crest directly above the Sciara, marked on the maps as Sierra d'i Capri (Serro delle Capre), with the crest known as the Fili di Baraona, forms the southern border of the Sciara.

The northern border is called Filo del Fuoco. Climbing up among the cistus and caper bushes, more trails begin to appear going off in all directions. Just keep going up. The very steep terrain (an elevation change of 650m in just more than 1km) is made up of volcanic sand and gravel which is very unstable. The low-growing vegetation helps in getting a foothold, but it is important to remember also that every one of these plants is serving a precious purpose. In spring you might come across huge round mushrooms, as big as coconuts, called *Balle di Lupo*. Climbing up near the crest, at an altitude of 300m, you'll reach a lookout from where you can see all the other Isole Eolie lined up to the south: going east to west they are Vulcano, Panarea, Lipari, Salina, Filicudi and Alicudi. Ascend along a steep tract of shifting gravel to about 400m and another lookout.

The next tract is even steeper, going up to about 600m, where there is a pile of rocks called an *ometto* which acts as a point of reference. After the ometto the incline becomes a bit gentler for a moment and then immediately formidable again, on unstable sandy ground which forces you to go up in zigzag fashion. Soon a vista opens on to the enormous, dark expanse of the Sciara. Continue climbing the bizarre terrain, which is now devoid of vegetation – the sound produced by your footsteps is not unlike crunching on a bed of Corn Flakes, but as you climb higher, the sound of the eruptions grows louder and louder. Ahead, on the trail, there is an enormous pudding-like cushion of solid lava, where you ascend with less difficulty up to 757m and the saddle of Purtedda d'a'Ginostra (two hours).

You are finally facing the summit of the volcano, completely without vegetation. On your left there is a series of dunes of various sizes formed by the accumulation of sand, stones and volcanic pyroclastic materials. This desert is made up of stones, big and small, that have been falling from above since ancient times. You are on the external edge of the craters that are about 500m from you to the north-east. A crest with some fortini facing the craters ascends directly up to the Pizzo o Sopra La Fossa, now visible to the north-east.

The route along the crest is the most direct but, obviously, also the most exposed to unexpected eruptions. It is better to descend east into the depression of the Fossiciedda (Fossetta), also known to locals as the Valle della Luna (Valley of the Moon), to the foot of the beautiful rocky crest of the paleocrater of the I Vancori (924m). Here a clearly visible horizontal trail about 600m long traverses the sandy slope of the depression, connecting the Purtedda d'a'Ginostra (Portella di Ginostra) with the Purtedda di Cruci (Le Croci). From the pass at Le Croci do not descend on the scree to the east of Rina Ranni (Rina Grande), instead, go up the last few metres to the north on a clearly visible trail that will soon lead to the Pizzo (918m, 45 minutes).

From the Pizzo you overlook the spectacular area of the eruptions 200m below. Tourists arrive in throngs along the normal route up the north face of Stromboli. It's a long, narrow, crest that has been transformed over the years by the thousands of visitors into a natural lookout point. The authorities that forbid the ascent without a guide haven't yet thought of installing any hygienic services. Consequently, there is a virtual 'minefield' on the south-east side of the Pizzo. The resulting unpleasant odours mix (fortunately or otherwise) with the periodic gusts of

VOLCANOES

sulphur vapours, rumblings and fire-sprays from the north-west face.

Stage 2: The Pizzo to Stromboli Town

After a rest while waiting to see an explosion, go back down to Le Croci (about 800m altitude – 10 minutes). When you come to the pass you will see below you to the southeast the great sand scree of Rina Grande, from where you comfortably descend east along the normal route. Be careful to keep to the trail, which can disappear after heavy rain or on windy days. In another 10 minutes you'll have descended to 700m, just under a group of large brown rocks that, at dawn, seem dusted with talcum powder. Here you turn right, to head south south-east (if you were to go straight you would continue along the normal return route known as *del canneto*). After a few minutes, when you reach 600m, follow the trail as it turns left and heads east. It is imperative that you don't continue the descent into the valley to the south, because you would quickly arrive at a sheer drop.

The trail heads toward a small vegetation-covered knoll, and another, smaller one to the left. When you reach 520m altitude, turn slightly to the right in the direction of the knoll, going around some bushes and watching your footing on the sheet of yellow rock camouflaged in the soft sand. At 460m, you reach the base of the knoll where, in between it and the scree, you may find a suitable place to lay your sleeping bag down. You are far enough away from the crater for safety and you are not breaking local restrictions on access to the summit. You are 30 minutes from the Pizzo.

The next day, or the same one after a rest, set off to the south-east with the gorgeous and distant rocky walls of the south-east face of the Pizzo at your back. A stone ometto clearly marks the trail to your left that passes between two powder-coloured boulders. It is important to find this exact trail and successive ones because any other trail (of some rabbit hunter for example) could lead to sheer drops. Following this trail, you soon reach a small green valley between high rocky cliffs where you find another passage

through the rock. This is the a Schicciula (Le Schicciole), where there is a natural spring, but where you cannot always find water. Le Schicciole is a canal, very deep in places, formed by rainwater erosion. Descend into the canal, passing first along its left bank and then walking inside the canal itself.

The terrain is sandy and very crumbly and the canal is steep and heavily overgrown, which makes it difficult to get a foothold – there is a short jump that is steep and could be dangerous at night. In a few minutes you'll have descended to 320m, where an easily distinguishable trail leaves the canal and goes off to the left passes beyond some bushes and leads you into the middle of the summit area of the great black sand scree of the Forgia Vecchia, under the cliffs of the Ròccazza. Downhill there is a pebbly beach and the sea, where you'll be able to take a refreshing dip. You could run and jump from the scree – pretty exhilarating if you know how to do it.

You can reach Stromboli easily by walking north along the shore (30 minutes).

Vulcano

> **Duration** 3 to 4 hours
> **Standard** Easy
> **Start/Finish** Porto di Levante
> **Permits Required** No
> **Summary** An easy walk on which you could even take mum, dad and the kids, as long as you take care to avoid the fumaroles, which spew out smelly sulphurous gases. Thrillseekers can walk down into the actual crater – remembering though, that it is an active volcano.

THE WALK

From the hovercraft mooring in Porto di Levante, follow the narrow asphalt road that heads south-west towards Vulcano Piano. The massive body of the crater is on your left. This is a relatively small volcano, its highest point being 391m. Its lower part is

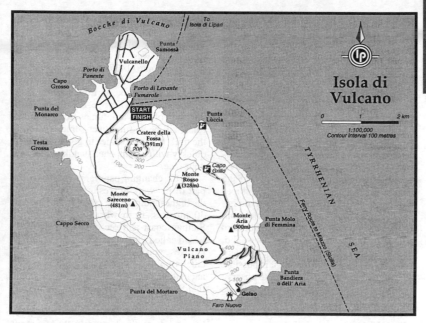

Isola di
Vulcano

0   1   2 km

1:100,000
Contour interval 100 metres

covered by a mantle of shrubbery that, when it flowers in May/June, sweetens the landscape with a beautiful yellow flower and an intense perfume. It is easy to spot large imperial crows, with their shiny black plumage, and white and grey royal seagulls circling over the crater. On your right, there is a little restaurant *Al Cratere*, with a convenient panoramic terrace on the roof, and a supermarket on the left, useful points of reference for organising meals

After a 10 minute walk along the road, flanked by wild geraniums and enlivened by the songs of blackbirds, serins, cardinals and sparrows, you come to a sign that reads 'Accesso al Cratere' (Access to the Crater). From this point, a trail heads uphill to the left among some brushwood; this is a short cut which, in five minutes, links up with the main trail. (The main trail ascends from the same road about 200m ahead of where you took the short cut and is marked with a sign reading 'Cratere'). When you reach the main

trail go up to the left (east) until you come to a sharp curve to the right, where a municipal sign in four languages announces the dangers of the crater. If you proceed (which everyone does), you won't have any problems with officialdom, but you need to be aware that Vulcano is only sleeping and is an active volcano.

Shortly after, the trail turns again to the left. The terrain which, until this point, has been made up of a small, dark volcanic gravel, now becomes a sandy colour. The trail takes on an impressive look of a deep erosion furrow, a bizarre, airy canal that ascends across the slope, forcing you to perform little acrobatic feats. At the end of this canal you reach a sort of wide, flat clearing of lava pebbles from which several trails depart. Ascend again to the left, following the southeast trail. In three minutes you'll be at the lowest point of the crater's edge (290m – 45 minutes from the point of departure), from where you can take a look inside!

To your left, the inside wall of the crater is full of countless fissures, covered in splendid yellow/orange crystals, that let off columns of sulphurous gases. These emissions are accompanied by an unnerving hiss like that of a pressure cooker.

Breathing in these fumes is certainly not pleasant, but over brief periods, is not dangerous. The bottom of the volcano is clearly visible less than 50m below, formed by two 'cold' (inactive) calderas, adjacent and at the same level – two perfectly circular and perfectly level intersecting spaces covered by a layer of solid sun-dried mud. Some of the many stones that have rolled down the slopes have been used by the more inventive visitors to compose messages, readable from above. A steep trail descends to the bottom in three minutes. Many go down, as we did, for an unconventional walk along the hard crater floor. Once at the bottom it is possible to get close, downwind of course, to observe the bizarre, needle-shaped sulphuric crystals of a vivid mineral yellow rarely seen in nature (see the 'At the Door to Hades' boxed text below).

Walk around the crest of the crater, from where you have a stunning 360° view of the Isole Eolie lined up to the north. From left to right they are Alicudi, Filicudi, Salina peeking out from behind Lipari, beyond the little crater of Vulcanello, then to the northeast Panarea and the dark and distant smoking cone of Stromboli. To the south, from east to west, you can see Calabria with its Aspromonte (1437m) and on clear days a long piece of the Sicilian coast dominated by the imposing bulk of Etna (3330m), the highest volcano in Europe. Depending on the direction of the wind, fumes from the fumaroles will be wafting over some sections of the trail. It is a good idea to go through them quickly with a dampened handkerchief over your face.

It's the changing panorama that makes this part of the walk interesting. You can get to the highest point of the crest (391m) in about 30 minutes, from where you can see the Sicilian coast and see over the part of the island called Piano Grande (Great Plain). To the west you will note that the crest of the cliff is no more than a section of the great ancient volcano, eroded by the millennia, inside of which the present crater was formed.

Returning back down the volcano, you have no alternative but to take the same trail. Any deviations you might come across could present unexpected problems because of the extreme steepness and the instability of the crumbly soil. In any case, it is best to keep to the main trail to avoid damaging the rare

At the Door to Hades

It must be remembered that, although this volcano is sleeping, it is still carrying out its mysterious work. The great quantity of gas that it emits, especially among the fumaroles, creates large and small underground voids. While walking among the fumaroles on the interior slope searching out incredible sulphurous colours to photograph, the ground gave way and I sank a good 10cm. 'Big deal!' you'll say. But I immediately thought of all those films where the first 10cm are the beginning of the end. Here we are, inside – actually *inside* – a real volcano.

The mud floor looks like it gets softer in places and it is not difficult to imagine scenes of a sudden cave-in, where you drop directly into the inferno below. The ancients believed Vulcano was the entrance to Hades, the kingdom of the dead. In the Middle Ages, Christians also believed that the volcano was the entrance to Hell and inhabited by demons. Even Dante mentions it. However, there is no record of anyone ever being swallowed up by the volcano, which, in the last century, was frequented daily by prisoners who were forced to mine sulphur as part of their punishment.

As with all of the volcano walks in this chapter, we point you in the direction, but you must be aware of the potential danger of climbing an active volcano and, particularly, of descending into the crater. It's your decision!

Stefano Cavedoni

plants which are attempting to grow in this inhospitable land of lava.

OTHER WALKS

The visit to the crater of Vulcano takes up half a day. The north coast of Vulcanello, the little volcanic promontory to the north of the island, offers short walks to admire the splendid panorama over the *faraglioni* (rock stacks in the sea) of Lipari, in the area of the isolated and peaceful Hotel Arcipelago. You can also visit the little craters of Vulcanello (one hour).

If you want to spend another half day exploring the island, go back to the asphalt road at the beginning of the trail to Vulcano's crater. Go to the left towards Vulcano Piano and get lost in the countless little country roads beneath Monte Aria (500m), the highest point on the island. And to top it all off, follow the road that descends from the Piano to the extreme south of the island to reach the lighthouse at Gelso, from where there is a view across to the coast of Sicilia (three to four hours).

MT ETNA

Etna is a majestic mountain and a powerful, active volcano. Imposing and cloaked in myth, it has always been one of Sicilia's most fascinating symbols. Eruptions in modern times have been restricted to periodic lava flows which generally have not threatened the local population. There is also some modest explosive activity inside the craters, that only rarely becomes more intense.

The volcano and it slopes have since 1987 been part of a national park which covers 59,000 hectares in a territory that includes 20 communities. The park offers excursionists an extremely variable natural environment, ranging from the severe, almost surrealistic settings at the summit, rich in endemic life and breathtaking panoramas, to amazing lava deserts, crisscrossed by grottoes formed by lava flows. There are also ancient pine and birch forests – Etna is in fact the southern-most point where the birch is found in Europe.

A walkable trail, known as the *altomontana*, closed to private vehicular traffic and excellently maintained by the Guardia Forestale, offers the traveller a long semicircular route from Rifugio Brunek to the Rifugio Sapienza. It is a beautiful route that traverses the wooded slopes of the volcano at altitudes between 1300m and 1800m, crossing many ancient lava flows. There are several unstaffed, ranger-maintained rifugi along the way, that are used like the bivouacs (*bivacchi*) of the Alps. They are always open and are a good place to spend a night wrapped in a sleeping bag. They have a fireplace, raised slabs of stone or wood to lay your sleeping bag on and cisterns of non-drinkable water.

The Etna circuit walk described in this section utilises this trail. You can spend three days virtually isolated from the rest of civilisation, but you'll need to carry all of your food and water. At the beginning and end of the walk there are comfortable Alpine-style staffed rifugi offering food and accommodation. They can be used as bases to ascend to the craters from the north and south faces of the volcano.

HISTORY

In ancient times, Etna's summit was frequently lit up with the fires of eruptions. It was visible for hundreds of kilometres out to sea and was a visual reference point, even at night, for the ancient navigators of the Mediterranean – the Myceneaans, Phoenicians and Egyptians.

The classical world saw the volcano as the home of the god Plutone and of the Titans who had rebelled against Zeus. In the 18th century BC, Homer mentioned Etna in the episode of Ulysses and the Cyclops. In the 5th century BC, the historian Thucydides referred to the incredible eruptive activity of Etna. Aeschylus, who was at Syracuse in 472 BC, cited a 16th century BC legend in his *Prometheus*, where Etna is described as a 'column holding up the sky', with the giant Tifone (Typhoon) at its base, shaking his 100 heads and making the whole world tremble. Diodorus the Sicilian, who lived in the era of the Emperor Augustus, maintained that the people known as the Sicani, who had lived in the area many centuries before, were so terrified by the devastating fury of their pagan god, Vulcano, that they were forced to migrate to the opposite side of the island.

The first known visitor to Etna was Pietro Bembo in 1493, who wrote the Latin work, *De Aetna* telling of his adventures. This encouraged an influx of English, German, French, Dutch and Danish travellers. English physicist Patrick Brydone is considered the founder of the Sicilian 'Grand Tour'. In 1773 he published his *Tour through Sicily and Malta*, which was translated into French and German. His lyric and dreamy descriptions of the ascent to the crater inspired many aristocrats to visit Etna. Goethe was advised by an aristocratic guest at his inn to climb only the Monti Rossi of Nicolosi. The guest insinuated that Brydone had done the same thing.

It was a two-day mule ride to make the round trip with local guides from Nicolosi to see the sunrise at Etna's main crater. Among those who made the trip were Dumas, De Dolomieu, and the French landscape painter Jean Hovel. Already in the 19th century, Etna had a strong local economy founded on the presence of these travellers.

NATURAL HISTORY

Etna is the largest active volcano in Europe and one of the few large wilderness areas in Sicilia. It reaches an altitude of about 3330m. Its height has gone up and down during the past 100 years, in accordance with eruptions and the settlement of the soil. The area of volcanic material that surrounds Etna takes up 1260 sq km, and its base perimeter is 165km.

Geology

Etna is a multiple volcano made up of various eruptive channels, which began to spew magma, and thereby influence the geology of the area, about 600,000 years ago. The central eruptive channel, which corresponds to the present summit craters, is surrounded at various altitudes by hundreds

of major and secondary cones which dot the slopes of this enormous volcanic construction. The secondary cones are generally active on the occasion of one, single eruption.

The volcano was formed at the intersection of regional tectonic fractures along which the magma rises up from 100km beneath the earth's surface to be held in magma chambers about 20km under the ground. The magma varies in viscosity in relation to changes in pressure, temperature, chemical composition and the presence of volatile substances such as water and sulphur. More-fluid magma presents modest eruptive phenomena; magma with less fluid produces extremely violent eruptions.

Violent eruptions of this type took place on Etna until about 3000 years ago and it is probable that these were the phenomena reported by ancient historians. Recent eruptive activity has been relatively low key, with fluid magma flows at around 1100°C, which rarely cover more than 10km and travel at rates of 100 cubic metres per second to less than one cubic metre a second.

Etna has four live craters at its summit (one, the Bocca Nuova, was formed in 1968). Eruptions also occur on the slopes of the volcano, which is littered with crevices and old craters. In 1669, 16 small towns and the west side of the city of Catania were destroyed by lava flow so vast that it flowed for 1km into the sea. In 1843, the magma arrived at the town of Bronte. In 1928 another flow destroyed the town of Mascali. In 1971 an eruption destroyed the observatory at the summit, and another, in 1981, destroyed a few houses on the outskirts of Randazzo. A 1983 eruption finished off the old cable car and tourist centre. In the latest eruption (from 1991 to 1993), which began in the Valle del Bove, lava reached the Piano dell'Acqua on the outskirts of Zafferana Etnea.

Flora

The slopes of the volcano were once covered with huge forests that have been substituted today by plantations of citrus, grapes, olives, almonds, pistachio, apples, pears, hazelnuts and chestnuts.

In the lava areas, there are still patches of holm oaks (*Quercus ilex* – leccio), English oaks (*Quercus robur* – quercia), turpentine trees (*Rhamnus alaternus* – alaterno), which, grafted, gives us the pistacchio, hackberry trees (*Celtis australis* – bagolaro), olives (*Olea europaea sylvestris* – olivastro) and aspens (*Populus tremula* – pioppo tremulo). On the damper eastern slopes the manna ash (*Fraxinus ornus* – oniello), hornbeam (*Ostrya carpinifolia* – carpino nero) and maple (*Acer obtusatum* – acero) also grow.

Between 1000m and 1800m, the larch pine (*Pinus laricio* – pino laricio) performs an important role as a pioneer plant, recolonising lava flows. Higher up, on the cold north-west slopes up to 2000m, the copper beech (*Fagus sylvatica* – faggio) grows – this is the southernmost point in Europe where beech trees are found. A dwarf version can be found up to 2250m in the area of Punta Lucia. Etna's birch (*Betula aetnensis* – betulla dell'Etna) grows up to 2100m and is considered an endemic species, like the beech, left over from the last Ice Age. Birch grow mainly on the eastern slopes of the volcano, particularly above the Rifugio Citelli.

There is a species of broom, the ginestra dell'Etna (*Genista aetnensis*) which is endemic to Etna. It is dominant among bushes on Etna, and is found everywhere up to 1900m. It can reach up to 5m in height. In the lower areas you can also find patches of euphorbia (*Euphorbia dendroides* – euforbia arborea), scented broom (*Spartium junceum* – ginestra odorosa), citisus (*Cytisus villosus* – citiso), cistus (*Cistus salvifolius* – cisto) and juniper (*Juniperus hemisphaerica* – ginepro emisferico).

The most surprising vegetation formations are found at high altitudes beyond the forested areas. These are the surreal, pillow-shaped formations of thorntrees (*Astragalus siculus* – spino santo) another of Etna's endemic species that grows to 2450m. Inside, under its trusty thorns, the sweetly-scented chyrsanthemum grows protected from the wind and predators. Above 2500m, even the thorntree disappears and the only vegetation are the rumex and the odd Sicilian soapwort (*Saponaria sicula*) with its delicate little pink flowers.

Fauna

In the past Etna was home to wolf, wild boar, deer, roebuck, otter, marten and griffon. Today there are only three carnivores left: the fox, weasel and wild cat. They hunt rabbit, hare, mice and hedgehog. The porcupine is found along the trail and is the largest of the wild animal species on Etna. There are at least eight species of bat that inhabit the ravines and caves created by the lava. The largest is the rare molosso del cestoni. Among the birds of Etna, the royal eagle has recently returned to nest in the park. You'll also see sparrowhawk, buzzard, kestrel, peregrine falcon and nocturnal predators: the only Sicilian colonies of common owl, the tawny owl and the barn owl. In the woods and the high mountain areas there are many species of woodpecker, magpie, raven, dove, crow, the rare rock partridge and an infinite number of small birds.

There are numerous innocuous reptiles, but watch out for the viper, a poisonous snake found throughout Italy. You are more likely to meet the black coluber and the saettone coluber, but there are also ring snakes and the colourful leopard coluber.

CLIMATE

The climate on Etna varies according to altitude. At higher altitudes there is a mountain climate, becoming colder towards the summit area (above 2000m), which is exposed to strong, freezing winds. Snowfall is common from November to April. It is advisable to carry a compass, since there is the possibility of encountering sudden banks of fog, which make orientation difficult. At lower altitudes the climate becomes gradually more typical of the mild Mediterranean climate which characterises Sicilia. There is also climatic variation between the different faces of the mountain.

INFORMATION

Rifugio Sapienza, at an altitude of 1900m on the south face, is the closest to Catania and to the coast near Taormina. As a result it is crowded in all seasons. In winter, skiers take off from here for the numerous ski lifts. The rifugio is open all year and is easily accessible from Nicolosi, Catania and Zafferana Etnea. Many tour buses arrive daily and the local bus company, AST (☎ (095) 746 10 96), makes one daily run each way (see Getting To/From the Walks later in this section).

In summer, many tourists use the SITAS cable car service (☎ (095) 91 11 58) to reach 2500m. They are then taken by 4WD to 3000m, just below the summit. From there, local guides take them higher on foot – but they are not authorised to bring people to the edge of the crater to look in. The total cost is L58,000 return.

An identical service, for the same price, is offered on the north face of the volcano by the STAR bus company (☎ (091) 64 31 80) which takes tourists from Piano Provenzana (1810m) up to 3000m by 4WD. There are ski slopes and hotels at Piano Provenzana, but the area is not served by public bus. However, nearby in the peaceful Ragabo pine forest is Rifugio Brunek, a comfortable Alpine-style refugio, as well as Clan dei Ragazzi, a nearby camping ground and bungalows. Due to the lack of public transport, the managers of the rifugio and camping ground will pick up guests at Linguaglossa (easily accessible from Taormina). They will also ferry guests to Piano Provenzana and to Rifugio Citelli, which is on the route descending from the craters described in this section and is also operated by amiable young people.

We recommend making either the Rifugio Brunek or Rifugio Citelli your base (see Places to Stay & Eat later in this section) for the beautiful ascent to the craters from the northern face – the environment here is much better preserved than on the other side of the volcano.

The three-day, semicircular high mountain route, which can be added to the one-day visit to the craters, departs from Rifugio Brunek. Both the Brunek and the Citelli offer multiple-day guided walks and treks. The Brunek has a rockwall fitted out for free

climbing, offers horse riding and excursions to the lava flow caves with caving equipment, it also rents out mountain bikes and, in winter, offers ski tours and dog-sledding pulled by real Huskies!

The telephone code for Etna's southern slopes is ☎ 095 and the code for its northern slopes is ☎ 091.

Information Sources

The office of the Parco Regionale dell'Etna (Etna Regional Park) (☎ (095) 91 45 88; fax 91 47 38), Via Etnea 107/a, 95030 Nicolosi (Catania), will send free information on request regarding the park with a very good map (1:50,000) produced by the Touring Club Italiano. This is the best map available for the walks in this chapter. The same booklet with map is available free at park offices on Etna, or can be bought in bookshops in Catania for L15,000.

APIT (☎ (095) 730 62 33 or 730 62 22; email apt@apt-catania.com.it), Via Cimarosa 10, Catania, is the provincial tourist office. It supplies a useful map of Etna (1:50,000), a map and guide for Catania, a map (1:175,000) of the Province of Catania and brochures on the province and the city of Catania, in English. There are APIT offices at Catania's train station (☎ (095) 739 62 55) and at the Fontanarossa airport (☎ (095) 730 62 66). It also has a very useful directory of hotels, refugi, camping grounds and agriturismo establishments and information on transport etc, which they will send overseas on request.

The Azienda Soggiorno e Turismo (☎ (095) 91 15 05), Via Etnea 32, Nicolosi, also has information in English. You can pick up the Touring Club Italiano map (1:50,000) from here.

N. e T. – Natura e Turismo (Nature & Tourism) (☎ (095) 33 35 43; fax 53 79 10; email natetur@tim.it), Via R Quartarano 11, 95125 Catania, is an efficient organisation of highly motivated, university-prepared tourist and environmental guides who can offer advice and information in English, French, German and Spanish, on meteorological conditions and the behaviour of the volcano.

It also organises farm holidays that include the assistance of nature guides.

Other places where you can get information locally include: the Linguaglossa Pro Loco (tourist office) (☎ (095) 64 30 94) and the Distaccamento Forestale di Zafferana Etnea (regional forest rangers) (☎ (095) 7 08 20) although it is unlikely you'll find anyone who speaks English.

Scuola Italiana Sleddog (☎ (095) 64 30 15), near Rifugio Brunek on the way to Piano Provenzana, has information (also in English) on excursions, sporting activities, weather conditions and the behaviour of the volcano.

Permits

No permits are needed to walk on Mt Etna, but for safety reasons it is forbidden to ascend past 2900m without an authorised guide. However, there is little surveillance and the decision to go up to the craters alone is basically left up to individual walkers – just remember that it is potentially very dangerous and you were warned! Several people have been killed this century – see Warnings below.

Because of recent cave-ins, it is also forbidden to enter the Grotta del Gelo (Ice Cave). Park regulations forbid the collection of rocks and minerals as well as the disturbance, capture or harming of animals or plants. It is also forbidden to light fires, to litter or to camp outside designated areas.

Warnings

The ever-present danger of eruption, combined with extreme weather conditions at the summit, means that Etna should be approached with caution. Local guides, as well as the park offices, will be able to provide information about the volcano's current behaviour, as well as weather forecasts.

If you choose to make the ascent to the summit craters, you must accept responsibility for the risk. The eruptive activity of the craters is usually relatively moderate, thus permitting the curious to walk around the crater edges. However, this moderate activity can intensify suddenly and without warning, with potentially catastrophic results. In 1979

nine tourists, part of a larger group, were killed, surprised by an unusually large eruption at the south-east crater. In 1987 two were killed and 10 people were injured in an explosion at the same crater.

It is very important to consider the altitude (3330m at the summit) with the constant presence of strong winds, low temperatures and frequent fog. Watch out also for sulphur fumes – not lethal, but pretty unpleasant. If you see long, longitudinal fissures in the earth around the edge of a crater, keep well away: they can signal unstable ground and could give way to the inferno below.

Emergency

The soccorso alpino (Alpine rescue service) of the Guardia di Finanza (☎ (095) 791 60 69) is a special unit which operates from Nicolosi and also makes helicopter rescues. You can also call the nationwide emergency numbers for the police (☎ 113) or carabinieri (☎ 112) to reach this rescue unit.

The Guardia Forestale (forest ranger service) has a base in each of the towns which ring Mt Etna. They patrol the trails and rifugi of the park in their 4WDs and have keys to the various gates closing off access roads. They will intervene in cases of need. The rangers of the Guardia Forestale are competent and very willing to help out with advice or assistance, so don't hesitate to contact them if you need to at the following bases: Zafferana Etnea (☎ (095) 708 20 65); Linguaglossa (☎ (095) 64 31 12); Randazzo (☎ (095) 92 11 24); Nicolosi (☎ (095) 91 13 60); Bronte (☎ (095) 69 11 40); Adrano (☎ (095) 68 47 08). In Catania, the guardia forestale office can be contacted on ☎ (095) 44 70 84.

ACCOMMODATION & SUPPLIES

Catania is the nearest main town to Etna. If you plan to stay there, try the *Hotel Trieste* (☎ (095) 32 71 05), near Piazza Bellini in the town centre, at Via Leonardo 24. It charges around L25,000 per person. *Hotel Rubens* (☎ (095) 31 70 73), Via Etnea 176, has singles/doubles for L34,000/L50,000.

There is a fresh produce *market* in Catania's

Piazza Carlo Alberto every morning except Sunday where you can pick up food supplies.

Supplies

In Catania, you can stock up on walking and camping supplies at Canoa e Avventura (☎ (095) 50 30 20), Via A Longo 74. There is a sport and mountain equipment shop at Linguaglossa called Simone Sport (☎ (095) 64 32 52), Via Roma 145. If you're really desperate, you might be able to rent trekking shoes at Piano Provenzana.

PLANNING
When to Walk

The best periods for walking on Etna are April/May and September/October, when the weather is mild and there's the added incentive of the special colour effects of the vegetation. From November to the end of April the summit areas are covered in snow, but off-run skiing and other snow activities are possible. In the middle of summer the weather is very hot, making walking difficult and unpleasant – July and August are to be avoided, as much for the sun as for the huge number of tourists crowding the volcano.

Maps

The best available map is the Touring Club Italiano (1:50,000), available free from the Etna Regional Park office in Nicolosi and from the APIT provincial tourist office in Catania (see Information Sources earlier in this section). The APIT also distributes a map at 1:175,000 scale of the Province of Catania. There are Istituto Geografico Militare (IGM) maps of the area in 1:25,000 scale. However, they are 40 years old and show some trails that don't exist any more, while not showing other, newer trails, including the one recommended in this chapter for the ascent to the main crater.

In Catania the best places to buy maps, including IGM maps, are Libreria Cavalotto (☎ (095) 31 04 14), Corso Sicilia 91, and La Paglia (☎ (095) 44 66 40), Via Etnea 393.

What to Bring

The choice of equipment depends on the altitude you intend to walk at, and the season. The scarce shade and the hot, strong sun necessitate sunglasses and a hat. If walking only at low altitudes, you will need light clothing, with pants suitable for possible passages through spiny bushes. You will also need to carry a good supply of drinking water. A rain poncho is very light and could come in handy.

Those who do the three-day walk on the high mountain trail should have a comfortable backpack, with a sleeping bag, matches or lighter to make a fire and a battery-powered torch (indispensable in the refugi). You will need warm clothing at night when the temperature drops (see What to Bring in the Facts for the Walker chapter). It is necessary to bring all food and water for the three days. The water at the rifugi is often not drinkable.

Those who want to ascend above 2000m will find themselves, even in the summer, exposed to a mountain climate with very strong winds. A wind jacket is essential, along with warm headgear and gloves. Up on the craters, a scarf or handkerchief can be useful as a filter in the case of a sudden cloud of sulphur vapours.

Solid, comfortable walking shoes are advised for walking on Etna, above all for walking on the lava and for a descent over the scree. On the snow, waterproof trekking boots are indispensable.

You should also carry a good map, as well as a compass and an altimeter, which become essential in the case of fog. In case of emergency, carry a thermal blanket or bivuoac bag and a whistle to signal for help.

Guided Walks

The N. e T. – Natura e Turismo guides group (see under Information Sources for how to contact them) are well-prepared guides who organise nature walks and more challenging excursions.

Montagna e Vita (Mountain & Life) and the Scuola Italiana Sleddog Linguaglossa (☎ (095) 64 30 15) are two organisations connected with Rifugio Brunek and the Clan dei Ragazzi. They organise guided walks of more than one day, caving excursions and horse riding treks. They have a rockface outfitted for free-climbing, rent mountain bikes and, in the winter, organise alpine ski tours, snow shoeing and dog sledding.

Associazione Le Betulle (The Birches) (☎ (095) 96 81 28), based at Rifugio Citelli, is a group of young, environmentalist guides offering a range of excursions. Other guide groups for transport to the craters are: the Gruppo Guide Alpine Etna South (Rifugio Sapienza) (☎ (095) 91 41 41) and the Gruppo Guide Alpine Etna North (Piano Provenzana) (☎ (095) 64 34 30).

PLACES TO STAY & EAT
On the Walk

Camping Clan dei Ragazzi (☎ (095) 64 36 11) is about 1km from Rifugio Brunek and is run by the same group of young people. Bungalows cost the same as rooms at the Brunek and space for a tent costs L5000 per person.

Rifugio Sapienza (☎ (095) 91 10 62), near the big, open area of the Etna Sud-Nicolosi funivia, has an air of neglect, but its restaurant is good. *Rifugio Brunek* (☎ (095) 64 30 15; mobile (0360) 85 98 26) is in a quiet spot in the lovely Pineta Ragabo (pine forest) on the road 5km from Piano Provenzana. It is well maintained with very pleasant rooms and is recommended as a base for the trek. The owner is a passionate mountaineer who loves to cook for his guests and invite them to dine together around a large table. B&B is L35,000 and half board is L55,000 per person.

Rifugio Citelli (☎ (0368) 66 23 45 or (0330) 96 42 34) is another rifugio which is recommended as a base for the Etna trek. About 7km south of Rifugio Brunek, in the Etna north area, it is in an isolated position in the typical volcanic environment of Etna. B&B costs L35,000, half board is L50,000 per person and full board is L60,000.

Other Options

Camping Etna (☎ (095) 91 43 09) at Nicolosi, is in the Monti Rossi pine forest. Tent sites cost L14,000 a day, plus L7000 per person.

Rifugio Nord Est (☎ (095) 64 79 22) is one

of the less expensive hotels at Piano Provenzana. B&B costs L35,000 and half board is L60,000. At Nicolosi there are the hotels *Biancaneve* (☎ (095) 91 11 76) and *Gemellaro* (☎ (095) 91 13 73), at Via Etnea 160 and 163. Singles/doubles cost L80,000/L140,000. At Linguaglossa is the *Happy Day* (☎ (095) 64 34 84), Via Mareneve 9, with singles/doubles for L70,000/L100,000.

At Zafferana Etnea, try *Villa Pina* (☎ (095) 708 10 24), Via dei Gerani 19. Singles/doubles start at L50,000/L60,000. At Randazzo the only hotel is *Hotel Scrivano*, Via Bonaventura, near the train station and the stop for the inter-urban bus. Singles/doubles are from L40,000/L70,000. At Bronte, there is only *Parco dell'Etna* (☎ (095) 69 19 07) in the area known as contrada Borgonovo. Singles/doubles are from L45,000/L75,000.

GETTING TO/FROM THE WALKS

If you are coming from the Isole Eolie, there is a bus service from the port of Milazzo to Messina run by Giuntabus (☎ (095) 67 37 82). It runs a rapid service from 6.30 am to 6.30 pm Monday to Saturday and on Sundays and public holidays at 8 and 9.30 am and 3, 5.30 and 6.30 pm.

The train connecting Milazzo and Messina is slower and less convenient, since Milazzo's station is a few kilometres from the port. To reach Etna from Messina, catch one of the frequent trains for Catania and get off at Giarre. Once at Giarre, transfer to the Circumetnea train station and catch a train to Linguaglossa (40 minutes from Giarre, eight trains a day, every two hours, terminating at Catania).

Both walks start at Rifugio Brunek and if you give the staff a day's notice, they will pick you up at Linguaglossa.

If you are coming from Catania, catch the Circumetnea train to Linguaglossa (two hours and 40 minutes, five trains a day). The train partially circles Etna, running through numerous towns including Adrano, Bronte, Maletto and Randazzo, terminating at Riposto. The Circumetnea train station in Catania is in Corso delle Province and is accessible from the city's main train station on bus Nos 628, 448 or 401.

Zappalà and Torrisi buses (☎ (095) 764 71 39) connect Catania with Giarre and Zafferana Etnea. It stops in Giarre's so-called Piazza del Monumento four times a day at 8.30 and 11.30 am and 1.30 and 6 pm.

To get from Catania to Nicolosi, catch one of the frequent AST buses (☎ (095) 746 10 96). AST also runs a daily service at 8.15 am from Catania to Rifugio Sapienza, via Nicolosi (returning at 4 pm). The AST buses leave from the large piazza in front of Catania's main train station.

Ascent to the Craters

> **Duration** 9½ to 11½ hours
> **Standard** Medium
> **Start** Rifugio Brunek
> **Finish** Rifugio Citelli
> **Closest Towns** Linguaglossa
> **Permits Required** No
> **Public Transport Access** Yes
> **Summary** This is a long approach to the volcano's main craters; can be done over two days with a night of 'roughing it'.

Total time needed from Piano Provenzana to Rifugio Citelli, with a rest-stop at the craters, is 9 to 11 hours, which can be reduced to 8 to 10 hours if you use the 4WD service. The walk is divided into two stages – you can do it all in one long day, or opt to sleep out at the vulcanological observatory.

THE WALK
Stage 1: Rifugio Brunek to the Craters
5 to 6 hours plus 1 hour to visit the craters; 12km, 1880m ascent
From Rifugio Brunek (1380m), it is a 5km walk along the asphalt road to Piano Provenzana (1810m). It is better to organise in advance for the proprietors of Rifugio Brunek to take you by car to Piano Provenzana, since there is no public transport. If, however, you decide to walk, it will take about one hour and 20 minutes. Ignore the

turn-off to the left for Milo and Rifugio Citelli and continue to the right to Piano Provenzana.

In the main square of Piano Provenzana is the office of STAR (☎ (091) 64 31 80), which runs 4WD excursions up to the craters on the north face of the mountain (L58,000 return). By law, the company cannot offer one-way fares to the craters; however, it is possible to catch a ride as far as Monte Pizzillo (2400m) (L15,000 one way). It is advised that you use the 4WD service (it leaves from behind Hotel Le Betulle), otherwise you'll need to make most of the walk on the same steep, dirt road used by the 4WDs.

If you do decide to walk, there is a short cut that crosses the first series of sharp curves. Behind the souvenir stalls in the main square of Piano Provenzana is a field with a shrine – the trail departs from there, indicated by yellow-tipped markers. It ascends to the small lava rocks – in May and June they are dotted with delicate tufts of *Viola etnensis*, a flower endemic to Etna. It takes 10 minutes to cover the 300m distance of the short cut and reach the very steep dirt road. Head up to the left (south-west). After about 4km you encounter the last station of a ski-lift and then, immediately after, the impressive vents of the eruption of 1809 under Monte Pizzillo (about 2400m – one hour 40 minutes). If you had caught the one-way STAR 4WD service, this is where it would have let you off.

Continue to ascend for about 3.5km along the dirt road, which now bends south, among old lava flows and expanses of volcanic sand. There's no shade, so you'll need your hat. The road takes you up to 2800m and a wide, sandy high-plain called Piano delle Concazze, dominated by Etna's north-east crater. From the high plain you can note to the left (south-east) the short track to reach the Osservatorio Vulcanologico (vulcanological observatory, 2818m). Although always closed, the observatory could provide shelter from rain and wind and is a point of reference for the trip back across the Pizzi Deneri.

If you intend to go up to the craters, leave

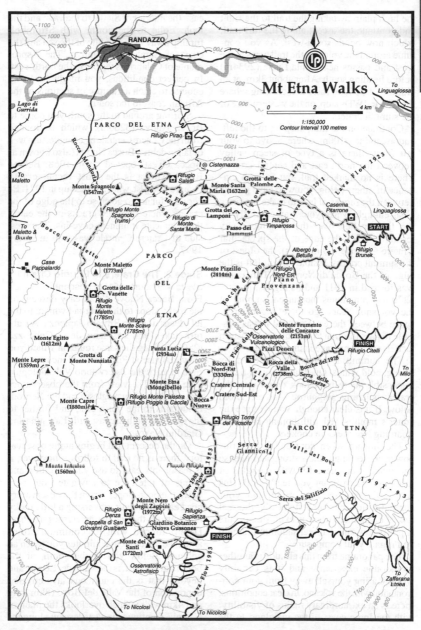

Mt Etna Walks

0   2   4 km

1:150,000
Contour Interval 100 metres

To Linguaglossa

RANDAZZO

Lago di
Gurrida

PARCO DEL ETNA

Rifugio Pirao

To Maletto

Monte Spagnolo
(1547m)

Rifugio Monte
Spagnolo
(ruins)

Bosco di Maletto

To Maletto &
Bronte

Case
Pappalardo

Monte Maletto
(1773m)

Grotta delle
Vanette

Rifugio
Monte
Maletto
(1785m)

Rifugio
Monte Scavo
(1785m)

Monte Egitto
(1612m)

Grotta di
Monte Nunziata

Monte Lepre
(1559m)

Monte Capre
(1880m)

Rifugio Galvarina

Monte Intraleo
(1560m)

Lava Flow 1610

Rifugio
Denza

Cappella di San
Giovanni Gualberto

Monte Nero
degli Zappini
(1972m)

Rifugio
Sapienza

Giardino Botanico
Nuova Gussonea

Monte dei
Santi
(1720m)

Osservatorio
Astrofisico

To Nicolosi

To Nicolosi

Rocca Mandonia

Lava Flow

Lava Flow 1981

Rifugio
Saletti

Cisternazza

Rifugio Santa
Maria (1632m)

Grotta dei
Lamponi

Rifugio di
Monte
Santa Maria

Passo dei
Dammusi

PARCO

DEL

ETNA

Monte Pizzillo
(2414m)

Punta Lucia
(2934m)

Monte Etna
(Mongibello)

Rifugio Monte Palestra
(Rifugio Poggio la Caccia)

Bocca di
Nord-Est
(3330m)

Cratere Centrale
Cratere Sud-Est

Bocca
Nuova

Rifugio Torre
del Filosofo

Piccolo Rifugio

Lava Flow 1985

Lava Flow 1983

FINISH

Grotta delle
Palombe

Lava Flow 1947

Lava Flow 1879

Lava Flow 1911

Lava Flow 1923

Caserma
Pitarrone

To
Linguaglossa

Rifugio
Timparossa

Pineta Ragabo

START

Rifugio
Brunek

Albergo le
Betulle

Rifugio
Nord-Est

Piano
Provenzana

Bocche del 1809

Piano delle Concazze

Osservatorio
Vulcanologico

Pizzi Deneri

Monte Frumento
delle Concazze
(2151m)

FINISH

Rifugio Citelli

Rocca della
Valle
(2738m)

Bocche del 1925

Valle del Leone

Serra delle
Concazze

Tn
Milo

PARCO DEL ETNA

Serra di
Giannicola

Valle del Bove

Lava flow of 1991-93

Serra del Salifizio

To
Zafferana
Etnea

the high plain by taking the trail to the right and continue the ascent along the dirt trail, which now bends south-west. As you continue around the volcano, the trail turns to the west and passes near Punta Lucia (2934m) before heading south. After about 3km, at an altitude of 3050m, there is a clearing where the STAR 4WDs stop, on the western face of the summit craters.

Continue on the trail, keeping to the left, and ascend to 3100m, where, above to your left (east) there is a type of steep valley between the north-east and central craters. There is no marked trail, but enough evidence of others before you who have passed between the blocks of lava to make the route clear enough. Make your way carefully up the little valley over the unstable rocky terrain to reach the edge of the spectacular Cratere Centrale (20 minutes), the oldest of the summit craters. Visible to your left is the edge of the Bocca di Nord-Est .This crater was formed in 1911 and its highest point – 3330m – constitutes the current summit of the volcano. Years ago there was a larger space between these craters and it was possible to pass through to the volcano's eastern face. Now the passage is impossible.

The summit is constantly whipped by strong, cold winds. Once there you'll find it impossible to resist a look down into the crater, belching sulphurous fumes, 150m below. If it is clear enough, you will see the crater's mouths, red with boiling lava, and steaming like pressure cookers.

The impact when confronted with this powerful, sleeping giant is strong and intense and makes your head fill with thoughts of just how insignificant you really are! This sense of powerlessness might get your adrenalin flowing, but statistically, the real risk of being there when an explosion occurs is pretty low and that realisation might help you regain your composure.

The panorama from this altitude is another memorable experience and it is certainly worth tearing yourself away from your confrontation with the volcano. In clear conditions, there is an extraordinary radius of visibility: with the Ionic coast of the mainland to the

east, the interior of Sicilia to the west and the Isole Eolie to the north, with Stromboli fuming away in the middle of the sea and the coast of Campania behind it. The Aspromonte of Calabria is visible to the north-east. In perfect conditions, you might be lucky enough to catch a glimpse of sections of the African coast to the south.

Skirting around to the south you come to Bocca Nuova (3260m), which is divided from the Cratere Centrale by a fragile, thin wall of fallen debris. Bocca Nuova (also known as Bocca Ovest) opened up in 1968. Behind Bocca Nuova is the most recent crater, Cratere Sud-Est, which opened up in 1971. Be very careful not to go close to the edge of the craters where there are cracks in the earth, these indicate imminent cave-ins. The west side of Cratere Centrale was safe in spring 1997.

Stage 2: The Craters to Rifugio Citelli
3½ to 4½ hours, 1515m descent

From Bocca Nuova it's an easy descent on the rocky slope to the dirt road which, to the left, leads down to Rifugio Sapienza. A right turn takes you to Piano delle Concazze (2800m) along the same route on which you arrived. Once at Piano delle Concazze, turn right to reach the Osservatorio Vulcanologico (one hour). The view from the observatory terrace takes in Linguaglossa and the Nebrodi mountains to the north-east, and further to the right the Sicilian coast with Taormina and Giardini Naxos.

On the descent that begins at the observatory, there is no trail to follow – however, it is reasonably easy to use your intuition and points of reference to navigate your way down the open slopes. From the observatory head east south-east, traversing a little rocky hill, towards the undulating crest of the Pizzi Deneri topped with telecommunications antennae. In about five minutes you reach an antenna. Below you to the south, at the bottom of the cliff, is the Valle del Leone, and beyond that is the enormous lava-covered depression of the Valle del Bove (8km long and 4km wide) which overlooks the plain of Catania. Continue the easy descent along the crest up to its last rocky peak (at the time of writing there was an antenna on this last peak), which comes before the leap to the peak of Rocca della Valle (2738m), which is marked on the map (30 minutes from the observatory).

From this point you have an even better view of the Valle del Bove to the south, enclosed by the Serra delle Concazze to the left and the Serra di Giannicola to the right. To the east is Giarre and the port of Riposto and, running your eyes up the coast to the north-east, is the gulf of the Giardini Naxos at the foot of Taormina. To the north is Linguaglossa.

From this point don't continue along the crest towards the peak of Rocca della Valle. Instead, change direction and begin the descent to the left (north-east) along another steep ridge, heading for (if it is visible), the gulf of Giardini Naxos. You'll change altitude very rapidly, passing from the ridge and going left into a canyon of volcanic debris which heads straight for Monte Frumento delle Concazze (2151m), a secondary volcano with its unmistakable conc-shape covered in pincushion-like shrubs. If you had continued straight along the ridge, it would have taken you down to the precipices of the eruption vents of 1928.

As you descend, you can see in the distance Rifugio Citelli on the right and the buildings of Piano Provenzana on the left. About 400m before the base of the cone of Monte Frumento delle Concazze, you'll find yourself in the thick of some quite surrealistic Spino Santo (thorntree) bushes, shaped like semi-spherical green pincushions (altitude 2300m). At this point cut to the right (east), crossing the open slopes diagonally in the direction of Rifugio Citelli. Along this undulating route, the vegetation grows thicker and you eventually reach the lava flow of the 1928 eruption (Bocche del 1928). Descend along its right edge through a patch of birch trees to reach the road, where you ascend to the right for the rifugio.

Alternatively, you could also cross over the lava flow and head for the small grassy volcanic cone with a birch covered crater. Go around the little crater to the right and walk through a thick birch forest to reach the road. Go uphill to the right for Rifugio Citelli (1746m), from where you can enjoy the magnificent views. The rifugio offers meals and a bed for the night (see On the Walk under Accommodation & Supplies earlier).

Mt Etna Circuit

Duration 3 days
Standard Medium
Start Rifugio Brunek
Finish Rifugio Sapienza
Closest Towns Linguaglossa, Nicolosi
Permits Required No
Public Transport Access Yes
Summary You'll need to be self-sufficient on this walk, carrying your own food, water, sleeping bag etc, but it is possible to stay in rifugi forestali, which are basic but adequate shelters. You'll walk around the volcano through forests and over old lava flows.

THE WALK
Day 1: Rifugio Brunek to Rifugio Forestale Saletti
4½ hours, 14km

From Rifugio Brunek (1380m) take the dirt road which heads north-west through the Ragabo pine forest towards the Caserma Pitarrone carabinieri barracks. In just more than 1km you'll pass a turn-off to the right, which heads to the barracks. Stay on the dirt road, following it to the left, and climb over a gate that keeps cars from entering this *pista forestale altomontana*, a mountain trail maintained by forest rangers. The trail crosses a series of old lava flows – the 1923 eruption, followed by 1911 and finally 1879.

Shortly after crossing the 1879 lava flow, you'll pass two deviations to the right for the Grotta delle Palombe. Ignore them and continue along the trail, crossing the lava flow of the 1947 eruption: you'll reach a trail junction at Passo dei Dammusi (1709m – 7.5km from Rifugio Brunek – two hours).

The trail heading uphill to the left leads to Rifugio Timparossa (1838m – not useable), a distance of about 3km. A sign for Linguaglossa-Pittarrone/north-east indicates the direction you have just come from, and the sign for Monte Spagnolo/west indicates the direction you are going in.

To the south a faint trail across the lava is indicated by a sign for the Grotta del Gelo e dei Lamponi. It is worth visiting the Grotta dei Lamponi (Cave of the Raspberries) which is very close. To reach the Grotta del Gelo you have to cross 4km over lava where orientation becomes difficult. In any case, this cave was closed at the time of writing.

However, if you want to visit the Grotta dei Lamponi, ascend to the south across bizarre lava *cordate*, which look like huge coils of rope, and after 50m you'll come to an opening which is actually the cave exit. It is better to continue your ascent to the left of the opening for another 100m along the trail, which is marked by piles of stones, to reach the cave's entrance. Once inside the cave, head south along the tunnel for about 100m – you'll pass two lovely pools of light framed by delicate grasses which correspond to two places where the roof of the cave has fallen in. Once at the end of the cave you'll notice a tongue-shaped strip of lava.

Go back the way you came and, just before reaching the cave entrance, you'll find a small tunnel on the left. A bit narrow at first, it then widens, bypasses the point where you entered the cave and opens onto the main tunnel. Go in and descend for about 300m, passing carefully over a large landslide, to reach the cave exit – this is the opening you passed earlier on your way to the cave. The tunnel actually continues its descent underground to the north, but there is danger of cave-ins and it is not recommended that you continue.

Go west along the dirt road in the direction of Monte Spagnolo, descending among beech trees and the rope coil-like lava flows until you reach Rifugio di Monte Santa Maria (1620m – 20 minutes) where there is a fireplace, but no water. It is recommended that you continue downhill for another 4.5km to the cosy Rifugio Saletti. Skirt the base of Monte Santa Maria, avoiding a deviation to the right for the Cisternazza (you can exit from the walk here; see Walk Exit Option following), and after 2.5km you'll find a very small bivacco (bivouac) at 1493m. You don't want to stay here, but it might be a useful shelter in the event of bad weather.

Continue the descent over the lava flow of the 1614 eruption. After a double curve in the road, it makes a sharp curve to the right and heads north-east. At this point, note the dirt road heading off to the west: it is a 1km-long short cut that becomes a trail over the lava which covered the altomontana road in 1981. The trail leads to the dilapidated Rifugio Monte Spagnolo and then reconnects with the new section of the altomontana. This is the

Grotta del Gelo

Gelo means 'intense cold' and the Grotta del Gelo is so called for its natural perennially iced interior. It is the most southern of its kind in Europe and certainly an unusual sight in sunny Sicilia. In recent years the ice has started to melt and there have been cave-ins, so the authorities have closed the cave to visitors.

Also known as the Grotta dei Lamponi (Cave of the Raspberries), the 900m-long cave is one of the longest flow tunnels, where the molten lava, kept hot and fluid inside the tunnel, flowed downhill during an eruption. The tunnel itself was formed by the flow of the lava which, as it cooled on the outside upon contact with the air, solidified around the central lava stream, which maintained its heat and fluidity.

At the bottom of the cave, where the tunnel is interrupted, you can see the solidified lava tongue of the internal lava stream. For some reason it cooled, blocking the flow. The tunnel, with further cooling, became hardened, petrifying the imprint of the flowing lava along its floor and walls – creating a kind of fossil lava flow.

Stefano Cavedoni

short cut described in day two of this Etna circuit walk (see under Short Cut in Day 2 following).

From the sharp curve at 1444m descend north-east along the dirt road for about 1km to Rifugio Saletti (1373m). This small, unstaffed rifugio is usually clean and un-crowded. You can spend the night here. The next closest *rifugi forestali* (bearing in mind that Rifugio Monte Spagnolo is ruined) are Monte Maletto (10km away) and Monte Scavo (12km away).

Walk Exit Option The dirt road that descends to the right as you skirt the base of Monte Santa Maria leads to the Cisternazza (just under 1.5km from Rifugio Saletti), a quaint cistern covered by a round building. From here the road continues to Rifugio Pirao, which is not open to the public. From Rifugio Pirao, the town of Randazzo is only 6km away on the normal paved road. At Randazzo, there are restaurants and the *Hotel Scrivano* (☎ (095) 92 11 26), Via G Bonaventura. The hotel is next to the SAIS bus stop for Giarre-Taormina and not far from the Circumetnea train station (see Getting To/From the Walks earlier in this section).

Day 2: Rifugio Saletti to Rifugio Monte Scavo
4 hours, 12km
From Rifugio Saletti there are two options including a short cut described below. The route is fine, but you might have to deal with fog. If you don't want to take the short cut, follow the indications for Nicolosi-Monte Spagnolo to the west, avoiding the turn-off to the right after less than 1km for Rifugio Pirao and Randazzo town. After the turn-off, the road begins to ascend, crosses the lava flow of the 1981 eruption and meets the startling vents thrown up by that eruption, before reaching the ruined Rifugio Monte Spagnolo (3km from Rifugio Saletti). Opposite there is a small, badly maintained bivouac, which is useful only as an emergency shelter.

Short Cut From Rifugio Saletti, retrace your

steps back to the sharp curve (see Day 1 section) at 1444m and turn west on to the dirt road. After walking through a forest, you'll encounter dried-out beech trees with white trunks. Traverse the slope of the lava, still going west. Try to maintain a constant altitude and keep to the trail.

Take a few minutes to see the breaks in the lava which, since 1992, have begun to steam again. In 1981, the lava flow that erupted from this break reached the town of Randazzo, destroying houses, roads and the railway line, eventually flowing into the Alcantara River.

Once past the lava flow, you'll find the old altomontana dirt road, which continues for about 200m through a lovely forest to join up with the new dirt road. Here you turn left for the ruined Rifugio Monte Spagnolo (1440m), 1km from the curve at altitude 1444m, 3km from Rifugio Saletti.

At this point the two routes rejoin. From Rifugio Monte Spagnolo continue west along the dirt road through an area reafforested with cedar pines, to the south of the little Monte Spagnolo volcano (1547m). You'll pass two deviations to the right, one immediately after the mountain and another about 1km from Rifugio Monte Spagnolo. (Both lead to Rocca Mandorla and Randazzo, about 8km away). After 2km, you'll pass another turn-off to the right, this time for Bosco Nave which heads west to Maletto, about 8km away. Ignore this and continue on the dirt road which now ascends to the south.

Walking for another 3km, you'll pass through Bosco di Maletto and under the vol-canic cone of Monte Maletto (1773m) before reaching a turn-off to the left for Rifugio Monte Maletto (1701m), which is just more than 1km from the turn-off, immersed in a thick and isolated forest. The refugio, which is near the Grotta delle Vanette, doesn't offer any views but is very romantic and among the least frequented on Mt Etna. This could be an alternative point at which to end this leg of the walk, although the next rifugio at Monte Scavo is only a bit more than 3.5km away. (Rifugio Monte Scavo marks the half-way point on the Etna circuit and is among the most frequented of the volcano's rifugi, especially on weekends and often by boy scouts.)

If you prefer to continue to Rifugio Monte Scavo, ignore the turn-off for Rifugio Monte Maletto and continue the ascent south on the dirt road. After 200m there is a deviation to the right for Case Pappalardo, from where you can reach Maletto or Bronte. There are no hotels in Maletto, but you could try *Hotel Parco dell'Etna* (☎ (095) 69 19 07) in the Borgonuovo neighbourhood of Bronte.

After walking for just less than 2.5km, you'll reach the spacious *Rifugio Monte Scavo* (1785m) where a huge round table in the centre of a vast dining room welcomes hungry visitors – although you'll have to cook your own food, since the rifugio is unstaffed. There are panoramic views from the rifugio.

Almost 4km beyond Rifugio Monte Scavo is another rifugio forestale, the Monte Palestra, also known as Poggio la Caccia (1917m).

If you still have some energy, make the two-hour return walk to Monte Egitto through an immense, dramatic desert of lava formations. Be careful of vipers in this area.

Day 3: Rifugio Monte Scavo to Rifugio Sapienza
5 hours, 14.5km

Walk south on the dirt road again from Rifugio Monte Scavo. Avoid a deviation on the left that peters out on the slopes of the volcano. Just more than 1km from the refugio, on the right-hand side of the road, note the chasm of the Grotta di Monte Nunziata which, in the past, was filled with snow in winter by the people of Bronte so they could have ice in summer.

After another 900m, in a forest of birch trees, you'll come to a pagliara, a typical conical shelter for workers producing charcoal, built of branches and earth. Just less than 2km further on is the small and gracious *Rifugio Monte Palestra* (1917m on the IGM map). Pass a turn-off to the right for the lava-covered areas around the volcanic

cones of Monte Capre, Monte Lepre and Monte Intraleo. You will soon reach Rifugio Galvarina, the last of the unstaffed bivouac-style rifugi on the circuit. At the time of research, the fireplace was out of order and the place was depressingly neglected. To the right of the rifugio is another trail which connects with the trail for the volcanic cones mentioned previously.

Continue on the dirt road for 4km, across large fields of lava from various epochs, including the 1610 eruption. Ignore the minor, lateral roads and keep going until you reach the asphalt road, near Rifugio Denza (1740m – uninhabitable and always closed). Go right here and the road turns almost immediately to the left and you will soon see the Cappella di San Giovanni Gualberto on the left. Continue along the asphalt for almost 2km, crossing a little bridge, immediately after which you'll see the entrance to the **Giardino Botanico Nuova Gussonea** (botanical gardens) on the left.

Keep going straight and you'll soon find a turn-off to the left, onto a smaller asphalt road, closed off by a green bar (1701m on the IGM). A sign indicates the Osservatorio Astrofisico (astrophysics observatory). Monte dei Santi (1720m) is on the right – a little volcanic cone covered with larch trees, which really stands out in the middle of all that lava.

This road is a short cut alternative to the longer main route to Rifugio Sapienza. The short cut heads east corresponding to a section of the Monte Nero degli Zappini nature trail. Pass the observatory which is some distance off to your right, and avoid all subsequent deviations. After about 1.5km you come out on to provincial road No 92, which connects Nicolosi, Rifugio Sapienza and Zafferana Etnea.

Turn left and walk uphill, avoiding the sharp curves of the road by taking advantage of the clearly visible trails across the recent lava flows of 1983. After about 3km you'll reach the big, open square of *Rifugio Sapienza*. You can eat a hot meal and spend the night at this staffed rifugio, operated by the Club Alpino Italiano, or catch an AST bus to

Nicolosi or Catania (the bus leaves daily at 4 pm – see Getting To/From the Walks earlier in this section).

From the rifugio, you can take the cable car up the first section of the crater ascent (L58,000 – SITAS; ☎ (095) 911 15 58), which includes a section in 4WD and a section on foot.

Amalfi Coast & Sorrento Peninsula

From a distance, the rugged Amalfi Coast-Sorrento Peninsula does not look as though it has much to offer walkers – perhaps just a few paths to the main summits. Yet this 25km long peninsula, rising to more than 1400m along its crest, has an extensive web of paths, many of ancient origin. Once the lifelines between settlements and remote monasteries and convents, these paths now provide abundant opportunities for a distinctive style of walking. Contrasts are of the essence – between busy coastal towns, hamlets and isolated farms on the mountainsides and the wild country beyond. The setting is colourful in a very Mediterranean way – no soft tones but every conceivable shade of blue and green, stark white in the vast rockfaces and all colours of the rainbow in the plentiful wild flowers.

Walking trips could easily be combined with a beach holiday at one of the Amalfi Coast's picturesque resorts such as Positano, Amalfi or Atrani. Vesuvio (Mt Vesuvius) is close by if you're interested in tackling the walk described in the Volcanoes of Southern Italy chapter of this book.

HISTORY

Greek settlements appeared along this coast in the 8th century BC, although it is likely that the Greeks were far from being the first to settle here. The area became part of the Roman Empire in 344 BC, and was favoured by the elite as a summer retreat. Trade with eastern countries following the fall of Roma (Rome) brought great wealth, especially to towns along the south coast. In the 11th century the Normans took the peninsula into the Kingdom of Napoli (Naples) and Sicilia (Sicily). Founded in the 9th century, the town of Amalfi became a supreme naval power, at its peak rivalling the maritime republics of Pisa and Venezia (Venice). Its navigation tables, the *Tavole Amalfitanae*, formed the world's first maritime code and governed all

HIGHLIGHTS

SANDRA BARDWELL

- The scenic Amalfi Coast with its incredibly steep, densely wooded hillsides soaring to precipitous, craggy peaks
- The well-known Sentiero degli Dei, a connoisseur's walk of great beauty
- Magnificent views of Capri on the Punta Campanella walk
- Rambling through timeless villages, olive and citrus groves among abundant wild flowers

shipping in the Mediterranean for centuries thereafter.

The peninsula's attractions drew people on the Grand Tour from the 18th century onwards and was the beginning of the area's enduring popularity with tourists, who now possibly provide the mainstay of its economy.

NATURAL HISTORY

The peninsula is essentially the Monti Lattari range, which extends south-west from the fringes of the Picentini Range into the Tyrrhenian Sea, separating the Golfos di Napoli and Salerno. This rugged mountain

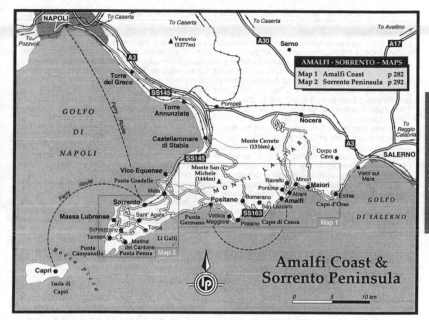

range has several summits above 1000m, the two highest being Monte San Michele (1444m) and Monte Cerreto (1316m). The range drops steeply on all sides, almost directly to the sea in the south, while in the north a relatively gentle coastal plain separates the foot of the range from the shores of the Golfo di Napoli. The range is composed of a marine type of limestone, which was compressed and upended after being laid down in the Mesozoic era; there are also outcrops of intensely fractured dolomite. The permeability of the rock is responsible for the many deep, steep sided valleys, notably to the south of the main ridge. The peninsula changes at the western or Sorrento end, with a much lower profile and generally more rounded hills.

The vegetation is very diverse, reflecting the dissected nature of the terrain – in places providing shelter from the influence of the sea, in others exposing the ground to the full blast of salt-laden winds. At the lowest levels, cultivation of citrus, vines and olives is dominant, often extending up the mountainsides on skilfully built terraces. In an intermediate zone, away from cultivated ground, holm oak and small shrubs are found.

At higher levels, up to the tree line, chestnut and alder dominate, with ash and beech in places, although beech, having been commercially exploited in the past, is now rare. Chestnut is an important resource in this area and is harvested for use in citrus and vine groves. On the Sorrento Peninsula, the hardy macchia community of plants, adapted to the extremes of heat and drought, clings tenaciously to the rocky hillsides. Wild flowers are abundant everywhere; rock roses, cyclamens, orchids, lilies, broom, honeysuckle, poppies, – the list is almost endless.

Unfortunately fauna – mammals or birds – is rare; the number of spent cartridges seen on the ground suggests one major reason for this.

Coastal Torre

One of the most eye-catching features of the peninsula's coastline is the *torri* (towers) in various stages of decay. Dotted along the coast on narrow promontories or headlands, and always with an unimpeded strategic outlook, they are squat, plain structures, either rounded or angular, rather like a cross between a largish house and a purely defensive tower. There are at least two torre between Vietri sul Mare and Punta Campanella, plus two on the coast facing Capri and one at Punta del Capo, just north-west of Sorrento.

All of the coastal walks from Marina del Cantone pass close to a torre, which are prominent in coastal views from almost anywhere on the peninsula. There is one near the camp site at Praiano – Torre a Mare; where a large sign (in Italian) at the entrance explains something of the history of the torri.

The torri originated in the 16th century when the Ottoman empire had designs on the peninsula, which was part of the Spanish empire at the time. Following a devastating Ottoman raid on Sorrento and Massa Lubrense in 1558, the local Viceroy ordered the building of towers. These were to be fairly closely spaced along the coastline, especially near likely or existing landing places (such as near Vettica Maggiore and at Marina di Praia just east of Praiano) and in some cases, using sites occupied by fortresses since about the 10th century. An earlier edict by Emperor Charles V was already in force requiring the construction of square or cylindrical towers armed with cannons.

By the 18th century the torri had become redundant as defences; some fell into disuse, some were leased others were sold and some even became state property.

Torre a Mare at Praiano, in its peaceful role, initially served the local fishing industry, then a countess set about making it a habitable residence. She replaced the small seaward window with a larger one enabling her to better enjoy the view of the Golfo di Salerno. Various other modifications have been made over the years and the torre is now a private residence and art gallery.

Sandra Bardwell

CLIMATE

Hot, dry summers and cool, damp winters are the hallmarks of the Mediterranean climate experienced by the Amalfi-Sorrento Peninsula. The decisive influence on this pattern is the movement of Atlantic weather fronts. In summer, the few fronts that approach the western Mediterranean are pushed aside, to the north and south, by a subtropical anticyclone anchored near the Azores. Usually at least one month during summer is rain-free, and rainfall overall between June and September is minimal. Sunshine is the norm and temperatures are high, often intensified by hot winds from northern Africa.

The average summer temperature on the Amalfi Coast is 25°C, Sorrento's is slightly lower, while in Napoli, the average maximum in July and August is around 29°C. During autumn (September to November) the Atlantic depressions begin to infiltrate the western Mediterranean, bringing changeable and cloudy, though still mild, weather. Rainfall is much higher, coming in short, sharp showers but is still confined to about 100 days in any one year. Along the coast, the total annual rainfall is 1000mm, while inland it is 1500mm. Mean temperatures during winter (December to February) reach only 10°C on the Amalfi Coast and 8.5°C on the Sorrento Peninsula.

INFORMATION

Maps

The *Campania, Basilicata* sheet in the Touring Club Italiano's 1:200,000 series covers the Sorrento Peninsula and costs L9500. *Monti Lattari, Peninsula Sorrentina, Costiera Amalfitana: Carta dei Sentieri* (1:30,000, 25m contours) by the Club Alpino Italiano (CAI), Napoli and Cava dei Tirreni sections, and the Comunità Montana 'Penisola Amalfitana', 1997 edition, is the best map for the whole area (although the small type is not particularly easy to read). Inaccuracies are few, but include the misleading marking of the Alta Via route, path 00, east of Torca village on the Sorrento Peninsula. Accompanying notes cover climate, flora, fauna and geology; there is also a handy list of marked walks. It is priced at L15,000; you could try contacting the CAI, at Casella Postale 148, 80100 Napoli CC, postale n.19756808, for a copy (add L5000 per copy for postage and handling). Preferably, visit La Capsa bookshop, on Corsa Italia, Sorrento, a short distance east of the side road leading to the train station. This gold mine of a bookshop has a good stock of maps and guides for the area.

Penisola Sorrentina, Costiera Amalfitana, Vesuvio-Pompei-Salerno-Sorrento (1:50,000, 100m contours, Kompass map No 682) is fine for general planning and orientation but is of extremely limited use for walking: some of the paths shown do not exist on the ground or are inaccurately mapped. It does have adequate maps of the main towns plus notes about their history and attractions in English, German, Italian and French. It is widely available for L9500.

Information Sources

The AAST di Salerno (☎ (089) 22 47 44; fax 25 25 76), at Via Roma 258, 84100 Salerno, issues a detailed town map, an accommodation list and some basic information about the Amalfi Coast. The regional EPT office (☎ (089) 23 04 11; fax 25 18 44) also has an email address, eptinfo@xcom.it, and a useful Web site: http://www.crmpa.it/EPT.

The AAST in Sorrento (☎ (081) 878 22 29; fax 877 33 97) is open from 8.30 am to 2 pm and 4.30 to 7.30 pm, Monday to Saturday throughout the year. The office, in the Circolo dei Forestieri (Foreigners' Club) at Via Luigi de Maio 35, 80067 Sorrento, issues a detailed accommodation list for the town and environs and can provide transport information.

Book

Landscapes of Sorrento and the Amalfi Coast by Julian Tippett is an invaluable guide to the area, with clear descriptions of more than 60 easy and moderate walks on the peninsula, though very few venture into the more remote country. It is well researched and reliable; the clear town maps are particularly useful. It is available locally for L27,000.

Warning

Vociferous, boisterous and occasionally aggressive dogs guard just about every farm, citrus grove and house away from the town centres. Make sure your tetanus inoculation is up to date before arriving in the area – it is a comforting thought as you run the gauntlet of several sets of snapping jaws!

ACCOMMODATION & SUPPLIES

Sorrento

This town could serve as a base for the walks on the Sorrento Peninsula. Apart from the huge number of hotels in and around the town, many geared to the package tour industry (a guide to which is available from the AAST – see Information Sources on this page), there are two camp sites on the Sorrento-Massa Lubrense road. Of these, *Nube d'Argento* (☎ (081) 878 13 44) has a good outlook over Sorrento and the mountains beyond.

In the town, *La Caffeteria Hostel* (☎ (081) 807 29 25) offers beds in dormitories for L23,000, including breakfast, or singles/doubles with private facilities for L46,000/L76,000. The entrance is next to La Caffeteria at Via degli Aranci 160, about 500m from the train station – walk east along Corsa Italia, immediately north of the station, take the first right and Via degli Aranci is around the corner. Note that the hostel is not an IYH establishment.

Salerno

This is more convenient as a staging post than as a base for the Amalfi Coast, but it's also worth spending some time here exploring the town in its own right. *Irno Youth Hostel* (☎ (089) 79 02 51; fax 25 26 49) is at Via Luigi Guernico 112; the entrance, in a narrow lane, is signposted off Via S Baratta. From the train station head east for about 700m then turn north. The tariff is L15,500 including breakfast and a sheet; a simple but adequate three-course dinner costs L10,000. There are several hotels in Salerno (a list is available from the AAST – see Information Sources on this page) but there are no camp sites.

GETTING THERE & AWAY

This region is very accessible both by public and private transport. Information about transport and access locally is given in the relevant Getting To/From the Walk sections later in this chapter.

Bus

There is a daily SITA bus service (☎ (081) 552 21 76) from Napoli (Via Pisanelli) to Sorrento, Positano and Amalfi. From Salerno, there are frequent SITA services (☎ (081) 22 66 04) to Positano and Amalfi, and at least three buses daily to Sorrento. Buses from Salerno depart from Piazza della Concordia on the sea front. Buy tickets from the SITA office in Via S Martiri, just west of Piazza della Concordia, near the corner with Lungomare Trieste. The fare to Amalfi is L2800 one way.

Train

The privately run Circumvesuviana (☎ (081) 779 24 44) from Napoli to Sorrento provides a frequent rail service. In Napoli, the station is in Corso G Garibaldi, about 400m southwest of Stazione Centrale via a covered path. The fare is L4200 one way. On the state system, there are reasonably frequent intercity, direct or regional train services between Napoli Central station and Salerno.

Car

To get to Sorrento by car, leave the A3 at the Castellammare exit and follow the SS145 (known as Sorrentina) to Sorrento. To get to the Amalfi Coast from Sorrento, continue along the SS145, following the signs for the Amalfitana (road) and Fontanelle, continue via Sant'Agata to the coast and the SS163 (Amalfitana) junction. Amalfi is 25km east along a most amazing – or alarming – winding road. Coming from Salerno, take the Vietri sul Mare or Amalfi turn-offs from the A3, to join the SS163, which snakes along the coast to Colli S Pietro, west of Positano. Here it meets the SS145 which leads to Sorrento. To take a short cut across the peninsula and to avoid Sorrento, turn north at Colli S Pietro towards the town of Meta, which lies east of Sorrento.

Ferry

The most impressive – and expensive – means of reaching the peninsula is by sea. From Napoli, you can reach Sorrento with Navigazione Libera del Golfo (☎ (081) 552 72 09) or Alilauro (☎ (081) 807 30 24). Alilauro also runs a service from Salerno to Amalfi and Positano.

AMALFI COAST

From the slender strip of the Amalfi Coast, incredibly steep, densely wooded mountains rise to become precipitous, craggy peaks. Many are surprised to discover that there is an extraordinary network of paths here, linking towns, villages and terraced mountainsides. These paths climb high above the coast to religious retreats and mountain summits through wild and beautiful valleys. Throughout the Amalfi Coast walking is a fascinating experience, culturally and scenically. It is also a very energetic one, as it is almost impossible to avoid climbing considerable distances, along paths, most of which are well made, and up long flights of steps.

Any of the coastal towns can serve as a base for the walks described here, depending on your accommodation preference, as the area is linked by excellent local bus services. Apart from Positano and Amalfi most of the towns are still largely unspoiled and uncluttered by a surfeit of concessions to modern tourism.

HISTORY

The Greeks, then the Romans, colonised the coast; in the 1930s the substantial remains of a Roman village, the summer residence of wealthy nobility, were uncovered in Minori. After the fall of the Roman Empire, Amalfi led the way in re-establishing relationships between east and west by importing exotic goods – carpets, coffee and paper. Great prestige and wealth flowed from this enterprise and Amalfi grew to match the sea power of Pisa and Genoa (Genova); its maritime law, the *Tavole Amalfitanae*, was the ultimate authority in the Mediterranean for centuries. Amalfi was also the home of Flavio Gioa, the inventor of the maritime compass. The town became a centre for paper making from the 13th century, deriving from its experience in trading with Mediterranean countries. Factories were built near rivers in villages along the coast – Maiori, Minori and Atrani. Although little remains of the old factories, the tradition has been maintained and handmade paper from Amalfi is internationally renowned.

Positano was once an isolated fishing village where lemons and olives were cultivated on nearby terraced fields. During the 16th and 17th centuries, like its neighbour Amalfi, it thrived on trade with the Middle East. The town has long been a favourite among artists, musicians and writers and it continues to uphold its traditional role as a centre of fashion.

NATURAL HISTORY

From the coast between Amalfi and Atrani deep valleys cut back towards the spine of the Monti Lattari range. It's here that the Valle delle Ferriere reserve harbours plants usually found in Africa and South America and a rare fern – *Woodwardia radicans*. Everywhere lush woodlands and dense vegetation of the valleys, and especially the beautiful slender Italian cypresses, contrast with the open, sparsely vegetated slopes above.

INFORMATION

Of the AASTs in the area, only the Positano office (☎ (089) 87 50 67; fax 87 57 60) can provide any useful information about local walks, in the form of a brochure with notes and a map. A local accommodation list is also available. The office is open from 8 am to 2 pm year round and is at Via del Saracino 4, 84107, close to Santa Maria Assunta, the large church on the beach side of town. The Web site for Positano Commune – http://www.starnet.it/positano/welcome.html – is in several languages and includes some basic background information and a limited accommodation guide.

In Amalfi, the AAST office (☎ (089) 87

11 07; fax 87 26 19) on Corso Repubbliche Marinare is open year round between 8 am and 2 pm from Monday to Friday and 8 am and 1 pm on Saturday. During summer the office also opens during the late afternoon from Monday to Saturday. It issues a brief accommodation list, brochures about local attractions and *E'costiera*, a useful monthly magazine which has articles (in English and Italian) about local history, attractions and accommodation information.

Basic information about the Agerola area (north-west of Amalfi) is available from Pro Loco Agerola (☎ (081) 879 10 64), at Viale delle Vittoria, 80051 Santa Maria.

PLANNING
When to Walk

Autumn, winter and early spring are the least crowded and most peaceful times on this part of the peninsula, and the weather is usually ideal for walking; from early March until late May the displays of wild flowers are superb. If possible, avoid the period between late May and early September when daily temperatures may be too high for comfortable walking (unless you usually live in a warm climate). The wild flowers have generally passed their best by late spring. From mid-June to the end of August, the coastal towns are overflowing with tourists and getting about becomes extremely time consuming.

Maps & Book

The CAI's *Monti Lattari* 1:30,000 sheet is the map to use for walking, while Julian Tippett's book *Landscapes of Sorrento and the Amalfi Coast* describes more than 40 walks around the Amalfi Coast (see Book in the Information section earlier in this chapter). *Positano, Citta Romantica: Sui Sentieri degli Dei, Passeggiando per i Monti Lattari*, published by the AAST, Positano, is a brochure with a planimetric map of the area showing six itineraries to the major features. The very brief notes in Italian and English are not much help in following the walks on the ground. However, with details of bars, cafes, and gradient profiles of the itineraries, it is useful for planning walks in conjunction

AMALFI COAST

with other references. *Penisola Sorrentina* (1:50,000, Kompass map No 682) is also handy, but for planning purposes only.

What to Bring

No special equipment is needed for any of the walks described in this chapter. Most follow well-defined paths, where strong, well made walking shoes or trainers would be suitable. Walking boots are recommended for the longer walks and for those which include sections along rough paths. The support of walking poles may be appreciated on the steeper descents. Sunscreen and a shady hat are essential during spring and summer, and a water bottle of at least 1L capacity is indispensable; surface water is virtually non-existent away from the towns and villages with their customary fountains and bars. If you are planning to camp, bear in mind that gas (for small stoves) is not readily obtainable.

PLACES TO STAY & EAT

There are precious few inexpensive places to stay along the Amalfi Coast, so the few in this category are much sought-after, and even then are pricey compared with hostels and camp sites elsewhere. The abundance of excellent fresh produce – fruit, vegetables, cheese, bread and wine, make al fresco dining a very attractive alternative to pizzerias and the like. Free camping is not a feasible option; apart from the problem of finding out who owns a particular piece of land, the absence of fresh surface water is a drawback, as is the dearth of flat, scrub and stone-free pitches.

Atrani

A'Scalinatella/Ristorante La Piazzetta (☎ (089) 87 14 92 or 87 19 30) is more a hostel than a pensione. For L30,000 you get to stay in a bed in a two or four-bunk room, disconcertingly lacking a proper window; the tariff includes sheets, an excellent breakfast and free pasta at dinner. A room with private facilities, four beds and a window costs L50,000 per person. A washing machine is available for guests' use. To find the reception and the friendly English speaking host Phillipe, walk up Via dei Dogi from Piazza

Umberto (which is also the address of the place), go under an arch, follow the signs to the hostel for about 150m and then turn right up the winding steps. Dinner at La Piazzetta is good value. The free pasta course is worth between L8000 and L12,000; in addition, there is a selection of salads, fish, omelettes and desserts as well as wines, beers (especially the excellent Baffo d'Oro), the local lemon liqueur and coffee. You could spend up to L20,000 but you would be well fed and watered for L12,000.

There is nowhere else to stay in Atrani. Amalfi, the nearest alternative, has mainly three and four-star hotels; an accommodation list is available from the AAST (see Information Sources earlier in this section).

Praiano

It is worth paying the outrageous tariff at *La Tranquillata* camp site (☎ (089) 87 40 84; fax 87 47 79) for the view across the Golfo di Salerno from the terraced pitches. The site, at Via Roma 21, 84010 Praiano, is attached to the *Continentale Pensione* on the SS163, the main coastal road. It costs L14,000 per tent then there's an additional charge of L12,000 per person; the facilities are spartan: one cold shower and one short-lived hot one, toilets, basins and a clothesline. Cabins are also available on a weekly basis. Singles with private facilities in the two-star pensione start at L40,000, plus breakfast, which costs L8000. The SITA bus stops outside the pensione. The only other local hotel in the same price range is *Casa Alfonsa* (☎ (089) 87 40 48), a one-star establishment at Via Umberto I 113. Single/double rooms with bath start at L40,000/ L80,000 and breakfast is an additional L8000. Further west, and nearer Vettica Maggiore than Praiano is the one star *Aquila Pensione*, Via Ulivi 84010, where prices for singles/ doubles with bath start at L16,000/L40,000.

There are several attractive waterfront restaurants near La Tranquillata camp site, access to which is down the steps about 100m along the main road to the east of the camp site. *Tutti per Tutti, Marino* is a good *alimentari* (delicatessen/grocery store) in Praiano proper (Via Umberto 1) above the main road.

Positano

This place is generally on the serious side of expensive. There are a few one-star hotels with doubles (private facilities) starting at L80,000 in the low season; at the top of the range you would have to pay at least L300,000 for a double. The pick of the cheaper hotels is *Villa Maria Luisa* (☎ (089) 87 50 23), Via Fornillo 40, which has large doubles with terraces and magnificent views for L80,000.

GETTING TO/FROM THE WALKS
Bus

The blue SITA buses are the lifeline of the area, providing frequent, inexpensive and reliable links between the coastal towns and some of those inland. Tickets must be bought before boarding, either at one of the SITA offices or at bars or *tabacchi* (tobacconists) displaying a SITA sign close to the local bus stops (clearly indicated by a blue and white Fermata sign). They must then be validated in the machine on the bus. It's a good idea to buy tickets well in advance, especially for the day's return journey, to save being caught by closed doors between early afternoon and about 4 pm. In Atrani, buy tickets from the newsagent in Piazza Umberto I; in Positano, from the bar in Piazza dei Mulini; and in Praiano, from the tabacchi just west of the Continentale Pensione. L1500 will get you from Praiano to Positano and from Atrani to Minori or Praiano, while the fare from Atrani to Erchie (see Monte dell' Avvocata walk later in this section) is L2000. In Amalfi, buses depart from Piazza Flavio Gioia which overlooks the marine and ferry port; obtain a timetable and buy tickets from the SITA office opposite. Apart from bus services along the coast and through to Sorrento, local runs from Amalfi include Ravello, via Atrani and Scala, and Bomerano and San Lazzaro. There is also a handy service run by the Positano town bus service, between Positano and Montepertuso. Buses leave from Piazza dei Mulini, via Bivio Montepertuso, at the junction of the coast road and the Montepertuso road. In Montepertuso, the bus stop is on the main road opposite the piazza. Purchase tickets on board.

Ferry

Ferry services between Amalfi and Positano only run during the summer and are more expensive than the bus. At least two companies operate such a service: Navigazione Libera del Golfo (☎ (081) 807 18 12) and Amalfi Navigazione (☎ (089) 87 31 90).

Monte dell'Avvocata

Duration 7 to 7½ hours
Ascent 1014m
Standard Hard
Start Between Capo d'Orso and Erchie
Finish Maiori
Closest Towns Sorrento, Salerno
Permits Required No
Public Transport Access Yes
Summary An outstandingly scenic walk to Monte dell'Avvocata and the nearby monastery, with extensive views and an abundance of wild flowers.

This walk is best done from east to west, as it is more convenient for bus travel – it's better to finish in Maiori (where there are bars, cafes and seats on the promenade) than by the road, at nowhere in particular, between Capo d'Orso and Erchie (even if the Capo d'Orso hotel is nearby). On the outward journey, ask the driver for the stop at the walk to Avvocata, but to be on the safe side, watch for the Capo d'Orso hotel and be ready to get off, just after passing it as you come from Maiori.

It's advisable to make an early start so that most of the climbing is out of the way before the day warms up. A return to base by bus from Maiori is recommended – it takes another two or more hours to walk from Maiori to Atrani. There are springs and small streams along the way, but carry water all the same. Much of the walk follows rather rough paths, partly overgrown in places on the ascent, and flights of steps. Marking is variable, but as always, it pays to be vigilant. This walk should be well within the range of moderately fit walkers.

THE WALK

From the bus stop on the SS163, walk up the nearby steps flanked by a timber rail then head along the rough path with a stone wall on the right; red and white markers will guide you for most of the walk. The well-graded path then skirts the head of a valley. After about 40 minutes you will see a few ruined buildings, continue past these for about 40m and fork left uphill, after another 15 minutes follow the markers heading uphill to the left. Soon you'll pass near some picnic tables, continue directly ahead on a broad rising path. Beyond a level stretch, you will cross a small stream, keep going ahead on the stony path leading uphill through trees (no markers). The path then winds uphill, beside a grove of trees, through clumps of broom. The next turn is not obvious: it leads back at an angle between two tall trees, then climbs steadily (in places partly hidden beneath bushes) up the prominent spur to the ridge above. You should reach the ridge about an

hour after crossing the stream. Turn left at a T-junction, head along the wide path and, further on, bear right past a fragmentary ruined wall. Shortly past the wall, bear left up a narrow path marked with a red arrow which will take you to the summit of **Monte dell'Avvocata**. The path leads through trees and out into the open. Make a mental note of where you emerge (you will be returning by this route) because the path to the top (three to 3½ hours from the start) becomes rather vague cutting across the rocky ground and through a profusion of wild flowers. The panoramic view from here embraces Vesuvio, the Picentini Range inland, the Golfo di Salerno and the Amalfi Coast as far as Capo di Conca.

After absorbing the view return to the main path and turn left towards the monastery. Unfortunately this place is all too popular with picnickers, who pay little heed to the practice of carrying out what they carry in. Nevertheless, there are fine views

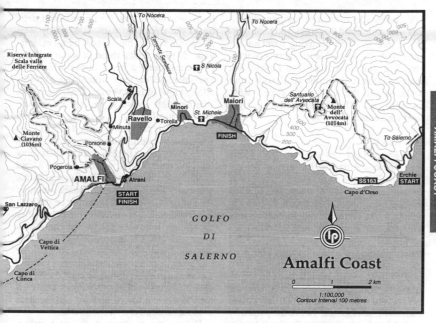

AMALFI COAST

from the seaward side of the walled area enclosing the monastery buildings. Walk around the outer perimeter and, close to the south-western corner, follow a narrow rocky path leading down through an elongated cave, formed by an overhanging cliff. The path continues through woods, past a couple of picnic sites, then skirts the remains of a large lime kiln. Soon you will reach the next ruin from where there is a good view of the coast. Follow a narrow path to the right of the building and continue down – and down. From the a pink and white building on the right, guarded by large cacti, descend the steps and continue along through a succession of terraces passing through minor junctions. When you reach **Maiori**, head down the steps between houses for about 200m and then turn right at a junction where there is a drinking fountain; 100m further on you turn left into Via de Iosola which leads to a road which runs through to the beach front.

Valle delle Ferriere

Duration 5½ to 6 hours
Ascent 500m
Standard Medium
Start/Finish Atrani or Amalfi
Closest Towns Sorrento, Salerno
Permits Required No
Public Transport Access Yes
Summary Traditional unspoiled local villages, breathtaking limestone cliffs in a nature reserve and spectacular coastal views.

You can start this walk from either Atrani or Amalfi (though the half-hour walk between the two is well worth doing). It's best done clockwise, as described, so that you descend the seemingly endless steps from Pogerola rather than toil up them. The walk should fit comfortably into a day, allowing time for wild flower identification, sampling of the bars in Pontone and Pogerola, and photography. There are some drinking fountains en route, but it's advisable to carry water as well. The bus from Amalfi to Ravello via Scala could save the climb to Minuta; from Scala, to join the walk as described, walk south for about 1km up the road to the tight bend where there is a tele

THE WALK

From Piazza Umberto in Atrani, walk along Via Campo, the narrow passage by the red post box. Turn left at a T-junction and head up the steps, turn left at house No 18, then head up more steps between the houses. Go right into Via Torricelli and you will shortly reach another T-junction, turn left into Via S Sebastiano. This route winds between and under houses, out onto a balcony path with good coastal views, before winding down onto the main road in Amalfi. Bear first right, through a small square followed by another, from where a passage in the far left corner leads to Piazza Duomo. Leave the piazza by the left-hand side (with the Banco di Napoli on the right) and walk along Via Lorenzo d'Amalfi. About 50m beyond the point where it widens, head to the right up some steps and through a tunnel. Further on the path forks (at a house with a fine mural) – bear right here. Flights of steps, linked by paths, lead on and up through citrus groves; keep walking more or less directly ahead at a three-way junction and continue up to the piazza (with a drinking fountain and bar) in **Pontone**.

With Bar Luca on your right, climb up the steps ahead of you, first under the church, then up past a good viewpoint to a junction where you should bear left, up some wider steps towards a square at Minuta in front of a church. From there, more steps lead up to the road from Scala, at a tight bend from where there are good views across Ravello to the hills above Minori. From the apex of the bend, follow the steps heading steeply to the left. At a four-way junction turn left along a level path, which winds around an intensively terraced hillside, before heading down

into a pine wood. Pass the fountain and steps up to the right; the path, flanked by well made stone walls, has seats at frequent intervals. It then leads through a tunnel and continues round a bend, above which is a prominent yellow tank, from where a breathtaking view, of near vertical limestone cliffs soaring high above steep wooded slopes, presents itself.

The rough path, now in the Riserva Integrale Scala Valle delle Ferriere, miraculously finds a way along the base of the cliffs (now the CAI path No 57, marked on the *Monti Lattari* map; see Maps & Book earlier in this section). The crossing of the main stream in the valley is safe and might only be difficult if it was flooded. Bear left immediately after the stream, following the O-1 markers, on a clear path along limestone ledges in luxuriant woodland. No more than 150m further on, after another smaller stream crossing, follow the markers uphill, along the path that eventually leaves the trees behind. The track then levels out, more or less, and the path contours around the steep hillside.

Follow the markers at the next stream crossing, which has a fine waterfall above it. Continue along the shady path and at a marked junction, bear left and head downhill. The path then leads past abandoned and overgrown terraces, across open hillsides, and passes just below the cliffs. Suddenly you arrive in **Pogerola**, go down the first alley you come to, between the houses and terraces from where you continue to the main square.

Turn your back on the square and continue down an alley opposite, by a triple street lamp and turn right, passing an alimentari. The well-made path with wide steps winds down to Amalfi and brings you to a road by the Scuola Media. Continue downhill and around a bend which goes past the *carabinieri* (police). Turn right at the next junction, pass through the tunnel and rejoin the outward route at the foot of the steps in Via Lorenzo d'Amalfi; continue down to Piazza Duomo. If you are returning to Atrani, it's simply a matter of retracing your steps back to Piazza Umberto.

Capo Muro

Duration 8½ to 9 hours
Ascent 1072m
Standard Hard
Start Praiano or Bomerano
Finish Positano or Montepertuso
Closest Towns Sorrento, Salerno
Permits Required No
Public Transport Access Yes
Summary A superb high-level walk, beneath limestone cliffs with panoramic coast and mountain views.

The Capo Muro walk rivals the Sentiero degli Dei walk scenically and in the adrenalin-producing quality of the paths. It could be done in either direction, though it is perhaps more satisfying to traverse Vallone Porto later in the day for coolness and lighting effects. Catching the Montepertuso-Positano bus (see Getting To/From the Walks earlier in this section) could take an hour or so off the walk. It is also possible to do the walk direct from Amalfi, by catching the bus to Bomerano, and returning by bus from Positano.

Carry enough water for the duration of the walk. Refreshments are available in Bomerano; the next watering place after this is Montepertuso, a few hours further on. Except for a stretch beyond Capo Muro, paths are good and generally well marked. This walk makes for a long, but most rewarding day.

THE WALK

From Tutti per Tutti alimentari in Praiano, walk west up Via Umberto I to a T-junction, turn right for about 35m and then take another sharp turn to the right. From the end of the road continue through the tunnel to the piazza by the imposing church of San Luca. Go between the church and bell tower, and head left up Via Lama to another T-junction. From there head right, through an archway and take the steps on the left up to the road. Then, it's left again for about 50m to steps (with a railing) which rise steeply; after climbing the

steps bear left behind a house, along a narrow path to a clearing with good views. Turn right here along the good path, with steep cliffs on the right, and continue up to **Colle la Serra**.

Follow the path leading north, passing a ruin on the left. There are good views of the intensively terraced slopes of Vallone di Praia below. The path follows the contours of the spectacular valley; below sheer limestone crags, through luxuriant woodlands, past disused terraces and on to Grotta Biscotta – a huge overhang sheltering disused cliff houses. Continue to a bitumen road and follow it for about 500m to the rough concrete steps on the right, almost opposite a two storey white house. Take the steps down to a rough track; cross the bridge and turn left up the path which leads into the piazza in **Bomerano** (about two hours from Praiano).

From the piazza, go along the road to the right, as you face the church, as far as Via Iovieno. Turn left and follow that road to the next left turn, where there is a stone wall on the corner. Take the left turn then go straight through an intersection, continuing along the road and round a bend for about 200m. From here head up the steps between the terraces on the right. Cross the road and climb up some more, rougher steps with woodland on the right, until you meet the road then bear left. Further on, at a left bend in the road, take a short cut by following rough steps up to the saddle, then drop back down to the road. The views along the peninsula here are stunning. From the end of the road a rough track continues for a few hundred metres until the start of a path (marked) which leads straight on for a short distance before swinging sharply right. From here it's an uphill climb to **Capo Muro** (about two hours from Bomerano). The view from Capo Muro includes Monte dell' Avvocata to the east.

About 500m beyond Capo Muro, there is a stretch which demands considerable vigilance in following the markers through the maze of mule tracks in dense thickets on the steep mountainside. The route is well marked as it descends for about 500m, but always keep the red and white/red markers in your line of sight and don't move on until

Chestnut Poles & Mules

All the walks in this chapter pass citrus or olive groves, with their elaborate arrangements of timber poles, sometimes held together only by good luck or divine intervention. These are used partly to support the trees and partly to hold up netting which protects them from predators.

The timber used for these poles is usually sweet chestnut, occasionally alder, both of which are harvested locally. The tall spindly trees, which seem to thrive in the thin soils of the steep hillsides, are coppiced (cut so that they will regrow many times over) in careful rotation, as the patchwork of open and wooded ground, visible in many places throughout the peninsula, testifies.

Chainsaws are used to fell the trees which are then stripped of their bark and branches on site before being skilfully loaded, about seven at a time, into specially designed wooden and leather harnesses on the backs of strong, patient mules. A quiet command sends the mule off along a well-worn path crossing the hillside to wherever the poles, between 2m and 3m long, are being stacked. The mule carefully judges its pace to ease the load up and over small bumps and to keep control over the downhill side. Once the poles have been unloaded, the mule returns to repeat the journey. A team of mules works at the site, so each animal is regularly rested during the day. In the evening you may hear the jingling of the bells on their harnesses as they are brought back down to a nearby village or farm for the night.

It seems that vehicles are only used to transport workers to and from the site and to bring the poles down from where they have been stacked.

Sandra Bardwell

you have the next one in view. About 45 minutes from the viewpoint you reach a distinct path entering **Vallone Porto**. The path winds around several small, dry canyons (tributaries of the main valley), in and out of tall woodlands and past soaring crags and isolated rock pinnacles. The drop to the left is very steep, but is well screened from the edge of the narrow path by dense bushes. Just under two hours from Capo Muro, you reach Caserma Forestale (Forestry Barracks), a substantial stone building.

From a position facing south, go down the path to the left of the caserma descending all the way to the road before turning right into **Montepertuso**. Follow the road around past a soccer pitch, around a slight corner and past a small piazza on the right. Continue down through a right-hand bend until you reach a shrine. Opposite the shrine take the steps to the left, and wind down – and down – to the outskirts of **Positano**. At the T-junction, bear left for about 100m to a footbridge and cross it to the steps which descend to a pedestrian crossing on the main road. To reach the Sponda bus stop, for services along the coast, it is safest to walk along the road to the left for 20m and go down the steps to Via Cristoforo Colombo – the bus stop is up to the left where the via meets the main road.

Sentiero degli Dei

Duration 5 to 5½ hours
Ascent 770m
Standard Medium
Start Positano
Finish Praiano
Closest Towns Sorrento, Salerno
Permits Required No
Public Transport Access Yes
Summary The classic walk on the peninsula: fine paths clinging to near vertical mountainsides with wide panoramic views and beautiful stands of Italian cypresses.

The route described includes the Sentiero degli Dei (Path of the Gods), probably the best known walk on the peninsula. It can be modified either to be shorter or spread over two separate days, by making use of the local bus service between Positano and Montepertuso (see Getting To/From the Walks earlier in this section).

The generally excellent paths are extremely narrow and slightly exposed in some places, so you must take care if you don't have a good head for heights. Refreshments are available in Montepertuso and at the *Trattoria Santa Croce* in Nocelle (for which reservations for lunch and dinner in summer are essential (☎ (089) 87 53 19). Nocelle is a bit less than 1km from the end of the road near Montepertuso and is accessible only by foot on a well-made path. Carry enough water for the duration of the walk which can be done in either direction, depending on personal convenience. If you arrive at Positano by bus, alight at the Bar Internazionale stop above the western side of the town.

THE WALK
From the Bar Internazionale on the western side of Positano, go up Via Chiesa Nuova towards the church. Walk around the right-hand side of the church into a small piazza before continuing along the lane and up the steps to a road. Cross over the road and climb the steps just to the left; faint red and white markers indicate the route. As you gain height there are good views of the hole in the cliff which gives Montepertuso its name. After about 45 minutes, where a path marked Montepertuso goes straight ahead, take a sharp left turn and continue ever upwards, passing a minor path to the left. The beautifully built path ends at the foot of cliffs then crosses more open ground. Near the top of the plateau, in grassland and about 40m before a small promontory (from where there is an excellent view of Positano), look for markers on the rocks to the left. Follow the markers up through rocky ground and grassland onto a minor road where signs point left to Positano and Monte Commune. Continue more or less straight ahead then turn right at the crossroads to the large church on the edge of the hamlet of Santa Maria del Castello.

From there, walk north down the road, past a Circumvesuvio bus stop. After about 10 minutes you come to a concrete road on the right, with a clutch of signs to various destinations including Sentiero degli Dei (which is beyond Nocelle). Walk down the concrete road and onto a slightly overgrown path beside terraces, which shortly becomes much clearer and leads into groves of superb Italian cypresses. This truly spectacular path winds around the precipitous hillside, often on narrow ledges with a stunning array of wild

flowers, and on to Caserma Forestale (about 1¼ hours from Santa Maria del Castello).

Facing seawards, continue down the path to the left of the caserma, which winds through cypress woodlands, making generous use of steps, and onto the road near Montepertuso. Bear left at this road and walk uphill, away from Montepertuso. About 50m beyond a bridge, head to the right, down to a path where there is a sign to Nocelle. Clearly the people of Nocelle will have to wait for the final section of road to be completed which will link them with the rest of the world.

The path winds around the precipitous, well-wooded mountainside, and passes the aerial cableways used to bring supplies up to the village. Turn left along a laneway and emerge at an intersection with a shrine on the left. From here climb the steps to the left (marked as route No 27), then take the first right through the village. Just past the remains of a lime kiln, ignore the path to the left and keep heading straight on. The Sentiero degli Dei stretches ahead, in places defying normal expectations of where a path can go, across the near-vertical mountainside and beneath towering cliffs. It passes beneath a group of stone huts or shelters built into the base of the cliffs, then past terraces still in use – follow the slightly obscure markers carefully here. Climb up to a clear path which leads up to the left, via steps, to Colle la Serra.

From the Colle, descend between the terraces for 100m and bear left at the T-junction. Continue down to a three-way junction and go straight ahead, down the steps guided by red markers. Bear right down more steps, by a tall transmission pole, through a high narrow archway to a road; cross the road and descend the steps to the right winding down to an alley, making right-left and left-right turns en route. Turn left into the alley, then head down Via Lama, followed by another left (downhill) at a T-junction and downhill. Then bear right to descend to the road, Via Umberto I, in Praiano. The alimentari is along to the left. To reach the camp site from here, continue round the bend and head left down Via San Giovanni; descend the steps to a T-junction, bear left and when you are almost at the end of the lane, turn right and keep going until you reach steps on the right, opposite a shrine. These steps finally lead down to the main road and emerge almost directly opposite Continentale pensione.

Other Walks along the Amalfi Coast

SAN NICOLA
This 17th-century convent overlooking Minori provides a worthwhile objective for a moderate walk from Minori, entailing a 500m ascent and taking about five hours to complete the round-trip. The views are splendid and Santuario dell'Avvocata is clearly visible from the convent.

From the eastern end of Minori's promenade, walk under the tower of the basilica. After passing a modern school on the right, follow the signposted Passegiata Panoramica up to a junction. Turn right towards S Nicola and head up to the church of S Michele in the hamlet of Torre. Pass to the left of the church and veer left up the steps to a junction by some railings. Tall power poles mark the next turn left, inevitably up steps. Eventually the steps reach a spur; and further on, at a path junction, follow the sign to S Nicola. To vary the return, walk back to the path junction and go half right. Three hundred metres further on, at a ruined house, turn left and head down to cross two streams, before climbing up some steps to a road. Head left to a bus stop (about 400m), and after 25m bear left again down a concrete drive (Via Riola). From here follow a path to steps which in turn lead to another, rough path; cross a stream and continue down to a road which leads to the centre of Minori.

SAN DOMENICO
From the small town of Vettica Maggiore, a couple of kilometres west of Praiano, there is a scenic half-day walk (two to 2½ hours return; 250m ascent) to San Domenico monastery, perched on the steep mountainside

north-west of the town. From Piazza Gagliano on the main road, climb steps (Via Russo). After about 40m, turn left into an alley and go up to another T-junction where you turn left again up more steps, then head along Via Croce. At the last house is the first of the 14 stations of the Cross leading, along a well-used path, to the monastery. About 100m beyond the house, follow the steps up to the right; the route from there is straightforward, passing by the stations, old terraces, caves and limestone crags. At the monastery the best view is from the piazza opposite the main door on the western side.

VALLONE DI PRAIA
This deep, steep valley just north-east of Praiano shelters perhaps the best concentration of terracing in the area. It is readily accessible from Praiano, and the route leads on from the Vallone to the small town of Bomerano. Allow about three hours (about 640m climbing). The route, which initially is the same as that to Colle la Serra (see Sentiero degli Dei walk earlier in this chapter), is described in Julian Tippett's book *Landscapes of Sorrento and the Amalfi Coast* (see Book in the Information section earlier in this chapter).

From there you could return to Praiano via Grotta Biscotta and Colle la Serra (see Capo Muro walk earlier in this section), which would make for a fairly full day's walk. Alternatively, to make the walk shorter you could use the bus service between Bomerano and Amalfi.

ATRANI TO MAIORI
This walk via Torello and Minori takes no more than three hours direct (involving a 370m ascent), but could be spread over a day for a pleasantly easy walk, by spending time exploring the towns and villages en route. The somewhat complicated but very enjoyable route, through citrus groves, hamlets and villages, is adequately described in Julian Tippett's book *Landscapes of Sorrento and the Amalfi Coast* .

ATRANI OR AMALFI TO RAVELLO
A network of old stone steps leads up from the seaside town of Atrani to the fine mountain-

STEFANO CAVEDONI

DOTT. SANDRO PRIVITERA

DOTT. SANDRO PRIVITERA

STEFANO CAVEDONI

STEFANO CAVEDONI

Sulphur-encrusted rocks on the lip of the Cratere della Fossa, Vulcano (top left). Dramatic evidence of the 1983 eruption on Etna's southern slopes (top right), and the view from the Cratere Centrale towards Bocca Nuova (middle). On Stromboli, looking south to I Vancori from the Pizzo (bottom left), and morning sun striking campers at Le Croci (bottom right).

SANDRA BARDWELL

SANDRA BARDWELL

SANDRA BARDWELL

Top: Santuario dell'Avvocata, a former monastery high above the Amalfi Coast near Maiori
Middle: Looking westwards across the Sorrento Peninsula to Isola di Capri, with picturesque
　　　Positano far below to the left
Bottom: Baia di Ieranto and Punta Penna from near Punta Campanella, Sorrento Peninsula

top village of Ravello. The difference in altitude is about 360m and you'll need to allow about 1½ hours to make the climb past villas, vegetable gardens, olive groves and vineyards. Ravello's attractions, including a handsome Romanesque cathedral and the gardens of the Villas Rufolo and Cimbrone make it well worth the effort. The trail begins in Piazza Umberto in Atrani. Allow three to four hours for the round trip, including the time needed to visit Ravello and to drink coffee in one of the cafes in the main piazza. For the return, retrace your steps or you can catch a bus down to Atrani from the piazza just through the tunnel to the right as you face the cathedral. The trail is clearly described in Julian Tippett's book *Landscapes of Sorrento and the Amalfi Coast.*

ALTA VIA DEI MONTI LATTARI

This is an eight-day walk devised, mapped and marked (as route 00) by the CAI. It starts at Corpo di Cava (about 5km north-east of Maiori) and generally follows the watershed of the Monti Lattari range to Punta Camanella, the westernmost point on the peninsula, finishing at the small town of Termini. Experience suggests that the marking is anything but consistent and easy to follow. In theory this would be a magnificent walk, were it not for the considerable problems encountered finding reliable accommodation. Wild camping is not practical due to the shortage of surface water and scarcity of suitable pitches. However, if you have plenty of time to spare, it could well be worth some serious investigation.

SORRENTO PENINSULA

The relatively gentle contours of the populous Sorrento Peninsula contrast strikingly with the rugged mountainous country along the Amalfi Coast. Yet there is a surprisingly wide variety of walks on the peninsula, linking wild, beautiful coastline and the rural hinterland of terraces and olive groves. An excellent network of bus services makes the planning of walks, from any one of several bases, easy; Marina del Cantone has been chosen as a base for this section for its proximity to the western end of the peninsula and its relative peace and quiet.

HISTORY

Greek civilisation left enduring marks on the Sorrento Peninsula in the form of place names, the remains of temples and in myths and legends. Thanks to its favoured location on the southern shore of the Golfo di Napoli, the peninsula flourished during the Roman empire. The trade route between the Golfos di Napoli and Salerno crossed the peninsula via Sant' Agata, a network of roads was built in the area and Sorrento became a favoured retreat of emperors and the wealthy.

Sorrento and Massa Lubrense were sacked in the 16th century; some of the torri that were built in the aftermath can still be seen around the coast (see Coastal Torre boxed text earlier in this chapter). The area was popular with Europe's leisured classes during the 18th century and Sant'Agata became a stop on the Grand Tour; English writer Norman Douglas stayed at Villa Rosa near Marina del Cantone and wrote glowingly of Baia di Ieranto in *Land of the Sirens*.

NATURAL HISTORY

The cultivation of citrus and olive groves, grapevines, fruit and vegetables, and the fishing industry have long been mainstays of the local economy, but are now considerably supplemented or replaced by tourism. Sorrento in particular is a very popular destination for package tours from Britain.

A line of cliffs extending south-east from Punta Gradelle on the Golfo di Napoli to near Punta Germano in the south, forms a clear dividing line between the gentle hills of the peninsula and the mountains above the Amalfi Coast. The highest point on the gently undulating ridge extending southwest from the cliffs to Punta Campanella, the western tip of the peninsula, is at Monte Tore (528m), near Sant' Agata. Surface water is sparse, though stream courses cut deep into the limestone rocks.

AMALFI COAST

On the intensively cultivated peninsula, only pockets of the once widespread oak and chestnut woodlands survive. In uncultivated areas an association of small evergreen trees and shrubs known as *macchia* or *maquis* thrives, well adapted to poor, rocky soil and the long summer drought. Abandoned ground, formerly under cultivation, eventually reverts to a type of vegetation known as garrigue, typified by many colourful dwarf shrubs. A special reserve set up by the Worldwide Fund for Nature (WWF) near Monte Tore serves to protect and draw attention to the native vegetation of the peninsula.

INFORMATION

Massa Lubrense Comune's tourist office (☎ (081) 808 95 71), Viale Filangiori 11, 80061, publishes a general guide to the area; an accommodation list for the town and environs, including Sant' Agata and Marina del Cantone. For facilities in Sorrento see earlier in this chapter.

To find out more about the Riserva Naturale di Ieranto (see the Punta Penna walk later in this section) contact the Delegazione Fondo Ambiente Italiano (☎ (081) 76 17 32), Via Caracciolo 13, Napoli.

PLANNING
When to Walk

The best times to visit the western end of the peninsula are during late autumn, winter and early spring when the wild flowers are in bloom. Although this is the 'rainy' season (see Climate section earlier in this chapter), wet days are not too frequent. From mid-May to early September the usual daily maximum temperatures, frequently in the high 20s, are less than ideal for walking. Rainfall is minimal so the grasslands on the open hillsides are bare and parched and far less attractive than at other times. The dense crowds frequenting the beaches make getting about an endurance test and accommodation is difficult to find without booking well in advance.

Maps & Book

A Passeggio con le Sirene: 13 Itinerari turistici pedonali da Sant' Agata per Sorrento,

Termini e Massa by Associazione Culturale Il Vadabillo, is a map at 1:15,000 with 50m contour intervals. It has accompanying notes, in English, French and German, on the walks and historical and other features, as well as a list of facilities and attractions and a map of Sant'Agata. Priced at L5000, it is available from La Capsa bookshop, Sorrento (see Maps section earlier in this chapter). It is very useful for routes through towns and villages, but not much help where the route in question does not follow a proper path.

Massa Lubrense, Sorrento, Sant'Agata by EIDOS, 1:10,000 with 25m contours, is a map of the roads and footpaths in this area with descriptions in English of eight itineraries and the main places of interest. It's priced at L5,000 and is also available from La Capsa. There are few true footpaths in this area, but there is plenty of scope for relatively gentle walks. This map seems to be reliable though it was not extensively tested. *Penisola Sorrentina* (1:50,000, 100m contours, Kompass map No 682) costs L9500 and is helpful for planning purposes only.

The CAI's *Monti Lattari* (1:30,000, 25m contours) map costs L15,000 and is a useful companion to the two local maps listed above.

Julian Tippett's *Landscapes of Sorrento and the Amalfi Coast* describes nearly 20, mostly short walks in the area. Both Kompass and Tippett use the spelling Marine di Cantone; the local maps use Marina del Cantone, the spelling adopted here.

What to Bring

No special equipment is needed for any of the walks described here – see under What to Bring earlier in this chapter for general advice. If you are planning to camp, come with your own supply of gas as it is not readily obtainable, although Articolo Sportivi, a small shop in the main piazza at Massa Lubrense, may be able to help.

PLACES TO STAY & EAT

Villaggio Turistico Nettuno (☎ (081) 808 10 51; fax 808 17 06), Via A Vespucci 39, Marina del Cantone, 80061 Massalubrense, has shady, if rather hard, level camp sites, most with a sea view, which are separated by trees or stands of bamboo. Prices per person are L12,000 during low season and L24,000 in high season. There is an adequately stocked shop, a bar (which can be noisy if bus loads of tourists are being entertained) and a *ristorante* on site. Take-away meals are generous and good quality, and include pizza for L5500 and under, pasta from L4000 to L9500, fish at L12,000 or less, and even chips at L2500. The facilities are more than adequate. Cabins with two to five beds can be hired by the week, starting from L400,000 for the smallest in low season, to L1,000,000 for the largest in high season. The bus stop for the camp site is in the piazza near the beach, 200m down the road from the villagio entrance. The beachfront hotels and pensioni in Marina del Cantone certainly have uninterrupted sea views, but are quite expensive: doubles with private facilities start at about L80,000.

GETTING TO/FROM THE WALKS

SITA buses provide frequent and cheap links between Sorrento and the towns and villages on the peninsula. As elsewhere, tickets must be purchased before boarding the bus, either at a SITA office, or at bars or tabacchi displaying a SITA sign near the local bus stop. Tickets must then be validated in the machine on board. Remember to buy some in advance, especially for the day's return journey, as shops generally close from early to late afternoon. Bus stops are distinguished by a blue and white 'Fermata Sita' sign. A timetable is available from the AAST office in Sorrento (see Information Sources earlier in this chapter). Buses depart from outside Sorrento's Ciroumvesuviana station. Tickets are sold at the bar at the station; in Marina they are available at the tabacchi near the bus terminus.

There are plenty of buses between Sorrento and Sant' Agata, and Sorrento and Nerano; there is an extension of the latter route down to Marina del Cantone but it is less frequent. The fare for the Sorrento-Marina journey is L2000. Sorrento and Amalfi are also linked by a service via Meta, Positano and Praiano; the fare from Sorrento to Praiano is L2800.

Punta Penna

Duration 4½ to 5 hours
Ascent 150m
Standard Easy
Start/Finish Marina del Cantone
Closest Towns Sorrento, Salerno
Permits Required No
Public Transport Access Yes
Summary An easy and scenic walk, mostly along good paths, past the Grotta delle Noglie, to a secluded bay.

The Punta Penna walk is an excellent introduction to the area. It follows a there-and-back route, with the optional extra of a rougher tramp right up to the heights of Punta Penna. Make sure you carry drinking water for this walk, which could be shortened by about half an hour by catching the public bus up to Nerano from Marina del Cantone.

THE WALK

The path up to Nerano starts from the north-western corner of the large car park on the beachfront in Marina, and has red and white markers indicating the route which mostly passes between houses and their gardens. Keep heading straight along Via Cantone, past the first and second road crossings. Further on, a high-walled alley leads around and up to the road in Nerano, emerging by the large church of San Salvatore. Continue left (south) along the road for about 50m then bear right along Via Ieranto, still following the red and white markers. The wooded slopes of Monte San Costanzo rise steeply on the west as views of Nerano and the coastline, against the backdrop of the distinctive Sant' Angelo a Tre Pizzi of the Monti Lattari range, open up to the east. The wide path leads through an archway and shortly passes a flower-decked shrine at the entrance of the small Grotta delle Noglie (Cave of the Cats), where skinny, long-legged cats are regularly fed by local people.

Soon you are out in open grassland and

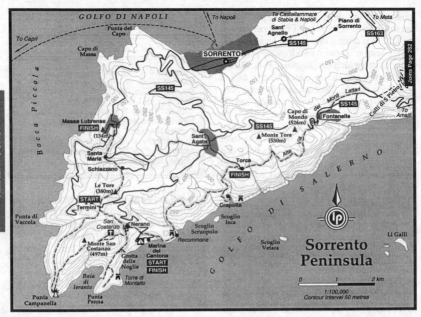

scattered terraces; Capri, with its 'teeth', floats on the horizon ahead, across the Bocca Piccola. Downhill, past a house and garden on the left, is a junction; to continue towards Punta Penna, bear left down the rocky path to a gate where there is a sign marking the boundary of the Riserva Naturale di Ieranto. This reserve is the responsibility of the Fondo Ambiente Italiano, and is set aside to protect the rare plant species of the fragile coastal ecosystem. About 12m before the gate, there is a path, between fences, leading to the left (east) following an old stone wall. From the corner of the wall, a line of markers leads to Torre di Montalto; its crumbling interior is virtually inaccessible and the walls look very unstable, but there is a good view from there. Return to the wall corner and head south up the slope for no more than 30m to a blue and green marker (these are now more or less in line of sight), head right for about 25m and left again, angling up to olive and fig groves. Aim for a shack below on the right

(west) and continue to the north-east side of the saddle between the two bumps which give the headland its distinctive profile.

The high point above Punta Penna is a tempting climb, the only price for yielding being socks full of sticky burrs. There is no clear path, but it is not difficult to climb the seaward side of the bushy, grassy slope, keeping well away from the sheer drop to the turquoise waters below. The reward is a fantastic view of **Baia di Ieranto** and Capri, a magnetic attraction for a constant procession of vessels, from small yachts to luxury liners. It's easy to retrace your steps back up to the path junction near the house and garden, either to return to Marina or for a side trip to the beach.

The beach at Baia di Ieranto (signposted 'Spiaggia', which is Italian for beach) is well worth the extra half hour or so detour from here. Go straight ahead from the corner of the wall around the house, take the rocky path followed by a long flight of rough steps down to a T-junction. The path to the left leads to a gate and fence where there are FAI signs and, beyond, some fortress-like buildings. Take the right turn to reach the tiny shingle and sand beach, and a slightly ramshackle timber beach house. Retrace your steps back to Nerano for the bus or make the last 15 minute walk down to Marina, via the path near the large church.

Punta Campanella

Duration 5 to 5½ hours
Ascent 500m
Standard Medium
Start/Finish Marina del Cantone
Closest Towns Sorrento, Salerno
Permits Required No
Public Transport Access Yes
Summary Panoramic views from the south-western extremity of the Sorrento Peninsula, and from Monte San Costanzo, perched high above Marina del Cantone.

The Punta Campanella walk could well be a fitting conclusion to your visit to the Sorrento Peninsula; the views of the Monti Lattari range and Capri are inspirational. Carry enough water for the duration of the walk. Refreshments are available in Termini. You could take advantage of local buses to shorten the walk by two hours and only 200m ascent, by starting from Termini.

THE WALK
Walk up to Nerano as described for the Punta Penna walk earlier in this section. From the church of S Salvatore continue to Termini by crossing the road and climbing the steps of Via Fontana Nerano, beside a superalimentari. Blue and green markers guide the way, between houses and through the welcome shade of olive and fig groves. Bear left at a fork, and follow the narrower concrete-paved road to Piazza San Croce in Termini (there is a *gelateria* nearby). Walk up Via Campanella to the left (south) for about 200m, then turn right downhill into a narrow lane, indicated

by blue and green markers and a sign to Punta Campanella. At the first sharp right-hand bend, follow another sign to the Punta and continue past the turn-off to Mitigliano. The islands of Capri and Ischia are now in view through the olive groves to the west. Several hundred metres further on, beyond a wayside shrine, the minor road becomes a broad path, leading across a sparsely vegetated, rocky hillside, with the aquamarine waters of the narrow inlet of Fossa di Papa below. Punta Campanella is a suitably spectacular terminus to the peninsula, with magnificent views of Capri to the west and the Baia di Ieranto and the mountains beyond to the east. The modern lighthouse stands close to the ruins of the legendary temple of Minerva; there are also scant remains of a Roman villa here which are difficult to identify.

From the lighthouse walk about 400m back along the track to a broad path on the right, where there is a red and white marker. Follow this path up and across the steep hillside to the crest of the ridge.

The popularity of the Baia di Ieranto is clear to see – at least 20 vessels were anchored here one afternoon in late May, well before the onset of the busy season. There are markers along the narrow path which climbs, steeply at first, along the ridge crest through scratchy vegetation.

Approaching the summit, the path leads through an area which, judging by the pattern of dry stone walls and curious stone cells (at least one of which is still roofed with huge flat stones), must have once been cultivated. Although the summit of **Monte San Costanzo** is monopolised by a fenced off military installation, the outlook to Capri and across the Golfo di Napoli is virtually unspoiled. Keep to the south-eastern side of the compound and shortly a splendid new vista opens up: the rugged peaks of the Monti Lattari range towering above the gentler slopes of the Sorrento Peninsula. Follow the path down to the road and turn right; just around the first bend, where there is an informal parking area on the right, turn off along the path leading north-east through the trees. Blue and green markers show the way to the steps up to a prominent, plain white building – the church of San Costanzo – the site of yet another superb viewpoint.

Return down the steps to the path junction, among the pine trees on the south-western side of a saddle and follow the red and white markers leading down to the left across the grassy hillside, past ruinous small terraces. Approaching some cultivated olive groves, the markers all but disappear, but the path remains clear enough. Keep just below the eastern side of the groves, and then swing round to the north, past a small ravine on the right. A steep descent through trees brings you to the Punta Penna path; bear left and continue into Nerano from where you can head back to Marina by bus or on foot (see the Punta Penna walk earlier in this section for details).

Other Walks on the Sorrento Peninsula

Paths and minor roads between the small towns and villages south of Massa Lubrense and Sant' Agata provide several other easy to moderate walks through intensively cultivated, terraced farmland, woods and open coastal hillside. With careful map reading, diligent observation of markers and a certain amount of intuition, the routes shown on the local maps can be followed with cautious confidence.

TERMINI TO MASSA LUBRENSE
This walk, via Schiazzano and Santa Maria, takes about an hour and is actually downhill (200m descent). The views of Capri are exceptional. To get to Termini from Marina, follow the route described in the Punta Campanella walk earlier in this section. From the piazza in Termini, walk along Via delle Tore. Bear right up the steps just past Caseria Sorrentina; blue-yellow and green-yellow markers appear along the way. Continue over the open hill of Le Tore and down to a road. Go right for 100m, then head left down to Schiazzano. From the church in

Schiazzano, go left down Via S Maria and on to Santa Maria. From Santa Maria, bear right down a cobbled street in front of the church, around a bend and down some wide steps, continue left along Santaniello Vecchio (now with red and yellow markers) through olive groves and past scattered houses. Keep going straight ahead at the junction, continuing down between the houses. Keep going straight ahead, through the next junction, until you reach a fork (about 30m). Turn left at this fork, then left again, before turning right into Massa.

ALTA VIA DEI MONTI LATTARI
The early stages of the CAI's Alta Via dei Monti Lattari (marked as route 00) pass through the wildest, most remote part of the Sorrento Peninsula. The paths are obscure in places but the coastal views are outstanding. Crapolla, a very old fishing village in an improbable location at the foot of vertical cliffs, is only about half a kilometre from the Via. A fairly strenuous walk from Marina to Crapolla and on to the village of Torca would take about three hours with a 500m ascent. It's possible to return by bus from Torca to Sant' Agata where you can connect with buses to Massa and Marina. Carry water with you.

From the eastern end of the beach in Marina, walk around the headland to the sheltered inlet at Recommone. Continue along the narrow road until you reach the end of the stone wall with the narrow path opposite. This steep, somewhat overgown, but adequately marked path diverges to the right, through the trees, and leads up to a rough track. Turn left and go uphill for no more than 50m, then turn right. Beyond a scrubby gully, the path levels out and leads through open grassland, across three more shallow valleys, around the edge of an olive grove, and east to a concrete track. Follow the track to the right (the markers here are sparse) until it ends. From here there is a faint path leading ahead into tall grass, which then heads down past olive groves. The next turn is from the corner of a grove, where you should turn right into more tall grass. Continue through here for about 60m, then turn left through

AMALFI COAST

Crapolla, an Ancient Settlement

The siting of houses, even of whole towns or villages, throughout the Amalfi Coast-Sorrento Peninsula, often seems to have been achieved despite the daunting difficulties involving access and safety – houses on vertiginous hillsides and coastal torri on the edge of vertical cliffs.

Nowhere does improbability seem to have been as boldly defied as at Crapolla, a tiny inlet on the south coast, below the village of Torca.

The entrance to the inlet is barely 30m wide between vertical cliffs, and the shingle beach is no more spacious; even in the calmest weather the sea surges in vigorously.

It is thought that the name Crapolla may derive from the Greek *Akron Apollinis*, suggesting that it was the site of a Greek temple. A Roman road may have been built leading down to the inlet from Torca, and there are certainly some ruins of Roman origin there. It is one of the relatively few moorings on the south coast of this peninsula and was considered to be safe from attack.

The origins of the inlet's use for fishing seem to be unknown. The extraordinary collection of stone buildings, fitted into hollows and crevices and beneath overhangs at the base of the cliffs, seems to be very old. Some were, and still are, used for storage of gear and fish, others for shelter. A plaque on one wall indicates that they were restored in 1968.

An excellent stone path and flights of steps now lead down to the inlet. On a shelf above the last flight of steps down to the beach are the scant remains of an old abbey dedicated to St Peter, where a small chapel now stands. The chapel was apparently built by the people of Torca in 1949. The remains of a 16th-century torre stand just to the east of the mouth of the inlet.

Sandra Bardwell

grass and broom towards a flight of steps. Crapolla is down the steps to the right.

To continue to Torca from the inlet, go back up the steps. Head along the path up the wooded valley, across a stream, and bear left. Shortly, just before a second stream, go right along a narrow path which continues up some steps. At a fork, go more or less straight ahead, past terraces and between houses. Turn right beyond an archway, up to a T-junction, right again, and on to Piazza S Tommaso Apostolo in Torca.

That Way
This Way

Toscana

It can be rightly claimed that Toscana (Tuscany) has the best of everything – art, architecture, some of Italy's finest fresh produce and best known wines, and beautiful countryside which has captivated artists and tourists alike for centuries.

It was in Toscana, about 600 years ago, that the Renaissance was born – a period of unparalleled creativity and visionary accomplishments, which has had long-lasting effects on European culture. The works of Michelangelo, Donatello and other Toscan masters of the 15th and 16th centuries continue to influence artists worldwide. Toscan architects – notably Brunelleschi, responsible for the magnificent dome of Firenze's (Florence's) cathedral, and Leon Battista Alberti, largely responsible for designing the façade of the Chiesa di Santa Maria Novella – have influenced architects through the centuries.

Most travellers are drawn to Toscana by the artistic splendour of Firenze and Siena, or to see the Leaning Tower of Pisa. Others come to sample the wines of Chianti, while perhaps spending a few weeks in a country villa. You can certainly programme a few wine-tastings and a villa into your amblings through the Chianti hills while following the trails of the Chianti Classico walk.

The region also has some of Italy's most impressive medieval hill towns, including San Gimignano, Volterra and Certaldo, which are featured in the Medieval Hills walk.

If you prefer more challenging mountain walks, but at lower altitudes than in the Alps proper, you'll want to head for the Alpi Apuane, bordered on one side by the Toscan coastline and on the other by the vast valley of the Garfagnana. The Alpi Apuane have been mined for their precious marbles since Roman times and nearby is Carrara, where Michelangelo selected white marbles, known for their unrivalled texture and purity. A regional park regulates land use here to some extent, but the landscape in some parts of the mountains has been utterly destroyed by

HIGHLIGHTS

NICK TAPP

- Exploring the medieval hill towns of San Gimignano, Volterra and Certaldo
- Strolling through Chianti and admiring the charm, grace and soothing peaceful atmosphere
- Grand panoramas from the summit of Pania della Croce
- Superb mountain and coastal views on the Pizzo d'Uccello walk

mining. As in many other parts of Italy, the extent of the interference in the natural landscape has created a new environment with a certain aesthetic appeal. The walks in this chapter go to both spoiled and unspoiled parts of the Alpi Apuane, and readers may judge for themselves which they prefer.

Travelling in Toscana is easy and all the walks detailed in this chapter are easily accessible by public transport. It pays to remember, however, that the region's popularity with tourists can make accommodation hard to find in peak periods (particularly during summer). It is best to book in advance, especially if you plan to tackle the Chianti Classico trek.

CHIANTI

A gentle and docile land where nature has been graciously domesticated, Chianti is nonetheless a place of intense atmosphere. Its panoramas are like patchwork quilts of vineyards, fallow fields and olive groves, interwoven with stands of cypresses and pines and dotted with medieval castles and villages, Romanesque churches and monasteries.

Chianti is that bit of countryside between Firenze and Siena, renowned the world over for its excellent wine and olive oil, where an ever increasing number of tourists come each year in search of a peaceful holiday in a villa, an elegant farmhouse, a quaint village, or even in a winery. Although prices tend to be high, the area does offer an unusually high concentration of art and history, as well as plenty of opportunities for romantic walks.

In this section, we describe two easy walks of three days each, which are suitable for the whole family. The first walk is through the countryside of Chianti Classico and the second connects the towns of Certaldo, San Gimignano and Volterra. The charm of the landscape and the lodgings along the way, in

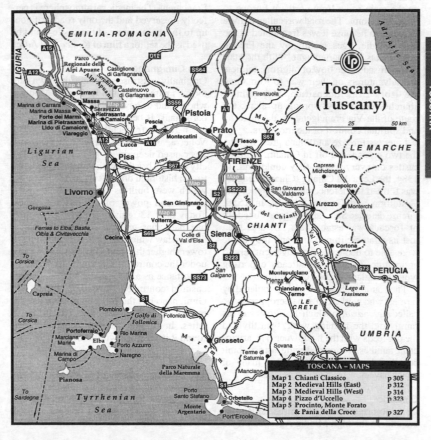

TOSCANA

TOSCANA – MAPS	
Map 1 Chianti Classico	p 305
Map 2 Medieval Hills (East)	p 312
Map 3 Medieval Hills (West)	p 314
Map 4 Pizzo d'Uccello	p 323
Map 5 Procinto, Monte Forato & Pania della Croce	p 327

hotels or *agriturismo* (farm) establishments, make them long, relaxing rambles, enriched by the beauty of ancient *borghi*, churches and medieval castles, and the possibility to try excellent food and wine along the way. The walks could also be adapted for cyclists, since they are mainly on dirt roads.

HISTORY

Etruscan civilisation blossomed in these valleys from the eighth century BC until it was absorbed by the expansion of Roma (Rome). The Etruscan museums in Volterra and San Gimignano have interesting collections. In medieval times, the Chianti area was on the main route from northern Europe to Siena and Roma. The road was called the Via Francigena because it was frequented in the high Middle Ages mainly by the French compatriots of Charlemagne. With the start of the crusades, the flow of pilgrims, soldiers and adventurers on their way to Roma and the Holy Land intensified, and country churches and abbeys sprung up along the route of the Via Francigena for the material and spiritual comfort of the travellers.

Later, as Firenze and Siena grew in size, the two cities faced off in Chianti, building castles on every hilltop they could find. In 1384, the Lega del Chianti (Chianti League) was formed for defence purposes by Radda, Castellina and Gaiole. Finally, in 1550, Firenze defeated Siena and the great dukedom of Toscana was established. The area then lost its strategic importance and the people were able to dedicate themselves entirely to agriculture. Chianti was already exporting wine to England in the 16th century.

The countryside was densely populated by farmers who worked on a sharecropper basis, called *mezzadria*, in which the farmer and his family did the farming work, then divided the proceeds with the landowner. The aristocratic families, who owned entire districts, built countless luxurious country villas, many of which have now been reborn as wineries.

Certaldo

Certaldo originated in the Etruscan/Roman era and, in the high Middle Ages, belonged to the Conti Alberti (counts of the Alberti family), who built their palace/castle in the town in the 12th century. It later became known as Palazzo Pretorio when the fiefdom passed to the Republic of Firenze at the end of the 13th century. Preserved in Certaldo are the house and tomb of Giovanni Boccaccio (1313-75), the celebrated author of the *Decameron*, one of the first poetic works in vernacular Italian, as opposed to Latin, which until then had been the language of literature.

The historic section of town is surrounded by defence walls and sits high on a hill overlooking the Val d'Elsa and the Via Francigena. The medieval atmosphere is perfectly preserved and the only road that goes up to the main square of the castle could be used as the set for a film of *Romeo and Juliet*.

San Gimignano

Originally an Etruscan village, the town later took its name from the Bishop of Modena, who is said to have saved the city from the barbarians. It became a commune in 1199, but it fought frequently with neighbouring Volterra, and internal battles between families caused deep divisions in the town. The city literally bristled with towers in medieval times: historical documents record some 76, which were built as status symbols of the wealth and power of the city's families. Today only 13 remain. In the 13th century one particular *podestà* (town ruler) introduced a law which prohibited the building of towers higher than his (51m). The town came under the control of Firenze in 1353, but its importance as a stop on the Via Francigena ensured continued prosperity. Today San Gimignano has the feel of a museum and is one of Europe's best-preserved medieval cities. In summer and at weekends year-round it is crowded with tourists.

Volterra

The Etruscan settlement of Velathri was an important trading centre, a status that continued under the Romans, who renamed the city Volaterrae. A long period of conflict with Firenze starting in the 12th century ended when the Medicis took possession of the city in the 15th century. Perched on top of a huge plateau, the city looks almost forbidding because of its well-preserved medieval ramparts, which housed a national penitentiary for many years. The city has long had a strong alabaster industry.

NATURAL HISTORY

The Chianti ridge is a system of harmonious wooded hills broken up by an elegant patchwork of vineyards, olive groves and fields of corn and wheat. It lies between Firenze and Siena in the area made up of the Val d'Arno to the east and the Val d'Elsa and Valle di Pesa to the west. The highest area is the eastern crest known as Monti del Chianti (the highest point of which is Monte San Michele at 892m). The Chianti area slopes down to the west in a sequence of valleys mostly oriented from the north-west to the south-east (where the crests maintain a height of between 300m and 500m). To the west of the Val d'Elsa are the hilltops of the so-called *dorsale medio-toscana* with more extensive wooded areas and a microclimate that favours the cultivation of cereals.

Geology

Chianti is made up predominantly of sandstone or clay-type sedimentary rock, and of layers of sand and gravel. In fact, 200 million years ago the area was covered by a sea. Starting in the Miocene (20 million years ago) the pressure of the African plate on the Euroasiatic plate began to push up the land, forming hills where even today, in some areas, you can still find marine fossils. Where the sea was shallow, near present-day Volterra, the evaporating water left gypsum crystals, one variety of which is the alabaster now mined in the area, and another of which is rock salt which gives us our common salt. Erosion has created the forms we see today, distorted in some areas by landslides. Thermal baths rich in alkaline and bicarbonate salts are found in the area of Gambassi.

Flora

The woods are dominated by four species of oak tree, including the holm oak. There are also maples, chestnuts, hazelnuts, alders, stone pines, cluster pines and black pines. In the areas of Mediterranean scrub there are the typical gum tree, strawberry tree and myrtle associated with the holm oak. Elegant rows of cypresses, noble grape vines and olive trees complete the picture.

Fauna

The largest mammal in the wood is the *cinghiale*, or wild pig, stalked intensively by its only dangerous predator – the Toscan hunter – who is also fond of the resident pheasant, hare and wild rabbit, fox, badger, weasel, beech-marten, squirrel and the bizarre istrice (porcupine), a threatened species which was imported from Africa by the ancient Romans. Among the birds there are many migratory and a good number of stationary species such as the woodpidgeon, jay, blackbird, hoopoe, kestrel, buzzard, crow and tit. Among reptiles there is the lizard, ever-present in summer, and the innocuous water snake. In rocky areas you can run into poisonous vipers.

CLIMATE

The climate of Chianti and of the Val d'Elsa is mild and temperate. Summer is the least suitable for walking due to the sultry heat. In spring and autumn the climate is sunny and mild and the palettes of seasonal colours are wonderful. The average annual temperature is around 14°C to 15°C, with peaks of 35°C in summer and the rare sub-zero winter day. Snow and fog occur only in exceptional cases.

INFORMATION

Maps

A good map is the 1:70,000 scale *Il Chianti, cartoguida turistica*, published by SELCA for the Firenze APT (tourist office), and is enough for the easy navigation of the country roads and few trails of the Chianti Classico trek. It is distributed in the tourist offices of the towns in the Chianti area. The excellent Kompass maps No 660 *Firenze-Chianti* and No 661 *Siena-Chianti-Colline Senesi* at 1:50,000 scale, together cover the entire

TOSCANA

Chianti Classico trek. They are sold in book-shops and at newsstands (L8000).

Firenze Edi Libra publishes a good guide-book (L28,000) with a trail map at 1:50,000 scale for the area of Certaldo, San Gimignano and Volterra, ideal for the Medieval Hills trek. It is called *Dolce Campagna, Antiche Mura* and describes some lovely routes, as well as providing interesting information about the area. A less expensive edition is due to be published.

The IGM maps at 1:25,000 and 1:50,000 scale are difficult to find and are not really necessary for walking in Chianti.

Information Sources

Firenze The APT office (☎ (055) 29 08 32; fax 276 03 83) is just north of the *duomo* (cathedral) at Via Cavour 1r. The office opens Monday to Saturday from 8.15 am to 7.15 pm, and Sunday from 8.45 am to 1.45 pm, from April to October. At other times of the year, opening hours are a bit shorter. There are other information offices in Firenze, but this one should have everything you need.

Siena The APT office (☎ (0577) 28 05 51; fax 27 06 76), Piazza del Campo 56, is open Monday to Saturday from 8.30 am to 7.30 pm in summer, and from 8.30 am to 1 pm and 3.30 to 6.30 pm Monday to Friday (to noon on Saturday) for the rest of the year.

Greve in Chianti About 20km south of Firenze on the SS222 road, served by SITA buses, Greve is the first base for the Chianti Classico walk. There is an information office (☎ (055) 854 52 43), at Via Cini 1, about 500m east of Piazza Matteotti, the town's main square. It opens in summer from 10 am to 1 pm and 4 to 7 pm (shorter hours at other times of the year) and can provide maps and informative materials in English.

Castellina in Chianti This town is in the Sienese part of Chianti and is very touristy, with plenty of hotels and restaurants. Its Tourist Information Office (☎ (0577) 74 02 01) is at Piazza del Comune 1 in the town centre.

Radda in Chianti Radda is 13.5km east of Castellina and is a genuine old village and a good base from which to reach some of the best spots in Chianti. The tourist information office (☎ (0577) 73 84 94), Piazza Ferrucci 1, has an enthusiastic and helpful staff and plenty of information about hotels, country villas and agriturismo establishments. It also has information on cultural and recreational activities, including suggestions for independent walking tours or organised guided tours to the wineries. Ask for Gioia Milani – you'll be hard pressed to find a more organised, enthusiastic person working in tourism in the area. The office has a Web site at http://www.chiantinet.it and its email address is staff@chiantinet.it.

Certaldo Certaldo overlooks the Val d'Elsa between Empoli and Poggibonsi, about 40km from either Firenze or Siena. The information office is in the new town at Piazza Macelli (☎ (0571) 66 49 35), just next to the bridge over the Agliena stream. It is open from April to October from 9.30 am to 1.30 pm and from 4.30 to 7.30 pm.

San Gimignano The office of the Associazione Pro Loco (☎ (0577) 94 00 08; fax 94 09 03) is in the Piazza Duomo 1 and offers exhaustive information on hotels and lodgings of all types, including farm holidays and house rentals. In addition the office gives information on transport, museums, guide services for the city and for naturalistic excursions, car, motorcycle, horse and bicycle rentals and many other services. Its Web site is at http://web.tin.it/sangiminiano and its email address is prolocsg@mbox.vol.it.

Volterra The tourist office (☎ (0588) 86150) is at Via Turazza 2, just off the town's main square, Piazza dei Priori.

Permits

In some areas it is necessary to obtain a permit from the local tourist office to gather mushrooms.

Warnings

It's hard to imagine the gentle landscapes of Chianti presenting any problems. Unfortunately, at certain times of the year it is infested with hunters. They are particularly numerous in the forested areas between Certaldo and Volterra. If you see or hear hunters in the area, make your presence known by making plenty of noise. The hunting season is from the end of September to March.

You could come across vipers, which are poisonous, but not aggressive. Wild pigs, even in numbers, tend to run away, but the female can become aggressive if she senses that her young are threatened or if cornered.

ACCOMMODATION & SUPPLIES

Both Firenze and Siena have extensive accommodation facilities, but they can be quickly booked out in peak seasons. The tourist offices in both cities are very helpful and will usually be able to locate a room for you. In Firenze, there is a HI hostel, *Ostello Villa Camerata* (☎ (055) 60 14 51), Viale Augusto Righi 2-4. B&B is L25,000 and a meal is L15,000. Catch bus No 17b from the right of the main train station as you leave the platforms. There is a *camping ground* (☎ (055) 61 03 00) next to the hostel. In town, *Ostello Archi Rossi* (☎ (055) 29 08 04), Via Faenza 94r, has beds in dorm rooms. *Albergo Azzi* (☎ (055) 21 38 06), Via Faenza 56, is a pleasant, simple hotel, with singles/doubles from L55,000/L85,000. *Brunori* (☎ (055) 28 96 48), Via del Proconsolo 5, is near the duomo and charges from L40,000/L75,000.

In Siena, there's a non-HI hostel called *Guidoriccio* (☎ (0577) 52212), at Via Fiorentina, località Stellino, about 2km northwest of the city centre. *Colleverde* camping ground (☎ (0577) 28 00 44) is north of the historical city centre at Strada di Scacciapensieri 47 (take bus No 3 from Piazza Gramsci in the town centre) and remains open from late March to early November. For a hotel, try *Tre Donzelle* (☎ (0577) 28 03 58), Via delle Donzelle 5, off Banchi di Sotto, north of the Campo – but you'll need to book in advance.

Chianti Classico

Duration 3 days
Distance 35km (approximately)
Standard Easy
Start San Fabiano
Finish Vagliagli
Closest Towns Firenze, Siena
Permits Required No
Public Transport Access Yes
Summary Long, pleasant walk mainly on country roads, up and down the vineyards, olive groves and medieval *borghi*, through evocative valleys and forests. Of great interest are the visits to Badia a Passignano at Montefioralle, Castello di San Polo in Rosso and Certosa di Pontignano.

PLANNING

When to Walk

Spring and autumn are the best times to walk in the Toscan hills. At the end of September and beginning of October, there is the *vendemmia* when the grapes are gathered. Winter can also be mild and sunny. Avoid the summer as it is too hot and sultry for enjoyable walking.

What to Bring

You'll need comfortable clothes, appropriate to the season, a small backpack, a rain poncho or jacket, hat, sunglasses and sunblock. Some comfortable runners (trainers/sneakers) are ideal for these walks, although you might encounter some mud after rainfall, as well as the occasional difficulty in traversing undergrowth. A walking stick is always useful, along with a compass – which should be your habitual companion on any of walk.

Guided Walks

There are no professional organisations based in the Chianti area with fixed programmes. Tours and walks are organised by companies outside the area, usually outside Italy. However, some private organisations do organise the occasional excursion in

Chianti. You can get up-to-date information at the information office of Radda in Chianti, or from the Gruppo Trekking Firenze (☎ (055) 58 53 20), Piazza Gervasio 12, Firenze. You can also get information and suggestions from the Club Alpino Italiano (CAI) in Firenze (☎ (055) 21 17 31), Via Studio 5, or in Siena (☎ (0577) 27 06 66),Viale Mazzini 95.

In Fiesole, near Firenze, I Bike Italy (☎ (055) 234 23 71) offers well-organised bike tours in the area of Fiesole and in the Chianti area, with an English-speaking guide.

PLACES TO STAY & EAT
Most hotels and agriturismo establishments are oriented towards a demanding clientele willing to spend from L100,000 a day, for three days to a week, depending on the period. Therefore, finding a place to sleep is a real problem when you have to change location from day to day while trekking. The minimum cost per person per night in a hotel is L50,000 for something very simple, and in some towns minimum prices are even higher.

We list several possibilities along the route, but you'll need to plan and book well ahead of time, making use, for instance, of the tourist office in Radda.

There is no problem, on the other hand, when it comes to eating. The area is rich in restaurants, all at a medium to high level in quality and price.

Greve in Chianti
The two hotels in town are in the main piazza (Piazza Matteotti). *Giovanni da Verrazzano* (☎ (055) 85 31 89), at No 28, charges L110,000/L130,000 for a single/double in high season. This hotel has a restaurant with a beautiful terrace overlooking the piazza. *Del Chianti* (☎ (055) 85 37 63), at No 86, charges L180,000 a double.

Panzano in Chianti
Accommodation here is expensive. The elegant *Villa Sangiovese* (☎ (055) 85 24 61), in Piazza Bucciarelli 5, is a refined three-star hotel where a double costs from L160,000 to

L240,000, depending on the season. It closes from mid-December to March.

Radda in Chianti
One of the cheapest options is to rent a room in a private house. *Da Giovannino* (☎ (0577) 73 80 56), Via Roma 6-8, is a real family house in the centre of Radda. It charges L50,000/L80,000 for single/double rooms. Otherwise, splurge on a small apartment in one of the delightful old farmhouses in the area – most set in picturesque vineyards. There is a minimum two-night stay and the starting cost is L100,000 per night for a small apartment. Check all the possibilities with Gioa Milani at the Radda tourist office – she'll find you a solution for sure.

Hotel/restaurant *Albergo Villa Miranda* (☎ (0577) 73 80 21) is at the beginning of the third and final section of the Chianti Classico trek, in the locality of Villa Radda. A double room costs L120,000 to L150,000.

Poggio San Polo
In Poggio San Polo, halfway along the route on the third day of the trek, there is no accommodation for travellers just passing through, but there is a good restaurant, *Il Poggio* (☎ (0577) 74 61 35) which is closed on Mondays and in December and January. A meal will cost around L40,000 without wine.

San Polo in Rosso
The castle of San Polo in Rosso (☎ (0577) 74 60 45) is a winery, where you can visit the cellars and taste the produce (see Day 3: Radda in Chianti to Vagliardi (Siena) of this trek for details). You can also rent rustic apartments in the area for a minimum of one week, from L1,100,000 a week for two people.

Fattoria Dievole
You'll reach the *Fattoria Dievole* (☎ (0577) 32 26 13) on the third day of the trek. It is an excellent place to stop off if you want to spend some leisurely days among the hills and vineyards of Chianti. A room with two

beds costs from L140,000 to L210,000 a day. A room with three beds costs up to L240,000.

Corsignano

In Corsignano, 3.5km from Vagliagli along the main road and 7km from Siena, there is the hotel *Casa Lucia* (☎ (0577) 32 25 08). A double room costs between L98,000 and L140,000.

Miscianello

This is a rustic agriturismo establishment (☎ (0577) 35 68 40) with a view over the Certosa di Pontignano. It is on the ridge between Ponte a Bozzone and Vagliagli, in an area not served by public transport. If you book ahead, you can arrange to be picked up at Vagliagli, depending on the season and the number of people. A double room costs from L70,000 to L90,000.

GETTING TO/FROM THE WALK

Chianti is between Firenze and Siena and is accessible by bus from either city. You can reach Firenze by train from any major city in Italy. Siena is not on a major train line. If you're coming from Roma, change at Chiusi, or from Firenze change at Empoli. There are also direct bus services from Roma to Siena run by Sena (☎ (06) 474 28 01) and to Firenze, run by Lazzi (☎ (06) 884 08 40). Both services depart from Piazzale Tiburtina in Roma, accessible from Roma's main train station, Termini, on the Metro Linea B (get off at Stazione Tiburtina).

Chianti is accessible by SITA bus from Firenze and by Ta-in bus from Siena, mainly running along the Chiantigiana road SS222, which connects Firenze and Siena. The SITA terminal is in Via Santa Caterina da Siena, near the main train station in Firenze. Ta-in buses depart from Piazza San Domenico in Siena.

To get to the start of the trek at the village of San Fabiano, about 8km south-east of Mercatale in Val di Pesa, take the SITA bus from Firenze. On weekdays and Saturday there are buses at 7.15 and 9.15 am and 12.55 and 1.50 pm. There is only one bus at 9.15 am on Sundays and holidays. It takes one

hour to get to San Fabiano, which is the end of the line. Check at the SITA ticket office (☎ (055) 478 22 31), or on the information number ☎ (166) 84 50 10.

To go by bus from Greve to the starting point of the second day of the trek at Pieve di Panzano, take the SITA bus and get off after Panzano at Pieve di Panzano (also called San Leolino). It leaves Greve at 8 and 10.30 am except Saturdays; on Saturdays there is only one bus at noon. Check the day before leaving.

A Ta-in bus No 34 leaves for Siena from Vagliagli, about 10km north of Siena. This bus will also take you to Corsignano and Ponte a Bozzone, but only on weekdays and Saturdays. In the afternoon and evening buses leave at 1.50, 2.25, 4.10 and 7.15 pm from the town piazza and take about 40 minutes to reach Piazza Gramsci in Siena, by way of Pontignano. Check at the Ta-in information office (☎ (0577) 20 42 45).

THE WALK

Day 1: San Fabiano to Pieve di Panzano
3 hours 40 minutes

This three-day walk in the heart of Chianti starts off at San Fabiano, a tiny *borgo* (hamlet) of only four or five simple houses well positioned in the northern Chianti hills. It is worth the short time needed to explore San Fabiano, in particular to find the Romanesque façade, which is all that remains of the local church.

Frequent buses from Firenze take one hour to bring you to San Fabiano and allow you to bypass the city's rather anonymous suburbs.

From San Fabiano head back along the road towards Firenze – being careful not to get run over while you admire the splendid view. After walking about 250m, leave the asphalt and turn left into Via Fornace Casavecchia, a dirt road which passes through picturesque olive groves. At last you're in the country – among warbling birds and furtive lizards!

Below, to the right, is the Palagio, a small, medieval castle, and further ahead you can see the Romanesque bell tower of the Pieve di Santo Stefano a Campoli , built in 900 AD. From where you are, you have a panoramic view to the hills across the Val di Pesa.

In 10 minutes you reach the ancient kiln (*fornace*) from which the road takes its name; to the left of the kiln there is a small house – its roof supported by unusual terracotta columns. The dirt road leads you south into the trees and skirts a fine *casale* and fountain.

After another 10 minutes you reach the group of buildings known as La Cava. From here you can make a brief detour to the Romanesque Pieve di Santo Stefano a Campoli. Head for the shrine at the corner of the casale and follow the road to the right, through the yards of two casali. In about five minutes you'll reach the pieve. The grassy churchyard surrounded by cypresses provides a pleasant setting for the contemplation of the pure Romanesque structure of this ancient country church.

If you decided to make the detour, return to the shrine and continue on between the houses of La Cava. After turning the corner (left), go up the tractor trail straight in front of you, through an olive grove. After a few minutes of rigorous climbing you reach a small clearing under a group of cypresses (420m, 30 minutes from the start). Take a minute to catch your breath, then turn right onto the path that traverses the slope of a small valley.

The path narrows and becomes muddy going into the woods. Go straight ahead, trying to avoid getting snagged in the blackberry bushes. Be sure to ignore all the deviations, among which is a tractor trail that goes up to the left into the woods. Here it is probably a good idea to go a few metres out of your way to avoid a large patch of blackberry bushes on the path. Once back on the path, the blackberry bushes will continue to impede your progress. After another five minutes you'll pass a large abandoned shrine, about 10m up the slope to your left. From here you can continue more easily along the path.

After another eight minutes you begin to skirt an olive grove blighted by a high tension pylon. Here the path leads back down into the woods and blackberry bushes. After

a short distance the path is completely swallowed up by the blackberry bushes: if this situation hasn't changed, follow the detour up to the left, which then turns right, levels out and continues south, parallel to the actual path just below.

Finally you'll reach an olive grove and, on walking through it, you'll find a path on the right which leads down to a vineyard. Skirt the vineyard until you come to a dirt road that comes from villa Tignanello. Your bit of Toscan jungle exploration has taken all of 15 minutes!

Turn left and walk uphill on the dirt road, skirting the fascinating ruins of the Case di Podere Casacce (Casacce farm) farm. Notable in the structure of the façade is a chapel that confirms the 'lordly' status the farm once enjoyed. The road ascends and bends to the right and levels out as it skirts a vineyard. After 200m you'll leave this path (which continues on to Poggio La Croce) at the point where you find a barely visible, faded red triangle painted on a rock to your left. On the right, a passageway through the blackberry bushes leads you downhill, past the vineyard to a dirt road. Cross the road and continue going downhill, roughly following the edge of another vineyard.

Cross the valley along the banks of the artificial lake and then follow the dirt road downhill to the right. You'll reach a gate bearing 'Private Property' signs. It may well be closed to keep the grazing cows in, but don't be discouraged – locals say it is fine to climb over it but don't open it. Passing by another vineyard, you'll reach a cemetery, and the road from Santa Maria Macerata, which you can see on the hilltop to the right. A shrine among the cypresses marks the place where the asphalt turns into dirt road (350m, 1 hour).

Follow the dirt road down to the left and then make the steep ascent to the turn-off to the left for Valigondoli (443m) marked by an oak tree. Take the fork to the right: the road soon begins to descend, affording a view of the Badia a Passignano. The abbey is among the most beautiful in Toscana, majestic and evocative with its two crenellated towers

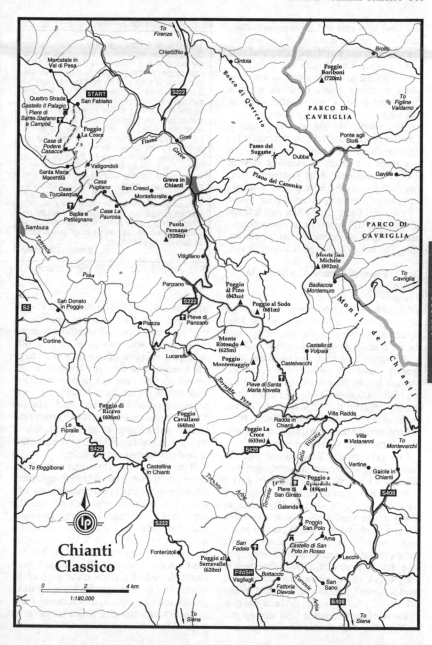

TOSCANA

Chianti
Classico

0   2   4 km

1:180,000

defended by a ring of lush cypresses. Continue past the tower-house of the working Tracolle farm and you'll reach the paved road near the abbey (Casa Torcilacqua, 354m).

To visit the abbey go down to the right, past the ancient casali, until you get to a crenellated tower which is softened by an elegant pointed arch of grey stone.

After visiting the abbey, return uphill to Casa Torcilacqua and take the dirt road to the right for Greve in Chianti. The road ascends to a ridge and offers an excellent view of Badia a Passignano. After passing the Casa Pugliano you reach the paved road that links the town of Mercatale in Val di Pesa; follow it to the right and after 200m turn left and head downhill towards Greve. There are panoramic views of the valley and the Chianti hills. The town below you is Montefioralle.

Day 2: Pieve di Panzano to Radda in Chianti

4 hours

Take the 8 am SITA bus from Greve and get off at the Pieve di Panzano stop, just after Panzano. On the opposite side of the road there's a small paved street which leads up to the borgo, then continues up to the 10th-century pieve and 16th-century colonnade (457m). Inside, there is a 12th-century painting of the *Madonna Enthroned* and a 14th-century triptych by the Master of Panzano showing the Madonna & Child with SS Peter & Paul; outside there is a splendid panoramic view of the Val di Pesa to the west.

Go back towards Panzano and take the fork heading slightly uphill to the right; pass Hotel Villa Barone and continue on past a cemetery until you come to a stop sign (20 minutes). Go right towards Montemaggio along a dirt road with a wide panorama looking south. After about 800m you pass a shrine on the right and, going down towards some cypresses, some wonderful vistas open up to the north as well. Shortly after there is a triple fork where you take the central uphill road towards Castelvecchi. The road snakes off into the woods, passing the large iron gate of the working Cennatoio farm on the right.

You soon reach a meadow with a pine tree

The Badia a Passignano

Going up the ramp among the cypresses you will come to the church and the portal of the imposing monastery, probably founded by the Lombard Kingdom. Here rest the remains of San Giovanni Gualberto, who started the monastic reform of Vallombrosa in the first half of the 11th century. The monastery can be visited only on Sunday from 3 to 5 pm or by appointment (☎ (055) 807 16 22). In the dining hall is a precious fresco of The Last Supper painted by Ghirlandaio in 1476; the chapel of San Michele Archangelo in the church was painted in 1598 by Domenico Cresti, called *il Passignano* for his having been born and raised in the nearby house of Pugliano. Notable also are the 1470 cloister and the imposing 14th-century fireplace in the monk's kitchen. There are some places to eat in the village which surely merits a visit for its incomparable atmosphere and its 'poor' little church of San Biagio (341m).

Stefano Cavedoni

which is aptly marked on the map as Poggio al Pino (643m). Pass a stand of pine trees on your right and continue comfortably along level ground with extensive views south. After passing a row of cypresses and a large oak tree on your left, you come to a fork among the fields and oak trees of Poggio al Sodo (681m). Take the fork to the right and begin the descent into the woods towards Montemaggio, marked SP 114 Traversa del Chianti. After 300 m, at another fork, follow the signs to Radda in Chianti as you continue to descend, keeping to the right.

Here the road narrows and after about 800m you'll come to the Montemaggio turn-off, but you continue your descent to the left, keeping to the main road. After 2.5km the pine wood is interrupted by some cypresses and then thins out into some beautiful meadows and cultivated fields, arriving at the romantic borgo of Castelvecchi. You can see Castello di Volpaia off to the left, built castle-like into the slope at the edge of the wood. The road twists down among olive groves and vineyards to the charming Pieve di Santa Maria Novella, which preserves its original Romanesque structure of three apses

TOSCANA

and internal columns with their original 12th-century capitals. From the grassy churchyard, there is a view south over Radda and the hills of the Sienese Chianti (478m).

The descent gets steeper here and leads down to a little artificial lake overlooked by an attractive roof-terraced building of the Castellino estate. Shortly after there is a fork in the road. You go to the right for Radda, cross the bridge over Torrente Pesa, and head uphill to the road for Lucarelli and Panzano. There you go left towards Radda. You'll need to walk 1.7km on this busy road until you come to an unusual red-brick bridge. Pass under it and immediately turn off to the left to cross the bridge for Radda, which is now only 700m away.

If you plan to sleep at Albergo Villa Miranda (see the earlier Places to Stay & Eat section), don't take the turn-off. Instead, go straight ahead to the village of Villa Radda: the hotel is on the right. Note the red-and-white sign painted on the left-hand angle of the hotel, marking trail No 68 for San Giusto – the next leg of the walk departs from here.

Day 3: Radda in Chianti to Vagliagli (Siena)
4½ hours

As already mentioned, this leg starts off at the Albergo Villa Miranda. Trail No 68 is actually a pleasant little country road which heads south into a small cultivated valley. Following the red-and-white signs, you'll pass the ancient tower of Canvalle on the right as you head up the other side of the valley. Almost immediately after reaching the ridge, you'll come to a three-pronged fork near the Casa Beretuzzo; go right, then straight, maintaining level ground until you reach a wooden cross encircled with cypresses. Take care to stick to the marked trail because there are numerous deviations along the ridge. After a few metres you can enjoy the view over the territory of Radda to the right and, to the left (south-east), the towers of Vertine and the 16th-century villa Vistarenni.

Continue through a wide, grassy clearing and then follow the dirt road downhill and turn right at the T-intersection (460m).

Shortly afterwards, you'll see the elegant Romanesque bell-tower of Pieve di San Giusto peeping out of the trees on the other side of the valley. The road now descends in steep curves through fields and cypresses, crosses a little bridge over a stream and leads to the paved road at the valley bottom, where you will turn left (378m, 1 hour).

About 100m along the road, there's a turn-off for Vagliagli-San Fedele on the right. Ignore it and continue on the paved road: you'll cross a bridge over Torrente Fosso delle Filicaie and after walking another 200m turn right onto the cypress-lined dirt road to reach Pieve di San Giusto. This 11th-century tri-apsed church is marvellously positioned among the ancient farmhouses, grassy courtyards and centuries-old trees of a tiny borgo. Continue past the church and walk uphill until you meet up with a tractor trail, marked by a red-and-white sign on a tree, where you turn left.

Continue among the vineyards and forest and you'll reach a three-pronged fork where you turn off to the right for Ama. The path follows an ancient stone wall and winds downhill leading you to another three-pronged fork: you take the path in the middle, which is marked by a red-and-white sign. At the next fork follow the red-and-white signs to the right and head downhill into the forests. After crossing the shallow stream, follow the path uphill to reach Galenda, a delightful rural borgo where you can make a pleasant rest-stop among the cypresses (485m).

Leave the borgo through the vaulted passageway between the houses and, heading south, follow the grassy path that traverses the side of the slope among the fields. Don't worry about the protests of the dogs, which (at least when we passed through) are safely restrained behind a metal fence. Note the small shrine on your right. The ancient retaining wall, now in ruins, is testimony to the importance once enjoyed by this route which today is abandoned among the fields, to the great pleasure of walkers.

Continuing downhill, you'll come to a fenced-in electricity exchange, and its dirt serviced roads. You'll no doubt be struck by

TOSCANA

the disharmony of this scene with the gentle slopes, vineyards and olive groves you've just passed. Best to just ignore it, cross the stream and continue to follow your path, which, at this point, starts to head uphill again into a group of bushes. When you reach an iron gate go to the right and follow the fence, maintaining your direction as you ascend: Poggio San Polo is in front of you and Galenda is behind. At this point the red-and-white markings have disappeared.

Walk downhill along the edge of the vineyard, then continue uphill along the grassy tractor trail – taking the brief detour around a blackberry patch – until you reach the small modern house. Here you find a little road on the left which takes you among the lovely houses of Poggio San Polo. Of interest is the ancient *parata*, a kind of garage for housing farm equipment, which has been transformed, into an elegant country home. You will once again find the CAI markings along the paved road. There is a restaurant here, *Il Poggio* (☎ (0577) 74 61 35) (see Places to Stay & Eat), where you can enjoy an excellent meal.

Continue your descent on the asphalt road towards Castello di San Polo in Rosso, now following CAI route No 66 instead of No 68. The road becomes a pleasant cypress-lined dirt road which passes through a forest and leads to a small cemetery. There is a splendid view of San Polo in Rosso and the Sienese Chianti.

Pass an elegant casale with a portico surmounted by a rustic, double-arched window. You then reach the ancient Castello di San Polo in Rosso, founded in 1000 AD as a pieve, fortified in the 13th century and later embellished with a Renaissance *loggia*, and the palace of the *padrone* (owner) in the 19th century (456m). The pieve and adjacent buildings are now part of a working farm and vineyard, which produces an excellent Chianti DOCG. It offers accommodation for a minimum of one week in farm-holiday facilities (see Places to Stay & Eat). It is advisable to book your visit with wine-tasting ahead of time by calling ☎ (0577) 74 61 22 or ☎ (0577) 74 60 45 during working hours. If you arrive without having

booked a visit, go through the beautiful Gothic portal into the medieval cloister. Nobody will mind as long as you behave courteously.

To resume the walk, take the trail which heads downhill beside the parking area (it is marked with a red-and-white sign), skirting the retaining wall of the garden, and passing a house with a lovely staircase supported by a column. The trail veers to the left and then winds down into the forest, affording a view of the pieve from the south. The trail continues its long descent through the forest towards Torrente Arbia and you'll begin to notice the rich birdlife of the area.

When you start to hear the gurgling of the river, you'll note the red-and-white sign on a rock to your right and then another one on a tree to your left (if you're walking during summer the river could be dry). Follow the red-and-white trail markings along the sharp curves that descend to Torrente Arbia, ignoring the various deviations. Notice on your left the evocative ruins of a medieval mill, with its solid arches swallowed up in the creeping ivy.

Immediately after this, the path crosses over a little grassy bridge spanning a stream blocked with debris, and continues among the poplars, curving to the left and maintaining a distance from the east side of the river. You will come to a junction marked with a small shrine, where you turn right. Pass the ruins of a house on the right (marked with a danger sign) and you'll come to a field where

---

A Taste of Toscana

The Dievole farm is at the centre of extensive vineyards and produces an excellent Chianti DOCG. The panorama here is among the most beautiful in Toscana. Call ahead on ☎ (0577) 32 26 13 to organise a wine tasting. You'll be welcomed by Andrea Annichini, the courteous sommelier of the farm. While recounting the history of Dievole and its wine, he will guide you through the cellars, sustaining you with sips of the various reds and whites, as well as some snacks. The farm has a swimming pool and guest rooms and the minimum stay is two days. This place is definitely worth a stopover after your long walk.

Stefano Cavedoni

Certosa di Pontignano

The bus from Vagliagli to Siena passes by the Certosa di Pontignano, a stupendous monastic complex built in 1343 which today serves as the perfectly restored university residences of the Siena University. The complex, accessible to all, comprises a church and two great cloisters, lined externally with the cells of the Certosan monks, each with its own vegetable patch. There are also some magnificent gardens at the back. For information call ☎ (0577) 35 68 51.

Stefano Cavedoni

the trail becomes less clearly defined. It winds around some piles of earth and then passes through the trees towards the river. After a few metres you reach an abandoned bridge, which is partially destroyed by floods.

Sections of the guard rail are missing, so take care when crossing the bridge, particularly in the event of poor visibility due to fog or failing light, or if you are walking with children. On a poplar on the left you will note the metallic marker for CAI route No 66.

After crossing the bridge, go uphill to the left, following the indication for Vagliagli. The old road, passable for vehicles until 20 years ago, is now a path consumed by rain waters that ascends into the forest in steep, sharp curves. You'll pass a dilapidated house in a field to your left (to your right there's a view of casali among the vineyards) before reaching a great oak tree where the path forks. Veer left and continue walking uphill until you reach a beautiful casale with a double parata next to the entrance, and a stone canopy at the back from where you can enjoy the north-west panorama with San Sano nestled among the vineyards.

As you ascend, you have Vagliagli before you and San Polo in Rosso behind. At a fork in the path, marked by a tree, go right and after passing a high wall take the steps to the left to reach the courtyard and Renaissance chapel of the tiny borgo of Bottaccio. As you continue uphill you now have a view of the remarkably beautiful Crete Senese, an area of vast pale clay fields.

You'll note the red-and-white markings of the CAI trail No 66 on a pole, before the path levels out on the ridge. Follow the road on the ridge, ignoring the first deviation to the left and after a few metres you'll reach a semi-circle of cypresses. Here you can take the dirt road to the left descending to the elegant manor house of the Dievole farm, adorned with a little 17th-century chapel as elegant as it is tiny (429m, 50 minutes). (See 'A Taste of Toscana' boxed text on the opposite page).

Otherwise, if you're heading for Vagliagli, make sure you stay on the road following the ridge and when you reach the asphalt road, turn right for Vagliagli.

If you go on to Siena, go up to the dirt road along the crest. Follow it to the left until you reach the asphalt of the provincial road where, to the right, you soon come to Vagliagli, where the bus for Siena leaves, which also goes to Corsignano (where there is a hotel) and to Ponte a Bozzone. There you can get to the agriturismo establishment of Miscianello.

Medieval Hills

Duration 3 days
Distance 43km
Standard Easy
Start Certaldo
Finish Volterra
Closest Towns Florence, Siena
Permits Required No
Public Transport Access Yes
Summary Pleasant route on peaceful and panoramic dirt roads and trails. The tract between San Gimignano and Volterra is without places to stay, so you'll need to camp out on the second night or tackle a 22km walk on the third day. Beautiful views of 14th-century cities and the unmatched atmosphere of ancient *borghi*, patrician villas, solitary country churches and the abandoned medieval fortress of Castelvecchio.

This is described as a three-day walk, but it can be made longer or shorter. Stopping the second day at San Donato, you could finish off the day by continuing into the woods and

TOSCANA

across the valley up to the turn-off for the fascinating ruins of Castelvecchio (4km from San Donato, three hours return) where it is pleasant to wander around exploring at your leisure. The third day can be cut to 4½ hours if you stop off at the comfortable Villa Palagione, 7km from Volterra, and walk the remaining distance to Volterra the following day. It is also possible to cut the trek to two days by getting to San Donato or Voltrona on the first day, coming from Certaldo, after a well-earned rest at San Gimignano (Certaldo-San Gimignano: 14km, four hours; San Gimignano-San Donato: 7km, 2½ hours).

PLANNING
See the Planning section in the Chianti Classico trek for details about when to walk and what to bring.

Guided Walks
At Certaldo, the Associazione Anthos (☎ (0571) 66 85 34) organises periodic guided excursions in the area and can give information on routes. The Gruppo Trekking Firenze (☎ (055) 58 53 20), Piazza San Gervasio 12, in Firenze, also organises periodic guided walking tours. In San Gimignano and Volterra there are guides for the cities and environmental guides for excursions, sometimes even on bicycle. Ask for information at the local tourist offices (see Information earlier in this chapter).

PLACES TO STAY & EAT
Certaldo
The *Fattoria Bassetto* (☎/fax (0571) 66 49 45; email bassetto@dedalo.com), a couple of kilometres from the town centre, just off the main road to Poggibonsi, is a 14th-century Benedictine convent, transformed over time by the Guicciardini counts into a beautiful farm with a manor house and garden. The owners, Daphne and Francesco, have converted a section of the ancient convent into travellers' lodgings, with rooms that sleep four to six people, an external bathroom and a communal kitchen. You'll pay L30,000 per night per person. In the

adjacent 19th-century manor house, once home of the Guicciardini duchess, there are romantic rooms replete with antique furniture and adjoining bathrooms for L100,000 per person. Advance booking is recommended. You can reach the Fattoria Bassetto on foot from the Certaldo train station, or contact the owners and arrange to be picked up.

In Certaldo's historic centre, next to the Palazzo Pretorio, is *Osteria del Vicario* (☎ (0571) 66 82 28), Via Rivellino 3, which has singles/doubles with bathroom for L65,000/L95,000. Its excellent restaurant boasts a magnificent terrace on the bastions of the ancient walls and a meal costs from L40,000. *Il Castello* (☎ (0571) 66 82 50), at the other end of the historic centre, at Via della Rena 6, has singles/doubles with bathroom for L70,000/L120,000. Half board costs L95,000. A meal in the restaurant costs from L25,000. In the new town is *Il Delfino* (☎ (0571) 62 27 47), Via Roma 83, a pizzeria/spaghetteria where pizzas start at L8000.

San Gimignano
The camping ground *Il Boschetto di Piemma* (☎ (0577) 94 03 52) is open from Easter to mid-October. It is 2km south of San Gimignano's Porta San Giovanni, towards Santa Lucia, on the actual walk route. The non-HI hostel *Ostello della Gioventù* (☎ (0577) 94 19 91), Via delle Fonti 1, is at the northern edge of town inside the walls. B&B is from L20,000. Lock-out is from 9 am to 5 pm and curfew is 11.30 pm. *Hotel La Cisterna* (☎ (0577) 94 03 28; fax 94 20 80), in the magnificent Piazza Cisterna, has singles/doubles from L108,000/L141,000. Ask for a room in the medieval section, with a view.

Volterra
The best deal is at the non-HI *Ostello della Gioventù* (☎ (0588) 85577), Via Don Minzoni near the Guarnacci Etruscan Museum, which has beds for L20,000 and doubles for L50,000. The house rules are the same as those at Ostello della Gioventù in San Gimignano. *Seminario Vescovile* (☎ (0588) 86028), in the Monastero di Sant'Andrea, Viale Vittorio Veneto, is a religious institution which

offers excellent rooms at reasonable prices. Rooms are large, clean and have bathrooms. They cost around L50,000 for a double. *Albergo Etruria* (☎ (0588) 87377), Via Matteotti 32, has singles/doubles with bathroom for L85,000/ L110,000. *Ristorante La Pace*, Via Don Minzoni 55, is a lovely restaurant with a friendly atmosphere and great food near the town walls. A full meal costs around L30,000.

On the Walk

There are several agriturismo establishments and villa-hotels along the route. The starting price per day is L50,000 and, as in Chianti, not all will take visitors for just one night, especially in high season and weekends. Some rent only by the week. It is recommended that you book well ahead to be sure of availability, especially in high season.

On the second day of the trek, even though you'll have covered less than one third of the long walk from San Gimignano to Volterra, you should consider staying at either the Fattoria Voltrona or at San Donato (see below). These are your last options until the Villa Palagione, which is under Monte Voltraio, 15km from San Donato and 7km from Volterra.

At Pignano, a very charming borgo with a luxurious manor house, only expensive apartments are rented out by the week, but it doesn't hurt to try. You may be able to make a deal for less time off-season. On the ridge north of the one between Pignano and Monte Voltraio which we follow on our route to Volterra, there are agriturismo establishments – Sant'Antonio in Sensano and San Michele in Ulignano. The only other option is to camp out (you'll need a tent) in the area of Castelvecchio or Bosco delle Volpaie.

If you plan to stay in any of these places, plan well ahead. They are as follows:

Pancole
 Cesani Vincenzo (☎/fax (0577) 95 50 84), Pancole 82/D
 Fratelli Vagnoni (☎ (0577) 95 50 77; fax 95 50 12), Pancole 82
Montauto
 Vallebuia di Montauto (☎ (0577) 94 12 39), Vallebuia 13

 Borgo Montauto (☎ (0577) 94 10 54), Montauto 9
 Montauto Vacanze (☎ (0577) 94 08 38; fax 93 82 14), Montauto 6A
 Fattoria Voltrona (☎ (0577) 94 31 52), Montauto 50
San Donato
 Fattoria San Donato (☎/fax (0577) 94 16 16)
Pignano
 Pignano appartamenti vacanze (☎ (0588) 35007) – only by the week
Sensano
 Sant'Antonio (☎ (0588) 42090)
Ulignano
 San Michele (☎ (0588) 42062)
Palagione
 Villa Palagione (☎ (0588) 39014; fax 39129)
Strada
 San Lorenzo (☎ (0588) 39080; fax 39090) – apartments by the week only

GETTING TO/FROM THE WALK

Certaldo is easily accessible from both Firenze and Siena by train (there are about 20 each day). The SS429 road, which runs along the Val D'Elsa connects Poggibonsi with Empoli passing by Certaldo.

San Gimignano is connected by bus to Certaldo (three per day excluding Sundays) and to Poggibonsi (16 per day) where you can catch a bus or train for Firenze and Siena.

Buses connect Volterra to Firenze (five per day), Siena (four per day) and San Gimignano (four per day). Trains connect Volterra and Cecina on the Tyrrhenian coast.

THE WALK
Day 1: Certaldo to San Gimignano
3¾ to 4½ hours, 14km

The actual start of the Medieval Hills trek is about 1km from Certaldo. To get to the starting point from the centre of Certaldo Nuovo follow the indications for San Gimignano. Cross a bridge and then immediately after a second bridge go left on the asphalt road for San Gimignano. After less than 1km, you'll come to an ERG petrol distributor and a dirt road on the right, with a blue sign indicating Pancole and Fattoria del Monte (Villa del Monte). The walk follows this road.

From Strada, at the end of the trek, there is a bus for Volterra four or five times per day.

TOSCANA

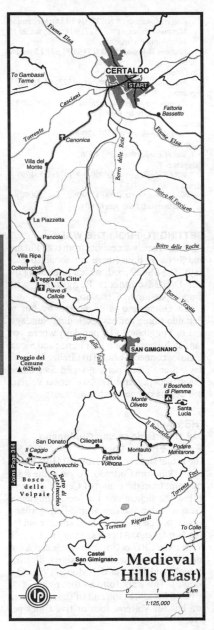

TOSCANA

Medieval
Hills (East)

0   1   2 km
1:125,000

The dirt road for Pancole rises gently
south-east among vineyards and olive groves
and immediately affords a beautiful view of
San Gimignano to the left, our destination for
the day. After about 2km of walking uphill
along the ridge, you come to the little church
of Canonica where a double row of cypress
trees begins and lines the road up to the
majestic Villa del Monte (202m) from where
you can enjoy a wide panorama east over Val
d'Elsa and the hills of Chianti. The undulating dirt road continues for 2.5km up to the
quaint borgo of La Piazzetta, and then
reaches the church and borgo of Pancole
(272m), a 17th-century sanctuary rebuilt
after WWII. The road passes through an
arched entrance and in among the houses of
Pancole. After a little more than 1km, at a bus
stop with a red-and-white trail marker, you
leave the road and turn right for Colle-
mucioli. Take the next fork to the left and
follow the dirt road that goes around the
recently restored ancient borgo, with its
lovely tower. Continue along, passing under
an archway, and heading uphill on the dirt
road – at this point there is a beautiful view
of San Gimignano, before you come to a
wide clearing across from the splendid Pieve
di Cellole (45 minutes from Pancole). The
little church, unfortunately open only on
Sundays and holidays from 10 am to noon,
has rows of cypresses in front of its elegant
13th-century façade. It was a very important
church in the Middle Ages due to its location
on the Via Francigena, which was the principal pilgrimage route from northern Europe
(France especially) to Roma and the departure points in Apulia for the Holy Land.
Fourteen minor churches in the surrounding
area were subordinate to it and it was long
contested by the bishops of Volterra and the
jurisdiction of San Gimignano.

From the piazza in front of the church,
with the church behind you, descend to the
left, heading south on the little road that,
after 300m meets up with the provincial road No
63, where you turn left. Being careful of the
traffic, walk the 3.5km to San Gimignano
where you can spend the night.

Alternatively, if you want to do the trek in

only two days, you could continue on past San Gimignano, following the directions for San Donato outlined for day two. This is a two to three-hour walk and, if you book ahead, you can stay in the delightful little borgo of San Donato.

Day 2: San Gimignano to San Donato
2½ to 3 hours, 7km

After leaving San Gimignano by Porta San Giovanni, going south, and descending to the right. At the intersection, turn right onto the road for Volterra and almost immediately turn left for the village of Santa Lucia and the camping ground. After less than 1km, you'll pass the convent of Monte Oliveto on the right and soon after you'll see the entrance to Il Boschetto di Pienna camping ground to the left. Santa Lucia is another half a kilometre further along the road. Note that you can get from San Gimignano to the camping ground Il Boschetto di Pienna by the city bus for Santa Lucia. The bus stops almost in front of the entrance to the camping ground. A visit to the ruins of Castelvecchio is highly recommended. (See the 'Castelvecchio' boxed text below).

About 200m towards Santa Lucia, there is dirt road on the right, marked with a red-and-white trail marker. Take this road and after

---

Castelvecchio
Castelvecchio probably originated as the Etruscan temple of an agricultural community which, after the Roman era, fortified the rockface. In the 13th century it was one of 20 castles that formed a defensive belt around San Gimignano. The only entrance, on the western side, was protected by a huge tower that exists even today. The population was no greater than 100 people who lived in the area between the tower and the church of San Frediano. The fascinating ruins of the church are still visible in the little square near the grain deposit. Farm animals and vegetable gardens were kept on the far eastern end of the cliff. Up to the 15th century the fortress was strategically important, but gradually fell into disuse and was ultimately abandoned after a plague epidemic. There are periodic attempts at excavations. ■

30m you reach an old shed. Do not continue to follow the dirt road that turns right, but descend straight into the woods between the shed and an iron gate on a steep, rambling trail marked with a red-and-white trail marker (south). After about 50m you come to a T-junction, where you go left – you'll reach a dirt road where you turn right and make the wide, curving descent into the valley.

The road ends in the courtyard of an old mill, which has been restored as a vacation home (180m). Descend to the left of the building and its lovely garden, (there is a red-and-white trail marker) and after a few metres, you reach the shady ford over Il Borratello – which you can jump over. On the other slope, to the south, follow the marked trail which ascends and soon comes out of the woods. You'll pass through a vineyard and reach a dirt road at the beautifully restructured Vallebuia agriturismo. Follow the cypress-lined dirt road that ascends to the ruins of Podare Montarone (229m), where the dirt road makes a right angle. Continue to ascend among vineyards and olive trees to the little church in the tiny, peaceful borgo of Montauto (277m), where you can find accommodation in either of two farm holiday centres (see Places to Stay & Eat earlier).

From Montauto, take the dirt road down to the left of the church and after about 300m leave the main dirt road, which goes north to San Gimignano, and turn left onto the dirt road marked with a trail map on a signpost. After 50m, there is another deviation marked by a similar signpost, as well as an indication for the Azienda Agricola Casavecchia. Turn right here and follow the dirt road for 1km. Among a group of houses, the road becomes little more than a tractor trail. Continue along this marked trail and after 30m, go left and descend sharply south into the valley, skirting a vineyard. After two curves, one left and one right, around the vineyard, the trail finally veers right and enters among the trees (marked with a trail marker), crosses a sandy creek bed, which is usually dry, and climbs up the other side among the fields, continuing south.

You'll pass two houses before reaching the *Fattoria Voltrona* near a small lake. As

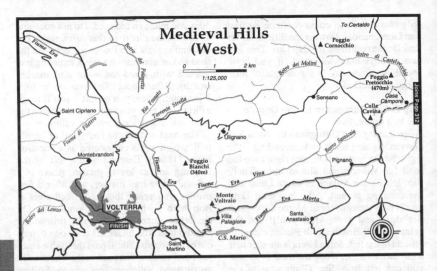

Medieval Hills (West)

you continue along the dirt road, you can see the profile of Castel San Gimignano. Pass the Podere Ciliegeta and you'll soon arrive at the delightful little borgo of San Donato (349m). A section of this tiny medieval village operates as the Fattoria San Donato, where you can spend the night (see Places to Stay earlier).

If you have the energy, you can follow the directions for the third day to reach the ruins of Castelvecchio and then return to San Donato (three to four hours).

Day 3: San Donato to Volterra
6½ to 7 hours, 22km
From the elegant little Romanesque church of San Donato, head south-west in the direction of Castel San Gimignano to reach the provincial road – where you will notice a lamppost marked with a trail marker. Turn right onto the road and ascend, following the trail marker. The dirt road goes into thick woods, and when it emerges onto a rocky crest, you can see the ruins of Castelvecchio beyond the narrow wooded valley. Shortly after, the dirt road descends steeply and then goes uphill to a clearing in the woods in front of the atmospheric, abandoned farm of Il Caggio (30 minutes from San Donato). From

here, descend south-east on the steep, sharply curving trail (marked as No 18) to reach the ford over Botro di Castelvecchio stream where you take the trail up to the west on the other slope. After a brief but tiring climb, you come to a clearing where there is a dirt road closed with a chain. If you want to visit the interesting ruins of Castelvecchio, turn left and hop over the chain. The ruins are about 600m away and you'll need about 30 minutes for a decent exploration. Parts of the ruins were being excavated at the time of writing.

If you don't want to visit the ruins, turn right (west) at the clearing and ascend on the dirt road that crosses through the woods, avoiding all turn-offs, until you reach a plain. Shortly after, the road passes under some high tension wires, veers left and gradually descends until it reaches the intersection with the access road for the Casa Campore (440m) on your right. Follow the main dirt road to the left (west) and after just more than 1.5km you'll reach the provincial road No 62 (locally known as *di Poggio Cornocchio*) near Colle Carina. Turn left and walk along the road (watch out for cars) and along the panoramic crest towards Volterra for about 1km. Here you'll find a dirt road on the right (west), marked with a stone wayside post and a trail marker, that descends among the trees and soon meets another dirt road, where you head to the right. Follow this lovely, cypress-lined walk up to the stupendous borgo of **Pignano**, with its lovely, 12th-century Romanesque church with a double access ramp, adorned with a palm and a cherry tree.

From here follow the main dirt road which descends sharply south-west, offering a very wide panorama over the wooded territory south of Volterra. The route continues west on this panoramic road slightly descending along the ridge to the Medici-style villa, known as Villa Palagione (337m, two hours from Pignano). Built in 1598 right under the rocky hump of Monte Voltraio, it is today a cosy and well-organised holiday centre (☎ (0588) 39014; fax 39129) and an option for an overnight stay on this walk. If you have the energy, you might like to climb Monte Voltraio (see the 'Monte Voltraio' boxed text below).

From Villa Palagione, continue on the dirt road (which descends in steep, sharp curves) for Volterra, cross a bridge over the Era Morta River and you'll reach the SS439 road, with indications for Pontedera on the right and for Saline di Volterra on the left (3km from Villa Palagione). From here, to cut down the kilometres and to avoid walking along this busy road all the way to Volterra, we recommend a pleasant shortcut. Turn left

on to the curving state road and after about 20m, you'll note trail markers on the guard rail and on a tree, indicating trail No 21 to the right. The trail is actually a bit difficult to see because it is hidden by the undergrowth.

Ascend through the thick vegetation and annoying prickly bushes for about 300m, until you reach a junction with a narrow paved road. If you go right, it will lead you to the elegant Agriturismo San Lorenzo (☎ (0588) 39080), with a little 13th-century church. The establishment rents apartments by the week only, but perhaps in the low season you can make a deal.

If, instead, you want to continue on to Volterra, don't turn off for San Lorenzo, but go straight and ascend among the fields until you reach a junction with another narrow paved road. Turn left and, in a few metres, you'll be on the SS68 road for Colle Val d'Elsa in the locality of Strada, where buses pass frequently.

Turn right and after 2km you'll reach Volterra, passing under the old Medici fortress now used as a prison.

ALPI APUANE

The sub-Apennine range known as the Alpi Apuane (Apuan Alps), in the far north-western corner of Toscana, has given the western world the raw material for some of its grandest monuments and works of art. The pure white marble of Carrara and Massa, and the many other marbles of other shades extracted from different parts of the Alpi Apuane, have been favoured for buildings and sculpture since the days of the Roman Empire. Most famously, Michelangelo travelled to the quarries behind Carrara to select the blocks of stone from which he carved many of his greatest works.

The Apuane are also a range of real natural beauty. They form a continuous ridge approximately 30km in length, but a ridge which divides here and there and wanders from its main axis. They include as well almost disconnected peaks such as Monte

---

Monte Voltraio

Upon this strange mountain, shaped like a truncated cone, and rich in fossils, there once stood a fortress. Built late in the 1st century AD, it was where the bishops of Volterra hosted the powerful men of the time. Of the fortress there remains only a few evocative traces, but it is worth the climb to enjoy the view from the summit (there is a path just across the road from the entrance to Villa Palagione – 50 minutes return). At the foot of the mountain you can see a few carved stones strewn about which were once part of the façade of the 13th-century church of San Giovanni.

Stefano Cavedoni

The Price of Glory

If the Alpi Apuane have indirectly achieved fame and glory, and contributed to some of the highest achievements of western civilisation, by serving for centuries as a source of fine marble, the cost to the natural environment has been high. Commentators wax lyrical about sunsets on the Alpi Apuane, seen from the coast, when the warm rays are reflected from vast slopes of cast-off marble scraps as though they were covered in snow. Nor is there any denying the beauty of a smooth, cool cut facet of marble, as can be seen in 300 or more quarries, large and small, throughout the range. But there's beauty, if you focus narrowly enough, in the rings of a sawn-off forest giant or the reflections in the surface of the reservoir that drives a hydroelectric power station. A marble quarry enhances the Alpi Apuane the way a hillside of tree stumps enhances a forest or a concrete dam improves a river valley. Glowing sunsets and sculpted masterpieces have their price.

Nick Tapp

Pisanino, the highest in the range at 1947m. The peaks are often described as 'dolomitic' in appearance and are separated in many cases by deep valleys. They rise in the space of 20km from the Ligurian Sea to nearly 2000m. Their valleys and slopes support a wide range of habitats, from dense beech and chestnut forests to low-growing alpine vegetation. Below the surface is Italy's largest cave network.

Two longish walks, known as Apuane Trekking and Garfagnana Trekking, cover much of the best ground in the Alpi Apuane. The latter also explores the Garfagnana valley, east of the Alpi Apuane, and the Orecchiella mountains further inland again. Both trails link a series of *rifugi* (refuges) and other cheap places to stay, but many of these are open only for a limited period during summer, and outside this time it is much harder to do a long walk.

Wild camping is not permitted within Parco Regionale delle Alpi Apuane. We describe two walks, of two and three days, respectively, which incorporate the spectacular formations of Monte Procinto and Monte Forato and the grand summit of Pania della Croce (1858m) in the southern part of the park, and the precipitous Pizzo d'Uccello (1781m) further north. These walks can be done from the beginning of June to the middle of September; at the height of the summer they could be combined into a very rewarding walk of seven days or more along the Apuane Trekking route.

NATURAL HISTORY

The 543 sq km Parco Regionale delle Alpi Apuane was established in 1985 with the aim of managing the difficult balance between environmental values and the long established human activities – principally, the extraction of marble – in the region. Approximately 22,000 people live inside the boundaries of the park. There are three levels of legislative protection for the different parts of the park, under which scenic, economic and natural values, respectively, take precedence. An area of 124 sq km within the park is administered as a series of *riserve naturali* (natural reserves).

Geology

More than anything else, it is the geology of the Alpi Apuane that has made them famous. The raw materials of today's marble, limestone and sandstone were laid down on the sea bed during hundreds of millions of years and underwent severe compression and folding during the Tertiary Period (beginning about 60 million years ago). At one time covered by a layer of sedimentary rock known as the Falda Toscana (Tuscan Layer), the Alpi Apuane, now metamorphosed, were pushed up and the Falda Toscana slid off and became the Appennino Tosco-Emiliano. The elements, principally water in the form of rain and then ice (during the last glacial period, which ended about 10,000 years ago), carved the new range into something like the shape it now possesses.

TOSCANA

This modelling by water went on, and still goes on, below ground as well as above. Under the Alpi Apuane is the largest cave system in Italy, and one of the largest in the world. It contains a number of deep, predominantly vertical *abissi* (one of these, the Abisso Olivifer, is the deepest cave in the country at 1215m), the extensive complex of Antro del Corchia, and many caverns rich in beautiful formations. Some of the finest examples are accessible to the general public in the Grotta del Vento, near Fornovalasco.

One peculiarity of the geology of the Alpi Apuane is that the predominantly calcareous rock quickly absorbs most of the plentiful rain that falls and feeds it into underground watercourses, leaving the surface comparatively arid and almost without permanent running water. This has practical implications for walkers, who must as a rule carry all the water they will need during a day's walk.

Flora

Because they range from sea level on the Mediterranean coast to a height of nearly 2000m in the space of less than 20km, and because of their geological diversity, the Alpi Apuane contain a great variety of plant communities. Species of the Mediterranean *macchia* or coastal scrub give way over a relatively short distance to alpine varieties. Vegetation types can also change, quite discernibly to the experienced eye, at the boundaries between different geological zones. On top of all this, human activities over the centuries (even leaving aside quarrying for marble) have had a significant impact on the original vegetation.

In the lower valleys, up to an altitude of about 800m, the sweet chestnut (*castagno*) tends to dominate. While originally a naturally occurring species, the chestnut was spread during centuries of cultivation by local people, who depended on it for sustenance and income. Though cultivation has all but ceased since WWII, and the tree's numbers have been reduced by disease, chestnut forests now cover something like 20% of the Alpi Apuane. On seaward slopes

at these altitudes, the cluster pine (*pino marittimo*) is more common.

The most common tree of the higher slopes, from 800m to 1700m or so, is the beech (*faggio*). Birches and oaks are also found in this altitude band. While human intervention long favoured the spread of the chestnut, the beech, by contrast, was often exploited for firewood and is believed to cover less of the Alpi Apuane now than it once did. At the upper limit of its range, cutting of the beech has led to an increase in the area covered by grassland. Grasses and other low-growing species, a number of them endemic to the Alpi Apuane, occupy the highest slopes and cling to cracks in the cliffs.

In spring and summer the forest floors and upper slopes support magnificent displays of wild flowers, including jonquils, crocuses, anemones, gentians and a number of orchid species, and, late in summer, pink cyclamens.

Fauna

Badger, marten, fox and other small mammals live in the Apuan forests, but are seldom seen. A variety of small forest birds also live here, and above the tree line walkers may see choughs in large colonies, falcons and the occasional majestic golden eagle.

CLIMATE

The Alpi Apuane are among the rainiest places in Italy, with an annual rainfall in some areas of more than 3000mm. The two sides of the range, however, receive very different weather. The south-western slopes enjoy mild, humid Mediterranean conditions, with warm summers and mild winters. On the landward north-eastern side of the range, summers are hot, and winters are cold, with significant snowfalls.

INFORMATION
Maps

To help with planning and give you a good overall picture of the layout of the Alpi Apuane, a map such as the Touring Club Italiano *Toscana* (1:200,000), widely available in bookshops throughout much of Italy for

TOSCANA

L9500, may be useful. For larger scale maps showing the walks in detail, see under Maps in the relevant walks sections throughout this chapter.

Information Sources

The Parco Regionale delle Alpi Apuane has three main visitor centres: in the former *filanda* (cotton mill) just above Forno (☎ (0585) 31 53 00); at Via Corrado del Greco 11, Seravezza (☎ (0584) 75 61 44); and at Piazza delle Erbe 1, Castelnuovo di Garfagnana (☎ (0583) 64 42 42).

Further information of a more general kind is available from tourist offices such as the APT at Viale Amerigo Vespucci 24, Marina di Massa (☎ (0585) 24 00 63), or at Viale XX Settembre, between Carrara and Marina di Carrara (☎ (0585) 84 57 46). Behind the Carrara office is the well set up Museo del Marmo (Museum of Marble), with photographs, displays and examples of marble. Admission is L6000.

Books

There are few books published in English on the Alpi Apuane but many in Italian. Two which contain handy background information if your Italian is up to it are *Alpi Apuane: Guida al territorio del Parco* by Frederick Bradley & Enrico Medda and *Alpi Apuane* by F Ravera. Both are well illustrated and cover the human history of the Apuane in some detail; the first is perhaps the stronger on natural history. *Wild Italy* by Tim Jepson has a section on the Alpi Apuane and goes into some detail on natural history.

Emergency

The numbers to call if you strike trouble (and can get to a telephone) in the mountains are ☎ 112 (for the *carabinieri*), ☎ (0585) 31 53 17 (Massa branch of the Corpo Nazionale Soccorso Alpino) or ☎ (0585) 84 19 72 (Carrara branch). These numbers change, so it would pay to check them before you head off.

Leaving Luggage

You can leave excess gear at any train station while you walk, though, at L5000 for each item per 12 hours or part thereof, this is an expensive business.

ACCOMMODATION & SUPPLIES

The major towns in the region are those on the coastal plain at the foot of the Alpi Apuane: Carrara, Massa and Pietrasanta. All are well supplied with places to stay and shops where you can buy lunches and snacks. Further inland, Castelnuovo di Garfagnana gives access to walks in the Garfagnana valley and the Orecchiella mountains not described here.

Carrara

There is any amount of reasonably priced accommodation by the sea in Marina di Carrara, including two camping grounds, the huge *Carrara* (☎ (0585) 78 52 60), on Via Carlo Fabbricotti, and the smaller *Bungalows Club* (☎ (0585) 63 22 31), Viale Giovanni da Verrazzano 29. These are open from April to September. Not far from the train station (follow the signs in the entrance hall), the *youth hostel* has beds from L14,000 and comes strongly recommended. *Hotel Anna* (☎ (0585) 78 02 08), a couple of blocks back from the beach at Via Venezia 2, Marina di Carrara, has singles/doubles with bath from L30,000/L60,000. In central Carrara, *Albergo da Roberto* (☎ (0585) 70634), Via Apuana 3B, has rooms with bath from L50,000/L80,000 in the high season, and an excellent restaurant.

Massa

Most of Massa's budget accommodation is near the coast at Marina di Massa. There are dozens of *camping grounds*; you could try calling the office of the Associazione Gestori Parchi di Campeggio (☎ (0585) 63 31 15). The youth hostel, *Ostello della Gioventù* (☎ (0585) 78 00 34), Via delle Pinete 237, charges L14,000 for a bed. Marina di Massa is awash with one, two and three-star hotels. The comfortable, two-star *Hotel Frjsco* (☎ (0585) 24 22 35), Viale Roma 410, charges from L40,000/L65,000 for a single/double with private bathroom, and *Hotel Parmamare*

(☎ (0585) 24 10 44), Via delle Pinete 102, charges from L35,000/L50,000 for a single/double. Both are open all year. At *Hotel Annunziata* (☎ (0585) 41023), Via Villafranca 4, in Massa itself, a single/double with bath starts at L60,000/L90,000 and there are rooms without bath for L35,000/L65,000.

Pietrasanta

Again, the seaside is the spot for a wide selection of digs. *Hotel La Pigna* (☎ (0584) 74 58 88), Via Don Bosco 15, Marina di Pietrasanta, charges from L65,000/L70,000 for a single/double with bath and is recommended. Two blocks from the bus station in Pietrasanta proper, *Da Piero* (☎ (0584) 79 00 31), Via Traversagna 25, has rooms without bath from L30,000/L50,000 and with bath for L10,000 extra. Closer to the train station, *Hotel Palagi* (☎ (0584) 70249), at Piazza Carducci 23, with rooms starting at L65,000/L100,000, might be worth a splash if only for the magnificent breakfast.

Rifugi

Wild camping is not permitted in Parco Regionale delle Alpi Apuane, and accommodation on the walks in this chapter is in rifugi run by the Club Alpino Italiano (CAI). There is a rifugio at the end of each day's walk described, and other rifugi make variations on these walks possible during the summer months when they are open. Costs and other details are similar to those outlined in the Alpi Marittime chapter. As is *always* the case, phone ahead, or have someone phone for you, to make sure the rifugi you plan to stay in are open and have room for you.

GETTING THERE & AWAY

Carrara, Massa and Pietrasanta are all on the train line between Pisa and La Spezia. Some trains on the busy line speed through, but several a day stop. Lazzi buses also call in here. All three towns are accessible by car from the A12 and the S1 (Via Aurelia). See the individual walks sections for how to get from these towns to the start of the walks and back from the other end.

Pizzo d'Uccello

Duration 2½ days
Standard Medium
Start Reseto
Finish Castelpoggio
Closest Towns Massa, Carrara
Permits Required No
Public Transport Access Yes
Summary Beech forests and marble quarries highlight the ancient conflict in the Alpi Apuane – natural treasure and commercial resource. Fine views of the sheer north face of Pizzo d'Uccello and an optional, challenging side trip to its airy summit.

At just 1781m, Pizzo d'Uccello is not the highest peak in the Alpi Apuane, but its isolated position at the north-western end of the range and the steepness of its faces and ridges make it undoubtedly one of the most imposing. Pizzo d'Uccello's north face, which drops approximately 700m from the summit, appeared in the records of English mountaineer FF Tuckett in 1883. He apparently considered it one of the most impressive rock walls in the Alps, but at least four decades were to pass before it was first climbed. Opinion differs on whether the honour went to two *genovesi* in 1927 or two *milanesi* in 1940. Today, the face sports many Alpine rock climbing routes. Among them are some of Italy's hardest, and repeat ascents are few.

This walk views the north face of Pizzo d'Uccello from close range and includes the option of a side trip to its airy summit by the easiest route. This calls for a steady head but no special skills as a rock athlete. Walkers approach the peak through the renowned Orto di Donna beech forest, a botanists' paradise and, in spring, a mass of wild flowers. They come face to face with the scourge of the Alpi Apuane environment, the marble extraction industry, at Passo della Focolaccia, on the Cresta Garnerone and at Foce di Pianza. They also enjoy many of the glorious views, both mountainous and coastal, for which the Alpi Apuane are, in their own small way, justly famous.

The walk begins in the hamlet of Resceto, 10km north-east of Massa, and finishes in Castelpoggio, 9km north-west of Carrara. As described, the walk is in three stages, but the Day 3: Campocecina to Castelpoggio walk is short and allows you to be back in to Carrara by lunch time. The walk could be extended and made into a circumnavigation of Pizzo d'Uccello with additional overnight stops in Ugliancaldo and Vinca. Alternatively, it could be extended south past Monte Tambura to link up with the southern part of the Apuane Trekking route and the Procinto, Monte Forato & Pania della Croce walk described later in this chapter.

NATURAL HISTORY

Pizzo d'Uccello (1781m) is the northernmost of the major peaks in the Apuan chain. It takes the form of a triangular pyramid, the most impressive feature of which is its sheer north face.

Val Serenaia, where Rifugio Donegani sits, is one of the most extensive glacial valleys in the Alpi Apuane and is enclosed by the major peaks of the northern Apuane: Pizzo d'Uccello, Monte Pisanino (1947m), Monte Cavallo (1888m), Monte Contrario (1790m) and Monte Grondìlice (1805m). Its upper reaches, in particular the area covered in beech forest known as Orto di Donna (Lady's Garden), are rich in plant species.

As elsewhere in the Alpi Apuane, the marble industry has made an indelible mark on the landscape. Around Passo della Focolaccia, along the eastern slopes of Cresta Garnerone and at Foce di Pianza, working quarries highlight the scant official protection from commercial exploitation that parts of this important park enjoy.

PLANNING

When to Walk

Rifugi and some other places to stay in the Alpi Apuane remain open continuously from the beginning of July until mid-September, and bus companies operate to an expanded summer timetable for the same period, making this the most convenient period to walk.

Maps

The most detailed map of walking tracks and rifugi in the Alpi Apuane is the Edizioni Multigraphic No 101/102 *Alpi Apuane: Carta dei Sentieri e Rifugi* (1:25,000). The Edizioni Multigraphic *Parco delle Alpi Apuane: Carta Turistica e dei Sentieri* (1:50,000) is less detailed, but the fact that the entire range is displayed on one sheet makes it easier to use. Both maps list telephone numbers and other details for rifugi. Both are available for L10,000 from bookshops in the major towns in the area as well as in larger Italian cities.

What to Bring

Since each day's walk ends at a rifugio, where prepared meals and a bed, pillow and blankets are available at moderate cost, and since wild camping is not permitted within Parco Regionale delle Alpi Apuane, you can leave behind much of the equipment usually necessary on a walk of this length in mountainous terrain. There's no need to carry a tent, sleeping bag, stove, fuel, eating gear, or more food than snacks to eat during the day and perhaps some lunches. You should bring a sleeping sheet and a pair of light alternative footwear to put on when you remove your boots at the rifugio (though most rifugi have a supply of 'hut slippers'). Don't forget to bring enough cash to cover accommodation and meals. At most rifugi, staff will ask to see your passport when you arrive, and may keep it overnight.

GETTING TO/FROM THE WALK

Resceto and Castelpoggio are both accessible by CAT buses. Four a day (in summer) leave from outside the ticket office on Largo Matteotti, just off Viale Chiesa, in Massa heading for Resceto (L1800). At the other end of the walk, frequent buses connect Castelpoggio and the bus station in Carrara, near Piazza Allende, just off Via Don Giovanni Minzoni (L2000). Both trips take around half an hour.

Top: The setting sun slants through mist in the rugged chain of the Alpi Apuane.
Middle Left: The twin peaks of Monte Forato, with Monte Nona behind, Alpi Apuane.
Middle Right & Bottom: Fallow fields, fortified hill-top towns, vineyards, olive groves and
    cypresses all contribute to the charm of the Chianti countryside in Toscana.

Top Left & Right: Capo Testa, at Sardegna's northern tip, offers easy walking to beautiful, sheltered coves in a coastline of pink granite sculpted by wind and the sea.
Bottom: The wide, green Lanaittu valley, on the edge of the Supramonte in eastern Sardegna, is fringed by limestone peaks.

THE WALK
Day 1: Resceto to Rifugio Donegani
3½ to 4½ hours, 1185m ascent, 520m descent

From the car park just above Resceto where the bus from Massa turns around, an unsealed road continues up the valley of Canale di Resceto. Red-and-white paint markers label it as track No 35. Follow it northwards, past a junction where track No 170 heads off on the left towards Foce Vettolina. After 10 minutes or so, at a small quarry, the road gives way to a narrower but still impressive track, once a *via di lizza* down which marble blocks were lowered from the quarry above (see 'La Lizzatura' boxed text). A few hundred metres further on is another track junction. Here track No 35, the remarkable **Via Vandelli**, crosses Canale Pianone to the east and begins its zigzag ascent of nearly 1000m to Passo della Tambura.

Continue up the west side of the valley on track No 166 past yet another impeccably signposted track junction, this time where track No 166b departs on a higher route to Passo della Focolaccia. After a further half-hour of steady climbing, track No 163 heads off to the east at a clearly marked junction. Stay on track No 166, which heads left here and up some grassy slopes, then begins to negotiate gullies full of marble 'scree'. Cairns and painted markers, and the occasional stretch of well-engineered track, lead to the lower edge of Cave Magnani, a functioning marble quarry. The western slopes of Monte Tambura (1895m) loom across the valley to the east.

The final climb to the pass follows the zigzagging road through the quarry – interesting if unattractive – past some buildings on the right and **Bivacco Aronte**, the oldest walkers' shelter in the Alpi Apuane, a short distance off to the left just below the pass. The rocky crest just west of Bivacco Aronte, including the elegant needle of Punta Carina, sports a number of classic rock climbs.

Although approaching it through a quarry is good mental preparation, **Passo della Focolaccia** (1642m) still comes as a shock. The original pass has disappeared, engulfed

La Lizzatura
The technique used to lower huge blocks of marble down the hillsides of the Alpi Apuane from the quarries where they were mined changed little between Roman times and the 1960s. At that time the road network that is used today began construction, and trucks took over much of the work. The old system, known as *lizzatura*, consisted of lowering the marble on a *lizza* or wooden sled, which slid over *parati* or rollers down a *via di lizza*, a kind of slipway constructed for the purpose.

The exercise was the work of a team led by a *capolizza*, who inserted the rollers under the sled and gave orders to a number of *mollatori*. These were the men who controlled the progress of the sled by means of ropes wound around *piri*, or wooden pegs, each hammered into a *foro da piro*, a square hole in the rock beside the via di lizza. Examples of fori da piro can be seen beside track No 166, a former via di lizza which climbs from Resceto to Passo della Focolaccia on the Pizzo d'Uccello walk. The team was completed by several men who retrieved the rollers from behind the sled as it made its way downhill and a specialist *ungino*, who greased the rollers before the capolizza reinserted them under the front of the sled.

These vie di lizza were often very steep – so steep that the roads that have replaced them often zigzag up hillsides with no room for a truck to turn, and the trucks that now carry the marble blocks down to the valley floor must alternate between forward and reverse gear all the way up and down.

Nick Tapp

by a huge pit from which slabs of the precious white stone are probably being carved out and carried away before your eyes. At the time of writing, the walking track continues to the right, smooth and white underfoot, around the main pit at the level of the road (appropriately, the red markers that show the way are daubed on a block of marble). It then drops and swings to the north-west. The gully to the north-east, below the road, is full of unwanted stone, which has been tipped over the edge to bounce and crash to rest. Above the quarry to the south-east, **Monte Tambura** wears a somewhat forlorn look.

Track No 179 leaves the road only a short distance beyond Passo della Focolaccia and contours to the north-west, but the start of it is not clearly marked. If you suspect you've missed it – in particular, if you reach the point where the road switches back to the south, downhill – head uphill from the road to regain the track and follow it to **Foce di Cardeto** (1670m). The lush Val Serenaia now lies ahead to the north-west, and towering beyond the valley is Pizzo d'Uccello. Your destination, Rifugio Donegani, is visible 2.5km away, just above the valley floor. All along the western side of the valley, reaching up to the rugged Cresta Garnerone, the effects of marble extraction are plain to see.

Take track No 180, the more northerly of the two options here. It descends to the north-west, staying above a couple of gullies, then heads down a spur to enter the beautiful beech forest of **Orto di Donna** (Lady's Garden). Though well marked and mostly well defined, the track takes a devious route through the forest, and it pays to be watchful. About 1km below Foce di Cardeto, at a clearly marked three-way junction, track No 180 goes left (west) across a gully system, then continues in a roughly northerly direction. It finally emerges from the forest an hour from the pass, and within a few more minutes reaches a made road. Just 250m north, on the east side of the road, is *Rifugio Donegani* (1150m), open from 1 May to 15 November and on weekends for the rest of the year, with bar, restaurant and 44 beds. To stay, phone ahead on ☎ (0583) 61 00 85.

Day 2: Rifugio Donegani to Campocecina

5 to 6 hours, 825m ascent, 655m descent

The most direct route to Campocecina heads from the rifugio straight to Foce di Giovo along track No 37. The route described here begins instead with a detour to Foce Siggioli for a spectacular view of the north face of Pizzo d'Uccello. If you plan to include the return trip to the top of Pizzo d'Uccello – hard to resist on a fine day – you should make a reasonably early start in order to reach Campocecina in good time.

Back out on the road in front of the rifugio, turn right (north), then follow the road as it bends back to the south after 500m, past a sign marking the boundary of the *cava di*

marmo (marble quarry). A short distance on, markers on rocks indicate the start of track No 187, which heads back towards the north-west at an acute angle from the road. Passing first through lovely beech forest, then angling up more open slopes with views to the right across the Alta Garfagnana, the track comes to **Foce Siggioli** (1386m), 40 minutes from the rifugio. The uninterrupted view from here of the sheer north face of Pizzo d'Uccello, just a stone's throw away, fully warrants the detour. A few metres north along the Cresta di Capradosso ridge is the top of a *via ferrata*, which offers those with the necessary equipment and experience a strenuous but spectacular route up to this point from the valley bottom more than 500m below.

The well-marked track No 181 now leads south along the picturesque ridge top for a couple of minutes, then leaves the crest and traverses steep hillsides, where beech forest alternates with rocky, open spurs and gullies. A few short sections of the track are somewhat exposed and are equipped with handrails – a kind of miniature via ferrata – but in good weather should not present problems to moderately experienced walkers. No special equipment or technical skill is required. After 30 minutes, the track regains the ridge top in a small saddle (1497m) where track No 191 heads down to the west and an unnumbered route leads north towards the summit of **Pizzo d'Uccello**. If it's a fine day, you'll probably be tempted to make a side trip to the top. See Side Trip: Ascent of Pizzo d'Uccello following for details.

To continue towards Campocecina, head easily south for 500m to **Foce di Giovo** (1500m), the main weakness in the ridge, the Cresta Garnerone, that connects Pizzo d'Uccello with Monte Grondìlice. A descent of less than 10 minutes to the north-west brings you to a track junction above the group of ruined buildings marked on some maps as 'Capanne del Giovo'. Ignore track No 175, which continues towards Vinca. Instead take No 37 on a long descending traverse to the south. After nearly 2km in the open below the rocky Cresta Garnerone, the

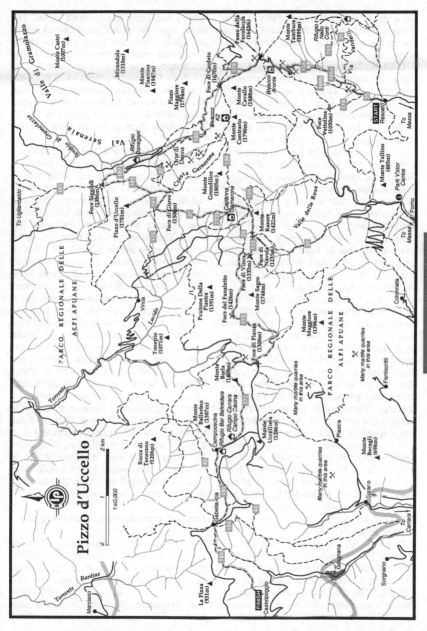

track enters mixed forest. Only a few minutes into the forest is the locked Capanna Garnerone, with reliable water from a pipe below the hut.

Track No 37 is now joined by No 173 from Vinca and continues, through dense undergrowth at first, in a forest now dominated by introduced pines. After 15 minutes track No 38 heads downhill on the right. To enjoy the scenic crest that connects Monte Rasore and Monte Sagro, continue uphill for another five minutes to the ridge top and a junction with track Nos 168 and 186. Follow No 37/173 west along the north side of the ridge, past a narrow gap where No 37 peels away to the south, then touching the crest at another low point, before reaching **Foce di Vinca** (1333m).

From here make your way attentively down to the north, bearing left at every opportunity, still on track No 173. This heads generally west, becoming more clearly marked and with spectacular views of Pizzo d'Uccello, crossing scree slopes and encountering abandoned machinery in a gully. A climb up this gully, steep and crisscrossed with fixed cables towards the top, leads to a ridge and a patch of eerie forest. The track swings to the west below the cliffs of Monte Sagro, and 1km from the top of the gully, after several sections equipped with fixed cables, emerges at the **Foce del Fanaletto** (1426m). The scene to the west is one of monumental destruction – or of busy production, depending on your point of view.

It is now necessary to skirt around the south side of the quarry that fills the intervening valley. Markers lead south at first, around the steep western slopes of Monte Sagro, then across the head of the valley, up onto a spur and along it, with excavations below on both sides, to meet the road through **Foce di Pianza** (1300m).

Cross the road and follow track No 173 north at first around the eastern flanks of Monte Borla. (Note that it is not necessary to walk along the road as some maps of the area indicate.) The final half-hour from Foce di Pianza is a pleasant coda to the day's exertions. Leave the rumble of heavy machinery behind and enter beech forest again. The broad, open slopes of Campo Cècina appear and quite soon the track crosses them, descending gently, to the scattered buildings of **Campocecina** village. Just above the road is *Rifugio Carrara* (☎ (0585) 84 19 72), open year round, with bar, restaurant and 36 beds. A couple of minutes further on, beside the road, *Rifugio Bar Belvedere* (☎ (0585) 84 19 73), is a possible alternative to put your feet up.

Side Trip: Ascent of Pizzo d'Uccello
1¼ to 1½ hours, 290m ascent & descent
Painted markers on rocks lead all the way up the south ridge of Pizzo d'Uccello from the saddle at 1497m. The gradient is gentle at first. As it steepens, the route seeks out the line of least difficulty and becomes less direct. The ridge is increasingly airy, and it is necessary to use your hands on a few of the steepest sections, and look carefully where you place your feet, but there is no great climbing skill required. The markers continue, so if faced with an impossibly sheer-looking stretch of rock, look about you for a splash of red paint. After an unhurried 45 minutes from the saddle, the summit cross appears ahead on a knoll. After a final clamber down into a dip and up the other side, you are there.

On a clear day, the summit of **Pizzo d'Uccello** or 'Bird's Peak', is a spectacular eyrie, with views of the snowcapped Alps away to the north and north-west, the Golfo della Spezia to the west and, closer at hand, the rest of the Alpi Apuane, including their highest point, Monte Pisanino, just across the valley to the east. With the benefit of familiarity, the descent to the saddle takes little more than half the time it took to get up there – but take your time and take care.

Day 3: Campocecina to Castelpoggio
1½ hours, 770m descent
This short, straightforward, downhill amble is a pleasant way to finish the walk. Follow the track from the front of Rifugio Carrara downhill to the north-west to meet the road opposite a car park. Continue past Rifugio Bar Belvedere, then, just before a little bridge, follow red-and-white markers down

the hill to the west. The track winds between fields, fences, caravans and buildings for a few minutes, then proceeds down the side of a ridge. Track No 40 joins in from the north, then a few minutes later departs to the south at a grotto. Follow track No 185, which swings north down a spur among interesting rock formations, including an archway which may be partly natural, before it meets a sealed road and the intersection of several walking tracks at Gabellaccia.

Cross the road and continue downhill to the west on track No 185. Track No 184 soon branches off south towards La Pianaccia and Gragnana, followed by No 46 towards Ponte Storto. After a gently descending traverse of a couple of kilometres, No 185 rounds a spur and passes beneath power lines, then merges with an unsealed vehicle track and makes its way into **Castelpoggio**, perched picturesquely on a spur. A small, white building bearing a red-and-white track marker, on the left as the sealed road begins, is that rare beast in Italy, a public lavatory. The CAT bus for Carrara departs frequently from opposite Bar Ricci, on the main street through the village.

Procinto, Monte Forato & Pania della Croce

Duration 2 days
Standard Medium
Start Stazzema
Finish Pontestazzemese
Closest Town Pietrasanta
Permits Required No
Public Transport Access Yes
Summary Glorious ridge-top walking to the 'queen of the Alpi Apuane'; spectacular formations of the Procinto and the 'mountain with a hole'; and a cosy mountain *rifugio*.

Pania della Croce (1858m), together with Pania Secca (1709m) and Pizzo delle Saette (1720m), forms the southernmost of the really big Apuan massifs. Its airy summit ridge is a magnificent place to be when the

light slants across the Alpi Apuane, either early or late in the day, and sets off the mountain peaks against the haze-filled valleys. The summit itself, topped by a massive iron cross, gives wonderful views up and down the crest of the range and across to the Ligurian Sea only 15km away.

This walk approaches Pania della Croce by way of two lower, but also noteworthy, mountains. Monte Procinto is a splendidly steep-sided, limestone pinnacle which juts from a ridge a little to the west of the main Apuan crest. Much commented on by poets and artists over the centuries, it was first climbed in 1879. A via ferrata makes the summit accessible to those who are properly equipped and with sufficient experience, even those who are not serious climbers, but it is beyond the scope of this book. All the other routes to the top of the Procinto are the province of rock climbers. Monte Forato is one of the strangest and most visible examples of the natural forces at play in the Alpi Apuane. Erosion by wind and water has worn a hole, 30m across, in the ridge and left a remarkable rock bridge between the two summits of the mountain.

The walk begins in the village of Stazzema – or, rather, just below Stazzema – 7km, as the crow flies, but further by road, from Pietrasanta. It finishes at Pontestazzemese, beside the Fiume Vezza on the valley floor below Stazzema. Walkers could choose to catch a bus back to Pietrasanta from Cardoso, 2km further up the valley, but bus services are less frequent than those to Pontestazzemese. The upper reaches of this valley were drastically affected in June 1996 by floods, the effects of which were still visible at the time of writing (see the 'Flood Damage' boxed text on the next page).

As described earlier in the chapter, it would be possible during summer to fill in the gaps between this walk and the Pizzo d'Uccello walk and combine the two into a long traverse of the entire Alpi Apuane. Such a walk might either follow closely the marked Apuane Trekking route from Pietrasanta to Carrara or vary it somewhat.

Pietrasanta, an excellent base for walks in

Flood Damage

In June 1996 severe floods destroyed much of the village of Cardoso and damaged settlements further downstream on the Fiume Vezza. Many lives were lost. Sections of walking tracks Nos 8, 12 and 124 were washed away and became impassable. At the time of writing, track No 8, from Cardoso to Foce delle Porchette, was open again, but walkers were still being advised to avoid Nos 12 and 124, south of Foce di Mosceta and below Monte Forato. For the most recent information, call the Parco Naturale delle Alpi Apuane information centre (☎ (0584) 75 73 61) at Seravezza or one of the local sections of the Club Alpino Italiano (CAI). ■

this south-eastern part of the Alpi Apuane, is a fascinating town in its own right for those with an interest in sculpture, especially in marble. Many sculptors have studios here, and each year sculptors and students of sculpture from abroad visit Pietrasanta to attend master classes and workshops. Exhibitions of sculpture are common. A day or two spent in Pietrasanta makes an interesting counterpoise to a walk in the Alpi Apuane amid the quarries where the marble comes from.

PLANNING

All the practical information given in the Pizzo d'Uccello section regarding what to bring and when to walk applies equally to this walk.

GETTING TO/FROM THE WALK

Stazzema and Pontestazzemese are served by CLAP buses. These depart from the bus station in Pietrasanta, on the other side of the railway line from the train station and accessible from the station by a pedestrian underpass. There are frequent services to Pontestazzemese (25 minutes, L3200) from Monday to Saturday and fewer on Sunday. Some of these buses continue to Cardoso. At least six a day (none on Sunday outside the summer months), leaving Pietrasanta at 6.10, 7.40 and 11 am and 1, 2 and 5 pm, turn up the hill to Stazzema (35 minutes, L3400).

THE WALK
Day 1: Stazzema to Rifugio Rossi alla Pania

4 to 5 hours, 1300m ascent, 90m descent

Track Nos 5, 5b and 6 set off from the last sharp bend in the road from Pietrasanta below the village of Stazzema. Monte Procinto (1147m) rises prominently above to the north-east. Markers lead at first up a made road towards Monte Procinto and Rifugio Forte dei Marmi. This climbs gradually around the hillside and switches back first to the west, then to the east again. In less than half an hour, at a signposted junction only a short distance after the second major bend, a marked walking track branches off on the south side of the road. Check the signs here for the latest on the state of tracks destroyed by floods (see the 'Flood Damage' boxed text).

A few hundred metres after it leaves the road, the walking track divides. Track No 6 goes left and is the more direct route to Monte Forato. It is worth going right and following No 5 for a further 30 minutes to meet track No 121. At the track junction is a stone shelter, and water fills a stone tank nearby. Two hundred metres to the right (south-east) from here, with a dramatic view of Monte Procinto, is *Rifugio Forte dei Marmi* (☎ (0584) 77 70 51), with bar, restaurant and 52 beds, open continuously from 15 June to 15 September and on weekends for the rest of the year.

From the track junction, follow markers uphill on track No 121 (not No 5b, which descends). This passes below the cliffs of **Monte Procinto** and around the western end of a group of smaller towers known as I Bimbi del Procinto. Monte Forato (1223m) and Pania della Croce (1858m) now dominate the view across the valley to the north. Track No 6 comes in from below, followed by No 8 from Cardoso (at the opposite angle to that shown on Multigraphic maps of the area); the latter soon splits off and climbs to Foce delle Porchette. Continue along track No 6, ignoring first No 124b on the left, then No 109 on the right and No 124 on the left, to **Foce di Petrosciana** (931m). Plans to build a road through this pass, connecting the

TOSCANA

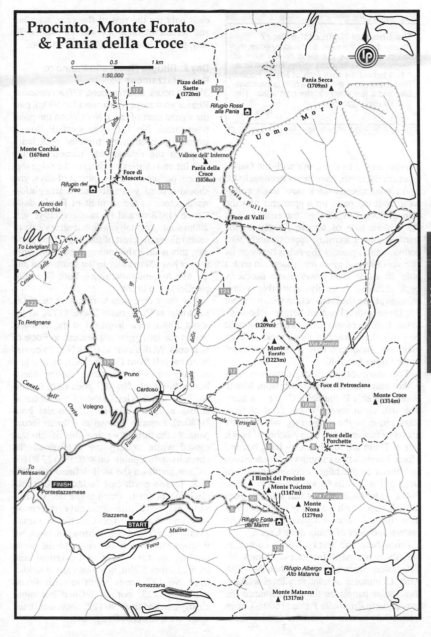

Procinto, Monte Forato & Pania della Croce

0   0.5   1 km

1:50,000

Monte Corchia (1676m)

Pizzo delle Saette (1720m)   [127]   [139]   Pania Secca (1709m)

Rifugio Rossi alla Pania

[126]   Uomo Morto

Vallone dell' Inferno

Foce di Mosceta   Pania della Croce (1858m)

Rifugio del Freo   [125]

Antro del Corchia   Costa Pulita   [7]

To Levigliani   [9]   Foce di Valli

[122]   Canale delle Volte   Canale delle Deglio

[123]   To Retignano   Canale delle Capriola

(1209m)   [12]

Via Ferrata

Monte Forato (1223m)   [124]

[122]   Pruno   [12]

Cardoso   [124]   Foce di Petrosciana

Volegno   Canale Versiglia   [124b]   Monte Croce (1314m)

Canale dell' Oreto   [109]   Foce delle Porchette

Fiume Vezza   [8]   [8]

To Pietrasanta   I Bimbi del Procinto

FINISH Pontestazzemese   [6]   Monte Procinto (1147m)

Via Ferrata

Stazzema   [5]   Monte Nona (1279m)

START   Rifugio Forte dei Marmi

Mulina   [121]

Fosso

Pomezzana   Rifugio Albergo Alto Matanna

Monte Matanna (1317m)

The Shortest Night of the Year?

On one day of the year, so the story goes, the sun sets not once but twice on the town of Barga, in the Garfagnana valley. The first time, it sets behind the rock arch of Monte Forato. Then it reappears through the hole in the mountain, and a few minutes later sets again. This time it's really goodnight.

Nick Tapp

Versilia region to the south with the Garfagnana to the north, have never been realised.

An unnumbered track now leads northwest from the pass, up a spur and past the start of a via ferrata, then traverses around the eastern side of **Monte Forato** to the startling natural archway, approximately 30m across, which pierces the ridge between its two summits and gives the 'mountain with a hole' its name. The lower, more northerly peak (1209m) is easily accessible a few minutes above the intersection with track No 12. Those with a head for heights who wish to take their lives into their own hands should be particularly wary of loose rocks as they make the obvious, narrow 'skyline traverse' to the higher summit.

The saw-toothed ridge, approximately 1.5km long, that extends north from Monte Forato towards Pania della Croce is a gem. The still unnumbered track, faint at first, stays close to the ridge top, which is by grassy, rocky and clad with patches of beech forest. There are lovely views back beyond Monte Forato's two summits to Monte Nona, and ahead to the huge, open south-eastern slope of Pania della Croce, known as 'Costa Pulita'. The track leads down through **Foci di Valli**, then north – a steady climb of more than 400m – across Costa Pulita to the eastern shoulder of Pania della Croce.

From here the track, No 7, continues roughly north, past junctions with track No 126 (tomorrow's route) and then No 139. After 15 minutes of relatively level walking some solar panels on the left announce the cosy *Rifugio Rossi alla Pania* (1609m), open from 1 July to mid-September and on weekends only for the rest of the year, with bar and restaurant facilities and 22 bunks. To stay, phone ahead on ☎ (0583) 71 03 86.

Day 2: Rifugio Rossi alla Panna to Pontestazzemese

3½ to 4 hours, 250m ascent, 1700m descent

Retrace your steps south-west for 500m, past the signed start of track No 139, to the point where track No 126 goes west. Follow it steeply up through the tumbled rock landscape of the evocatively named Vallone dell'Inferno (Valley of Hell) to the ridge top. Except perhaps on the windiest of days, you should reward yourself with a straightforward detour to the summit of **Pania della Croce** (1858m) and its massive cross, just 200m south (actually, a few degrees east of south) along the crest of the ridge. On a good day, this is an exhilarating viewpoint, with the sea just 15km away to the south-west and the Alpi Apuane stretching in both directions parallel to the coast.

The track descends north along the ridge top towards Pizzo delle Saette (1720m) for about 200m, then drops off to the west and begins the long, gradual descent to **Foce di Mosceta**. At this saddle, track No 125 comes in on the left from Foci di Valli, then, a few minutes on, where a stone shelter stands beside the track, No 127 goes right (north) and No 122 heads left (south). Straight ahead across a little gully is Rifugio del Freo (1180m), formerly known as Rifugio Pietrapana. At the time of writing, this rifugio was closed while undergoing extensions. To check its status, phone on ☎ (0584) 77 80 07.

Turn south on the well-defined track No 122. To the north-east is **Monte Corchia** (1676m), beneath which is the deepest and most extensive limestone cave system in Italy, known as Antro del Corchia. In a small saddle 1km from Foce di Mosceta, track No 9 drops steeply off the ridge to the west, heading for the village of Levigliani, and after a further 500m, in another small saddle, track No 122 heads south towards Pruno while No 123, not as defined but more clearly marked than No 122, continues to the south-west towards Retignano.

Leave the ridge on track No 122, which drops past some small clusters of decrepit buildings and one or two well maintained ones. Track markers are infrequent but the walking is easy. Half an hour from the ridge top the track joins a steep, winding, sealed road, but after only a couple of minutes leaves it again at a red-and-white marker painted on the corner of a building on the left. A further 15 minutes, mostly spent on a venerable stone-paved mule track, brings you to **Pruno**, where track No 122 descends

a flight of concrete steps to meet the asphalt at a car park and a park information board.

From Pruno it's sealed road all the way. In clear conditions Monte Forato is seen to good advantage above and to the east. Once on the valley bottom, which you reach at the lower end of Cardoso, it's an unappealing trudge of 2km down the valley past flood-damaged buildings to **Pontestazzemese**. The CLAP bus to Pietrasanta leaves from the main piazza, just near the turn-off up the hill to Stazzema.

Sardegna

The second largest island in the Mediterranean, Sardegna (Sardinia) has always been considered an isolated faraway land. Even today, its people and culture maintain a separate identity from the mainland, which they call *il continente* (the continent). This is despite the fact that the 180km stretch of ocean separating Sardegna from il continente can now be traversed in a few hours.

The inland areas of the island offer walkers spectacularly well-preserved semi-wilderness areas, the domain for centuries of shepherds living with their flocks in almost complete isolation. These areas are now protected by one national park, nine regional parks and 54 natural reserves recently instituted by the Italian government. Birdwatching, trekking and other kinds of outdoor activities have picked up and are not restricted to the summer. Warm weather usually lasts from April to October; in August, when it's too hot for walking, the beaches are packed with tourists from all over Europe. The landscape of the island ranges from the 'savage, dark-bushed, sky-exposed land' described by DH Lawrence, with incredibly beautiful gorges, highlands and mountains which are home to eagles and vultures, to the 1900km of unspoiled, magnificent coastline with clear waters, lovely sandy beaches, dramatic rocky stretches and salt lakes inhabited by herons and pink flamingos.

In 1700, the Jesuit priest, Francesco Cetti, one of the first naturalists to be attracted to this 'exotic island', wrote: 'What there is in Sardinia there is not in Italy, nor is there in Sardinia what there is in Italy'. This is true in every way for a walker. The extraordinary scenic and natural attractions of the island, including the walking routes, are decidedly special when compared with the Italian standard.

There is no system of managed or ranger-operated *rifugi* (refuges) in the mountains of Sardegna, as found in other areas of Italy. Walking here means bringing along all the necessities, including water.

HIGHLIGHTS

STEFANO CAVEDONI

- The scenic rocky coastline of the Golfo di Orosei
- Visiting ancient Nuraghic villages in Valle Lanaittu
- Exploring Gola di Gorropu and other gorges in the mountainous area of Barbagia
- Relaxing with a swim on the Capo Testa walk

The eastern mountainous area of Barbagia, for those who love to walk, is the most fascinating part of Sardegna and is the only expansive area of relative wilderness existing in Italy. The people of these mountains live in little towns, connected by a few roads and served by infrequent buses. Vast areas, where it is possible to travel only on foot, are inhabited exclusively by shepherds and their flocks. A network of trails, which are rarely marked, crosses the rocky limestone terrain of the highplains, with fantastic gorges where bizarre rock formations tormented by erosion have been colonised by the tough, evergreen vegetation typical of the Mediterranean.

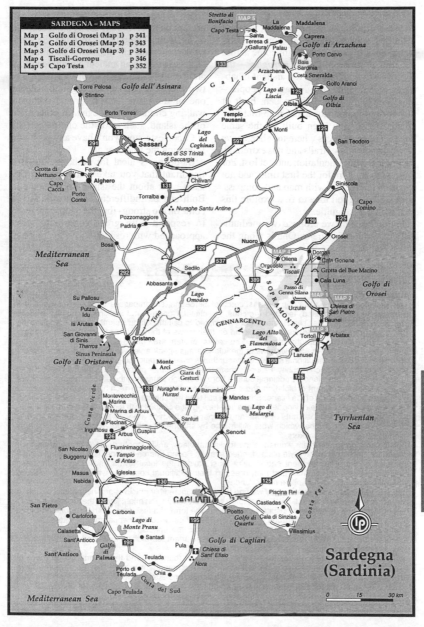

SARDEGNA – MAPS

Sardegna
(Sardinia)

SARDEGNA

0   15   30 km

Finding yourself immersed in this picturesque solitude, in a primordial silence disturbed only by the wind, you are catapulted back in time. You might come across the ruin of a Bronze Age *nuraghe* – the fortress-like dwellings of the ancient inhabitants of Sardegna, the Nuraghic people – alongside a traditional sheep pen, built of 10-year-old juniper logs, and note that they could almost have been built by the same hands. These are areas where the sheep have created a network of trails and it is extremely easy to lose your orientation and get lost. For those who are here for the first time, and not expert in navigation with map and compass, it would be a good idea to first explore this area with a local guide.

In the Barbagia we propose two medium-difficulty, three-day treks. One is along the coast, where orientation problems might present themselves only along short sections of the walk. The other is through the semi-wilderness area of the Valle Lanaittu and includes visits to an ancient Nuraghic village and the spectacular Gola di Goroppu. The two walks can connect at Dorgali to make up one of the most interesting and complete walking circuits in Sardegna. In other areas of the island, such as on the one-day circuit at Capo Testa, you won't have any problems following the tracks at all.

Sardegna is ideal for walking, but it is important that you take some time to first learn a bit about the island and its people. Both can be indifferent and hostile if you come on too strong – but the people are ready to respond with great generosity when approached with respect.

Nuoro Province

This province, about halfway up the east coast of Sardegna, encompasses the area known as the Barbagia. It has unspoiled, isolated beaches, spectacular gorges and walking routes, as well as important Nuraghic sites. The Romans were prompted to call the island's central-eastern mountains Barbagia (from the Latin for barbarian) based on their views of the lifestyle of the warrior/shepherds who wouldn't give up Nuraghic practices. The central-eastern area of the island is still known by this name and even today the Sardegnans of the inland areas speak a very ancient Latin-based dialect and are proud of their traditional social behaviour that is based on belonging, firstly to one's family and secondly to the village community. Probably more than in any other part of Sardegna, you will be able to get a sense of the island's traditional culture here. Although tourism in the area is increasing, there remains a strong element of isolation and a connection with traditions which have been swept aside by tourism in other parts of the island. Shepherds still tend their flocks in remote areas of the province, often living alone in stone or wooden shacks and having little contact with the outside world. However, the *pinnettas* (cone-shaped huts of stone and juniper wood) which are very similar in appearance to the ancient stone nuraghe, which were still in use by shepherds until about 10 years ago, are now used as rifugio huts by walkers.

It is common to see older women in the traditional black, ankle-length dresses of the area, their heads covered in Spanish-style black, fringed shawls. Spring (March to June) is a good time to visit the area as there are frequent patron saint feast days in the local towns and villages. On these occasions, the young women and men dress in their traditional costumes with beautiful coloured embroidery and perform traditional folk dances.

If you venture into the interior, you will find the people incredibly gracious and hospitable, although contact can be difficult at first. If you want to try what little Italian you might know, the locals will surely respond with enthusiasm and hospitality – mainly in the form of a first drink, then a second and then others until you are completely drunk. They have a deep affection for their apparently deserted territory. Theirs is a shepherd's society that, never having had the impulse to build magnificent cities or monuments, has saved the precious, unspoiled environment, carefully maintained for centuries by their shepherd's practices.

This is also an area long associated with *banditismo* (banditry) and the unfortunate practice of kidnapping – a long-time scourge on Italian society. It is important to note that Sardegnans have recently been turning out en masse at public demonstrations against the kidnapping of people from wealthy families, whereas 20 years ago they would have maintained a conspiratorial silence. ■

Sardegnan Cooking

The island's cuisine is as varied as its history. Along the coast most dishes feature seafood and there are many variations of *zuppa di pesce* (fish soup) and pasta. Inland you will find porcheddu (roast suckling pig), kid goat with olives and lamb trotters in garlic sauce. The Sardi eat *pecorino* (sheep's milk cheese) and the preferred bread throughout the island is the paper thin *carta musica*, also called *pane carasau*, often served sprinkled with oil and salt. ■

HISTORY

Sardegna is dotted with some 7000 nuraghe, cone-shaped megalithic fortresses that are the only remnants of the island's first inhabitants – the Nuraghic people. These people lived in separate communities led by warrior-king shepherds, and their culture flourished from around 1800 BC. Sardegna's coast was often visited by Greeks and Phoenicians, who came first as traders and later as invaders, before the island was eventually colonised by the Romans.

The Romans, in turn, were followed by the Pisans, Genovese, Spanish, Austrians and, finally, the Savoia royal family, whose possessions became the Kingdom of Sardegna prior to their eventual incorporation into the newly, though imperfectly, united Kingdom of Italy in 1861. Despite their history, it is often said that the Sardegnans, known as Sardi, were never really conquered; rather, they simply retreated into their villages to defend their culture.

Sardegna has many historical sights: the capital city, Cagliari, has a Roman amphitheatre, an interesting medieval centre and an important archaeological museum; the countryside offers isolated Pisan-style Romanesque churches, imposing Nuraghic royal fortresses (such as at Barumini) and Carthaginian towns such as Nora and Tharros on the west coast. Sardegna became a semiautonomous region in 1948, and the Italian government's Sardegnan Rebirth Plan of 1962 had some influence on the development of tourism, industry and agriculture.

NATURAL HISTORY

Sardegna is in the middle of the western Mediterranean, about 190km from the coast of Africa and 180km from the Italian peninsula. The island is separated from Corsica, to the north, by an 11km stretch of sea, known as the Stretto di Bonifacio. The island has a population of about 1.7 million, which equals an average of 68 people per square kilometre – making it a very scarcely inhabited region with respect to the Italian average (190 per square kilometre). The island is 68% mountainous, with plains making up only 18% of the territory. The Gennargentu, in the central-eastern part of the island, is the highest area with the 1834 m of Punta La Marmora. There are long sandy beaches between Buggerru and Montevecchio on the western coast, between San Teodoro and Capo Comino on the eastern coast, at Santa Maria Navarrese and Arbatax to the east and at the Poetto beach at Cagliari. The rest of the Sardegnan coastline is rocky. The western and southern coasts of Sardegna have preserved a rich heritage of coastal ponds and brackish lagoons which are an ideal habitat for many animals, especially birds, including the pink flamingo and the rare white-headed duck and purple gallinule. The ponds are also a strategic point of reference for migratory species using the island as a stopover between Africa and Northern Europe twice a year.

Geology

Millions of years ago Sardegna and Corsica broke off the southern coast of France, leaving behind the Côte d'Azur. Ancient volcanic phenomena, extinct for centuries, have left marked traces in the complex of Monte Ferru and the cones of the Meilogu and Monte Arci along the west coast; in the evocative granite formations of the Gallura to the north; and in typical flat basalt high plains like the Giara di Gesturi, inland from the Golfo di Oristano. The vast central-east limestone high plains that form the Supramonte of Orgosolo and Oliena are, on the other hand, originally sedimentary with numerous grottoes, underground streams

SARDEGNA

and deep gorges. A must-see are the remains of the fossil forest on the banks of the Lago Omodeo (Lake Omodeo), formed in the Miocene period when trees were covered by a shower of volcanic debris.

Flora

Sardegna's rich flora is conditioned by the typical Mediterranean climate and the generally arid and rocky terrain. Numerous species endemic to Sardegna and Corsica have evolved in this hard, dry environment, restricted at times to particular areas – such as Baleari boxwood in the area of Carbonia; horrid centaury, with its white, prickly bushes at Capo Caccia; filigree centaury of the coast of Baunei; morigian rushes on the Gennargentu; and Sardegnan currants of the Supramonte.

There are three prevalent landscape types: coastal, plain-hillside and mountain. On the eastern coast, where one of our treks will take you, the harmony created between the rock of the high cliffs and the vegetation owes a lot to the obstinacy and beauty of the typical low Mediterranean scrub. Cistus, myrtle and gum tree are often found together and offer a splendid, multi-coloured and perfumed floral spectacle in the spring and summer. Heather, euphorbia, rosemary and broom found here are often associated with the presence of trees such as the holm oak, juniper, strawberry tree, oleander and tamarisk.

The west coast is differently characterised by low sandy sediments with ground-hugging bushes, referred to as a *gariga*, of juniper, gum trees, rosemary, myrtle, asparagus, heather, lavender and cistus. A rare species of spontaneous European palm is the dwarf palm, or the palm of San Pietro, which is found also on the islands of San Pietro and Sant' Antioco. There are lovely forests of domestic pines in the area of Buggerru. In the many brackish ponds, the salt-wort flourishes, the only plant able to stand the salt, and then there is reed, bamboo, cat's-tails and tamarisk. Among the grasses there are the pot marigold, mugwort and verbena.

The plains and hillside are characterised by high patches of holm oak or laurel (the one used as bay leaf in cooking, which here grows to a height of up to 5m) along with durmast, olive, elder, blackberry, hawthorn, butcher's broom and strawberry trees.

In some areas there are patches of broom with their bright yellow flowers, of which there are six different species on the island. In the mountains from 500m to 800m, the holm oak is predominant, associated with the sugar oak. Above 800m we find the holm oak, the yew, the maple, the turpentine and the black hornbeam tree. Above 1100m, tree cover is limited to low growing species such as the dwarf juniper and the prostrate blackthorn found on the Gennargentu. Be careful in the underbrush of poisonous medicinal varieties such as the *Digitalis purpurea* and *Helleborus lividus*.

Flowers On the plains and among the rocks, the grassy vegetation offers the poppy, the violet, the gladiola, the yellow of the cane, the white of the daisy and the wild carrot, the blue of the periwinkle and lavender and the coloured mix of the irises and many species of orchid. On the Supramonte, the elegant rose-pink bloom of the peonies is justifiably famous.

Fauna

Mammals Although hunters and poachers have traditionally been active in Sardegna, some wildlife remains. The list includes the ever present wild boar (*Scrofa meridionalis* – cinghiale sardo), the mouflon (*Ovis musimon* – muflone) with its great curved horns, the endemic Sardegnan wild cat (*Felis silvestris* – gatto selvatico) and the Sardegnan deer (*Cervus elaphus* ssp *corsicanus* – cervo sardo). Fox, weasel, marten, hare and dormouse complete the list of wild terrestrial animals.

There are impressive populations of wild ponies, that have for centuries been raised on the Giara di Gesturi, and little groups of small white donkeys on the Island of Asinara – the island is not accessible to the public because of the presence of a high-security prison holding *mafiosi*. The Mediterranean monk seal (*Foca monaca* – bue marino) is extremely rare – perhaps only a few couples remain in the caves of the eastern coast.

Birds Sardegna is a paradise for birdwatchers – there are many species, some which are really spectacular – such as the flamingos (*Phoenicopterus ruber rosseus* – fenicottero) in the salt ponds near Cagliari and Oristano, and the colony of griffon vultures (*Gyps fulvus* – grifone) on the west coast near Bosa. More difficult to see are the black vulture (*Aegypius monachus* – avvoltoio monaco) and bearded vulture (*Gypaetus barbatus* – gipeto). Among the birds of prey, the golden eagle (*Aquila chrysaetos* – aquila reale) is easy to find throughout the Barbagia, while the smaller Bonelli's eagle (*Hieraaetus fasciatus* – aquila del Bonelli) nests in the coastal area of the Supramonte. It is easy to see the peregrine falcon (*Falco peregrinus* – falco pellegrino) and Eleanora's falcon (*Falco eleonorae* – falco della regina) along the rocky shores of the island.

You can see kestrels everywhere, holding themselves immobile against the wind on wings spread wide, eyeing their terrestrial prey. There are also buzzard, goshawk, sparrowhawk, swamp falcon and Sardegnan owl to be seen. Besides the barbary partridge, rock partridge (pursued by hunters), crow, jay, hoopoe and wood pigeon, there are many species to be found in the ponds. These include the rare purple gallinule and white-headed duck, waders like the grey heron, white egret, purple heron, night heron, water rail, little egret, curlew, avocet, black-winged stilt and other migratory species of duck and goose stopping off en route between Europe and Africa in February/March and September/October.

Reptiles Sardegna is the only region of Italy where there are no poisonous vipers. You might meet other species of harmless snake like the natrix viper, similar in appearance to the poisonous adder *(Vipera berus)*, the Sardegnan coluber and the endemic Sardegnan lizard. Interesting among amphibians is the Sardegnan newt which can be found inhabiting caves.

CLIMATE

High average temperatures and little rain mean that Sardegna has at least seven months of good weather each year. Average temperatures along the coast are 19°C in autumn, 10°C in winter, 12°C in spring and 22°C in summer. On the eastern coast, winds from the north create clear skies and a cool airflow, while winds from the south or east bring occasional rain which rarely lasts long. However, there can be strong winds which last for several days. Spring and autumn are the best seasons for walking.

INFORMATION
Maps

Ente Sardo Industrie Turistiche (ESIT) produces and distributes a good road map of the island (1:300,000 scale) which has maps of the major cities and some useful tourist itineraries. This map is available from most local tourist offices. At newsstands and in bookshops you can also easily find other editions of regional maps.

Information Sources

Cagliari The AAST information booth (☎ (070) 66 92 55) in Piazza Matteotti is open from 8 am to 8 pm daily during summer, and from 8 am to 2 pm in other months. It has a reasonable amount of information about the town and will advise on accommodation. There is also a provincial tourist information booth at the airport (☎ (070) 24 02 00) open from 8.30 am to 1 pm and 3.30 to 9 pm daily in the high season. There is an ESIT office, which covers all of Sardegna, at Via Goffredo Mameli 97 (green number ☎ 167-013153 from 8 am to 8 pm every day during summer). The office can be useful if you are starting your tour of the island at Cagliari.

Olbia The AAST office (☎ (0789) 24979) is at Via Catello Piro 1, off Corso Umberto, and is open daily from 8 am to 2 pm and 4 to 8 pm in summer. The staff speak English and are very keen to help and advise on places to stay and eat. They can also provide information about accommodation and places to visit throughout the rest of the island.

Nuoro The EPT office (☎ (0784) 30083) is at Piazza Italia 19 and is open Monday to Friday from 10.30 am to 1 pm. It also opens from 4 to 7 pm on Wednesday and Thursday.

Dorgali & Cala Gonone At Dorgali there is a Pro Loco tourist office (☎ (0784) 96243) in Via La Marmora, where you can pick up information about trails in the area, including an alternate route to the Nuraghic village of Tiscali if you don't want to tackle the walk detailed in this section. At Cala Gonone the tourist office (☎ (0784) 93387) in Viale del Bue Marino opens during summer only.

Oliena There is no official tourist office in Oliena, but this function is efficiently covered by Levamus Viaggi travel agency (☎ (0784) 28 51 90), on Corso Vittorio Emanuele 27.

Santa Teresa di Gallura Santa Teresa's AAST office (☎ (0789) 75 41 27), in the town centre at Piazza Vittorio Emanuele 24, is open daily during summer from 8.30 am to 1 pm and 3.30 to 8 pm. The helpful staff can provide loads of information and will assist in finding accommodation. It is possible to ring ahead to request information on hotels, rooms and apartments to rent, or you can write (in English) to: AAST, Piazza V. Emanuele 24, 07028 Santa Teresa di Gallura, Sassari.

Books

DH Lawrence, the English novelist and poet (1885-1930), wrote about Sardegna after he visited the island, on a one-week winter excursion from Sicilia (Sicily), in the early 1920s. The Penguin Travel Library edition *DH Lawrence and Italy* includes his interesting *Sea and Sardinia*.

Place Names

Place names on the IGM maps and on signs throughout the island are sometimes in local dialects and may differ slightly from those used in this book.

Warnings

Since you'll be walking in some very isolated areas, it's a good idea to notify someone of your route and destination before setting out. In case of an emergency, in some areas the lack of roads makes rescue operations very slow; a mobile telephone could resolve a lot of problems. Never underestimate the problem of orientation in the wilderness areas! You might also encounter problems crossing the limestone terrain of the Supramonte – it is full of deep holes and channels covered by vegetation and therefore it is not a good idea to leave the trail. If you do lose your trail – the best idea is to retrace your steps to find it. If you would like to explore the area, but doubt your orienteering abilities, hire a local guide for an initial exploration of the area. Compass and altimeter, an ample water supply, a good map, heavy shoes and sun protection should be the first things on your list of strategic items.

ACCOMMODATION & SUPPLIES
Cagliari

There are numerous budget hotels in the old city near the station. Try *Locanda Firenze* (☎ (070) 65 36 78), Corso Vittorio Emanuele 50, which has singles/doubles for L40,000/ L54,000. *Locanda Miramare* (☎ (070) 66 40 21), Via Roma 59, has singles/doubles for L50,000/L65,000. Nearby is *Albergo Centrale* (☎ (070) 65 47 83), Via Sardegna 4, which has rooms for L40,000/L60,000, and the pleasant *Albergo la Perla* (☎ (070) 66 94 46), Via Sardegna 18, with rooms for L44,000/L56,000. *Pensione Vittoria* (☎ (070) 65 79 70), Via Roma 75, is a very pleasant establishment, with rooms for L55,000/ L85,000, or L62,000/L99,000 with bathroom. *Hotel Italia* (☎ (070) 66 05 10), Via Sardegna 31, has more upmarket, comfortable rooms for L100,000/L135,000.

Olbia

Albergo Terranova (☎ (0789) 22395), Via Giuseppe Garibaldi 3, has singles/doubles for L38,000/L60,000. *Hotel Minerva* (☎ (0789) 21190), Via Mazzini 7, has doubles for L60,000, and singles/doubles with bathroom for L45,000/L70,000. *Hotel Gallura* (☎ (0789) 24648), Corso Umberto 145, is a pleasant place with singles/doubles with bathroom for L80,000/L110,000. Hotel Centrale (☎ (0789) 23017), Corso Umberto 85, has rooms for L100,000/ L140,000.

Arbatax

If you get stuck, try the *Il Gabbiano* hotel (☎ (0782) 62 35 12) in the Porto Frailis area, a few kilometres from Arbatax, which has singles/doubles with bathroom for L60,000/L85,000.

PLANNING
When to Walk

The best period for walking is in spring, from March to May, when the days are beginning to lengthen and the wild flowers are in bloom and not yet dried out by the summer heat. Autumn is also a pleasant time to walk. Winter is too cold and summer is far too hot for walking.

Maps

Unfortunately there are no modern editions of walking maps for Sardegna. It is necessary to use the Istituto Geografico Militare (IGM - see Maps in the Facts for the Walker chapter) maps at 1:25,000 scale. The new editions of the maps, called *serie* (series) 25 (L20,000), are current up to 1989-91. The old series 25/V editions (L11,000), which are still the most widely available, are based on surveys taken between 1958 and 1965 but are still usable.

What to Bring

Lightweight mountain climbing shoes with rigid soles, suitable for rocky terrain, are essential; light, season-appropriate clothing preferably with long pants which will help when crossing through thick spiny bushes; hat; sunglasses; sun block; a light rain-poncho; scarf for the wind; and insect repellent will all prove useful. If camping overnight you will also need a torch; sleeping bag; a lightweight tent, which is advisable if it isn't the middle of the summer; and a large canteen

(at least 2L capacity) as fresh springs are rare. A thermal cover and a whistle are useful in case of an emergency. A good map, compass and altimeter are all indispensable.

Guided Walks

Dorgali The Cooperativa Ghivine (☎ (0784) 96721 or 96623), Via Montebello 5, organises nature walks and archaeological, speleological (caving) and scuba excursions in the Dorgali area.

Oliena The mythical Murena (real name Vincenzo Tupponi) was the first walking guide to the Supramonte in the 1970s. He runs a speleological rifugio in the magical Valle Lanaittu and organises, along with his associates, interesting one-day and five to six-day walks, between the Supramonte and the coast. They visit the Nuraghic villages of Tiscali and Sos Carros in the Valle Lanaittu, the Gola di Gorropu and Badde Pentumas, the Supramonte of Oliena and Orgosolo, the Gennargentu and the gorges on the coast, known as *codule*. You can also talk to him about spending a night in the quaint shepherds' pinnettas. Information is available from Albergo Ci Kappa (☎ (0784) 28 87 33 or 28 80 24).

The Levamus travel agency (☎ (0784) 28 51 90; fax 28 87 77), Corso Vittorio Emanuele 27, offers 20 or so excursions and guided tours of one or more days duration. You can also rent tents, sleeping mattresses and gas lanterns from here, and they can organise transport for groups from Nuoro and to and from the start and finish of the treks by 4WD. Transport by 4WD to Scala è Pradu costs L50,000 regardless of the number of people travelling.

Barbagia Insolita (☎ (0784) 28 81 67) at Via Carducci 25 has guided tours to out-of-the-way areas by 4WD and on foot. You can choose between demanding walks or relaxing walks to places including Tiscali, the Gola di Gorropu, Monte Corrasi and the Codula di Luna.

The Cooperativa Turistica Enis (☎ (0784) 28 83 63; fax 28 84 73) operates a hotel/restaurant near Monte Maccione, 3km from Oliena on the slopes of Monte Corrasi. It organises guided daily excursions around

Oliena for groups of at least eight people and has nine-seater minibuses with driver available for hire. The ride to Scala è Pradu, for example, costs around L10,000/L20,000 per person, depending on the number of people travelling.

Urzulei The Società Gorropu (☎ (0782) 64 92 82 or (0368) 55 37 49), Via Cagliari 4, is an organisation of young, competent and environmentally motivated guides, which offers real walks in the Sardegna wilderness at good prices. They offer a variety of guided one-day walks that include 4WD transfers to the start of the walk. For groups of at least five people the cost is only L50,000 (guided walk and transfer) a head. This includes the descent of the Codula di Luna to the sea, a route along the edge of the same *codula* (gorge), the climb from the depths of the Gola di Gorropu up as far as possible, the exciting descent from the top of the same imposing gorge with sections of rappelling (abseiling), and the use of rubber dinghies to cross the lake (L70,000). They also offer three different five or six-day walks: from the Nuraghic village of Tiscali to Cala di Luna, from Monte Novo to Cala di Luna passing by Gorropu, and the codule walk from Cala di Luna to the Golgo di Baunei which is described later in this chapter. This particular walk, for groups of eight to 10 people, costs from L320,000 to L340,000 per person.

Baunei *Golgo* restaurant/camp site, on the high plain of the same name near the Chiesa di San Pietro, operates organised, guided walks of one or more days in the area of Baunei, with 4WD transfers and a rustic dinner with local shepherds, for L100,000 per person per day.

Emergency
Call ☎ 112 (carabinieri) or ☎ 113 (police) for emergency assistance. In Sardegna, the 8th group of the Corpo Nazionale del Soccorso Alpino (National Alpine Emergency Corps), a group of volunteers of the CAI, operates an emergency rescue service. Should you require first aid while on any of the walks in the mountains or caves around the Supramonte, call the regional head Giuseppe Domenichelli (☎ (070) 72 81 63) or the Nuoro station chief, Giuseppe Basolu (☎ (0784) 35930 or 20 43 93).

GETTING THERE & AWAY
Air
Airports at Cagliari, Olbia, Alghero and Arbatax-Tortolì link Sardegna with major Italian and European cities. For further information on domestic flights contact CIT or CTS, they have offices in all major Italian towns; for international flights contact Alitalia.

Sea
The island is accessible by ferry from Genova (Genoa), Civitavecchia, Napoli (Naples), Palermo, Trapani, Bonifacio (Corsica) and Tunisia, as well as Toulon and Marseille in France. The main embarkation/departure points in Sardegna are Olbia, Golfo Aranci, Palau and Porto Torres in the north, Arbatax on the east coast and Cagliari in the south.

The main ferry company is Tirrenia, although Ferrovie dello Stato (FS) runs a slightly cheaper ferry service between Olbia and Civitavecchia. Other companies include Moby Lines, also known as Sardegna Lines, which runs ferries between Sardegna and Corsica and between Livorno and Olbia. Brochures detailing Moby Lines and Tirrenia services are available at most travel agencies throughout the country. Note that timetables change dramatically every year and that prices fluctuate according to the season.

Tirrenia's offices can be found throughout Italy including: Roma (Rome) (☎ (06) 474 20 41), Via Bissolati 41; Civitavecchia (☎ (0766) 28801); and Genova (☎ (010) 25 80 41). They have an office in Cagliari (☎ (070) 66 87 88), at the Stazione Marittima (ferry terminal) and two more in Olbia at the Stazione Marittima (☎ (0789) 24691) and at Corso Umberto 17 (☎ (0789) 28533). Moby Lines has offices and agents throughout the island and Italy. In Livorno, it operates through the agency LV Ghianda (☎ (0586) 89 03 25) at Via Vittorio Veneto 24.

SARDEGNA

Tirrenia Ferry Services

Destination	Fares	Duration
Genova-Porto Torres or Olbia	L76,700/L97,600/L124,700	12½ hours
Genova-Cagliari	L102,900/L129,900/L170,900	19 hours
Civitavecchia-Olbia	L40,700/L56,000/L77,800	7 hours
Civitavecchia-Cagliari	L71,500/L89,500/L119,500	13½ hours
Naploli-Cagliari	L52,000/L72,000/L93,000	15 hours
Palermo-Cagliari	L47,000/L66,000/L85,000	12½ hours

Refer to the Tirrenia Ferry Services chart for details on Tirrenia ferry services. Fare prices are listed in the following order: *poltrona*; bed in a 2nd class cabin; and bed in a 1st class cabin.

The cost of taking a small car on the ferry was around L139,000 on all routes.

Moby Lines offer special fares for daytime passages in low season. At the time of research, this fare was L280,000 return (Livorno-Olbia) for a car and two people.

Golfo di Orosei

Duration 3 days
Distance 43km
Standard Medium
Start Cala Gonone
Finish Baunei
Closest Towns Olbia, Arbatax
Permits Required No
Public Transport Access Yes
Summary This beautiful, demanding and completely self-sufficient route covers a tract of rocky coast that is among the most scenic in Sardegna.

PLANNING
Maps

This walk is covered by the new series 25 maps as follows: 500 II *Dorgali*; 517 1 *Cantoniera Genna Silana*; 518 III *Capo di Monte Santu*; and 518 IV *Punta è Lattone*.

The old series 25/V maps that cover the walk are: 208 III SE *Baunei*; 208 III NE *Punta S'Abbadorgiu*; and 208 IV SE *Grotta del Bue Marino*.

PLACES TO STAY & EAT
Cala Gonone

Camping Cala Gonone (☎ (0784) 93165), Via Collodi 1, charges up to L24,900 per person. Hotels include *Piccolo Hotel* (☎ (0784) 93232), Via Cristoforo Colombo, near the port, which has very pleasant rooms for L60,000/L99,000 with bathroom. *Hotel La Playa* (☎ (0784) 93106), Via Collodi, is more upmarket; with rooms costing up to L95,000/L135,000. At *Pop Hotel* (☎ (0784) 93300), behind the port, half board is L105,000 and full board L125,000. It also has a reasonably priced restaurant. *Due Chiacchiere* is a trattoria/pizzeria overlooking the sea at Via Acquadolce 13, near the port in Cala Gonone; a full meal will cost around L30,000. More expensive is the nearby *Ristorante Il Pescatore*, where you will pay around L40,000 or more.

Dorgali

Just out of Dorgali, at Monte Sant'Elene, is *Hotel Sant'Elene* (☎ (0784) 94572) (see the Tiscali-Gorropu map later in this chapter), Località Sant'Elene, set in a panoramic position en route to the Gola di Gorropu. Singles/doubles/triples are L60,000/L110,000/L150,000. It also has an excellent restaurant with a reasonably priced tourist menu. In the town itself the only reasonable place to stay is the *San Pietro* hotel (☎ (0784) 96142), Via Lamarmora, which charges L30,000/L65,000 for a very basic single/double.

Baunei

There are no hotels or camping grounds in Baunei itself. However *Golgo* camping ground (☎ (0337) 81 18 28 from July to

September or (0782) 61 06 75 year-round) is
only 8km from Baunei and is open from
March to November. The staff of the coop-
erative-run restaurant can arrange 4WD
transport to Baunei (8km) which provides the
option of finishing the walk here. Another
option is to tackle the walk in the opposite
direction and use the transport to get from
here to Cala Sisine, thus shortening the route
by 15km. The *restaurant* offers excellent and
rich meals of local dishes and grilled meats
for about L40,000, drinks excluded. After
dinner you can arrange to pitch a tent and
sleeping bag in the courtyard, with full use
of the facilities, for an additional charge of
L7000 per person. It may be possible to
arrange the use of some of the facilities in the
off season, when it's normally closed, by telephoning a few days ahead.

GETTING TO/FROM THE WALK

This walk starts in Cala Gonone which is
served by local bus services. It is difficult to
get precise information on buses, especially
if you don't speak Italian. To give you a rough
idea of the services and schedules available
in this area, we have provided a summary of
the 1997 summer schedule following. These
schedules change very little from year to year
but naturally these details should be verified
before setting out on the trek.

Bus

Olbia ARST buses connect the port of Olbia
(leaving at about 7.25 am) with Lanusei
(arrives 12.20 pm), travelling along the
SS125 via Olbia, Siniscola, Orosei, Dorgali
(9.45 am), Baunei (11.10 am), Santa Maria
Navarrese and Tortolì.

ARST buses also connect Olbia port with
Oliena and Nuoro via Siniscola (they leave
after the landing of the ferry from Civitavecchia at about 7.25 am). A direct service
operates from Olbia to Nuoro daily at around
2 pm. There are another eight daily services
from Monday to Saturday, and five on
Sunday, between Olbia and Siniscola. From
Siniscola, there is also one service to Dorgali,
once a day at around 2 pm from Monday to
Saturday.

Nuoro There is a service from the Nuoro
ARST station which goes to Dorgali via
Oliena. These buses operate seven times per
day Monday to Saturday (6.20, 7.43 and 9.40
am and 2, 2.50, 4.40 and 7.50 pm) and four
times on Sundays (7.43 am and 2.50, 4.40
and 7.50 pm). This route is covered by an
additional three daily services during July
and August (8.50 am and 3.55 and 7.25 pm).
On some of these runs the bus continues on
to Cala Gonone: three times a day from
Monday to Saturday (6.53 am and 2 and 3.50
pm) and twice on Sundays (6.53 am and 2
pm). There are two additional runs during
July and August (8 am and 12.15 pm). There
are also direct services from Nuoro to
Dorgali four times a day from Monday to
Saturday (9.50 am and 1.10, 2 and 7 pm) and
one on Sundays at 7 pm. The 2 pm bus only
continues along the SS125 (via Baunei and
Tortolì) arriving in Arbatax at 4.55 pm.

Arbatax There is one run only from Arbatax
to Dorgali (via Tortolì), leaving the port following the arrival of the ferry, at
approximately 5.05 am from Monday to Saturday. The bus arrives in Dorgali at 7.10 am,
then continues to Oliena and arrives in
Nuoro at 8 am.

Baunei There are frequent buses from
Baunei heading south towards Tortolì and
Lanusei as well as a few going north to
Dorgali (5.55 am, Monday to Saturday only,
continues to Oliena and Nuoro; and 4.05 pm
daily, continues to Siniscola and Olbia on the
SS125).

Ferry

The Nuova Consorzio Trasporti Marittimi di
Cala Gorgone (☎ (0784) 93305) operates
large boats, back and forth along the coast,
several times a day from the end of March to
mid-November. The boats go to the Grotto
del Bue Marino (L17,000 return with a guided
visit to the caves), Cala di Luna (L9000 one
way to Cala Gorgone; L15,000 return), Cala
Sisine (L20,000 return) and Cala Mariolu
(L29,000 return). It's possible to catch this
boat directly to Cala di Luna – which

includes a visit to the Grotta del Bue Marino, a cave where a colony of the now very rare monk seal once lived – thus avoiding the first day of the walk. Alternatively, you can follow Day 1 of the trek as far as Cala di Luna, returning to Cala Gorgone by boat. The first boat, from Cala di Luna, departs around 9.30 to 10 am; check by phoning.

THE WALK
Day 1: Cala Gonone to Cala di Luna
3½ hours

From Cala Gonone head south along the asphalt coast road for about 3km. After about one hour you'll reach the deep fissure of the Codula di Cala Fuili, where the road ends at a parking area (one hour on foot). From here the stepped trail descends to cross the codula, a long gorge formed by water erosion, only tens of metres from the sea. The trail then climbs back up the opposite slope to continue on to a junction with a trail to the left that leads to Grotta del Bue Marino. This cave is more easily approached from the sea on the boat service from Cala Gonone. Bear right at the junction to begin a long ascent, at mid-slope, across a large, deep valley (131m altitude, one hour). After passing the valley, the trail begins to descend, still at mid-slope, and enters a little valley going south-south-east. When the little valley turns east, the trail continues south-south-east up to a plateau before quickly descending into a deep gorge, the Gola di Oddoana (21m altitude, 45 minutes). From the gorge, the trail ascends again to the south and passes the hill known as Fruncu Nieddu, crossing its eastern slope at about 100m altitude with a great view of the sea. The trail then begins a steep descent, with sharp turns, to the gravel riverbed of the magically beautiful Codula di Luna. Follow this majestic limestone canyon to the left, going east. About 45 minutes after leaving the Gola di Oddoana you should reach the low structure of the *Ristorante Su Neulagi* where they serve excellent meals. During the off season (September to June) you can ask to pitch a tent nearby for the night.

You are now separated from the sea only

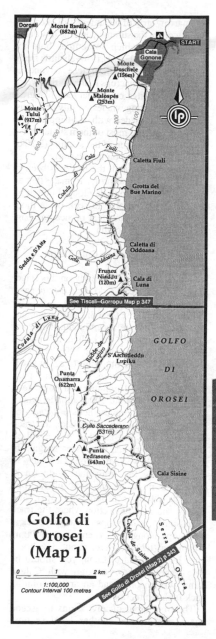

Golfo di Orosei (Map 1)

0   1   2 km

1:100,000
Contour Interval 100 metres

by a narrow strip of oleanders, full of colourful flowers in the summer, and the low dunes of the beach, which sometimes hold the water of the codula to form lovely little freshwater ponds. The beach stretches beyond the cliffs and rocky outcrops to the north towards a series of strange caves that look like great garages for resting whales. In July or August the beach is crowded with day-trippers from Cala Gonone, but most of them should leave with the last boat run of the evening (3.30 or 5.30 pm depending on the season).

You can also catch the last boat back to Cala Gonone if you prefer to make this an easy and pleasant one-day loop. In the high season, it is advisable to seek out a more discreet spot for your tent or sleeping bag, such as inside the codula.

Day 2: Cala di Luna to Cala Sisine
5 hours

It is advisable to set out early on this stage, since you will need to do some careful navigating in order not to lose the trail.

From behind the Cala di Luna restaurant, where the toilets are, ascend south along easy curves on a new dirt track about 2.5m wide. The track was constructed in 1996-7 over the traces of a pre-existing trail, to allow small three-wheeled service vehicles to pass through. After 20 minutes you come to a level section, at about 100m altitude, where you can enjoy the marvellous panorama of the coast to the south. From here, the track descends into the striking gorge called Badde de Lupiru and then ascends again in a south-south-west direction. Continue to ascend along the sunbeaten wide track, passing an imposing and atmospheric rock arch called S'Architieddu (365m), and finally you reach a section where the track veers south and develops into a level track at mid-slope along the eastern face of Punta Onamarra (622m). Here, about 1¾ hours after leaving Cala di Luna, you should be able to spot a stone on the right with 'Cala di Luna' written on it and an arrow pointing back in that direction.

The track immediately begins to ascend again and reaches another level section,

longer than the previous one, which soon crosses over the ridge and leads to the western face of Punta Onamarra – where there are exciting views inland and over the deep incision of the Codula di Luna. There are many interesting mineral formations along this section which are fairly easy to spot, however you will have to be vigilant along here as you approach a fundamental turn-off to the left which is quite difficult to see. Continue along the track, passing a small, circular grass clearing on the left which is bordered by stones – an old coal merchant's spot – the track now begins to ascend again with two sharp curves. Note that at the second curve there is a gap in the low stone wall that follows the track on the left. From this point ascend another 20m taking note of a small holm oak tree on the right-hand side which should have an obvious stone placed in the hollow of its branches (about 630m altitude, 45 minutes from Punta Onamarra). This stone is placed here to signal that, from this point, a faint trail goes off to the left heading eastwards into the vegetation, occasionally marked by stone *ometti* (cairns) on the ground. You are now leaving the easy track behind you and beginning your adventure into the fascinating nature of Sardegna. From here to Cala Sisine it is essential that you have an IGM map in 1:25,000 scale. Once on the trail, which ascends easily to the left (east) among the bush-covered rocky terrain, walk about 20m to 30m until you reach the flat area of the ridge where, on a stone on the left, you can see a red and white trail marker. If you can't find this marker within the first 30m, go back to the tree and recheck the directions.

Continuing, you hopefully find another two red and white markers on rocks, followed by others that lead down to a section that crosses through the bush, then veers right leading to a little rocky valley. The trail descends steeply with short curves crossing the little valley and reaching another circular, grassy coal merchant's clearing surrounded by stones. In the last few metres you should note the appearance of another type of marking in green spray paint.

From the coal merchant's circle, follow

the markings to the left heading into the bush and soon you'll reach the characteristic Cuile Saccerderano, an abandoned, cone-shaped shed made of juniper logs, with a goat pen alongside (531m altitude, 45 minutes from the turn-off). From the Cuile descend south-east over rocky terrain with twisted juniper trees for about 50m to reach a little open valley with lots of different and confusing trails in the low shrubbery. Descend east towards the low part of the valley where, at the edge of the valley, dense woods begin. Note the markers on the branch of a tree and then on a trunk. Enter the woods along a dried river bed descending along the trail which is sporadically marked. After about 20 minutes you will pass the base of a big white rock and shortly after that the trail begins to veer right along the rocky shoulder to the south. The trail then leaves the valley floor, rising gradually until it emerges from the woods, becoming a panoramic trail at mid-slope with breathtaking views of the northern coast and Cala Gonone. Continuing on, cross over the rocky shoulder to reveal the southern panorama opening up on the imposing cliff of Cala Sisine (45 minutes from Cuile Saccerderano).

For the next 45 minutes the, now more obvious, trail crosses over a landslide and re-enters a forest, descending in sharp curves among invasive vegetation. At the time of research, the red/white markers in this section were covered by camouflaging grey paint, but the green spray paint remained. Perhaps a jealous shepherd? Open sections across rocks alternate with sections through woods until you arrive above the large beach of Cala Sisine. The trail now descends diagonally towards the inside of the codula, then curves sharply to the left towards the beach, which you can reach via a steep descent near a small ruin.

Heading from the beach towards the inside of the codula on a gravel river bed for about 500m, you reach a restaurant on the left (south) side that is open during summer only. When the restaurant is open it is advisable to camp on the south side of the beach, which is secluded and often downwind. During the rest of the year, when the restaurant is closed, it is possible to set up your

bivouac overnight on its external cement skirting block, which is protected from the wind and the wild cows that live in the codula. There is no drinking water available here.

Day 3: Cala Sisine to Baunei
15km, 4½ to 5 hours

The distance covered on this stage is the greatest of any of the three days of the walk.

From the restaurant, ascend into the codula keeping to the trail on the left (south side) which, shortly after setting off, curves left at a junction with another codula, leading south into the Codula Sisine. About 30 minutes from Cala Sisine you will reach a dirt clearing where 4WDs stop in front of a large tormented-looking rock. A dirt road that goes up into the codula, often washed out by floods, starts here. Meander through the codula past a collection of atmospheric and bizarre architectural rock formations modelled by the wind. These structures, sheltered by

Golfo di Orosei (Map 2)

thick vegetation, are inhabited by many species of small birds. One hour from the start of the dirt road you will reach another steep dirt road as-cending to the right. This road was built in 1996 and is not always marked on maps, ignore it and continue on the main dirt road within the codula. After another 30 minutes of walking, ascend to the left following the steep, sharp curves to reach a junction on the high plain (about 270m altitude, one hour) where there is a road to the left leading northwards to Cuile Ololbizzi. Ignore this and continue south on the dirt road that, after a while, starts to descend, passing a turn-off to the right (which you shouldn't take) and then begins the long climb uphill. Continue on, one hour from the road to Cuile Ololbizzi you will pass another turn-off to the right where there's a signpost to a nuraghe, soon followed by a turn-off with a sign to Ispuligi to the left.

You will know that you are nearing your destination when you pass the interesting country church of San Pietro (385m altitude, 30 minutes from the nuraghe), above and to the right of the track. Slightly further on to the right, you'll find the little road that leads to the enclosed yard of the church, which is dominated by an enormous centuries-old tree. In front of the church entrance is an ancient Nuraghic *Betile* – a monolith of dark stone with the outlines of female attributes – a symbol of fertility. The wall that encircles the church, which is almost always closed, contains the shelters used by the pilgrims who have been gathering here for centuries on the annual feast of San Pietro on 28 and 29 June.

From the church, follow the main dirt road south and soon you will reach a crossroads with signs pointing to the left (east) for Su Sterru and Piscinas, and to the right (west) for the restaurant Il Golgo (430m), which is

Golfo di Orosei (Map 3)

Nuraghe Orgoduri
Chiesa campestre di San Pietro
See Golfo di Orosei (Map 2) p 343
Bacu Goloritzè
Golgo Restaurant
Bacu e Sterru
Su Sterru
Piscinas
Punta Giorgia (742m)
Bacu Indesuli
Monte Bissicoro (776m)
Planu Supramonte
Baunei
FINISH
Planargia
SS125

0   1   2 km
1:100,000
Contour Interval 100 metres

Exploring the Area

About 300m east of the crossroads you meet the impressive natural chasm of **Su Sterru**, a huge opening covered over with a net. It's a 280m sheer drop. A short distance to the south of the chasm are the Piscinas, atmospheric archaic tubs, where animals come to drink. It is worth spending an extra night at Il Golgo if only to visit the magnificent beach of Cala Goloritzè, a brief descent of 1½ hours away. To get to this beach from the crossroads, downhill from the restaurant, take the dirt road heading west towards and beyond Piscinas and, after crossing the dry Bacù e Sterru riverbed, continue north-west until you come to a parking area near a sheep pen. From here take the trail that ascends diagonally to the left among the rocks up to a level saddle (471m). Crossing over the saddle, you then enter the evocative **Bacu Goloritzè** gorge, which descends rapidly to the sea. The atmosphere is truly fairytale-like, with centuries-old oak and rocky ravines where the shepherds have built their unusual huts, evoking images of Homer's *Odyssey*. Still descending, you arrive at the beach with its imposing, 143m-high rocky spire, well-known among free-climbers. Along the rocky coast to the north are undersea freshwater springs, which are impressive but completely useless if you're thirsty. There are no other springs here so you will need to bring drinking water with you. The return trip to the crossroads obviously takes longer than the descent, allow about two hours. ■

about 300m away on the hilltop, and where it is advised that you spend the night in their camping ground (see Places to Stay & Eat earlier in this section for details). In fact, this area is so fascinating that we strongly suggest that you spend another night here to allow you to explore it fully (see 'Exploring the Area' boxed text on the previous page).

The closest town with public transport is Baunei to the south, 8km and a two-hour walk from the Su Sterru and Piscinas crossroads, carrying straight along the dirt road from Cala Sisine. This road has recently been paved from here to Baunei and has lost much of its charm. As Baunei can offer neither hotel nor camping facilities, it is advisable to spend the night at Golgo. The owners can also organise guided walks in the area, including an overnight stay and dinner at a shepherd's pinnetta (see Guided Walks earlier in this chapter).

Tiscali-Gorropu

Duration 3 days
Standard Medium
Start Oliena
Finish Dorgali
Closest Towns Nuoro, Olbia, Arbatax
Permits No
Public Transport Access Yes
Summary A fascinating walk along dirt roads and good trails at the unspoilt edge of the Supramonte.

The normal route does not present any particular difficulties. The alternative to the first day presents difficulties in orientation and should be tackled only by experts. This three-day route can be linked up with the three-day Golfo di Orosei walk along the coast.

PLANNING
Maps
This walk is covered by new series 25 maps: 500 III *Oliena* and 500 II *Dorgali*. Unfortu-

nately, the southernmost section of the trek, the entrance to the Gorropu Gorge, is divided for a few centimetres between the 517 IV *Funtana Bona* and 517 I *Cantoniera Genna Silana* maps. It isn't worth the L40,000 needed to buy them both just for this tract as it should present no serious orientation problem.

The walk is also covered by the following old series 25/V maps: 207 I NE *Nuoro*; 208 IV NE *Cantoniera Manasuddas*; 208 IV SO *Monte Oddeu*; and the less important 208 IV NE *Dorgali*.

PLACES TO STAY & EAT
The nights along the walk are spent in a sleeping bag and tent. There are comfortable hotels available in Oliena and Dorgali. Remember that it's important to bring at least 2L of drinking water for the walk.

Oliena
Hotel Ci Kappa (☎ (0784) 28 87 33 or 28 80 24), Via Martin Luther King 2, in the centre of Oliena is simple but comfortable and the *restaurant/pizzeria* is very friendly. It has singles/doubles for L60,000/L85,000. On the way to the Lanaittu valley, along the route of the first day of the trek, there is the convenient and luxurious *Hotel Su Gologone* (☎ (0784) 28 75 12). In a lovely setting, the elegant hotel is a good option for people wanting to enjoy easy explorations in the area, because it organises guided tours and walks and horse riding expeditions. Singles/doubles cost L105,000/L150,000 with bathroom, out of season, half board/full board costs up to L115,000/L145,000. The *restaurant* serves excellent, traditional local dishes and is justifiably renowned throughout the island. On the way up to the Scala è Pradu pass (on the alternative and demanding Day 1B route) about 3km from Oliena, is *Albergo Monte Maccione* (☎ (0784) 28 83 63) which charges L70,000/L82,000 (low/high season) for a double. Half board costs from L57,000 to L69,000.

Dorgali
See Dorgali under Places to Stay & Eat in

the Golfo di Orosei section earlier in this chapter.

Urzulei

Not really in Urzulei, but nearby, *Hotel Genna Silana* (☎ (0784) 95120) is a convenient base for walkers, on the SS125 above the Genna Silana pass, where the rare buses between Dorgali and Baunei stop. It's possible to reach the hotel from the northern area of the Gola di Gorropu, if you are willing to make the long, steep ascent from the gorge that scales the rock face up to the pass (650m altitude, two hours). Singles/doubles with private bathroom cost L40,000/L70,000. The hotel is sometimes closed in the off season so check in advance.

GETTING TO/FROM THE WALK

See the Getting To/From the Walk section under the Golfo di Orosei walk earlier in this chapter for details of transport to this area.

THE WALK
Day 1A: Oliena to Rifugio Lanaittu via Su Gologone
3 to 4 hours

Take the asphalt road from Oliena heading towards Dorgali and, after about 6km, turn off to the right onto another minor asphalt road with a signpost to Su Gologne. After another 2km, you'll reach the hotel/restaurant. It's also possible to cover this first section, as far as the turn-off, by bus. Go past the entrance ramp of the hotel and shortly after turn right onto the road that climbs a little valley. It may be worth taking the 300m detour straight ahead here to reach a pure, icy underground spring, called the Su Gologone, which gushes out in a strong jet from the mountain then flows into Fiume Cedrino. On the rock above the striking fissure is the little church of Nostra Signora della Pietà.

Back on the paved road which climbs the little valley, you will gain altitude and round a rocky shoulder to enter the fresh green

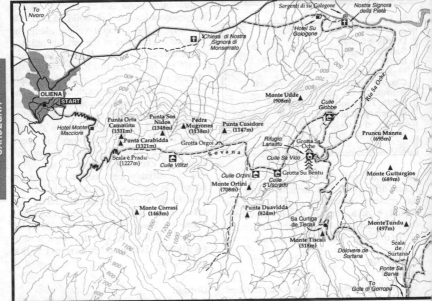

Nuraghic Village of Sos Carros

Three hundred metres north of Rifugio Lanaittu, on the wooded slope overlooking the bridge, is an important archaeological site with the remains of the Nuraghic village of Sos Carros. The area is fenced in but you can ask the guard, who is also the shepherd of the adjacent sheepfold, to let you in – entrance is free. You can see the remains of a small area where a family would have gathered together at an unusual circular stone seat, perhaps to perform some ancient ritual.

Stefano Cavedoni

valley of the Lanaittu, crowned by imposing limestone peaks as high as 1400m.

The road then descends towards Riu Sa Oche running alongside it until the road divides into two, one straight and to the left crossing a plateau of abandoned fields, and one to the right at mid-slope cutting through the

vegetation. Both reach the speleological Rifugio Lanaittu (at 145m altitude on the IGM map), built by the municipality of Oliena alongside the imposing entrance to Grotta Sa Oche (Cave of the Voice) named after the sound made by the large amounts of water which pour out of it when flooded. The rifugio is operated by Murena, the No 1 guide in the area, who can be contacted at Hotel Ci Kappa in Oliena (see Guided Tours earlier in this chapter). The road to the right may be a bit shorter and less confusing as it doesn't have any turn-offs. The road to the left follows a level section and a wide curve to the left, arriving at a fork where, to get to the rifugio, you must turn right. The rifugio is never open but you can always camp out in the courtyard.

Day 1B: Oliena to Rifugio Lanaittu via Scala è Pradu
6 to 7 hours

This alternative route is for experts only, since it presents some difficult sections in

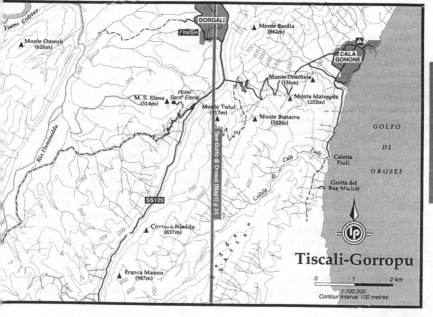

Tiscali-Gorropu

terms of orientation. You'll need the IGM map (see Maps in the Planning section earlier in this chapter) to follow the route via the Scala è Pradu pass (1227m altitude) and the Sovana high plain (650m altitude). The steep climb up to the pass can also be done in 4WDs (see Oliena under Guided Walks earlier in this chapter). Considering the length and difficulty of the route, it is recommended that you take advantage of this service in order to be fresh for the long descent.

From the centre of Oliena (350m altitude) follow the signs for Orgosolo, but before leaving the town take the road that ascends to the left with signs for Rifugio/Hotel Monte Maccione. The road ascends and turns again to the left, then, at an intersection, continues to the right, climbing in narrow switchbacks along the slope of the mountain under the majestic limestone face of Punta Carabidda, up to Rifugio/Hotel Monte Maccione (640m altitude, one hour from Oliena). From the turn-off for the hotel, continue at mid-slope on the now dirt road to the right, which begins a very demanding ascent. Avoid the deviation to the right for Fonte Daddana and keep going up the dirt road that climbs the practically vertical wall along horrible, scalloped curves that become narrower and narrower. You will leave the forests behind you to arrive at an arial panorama of the Scala è Pradu pass (1227m altitude, two hours from the rifugio). To the south-east of the pass you can take in the immense wilderness of the Supramonte, separating you from the sea; and to the north-west is Nuoro, with its ugly spaceship-like hospital right in the worst possible spot. A bit further south, the summit of Monte Corrasi (1463m), the highest point of the Supramonte, should be visible.

Here the difficult descent begins among the lovely but insidious pale rocks and the spiney vegetation, down towards Rifugio Lanaittu, directly east of the pass.

At the pass you will see a rectangular rock of grey granite on the left edge (north) of a clearing. Head north from this rock crossing a faint trail at mid-slope that then curves gradually to the east and leads to a wide saddle on the southern side of Punta Sos

Nidos. Pass by the grassy plateau of the saddle and continue east on open terrain, after 10 minutes you should reach a small valley with twisted junipers that descends south-east with a view of the large telecommunications antenna of Dorgali in the distance. Descend into the little valley, down to the single large holm oak, where you will find the well camouflaged Cuile Vilitzi (about one hour from the pass).

About 10m before the cuile to the left (east) there should be some faded red/white trailmarkers that lead towards an insignificant little rocky crest, following the route above the cuile which you must keep to your right.

The faint trail crosses the little crest and continues over the rocks, with widely-placed faded markings, almost lost within the lichen of the same colour. It's difficult not to lose track of these markings and if this does happen you should turn back, retrace your steps back to the last marker and try again. Attempting to descend south-east to the high plain of Sovana, which you can see from above, without following a trail is a very bad idea!

Within 35 minutes you will reach a ledge with grassy sections where the trail is clearer and which, 15 minutes later, takes you straight down to the plain of Sovana. On the north side of the saddle you should be able to spot the chasm of the Grotta Orgoi (50 minutes from Cuile Vilitzi).

Climb up to the right of the saddle along the grassy slope then descend to the east, among many interlaced tracks along a grassy sloped ledge, until the point where you veer right to the south, leaving the ledge to descend, on the usual numerous goat tracks, to a large isolated holm oak on the highplain of Sovana (30 minutes from the grotta). From the oak, continue across the charming plateau, which is a good place to stop for a while, towards its south-eastern wooded borders. Follow the trail that heads to a nearby fork with a stone *ometto* (cairn) where it ascends to the left (south-east) among the rocks and into the woods. The right fork leads to the Cuile Orzini several metres away.

Continue south-east, descending into a rocky area where the trail gets lost among many tracks, at mid-slope with the riverbed to your right, until you find the Cuile S'Uscradu (484m altitude). From here the trail curves to the left (north-east) and descends more clearly at mid-slope into the woods. You should pass by the Cuile Sa Vicu (400m altitude) and arrive at the Cuile Giobbe (about 247m altitude) where tractor tracks lead down to the right (south) to join up with the wide dirt road of the valley and the main route of the walk. Head right (south-west) and about one hour and 40 minutes after leaving the high plain you should reach Rifugio Lanaittu.

There is an alternative route, via steep shortcut (one hour) through the woods, from the Cuile S'Uscradu to the rifugio. This vague trail descends to the right (east) through the vegetation, passing in front of the entrance to the Grotta Su Bentu (Cave of the Wind) to arrive right inside the courtyard of the rifugio, next to the entrance to the Grotta Sa Oche (Cave of the Voice).

Day 2: Rifugio Lanaittu to Ponte Sa Barva & Gola di Gorropu
5 to 6 hours

The bridge known to locals as Sa Barva, three to 3¾ hours from Rifugio Lanaittu, is a good base from which to visit the Gola di Gorropu gorge, a magical place that deserves an extended stopover. Allow at least another four hours for the round trip to the gorge, including a quick stop of one hour in the gorge. This can be done on the same day as the walk to Sa Barva, or on the following day.

From Rifugio Lanaittu (145m altitude) follow the dirt road south which, after a few curves reaches a junction. Follow the dirt road to the right until you reach a small clearing then take the rambling, steep dirt road to the right which heads south-west out of the clearing. After about 15 to 20 minutes of hard climbing, you'll come to a boulder with a blue painted arrow: here you leave the dirt road and climb uphill to the left (south-east) into the forest, climbing the very steep slope until you come to the base of a rockface. To your left is an obvious and quite evocative split in the mountain, which you

climb into, one at a time, thankful that Sardegna isn't subject to earthquakes. After another short climb, you'll come out of the fissure onto a wide ledge. The end of the ledge is high on the western edge of the enormous *dolina* (sinkhole) where the village of Tiscali is, although you're unable to see the village at this point. To enter the dolina and reach the village, you need to go round to the east – head north and to the right – where you'll find a passage down through the rocks to the village (two hours from the rifugio).

After visiting Tiscali, return to the main track via the passage through the rocks, but instead of heading back the way you came, head right (south-east) into the scrub on a track which leads steeply downhill. Shortly after passing a small nuraghe, the track joins another climbing from the Valle Lanaittu to Campo Donanigoro (25 minutes from Tiscali). Go left and descend for a short distance to a grassy area (270m altitude), from where you go up to the right (east) into the gorge of the Dolovere di Surtana, continuing until you reach the pass (350m altitude, 45 minutes from the nuraghe).

From here, go downhill along the steep, narrow, rocky gorge of Scala è Surtana and once at the bottom, near the Riu Flumineddu, go right (south) to reach Sa Barva (190m altitude, 30 minutes from Dolovere di Surtana; total time from Rifugio Lanaittu 3¾ to four hours).

Tiscali: An Ancient Nuraghic Village
The natural karst environment of the enormous *dolina*, formed by a collapse of the limestone rock on a mountain crest, appears to have been utilised by the ancient Nuraghic inhabitants of the Valle Lanaittu as a hiding place from invading enemies. Sited on a crest, the village offered various possibilities for escape and received a constant supply of water, which dripped from the roof of the cave overhanging the settlement. Almost all of the buildings are incomplete ruins due to the meddling of human hands – and it is very sad to think that many were still standing only 10 years ago.
Stefano Cavedoni

Dorgali is 11km away to the north-north-east on the dirt road which starts at this bridge (the road becomes asphalt after 3.5km).

To reach the Gola di Gorropu, a natural spectacle with 400m of sheer rock walls so close together they almost touch, continue southwards on the dirt road to the west of Ponte Sa Barva. Follow the undulating river along the dirt road, leading to the very short and steep little path that takes you right down into the silent entrance of the gorge, a magical place that deserves an extended stopover (343m altitude, 1½ to two hours from the bridge).

About 1km south of the bridge is a grassy clearing off the dirt road, which we recommend as a good place to camp for the night as it has the advantage of fresh river water. Further ahead, towards the gorge, the banks turn damper, steeper and rockier, and are more exposed to possible landslides or falling rocks. The gorge itself is narrow and very rocky making it impossible to pitch a tent there.

A visit to the gorge should not be rushed. If you're tired from the day's walk or arrive at the bridge late in the day, it is recommended that you camp out at the clearing near the bridge and enjoy a stroll along the river. The

next day you will be refreshed and able to fully enjoy a visit to the gorge before returning unrushed to Dorgali.

If you would prefer more comfortable accommodation you can go back to the bridge and follow the dirt road to Dorgali for 8km (two hours) to reach *Hotel Sant'Elene* (3km before the town – see Places to Stay & Eat under the Golfo di Orosei Trek earlier in this chapter).

Another more strenuous option is to take the steep trail that climbs southwards from the limestone clearing at the gorge exit to the base of the rock face, ascending 650m up to the pass of Genna Silana on the SS125 (two to three hours from the gorge). There is a bus stop here, where the rare buses for Dorgali (4.30 and 4.50 pm) and Baunei (3.15 pm) leave from. There is also a cafe here and *Hotel Genna Silana* (see Places to Stay & Eat earlier in this section).

Day 3: Ponte Sa Barva to Dorgali
3 hours

This last day is easy and restful for those who have spent the night at the Sa Barva bridge. From the bridge, take the road (starts as dirt and then, after 3.5km, becomes asphalt)

Gola di Gorropu

Strangely, the noise of the water comes from outside the gorge. East of the entrance, beyond the enormous boulders and a lovely, little limestone clearing, the Riu Flumineddu gushes back out into the open after a journey of several kilometres underground. The clearing is an ideal place to enjoy the sun and a snack, alongside the gurgling, crystalline water. To the right of the clearing, looking downhill, you can see the start of the tough trail that ascends to the Genna Silana pass. A visit to the gorge is not complete without a walk through the narrow passageway overhung by high walls that are clogged with giant blocks of fallen rock moulded by water erosion. It's an exciting, unforgettable and humbling experience to climb among the deep channels of a river that isn't there, among powerful rocks covered in perennial shadow, being hit now and then by mysterious drips. Those who are able to get through the tricky grade-three mountaineering level passages can ascend the gorge to reach an uncrossable 20m gap. Very few plants are able to survive under these conditions; however, there are ferns and mosses taking advantage of the dampness and lack of light; and rare endemic insects who spend their whole existence in this vast underground system. During long periods of rain the water table rises and the gorge floods, a phenomenon that we recommend you avoid. Check with the local guides organisation or the tourist office at Dorgali for the status of the gorge before setting out.

Access to the gorge from the south is only possible with cables, rubber rafts and mountaineering experience. This usually takes two days and requires the presence of an expert guide. The Società Gorropu of Urzulei (see Guided Walks earlier in this chapter) is made up of young and competent fanatics who can assist in the organisation of this and similar kinds of excursions for a reasonable price.

Stefano Cavedoni

that follows the river and then heads towards the area of Hotel Sant'Elene (8km from the bridge). From the hotel take the little second-ary road that crosses the countryside to Dorgali (about 3km).

You can continue from Dorgali by bus to Cala Gonone where the Golfo di Orosei walk starts.

Capo Testa

Duration 3 hours	
Standard Easy	
Start/Finish Santa Teresa di Gallura	
Closest Towns Olbia, Sassari	
Permits No	
Public Transport Access Yes	
Summary This is a short and not too tiring walk exploring the soft and curvy profiles of the pink granite of Capo Testa.	

PLANNING

The seaside resort of Santa Teresa di Gallura, along with nearby Palau, about 26km east, has developed into an affordable alternative to the jet-set hang-outs on Costa Smeralda. This is a very pleasant spot to pass a few relaxing days, particularly if the magnificent coves, rock pools and small beaches of nearby Capo Testa appeal to you. From the town you can look across the Stretto di Bonifacio to Corsica, or even catch one of the regular ferries which make the crossing to Bonifacio on Corsica's southern tip.

When to Walk

This walk can be done year round, although the best time is from March to October, as there is the obvious advantage of swimming in the warmest months. However, in August the area becomes extremely overcrowded and therefore we recommended that you avoid it during this period.

Maps

This is a short walk which presents no orien-tation difficulties, so it is not really necessary to go to the trouble of ordering an IGM map. For those who do want a map, the old series 25/V sheet 168 IV SE *Santa Teresa* is good. It includes Capo Testa and Santa Teresa di Gallura. The new series 25 map 411 III *Capo Testa* includes only the cape and a lot of sea. The AAST office in Santa Teresa di Gallura distributes photocopied information about Capo Testa, including a rough map.

What to Bring

You'll need only comfortable clothes, suit-able for the season, and a picnic. In summer, make sure you bring along your swimming gear so you can take advantage of a swim in the cape's magnificent rock pools. At least 2L of drinking water is required for this walk.

PLACES TO STAY

Santa Teresa offers extensive accommodation possibilities, including rooms and apartments for rent (contact the tourist office). It is advis-able to book well ahead if you plan to arrive during late July or August. Camping facili-ties are all out of town. Try *La Liccia* (☎ (0789) 75 51 90), about 6km from Santa Teresa towards Palau, 400m from the beach; charges are L16,000/L11,500 per adult/child, which includes the cost of the site.

For hotels in town there is *Algergo Da Cecco* (☎ (0789) 75 42 20), Via Po 3 (take Via XX Settembre from the tourist office and turn right at Via Po), which has pleasant singles/doubles for L80,000/L110,000 with bath-room. *Hotel Bacchus* (☎ (0789) 75 45 56), Via Firenze 5, a quiet spot in the new town, known for its restaurant, has singles/doubles for L80,000/L100,000; half board is L135,000 per person. *Hotel del Porto* (☎ (0789) 75 41 54), Via del Porto 20, at the port has singles/doubles for L55,000/L80,000.

At Capo Testa, near the walking area, is the *Bocche di Bonifacio* (☎ (0789) 75 42 02) which has singles/doubles for L60,0000/ L85,000 and half board for L100,000 per person.

GETTING TO/FROM THE WALK

ARST buses regularly arrive in Via Eleonora d'Arborea (off Via Nazionale), a short walk

SARDEGNA

from the centre of Santa Teresa di Gallura, from Olbia, Golfo Aranci and Palau. There are also two buses a day to and from Sassari. Tickets can be purchased at the Black & White bar on Via Nazionale. Fares and timetable information can also be found at the Black & White bar.

Ferry Services to Corsica are run by two companies, Moby Line (☎ (0789) 75 52 60) and Saremar (☎ (0789) 75 47 88), both of which have small offices at the port. Both companies run several services a day.

THE WALK

From Santa Teresa di Gallura, walk 3km east up to the isthmus of Santa Reparata, the strip of land that connects the Cape to the mainland. During the tourist season there is the option of taking one of the buses that cover the first part of the walk to Capo Testa, departing every 15 minutes from Via Eleonora d'Arborea near the Santa Teresa di Gallura post office.

Just after the sandy isthmus, along the asphalt road to the lighthouse, you will note the Centro Nautico on the left, where you turn left into a dirt road that soon leads to a square with houses. A little before the square, turn right into another dirt road that passes through some shrubbery and leads to a parking area (20 minutes from the isthmus).

A trail through some thick vegetation starts here and descends towards the sea in a wide granite valley known to the locals as Fosso dell'Ea. Halfway along, the trail crosses an enormous block of granite divided in three parts displaying the strange indentations left by ancient Roman, or medieval Pisan, quarry workers. Split obelisks lay on the ground and, further ahead, there are some small caves, refuge to groups of hippies still in search of their little slice of paradise.

At the bottom of the valley to the left, is a beautiful little cove and in front of you on the right is another rockier cove. From this last cove, there is a passage through the rocks to the right, leading to the other side of the rockface that encloses the valley. After passing a wide break in the rocks you should find a very visible trail that ascends north-north-east. When you reach the rocky shoulder you should be able to see the old abandoned lighthouse and the white cliffs of the coast of Corsica at Bonifacio. From the saddle, there is a fork where you should descend to the left of the cove which is divided in two by an enormous 'sugarloaf'

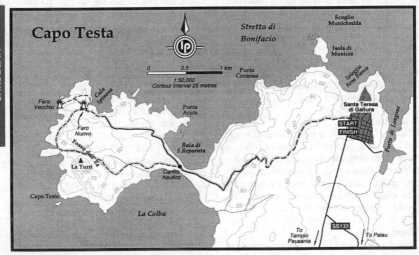

of granite. Pass a low stone wall and climb up a small valley, heading north-north-east, snuggled between the rocks that obstruct the view of the sea. At the saddle, you can go for a swim in the small cove, down to the left, with big horizontal slabs of sandstone immersed in it. Continuing on, go right, ignoring a turn-off towards the interior, onto the next shoulder. On the other side of the shoulder you cross another small valley at mid-slope to reach the ruin of a tiny military lookout post from where you can see the new lighthouse, not much beyond the old one (one hour from the parking area). From the ruin,

descend to the trail on the left among the cistus bushes, which opens up a passage to a small grassy clearing a short distance below. Twenty metres from the clearing turn left to descend, among more bushes, to the little valley below the two lighthouses. Down to the left, this little valley leads to another lovely cove next to the one with the sandstone slabs (10 minutes). Ascend to the right to the square on the asphalt lighthouse road, which will lead you back to the isthmus where you started out (30 minutes from the cove). It is recommended that you return to the mainland by the same route you came in on.

Long-Distance Walks

Italy is the ideal place for long-distance walks: it has two very extensive mountainous areas (the Alps and the Appennini), a wealth of existing paths, a strong tradition of walking and mountaineering, and far (but not too far) reaching roads and public transport routes.

Shorter long-distance walks are many and varied. They are based on topography: the numerous Alte Vie (high-level routes) in the Dolomiti (Dolomites), Monti Liguri, Valle d'Aosta and Lago di Como, for example; there are what might be called theme walks, such as Sentieri delle Pace (connected with wartime activities); and walks using historic or traditional routes, such as the Via dei Monti Lariani by Lago di Como. All these walks can be followed from end to end in as few as four days or up to two weeks, and it is eminently feasible to include at least one in a walking holiday in Italy.

But there is much more to long-distance walking in Italy than even this generous menu offers. The Grande Traversata delle Alpi (GTA) is an elongated web of paths through and around the outliers of the Western Alps, 1000km in all; the Grande Escursione Appenninica (GEA) is a 429km high-level route along the spine of the Appennini (Apennines) on the Toscana (Tuscany) and Emilia-Romagna border; and the E/1 (part of the European system of long-distance walks) currently covers 2000km or more, from the Swiss border at Lago di Lugano, south to Genova (Genoa), east via the Appennini and down into Umbria, in central Italy. And then there is the Sentiero Italia (SI), in a class all of its own – 5000km (ultimately) from Trieste in north-eastern Italy to Reggio Calabria, with extensions in Sicilia (Sicily) and Sardegna (Sardinia).

However, these seriously long walks would not fit into a conventional holiday so, for Italians and for visitors, they are an incentive to return many times to complete the full distance. On a practical note is the question of whether or not to carry a tent. Given the

SANDRA BARDWELL

HIGHLIGHTS

- Remote communities, abundant wildlife, towering peaks and deep valleys on the Grande Traversata delle Alpi
- The Grande Escursione Appenninica, one of the best known long-distance walks in Europe
- Sampling Italy's transitional route, the Sentiero Italia, in Lombardia
- Following the Italian leg of the Sentiero Europaeo, a route linking several European countries

plentiful availability of overnight accommodation along the paths, to some the weight of a tent, sleeping bag and cooking equipment is not justified, especially as days involving ascents of 1000m or more are not uncommon. Make inquiries in advance to ensure the advertised accommodation exists, is open, and that space is available.

It is worth noting that some walking along minor roads is probably unavoidable in areas where the overall route is compromised by topography (mountain passes in inconvenient places) or by modern road building.

LONG-DISTANCE WALKS – MAPS
Map 1 Grande Traversata delle Alpi p 358
Map 2 Grande Escursione Appenninica p 360
Long-Distance Walks
Grande Traversata delle Alpi (GTA)
Grande Escursione Appenninica (GEA)
Sentiero Italia (SI)
Sentiero Europaeo E/1
0 75 150 km
FRANCE
GERMANY
AUSTRIA
LIECHTENSTEIN
SWITZERLAND
SLOVENIA
HUNGARY
CROATIA
BOSNIA HERCEGOVINA
CORSICA (FRANCE)
ALGERIA
TUNISIA
LIGURIAN SEA
TYRRHENIAN SEA
ADRIATIC SEA
IONIAN SEA
MEDITERRANEAN SEA
GOLFO DI VENEZIA
GOLFO DI TARANTO
ROMA
Milano
Torino
Genova
Bologna
Firenze
Venezia
Napoli
Palermo
Cagliari
Trieste
Budapest
Ljubljana
Zagreb
Sarajevo
Bern
Vaduz
Tunis
Valletta
Monte Bianco (4807m)
Monviso (3841m)
Corno Grande (2914m)
Mt Vesuvio (1277m)
Mt Etna (3330m)
LONG-DISTANCE WALKS

Grande Traversata delle Alpi

The GTA is aptly described as a walking tour network of paths, rather than a single, continuous path, through the Western Alps from the Alpi Marittime (close to Liguria), and heading north to Valle Anzasca, between the Swiss border and Lago Maggiore (near Monte Rosa, 4434m). Some 1000km in length, it involves the equivalent of several ascents of Mt Everest – 67,000m of climbing. From the main route, there are many loops or side trips to enable walkers to explore particular areas more closely, notably in Valle di Susa.

More than 120 *posti tappa* or staging posts – simple, hostel-style accommodation – have been established on the route, each equipped with double-bunk beds, kitchen, water and power. Most are in villages where supplies and/or meals are available.

In establishing and maintaining the route, the Associazione Grande Traversata delle Alpi cooperates with several organisations: the Consortium of Mountain Communities; the provinces of Torino (Turin), Cuneo, Vercelli and Novara; and the Mountain Council and the Tourism and Cultural councils of the Piemonte (Piedmont) region.

INFORMATION
Maps

The IGC 1:50,000 series, 100m contours covers the full length of the GTA with the route specially marked, including the various alternatives. The nine sheets required, from south to north, are: No 8 *Alpi Marittime e Liguri*, No 7 *Grana-Stura*, No 6 *Monviso*, No 1 *Valle di Susa, Chisone e Germanasca* (including interesting background information, in Italian), No 17 *Torino-Pinerolo e Bassa Val di Susa*, No 2 *Valli di Lanzo e Moncenisio*, No 3 *Il Parco Nazionale del Gran Paradiso*, No 9 *Ivrea-Biella e Bassa Valle d'Aosta*, and No 10 *Monte Rosa, Alagna e Macugnaga*; the price per map is around L12,000. Part of the northernmost reaches of the GTA is also shown on two

sheets in the Kompass 1:50,000 series: No 88 *Monte Rosa* and No 97 *Omegna-Varallo, Lago d'Orta*; these cost L9500.

The IGC sheets are easy to read – the GTA stands out very clearly and the overnight stages are shown. However, in the Alpi Marittime, the accuracy of sheet No 8 proved to be unreliable.

Information Sources

The Associazione Grande Traversata delle Alpi (☎ (011) 567 44 77) issues two brochures which are useful for planning a walk: *Grande Traversata delle Alpi* has a map of nearly all the route and a summary list of *rifugi* (refuges) and other types of accommodation (in English) and, more helpfully, *Percorsi e posti tappa* which has the complete map of the

---

Parco Naturale Orsiera Rocciavrè
This Parco Naturale is a good example of the type of area served by networks of paths linked in many places to the core GTA, and one which deserves more time than the day or so it would take to traverse the park on the GTA.

Occupying nearly 11,000 hectares on the south-eastern slopes of Valle di Susa, it was established during the 1980s mainly to protect and conserve natural and historic features and to improve the quality of life of local people.

The park is essentially a mountainous area with the highest point being Monte Orsiera (2890m). Despite being close to Torino, it is an island of largely unspoiled wild country between Chisone, Susa and Sangone valleys. It stands in strong contrast to other mountainous areas in Piedmont, having escaped developments associated with mass tourism. Human activities are largely confined to agriculture and pastoralism in small settlements; there are also many which have been abandoned.

The park's fauna is typically alpine: chamois, marmots, ermines, hares, eagles and white partridges. Wild flowers are abundant, there are larch and pine forests, beech and birch trees in the valleys, and above the tree line, alpine tarns are overlooked by rocky mountain peaks.

This is a park for all seasons, for walking, mountaineering and ski mountaineering. There is a good network of marked paths, several rifugi and agriturismo establishments.

To find out more about the park and Valle di Susa contact the APT office (☎ (0122) 83 15 96), at Piazza Garambois, Oulx. ■

area on a larger scale and basic details of accommodation, access by public transport, and facilities for each of the 27 stages along the route. However, although the map shows the route going right round Val d'Ossola and finishing at Cannobio on Lago Maggiore, it ends (for the time being) in Valle Anzasca, some 20km south of Domodossola. The association's address is: Via Barbaroux 1, 10122 Torino.

The association or the APT office (☎ (011) 53 51 81) in Torino should be able to provide a list of rifugi and bivouacs in the Piemonte region. This information is no more detailed than that in the association's brochure, but the publication also lists mountain guides who work in the region and their contact numbers.

Local tourist information offices should be able to provide more comprehensive guides to accommodation and details of public transport. From south to north the contacts are:

APT delle Valli di Cuneo
    (☎ (0171) 66615), Corso Nizza 17, 12100 Cuneo
APT del Monregalese
    (☎ (0174) 40389), Corso Statuto 39, 12084 Mondovi
APT del Saluzzese
    (☎ (0175) 46710), Via Griselda 6, 12037 Saluzzo
APT del Pinerolese
    (☎ (0121) 79 40 03), Viale Giolitti 7/9, 10064 Pinerolo
APT della Valle di Susa
    (☎ (0122) 83 15 96), Piazza Garambois, 10056 Oulx
APT delle Valli di Lanzo
    (☎ (0123) 28080), Via Umberto I 9, 10074 Lanzo
APT del Canavese
    (☎ (0125) 61 81 31), Corso Vercelli 1, 10015 Ivrea
APT della Valsesia
    (☎ (0163) 51280), Corso Roma 38, 13019 Varallo
APT dell'Ossola
    (☎ (0324) 48 13 08), Corso Ferraris 49, 28037 Domodossola

Books

At the time of research, guides to the GTA in the provinces of Novara and Vercelli were being prepared; the association should be able to provide the likely publication dates.

Guides covering the provinces of Torino and Cuneo may be obtained from the association (price per guide including postage is L30,000), or from good bookshops. They include maps, background articles and details of the numerous rest areas.

ACCOMMODATION & SUPPLIES

The many specially designed shelters along the GTA have double-bunk beds, a kitchen and basic facilities. CAI and private rifugi serve 16 of the 27 stages of the GTA; of the remainder, several have a few hotels, others have inns or pensioni. Remember that rifugi are generally open only during the summer months. Experience at Palanfrè on the edge of the Alpi Marittime underlines the need to make sure in advance that a listed establishment will be open when you arrive, especially if there is no local alternative.

GETTING THERE & AWAY
Bus

Most of the valleys traversed by the GTA are served by bus routes, including services from Cuneo (Valle Gesso) and Domodossola (Valle Anzasca). More detailed information may be available from the APT offices serving the route of the GTA (see Information Sources earlier).

Train

Several services from Torino and linked stations actually cross the route of the GTA or pass reasonably close to it, including the line from Cuneo to Limone, and services from Torino to Susa, Aosta and Domodossola.

PLANNING
When to Walk

The availability of accommodation and the frequency of local bus services are decisive factors; for example, the bus service from Cuneo to Terme di Valdieri, close to the GTA, operates a summer timetable only during July and August (ie two or three buses daily instead of just one). Moreover, many of the rifugi are only open between June and September.

Grande Traversata delle Alpi

0   15   30 km

1:1,600,000

The route crosses some high passes, above 2500m, where snow may lie until well into summer.

What to Bring

All the usual protective clothing and similar equipment should be carried (see the 'Safety in the Mountains' boxed text in the Western Alps chapter); a sleeping bag may be needed if you plan to make use of the special shelters.

THE ROUTE

From Viozene in the south, the GTA keeps close to the French border and the main watershed, as far as the southern boundary of Valle d'Aosta and Parco Nazionale del Gran Paradiso. At Ceresole, it swings eastwards and then north to skirt these areas, and heads towards the Monte Rosa massif. Its final stretch leads away from the big mountains into the lower reaches of Valle Anzasca, east of Monte Rosa. The GTA crosses more than 20 major valleys, accounting for the 67,000m of climbing involved. It passes through two major reserves: Parco Naturale Alpi Marittime in Valle Stura and Parco Naturale Orsiera Rocciavrè in Valle di Susa.

In theory, the route is marked with the GTA logo and red-and-white markers, but where it coincides with other marked paths (eg in the Alpi Marittime), the GTA markers may be few and far between. The information in the Associazione Grande Traversata delle Alpi brochure, and the provision of the overnight shelters, is based on daily stages of five to seven hours walking with as much as 1000m ascent. Thus it would take at least four weeks of fairly solid walking to complete the full distance, without exploring any of the detours along the way. Whether there is anything to choose between a north to south, or south to north traverse is difficult to say. Apart from personal convenience, there is much to recommend the former – finishing in, or very close to, the splendid Alpi Marittime. Whatever your choice, part or all of the GTA offers abundant opportunities to discover remote communities where Alpine traditions are still maintained, to observe wildlife, and to pass through or very near to some of Italy's finest mountain areas.

Grande Escursione Appenninica

Since it was established in the early 1980s, the Grande Escursione Appenninica (GEA) has become one of Europe's best known long-distance walks. It follows an undulating route along the spine of the Appennini for more than 400km, passing through small towns, old villages, beech and birch forests, and crossing high Alpine areas.

The route really divides into two distinct sections: in the south-east, from Bocca Trabaria to Pracchia, there are many forests and wooded areas and numerous towns and villages, typical of the lower Appennini, where the climate is Mediterranean. The north-west section, from Pracchia to Passo dei Due Santi, is another world, with typically alpine features – high meadows and tarns, conifer and beech woodlands, and a central European climate.

There are several special reserves along the GEA, notably the Monte Falterona di Campigia e Parco Nazionale delle Foreste Casentinesi in the southern section, which is particularly important for fauna conservation. In recent years the populations of several species have increased in the park and in the other reserves (further north), notably the roe deer and wild boar, while marmots, normally found in alpine areas, have been successfully introduced. The park also protects fine beech forests. Between the forests and the highest areas human activity has had a marked impact on vegetation, although many pastures have long since been abandoned.

In the high Appennini, the annual rainfall can reach 2500mm, most of which falls in spring and autumn; summer and winter are relatively dry. Average temperatures range from 0°C in January to just above 20°C in July.

The CAI, Toscana's regional administration, and the local Mountain Community organisations have cooperated since early days in the establishment and maintenance of the GEA, and from time to time internationally renowned mountaineer, Reinhold Messner, has opened and walked new sections of the route.

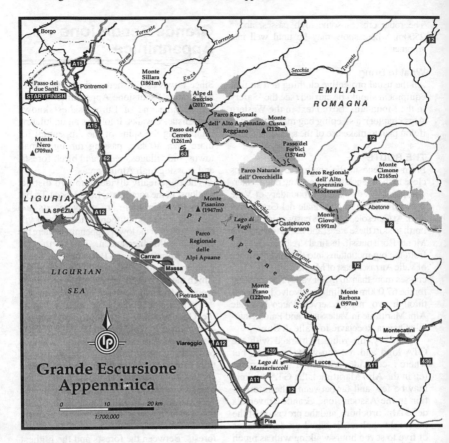

INFORMATION
Maps

The GEA is covered by more than 15 topographical maps from several publishers, ranging in scale from 1:15,000 to 1:70,000 – too many to list here. The 1:30,000 maps which accompany the guidebook (see the Books section below) are perfectly adequate for a few days walk, though the rather awkward format does not lend itself to extended use.

Information Sources

The Garfagnana tourist information office

(☎/fax (0583) 65 16 9), at Piazza delle Erbe 1, Castelnuovo Garfagnana, can provide information about the central section of the GEA, and has copies of the guide for sale (see Books). The office also has an email address: grfwz@garfprod.it. Otherwise, contact the APT offices in the town nearest to the section of the GEA you are planning to explore. In Arezzo at the eastern end of the walk, the office (☎ (0575) 37 76 78) is in Piazza della Repubblica; in Pistoia, close to the central part of the walk, the APT office (☎ (0573) 21 62 2) is in Piazza del Duomo.

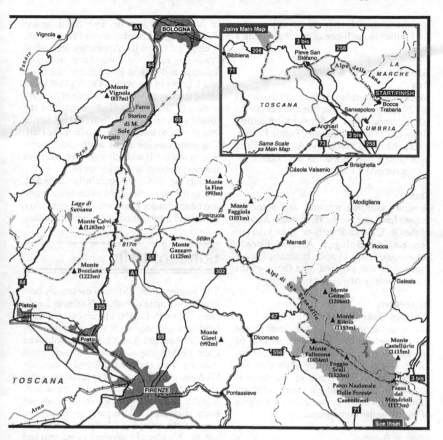

Books

GEA, Grande Escursione Appenninica by Alfonso Bietolini & Gianfranco Bracci is a beautifully produced, extremely comprehensive guide to the walk. Published by Tamari Montagna Edizioni, Padova, and priced at L32,000, it is exceptionally good value. It contains notes on flora, fauna and geology, advice and summary information about the walk for planning purposes, and an explanation of the grading and marking schemes. Description of the route is divided into seven sections with details of maps, and contacts for accommodation and informa-

tion (although bear in mind that it was published in 1993), as well as walk notes. The guide comes with two topographical maps at 1:30,000 with 25m contours covering the full length of the walk and showing the route, facilities at many towns and villages, and other linking footpaths. There are also gradient profiles, so you can be in no doubt about how much up and down there is ahead.

ACCOMMODATION & SUPPLIES

There is a good range of accommodation all the way along the route: rifugi, pensioni, hotels and camp sites. However, up-to-date accommodation lists from the appropriate APT office are indispensable for planning a walk.

GETTING THERE & AWAY
Bus
Numerous companies, both national (such as SITA) and local, provide direct access to the GEA, from cities and towns including Bologna, Firenze, Arezzo, Prato, Pistoia, Lucca, Modena, Parma and Aulla. Inquiries about routes and timetables are made at the appropriate APT office.

Train
Several main-line stations, and some on branch lines, are within reasonable distance of the GEA, either directly or by onward bus connections: Bologna, Arezzo, Firenze (Florence), Prato, Pistoia, Pracchia, Parma, Pontremoli and Modena, and those on the Lucca-Castelnuovo-Aulla branch line.

PLANNING
When to Walk
Spring and autumn are the best times for the GEA – before the heat and crowds of summer, and for the softer light and colourful deciduous forests during September and October. Most, if not all, of the route is accessible throughout the year, although snow and ice could be hazards in the depths of winter in the highest areas.

What to Bring
No special equipment is required for this walk. Boots are always preferable for any sustained walking, however good the paths; also take clothing to suit changeable weather, a hat in summer, and plenty of film for your camera. If you are planning to carry a tent, make sure you start with plenty of fuel for your cooking equipment – opportunities to replenish supplies are few and far between.

THE ROUTE
The GEA is 429km in length with 34,000m of climbing along paths, mule tracks and minor roads from Bocca Trabaria, north-east

of Arezzo, to Passo dei Due Santi on the Toscana-Liguria border, west of Pontremoli. It closely follows the Appennini watershed (and the regional boundary between Toscana, and Emilia-Romagna to the north and Liguria to the west). The highest point along the way is Monte Rondinaio (1964m), north of Castelnuovo Garfagnana, and the lowest is Pieve Santo Stefano (431m), north-east of Arezzo and about 30km from the start. The route crosses major north-south trans-Appennini roads and railway lines, but does not pass through any large towns.

Marking has been carefully designed. Along the walk, red signs indicate direction and time; at major junctions, larger signs have a map and information about local facilities.

Sentiero Italia

The Sentiero Italia (SI) will eventually be a continuous chain of paths, 5000km in length from Trieste to Calabria (with extensions to Sardegna and Sicilia). It will unite the Alps and the Appennini and create an unbroken route of 350 stages – a year's continuous walking. Two major established routes, the GTA and the GEA (see those sections earlier in this chapter), are important components, together with many other shorter, but yet long(ish) walks. All the paths are accessible most of the year, but ideally in spring and autumn. No special equipment is required and the paths are adequately marked and signposted.

The route is designed so that at the end of each stage there is somewhere to stay over-night. This could be a CAI or private rifugio, or a purpose-built shelter with basic but adequate facilities, especially in the Appennini and along the GTA. Very few walkers would be able to undertake the whole walk in one go; the idea is that walkers will do one or more sections at a time, choosing those which best suit their particular circumstances and interests, gradually joining them together. The SI project is inspired by several aims, briefly the protection of ecological and cultural features and the promotion of environmentally

Walking and the Environment

To an inexperienced outsider, Italy does not readily come to mind as a country with a strong environmental conscience, or an awareness of the benefits of protecting the natural environment – green tourism for example. Among other things, indiscriminate hunting is a prominent part of this negative image. However, as always, first-hand experience consigns the stereotypes to the bin pretty promptly, to be replaced by a more informed picture. The extent of national and natural parks helps to dispel the myths; learning about the philosophy behind the development of long-distance paths helps even more.

The Sentiero Italia (SI) project is inspired by several aims, which are shared by those responsible for the other three long-distance paths. These aims are:

- To bring to mountain areas an economic activity linked to tourism, which does not depend on major construction works and which does not compromise the natural and cultural heritage of these areas.

- To protect and respect the historic network of paths which originated with farming, forestry and pastoral activities, and their associated customs and traditions, and thus avert the terminal decline of mountain areas.

- To make society at large more aware of Italy's natural features, and minority cultural groups who may not be technologically advanced, but who nevertheless uphold worthwhile values, and in this way broadening popular conceptions of what Italy stands for.

- To educate young people in a better understanding of their country and to foster their commitment to conservation and protection of the environment.

- To promote the environmentally friendly activities of walking and trekking.

Sandra Bardwell

friendly recreation. Implementation of the SI is coordinated by a working group comprising members of the CAI and the Associazione Sentiero Italia (ASI), based at CAI's headquarters in Torino. The ASI is a group of experts in various fields and well-known authors of guidebooks, who promote the SI and provide information by way of publications, and at national and international conferences.

INFORMATION

Maps

Two special maps published by Kompass at 1:50,000 with 100m contours cover the route of the SI through Lombardia (Lombardy): No 676 *Le Tappe del Sentiero Italia, Tratto Lombardia Nord* and No 677 *Lombardia Sud*. The route of the SI is highlighted, there are gradient profiles of the walk, and each sheet is in fact two maps – one on each side. They come with a superbly produced booklet outlining the route of the path. Prices vary, but expect to pay L10,000/L14,000 per set.

Information Sources

The ASI (☎ (055) 58 53 20; fax 57 44 57), at Piazza S Gervasio 12, 50131 Firenze, is the best starting point for any detailed inquiries about the status of the SI. The association also has an office (☎/fax (011) 33 12 00) at Corso Rosselli 132, 10131 Torino.

Books

Two companion guides to the Kompass maps (see Maps section on this page) outline the route and include details of places to stay. Written by Giancarlo Corbellini, sponsored by the CAI and the ASI, and published by ITER in a convenient format, they cost L20,000 each.

THE ROUTE

A significant part of the SI comprises established long-distance walks. The GTA, in its fully planned length (continuing from Valle Anzasca to Cannobio on Lago Maggiore), links up with the Alta Via dei Monti Liguri, which in turn leads to the GEA, from the eastern end of which the E/1 reaches right down to Umbria and Le Marche (The Marches) in the Parco Nazionale dei Sibillini (see other sections in this chapter).

LONG-DISTANCE WALKS

From Cannobio it is possible to cross Lago Maggiore (see the Lake District chapter) to join the SI's Lombardia Nord route which leads westwards via Lago di Como to Passo del Tonale, north-west of Lago di Garda. This is but a part of a possible grand tour of Lombardia – the Lombardia Sud route links with the Nord route west of Lago di Garda. From there it can be followed generally westwards, via the Alpi Oróbie (Orobie Alps), to Brunate near the southern end of Lago di Como.

The Lombardia Nord walk, a distance of more than 500km divided into 36 stages, includes the Via Verde Varesina in the hills above the north-eastern shore of Lago Maggiore and the Via dei Monti Lariani along the western side of Lago di Como (see the Lake District chapter). The Lombardia Sud walk, in 21 stages, follows the Triangolo Lariano walk from Brunate to Bellagio, by Lago di Como (see the Lake District chapter), and from Valcamonica offers the choice of either a route generally northwards to Passo del Tonale or a walk east, via Valle del Singol to Limone sul Garda (see The Lake District chapter).

Sentiero Europaeo E/1

In 1969, walking and mountaineering organisations across Europe formally joined forces as the Federazione Europea Turismo Pedestre, to promote their activities, to protect the natural environment, to bring people closer together through walking and mountaineering, and to work for the removal of regulations inhibiting free movement between countries. The last of these aims has largely been achieved by the implementation of European Union policies.

The commitment to the original objectives has been sustained; 37 associations from 20 European countries now cooperate through the federation in the development and promotion of a network of 10 long-distance paths, which total about 20,000km across the length and breadth of Europe. These link existing paths within the various countries to make continuous routes, most of which are more than 2000km in length. Maintenance of paths within each country is the responsibility of the appropriate national organisations. In Italy, the paths are seen as playing a very important part in enabling people to gain a greater awareness of the natural world.

There are sections of two of these long-distance paths in Italy: the E/1 and the E/5. The latter, a mere 600km in length, extends from Lake Constance on the Swiss-German border to Venezia (Venice). The E/1 is in a different league. Essentially it links the North Sea to the Mediterranean. In outline, the route is from Flensburg on the Baltic Coast, near the Danish-German border, through Saxony, past Frankfurt and Freiburg, through the Black Forest, the Swiss Alps and beside Lago di Lugano, crossing into Italy at Porto Ceresio. Ultimately, the E/1 will start at Capo Nord at the top of Norway, and finish at Capo Passero di Siracusa in Sicilia – a total distance of 6000km.

INFORMATION
Maps

Four 1:50,000 maps published by Studio Cartografico Italiano cover the E/1, from Porto Ceresio to the crossing of the River Po. They are: No F16 *Lago Maggiore-Lago di Varese-Lago di Lugano*, No F15 *Il Parco del Ticino da Sesto Calende a Turbigo*, No F14 *Il Parco del Ticino da Galliate a Vigevano e Magenta* and No F13 *Il Parco del Ticino da Garlasco a Pavia*. Each one comes with an illustrated booklet describing features of the parks and reserves shown on the map, and outlining the stages along the E/1; they cost L15,000 and should be available at good local bookshops. In the same series, sheet Nos F11, F1 and F4 cover the E/1, and sheet No F6 covers the Alta Via dei Monti Liguri, from where you pick up the coverage of the GEA (see Maps under Grande Escursione Appenninica for the walk).

Information Sources

The best starting point to obtain up-to-date information about mapping, publications, and guides to accommodation is the Federazione Italiana Escursionismo (☎ (010)

697 07 93), Via E Salgari 1-20, 16156 Genova Pegli. The FIE was established by presidential decree in 1971 and is the main repository of information about the E/1. A free brochure, *La Valle del Ticino col Sentiero E/1*, is available from Il Parco Lombardo del Ticino (☎ (02) 97 21 01), Via Isonzo 1, 20013 Ponte Vecchio di Magenta.

THE ROUTE

As a long-distance walk in its own right, the E/1, between Lago di Lugano and Genova (a distance of at least 400km), is a walk of great variety – the lakes and the high plateau of Campo dei Fiori in the north, the flat Ticino and Po valleys, and back into the mountains with the Ligurian Alps. From Porto Ceresio on the southern shore of Lago di Lugano, the E/1 climbs to Parco Naturale Campo dei Fiori, passing close to the highest point (1226m) on the plateau, then descends to Gavirate on Lago di Varese. From there it heads south into the Parco Naturale della Valle Ticino. With an area of 90,640 hectares, this is the major river-based park in Europe and extends from Sesto Callende, where the River Ticino flows out of Lago Maggiore, right down to its junction with the River Po at Ponte della Becca, south-east of Pavia.

The E/1 stays within this park to near Bereguardo, 12km north-west of Pavia, then pursues a fairly direct southward course, through the Po valley to cross the Po near the small town of Cornale (about 30km north-east of Alessandria). Dodging the A7 and the A21, it continues south and eventually crosses the Ligurian Alps and descends to Genova Pegli, a few kilometres west of that city.

However, in pursuit of the aim to traverse the full length of Italy, the E/1 links with the Alta Via dei Monti Liguri at Passo Bocchetta, some 20km north of Genova. The Alta Via is another major long-distance walk, starting at Ventimiglia, on the Mediterranean coast in Liguria, heading generally eastwards through the mountains to Ceparana, not far north of La Spezia, a distance of nearly 450km. The 'AV', as it is known, joins the Grande Escursione Appenninica at Passo dei Due Santi. From the other end of the GEA, at Bocca Trabaria, the E/1 regains its identity and continues to the vicinity of Norcia and Parco Nazionale dei Sibillini, straddling the border between Umbria and Le Marche. Beyond that point the route is still in the planning stages, apart from a section of about 100km in the Monti Picentini range near Acerno, north of Salerno in southern Italy.

Glossary

abete – fir tree
abbazzia – abbey
alpeggio – summer base for making dairy products in the high mountain pastures
alpinismo – mountaineering, usually requiring some technical expertise
alta via – high-level walking route, which may follow a watershed or cross a series of high passes
alto – high

baita – refuge, building providing shelter, open to all, usually not at high altitudes
basso – low
becco – mountain peak with pointed profile
betulla – birch tree
bivacco – remote, high mountain shelter, sometimes kept locked except to those who have obtained keys from the custodian
bocca – mouth, entrance
borgo – hamlet
bosco – woodland, forest
burrone – cliff, precipice

caduta massi – falling rocks (a common roadside sign in the mountains)
cairn – a mound of stones erected as a memorial or marker
campeggio – camping area with facilities
campo – field
canale – rocky Alpine gorge, valley
canalone – large rocky Alpine gorge, valley
cappella – chapel
carreggiabile – trafficable, accessible by vehicle
carta/cartina – map
cascata – waterfall
castagno – chestnut or sweet chestnut
castello – castle
cattivo – bad, as in bad weather
cima – mountain peak
cipresso – cypress tree
colle – hill
commune – town council; the local government area for which it is responsible
conca – hollow

corno – mountain peak, usually steep-sided
crampon – one of a pair of spiked metal grids strapped to boots for climbing or walking on ice or snow
cresta/crinale – mountain ridge, the relatively high divide between streams
curva di livello – contour line

discesa – descent, downhill walk
dislivello – gradient, difference in altitude between two places
divieto d'accesso – keep out (see also *proprietà privata*)
divieto di sosta – no parking/stopping
doccia – shower (washing)

escursione – walk, hike, tramp
est – east

faggio – beech
ferrata – cord trail
fienile – haystack
fiore selvatico – wild flower
fiume – major river, larger than a *torrente*
forcella – col, saddle, low point on a ridge
frana – landslide
frazione – small town/large village
fulmine – lightning
funivia – cable car

galleria – tunnel
gestore – manager of a *rifugio*
gettone – token, sometimes required at a *campeggio* to operate shower
ghiacciaio – glacier
ghiaione – scree slope
gias – graziers' camp
gola – gorge
grotta – cave

inserimento – linking path between two other paths
itinerario – route rather than a formed path

laghetto – small lake
lago – lake

lama – very narrow mountain ridge
larice – larch, a deciduous conifer
letto – bed
locanda – country inn, smaller and simpler than a *pensione*

malga – Alpine hut where graziers make butter and cheese in summer
meridionale – southern
montagna – mountain
mulattiera – path (originally) used by mules, along which mules were led

nebbia – fog, mist
neve – snow
nord – north
nuvoloso – cloudy (weather)

occidentale – western
ometta – pile of rocks
oratorio – wayside shrine, often quite elaborate, with crucifix, statuette(s) of religious figures, paintings, flowers
orientale – eastern
osservatorio – observatory
ovest – west

paese – village, small town
parete (di roccia) – rockface
passerella – footbridge
passo – pass, usually in the mountains; low-level route between two valleys
pensione – small hotel, often with board
pericolosissimo – very dangerous
pericoloso – dangerous
pian/piano – plain, more or less level area
pineta – pine forest
pino – pine tree
pioggia – rain
piovoso – wet (weather)
prato – meadow, flat grassy area
previsioni del tempo – weather forecast
proprietà privata – private property (see also *divieto d'accesso*)
punta – mountain peak
pyroclastic – formed from the solid fragments ejected during a volcanic eruption

quercia – oak
quota – altitude, height above sea level

ricovero – fairly basic shelter in mountain areas
rifugio – mountain refuge, more like a one-star hotel with bunk rooms
rocca – ruined castle
rovina/rudere – ruin(s) of a building

salita – climb, ascent
scarpone – walking/hiking/mountain boots
scree – an accumulation of weathered rock fragments at the foot of a cliff or hillside
seggiovia – chair lift
segnale/segnaletica – signposting
sella – saddle, low place in a ridge
sentiero – footpath or defined walking route on formed path
settentrionale – northern
smottamento – scree (see also *ghiaione*)
soccorso – help, aid, assistance, especially as in *soccorso alpino*, or mountain rescue
sorgente – spring, often of mineral water
strada provinciale – provincial road
strombolian – describes explosive volcanic activity
sud – south
switchback – route, or road, that follows a zigzag course

tempesta – storm
tempo – weather
tempo di percorrenza – time needed to complete a walk
temporale – thunderstorm
tenda – tent
testa – head; mountain resembling a head in shape or position
tetti – small group of houses, hamlet
torre – tower, fortified tower-like building
torrente – small river, stream

valanga – avalanche, landslide
valle – valley
vallone – deep/large valley
vento – wind
vetta – mountain peak
via ferrata – steep route equipped with a fixed cable

zaino – rucksack

Index

TEXT

WALKS

From the Authors

Helen Gillman In addition to many of the people and organisations thanked by Stefano, I'd also like to thank Chris Klep, Nick Tapp, Justin Flynn and Andrew Smith at Lonely Planet, who were a great bunch of guys to work with on this guide. Thanks also to my parents for generally helping beyond the call of duty while I tried to pull it all together as the deadline came and went.

Sandra Bardwell Sally gave me leave from my part-time post with Historic Scotland; Anne readily deputised while praying that no-one in southern Highlands would bulldoze any scheduled ancient monuments during the summer. Alison, Roddy Maclean and Linda helped in various ways. In our village, thanks to Margaret, Lionel, Jan and the staff at the high school office. Thanks to Bill for help with email and computers. The prompt service provided by Stanfords, The Map Centre and the Met Office overcame the problems of living in the comparatively remote Highlands of Scotland.

In Roma, Helen, Stefano and Virginia's friendly hospitality was much appreciated, and Helen's advice about matters Italian, her introduction to the *International Herald Tribune* and her patient editorial guidance were a great help for a somewhat apprehensive first-time Lonely Planet author.

At Lonely Planet in Melbourne, thanks to former staff member Frith Luton, and to Nick and Chris, whose Australian-style informality refreshingly combined with their professional commitment to make the whole job more enjoyable.

Hal's cheerfully philosophical acceptance of my lengthy absence, and the consequent phone bill, and then his support and advice during the weeks of intensive writing up and map compilation (not to mention coming to terms with the arrival of Pegasus, the computer) made an already immensely enjoyable summer infinitely better.

The following organisations also provide me with valuable assistance: AASTs in Salerno, Amalfi, Positano and Sorrento; Comune Information Office in Massa Lubrense; IATs

in Limone, Luino and Menaggio – where special thanks are due for helpful advice; APT in Cannobio; Pro Loco in Stresa, Cannero, Maccagno, Aosta and Cogne; national park visitor centres in Degioz (Valsavarenche) and Chanavey (Val di Rhemes); national park information office in Villeneuve; Associazione Grande Traversata delle Alpi in Torino; Federazione Italiana Escursionismo in Genova; Comunità Montana della Garfagnana; CAI national library, Torino.

Stefano Cavedoni I would like to thank the following friends, tourist organisations and staff for their valuable assistance: my old friends Giovanni Cenacchi, Jimmy De Col, Mario Vianelli, Paul & Laura Loss, who showed me the way; my American friend Enrico Black for his refined explorer's talent; travelling companion Petra Kaminsky for her German seductiveness; my new Sicilian friends Dott. Sandro Privitera for his great enthusiastic competence and Ugo & Cinzia Esposito for their real love of nature and their generosity. Then there are the many other friends who affectionately helped me in my research: Roberta Rizzati; Massimo Masci; the Pisano family; Roberto, Lucina & Alice Terzani; Hans, Mariangela & Alba; Tato & Giuliana Rossi; Rosario & Lena Serra; Dafne & Francesco Canevaro; 'Ianez' Saverio Bessone, Fabio Giacotto and Paolo Fiore; Saro Cudda and Marco Ruscica; 'Murena' Vincenzo Tupponi.

Thank you to ENIT, in particular Gigliola Lantini and Sig.a Lodi; ESIT, in particular Mario Pinna and Marco Grippo; the AAST delle Isole Eolie (in particular Mimmo Zino) and at Stromboli Lorenzo Russo, Mario Zaia and 'Ulli'; Catania AAPIT (Dott. Sciacca, Fiorella Zappalà, Sig.ra Ali and Dott.ssa Violetta Francese); Comando Ripartimentale Foreste della Regione Sicilia (Dott. Riggi, Dott. Piccinini, Maresciallo Alfio Coco, Guardie Luciano Domanti and Carmelo Cavallaro); Corpo Forestale dello Stato of Caserta (Dott. Costantino and Ing. Zumbolo); Siracusa APT (Dott. Basso, Giusi Di Lorenzo); Ragusa AAPIT (Dott. Mannino, Signora Burgio); the APTs of Firenze and

Siena, the CAIs of Firenze (Dott. Aldo Benini, Sig. Piccini, Sig. Degli Innocenti) and Siena (Eolo Menchetti, Gianfranco Muschietti); the enthusiastic staff of the Tourist Office at Radda in Chianti (Gioia Milani and Patrizio Pagni); APT Dolomiti; Alto Adige Promozione Turismo; Associazione Turistica Sciliar-Castelrotto; Associazioni Turistiche dell'Alta Badia (in particular Dott. Damiano Dapunt); Napoli EPT (in particular the wonderfully dedicated Aldo Cianci) and Dott. Luigi Guido. A personal thank you to Helen, who had the temerity to risk life with me, and 1001 Italian kisses 'from here to dinosaurs' to my very special daughter Virginia.

A special thank you to Darragh Henegan, who endured more than most translators would be prepared to bear. Darragh translated Stefano's text, which was originally written in Italian, and both Stefano and Helen very much appreciate her work.

Nick Tapp Thanks to many people in various

Italian tourist offices, especially Simona Iorio of the APT in Cuneo, and to the *gestori* of the *rifugi* I stayed in, who were all, in their different ways, extremely helpful. Thanks also to the many walkers who took a friendly interest in my progress, especially Anna Arata and friends, who introduced me to *grolla* in Rifugio Genova-Figari; Christine & Kurt Bauer, who picked berries and rescued me from language fatigue; and Domenico and friends from Rifugio Rossi. Thanks to Helen, Stefano and Virginia for hospitality in Roma, and to Sandra for generous assistance. Thanks to Sue Galley for a great opportunity, to Chris Klep for holding the fort, and to numerous other colleagues in Lonely Planet's Melbourne office for making allowances while I did what a writer has to do. Thanks to all those friends who saw it as more than a junket and responded as friends do, especially Annie, Richard, Karen and Brian. Finally, thanks to Ely for putting up with it all.

Notes

Lonely Planet Guides by Region

Lonely Planet is known worldwide for publishing practical, reliable and no-nonsense travel information in our guides and on our Web site. The Lonely Planet list covers just about every accessible part of the world. Currently there are 16 series: Travel guides, Shoestring guides, Condensed guides, Phrasebooks, Read This First, Healthy Travel, Walking guides, Cycling guides, Watching Wildlife guides, Pisces Diving & Snorkeling guides, City Maps, Road Atlases, Out to Eat, World Food, Journeys travel literature and Pictorials.

AFRICA Africa on a shoestring • Botswana • Cairo • Cairo City Map • Cape Town • Cape Town City Map • East Africa • Egypt • Egyptian Arabic phrasebook • Ethiopia, Eritrea & Djibouti • Ethiopian Amharic phrasebook • The Gambia & Senegal • Healthy Travel Africa • Kenya • Malawi • Morocco • Moroccan Arabic phrasebook • Mozambique • Namibia • Read This First: Africa • South Africa, Lesotho & Swaziland • Southern Africa • Southern Africa Road Atlas • Swahili phrasebook • Tanzania, Zanzibar & Pemba • Trekking in East Africa • Tunisia • Watching Wildlife East Africa • Watching Wildlife Southern Africa • West Africa • World Food Morocco • Zambia • Zimbabwe, Botswana & Namibia
Travel Literature: Mali Blues: Traveling to an African Beat • The Rainbird: A Central African Journey • Songs to an African Sunset: A Zimbabwean Story

AUSTRALIA & THE PACIFIC Aboriginal Australia & the Torres Strait Islands •Auckland • Australia • Australian phrasebook • Australia Road Atlas • Cycling Australia • Cycling New Zealand • Fiji • Fijian phrasebook • Healthy Travel Australia, NZ & the Pacific • Islands of Australia's Great Barrier Reef • Melbourne • Melbourne City Map • Micronesia • New Caledonia • New South Wales • New Zealand • Northern Territory • Outback Australia • Out to Eat – Melbourne • Out to Eat – Sydney • Papua New Guinea • Pidgin phrasebook • Queensland • Rarotonga & the Cook Islands • Samoa • Solomon Islands • South Australia • South Pacific • South Pacific phrasebook • Sydney • Sydney City Map • Sydney Condensed • Tahiti & French Polynesia • Tasmania • Tonga • Tramping in New Zealand • Vanuatu • Victoria • Walking in Australia • Watching Wildlife Australia • Western Australia
Travel Literature: Islands in the Clouds: Travels in the Highlands of New Guinea • Kiwi Tracks: A New Zealand Journey • Sean & David's Long Drive

CENTRAL AMERICA & THE CARIBBEAN Bahamas, Turks & Caicos • Baja California • Belize, Guatemala & Yucatán • Bermuda • Central America on a shoestring • Costa Rica • Costa Rica Spanish phrasebook • Cuba • Cycling Cuba • Dominican Republic & Haiti • Eastern Caribbean • Guatemala • Havana • Healthy Travel Central & South America • Jamaica • Mexico • Mexico City • Panama • Puerto Rico • Read This First: Central & South America • Virgin Islands • World Food Caribbean • World Food Mexico • Yucatán
Travel Literature: Green Dreams: Travels in Central America

EUROPE Amsterdam • Amsterdam City Map • Amsterdam Condensed • Andalucía • Athens • Austria • Baltic States phrasebook • Barcelona • Barcelona City Map • Belgium & Luxembourg • Berlin • Berlin City Map • Britain • British phrasebook • Brussels, Bruges & Antwerp • Brussels City Map • Budapest • Budapest City Map • Canary Islands • Catalunya & the Costa Brava • Central Europe • Central Europe phrasebook • Copenhagen • Corfu & the Ionians • Corsica • Crete • Crete Condensed • Croatia • Cycling Britain • Cycling France • Cyprus • Czech & Slovak Republics • Czech phrasebook • Denmark • Dublin • Dublin City Map • Dublin Condensed • Eastern Europe • Eastern Europe phrasebook • Edinburgh • Edinburgh City Map • England • Estonia, Latvia & Lithuania • Europe on a shoestring • Europe phrasebook • Finland • Florence • Florence City Map • France • Frankfurt City Map • Frankfurt Condensed • French phrasebook • Georgia, Armenia & Azerbaijan • Germany • German phrasebook • Greece • Greek Islands • Greek phrasebook • Hungary • Iceland, Greenland & the Faroe Islands • Ireland • Italian phrasebook • Italy • Kraków • Lisbon • The Loire • London • London City Map • London Condensed • Madrid • Madrid City Map • Malta • Mediterranean Europe • Milan, Turin & Genoa • Moscow • Munich • Netherlands • Normandy • Norway • Out to Eat – London • Out to Eat – Paris • Paris • Paris City Map • Paris Condensed • Poland • Polish phrasebook • Portugal • Portuguese phrasebook • Prague • Prague City Map • Provence & the Côte d'Azur • Read This First: Europe • Rhodes & the Dodecanese • Romania & Moldova • Rome • Rome City Map • Rome Condensed • Russia, Ukraine & Belarus • Russian phrasebook • Scandinavian & Baltic Europe • Scandinavian phrasebook • Scotland • Sicily • Slovenia • South-West France • Spain • Spanish phrasebook • Stockholm • St Petersburg • St Petersburg City Map • Sweden • Switzerland • Tuscany • Ukrainian phrasebook • Venice • Vienna • Wales • Walking in Britain • Walking in France • Walking in Ireland • Walking in Italy • Walking in Scotland • Walking in Spain • Walking in Switzerland • Western Europe • World Food France • World Food Greece • World Food Ireland • World Food Italy • World Food Spain **Travel Literature:** After Yugoslavia • Love and War in the Apennines • The Olive Grove: Travels in Greece • On the Shores of the Mediterranean • Round Ireland in Low Gear • A Small Place in Italy

Lonely Planet Mail Order

onely Planet products are distributed worldwide. They are also available by mail order from Lonely Planet, so if you have difficulty finding a title please write to us. North and South American residents should write to 150 Linden St, Oakland, CA 94607, USA; European and African residents should write to 10a Spring Place, London NW5 3BH, UK; and residents of other countries to Locked Bag 1, Footscray, Victoria 3011, Australia.

INDIAN SUBCONTINENT & THE INDIAN OCEAN Bangladesh • Bengali phrasebook • Bhutan • Delhi • Goa • Healthy Travel Asia & India • Hindi & Urdu phrasebook • India • India & Bangladesh City Map • Indian Himalaya • Karakoram Highway • Kathmandu City Map • Kerala • Madagascar • Maldives • Mauritius, Réunion & Seychelles • Mumbai (Bombay) • Nepal • Nepali phrasebook • North India • Pakistan • Rajasthan • Read This First: Asia & India • South India • Sri Lanka • Sri Lanka phrasebook • Tibet • Tibetan phrasebook • Trekking in the Indian Himalaya • Trekking in the Karakoram & Hindukush • Trekking in the Nepal Himalaya • World Food India **Travel Literature:** The Age of Kali: Indian Travels and Encounters • Hello Goodnight: A Life of Goa • In Rajasthan • Maverick in Madagascar • A Season in Heaven: True Tales from the Road to Kathmandu • Shopping for Buddhas • A Short Walk in the Hindu Kush • Slowly Down the Ganges

MIDDLE EAST & CENTRAL ASIA Bahrain, Kuwait & Qatar • Central Asia • Central Asia phrasebook • Dubai • Farsi (Persian) phrasebook • Hebrew phrasebook • Iran • Israel & the Palestinian Territories • Istanbul • Istanbul City Map • Istanbul to Cairo • Istanbul to Kathmandu • Jerusalem • Jerusalem City Map • Jordan • Lebanon • Middle East • Oman & the United Arab Emirates • Syria • Turkey • Turkish phrasebook • World Food Turkey • Yemen **Travel Literature:** Black on Black: Iran Revisited • Breaking Ranks: Turbulent Travels in the Promised Land • The Gates of Damascus • Kingdom of the Film Stars: Journey into Jordan

NORTH AMERICA Alaska • Boston • Boston City Map • Boston Condensed • British Columbia • California & Nevada • California Condensed • Canada • Chicago • Chicago City Map • Chicago Condensed • Florida • Georgia & the Carolinas • Great Lakes • Hawaii • Hiking in Alaska • Hiking in the USA • Honolulu & Oahu City Map • Las Vegas • Los Angeles • Los Angeles City Map • Louisiana & the Deep South • Miami • Miami City Map • Montreal • New England • New Orleans • New Orleans City Map • New York City • New York City City Map • New York City Condensed • New York, New Jersey & Pennsylvania • Oahu • Out to Eat – San Francisco • Pacific Northwest • Rocky Mountains • San Diego & Tijuana • San Francisco • San Francisco City Map • Seattle • Seattle City Map • Southwest • Texas • Toronto • USA • USA phrasebook • Vancouver • Vancouver City Map • Virginia & the Capital Region • Washington, DC • Washington, DC City Map • World Food New Orleans **Travel Literature:** Caught Inside: A Surfer's Year on the California Coast • Drive Thru America

NORTH-EAST ASIA Beijing • Beijing City Map • Cantonese phrasebook • China • Hiking in Japan • Hong Kong & Macau • Hong Kong City Map • Hong Kong Condensed • Japan • Japanese phrasebook • Korea • Korean phrasebook • Kyoto • Mandarin phrasebook • Mongolia • Mongolian phrasebook • Seoul • Shanghai • South-West China • Taiwan • Tokyo • Tokyo Condensed • World Food Hong Kong • World Food Japan **Travel Literature:** In Xanadu: A Quest • Lost Japan

SOUTH AMERICA Argentina, Uruguay & Paraguay • Bolivia • Brazil • Brazilian phrasebook • Buenos Aires • Buenos Aires City Map • Chile & Easter Island • Colombia • Ecuador & the Galapagos Islands • Healthy Travel Central & South America • Latin American Spanish phrasebook • Peru • Quechua phrasebook • Read This First: Central & South America • Rio de Janeiro • Rio de Janeiro City Map • Santiago de Chile • South America on a shoestring • Trekking in the Patagonian Andes • Venezuela **Travel Literature**: Full Circle: A South American Journey

SOUTH-EAST ASIA Bali & Lombok • Bangkok • Bangkok City Map • Burmese phrasebook • Cambodia • Cycling Vietnam, Laos & Cambodia • East Timor phrasebook • Hanoi • Healthy Travel Asia & India • Hill Tribes phrasebook • Ho Chi Minh City (Saigon) • Indonesia • Indonesian phrasebook • Indonesia's Eastern Islands • Java • Lao phrasebook • Laos • Malay phrasebook • Malaysia, Singapore & Brunei • Myanmar (Burma) • Philippines • Pilipino (Tagalog) phrasebook • Read This First: Asia & India • Singapore • Singapore City Map • South-East Asia on a shoestring • South-East Asia phrasebook • Thailand • Thailand's Islands & Beaches • Thailand, Vietnam, Laos & Cambodia Road Atlas • Thai phrasebook • Vietnam • Vietnamese phrasebook • World Food Indonesia • World Food Thailand • World Food Vietnam

ALSO AVAILABLE: Antarctica • The Arctic • The Blue Man: Tales of Travel, Love and Coffee • Brief Encounters: Stories of Love, Sex & Travel • Buddhist Stupas in Asia: The Shape of Perfection • Chasing Rickshaws • The Last Grain Race • Lonely Planet ... On the Edge: Adventurous Escapades from Around the World • Lonely Planet Unpacked • Lonely Planet Unpacked Again • Not the Only Planet: Science Fiction Travel Stories • Ports of Call: A Journey by Sea • Sacred India • Travel Photography: A Guide to Taking Better Pictures • Travel with Children • Tuvalu: Portrait of an Island Nation

The Lonely Planet Story

L onely Planet published its first book in 1973 in response to the numerous 'How did you do it?' questions Maureen and Tony Wheeler were asked after driving, bussing, hitching, sailing and railing their way from England to Australia.

Written at a kitchen table and hand collated, trimmed and stapled, *Across Asia on the Cheap* became an instant local bestseller, inspiring thoughts of another book.

Eighteen months in South-East Asia resulted in their second guide, *South-East Asia on a shoestring*, which they put together in a backstreet Chinese hotel in Singapore in 1975. The 'yellow bible', as it quickly became known to backpackers around the world, soon became *the* guide to the region. It has sold well over half a million copies and is now in its 9th edition, still retaining its familiar yellow cover.

Today there are over 350 titles, including travel guides, walking guides, language kits & phrasebooks, travel atlases, diving guides and travel literature. The company is the largest independent travel publisher in the world. Although Lonely Planet initially specialised in guides to Asia, today there are few corners of the globe that have not been covered.

The emphasis continues to be on travel for independent travellers. Tony and Maureen still travel for several months of each year and play an active part in the writing, updating and quality control of Lonely Planet's guides.

They have been joined by over 120 authors and 280 staff at our offices in Melbourne (Australia), Oakland (USA), London (UK) and Paris (France). Travellers themselves also make a valuable contribution to the guides through the feedback we receive in thousands of letters each year and on our web site.

The people at Lonely Planet strongly believe that travellers can make a positive contribution to the countries they visit, both through their appreciation of the countries' culture, wildlife and natural features, and through the money they spend. In addition, the company makes a direct contribution to the countries and regions it covers. Since 1986 a percentage of the income from each book has been donated to ventures such as famine relief in Africa; aid projects in India; agricultural projects in Central America; Greenpeace's efforts to halt French nuclear testing in the Pacific; and Amnesty International.

LONELY PLANET OFFICES

Australia
Locked Bag 1, Footscray, Victoria 3011
☎ 03 8379 8000 fax 03 8379 8111
email: talk2us@lonelyplanet.com.au

USA
150 Linden St, Oakland, CA 94607
☎ 510 893 8555 TOLL FREE: 800 275 8555
fax 510 893 8572
email: info@lonelyplanet.com

UK
10a Spring Place, London NW5 3BH
☎ 020 7428 4800 fax 020 7428 4828
email: go@lonelyplanet.co.uk

France
1 rue du Dahomey, 75011 Paris
☎ 01 55 25 33 00 fax 01 55 25 33 01
email: bip@lonelyplanet.fr
www.lonelyplanet.fr

World Wide Web: www.lonelyplanet.com *or* AOL keyword: lp
Lonely Planet Images: lpi@lonelyplanet.com.au